THE SWAPMEET AND TOY FAIR CATALOGUE OF

BRITISH DIE-CAST MODEL TOYS

FIRST EDITION

A Swapmeet Toys and Models Ltd Publication
Lions Lodge, 10 High Rd West, Felixstowe, Suffolk,
England IP11 9JB

Distributed by:
RAVETTE LIMITED
12 Star Road, Partridge Green
Horsham, Sussex RH13 8RA
Tel: Horsham (0403) 710392

Compiled by John Ramsay

First published 1984

ISBN 0 9509319 0 X

Printed in Great Britain by W. S. Cowell Ltd, Ipswich

CONTENTS

The Swapmeet and Toy Fair Catalogue of British Die-Cast Model Toys

CHAPTER 3 MATCHBOX TOYS

CHAPTER 4 CORGI TOYS

NB GIFT SETS shown at end of each section.

CHAPTER 5 LLEDO 'Models of Days Gone'

THE COMPILER'S PERSONAL ACKNOWLEDGEMENTS

John Ramsay, the compiler of the catalogue, has received tremendous help and encouragement from many sources and would especially like to thank the following people without whose help the catalogue would never have been published.

To Paul Robinson of Felixstowe for all the hours spent drawing the Dinky Toys recognition diagrams.

To Peter Wheatley of 'Wheatleys', the specialist modern die-cast model shop in Hamilton Road, Felixstowe, for all his help and guidance on modern issues. Also for his photographic contributions.

To John Webb of 5 Boswell Drive, Lincoln, specialist Toyfair and mail order dealer in obsolete and current models, for his dealer's viewpoints on both the catalogue's content and title.

To Ian E. Clark of Walney Island, Barrow in Furness, for the invaluable assistance rendered in the preparation of the Spot On model listings.

To Mike and Sue Richardson of Mikansue, 15 Bell Lane, Eton Wick, Windsor, co-authors of 'Dinky Toys and Modelled Miniatures', for kindly allowing the compiler to use technical information from Cecil Gibson's 'History of British Dinky Toys 1934-1964'.

To Mr G. D. Hudson, the marketing director of Matchbox Toys, for granting permission to quote his company's trade names and for his kind offer of access to original photographic material.

To Mr M. Rosser, director of The Mettoy Company plc for granting permission to quote his company's trade names and to Corgi Marketing Manager, David Dooley, for his help in providing up-to-date model listings.

To 'Major Models' of 77 Wood Close, Windsor, Berkshire, the rare 'Models of Yesteryear' specialists and producers of the 'Models of Yesteryear' calendar, for guidance on the rare models of the series.

To Ray Bush, founder of the UK Matchbox Club for help and guidance on the content of Matchbox '1-75' Series and 'Models of Yesteryear' Series.

To Narisa Levy, director of the London Toy and Model Museum, October House, 23 Craven Hill, London W2, for permission to acknowledge that the source of much of the information concerning the early Dinky Toys was gained from the Dinky Toys Jubilee Exhibition held at the Museum.

To Swapmeet pal John Plume of Iver, Bucks, for providing original research material.

To Ron for great encouragement and understanding.

To Andrew Perkins of The Chimneys, Hall Road, Hemsby, Gt Yarmouth, Norfolk for the personal attention given to the model photography.

Lastly to the compiler's wife Sally and to his family, without whose total support this catalogue really would never have been published.

OFFICIAL COMPANY ACKNOWLEDGEMENTS

INTRODUCTION

'THE FIRST FIFTY YEARS 1933 – 1983'

There has been a tremendous growth in recent years in the fascinating pastime of collecting both past and present day toys. This upsurge has been particularly evident in the die-cast model sector. Just what has caused this phenomenon is of course a matter of conjecture. Most certainly ever since Frank Hornby's Dinky cars became a household name in the mid-thirties there has been an interest in collecting these delightful little models by boys of all ages.

Many of today's parents grew up in the fifties and sixties which was a golden era for British produced die-cast models. Possibly therefore for several of today's growing band of new collectors this hobby provides them with a nostalgic return to the memories of childhood. A return maybe to the days when two shillings and elevenpence could buy a beautifully made model of perhaps the car their father owned.

Perhaps again the recent demise of great names from the past such as Dinky has brought an increasing awareness of just how good these models were.

No doubt some of these new collectors have been pleasantly surprised to discover that it is still possible to build up an interesting collection without having to spend a fortune and furthermore that quality models are still being produced today by British manufacturers.

Whatever the reasons are for the growth in collecting die-cast models, there have been several indications that it is taking place.

One of these is the number and size of Swapmeets and Toy Fairs which are taking place all over the country — very often for the first time. Indeed a glance at the pages of the 'Antique Toy World' shows that there appears to be a similar trend in the USA as well. Toyfairs in Britain can vary in size from as few as twenty tables to as many as two hundred and fifty at the large established venues such as Gloucester and Windsor.

It is estimated that over four hundred such swapmeets a year now take place in venues ranging from local community and sports centres to great London hotels.

Similarly specialist collectors' shops have continued to open up offering a wide range of models for sale both to direct callers and by mail order.

In addition, the world famous London auction houses and provincial auctioneers hold regular sales of toys, of which a large section is devoted entirely to the sale of die-cast models.

Some of the prices paid over the past two years for early Dinky toys have been quite phenomenal, as the following examples show:—

28th July 1982. Phillips, the New Bond St, London, auctioneers, sold a 22b Dinky Toys Sports Coupe for £480.

20th May 1983. Sothebys, the New Bond St, London, auctioneers sold a 28 Series 1st Type 'Oxo' van for a world record price of £550.

1983 has seen the fiftieth anniversary of the formation of Dinky Toys. This Golden Jubilee was marked by a special exhibition at the London Toy and Model Museum.

Over 700 of the rarest models made up from several collections were on display. These included examples of all the rare pre-war models and sets plus the unique Model No 992, the Avro Vulcan Bomber of which only five hundred were reported made.

The compiler was able to gather much unique first hand information from this Exhibition and is delighted to express his appreciation both to the Museum and to Mike and Sue Richardson for putting the display together.

1983 has also seen the launch of a new British toy company, Lledo 'Models of Days Gone', by die-cast expert Jack Odell, one of the original founder directors of the Matchbox Toys company. The first models have been well received and it is to be hoped there are more to come.

As can be seen from the model listings, both Matchbox and Corgi have issued excellent new models during the year, so there is plenty to interest the increasing numbers of collectors of new issues.

Lastly 1983 has seen the preparation of this first edition 'The Swapmeet & Toy Fair Catalogue of British Die-cast Model Toys' which has taken three years to produce. The compiler hopes that its contents will both add to the enjoyment of existing collectors and that it will encourage others to take up the absorbing pastime of die-cast model collecting.

MARKET SURVEY

A Market Survey of the availability and prices of die-cast models has been undertaken by the compiler with two main objectives in mind.

Firstly, it was to obtain all the information required to produce in just one catalogue an up-to-date, comprehensive guide to the identification, rarity and likely asking prices in respect of a wide range of collectable die-cast models.

Secondly, it was to ensure that the information, once obtained, was presented in a simple factual manner, which would help identify models and closely reflect the results obtained by the survey.

This would then not only provide useful information for enthusiasts but would also provide a yardstick against which to measure changes in any future editions.

The information given in this catalogue therefore has been based on the results of a two year survey which took into account information from a variety of sources. These included many Toy Fairs and a large number of Mail Order Lists including some from the USA and Australia. In addition the marked up prices shown in collectors' shops were recorded together with the values realised in the auction rooms, particularly in respect of the rarer models.

The qualifying standards concerning model and box condition were as follows:—

Pre-War Models Fine — Good condition
1946-53 Models Good — Excellent
1953-83 Models Excellent Boxed to Mint Boxed

(See Section V classifying the condition of models and boxes.)

The survey recorded that prices for the same models varied from dealer to dealer on both Mail Order Lists and at the same Toy Fairs.

This is hardly surprising for asking prices are largely determined by, firstly, the demand a dealer is experiencing for a particular model and, secondly, by the cost of his overheads. These two factors coupled with a dealer's expertise at buying well and the natural laws of supply and demand result in varying prices being seen.

Consequently as a result of all these variables this catalogue has not shown an exact price for each model but has used the results of the survey to produce its own original rarity and price grading system as is explained in the next section.

THE MODEL RARITY AND PRICE GRADING SYSTEM

By using the information produced by the Market Survey it has been possible to develop a unique combined rarity and price grading system.

This has been based on the answers provided by the research information to the following questions:—

1. Availability of Models and Gift Sets
How often was a model encountered during the two year period in terms of:—
a) Was it always available?
b) Was it always reasonably available?
c) Was it only occasionally available?
d) Was it hardly ever or rarely seen?
e) Was it never seen?

2. The Asking Prices seen
What were the asking prices requested in respect of the same models in terms of:—
a) The highest asking price?
b) The lowest asking price?
c) The usual asking price?

3. The Auction Prices realised for Models
a) What prices were achieved at auction, particularly in respect of rare models?

Using the answers to these questions each model and gift set has been put into one of seven different grades.

1. NVE No Values Estimate
This coding has been shown alongside models and gift sets which were never encountered in the survey and about which no up-to-date asking price or auction value information was obtained. The value shown against the model therefore is the compiler's estimate of what it would fetch should it come onto the market. This grading particularly applies to many of the pre-war Dinkies and also to the Spot On model range.

Consequently because of rarity considerations, expect to see large price fluctuations occur over and above the catalogue estimate, especially at auctions.

2. GV Guidance Value
This coding has been shown alongside models which the survey found were only rarely available and about which only limited price and auction value information was obtained. The value shown against the model therefore reflects this limited information and has been given for guidance purposes only. Consequently because of rarity considerations, expect to see the occasional largish price fluctuation from the figure shown, especially at auctions.

3. NC Not Common
This coding has been shown alongside models which are fairly scarce but not rare and about which sufficient information was produced by the survey to give reasonable asking price guidance. Nevertheless expect to see asking price fluctuations from the figure shown because of scarcity.

4. MPR Market Price Range
eg £25-£30
This category is by far the most common grading used in the catalogue and applies to all those models which were found to be reasonably available most of the time. The two figures shown indicate the range of asking prices seen having discounted exceptionally high or low figures. Expect slight price fluctuations above and below the range shown in respect of the laws of supply and demand.

5. Current
This is shown alongside models which have usually been recently issued or for models which have yet to attain a real collectable value. One would not expect to see asking prices for models in this grade set higher than a few pounds unless a model happens to be particularly large, eg. a common gift set containing several models.

6. NVP No Values Possible
This is shown alongside models never encountered in the survey and about which there is doubt whether they were ever actually issued, even though it may have been pictured in a catalogue. This particularly applies to some of the Spot On models and the odd Dinky toy. Readers will appreciate that unlike postage stamps or coins, no birth records are available in respect of all the die-cast models issued.

7. NGPP No Grading Possible at Present
Where a model or gift set is particularly rare and no values information whatsoever is available, no rarity or price grading has been shown as the compiler believes this is carrying rarity and value grading into the realms of pure guesswork.

As and when information becomes available concerning these rarities it will be included in the catalogue.

This grading particularly applies to some of the very rare fairly recent 'Models of Yesteryear' issues, some of the very early Dinky gift sets and also to the Spot On gift sets.

AUCTION PRICES REALISED

Some of the price gradings shown have been supported by reports of the values actually realised at auction.

This has only been done in those instances where a model is either rare or is representative of a group of similar models eg. Dinky 28 Series Vans etc.

NB It cannot be over-emphasised that irrespective of any value guidance given in this catalogue, it would be inadvisable for readers to expect their local collectors shop or dealer to charge similar prices in every case.

As has been explained earlier, each dealer will base the price he charges on what he had to pay for the model in the first instance, coupled with the cost of his overheads and the demand for the model itself.

He will *not* be governed by any figures shown in this catalogue, nor could he be reasonably expected so to do.

CLASSIFYING THE CONDITION OF MODELS AND BOXES

The condition of a model and its accompanying box does of course have a direct bearing on its value which makes accurate condition grading a matter of key importance.

Unlike most other collecting hobbies such as stamps and coins, no one universal grading system is used to classify the condition of models and boxes.

Nevertheless whilst several variants exist there are really two main condition classification systems in operation in the UK as follows:—

1. The 'Specific Condition' Grading System

The following example is fairly typical of the types of descriptions and gradings seen on Mail Order Lists.

M	Mint
AM	Almost Mint
VSC	Very Slightly Chipped
SC	Slightly Chipped
C	Chipped
VC	Very Chipped

If a model is described as Mint Boxed, the condition of its box is not normally separately described. However it is expected to be in a first class and as near original condition as is possible, bearing in mind the age of the model concerned.

If a box is damaged the flaws are usually separately described. This method has always seemed to work out quite well in practice, for all reputable dealers automatically offer a 'sale or return if not satisfied' deal to their clients, which provides the necessary safeguard against the misrepresentation of a model's condition. The compiler would stress that the foregoing is only an example of a mail order condition grading system and stricter box grading definitions are known to exist.

2. The 'General Condition' Grading System

This method is often seen used by auctioneers, although it is seen used on the odd Mail Order Lists as well.

(M)	Mint
(E)	Excellent
(G)	Good
(F)	Fair
(P)	Poor

Usually these gradings are separately applied to describe firstly the condition of the model and secondly the condition of the box.

From our observations and purely for guidance purposes, we would suggest the following descriptions approximately represent the different grades.

a. Model Condition Gradings

1. MINT (M)
The model must be complete and as fresh, new and original in appearance as when first received from the manufacturers.

2. EXCELLENT (E)
The model is almost in mint condition and is only barred from this classification by having a few slight flaws — eg slight paintwork chipping in unimportant areas.

3. GOOD (G)
The model is in a complete and original condition and retains an overall attractive collectable appearance despite having a few chips or rubbed paintwork.

4. FAIR (F)
The model may not be in its original state eg. broken bumper, replacement radiator or windscreen, or have signs of metal fatigue. The paintwork may be faded, well chipped, retouched or repainted. There may be signs of rust. Unless the model is rare it is in a barely collectable condition.

5. POOR (P)
The model may be damaged, incomplete, repainted, metal fatigued, have bad rust on the base plate, or be heavily chipped etc. Unless the model is rare it has little real value to a collector other than as a candidate for a complete restoration or spares.

b. Box Condition Gradings

1. MINT (M)
The box must be complete both inside and out and contain all the original packing materials, manufacturer's leaflets and box labels. It should be as fresh, new and original in appearance as when first received from the manufacturers.

2. EXCELLENT (E)
The box is in almost mint condition but is barred from this classification by just the odd minor blemish eg. there may be slight damage to the display labels caused by bad storage. The original shop price label may have been carelessly removed and caused slight damage. The cover of a bubble pack may be cracked or there may be very slight soiling etc.

3. GOOD (G)
The box is complete both inside and out and retains an overall attractive collectable appearance. Furthermore despite showing a few signs of wear and tear it does not appear 'tired'.

4. FAIR (F)
The box will appear to be 'tired' and show definite signs of wear and tear. It may well be incomplete and not contain the original packing materials or leaflets. In addition it may not display all the exterior identification labels or they may be torn or soiled or it may have a box-end flap missing or be otherwise slightly damaged. In this condition unless the model is particularly rare, it will have only a small effect on a model's value.

5. POOR (P)
The box will show considerable signs of wear and tear. It will almost certainly be badly damaged, incomplete or heavily soiled and being in this condition, unless it is very rare, is of little value to a collector.

MODEL AND BOX VALUATION GUIDELINES

The research has produced the following comparative price information concerning the values of both unboxed models and separate boxes in the various condition classifications.

The guidelines have been based on the 'General Condition' grading system as described in the previous section. The percentage value ranges are designed to reflect the relatively higher values of the rarer models and boxes.

UNBOXED MODEL CLASSIFICATION	% VALUE OF MINT BOXED MODEL
Mint	65%-75%
Excellent	55%-65%
Good	35%-55%
Fair	15%-35%
Poor	0%-15%

BOX CLASSIFICATION	% VALUE OF MINT BOXED MODEL
Mint	15%-25%
Excellent	10%-20%
Good	5%-15%
Fair	5%-10%
Poor	0%- 5%

N.B. The same model may have been issued in two types of box eg. 'Yesteryears'. The model in the earlier box is normally more valuable.

Rare Models and Sets

The exceptions to the foregoing guidelines are in respect of rare models or boxes, or models seldom found in first class condition such as some pre-war Dinkies. In these situations rarity commands a premium and the asking price or the price realised at auction will almost certainly reflect it.

SELLING MODELS TO THE TRADE

The model value figures produced by the Price Grading System always refer to the likely *asking prices* for models.

They have been prepared solely to give collectors an idea of the amount they might reasonably expect to pay for a particular model.

The figures given are *not* intended to represent the value which will be placed on a model when it is offered for sale to a dealer. This is hardly surprising bearing in mind that the dealer is carrying all the expense of offering a collecting service to his customers which costs money to maintain.

Collectors should therefore not be surprised when selling models to the trade to receive offers which may appear somewhat low in comparison with the figures shown in the catalogue.

Dealers are always keen to replenish their stocks with quality items and will, as a result, normally make perfectly fair and reasonable offers for models. Indeed, depending on the particular models offered to them, the actual offer made may well at times exceed the levels indicated in the catalogue which are only *guidelines* and not firm figures.

THE MODEL DESCRIPTION AND ABBREVIATIONS SYSTEM

a. Lettering on Models
All lettering shown in CAPITAL LETTERS and *Italic* indicates the actual lettering on the model itself. It may appear in either the Model Type or Model Features column.

b. Abbreviations
To enable models to be described in as much detail as possible an abbreviation system has been devised and used throughout the catalogue.

Readers will find that many of the abbreviations are common to each manufacturer so that with a little use no difficulty whatsoever will be experienced.

Examples relating to the particular abbreviations in respect of individual manufacturers are shown at the beginning of each chapter.

For the purposes of quick model and rarity recognition the abbreviations have been divided into four sections.

i) The Model Rarity and Price Grading Abbreviations

GV	Guidance Value	
NC	Not Common	For Explanation see
NVE	No Values Estimate	Introduction Section
NVP	No Values Possible	Page 8
MRP	Market Price Range	
NGPP	No Grading Possible at Present	

ii) Colour Abbreviations

BLK	Black
CM	Camouflage
DK	Dark
GRN	Green
KH	Khaki
LT	Light
MRN	Maroon
Met	Metallic
MG	Military Green
MGC	Military Green Camouflage
MLCD	Multicoloured
MS	Many Shades
OC	Other Colours also thought to exist
SIL	Silver
TT	Two tone
TQ	Turquoise
VS	Various Shades
WH	White
YEL	Yellow

iii) Wheel Abbreviations

BGPT	Black or Grey Plastic Tyres
BPT	Black Plastic Tyres
BPW	Black Plastic Wheels
BRT	Black Rubber Tyres
BW	Bogey Wheel
CHS	Coloured Hubs Seen
CHT	Chain Tracks
CISPKW	Cast in Spoke Wheels
CTP	Correct Tyre Pattern
DSPW	Detachable Spare Wheel
DW	Double Wheels
EBD	Exposed Brake Drums
FMW	Front Metal Wheels
GBPW	Grey or Black Plastic Wheels
GMW	Grey Metal Wheels
GPT	Grey Plastic Tyres
GSBPW	Grey Silver or Black Plastic Wheels
GSPW	Grey or Silver Plastic Wheels
HLPW	High Lift Plastic Wheels
JW	Jockey Wheel
LRW	Large Racing Wheels
MGBPW	Metal Wheels or Grey or Black Plastic Wheels
MGPW	Metal Wheels or Grey Plastic Wheels
MGSBPW	Metal Wheels or Grey Silver or Black Plastic Wheels
MPSPKW	Metal or Plastic Spoke Wheels
MRW	Metal Roller Wheel
MSPKW	Metal Spoke Wheels
MSPW	Moulded Spare Wheel
MW	Metal Wheels
PBHW	Plastic Bolt Head Wheels — the number in brackets indicates how many bolts
PRW	Plastic Roller Wheels
PSPKW	Plastic Spoke Wheels — the number in brackets indicates how many spokes
PSWH	Plastic Spoked Wheel Hubs
PT	Plastic Tyres
PTR	Plastic Tracks
PW	Plastic Wheels
PWH	Plastic Wheel Hubs
RT	Rubber Tyres
RTR	Rubber Tracks
RTW	Retractable Wheels
RW	Racing Wheels
RWTS	Rear Wheel Treads on Some
SBPRW	Silver or Black Plastic Roller Wheels
SBPW	Solid Black Plastic Wheels
SBRW	Solid Black Rubber Wheels
SDWT	Straight or Diagonal Wheel Tread
SF	Superfast Wheels
SFMW	Solid Front Metal Wheels
SPKW	Spoke Wheels
SPT	Smooth Plastic Tyres
SPW	Spare Wheel(s)
SPWB	Spare Wheel on Bonnet
SPWBC	Spare Wheel behind Cab
SPWBD	Spare Wheel behind Driver
SPWH	Spare Wheel Housing
SPWR	Spare Wheel on Right
SPWRE	Spare Wheel at Rear
SPWS	Spare Wheel on Some
SPWW	Spare Wheel(s) in Wing
SRMW	Solid Rear Metal Wheel
SSW	Solid Spoke Wheels
SWRW	Solid White Rubber Wheels
SWS	Speedwheels
T	Tyres
TBPT	Treaded Black Plastic Tyres
THW	Thin Wheels
TOW	Take off Wheels
W	Wheel(s)
WDW	Wide Wheels
WHB	Wheel Hub(s)
WT	White Tyres
WWT	White Wall Tyres
WZW	Whizz Wheels

iv) Other Features & Word Abbreviations

A	Aerial
AB	Aveling Barford
AC	Aircraft
AD	Army Driver
ADS	Advertisements
A.E.C.	Not an abbreviation but the name of a vehicle type
AF	Aerofoil
AFO	Air Force
AFT	Adjustable Feet
ALU	Attendant Leans out
AM	Ambulanceman (men)
AN	Animal(s)
AP	Airport
AR	Authentic Radiator
ARB	Anti Roll Bar
ARBB	Anti Roll Bar and Bumpers
ARC	Armoured Car
AS	Adjustable Seats
ASM	Auto Steer Mechanism
ASR	Armstrong Siddeley Radiator
AUTO	Automobile
AV	Articulated Vehicle
AX	Axle
B	Body
BB	Black Base
BC	Black Crosses
BCR	Bedford Carrimore
BCV	Battery Cover
BD	Boiler Door
BEM	Bonnet Emblem
BK	Building Kit
BM	Bumper(s)
BMBP	Bare Metal Base Plate
BMS	Boom(s)
BN	Bonnet
BO	Battery operated
BOCTV	Battery operated Colour TV Set
BOF	Battery operated Features
BOFL	Battery operated Flashing Lights
BOMCA	Battery operated Micro-chip Action
BOWL	Battery operated working Lights
BP	Base Plate
BPCL	Black Plastic Coal Load
BPHS	Base Plate Holes in some models
BPBP	Black Painted Base Plate
BPS	Base Plate Solid
BPSW	Black Plastic Steering Wheel
BR	Bentley Radiator
BRB	Battery on Running Board
BRR	Brass Radiator
BRS	Bristol
BS	Bonnet Strap
BSR	British Salinson Radiator
BT	Boot
BU	Button Upholstery
BUP	Bubble Pack
BX	Boxed
CA	Crimped Axles
CCCH	Criss Cross Chassis
CCR	Cross Cross Radiator
CD	Civilian Driver
CDG	Corgi Dog
CDS	Conductress
CEM(S)	Company Emblem(s)
CF	Competition Finish
CFL	Cab Floor
CH	Chassis
CHEVVY	Chevrolet
CHIP	Chipperfields
CHVR	Combine Harvester
CI	Cast In
CIR	Circle
CL	Carriage Lamps
CMC	Command Centre
CMN	Camouflage Net
CMX	Concrete Mixer
CNP	Canopy
CNT	Container
CNTT	Container Truck
CO	Crane Operates
CP	Chrome Parts
CPC	Clear Plastic Cover
CPL	Cream Plastic Load
CPT	Carpeting
CR	Crane
CRA	Crimped or Rivetted Axles
CRV	Caravan
CRWH	Closed Rear Wheel Housing
CS	Cab Streamliner
CSP	Canopy Supports
CT	Contains
CTP	Collection Times Panel
CTS	Collapsible Tiers
CTW	Clear or Tinted Windows
CV	Convertible
CVB	Conveyor Belt
CW	Clear Windows
CWK	Catwalk
CWS	Celluloid Windscreen
D	Driver
DAT	Detachable Ammunition Trailer
DB	Dashboard
DBD	Destination Boards
DBL	Dozer Blade
DC	Die-cast
DCH	Detailed Chassis
DCFB	Dropping Cap Firing Bombs
DCI	Drive Cast In

DCNT	Detachable Container
DCR	Diecast Radiator
DCS	Decals
DCST	Driver Controlled Steering
DCV	Detachable Canvas
DD	Double Decker
DDB	Detailed Dashboard
DDC	Detachable Driver's Cab
DDR	Drop Down Ramp
DDTB	Drop Down Tailboard
DDTG	Drop Down Tailgate
DE	Detailed Engine
DEX	Detailed Exhaust
DH	Driver's Helmet
DHT	Detachable Hood and Tonneau
DI	Detailed Interior
DIIT	Detailed Interior includes Toilet!
DL	Double Line
DLD	Detachable Ladder
DLG	Detachable Luggage
DLRDD	Double Line Rear Door Design
DMB	Dumper Blade
DMP	Dumper
DPBA	Detailed Propshaft and Back Axle
DPHD	Detachable Plastic Hood
DR	Decal reads
DRAXW	Detachable Rear Axle and Wheels
DRF	Detachable Roof
DRL	Diesel Roller
DRMDW	Detachable Roof Mounted Driving Wheel
DS	Detailed Suspension
DSC	Driving School Car
DSI	Driver Slotted in
DT	Detail
DTA	Detachable
DTC	Detachable Truck Cover
DTH	Detachable Hood
DTR	Dump Truck
E	Engine
EBMS	Elevating Booms
EC	Engine Cover
EE	Exposed Engine
EG	Elevating Gun
EHBL	Equal Horizontal Bonnet Louvres
ELD	Extension Ladders
ELS	Electronic Siren
EM	Emblem(s)
ENR	Early models had no Rivets
EOI	Explodes on Impact
EQ	Equipment
ERE	Exposed Rear Engine
EX	Exhaust
F	Front
F&R	Front and Rear
FAS	Front Axle Swivels
FC	Forward Control
FCS	Filler Caps
FD	Fender(s)
FDR	Female Driver
FE	Fire Engine
FFS	Flat Float with Sides
FFWS	Flat Float without Sides
FHD	Folded Hood
FI	French Issue
fig(s)	figure(s)
FL	Flash
FLL	Flashing Light
FM	Fireman (men)
FMS	Fires Missiles
FN	Funnel(s)
FP	Fire Pump
FR	Front and Rear
FRK	Fires Rockets
FS	Fingertip Steering
FSH	Fires Shells
FT	Flat Truck
FW	Forward
FWL	Flywheel
FWM	Friction Wheel Motion
FWS	Folded Windscreen
FWT	Folding Wing Tips
G	Grille
GDR	Guard Rails
GEN	General
GJ	Golden Jacks — a jacking system
GL	Glass Load
GMS	Guided Missile
GS	Gift Set
H	Hook
HA	Handling Attachment
HB	Hatchback
HBD	Headboard
HBL	Horizontal Bonnet Louvres
HBR	Handbrake
HCLP	Hackney Carriage Licence Plate
HD	Hood
HDS	Hood Supports
HG	Headlight Guard
HH	Hooter Horn(s)
HL	Headlights
HLC	Helicopter
HLF	Hydraulic Lifter
HP	Hand Painted
HPC	High Peaked Canopy
HPS	Hinged Parcel Shelf
HRR	Half Ribbed Roof
HRS	Hinged Rear Shelf
HS	Horse
HSB	Horsebox
HSL	Headlights and Sidelights
HST	Hoist
HTBD	Hinged Tailboard
HVR	Humber Vogue Radiator

INT	Interior
INTER	International
JB	James Bond
K	Kangaroo
KB	Karrier Bantam
KC	Kings Cross
L	Lights
LB	Label
LC	Lead Construction
LD	Ladder
LDB	Lifting Dozer Blade
LFB	Large Front Bumper
LG	Luggage
LM	Lifting Mechanism
LMS	Lifting Mid Section
LOB	Lift Off Body
LORC	Large Open Racing Car
LP	Licence Plate
LPBP	Large Print on Base Plate
LR	Land Rover
LRP	Launching Ramp
LS	Loudspeaker(s)
LSM	Large or Small
LTR	London Transport
LTRL	Loading Trolley
LTS	Letters
LUS	Luminous Seats
LV	Later Version
LWB	Long Wheel Base
MB	Main Body
MBENZ	Mercedes Benz
MC	Motor Cycle
MCA	Micro Chip Action
MCB	Matchbox Collectors Badge included in box
MCBV	Minor Colour and Body Variations exist
MCH	Moulded Chassis
MDG	Mudguard
MECH	Mechanical
MF	Massey Ferguson
MGBN	MG Badge on Nose
MGM	MG Magnette
MH	Mechanical Horse
MIECI	Made in England Cast In
MK	Markings
MLG	Moulded Luggage
MLL	Machinery Low Loader
MNP	Military Number Plate
MOY	Models of Yesteryear
MPSW	Metal or Plastic Steering Wheel
MRER	Mobile Ram Expels Rubbish
MSW	Metal Steering Wheel
MTBP	Moulded Tinplate Base Plate
MTC	Monte Carlo
MTP	Metropolitan
N	Nose
NB	News Board
NCI	Number Cast In
NFB	No Front Bumper
NN	No Number
NP	Number Plates
OBB	Opening Bonnet and Boot
OBN	Opening Bonnet
OBNHB	Opening Bonnet and Hatchback
OBT	Opening Boot
OC	Other Colours also thought to exist
OCATD	Open or Closed Access to Top Deck
OCH	Open Chassis
OCP	Opening Cockpit Cover
OD	Opening Door(s)
ODBB	Opening Door(s), Bonnet and Boot
ODBN	Opening Door(s) and Bonnet
ODBNHB	Opening Door(s), Bonnet and Hatchback
ODBT	Opening Door(s) and Boot
ODHB	Opening Door(s) and Hatchback
ODS	Opening Dicky Seat
ODT	Opening Door(s) and Tailgate
OEC	Opening Engine Cover
OH	Opening Hatch
OHB	Opening Hatchback
OLF	Operating Lifting Forks
OOS	On Off Switch
OPC	One Piece Casting
OPWDS	Open Windows
ORC	Opening Rear Cover
ORD	Opening Rear Door
ORDBN	Opening Rear Door and Bonnet
OREC	Opening Rear Engine Cover
ORF	Opening Roof
ORG	Original Radiator Grille
ORGN	Other Registration Numbers
ORS	Opening Rear Shutter
ORWH	Open Rear Wheel Housing
OTE	Opening Tipper End
OTG	Opening Tailgate
OWD(S)	Opening Window(s)
OWP	Operating Water Pump
OWS	Open Windscreen
P	Plastic
PB	Propellor Blades
PBP	Plastic Base Plate
PC	Petrol Cap
PCH	Plastic Chassis
PCR	Police Crest
PDS	Press Down Start
PFC	Petrol Filler Cap
PH	Plastic Hook
PHD	Plastic Hood
PHT	Plastic Hard Top
PL	Plain
PLD	Plastic Ladder
PLP	Plastic Parts

PLR Plain Radiator
PM Policeman
PMG Plastic Mudguards
PN Painted
PNB Panelled Body
PP Plated Parts
PRB Plastic Running Board
PRL Plastic Roller
PRM Promotional Model
PRR Plastic Replica Radiator
PS Passenger
PSD Plastic Sliding Door
PT Plastic Tracks
PTF Plastic Trailer Fittings
PTK Petrol Tank
PTL Painted Tail Lights
PU Pick-Up
PUS Plastic Upper Section
PV Platform Vehicle

(R) Indicates the rarer colour issued
R Radiator
RA Rivetted Axles
RAHBP Rear Axle held by Base Plate
RAP Rear Axle Pillars
RAR Ribbed at Rear
RAXWR Rear Axle and Wheels Removable
RB Radiator Badge
RBD Ribbed
RBDB Ribbed Bed
RBT Ridged Boot
RC Racing Car
RCL Remote Control
RCD Racing Driver
RC(S) Red Cross(es)
RCTLD Remote Control Telescopic Ladder
RD Rear Door
RDD Rear Door Design
RDLS Roundels
RE Racing or Rally Emblem
REC Rear Engine Cover
RF Roof
RG Rungs
RGT Revolving Gun Turret
RH Roof Hatch
RHD Right Hand Drive
RHL Retractable Headlights
RHT Removable Hard Top
RL Rocket Launcher(s)
RLM Rolomatic
RM Routemaster
RN Racing or Rally number
RNB Running Board
RPR Replica Radiator
RR Roof Rack
RSJ Retractable Support Jacks
RT Route
RTB Rotating Barrel
RTR Rotating Turret
RTT Retractable
RV Reverse
RVD Revolving Drum
RVM Rear View Mirror
RVR Rover Radiator
RWD(S) Rear Window(s)
RWS Rear Window Slats

S Seats
SAA Self Adhesive Accessories
SAPM Same as Previous Model
SB Stake Body
SBL Slanting Bonnet Louvres
SBP Slots in Base Plate
SBMU Separate Bumper Unit
SC Sidecar
SCF Scaffolding
SCS Self Centering Steering
SD Side
SDB Strapped Down Bonnet
SDL Sidelights
SDW Side Windows(s)
SDWT Straight or Diagonal Wheel Tread
SE Shaded Edging
SF Steam Funnel
SGL Single Line
SGLRDD Single Line Rear Door Design
SGW Single Wheels(s)
SH Shells
SHOD Shields on Doors
SL Special Lights eg. jewelled headlights & emergency services roof lights
SLDS Soldiers
SLWS Solid Windscreen
SM Smooth
SMB Smooth Bed
SNP Snowplough
SOD Switch Operated Door
SP Spares
SQM Squadron Markings
SR Steering Rods
SRF Smooth Roof
SS Suspension
SSR Shield Shaped Radiator
SSW Separate Steering Wheel
ST Supertoy
STB Stabilizers
STC Steering Control
STR Stretcher
SW Steering Wheel
SWCI Steering Wheel Cast In
SWOS Steering Wheel Open or Solid
SWV Swivels

T Tyre(s)
TB Towbar
TBD Tailboard
TBDHD Tailboard Hinges Down

TBMS	Turntable Booms
TC	Tonneau Cover
TCB	Tilt Cab
TCC	Tinted Cockpit Cover
TD	Top Deck
TF	Touring Finish
TFN	Tailfin
TK	Not an abbreviation — a Vehicle type
TL	Tail Lights
TN	Tonneau
TOL	Trans-O-Lite — Corgi light ray system to illuminate headlights
TP	Tinplate
TPBP	Tinplate Base Plate
TPR	Tinplate Radiator
TPTR	Transporter
TR	Trim — this can include:— Radiator Shell, Head and Sidelights, Petrol Tank, Battery Cover, Bumpers, Outside Handbrakes and Horns, Spare Wheel Housing and Luggage Racks etc.
TS	Tilt Seats
TSP	Tommy Spot
TU	Trailer Uncouples
TUT	Turntable
TW(S)	Tinted Window(s)
UB	Unboxed
UDC	Undercarriage
UJ(S)	Union Jack(s)
UNP	Unpainted
UPF	Unpainted Plastic Figures
US	United States
USDW	Upper Side Windows
V	Vehicle
VADS	Various Advertisements
VB	Venetian Blinds
VBL	Vertical Bonnet Louvres
VD	Various Decals
VNS	Varying Number of Spokes
VRN	Various Rally Numbers
VW	Volkswagen
W	Wheel
WBL	Working Brake Lights
WCJ	Working Crane Jib
WDS	Windows
WGS	Wings
WH	Wire Hook
WHL	Working Headlights
WHS	White Horses
WM	Wing Mirrors
WO	Winch Operates
WPD	White Plastic Dogs
WPEM	Working Pallet Ejection Mechanism
WRL	Working Rear Lights
WS	Windscreen
WSW	Windscreen Wipers
WTF	Warrior Type Front
WW	With or Without
WWCLW	With or Without Crane Lattice Work
WWPTL	With or Without Painted Tailights
WWS	Wire Windscreen
YPCHBD	Yellow Pages correct on Headboard
YPRHBD	Yellow Pages in reverse on Headboard

SOURCE MATERIAL

Compiler's own collection.
Manufacturers' Issued Listings.
Mail Order Lists from dealers and private individuals in the UK plus some from the USA and Australia.
Information gathered from swapmeets and Toyfairs over a two year period.
Asking Price information from collectors shops and the realised sale prices at auctions both in London and in the provinces.
Pre-war and a post-war Meccano Magazines.
The Golden Jubilee Exhibition of Dinky Toys at the London Toy and Model Museum.
Cecil Gibson's 'History of British Dinky Toys 1934-1964'.
Information and guidance from those listed under the compiler's personal acknowledgements.

NB This catalogue has been prepared solely for use as a reference book and guide to the rarity and asking prices of die-cast model toys.

Whilst every care has been taken in compiling the catalogue, neither the compiler nor the publishers can accept any responsibility whatsoever for any financial loss which may occur as a result of its use.

CHAPTER I — DINKY TOYS

i) INTRODUCTION

Meccano Ltd introduced in 1931 a series of railway station and trackside accessories to accompany their famous 'HORNBY' train sets. These 'Modelled Miniatures' were in sets numbered 1-22 and included railwaymen, station staff, passengers and trains. Set number 22 was comprised of six vehicles which were representative rather than being replicas of actual vehicles. It was first seen advertised in the Meccano Magazine of December 1933.

At about this time 'Tootsie Toys' of America were importing model vehicles into the United Kingdom and they were proving to be very popular. Consequently Meccano Ltd decided to widen their range of products and issue a comprehensive series of models to include vehicles, ships and aircraft.

'Modelled Miniatures' therefore became 'Meccano Dinky Toys' and set number 22 the first set of 'Dinky Cars'. The first 'Dinky Toys' advertisement appeared in the April 1934 edition of the Meccano Magazine. The first actual Dinky car produced after the change of name, was 23a in April 1934. It was probably based on an early MG but was again more representative rather than being an actual replica.

Set 22 cost 4/- and consisted of 22a Sports Car, 22b Sports Coupe, 22c Motor Truck, 22d Delivery Van, 22e Tractor and 22f Tank and is today highly sought after.

The range of models produced quickly grew so that the Meccano Magazine of December 1935 was claiming that there were 200 varieties for sale.

Although the phrase 'Dinky Cars' became a household name, the actual range of models was of course far greater even including dolls house furniture.

Indeed by the time the famous Binns Road, Liverpool factory finally closed its doors in November 1979 over 1000 different designs had been produced, with a similar number emanating from the French factory outside Paris.

Today pre-war models are rare and fetch high prices which reflects how difficult it is to find a model in really good condition. This is because many pre-war models were made from an unstable alloy and have tended to crystallize and disintegrate.

Fortunately the post-war models do not suffer from the same problem and much of todays collecting interest is centred around the superb models produced in the fifties and sixties.

It has been said of Dinky Toys that if you love them you'll buy them. Nothing truer has ever been stated for in the eyes of all Dinky enthusiasts they really do seem to possess a delightful charm all of their own.

TYPICAL MODELS FOUND AT TOYFAIRS

No 261 Post Office Telephones

No 260 Royal Mail Van

No 40h Taxi
(Yellow/green version)

Unusual view of No 936
Leyland 8 wheel chassis

No 454 Trojan Van CYDRAX

No 471 Austin Van NESTLÉS

No 250 Streamlined Fire Engine
(Pre-war version had figures)

Dinky Dublo
No 067 Bedford Taxi
No 068 Royal Mail Van
Dinky Toy Club badge

PACKAGING

Pre-war Box (Blue)

Trade Box (Yellow or Brown)

1947-50 The 1st Supertoy Box
(Brown Cardboard)

The famous Blue
and White Striped Box

Multicoloured and in use 1965-70

1960-66 Yellow Dublo Dinky Box

1971-78 With clear plastic dome
and rather fragile

1977-79 The last type of window box.
Usually Blue/Yellow but all Silver for this special issue.

iii) MODEL IDENTIFICATION

Common Features
There are several common features which apply to the various groups of models and to avoid unnecessary repetition in the 'Features' column these have been shown below.

a Dinky Toys, Meccano Ltd or Meccano Dinky Toys
These wordings are to be found stamped on all post-war models and virtually all pre-war models. They are either on the Base Plate or chassis or in the case of the early models cast into the model itself. On the very early 22 Series Van the words HORNBY SERIES are cast in.

b Wheels
The Types of Wheels
It has been assumed that pre-war models have white tyres and post-war models black tyres unless otherwise described.

eg. MW Metal Wheels
SWRW Solid White Rubber Wheels
SBRW Solid Black Rubber Wheels
PW Plastic Wheels
SWS Speedwheels

c Wheel Hubs
Pre-war wheels have been assumed to have smooth wheel hubs and post-war ridged. This ridge or nave plate is clearly discernable on post-war models. A few of the smooth pre-war variety were issued in 1946, an example of this being 153A Jeep 1st issue.

Similarly it is generally accepted that a few ridged wheels may have been used pre-war.

Nevertheless smooth wheel hubs combined with the other identifying points given in the pre-war section should be sufficient to determine whether it is pre-war or not. One final point on smooth wheels is that if there is evidence of silver-plating on them the model is definitely pre-war.

d Wheel Construction
It is assumed that all wheels were of a die-cast mazuk construction until 1958/59 when a shiny spun metal type was introduced. Models issued in both the old type and new type wheels included 131, 178, 179, 180, 181, 182 and the 290 bus.

The exceptions to the foregoing are the 1st type 28 Series Vans which were of a lead alloy construction.

The die-cast wheels on the 230-235 racing cars were replaced by plastic wheels as were the normal wheels on Model No 183, the Fiat 600. Where they are known to have been fitted this has been indicated by (PW) Plastic Wheels.

e Speedwheels (SWS)
These were issued from the early seventies. Some models were issued with either Metal wheels or Speedwheels with the former being the more collectable.

f Model Number and Name
It has been assumed that all post-war models have either the model number or name or both stamped on the base plate or chassis.

Pre-war models usually had neither although some did eg. the 38 Series and 39 Series had the Model name on the base plate.

g Windscreens (WS)
Assumed to be Plastic unless otherwise described eg. celluloid Windscreen (CWS) Tinplate Windscreen (TPWS) Open or Solid Windscreen (Open/Solid WS) Open Windscreen (OWS) Solid Windscreen (SLWS).

h Base Plate (BP) and Chassis (CH)
All assumed to be of Tinplate or metal construction unless otherwise indicated. eg. PCH Plastic Chassis.

i Construction Materials
All models assumed to be constructed at least in part of a die-cast alloy. A few pre-war models were made of a lead alloy. eg. The 22 Series and 28 Series (Type 1) plus the odd models such as 23a Racing Car (1st casting) and 23m Thunderbolt Speed Car.

j Windows (WDS)
All the first models to have plastic windows fitted have been given the above abbreviation. The later issues have been assumed to have them fitted anyway.

k Axles
Assumed that all pre-war models had crimped axles as did the following post-war issues:— 23, 25, 280, 29, 30, 34, 35, 36, 37, 38, 39 and 40 Series, Otherwise models had rivet ended axles until the advent of Speedwheels.

l Length of Models
The pre-war measurements shown may include slight inaccuracies due to the measurement of models which have expanded in the course of time.

m 'Supertoys' (ST)
These were first introduced in 1947 when six large lorries plus the Shetland Flying Boat were announced. These models are easily identified having DINKY SUPERTOYS on the chassis. The large commercials should also have treaded tyres.

Scale Sizes of Dinky Toys
The original Dinky models were made to an approximate 1/48 scale. In the late sixties and early seventies the 1/43 and 1/36 scale were introduced much to the annoyance of collectors who found the larger size models didn't match up with their existing collection too well!

iv) CLASSIFYING THE EARLY MODEL TYPES

In addition to the details given in the earlier sections, the age and category of a particular model is determined by features such as:—

i) The type of chassis or Base Plate.
ii) The type of Radiator Shell and Bumper.
iii) Body features such as the front of a Lorry, Van or Bus.

These features were first categorised into types by Cecil Gibson in his excellent book 'History of British Dinky Toys 1934-1964' and readers requiring detailed information should obtain a copy from MIKANSUE, 15 Bell Lane, Eton Wick, Windsor, Berks.

A basic understanding of these types is necessary as models described for sale often refer to Cecil Gibson's original 'Type 1' etc gradings.

The following diagrams show details of the differences between the types:—

A. The Chassis Types 1934-1950

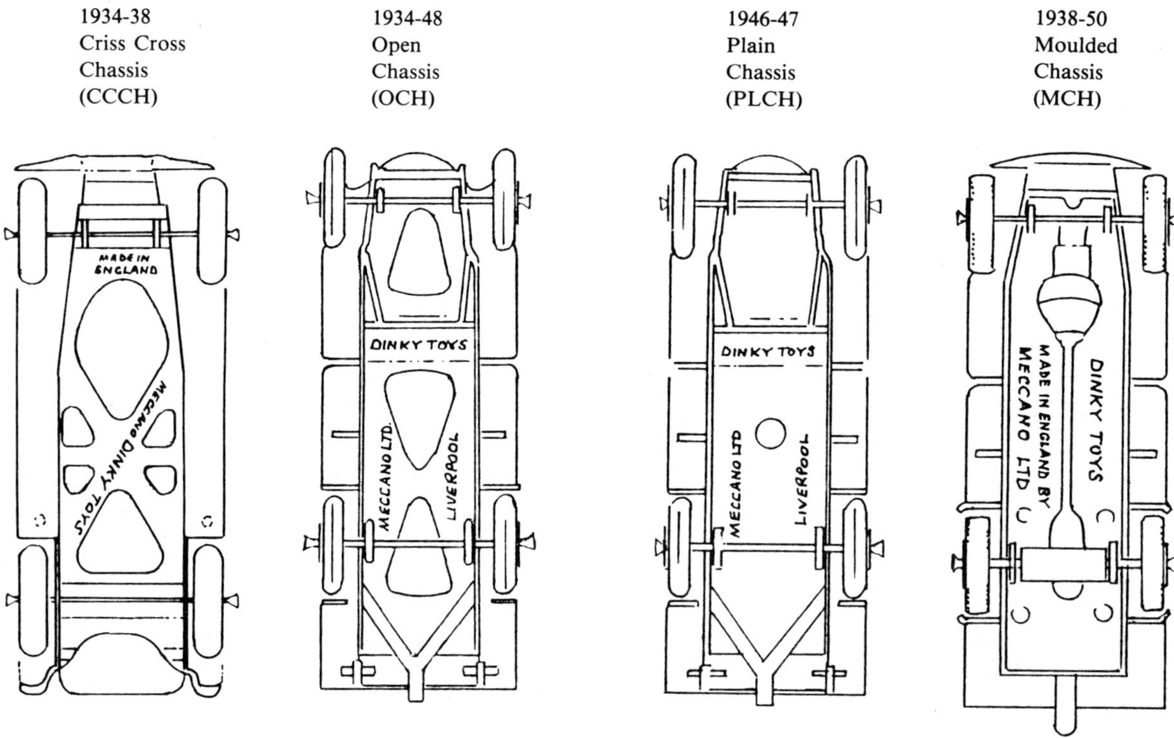

B. The Van Types 1934-1954

28 Series and 280 Series Castings.

1st Type
1934-36

2 Piece Lead Construction
Metal Wheels
Radiator not cast in.
No Headlights.

2nd Type
1936-38

One Piece Construction
Rubber Tyres (White)
Cast in Radiator
Made of Poor Metal
and liable to disintegrate.

3rd Type
1938-54

One Piece Construction
Rubber Tyres
Cast in Radiator
Front Bumper
Made of Poor Metal
and liable to disintegrate

C. The Lorry Types 1934-50

25 Series Commercials

1st Type
1934-1938

2nd Type
1938-1940

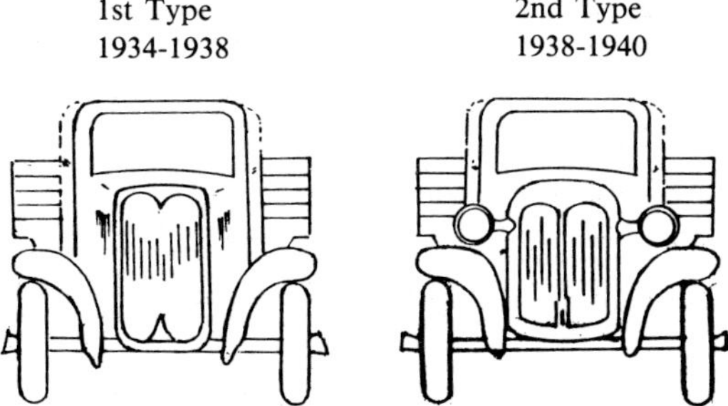

3rd Type
1946-47

4th Type
1947-50

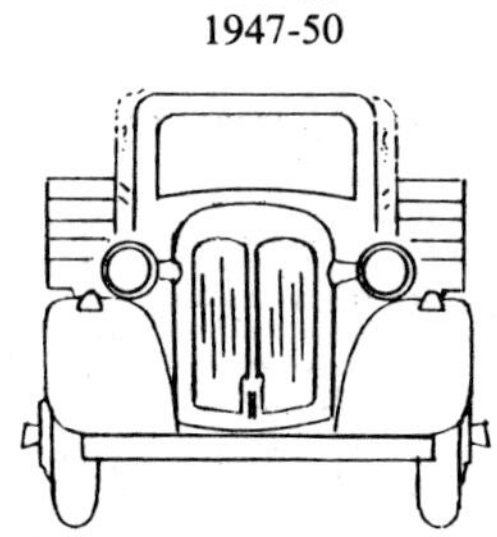

1st Type No Headlights on a tinplate Radiator, Open Chassis.
2nd Type Headlights on a die-cast Radiator, Open Chassis.'

3rd Type This model has the same lorry front as the 2nd Type but has a Plain Chassis.
4th Type Headlights on a die-cast Radiator plus the bumper.

D. The Heavy Commercial Types 1947-60

1st Type
Foden 1947-52

2nd Type
Foden 1952-55

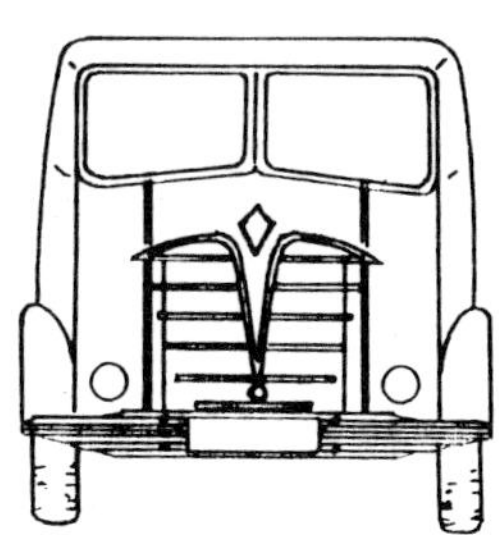

1st Type
Guy 1947-54

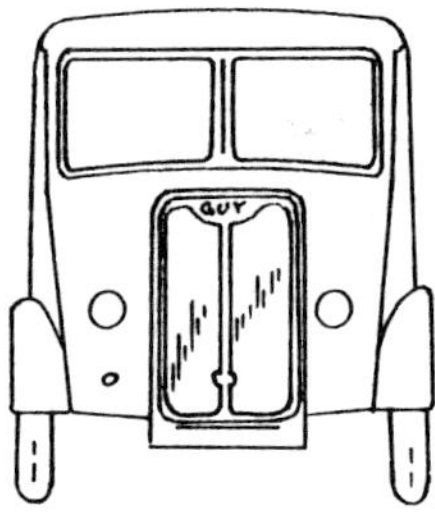

2nd Type
Guy 1954-58

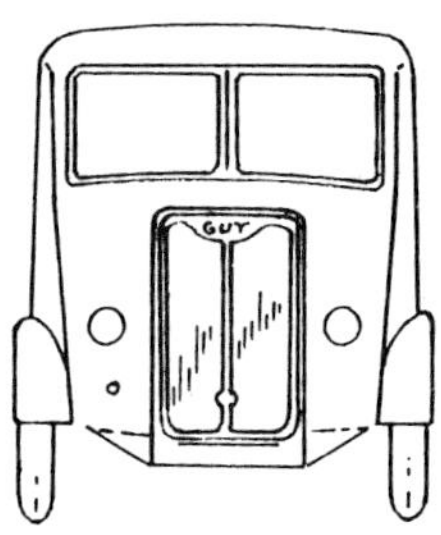

Warrior Type
1959-60

Note the slight difference in the casting around the area of the number plate between the 1st and 2nd Types of Guy Vehicles.

E. The Bus Types 1938-63

1st Type
AEC 1938-50

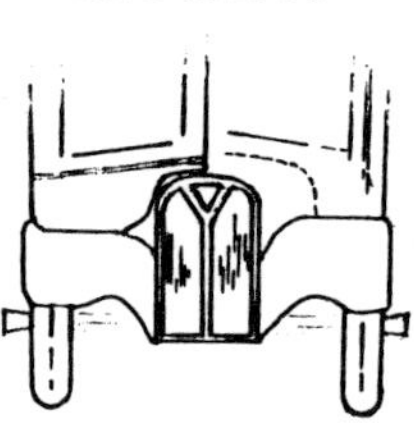

2nd Type
AEC 1950-57

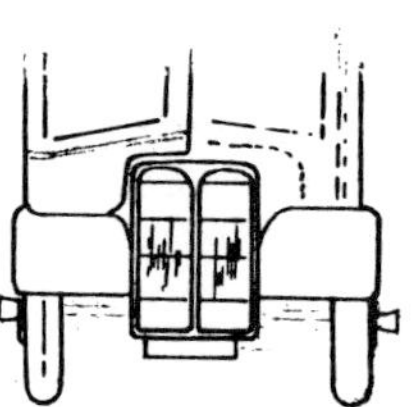

3rd Type
Leyland 1957-63

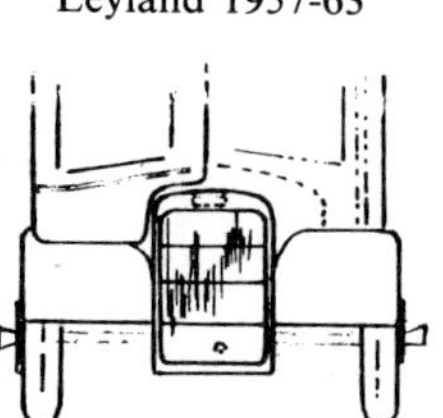

There are three main types although many slight variations in the castings are thought to exist.
Note the 2nd Type AEC is also referred to as a Guy at times.

v) PRE-WAR MODELS IDENTIFICATION FEATURES TO LOOK FOR:—

i) The wheel hubs were smooth and not ridged (see section 2a on wheels).
ii) Axles were crimped.
iii) Look for unpainted bare metal base plates.
iv) Look for early chassis types.
v) Only pre-war models had wing mounted spare wheels.
vi) Whilst tyres can be changed only pre-war models had white tyres.
vii) Slots in the chassis for the driver and passengers indicates that the model is from the pre-war 36 series.
viii) Look for the early van and lorry front types.
ix) Know your facts eg. only the pre-war Double Decker Bus of the 29 Series had stairs on the platform etc.
x) Thinner axles used pre-war eg 22 Series Trucks.

vi) ABBREVIATIONS EXAMPLES OF USE

i) Early Dinky Cars
Model 366 Bentley Two Seater Sports Coupe.
Yellow/Black or Cream/Black body, OC
SBL (3 + 9)/SBP/SDL/MCH/BR/1SDW/S

Non Abbreviated Form
Yellow and Black or Cream and Black body, other colours also thought to exist. Slanting bonnet louvres (group of three, plus a group of nine), Slots in Base Plate, Sidelights, Moulded Chassis, Bentley Radiator, one sidewindow, seats.

ii) Aeroplanes
The number of engines and the type of propellers each model has is described as follows:—
eg. 60a Imperial Airways Liner 4 × 2PB (PB — Propeller Blades). This means that the aircraft has four engines each of which has a propeller with two blades.

NB. Model Numbers Reference System
Because of the Dinky habit of renumbering their models when they were re-issued some models have two or three numbers shown.

1a Dinky Cars

Ref. No.		Model Type	Model Features and Size	Rarity and Price Grading	
Note. For a description and diagrams of the different Chassis Types see Section IV					
22a	1933-35	Sports Car	Orange/Cream body, Tinplate Radiator, Metal Wheels, No headlights. 82 mm.	£400	GV ☐
22b	1933-35	Sports Coupe	Cream body, Red roof and wings, gold metal wheels, TPR with No Headlights or Yellow/Green body. An identical model to this realised £480 on 28th July 82 Auction held by Phillips, New Bond St, London. 85 mm.	£400	GV ☐
22g	1935-40	Streamline tourer	Cream, Gold or Red body SSW and WS. 85 mm.	£125	NVE ☐
22h	1935-40	Streamlined Saloon	Red, Blue or Cream body, OPC. 85 mm.	£125	NVE ☐
23a	1934-35	Racing Car	Orange and Green body, No driver 4EX. 94 mm.	£100	NVE ☐
23a	1935-38	Racing Car	Blue and White body, driver, 6EX/RRD/RN. 94 mm.	£65	NVE ☐
23a	1938-40	Racing Car	Red body, Cream flash, D/6EX/RN. 94mm.	£55	GV ☐
23a	1946-48	Racing Car	Blue body, Silver flash DCI/No RN. 94 mm.	£40	NC ☐
23a	1949-52	Racing Car	Red body, Silver flash, Black circles RN '4' Driver cast in. 94 mm.	£18	NC ☐
23a	1953-54	Racing Car	Silver body, Red flash, Red circles RN '4', Driver cast in. 94 mm.	£15-£18	MPR ☐
23b	1935-40	Hotchkiss Racing Car	Blue body, white flash RN '5', OC. 100 mm.	£35	GV ☐
23b	1946-48	Hotchkiss Racing Car	Red or Silver body, Red RN '5'. 96 mm.	£19	NC ☐
23c	1936-40	Mercedes-Benz Racing Car	Red or Blue body, Yellow circle, RN '2' MTB/DCI/ENR. 92 mm.	£65	GV ☐
23c	1947-50	Mercedes-Benz RC 'Large Open Racing Car'	Blue or Silver body, RN/MTB/DCI. 92 mm.	£19	NC ☐
23d	1936-40	Auto Union Racing Car	Red or Blue body, White or Yellow Circles, RN, DSI/ENR. 100 mm.	£30	GV ☐
23d	1947-50	Auto Union Racing Car	Silver body, Red RN '2', No D/MTPBP. 100 mm.	£19	NC ☐
23e	1936-40	'Speed of the Wind' Racing Car	Blue, Red or Yellow body RN '1', ENR/MTB/DCI. 104 mm.	£45	GV ☐
23e	1946-49	'Speed of the Wind' RC	Red (R) or Silver body MTB/DCI. 104 mm.	£19	NC ☐
23e (221)	1950-54	'Speed of the Wind' RC	Silver body, Plain base plate, DCI. 104 mm.	£15-£19	MPR ☐
23f (232).	1952-54	Alfa-Romeo Racing Car	Red body, White RN '8' on tail, D/SWCI. 100 mm.	£18-£23	MPR ☐
23g (233)	1952-54	Cooper Bristol Racing Car	Green body, White RN '6' on tail, D/SWCI. 89 mm.	£18-£23	MPR ☐
23h (234)	1953-54	Ferrari Racing Car	Blue body, Yellow nose & RN '5' on tail Driver and steering wheel cast in. 100 mm.	£18-£23	MPR ☐
23j (235)	1953-54	H.W.M. Racing Car	Green body, Yellow RN '7' on tail Driver and steering wheel cast in. 99 mm.	£18-£23	MPR ☐
23k (230)	1953-54	Talbot-Lago Racing Car	Blue body, Yellow RN '4' on tail Driver and steering wheel cast in. 103 mm.	£18-£23	MPR ☐
23m	1938-40	Thunderbolt Speed Car	Light or Dark Green body, Union Jacks on tailfin, DCI/LC/Boxed. 126 mm.	£65	NVE ☐
23n (231)	1953-54	Maserati Racing Car	Red body, White flash, White RN '9' on tailfin, Driver and SW cast in. 94 mm.	£18-£23	MPR ☐
23p	1939-40	Gardners MG Record Car	Green body, White flash, *MG Magnette* and UJS on sides, MG badge on nose DCI. 104 mm.	£55	GV ☐
23p	1939-40	Gardners MG Record Car	SAPM but TPBP made from old Hornby carriages and overprinted by Dinky. Author has only seen one. 104 mm.	£75	GV ☐
23S	1938-40	Streamlined Racing Car	Silver body, DCI, Lead versions exist. 126 mm.	£30	GV ☐
23S (232)	1948-54	Streamlined Racing Car	Blue, Green or Silver body Green or Blue flashes. 128 mm.	£17-£24	MPR ☐
24a		See Ambulances			
24b	1934-38	Limousine	Maroon/Black or Maroon/ Grey body, OC/SPWW/3SDW/CCCH/Plain R/3HBL/ No SDL. 98 mm.	£145	GV ☐
24b	1938-40	Limousine	Blue body, yellow chassis, No SPW, OC, 3 SDW/CCCH/R badge/3 HBL/No SDL. 98 mm.	£120	GV ☐

Ref. No.		Model Type	Dinky Cars continued	Rarity and Price Grading	
24c	1934-38	Town Sedan	Blue or Cream Blue body, SPWW/1 SDW OC/Plain R/ CCCH/VBL/No SDL. 97 mm.	£140	GV ☐
24c	1938-40	Town Sedan	Blue or Red/Black body No SPW/1 SDW/OC/R Badge/ CCCH/VBL/No SDL. 97 mm.	£110	GV ☐
24d	1934-38	Vogue Saloon	Two tone Green or Green/Black body, OC/SPWW/ 1 SDW/CCCH/Plain R/VBL/No SDL. 107 mm.	£140	GV ☐
24d	1938-40	Vogue Saloon	Red/Grey or Brown/Green body OC/No SPW/1 SDW/ R badge/VBL/No SDL/CCCH. 107 mm.	£110	GV ☐
24e	1934-38	Super Streamlined Saloon	Two tone Red or Green/Red body, OC/No SPW/ 1 SDW/CCCH/Plain R/VBL/No SDL. 97 mm.	£140	GV ☐
24e	1938-40	Super Streamlined Saloon	Red/Black or Green Blue body, OC/No SPW/1 SDW/ CCCH/R Badge/VBL/No SDL. 97 mm.	£110	GV ☐
24f	1934-38	Sportsmans Coupe	White/Blue or Blue/Yellow body, OC/SPWW/1 SDW/ CCCH/Plain R/VBL/No SDL. At Phillips Auction on June 1st 1983 a similar model fetched £180. 100 mm.	£140	GV ☐
24f	1938-40	Sportsmans Coupe	Two tone Brown or Two tone Blue body 1 SDW/ No SPW/R badge/CCCH/VBL/No SDL. 100 mm.	£110	GV ☐
24g	1934-38	Sports Tourer 4 Seater	Yellow/Brown or Blue/Brown body, OC/SPWR/ Plain R/CCCH/OWS/VBL/No SDL. 104 mm.	£140	GV ☐
24g	1938-40	Sports Tourer 4 Seater	Black/Cream or Yellow/Blue body, OC/No SPW/ R badge/CCCH/SLWS/VBL/No SDL. 104 mm.	£110	GV ☐
24h	1934-38	Sports Tourer 2 Seater	Two tone Red or Two tone Green body, OC/SPWR/ Plain R/CCCH/OWS/VBL/No SDL. 98 mm.	£140	GV ☐
24h	1938-40	Sports Tourer 2 Seater	Black/Cream or Cream/Green body, OC/No SPW/ R badge/CCCH/SLWS/VBL/No SDL. 98 mm.	£110	GV ☐
			NB. The rarest models of the 24 Series have coloured tyres to match their body paintwork and can be expected to value higher.		
25j	1947-48	Jeep	Red or Green body LHD/SW/TPWS/SPWR Some issued with smooth pre-war hubs. 68 mm.	£23-28	MPR ☐
25y	1952-54	Jeep	Red body, LHD/SW/TPWS/H/SPW on side. 83 mm.	£15-£19	MPR ☐
27d (340)	1950-54	Land Rover	Green/Orange body, D/SW/TPWS/SPW BD. 90 mm.	£14-£17	MPR ☐
27d (344)	1950-56	Estate Car	Brown/Fawn body, Rear axle pillars. 105 mm.	£14-£17	MPR ☐
30a (32)	1935-40	Chrysler 'Airflow' Saloon	Blue or Green body, No chassis 3 side windows, separate Bumper unit. 103 mm	£135	NVE ☐
30a	1946-48	Chrysler 'Airflow' Saloon	Blue, Cream or Green body, No chassis 3 side windows, separate Bumper unit. 103 mm.	£75	GV ☐
30b	1935-40	Rolls Royce	Grey body or Dark Blue body, OC/2 SDW/SBL/ Open CH/No SDL. 101 mm.	£130	GV ☐
30b	1946-50	Rolls Royce	Blue/Black or Fawn/Black body, OC/2 SDW/SBL/ Open or Plain CH/No SDL. 101 mm.	£34	NC ☐
30c	1935-40	Daimler	Fawn or Light Blue body OC/2 SDW/Open CH/ No SDL. 98 mm.	£130	GV ☐
30c	1946-50	Daimler	Green/Black or Cream/Black body, OC/2 SDW/ Open or Plain CH/No SDL. 98 mm.	£32	NC ☐
30d	1935-38	Vauxhall	Brown or Green body, OC/SPWW/CCR/Open CH/ HBL/3 SDW/No SDL. 102 mm.	£145	GV ☐
30d	1937-38	Vauxhall	Cream/Brown or Blue/Black body, OC/No SPWW/ CCR/Open CH/HBL/3 SDW/No SDL. 102 mm.	£135	NVE ☐
30d	1938-40	Vauxhall	Maroon/Black or Yellow/Black body, OC/SPWW/SSR/ Open CH/HBL/3 SDW/No SDL. 100 mm.	£120	GV ☐
30d	1946-48	Vauxhall	Brown/Black or GRN/BLK body, OC/3 SDW/No SPW/ SSR/Open or Plain CH/HBL/No SDL. 98 mm.	£32	NC ☐
32 (30a)	1935	Chrysler 'Airflow' Saloon	See 30a for details. 103 mm.		MPR ☐
35a	1946-48	Saloon Car	Two tone blue or TT grey body, SBRW. 51 mm.	£30-£40	MPR ☐
35b	1936-39	Racer	Red body, Silver grille, No driver SWRW or SBRW. 61 mm.	£20	GV ☐
35b (200)	1939-40	Racer	Silver body, Brown D, Red grille, SBRW. 59 mm.	£20	GV ☐

Ref. No.		Model Type	Dinky Cars continued	Rarity and Price Grading	
35c	1936-40	MG Sports Car	Red, Green or Blue body, Silver Radiator, SWRW/SPW/WS/SW. 52 mm.	£45	NVE ☐
35c	1946-48	MG Sports Car	Red or Green body, Silver R, SBRW. 52 mm.	£40	NC ☐
35d	1938-40	Austin 7 Tourer	Blue, Green or Yellow body, Silver grille, SWRW/WWS/SW. 50 mm.	£30	NC ☐
35d	1946-48	Austin 7 Tourer	Fawn or Grey body, SBRW/No WS. 50 mm.	£20-£25	MPR ☐
36a	1937-40	Armstrong-Siddeley	Blue or Brown/Black body, 3 SDW/ASR/MCH/SDL/VBL (3×4)/SBP. 97 mm.		
			With driver and footman	£140	NVE ☐
			Without	£55-£65	MPR ☐
36a	1946-48	Armstrong-Siddeley	Blue, Green, Grey or Maroon/Black body, 3 SDW/ASR/VBL (3×4)/ No figures. 97 mm.	£32-£39	MPR ☐
36b	1937-40	Bentley Two seater Sports Coupe	Green/Black or Cream/Black body, OC/SBL (3+9)/SBP/SDL/MCH/BR/1 SDW/S. 100 mm.		
			With driver and passenger	£140	NVE ☐
			Without	£65	NC ☐
36b	1946-48	Bentley Two seater Sports Coupe	Green, Grey or Cream body, OC/1 SDW/SBL (3+9)/SDL/MCH/BR No figures. 93 mm.	£32-£39	MPR ☐
36c	1937-40	Humber Vogue	Grey/Black or TT Green body, OC/1 SDW/SDL/MCH/HVR/5 SBL. 100 mm.		
			With driver and footman	£150	NVE ☐
			Without	£65	NC ☐
36c	1946-48	Humber Vogue	Grey/Black or Green/Black body OC/1 SDW/SDL/HVR/5 SBL/No figures. 97 mm.	£32-£39	MPR ☐
36d	1937-40	Rover Streamlined Saloon	Two tone Red or Green/Black body, 2 SDW/SDL/RVR/MCH/12 SBL. 99 mm.		
			With driver and passenger	£150	NVE ☐
			Without	£65	NC ☐
36d	1946-48	Rover Saloon	Blue or Green body, black chassis, 2 SDW/SDL/MCH/RVR/12 SBL/ No figures. 94 mm.	£32	NC ☐
36e	1937-40	British Salmson (2 seater Sports)	Red/Black or Blue Black body, OC/SPWRS/MCH/BSR/13 VBL/SDL/SLWS. 98 mm.		
			With driver	£150	NVE ☐
			Without	£65	NC ☐
36e	1946-48	British Salmson (2 seater Sports)	Red or Blue body, Black chassis, OC/MCH/13 VBL/No SPW/SDL/BSR/No D/SLWS. 93 mm.	£35-£45	MPR ☐
36f	1938-40	British Salmson (4 seater Sports)	Red/Brown or Two Tone Green body, 13 VBL/SDL/MCH/No SPW/BSR/SLWS. 98 mm.		
			With driver	£150	NVE ☐
			Without	£65	NC ☐
36f	1946-48	British Salmson (4 seater Sports)	Green or Grey body, Black chassis, 13 VBL/SDL/MCH/SWCI/BSR/No D/SLWS. 96 mm.	£35	NC ☐
38a	1940	Fraser Nash (B.M.W.) Sports Car	Blue or Light Grey body, Blue or Fawn seats, Silver Trim, CWS/BMBP. 82 mm.	£65	NC ☐
38a	1946-49	Fraser Nash (B.M.W.) Sports Car	Blue or Green body, Matt Black or Khaki seats, SWOS/BPBP. 82 mm.	£29	NC ☐
38b	1940	Sunbeam Talbot Sports	Green/Brown body CWS/BMBP/OC. 92 mm.	£65	GV ☐
38b	1946-49	Sunbeam Talbot Sports	Blue or Green body, Matt Blue or Maroon tonneau cover SWOS/BPBP. 92 mm.	£28	NC ☐
38c	1946-50	Lagonda Sports Coupe	Green or Grey body, Matt Black or Grey seats, SWOS/BPBP. 102 mm.	£28	NC ☐
38d	1940	Alvis Sports Tourer	Green body, Brown seats and hood, OC/SW/BMBP/CWS. 95 mm.	£65	NC ☐
38d	1946-49	Alvis Sports Tourer	Blue/Grey body OC/SWOS/BPBP. 95 mm.	£32	NC ☐
38e	1946-49	Armstrong Siddeley Coupe	Cream or Light Grey body, Blue seats, SW/BPBP/WS. 96 mm.	£32	NC ☐
38f	1940-46	Jaguar Sports Car	Khaki/Blue body, 2WS/BMBP. 80 mm.	£65	GV ☐
38f	1946-49	Jaguar Sports Car	Red or Blue body, 2 WS/BPBP/OC. 80 mm.	£32	NC ☐
39a	1940-41	Packard Super 8 Tourer	Brown or Grey body, Silver Trim, Moulded Spare Wheel, OC/BMBP. 107 mm.	£80	GV ☐
39a	1946-50	Packard Super 8 Tourer	Brown or Green body, Silver Trim, Moulded Spare Wheel, OC/BPBP. 107 mm.	£35	NC ☐

Ref. No.		Model Type	**Dinky Cars continued**	Rarity and Price Grading		
39b	1940-41	Oldsmobile 6	Blue or Green body, Silver Trim Bare Metal Base Plate OC. 100 mm.	£80	GV	☐
39b	1946-50	Oldsmobile 6	Blue, Green or Brown body, Silver Trim OC/BPBP. 100 mm.	£35	NC	☐
39bv	1950-54	Oldsmobile Sedan US Issue	Two tone Blue or Two tone Sand body, BPBP. 100 mm.	£35	GV	☐
39c	1940-41	Lincoln Zephyr	Grey, Brown or Cream body Silver Trim, OC/BMBP. 106 mm.	£80	GV	☐
39c	1946-50	Lincoln Zephyr	Grey or Brown body, Black chassis, black painted base plate OC. 106 mm.	£35	NC	☐
39cu	1950-54	Lincoln Zephyr US Issue	Two tone Red or Two tone Tan body, Black painted base plate. 106 mm.	£37	NC	☐
39d	1940-41	Buick Viceroy	Grey or Maroon body, Silver trim, OC/BMBP/MSPW. 103 mm.	£80	GV	☐
39d	1946-49	Buick Viceroy	Brown, Green or Maroon body, Silver trim, OC/BPBP/ MSPW. 103 mm.	£37	NC	☐
39e	1940-41	Chrysler Royal	Yellow or Green body, Silver trim, OC/BMBP/MSPW. 106 mm.	£80	GV	☐
39e	1946-49	Chrysler Royal	Blue or Cream body, Silver trim, OC/BPBP. 106 mm.	£37	NC	☐
39ev	1950-54	Chrysler Royal US Issue	Yellow/Red on Two tone Green body, Black painted base plate. 106 mm.	£37	NC	☐
39f	1940-41	Studebaker State Commander	Green or Dark Grey body, Silver trim, OC/BMBP. 103 mm.	£80	GV	☐
39f	1946-49	Studebaker State Commander	Brown or Green body, Silver Trim, OC/BPBP. 103 mm.	£37	NC	☐
40a	1947-55	Riley Saloon	Blue, Cream, Green or Grey body, BPBP/SPEV. 93 mm.	£19-£23	MPR	☐
40b	1948-49	Triumph 1800	Blue, Fawn or Grey body, RAP. 91 mm.	£22-£27	MPR	☐
40b (151)	1949-55	Triumph 1800	Blue, Fawn or Grey body, RAHBP. 91 mm.	£22-£27	MPR	☐
40d (152)	1949-54	Austin Devon	Blue Green/Black or Maroon body. 85 mm.	£19-£23	MPR	☐
40e	1948-50	Standard Vanguard	Brown or Maroon body, SPBP/ORWH. 91 mm.	£24	NC	☐
40e (153)	1950-55	Standard Vanguard	Fawn or Maroon body, SPBP/CRWH. 91 mm.	£22-£27	MPR	☐
40f (154)	1951-55	Hillman Minx	Lt or Dk Green or Lt or Dk Brown. 88 mm.	£22-£27	MPR	☐
40g (159)	1950-55	Morris Oxford	Green or Grey/Fawn body. 93 mm.	£19-£23	MPR	☐
40j (161)	1949-55	Austin Somerset	Blue, Red or Blue/Maroon body. 89 mm.	£19-£23	MPR	☐
101	1957-60	Sunbeam Alpine (TF)	Blue or Pink body, CD/SW/W/No RN. 94 mm.	£24	NC	☐
102	1957-60	MG Midget (TF)	Yellow or Green body, CD/SW/WS/No RN. 83 mm.	£24	NC	☐
103	1957-60	Austin Healey 100 (TF)	Red or Cream body, CD/SW/WS/No RN. 87 mm.	£24	NC	☐
104	1957-60	Aston Martin (TF)	Blue or Pink body, CD/SW/No RN. 87 mm.	£22	NC	☐
105	1957-60	Triumph TR2 SC (TF)	Yellow or Grey body, CD/SW/WS/No RN. 84 mm.	£22	NC	☐
106	1954-58	Austin A90 Atlantic	Blue or Pink body WS/SW. 95 mm.	£20	NC	☐
107	1955-59	Sunbeam Alpine (CF)	Blue body, RN '26', or Pink body RN '34', RCD/SW/ WS. 94 mm.	£22	NC	☐
108	1955-59	MG Midget (CF)	Red body, RN '24', or White body RN '28', RCD/SW/WS. 83 mm.	£22	NC	☐
109	1955-59	Austin Healey 100 (CF)	Cream body, RN '23', or Yellow body RN '21', RCD/ SW/WS. 85 mm.	£22	NC	☐
110	1966-70	Aston Martin DB5	Red/Black body, SS/SW/TS/OBN/WS. 111 mm.	£9-£12	MPR	☐
111	1956-59	Triumph TR2 (CF)	Pink body, RN '29', or Turquoise body RN '25', RCD/ SW/WS. 84 mm.	£24	NC	☐
112	1961-66	Austin Healey Sprite II	Red body, SS/SW/WS/FS/S. 78 mm.	£16	GV	☐
113	1962-68	M.G.B.	Cream body, CD/SW/SS/FS/WS/OD. 85 mm.	£16-£19	MPR	☐
114	1963-71	Triumph Spitfire	Gold, Red, Grey or Purple body Lady driver SS/OD/ WS/S/SW/SPKW. 88 mm.	£11-£14	MPR	☐
115	1967-68	Plymouth Fury Sports	Silver body D/PS/SW/SS/FS/SL/WS. 122 mm.	£9-£12	MPR	☐
116	1966-71	Volvo 1800 S	Red body, SS/TS/FS/SL/ODBB. 105 mm.	£8-£11	MPR	☐
120	1962-67	Jaguar 'E' Type	Red or Blue body, Black roof DHT. 91 mm.	£13-£16	MPR	☐
122	1977-79	Volvo 265 DL Estate	Blue body SS/ORD/PW. 141 mm.	£3-£5	MPR	☐
123	1977-79	Princess 2200 HL	Bronze or White body, Black roof SS/PW. 128 mm.	£3-£5	MPR	☐

Ref. No.		Model Type	**Dinky Cars continued**	Rarity and Price Grading	
124	1977-79	Rolls Royce Phantom V	Met Light Blue body, SS/OD/PW/OBT/D. 141 mm.	£4-£6	MPR ☐
127	1964-66	Rolls Royce Silver Cloud Mk 3	Gold body, SS/FS/SL/TS/WDS/ODBN. 125 mm.	£13-£16	MPR ☐
128	1964-73	Mercedes Benz 600	Met Red body, D/LHD/SS/ODBB/LG/FS. 147 mm.	£12-£15	MPR ☐
128	1974-79	Mercedes Benz 600	Met Blue body, SW/SS/ODBB/PW. 147 mm.	£5-£7	MPR ☐
129	1968-74	1300 Volkswagen Sedan	Blue body, SS/FS/SL/OWDS/ODBB. 100 mm.	£8-£10	MPR ☐
130	1963-68	Ford Consul Corsair	Red body, OC/SS/FS/SL/OWDS/OBN. 108 mm.	£10-£13	MPR ☐
131	1956-62	Cadillac Eldorado	Pink body, OC/D/LHD/SW/WS/OBT/SPKW. 118 mm.	£14-£17	MPR ☐
132	1968-74	Jaguar 'E' Type 2+2	Met Red, Blue or Bronze body, OC/TS/SS/ODBB/SPKW. 112 mm.	£12-£15	MPR ☐
			Speedwheels version	£8-£11	MPR ☐
132	1955-60	Packard Convertible	Fawn or Green body, D/LHD/WS. 114 mm.	£15-£18	MPR ☐
132	1967-71	Ford 40 RV	Blue or White body, SL/SPKW/OBT. 100 mm.	£8-£10	MPR ☐
133	1955-60	Cunningham C5R	White/Blue body, D/LHD/SW/WS. 99 mm.	£16-£19	MPR ☐
133	1964-68	Ford Cortina	Met Yellow, SS/FS/SL/OD/WDS. 102 mm.	£10-£13	MPR ☐
134	1964-67	Triumph Vitesse	Met Green or Met Blue body SS/WDS/SW. 87 mm.	£14-£17	MPR ☐
135	1963-68	Triumph 2000	Blue/White body, OC/SS/FS/OD/LG/WDS. 107 mm.	£13-£16	MPR ☐
136	1964-72	Vauxhall Viva	Blue or White body, SS/FS/OD/WDS. 94 mm.	£8-£11	MPR ☐
137	1963-65	Plymouth Fury CV	Met Grey body, OC/LHD/SS/FS/SW/WS/OBN. 122 mm.	£11-£15	MPR ☐
138	1963-72	Hillman Imp	Met Green or Blue body, SS/SL/ODBT/LG. 86 mm.	£6-£9	MPR ☐
139 (170)	1949-54	Ford Fordor Sedan	Red or Brown body. 102 mm.	£16-£21	MPR ☐
139 (171)	1950-54	Hudson Commodore	Maroon/Fawn or Fawn Blue body. 111 mm.	£16-£21	MPR ☐
139	1963-64	Ford Cortina	Met Blue body SS/FS/OD/WDS. 102 mm.	£13-£16	MPR ☐
140	1963-68	Morris 1100	Blue body SS/OBT/WDS/FS. 87 mm.	£9-£12	MPR ☐
141	1963-67	Vauxhall Victor EC	Yellow body SS/FS/ORD/WDS. 92 mm.	£8-£12	MPR ☐
142	1962-68	Jaguar Mark 10	Met Blue body SS/FS/OD/WDS. 106 mm.	£11-£14	MPR ☐
143	1962-66	Ford Capri	Green/White body SS/FS/WDS/LG. 90 mm.	£9-£12	MPR ☐
144	1963-66	Volkswagen 1500	White body, SS/FS/OBN/WDS/LG. 88 mm.	£8-£11	MPR ☐
145	1962-66	Singer Vogue	Met Green body SS/FS/WDS. 93 mm.	£11-£15	MPR ☐
146	1963-66	Daimler 2½ litre V8	Met Green body SS/FS/WDS. 95 mm.	£18-£22	MPR ☐
147	1962-68	Cadillac 62	Met Green body LHD/SS/FS/WDS. 113 mm.	£12-£15	MPR ☐
148	1962-65	Ford Fairlane	Met Green body LHD/SS/FS/WDS. 111 mm.	£10-£12	MPR ☐
149	1971-74	Citroen Dyane	Gold/Black body LHD/SS/ORDBT/WDS/SWS. 91 mm.	£5-£7	MPR ☐
150	1959-66	Rolls R Silver Wraith	Grey/Dark Grey body SS/WDS/CP. 117 mm.	£17-£21	MPR ☐
151 (40b)	1954-60	Triumph 1800	Blue or Brown body. 91 mm.	£17-£22	MPR ☐
151	1966-68	Vauxhall Victor 101	Yellow or Red body, OC/SS/FS/SL/OBB. 105 mm.	£9-£12	MPR ☐
152	1967-75	Rolls Royce Phantom V	Dark Blue body D/SS/SC/ODBB/WDS. 141 mm.	£8-£11	MPR ☐
			Later Metallic Blue version	£5-£7	MPR ☐
152 (40d)	1954-56	Austin Devon	Maroon or Blue body	£18-£22	MPR ☐
152	1956-60	Austin Devon	Blue/Yellow or Grey/Cerise body. 86 mm.	£15-£18	MPR ☐
153 (40e)	1954-60	Standard Vanguard	Blue, Cream or Fawn body, LPBP/RBT. 91 mm.	£17-£23	MPR ☐
153	1966-71	Aston Martin DB6	Blue or Green body, SS/FS/SL/TS/ODBB. 111 mm.	£8-£11	MPR ☐
154 (40f)	1954-56	Hillman Minx	Green or Brown body. 87 mm.	£16-£21	MPR ☐
154	1956-58	Hillman Minx	Green/Yellow or Cerise/Blue body. 87 mm.	£14-£19	MPR ☐
154	1966-68	Ford Taunus	Yellow/White body, LHD/SS/FS/TS/WDS. 110 mm.	£7-£10	MPR ☐
155	1961-64	Ford Anglia	Blue body, SS/WDS. 81 mm.	£9-£13	MPR ☐
156 (140b)	1954-56	Rover 75	Cream body. 101 mm.	£20-24	MPR ☐
156	1956-60	Rover 75	Blue/Cream or Two tone Green body. 101 mm.	£19-£24	MPR ☐
156	1968-70	Saab 96	Red body SS/TS/OD. 98 mm.	£7-£9	MPR ☐
157	1954-56	Jaguar XK120	Green, White or Yellow body. 97 mm.	£21-£26	MPR ☐
157	1956-62	Jaguar XK120	Red or Green body or Cerise/Yellow or Grey/Yellow body. 97 mm.	£18-£23	MPR ☐
157	1968-71	BMW 2000 Tilux	Blue/White body SS/SL/WDS. '1st AGAIN! FLASHING INDICATORS'. 121 mm.	£7-£11	MPR ☐
158	1954-60	Riley Saloon	Blue or Cream body LPBP. 93 mm.	£19-£24	MPR ☐

Ref. No.		Model Type	Dinky Cars continued	Rarity and Price Grading		
158	1967-72	Rolls Royce Silver Shadow	Met Red body SS/ODBB/WDS. '1st AGAIN! 4 OPENING DOORS'. 125 mm.	£9-£12	MPR	☐
			Later Met Blue version	£5-£7	MPR	☐
159 (40g)	1954-56	Morris Oxford	Fawn or Green body. 93 mm.	£19-£24	MPR	☐
159	1956-60	Morris Oxford	Green/Cream or White/Red body. 93 mm.	£27-£34	MPR	☐
159	1967-69	Ford Cortina	White body, SS/ODBB/WDS/FS/TS. 105 mm.	£9-£12	MPR	☐
160	1967-70	Mercedes Benz 250 SE	Met Blue body, LHD/FS/SS/SL/WDS. '1st AGAIN! STOP LIGHTS'. 117 mm.	£9-£12	MPR	☐
161 (40j)	1954-56	Austin Somerset	Blue body. 89 mm.	£19-£24	MPR	☐
161	1956-60	Austin Somerset	Black/White or Yel/Red body. 89 mm.	£18-£22	MPR	☐
161	1965-72	Ford Mustang	White or Yellow body SS/FS/SL/TS. 111 mm.	£7-£10	MPR	☐
162	1956-60	Ford Zephyr	Cream/Green or TT Blue body. 96 mm.	£17-£20	MPR	☐
162	1966-69	Triumph 1300	Blue body, SS/FS/SL/OBB. 92 mm.	£10-£12	MPR	☐
163	1956-60	Bristol 450	Green body, Black circle with RN. 98 mm.	£20	NC	☐
163	1966-69	Volkswagen 1600 TL	Red body, SS/SL/TS/ODBB. 102 mm.	£10-£13	MPR	☐
164	1957-60	Vauxhall Cresta	Maroon/Cream or Green/Grey body. 96 mm.	£18-£23	MPR	☐
164	1967-71	Ford Zodiac Mk IV	Silver body, SS/FS/SL/ODBB. '1st AGAIN! 4 OPENING DOORS'. 114 mm.	£8-£12	MPR	☐
165	1959-63	Humber Hawk	Maroon/Fawn or Green/Black body, WDS. 102 mm.	£15-£18	MPR	☐
165	1969-74	Ford Capri	Green or Met Purple body SS/OD/SWS. 102 mm.	£6-£10	MPR	☐
166	1958-63	Sunbeam Rapier	Cream/Orange or TT Blue body WDS. 89 mm.	£16-£19	MPR	☐
166	1967-69	Renault R16	Blue body SS/OD/FS/TS/OD. 86 mm.	£8-£11	MPR	☐
167	1958-63	A.C. Aceca	Red/Grey or Cream/Brown body WDS. 89 mm.	£20	NC	☐
168	1959-63	Singer Gazelle	Cream/Brown or Grey/Green body. 92 mm.	£20	NC	☐
168	1968-76	Ford Escort	Blue or Red body, OD/TS/PW later/BUP. 97 mm.	£5-£7	MPR	☐
169	1958-63	Studebaker Golden Hawk	Green/Fawn or Fawn/Red body WDS. 106 mm.	£14-£18	MPR	☐
169	1967-69	Ford Corsair 2000E	Silver/Black body SS/FS/SL/OD. 108 mm.	£7-£11	MPR	☐
170	1954-56	Ford Fordor	Yellow or Red body. 102 mm.	£17-£20	MPR	☐
170 (139a)	1956-59	Ford Fordor	Cream/Red or Pink/Blue body. 102 mm.	£14-£18	MPR	☐
170	1964-69	Lincoln Continental	Blue body, White roof, OC/OC/SL/LHD/SS/FS/OBN/WDS/CP. 127 mm.	£10-£13	MPR	☐
170	1979	Granada Ghia	Never issued on general release. 127 mm.	—	MPR	☐
171 (139b)	1954-56	Hudson Commodore	Maroon/Fawn or Fawn/Blue body. 111 mm.	£15-£21	MPR	☐
171	1956-58	Hudson Commodore	Red/Blue or Blue/Grey body. 111 mm.	£23-£28	MPR	☐
171	1966-69	Austin 1800	Blue body, SS/FS/SL/OBB. 101 mm.	£10-£13	MPR	☐
172	1954-56	Studebaker Land Cruiser	Green or Blue body. 107 mm.	£17-£22	MPR	☐
172	1956-58	Studebaker Land Cruiser	Maroon/Cream or Fawn/Brown body. 107 mm.	£15-£19	MPR	☐
172	1965-68	Fiat 2300 Station Wagon	Blue body, SS/FS/SL/TS/OBRD. 108 mm.	£10-£13	MPR	☐
173	1958-62	Nash Rambler	Green/Cerise or Pink/Blue body, WDS. 101 mm.	£14-£17	MPR	☐
173	1968-73	Pontiac Parisienne	Maroon body, FS/SS/SWS/2A. '1st AGAIN! RETRACTABLE AERIALS'. 132 mm.	£7-£9	MPR	☐
174	1958-63	Hudson Hornet	Red/Cream or Yel/Grey body, WDS. 111 mm.	£14-£18	MPR	☐
174	1969-72	Ford Mercury Cougar	Blue body, SS/OD/SWS/2A. 122 mm.	£7-£9	MPR	☐
175	1958-61	Hillman Minx	Pink/Green or Grey/Blue body, WDS. 88 mm.	£15-£18	MPR	☐
175	1969-72	Cadillac Eldorado	Purple/Black body, OC/SS/OD/SWS. 133 mm.	£7-£9	MPR	☐
176	1958-63	Austin A 105	Grey/Red or Cream/Blue body, WDS. 102 mm.	£16-£19	MPR	☐
176	1969-73	N.S.U. R 080	Maroon or Green body, LVS/SS/SL. 90 mm.	£6-£8	MPR	☐
177	1961-67	Opel Kapitan	Blue body, LHD/FS/SS/WDS. 100 mm.	£11-£14	MPR	☐
178	1959-63	Plymouth Plaza	Light Blue body, White roof, WDS. 108 mm.	£25	GV	☐
			Light Blue body, Dark Blue roof, WDS	£17	NC	☐
178	1974-80	Mini Clubman	Bronze body, OD/WDS. 75 mm.	£3-£5	MPR	☐
179	1958-63	Studebaker President	Blue body, Blue FL, or Yel body, BL FL. 108 mm.	£16	NC	☐
179	1971-74	Opel Commodore	Blue/Black body, OC/SS/ODB/SWS. 107 mm.	£5-£7	MPR	☐
180	1958-63	Packard Clipper	Fawn/Pink body, OC/WDS. 112 mm.	£16	NC	☐
180	1978-79	Rover 3500	White body, OC/OD/PCH/PW. 131 mm.	£3-£5	MPR	☐
181	1956-69	Volkswagen	Grey, Green or Blue body. 90 mm.	£11-£14	MPR	☐

Ref. No.		Model Type	Dinky Cars continued	Rarity and Price Grading	
182	1958-66	Porsche 356A Coupe	Blue or Cream body, WDS. 89 mm.	£11-£13	MPR ☐
183	1958-60	Fiat 600	Green or Red body, PW seen. 71 mm.	£13-£16	MPR ☐
183	1967-74	Morris Mini Minor	Blue/Black or Red/Black, OD/TS/SL. 75 mm.	£6-£8	MPR ☐
184	1961-64	Volvo 122S	Red body, SS/WDS/SS/S/SW. 97 mm.	£7-£9	MPR ☐
185	1961-63	Alfa Romeo 1900	Red or Yellow body, LHD/SS/FS/S/WDS. 102 mm.	£11-£14	MPR ☐
186	1961-66	Mercedes Benz 220SE	Blue body, LHD/SS/FS/WDS/CP. 102 mm.	£11-£14	MPR ☐
187	1959-63	VW Karmann Ghia Coupe	Red/Black or Cream/Green body, SS/WDS. 96 mm.	£9-£12	MPR ☐
188	1968-74	Jensen FF	Yellow or Green body, ODBN/SS/FS/SL/TS. 121 mm.	£6-£8	MPR ☐
189	1959-63	Triumph Herald	Green/White or Blue/White body. 86 mm.	£14-£17	MPR ☐
189	1969-77	Lamborghini Marzal	Red or Green body, DD/SWS. 108 mm.	£4-£6	MPR ☐
190	1971-73	Monteverdi 375L	Red body, OD/SWS. 116 mm.	£4-£6	MPR ☐
191	1959-64	Dodge Royal Sedan	Cream/Brown body, OC/WDS. 111 mm.	£17	NC ☐
192	1958-63	De Soto Fireflite	Grey/Red or Green/Fawn body, WDS. 114 mm.	£13-£16	MPR ☐
192	1971-79	Range Rover	Bronze or Yellow body, OD/SWS. 109 mm.	£3-£5	MPR ☐
193	1961-68	Rambler Cross Country	Yellow/White body, SS/FS/WDS/CP. 102 mm.	£14-£17	MPR ☐
194	1961-66	Bentley 'S' Coupe	Grey body, Red seats, Brown DB, Grey D, or Gold body, Cream seats, SS/FS/CP. 113 mm.	£19-£23	MPR ☐
195	1960-66	Jaguar 3.4 Mk II	Maroon, Cream or Grey body, SS/FS. 97 mm.	£15-£18	MPR ☐
196	1963-69	Holden Special Sedan	Bronze/White body, SS/FS/ODBN/WDS. 108 mm.	£8-£11	MPR ☐
197	1961-70	Morris Mini Traveller	Cream or Green body, SS/FS/WDS. 73 mm.	£10-£13	MPR ☐
198	1962-68	Rolls Royce Phantom V	Green/Cream or Two tone Grey body, D/SS/FS/OD/SL/CP/OWDS. 125 mm.	£19-£23	MPR ☐
199	1961-70	Austin 7 Countryman	Blue body, Wood TR, SS/FS/WDS. 73 mm.	£8-£11	MPR ☐
200 (356)	1954-57	Midget Racer	Red or Silver body. 57 mm.	£12-£16	MPR ☐
201	1979	Plymouth Stock Car	Blue body, RN '34' PW. 134 mm.	£3-£5	MPR ☐
202	1971-74	Fiat Abarth	Red/White body, OD/SWS. 91 mm.	£5-£7	MPR ☐
202	1979-80	Customised Land Rover	Black/Yellow body, PCH/PB. 115 mm.	£4-£6	MPR ☐
202	1978-79	Customised Land Rover	Black body, Yel Labels/LRW/PCH. 110 mm.	£4-£6	MPR ☐
203	1978-79	Customised Range Rover	Black body, PCH/LRW. 109 mm.	£3-£5	MPR ☐
204	1971-74	Ferrari 312P	Red body, OD/SWS RN '60'. 99 mm.	£5-£7	MPR ☐
205	1962-64	Talbot Lago	Blue body, BUP/PW. 103 mm.	£9-£12	MPR ☐
205	1968-71	Lotus Cortina Rally	White/Red body, RN '7' ODBB/SS/FS/TS. 105 mm.	£11-£14	MPR ☐
206	1962-64	Maserati	Red/White body, BUP/PW. 94 mm.	£9-£12	MPR ☐
206	1978-79	Customised Sting Ray	Red/Yellow body, PCH/PW. 113 mm.	£2-£4	MPR ☐
207	1962-64	Alfa Romeo	Red body, BUP/PW. 100 mm.	£8-£12	MPR ☐
207	1977-79	Triumph TRT Rally	White/Red/Blue body RN '8' PW/PCH. 98 mm.	£3-£5	MPR ☐
208	1962-64	Cooper Bristol	Green body, BUP/PW. 89 mm.	£8-£12	MPR ☐
208	1971-74	V.W. Porsche 914	Yellow or Blue body. 89 mm.	£4-£7	MPR ☐
209	1962-64	Ferrari	Blue/Yellow body, BUP/PW. 101 mm.	£9-£12	MPR ☐
210	1962-64	Vanwall	Green body, BUP/PW. 95 mm.	£9-£12	MPR ☐
210	1971-73	Alfa-Romeo 33	Blue body RN '36', SWS. 107 mm.	£6-£8	MPR ☐
211	1972-79	Triumph TR7	Red body, OC/OD/PW. 98 mm.	£3-£5	MPR ☐
212	1967-69	Ford Cortina Rally	White/Black body, *Castrol* RN '8' SS/FS/SL. 102 mm.	£9-£12	MPR ☐
213	1971-74	Ford Capri Rally	Red/Black body RN '20', OD/SWS. 102 mm.	£5-£7	MPR ☐
214	1967-68	Hillman Imp Rally	Blue body RN '35', SS/FS/SC/OBB. 86 mm.	£8-£10	MPR ☐
215	1967-74	Ford GT Racer	White body RN '7', OBN/SL/DE. 96 mm.	£6-£8	MPR ☐
216	1967-74	Dino Ferrari	Blue or Red body, SPW. 98 mm.	£6-£8	MPR ☐
217	1968-73	Alfa Romeo Searabeo OSI	Red body, OD/SWS/OEC. 90 mm.	£6-£8	MPR ☐
218	1970-74	Lotus Europa	Yellow/Blue/Black body, SWS. 96 mm.	£6-£8	MPR ☐
219	1978	'Leyland' Jaguar XJ5-3 Coupe	Purple/White/Red body RN '2'. 137 mm.		NVP ☐
219	1978-79	Jaguar XJ5 3 litre	White body, Cat decal, No BX. 137 mm.	£3-£5	MPR ☐
220 (23a)	1954-55	Small Open Racing Car	Silver/Red body, RN '4'. 94 mm.	£18-£23	MPR ☐
220	1970-74	Ferrari P5	Red body, OD/SWS. 96 mm.	£5-£7	MPR ☐
221 (23e)	1954-57	Speed of the Wind Racing Car	Silver body Plain BP. 104 mm.	£16-£19	MPR ☐
221	1970-78	Corvette Stingray	Brown/Orange body, OD/SWS. 113 mm.	£3-£5	MPR ☐
222 (23s)	1955-57	Streamlined Racing Car	Silver or Green body, Red or Blue trim. 126 mm.	£16-£19	MPR ☐
222	1978-79	Hesketh 308E	Blue body, RN '2', PCH/SWS. 132 mm.	£3-£5	MPR ☐
223	1971-74	McLaren M8A Can-Am	White/Green body, RN '5', SWS, OC. 94 mm.	£5-£7	MPR ☐

Ref. No.		Model Type	**Dinky Cars continued**	Rarity and Price Grading		
224	1970-73	Mercedes Benz C111	Met Dark Red body, ODBT/SWS. 102 mm.	£5-£7	MPR	☐
225	1971-77	Lotus F1	Red or Blue body, RN '7'. 127 mm.	£3-£5	MPR	☐
226	1978-79	Ferrari 312/B2	Red or Gold body RN '5'. 121 mm.	£3-£5	MPR	☐
227	1975-77	Beach Buggy	Yellow body, White detachable roof. 105 mm.	£4-£6	MPR	☐
228	1970-72	Super Sprinter	Blue/Silver body, SWS/SS. 113 mm.	£5-£7	MPR	☐
230 (23k)	1954-64	Talbot Lago RC	Blue body, Yellow RN '4', DCI. 102 mm.	£14-£17	MPR	☐
231 (23n)	1954-64	Maserati RC	Red body, White flash, RN '9', DCI. 92 mm.	£14-£17	MPR	☐
232 (23p)	1954-64	Alfa Romeo RC	Red body, White flash, RN '8', DCI. 102 mm.	£14-£17	MPR	☐
233 (23g)	1954-64	Cooper Bristol RC	Green body, White flash, RN '6', DCI. 89 mm.	£14-£17	MPR	☐
234 (23h)	1954-64	Ferrari RC	Blue body, Yellow RN '7', DCI, LV had Yellow triangle OL nose. 99 mm.	£14-£17	MPR	☐
235 (23j)	1954-60	H.W.M. Racing Car	Green body, Yellow RN '7', DCI. 99 mm.	£14-£17	MPR	☐
236	1956-59	Connaught RC	Green body, RN '32', White RCD. 96 mm.	£15-£18	MPR	☐
237	1957-68	Mercedes Benz RC	White body RN '30', Blue RCD. 96 mm.	£12-£15	MPR	☐
238	1957-64	D-type Jaguar	Turquoise body, White RCD. 87 mm.	£14-£17	MPR	☐
239	1958-66	'Vanwall' RC	Green body, White RN '35', RCD. 95 mm.	£11-£14	MPR	☐
240	1963-69	Cooper Racing Car	Blue/Green body, RN '20', SS/WS/OEC/DE. 80 mm.	£8-£11	MPR	☐
241	1963-69	Lotus Racing Car	Green body, RN '24', SS/WS/OEC/DE. 80 mm.	£8-£11	MPR	☐
242	1963-69	Ferrari Racing Car	Red body, RN '36', SS/WS/OEC/DE. 89 mm.	£8-£11	MPR	☐
243	1964-71	B.R.M. Racing Car	Green/Yellow body, RN '7', SS/WS/OEC/DE. 83 mm.	£8-£11	MPR	☐
342	1967-74	Austin Mini-Moke	Green/Fawn body, BVP/WS/OD/PW. 73 mm.	£4-£6	MPR	☐
344	1970-77	Land Rover (Pick Up)	Blue/Silver body, SWS/BVP. 108 mm.	£4-£6	MPR	☐
405	1955-66	Universal Jeep	Red/Green body, LHD/TPWS. 83 mm.	£9-£12	MPR	☐
518	1962-65	Renault	Brown body, FI/LHD/SS/FS/WDS. 85 mm.	£9-£12	MPR	☐
535	1962-65	2CV Citroen	Blue body, FI/LHD/SS/FS/WDS. 88 mm.	£9-£12	MPR	☐
550	1962-65	Chrysler Saratoga	Pink/White body, FI/LHD/SS/FS/WDS. 129 mm.	£9-£12	MPR	☐
553	1962-65	Peugeot 404	Green body, FI/LHD/SS/FS/WDS. 102 mm.	£9-£12	MPR	☐
555	1962-65	Ford Thunderbird CV	White body, FI/LHD/SS/CD/WS/FS. 121 mm.	£15-£18	MPR	☐

Gift Sets — Dinky Cars

Ref. No.		Model Type	Model Features and Size	Rarity and Price Grading		
	1933-40	22 Series Set	Contains 22a, 22b, 22c Motor Truck, 22d, Delivery Van, 22e Tractor, 22f Tank		NGPP	☐
	1936-40	23 Series Set	Contains 23c, d, e,	£125	NVE	☐
	1934-40	24 Series Set	Contains 24a Ambulance 24b, c, d, e, f, g, h		NGPP	☐
	1935-40	30 Series Set	Contains 30a, b, c, d, 30e Breakdown Van, 30f Ambulance		NGPP	☐
	1938-40	36 Series Set	Contains 36a, b, c, d, e, f, plus figures		NGPP	☐
	1938-40	38 Series Set	Contains 38a, b, c, d, e, f		NGPP	☐
	1940-41	39 Series Set	Contains 39a, b, c, d, e, f		NGPP	☐
No 3	1952-55	Passenger Cars	Contains 27f, 30h, 40c, 40g, 40h, 140b	£125	NVE	☐
No 4	1953-55	Racing Cars Set	Contains 23f, g, h, j, k, n	£75	GV	☐
118	1965-66	Towaway Glider Set	Contains 135 and trailer	£32	GV	☐
121	1964-67	Goodwood Racing Set	Contains 112, 113, 120, 182 (9 figs)	£65	NVE	☐
122	1963-65	Touring Gift Set	Contains 188, 193, 195, 270, 295	£75	NVE	☐
123	1963-65	Mayfair Gift Set	Contains 142, 150, 186, 194, 198, 199 (4 figs)	£120	NVE	☐
124	1964-66	Holiday Gift Set	Contains 952, 137, 142, 796	£40	NVE	☐
125	1964-66	Fun-A-Hoy Set	Contains 130, 796	£25	NVE	☐
126	1967-68	Motor Show Set	Contains 127, 133, 151, 171	£65	NVE	☐
149	1958-61	Sports Cars Set	Contains 107, 108, 110, 111	£75	NVE	☐
201	1966-68	Racing Cars Set	Contains 240, 241, 242, 243	£75	GV	☐
245	1969-73	Superfast Gift Set	Contains 131, 153, 188	£30	GV	☐
246	1969-73	International Gift Set	Contains 187, 215, 216	£22	GV	☐
950	1969-70	Car Transporter Set	Contains 974 Transporter 136, 138, 162, 168, 342	£80	NVE	☐
990	1956-58	Car Transporter Set	Contains 982 Transporter 154, 156, 161, 162	£85	NVE	☐

1b Dinky Commercial and Utility Vehicles

Ref. No.		Model Type	Model Features and Size	Rarity and Price Grading	
For descriptions of the different commercial Types and Chassis see section IV					
14a (400)	1949-60	B.E.V. Truck	Blue or Grey body. 85 mm.	£5-£7	MPR ☐
14c (401)	1949-64	Coventry Climax Fork Lift	Green/Orange body. 108 mm.	£5-£7	MPR ☐
22c	1933-35	Motor Truck	Red/Blue body. No HL on TPR. 90 mm.	£250	NVE ☐
22c	1935-40	Motor Truck	Red, Green or Blue body, Rear Window. 84 mm.	£35	GV ☐
22c	1946-50	Motor Truck	Red, Green or Brown body, No Window. 84 mm.	£15-£22	MPR ☐
25a	1934-38	Wagon	Red, Blue body, Type 1, OCH/No HL or TPR. 108 mm.	£35	NVE ☐
25a	1938-40	Wagon	Blue, Red body, Type 2, OCH/HL or DCR. 105 mm.	£35	NVE ☐
25a	1946-47	Wagon	Grey body, Type 3, Plain CH/DCR with HL. 105 mm.	£15-£20	MPR ☐
25a	1947-50	Wagon	Red body, Type 4, OC/MCH/DCR with HL and B. 110 mm.	£15-£20	MPR ☐
25b	1934-38	Covered Wagon	Blue or Cream body, Type 1/OCH/TPR/NoL. 105 mm.	£45	NVE ☐
25b	1938-40	Covered Wagon 'HORNBY TRAINS'	Grey/Cream body, Type 2, OCH/DCR/L/H, Gold Logo. 105 mm.	£125	NVE ☐
25b	1938-40	Covered Wagon 'MECCANO'	Green/Cream body, Type 2, OCH/DCR/L/H, Red/Black logo, *Engineering For Boys.* 105 mm.	£125	NVE ☐
25b	1938-40	Covered Wagon 'CARTER PATERSON'	Green/Red body, Type 2, OCH/DCR/H, White logo *Express Carriers London.* 105 mm.	£125	MPR ☐
25b	1946-47	Covered Wagon	Green or Grey body, Type 3/Plain CH/DCR/L/H. 105 mm.	£15-£20	MPR ☐
25b	1947-50	Covered Wagon	Yellow/Blue body, OC/Type 4/MCH/DCR/L/BM/H. 105 mm.	£15-£20	MPR ☐
25c	1934-38	Flat Truck	Grey or Red body, OC/Type 1/OCH/TPR/No L/H. 105 mm.	£40	GV ☐
25c	1938-40	Flat Truck	Grey or Blue body, OC/Type 2/OCH/H. 105 mm.	£30	GV ☐
25c	1947-50	Flat Truck	Green or Orange body, Type 4/MCH/DCR/L/BM/H. 105 mm.	£12-£17	MPR ☐
25a	1934-38	Petrol Tank Wagon	Red or Green body, Type 1/OCH/TPR/No L. 108 mm.	£125	NVE ☐
25a	1936-38	'SHELL BP' Wagon	Red body, Type 1/OCH/TPR/No L. 108 mm.	£125	NVE ☐
25d	1938-40	'PETROL' Wagon	Red or Green body, Type 2/OCH/DCR/L. 104 mm.	£110	NVE ☐
25d	1939-40	'SHELL BP' Wagon	Red body, Type 2/OCH/DCR/L. 107 mm.	£110	NVE ☐
25d	1936-40	'TEXACO' Wagon	Red body, Type 2/OCH/DCR/L. 107 mm.	£110	NVE ☐
25d	1939-40	'POWER' Wagon	Green body, Type 2/OCH/DCR/L. 107 mm.	£110	NVE ☐
25d	1939-40	'ESSO' Wagon	Red body, Type 2/OCH/DCR/L. 107 mm.	£110	NVE ☐
25d	1939-40	'MOBIL OIL' Wagon	Red body, Type 2/OCH/DCR/L. 107 mm.	£110	NVE ☐
25d	1939-40	'CASTROL' Petrol Wagon	Green body, Type 2, OCH/DCR/L, Red logo. 107 mm.	£110	NVE ☐
25d	1939-40	'POWER' Petrol Wagon	Green body, Type 2, OCH/DCR/L, Gold logo. 107 mm.	£110	NVE ☐
25d	1939-40	'REDLINE GLICO' Petrol Wagon	Blue/Red body, Type 2, OCH/DCR/L, Gold logo. 107 mm.	£110	NVE ☐
25d	1939-40	'SHELL BP' Petrol Wagon	Red body, Type 2, OCH/DCR/L, Gold logo. 107 mm.	£110	NVE ☐
25d	1939-40	'TEXACO' Petrol Wagon	Red body, Type 2, OCH/DCR/L, White logo. 107 mm.	£110	NVE ☐
25d	1939-40	'MOBIL OIL' Petrol Wagon	Orange body, Type 2, OCH/DCR/L, Bl/Wh logo. 107 mm.	£110	NVE ☐
25d	1940-41	'POOL' Petrol Wagon	Grey body, Type 2, OCH/DCR/L, White logo. 107 mm.	£110	NVE ☐
25d	1946-47	'PETROL' Wagon	Green body, Type 3, Plain CH/DCR/L. 107 mm.	£35	GV ☐
25d	1947-50	'PETROL' Wagon	Red body, Type 4, MCH/DCR/L/BM. 107 mm.	£25	GV ☐
25e	1934-38	Tipping Wagon	Maroon/Yellow body, Type 1/TPR/No L/H	£45	GV ☐
25e	1938-40	Tipping Wagon	Fawn body, Type 2, OCH/DCR/L/H. 105 mm.	£35	GV ☐
25e	1946-47	Tipping Wagon	Grey body, Type 3, Plain CH/DCR/L/H. 105 mm.	£16-£20	MPR ☐
25e	1947-50	Tipping Wagon	Brown body, Type 4, OC/MCH/DCR/L/BM/H. 110 mm.	£11-£15	MPR ☐
25f	1934-38	Market Gardeners Lorry	Green body, Type 1, OCH/TPR/No L/H. 107 mm.	£45	GV ☐
25f	1938-40	Market Gardeners Lorry	Green body, Type 2, OCH/DCR/L/H. 105 mm.	£35	GV ☐
25f	1946-47	Market Gardeners Lorry	Green body, Type 3, Plain CH/DCR/L/H. 105 mm.	£16-£20	MPR ☐
25f	1947-50	Market Gardeners Lorry	Yellow body, Type 4, MCH/DCR/L/BM/H. 110 mm.	£11-£15	MPR ☐
25g	1935-40	Trailer	Green body, Tinplate Towbar H. 69 mm.	£3-£4	MPR ☐
25g	1947-54	Trailer	Green or Red body, Wire Towbar H. 69 mm.	£2-£3	MPR ☐
25m (410)	1948-54	Bedford End Tipper	Orange body, OC/handle crank tipper. 98 mm.	£13-£16	MPR ☐

Ref. No.		Model Type	**Dinky Vehicles continued**	Rarity and Price Grading		
25r (450)	1948-50	Forward Control Lorry	Red, Green or Grey body. 107 mm.	£16-£19	MPR	☐
25s	1937-40	Six Wheeled Wagon	Brown body, SWC1/H/holes in seat. 101 mm.	£40	GV	☐
25s	1946-48	Six Wheeled Wagon	Green body, SWC1/H/holes in seat. 101 mm.	£16-£20	MPR	☐
25v	1948-54	Bedford Refuse Wagon	Fawn and Grey body OD. 107 mm.	£16-£19	MPR	☐
25w (411)	1949-54	Bedford Truck	Green body, Hook. 104 mm.	£16-£19	MPR	☐
25x (430)	1949-54	Breakdown Lorry	Orange/Green body, WO/H. 123 mm.	£16-£19	MPR	☐
30j (343)	1950-54	Austin Wagon	Blue or Brown body, Hook. 104 mm.	£16-£19	MPR	☐
30e	1936-40	Breakdown Lorry	Red or Green body, Blk Wings, RWD/WH. 92 mm.	£75	NVE	☐
30e	1946-48	Breakdown Lorry	Red or Green body, Blk Wings, No RWD/WH. 92 mm.	£17-£20	MPR	☐
30m (414)	1950-54	Rear Tipping Wagon	Orange body, *Dodge* on BP. 99 mm.	£14-£17	MPR	☐
30n	1950-60	Farm Produce Wagon	Green/Yellow or Blue/Red body, H. 107 mm.	£17-£20	MPR	☐
30p	1952-54	'PETROL' Tanker	Red body or Green body. 112 mm.	£32-£37	MPR	☐
30p (440)	1952-54	'MOBILGAS' Petrol Tanker	Red body. 112 mm.	£28-£34	MPR	☐
30pa (441)	1952-54	'CASTROL' Petrol Tanker	Green body. 112 mm.	£28-£34	MPR	☐
30pb (442)	1952-54	'ESSO' Petrol Tanker	Red body *Esso Motor Oil Petrol.* 112 mm.	£28-£34	MPR	☐
30r (422)	1951-54	Fordson Thames Flat Truck	Red or Green body, Hook. 112 mm.	£15-£18	MPR	☐
30s (413)	1950-54	Austin Covered Wagon	Maroon/Fawn or two tone Blue, H. 104 mm.	£17-£21	MPR	☐
30w (421)	1952-54	Electric Articulated Vehicle	Maroon body *British Railways* TV/H. 85 mm.	£17-£21	MPR	☐
33a	1935-40	Mechanical Horse	Green or Blue body, Silver trim. 65 mm.	£25	GV	☐
33b	1935-40	Flat Truck Trailer	Grey or Green body, no sides. 64 mm.	£16	NC	☐
33c	1935-40	Open Truck Trailer	Blue or Green body, with sides. 64 mm.	£16	NC	☐
33d	1935-40	Box Van 'Trailer MECCANO'	Green body, Red and Black logo *Engineering For Boys.* 70 mm.	£50	NVE	☐
33d	1935-40	Box Van Trailer 'HORNBY TRAINS'	Dark Blue body, Gold logo.	£50	NVE	☐
33e	1935-40	Refuse Wagon Trailer	Blue/Yellow body. 64 mm.	£20	GV	☐
33e	1946-47	Refuse Wagon Trailer	Grey or Red/Blue body. 64 mm.	£17-£21	MPR	☐
33f	1937-40	Petrol Tank Trailer	Green/Red body, no logo. 61 mm.	£22	GV	☐
33f	1937-40	Petrol Trailer and Tug 'ESSO'	Green/Red body, Gold logo. 61 mm.	£50	NVE	☐
33f	1937-40	Petrol Trailer and Tug 'WAKEFIELD CASTROL MOTOR OIL'	Dark Green and Red body. 61 mm.	£50	NVE	☐
33w (415)	1947-50	MH and Open Wagon	Blue/Cream body, Two tone Green, OC. 102 mm.	£15	NC	☐
60y	1938-40	Thompson Aircraft Tender	Red body, *Shell Aviation Services* in Gold.	£200	GV	☐
107a (385)	1949-54	Sack Truck	Blue body. 65 mm.	£11-£15	MPR	☐
151b	1938-40	Six W Covered Transport	Green body, holes for PS, SPW. 100 mm.	£35	NC	☐
252 (25v)	1954-64	Bedford Refuse Wagon	Fawn/Green body, body tips, OD. 107 mm.	£16-£19	MPR	☐
252	1960-65	Refuse Wagon	Fawn/Green body, OC/WDS. 107 mm.	£12-£16	MPR	☐
402	1966-69	Bedford TK Lorry	Red/White body, *Coca Cola* Crate load (6). 121 mm.	£28	NC	☐
404	1968-79	Climax Fork Lift	Red/Yellow body, *CG4 Conveyancer.* 97 mm.	£4-£6	MPR	☐
407	1966-69	Ford Transit Van	Blue/White body, *Kenwood* decals. 129 mm.	£11-£15	MPR	☐
407	1970-73	Ford Transit Van	Yellow body, *Hertz Truck Rental* decals. 129 mm.	£8-£12	MPR	☐
407	1970-73	Ford Transit Van	Red body, *Avis Truck Rental* decals. 129 mm.	£8-£12	MPR	☐
407	1970-73	Ford Transit Van	White body, *Rediffusion Colour TV* decals. 129 mm.	£8-£12	MPR	☐
408 (922)	1956-63	Big Bedford Lorry	Maroon/Fawn or Blue/Yellow body, H. 146 mm.	£17-£22	MPR	☐

Ref. No.		Model Type	Dinky Vehicles continued	Rarity and Price Grading		
409 (921)	1956-63	Bedford AV	Yellow body, SPW/H. 166 mm.	£18-£23	MPR	☐
410	1972-76	Bedford Van	Black/Red body, *Simpsons* decal and motif. 90 mm.	£12	GV	☐
410		Bedford Van	Blue body, *John Menzies* decals. 90 mm.	£6-£8	MPR	☐
410		Bedford Van	Bronze/Black body, *Belaco* decals. 90 mm.	£7-£9	MPR	☐
410		Bedford Van	White body, *M J Hire Service* decals. 90 mm.	£4-£6	MPR	☐
410		Bedford Van	Red body, *Marley Building Supplies* decals. 90 mm.	£6-£8	MPR	☐
410		Bedford Van	White body, *Modellers World* decals. 90 mm. All 410 Bedford Vans have BUP/WDS/PW	£15	GV	☐
410 (25m)	1955-63	Bedford End Tipper	Brown/Yellow or Blue/Yellow. 97 mm.	£14-£18	MPR	☐
410	1962-63	Bedford End Tipper	Red/Cream body, WDS. 97 mm.	£14-£18	MPR	☐
411 (25w)	1954-60	Bedford Truck	Green body. 104 mm.	£11-£14	MPR	☐
412 (30j)	1954-60	Austin Wagon	Blue/Mrn or Yel/Blue body. 104 mm.	£11-£14	MPR	☐
413	1954-60	Austin Covered Wagon	Blue or Maroon body. 104 mm.	£15-£19	MPR	☐
414 (30m)	1954-64	Dodge Rear Tipping Wagon	Green/Orange or Grey/Blue body. 99 mm.	£16-£20	MPR	☐
415 (33w)	1954-59	Mechanical Horse and Wagon	Blue/Cream body, open wagon. 102 mm.	£15-£18	MPR	☐
417	1956-59	Leyland Comet Lorry	Blue/Yellow body, Hook. 144 mm.	£29	NC	☐
418 (532/932)	1956-59	Leyland Comet with Hinged Tailboard	Green/Orange body. 142 mm.	£32	NC	☐
419 (533/933)	1956-59	Leyland Comet Cement Lorry	Yellow body, *Ferrocrete* and *Portland Cement,* ST/SPW. 142 mm.	£34	NC	☐
420 (25r)	1954-61	Leyland Forward Control Lorry	Red, Grey or Blue body, Hook. 107 mm.	£16-£21	MPR	☐
421 (30w)	1955-59	Electric Articulated Vehicle	Maroon *British Railways*, Hook. 135 mm.	£16	NC	☐
422 (30r)	1954-60	Thames Flat Truck	Green or Red body, WDS/Hook. 112 mm.	£18-£22	MPR	☐
424	1963-66	Commer Convertible Articulated Vehicle	Yellow body, Blue detachable cover, 2 White plastic TRL fittings, SPW. 171 mm.	£35	NC	☐
425	1964-67	Bedford TK Coal Wagon	Red body, *Hall & Co* etc, coal bags/scales. 121 mm.	£30	GV	☐
428 (551/951)	1955-64	Large Trailer	Grey body, front axle swivels, Hook. 105 mm.	£4-£6	MPR	☐
430 (25x)	1954-64	Commer Breakdown Lorry	Green/Black body, *Dinky Service,* WO/H. 123 mm.	£14-£19	MPR	☐
431 (911/511)	1956-58	Guy 4 ton Lorry	Two tone Blue, 2nd type SPW/H. 132 mm.	£29	NC	☐
431	1958-64	Guy Warrior 4 ton Lorry	Green/Fawn body, *Warrior* type, WDS/SPW/H. 136 mm.	£65	GV	☐
432 (912/512)	1956-58	Guy Flat Truck	Blue/Red body, 2nd type, SPW/H. 132 mm.	£32	NC	☐
432	1955-58	Guy Warrior Flat Truck	Red/Cream, *Warrior* type, WDS/SPW/H. 136 mm.	£100	GV	☐
432	1977-79	Foden Tipping Lorry	White/Red/Yellow body. 175 mm.	£6-£8	MPR	☐
433 (913/513)	1955-58	Guy Flat Truck with Tailboard	Green/Yellow body, 2nd type, H. 132 mm.	£32	NC	☐
435	1964-68	Bedford TK Tipper	Grey/Blue/Orange body, OC/WDS. 120 mm.	£12-£15	MPR	☐
438	1970-74	Ford D800 Tipper Truck	Red/Black body, Yellow tipper. 132 mm.	£7-£9	MPR	☐
439	1971-74	Ford D800 Snow Plough/Tipper	Blue body, Yellow plough, OC. 194 mm.	£12-£15	MPR	☐
440	1977-79	Ford D800 Tipper Truck	Red body, Yellow tipper. 132 mm.	£7-£9	MPR	☐
440 (30p)	1956-61	Petrol Tanker 'MOBIL GAS'	Red body. 112 mm.	£30-£35	MPR	☐
441 (30pa)	1954-60	Petrol Tanker 'CASTROL'	Green body. 112 mm.	£30-35	MPR	☐
442	1973-79	Land Rover Breakdown Crane	Red/White body, *Motorway Rescue,* WO.	£5-£7	MPR	☐
442 (30pb)	1954-60	'ESSO' Petrol Tanker 'MOTOR OIL PETROL'	Red body and Hubs, Blue, White and Red Logo, Silver trim. 112 mm.	£30-£35	MPR	☐

Ref. No.		Model Type	**Dinky Vehicles continued**	Rarity and Price Grading		
443	1957-58	Petrol Tanker 'NATIONAL BENZOLE MIXTURE'	Yellow body and Hubs, Black Logo, Silver Trim. 112 mm.	£45	NC	☐
448	1963-67	Chevrolet El Camino Pick-Up and 2 Trailers	TQ/WH/Red B, CEM on BOX TRL *Acme Trailer Hire* (3 parts). 256 mm.	£18	NC	☐
449	1963-67	Chevrolet El Camino PU	GR/WH or Red/Yel, LHD/SS/FS/SW/WDS. 111 mm.	£10-£12	MPR	☐
449	1971-79	Johnston Road Sweeper	Green/Orange with OD (1971)	£9-£12	MPR	☐
(451)			LV Green/Orange OC/No OD. 142 mm.	£6-£8	MPR	☐
501	1947-52	Foden 8 Wheel Diesel Wagon	Red/Fawn 1st type, OC/ST/SPW/H. 188 mm.	£50	NC	☐
501 (901)	1952-55	Foden 8 Wheel Diesel Wagon	Brown or Blue 2nd type, OC/ST/SPW/H. 188 mm.	£43	NC	☐
502	1947-52	Foden Flat Truck	Red/Blue 1st type, OC/ST/SPW/H. 188 mm.	£32	NC	☐
502 (902)	1952-55	Foden Flat Truck	Orange/Green 2nd type, OC/ST/SPW/H. 188 mm.	£32	NC	☐
503	1947-52	Foden Flat Truck with Tailboard	Red/Blue body, 1st type/ST/H. 188 mm.	£36	NC	☐
503 (903)	1952-55	Foden Flat Truck with Tailboard	Blue/Orange body, 2nd type/ST/H. 188 mm.	£36	NC	☐
504	1948-52	Foden 14 ton Tanker	Grey/Red body, or Blue 1st Type, ST/SPW/H. 188 mm.	£60	NC	☐
504	1953-54	Foden 14 ton Tanker	Two tone blue 2nd Type, ST/SPW/H. 188 mm.	£60	NC	☐
504 (941)	1953-54	Foden 14 ton Tanker	Red body, *Mobilgas*, CEM/ST/SPW/H. 188 mm.	£100	NC	☐
505 (905)	1952-55	Foden Flat Truck with Chains	Green or Maroon body, 2nd type, SPW/H. 188 mm.	£38	NC	☐
511 (911/431)	1947-55	Guy 4 ton Lorry	Two tone Blue body, 1st type, OC/ST/SPW/H. 132 mm.	£32	NC	☐
512 (912/432)	1947-54	Guy flat Truck	Maroon body, 1st type, ST/SPW/H. 132 mm.	£32	NC	☐
513 (913/433)	1947-54	Guy Flat Truck with Tailboard	2 tone Green, 1st type, OC/ST/SPW/H. 132 mm.	£34	NC	☐
521	1948-54	Bedford AV	Maroon/Fawn body, ST/H. 166 mm.	£30	NC	☐
522 (922/408)	1952-54	Big Bedford	Blue/Yellow or Maroon/Fawn, SPW/H. 146 mm.	£30	NC	☐
531 (931/417)	1949-54	Leyland Comet	Blue/Yellow body, ST/H. 144 mm.	£29	NC	☐
532 (932/418)	1953-54	Leyland Comet	Green/Orange body, ST/HTBD. 142 mm.	£32	NC	☐
533 (933/419)	1953-54	Leyland Comet Cement	Details as for Model 419. 142 mm.	£34	NC	☐
551 (951/428)	1948-54	Trailer	Grey, front axle swivels, H. 105 mm.	£4-£6	MPR	☐
571 (971)	1949-55	Coles Mobile Crane	Yellow/Black body, ST/CO. 160 mm.	£12-£16	MPR	☐
579	1961-63	Simca Glaziers Lorry 'SAINT-GOBAIN' & 'MIROITIER'	Grey/Green body, Mirror load FI	£28	NC	☐
			LV Yellow/Green body	£22	NC	☐
581	1962-64	Berliot Flat Truck	Red/Grey body, FI/6W/SPW/H/C. 130 mm.	£16	NC	☐
581	1953-54	'EXPRESS' Horse Box	Maroon body, *British Railways* OD. 175 mm.	£25	NC	☐
582	1953-54	Pullmore Car Transporter	Blue/Grey body, AV/DDR *Dinky Toys Delivery Service.* 250 mm.	£18-£24	MPR	☐
591	1952-54	A.E.C. Tanker	Red/Yellow body, *Shell Chemicals Ltd.* 151 mm.	£24	NC	☐
893	1962-64	Unic Pipe Line TPTR	Sand body, FI/AV/SPW/6 Pipes. 215 mm.	£26	NC	☐
894	1962-64	Unic Boilet Car TPTR	Grey body, *Dinky Toys Service,* FI/AV. 325 mm.	£45	NVE	☐
901 (501)	1955-57	Foden 8 Wheel Diesel Wagon	Red/Grey body, 2nd type, ST/SPW/H. 188 mm.	£36	NC	☐
902 (502)	1955-60	Foden Flat Truck	Orange/Green body, 2nd type, ST/SPW/H. 188 mm.	£30	NC	☐
903 (503)	1955-60	Foden Flat Truck with Tailboard	Blue/Orange body, 2nd type, ST/SPW/H. 188 mm.	£35-£45	MPR	☐
905 (505)	1955-64	Foden Flat Truck with chains	Green body, 2nd type, ST/SPW/H. 188 mm.	£55	NC	☐
908	1962-66	Mighty Antar with Transformer	Yellow cab, Red/Grey Trailer, ST/DDR/AV/CD/WDS/SPW. 337 mm.	£75	GV	☐

Dinky Vehicles continued

Ref. No.		Model Type		Rarity and Price Grading	
911 (511/431)	1954-56	Guy 4 ton Lorry	Two tone Blue body, 2nd type, ST/SPW/H. 132 mm.	£30	NC
912 (512/432)	1954-56	Guy Flat Truck	Blue/Orange body, 2nd type, ST/SPW/H. 132 mm.	£30	NC
913 (513/433)	1954-56	Guy Flat Truck with Tailboard	Blue/Orange body, 2nd type, ST/SPW/H. 132 mm.	£33	NC
914	1967-70	A.E.C. A.V. Lorry	Red/White body, *British Road Services* SL. 210 mm.	£28	GV
915	1973-74	A.E.C. with Flat TRL	Orange/White body, *Truck Hire Co Liverpool.* 210 mm.	£11-£14	MPR
915	1973-74	A.E.C. with Flat TRL	Orange/White body *Thames Board Mills* BUP. 210 mm.	£13-£17	MPR
917	1968-74	Mercedes Truck and TRL	Blue/Yellow/White body, IS/SL/ODB. 397 mm.	£16-£19	MPR
921 (521/409)	1954-60	Bedford Articulated Vehicle	Yellow body, ST/ODB/SPW/H. 166 mm.	£32	NC
922	1954-56	Big Bedford Lorry	Maroon/Fawn, SPW/H. 146 mm.	£32	NC
925	1967-69	Leyland Dump Truck	Silver/Red, Cab Tilts *Sand Ballast Gravel* on Tipper flap. 192 mm.	£24	NC
931 (531/417)	1955-56	Leyland Comet Lorry	Blue/Yellow body, ST/H. 144 mm.	£29	NC
932 (532/418)	1954-56	Leyland Comet with Hinged Tailboard	Green/Orange body, ST. 142 mm.	£32	NC
933 (533/419)	1954-56	Leyland Comet Cement Wagon	Details as for Model 419. 142 mm.	£34	NC
934	1954-64	Leyland Octopus Wagon	Yellow/Green body, ST/SPW/H. 194 mm.	£39	NC
935	1964-66	Leyland Octopus with Chains	Green/Grey body, ST/SPW/H. 192 mm.	£39	NC
936	1964-69	Leyland 8 Wheel Chassis	Red/Silver body *Another Leyland on Test* 3×5 ton weights. 197 mm.	£33	NC
940	1977-79	Mercedes Benz Truck	White body, Grey tarpaulin. 200 mm.	£6-£8	MPR
941 (504)	1955-57	Foden Tanker 'MOBILGAS'	Red body, *Mobilgas* 2nd type, CEM/ST/SPW/H. 188 mm.	£100	NC
942	1955-57	Foden Tanker 'REGENT'	Red/Blue/White body, CEM *Regent* in Gold, 2nd type, ST/SPW/H. 188 mm.	£100	NC
943	1958-64	Leyland Octopus Tanker 'ESSO PETROLEUM'	Red/White body, *Esso Petroleum,* CEM/ST/SPW/H. 192 mm.	£70	NC
944	1963-65	4000 gallon Tanker 'SHELL BP'	Yellow/White body, ST/SPW/H *Shell BP* & CEMS on sides. 192 mm.	£45	NC
945	1966-67	A.E.C. Fuel Tanker 'ESSO'	White body, *Esso* tiger on tank AV/TV. 266 mm.	£20	NC
			Later version with no tiger	£11-£14	MPR
945	1978	A.E.C. Fuel Tanker 'LUCAS'	Green body, Black CH, White *Lucas Oil Company,* AV/PRO. 266 mm.	£20	NC
948	1961-67	Tractor TRL 'McLEAN'	Red/Grey body, *McLean Winston,* ST/AV/TV. 290 mm.	£55	NC
950	1978-79	Foden Tanker 'BURMAH'	Red/White/Black body, *Burmah* AV/TV, LV has Cream wheels and Silver PFC. 266 mm.	£10-£12	MPR
950	1978-79	Foden Tanker 'SHELL'	Red/White/Black body, *Shell* AV/TV. 266 mm.	£19	GV
951 (551/428)	1954-55	Trailer	Grey body, Hook. 105 mm.	£4-£6	MPR
958	1961-66	Guy Warrior Snow Plough	Yellow/Black body, ST/SPW. 195 mm.	£35	NC
967	1959-64	BBC TV Control Room	Green body, *BBC Television Service,* ST/WDS. 149 mm.	£30	NC
968	1959-64	BBC TV Roving Eye V	Green body, B.B.C. crest, camera/ST/WDS. 110 mm.	£22	NC
969	1959-64	BBC TV Extending Mast V	Green body, B.B.C. crest, ST/WDS/A. 165 mm.	£30	NC
970	1967-74	Jones Cantilever Crane	Red/White body, *Jones Fleetmaster* Co. 174 mm.	£11-£15	MPR
971	1955-66	Coles Mobile Crane	Yellow/Black body, ST/D/CO. 162 mm.	£9-£13	MPR
972	1955-69	Coles 20 ton Crane	Yellow/Orange/Black body, ST/2D/CO. 240 mm.	£11-£15	MPR
974	1969-74	A.E.C. Hoynor TPTR	Blue/Yellow body, *Silcock & Colling Ltd.* 322 mm.	£25	NC
977	1960-64	Servicing Platform Vehicle	Red/Cream body, platform operates, SPW. 130 mm.	£16	NC
978	1964-79	Bedford Refuse Wagon	Green/Grey body, Bins/OD/Tips.	£6-£8	MPR
			Later version Yellow/Grey body.	£4-£6	MPR
979	1961-64	Racehorse Transport	Grey/Yellow body, *Newmarket Racehorse Transport Service Ltd,* 2 HS/ST/ODB. 175 mm.	£70	NC
980	1974-79	Coles Hydra Truck	Yellow/Black body, crane elevates. 210 mm.	£5-£7	MPR
981 (581)	1955-61	'EXPRESS' Horse Box	Maroon body *British Railways.* 175 mm.	£25	NC

Ref. No.		Model Type	Dinky Vehicles continued	Rarity and Price Grading		
982 (582)	1954-63	Pullmore Car Transporter	Blue body, *Dinky Toys Delivery Service.*	£18-£24	MPR	☐
983	1958-63	Car Carrier and Trailer	Red/Grey body, *Dinky Toys Delivery Service* (984 and 985), ST. 196/240 mm.	£80	GV	☐
984	1958-63	Car Carrier	Red/Grey body, *Dinky Auto Service*, ST. 240 mm.	£35	GV	☐
985	1958-63	Car Trailer	Red/Grey body, *Dinky Auto Service*, ST. 196 mm.	£16	NC	☐
986	1959-64	Mighty Antar with Propellor Load	Red/Grey body, Driver, ST/AV. 305 mm.	£60	NC	☐
987	1962-69	TV Control Room 'A-B-C TELEVISION SERVICE'	Blue/Grey body, Red stripe, CEM/ST, white logo, camera and operator. 151 mm.	£30	NC	☐
988	1962-69	TV Transmitter Van 'A-B-C TV'	Blue/Grey body, Red stripe, CEM/ST, revolving dish, white logo. 113 mm.	£25	NC	☐
989	1963-69	Car Transporter 'AUTO TRANSPORTERS'	Yellow cab, Grey body, Blue tier, Red hubs and logo, DDR/ST. 240 mm.	£55	GV	☐
991 (551)	1955-58	A.E.C. Tanker	Red/Yellow body, *Shell Chemicals Ltd*, ST. 151 mm.	£28	NC	☐

Dinky Commercial and Utility Vehicles Gift Sets

25 Series	1934-40	Type 1 Gift Set	Contains 25a, b, c, d, e, f		NGPP	☐
33 Series	1935-40	33 Series Gift Set	Contains 33a, b, c, d, e, f		NGPP	☐
No 2	1952-53	Commercial Vehicles Set	Contains 25m, 27d Land Rover 30n, 30p, 30s	£125	NVE	☐

1c Dinky Vans

Ref. No.		Model Type	Model Features and Size	Rarity and Price Grading	
Note for descriptions of Types 1, 2 and 3 see Section IV					
22d (28n)	1934-36	Delivery Van	Orange/Blue body, *Hornby Series* or LV, *Dinky Toys* cast in. Type 1. 83 mm.	£350	GV ☐
22d	1934-36	Delivery Van 'MECCANO'	Yellow body, Red/Gold letters *Meccano Engineering for Boys* Type 1. 83 mm.	£500	GV ☐
28a	1936-40	Delivery Van 'HORNBY TRAINS'	Yellow body, Gold letters, *Hornby Trains British and Guaranteed.*		
			Type 1. 83 mm.	£500	GV ☐
			Type 2. 81 mm.	£250	GV ☐
28a	1936-40	Delivery Van 'GOLDEN SHRED'	Cream body *Golden Shred* in Red/Blue.		
			Type 2. 81 mm.	£250	GV ☐
			Type 3. 83 mm.	£175	GV ☐
28b	1934-36	Delivery Van 'PICKFORDS'	Blue body, Gold letters, *Pickfords Removals and Storage Over 100 Branches.*		
			Type 1. 83 mm.	£500	GV ☐
			Type 2. 81 mm.	£250	GV ☐
28b	1936-40	Delivery Van 'SECCOTINE'	Blue body, Gold letters *Seccotine Sticks Everything*		
			Type 2. 81 mm.	£250	GV ☐
			Type 3. 83 mm.	£175	GV ☐
28c	1934-40	Delivery Van 'MANCHESTER GUARDIAN'	Blue body, Gold letters *The Manchester Guardian.*		
			Type 1. 83 mm.	£500	GV ☐
			Type 2. 81 mm.	£250	GV ☐
28d	1934-40	Delivery Van 'OXO'	Blue body, Gold letters, *Oxo Beef in Brief* and *Oxo Beef at its Best.*		
			Type 1. 83 mm.	£500	GV ☐
			Type 2. 81 mm.	£250	GV ☐
			Type 3. 83 mm.	£175	GV ☐
			N.B. World Record Auction Price of £550 for a single model was paid at Sotheby's Auction at New Bond St London, on 20th May 1983 for a Type 1, 28 series van with *Oxo* decals.		
28e	1934 only	Delivery Van 'ENSIGN'	Orange body, Gold letters, *Ensign Lukos Film* and *Ensign Cameras* Type 1.	£500	GV ☐
28e	1934-40	Delivery Van 'FIRESTONE'	White body, Gold letters, *Firestone Tyres.*		
			Type 1. 83 mm.	£500	GV ☐
			Type 2. 81 mm.	£250	GV ☐
			Type 3. 83 mm.	£175	GV ☐
28f	1934-37	Delivery Van 'PALETHORPES'	Light Grey body, Blue and Red letters, Pink sausage decal *Palethorpes Royal Cambridge.*		
			Type 1. 83 mm.	£500	GV ☐
			Type 2. 81 mm.	£250	GV ☐
28f	1937-40	Delivery Van 'VIROL'	Yellow body, Black letters *Give Your Child a Virol Constitution.* Type 2. 81 mm.	£250	GV ☐
28g	1934-40	Delivery Van 'KODAK'	Yellow body, Red letters, *Use Kodak Film* and *To Be Sure.*		
			Type 1. 83 mm.	£500	GV ☐
			Type 2. 81 mm.	£250	GV ☐
			Type 3. 83 mm.	£175	GV ☐
28h	1934-36	Delivery Van 'SHARPS'	Red/Black body, Gold letters, Yellow *Sharps Toffees Maidstone.* Type 1. 83 mm.	£500	GV ☐
28h	1935-40	Delivery Van 'DUNLOP'	Red body, Gold letters *Dunlop Tyres.*		
			Type 2. 81 mm.	£250	GV ☐
			Type 3. 83 mm.	£175	GV ☐
28k	1935-40	Delivery Van 'MARSH'S'	Green body, Gold letters, Pink *Marsh's Sausages* and design, MW on Type 1.		
			Type 1. 83 mm.	£500	GV ☐
			Type 2. 81 mm.	£250	GV ☐
			Type 3. 83 mm.	£175	GV ☐

Ref. No.		Model Type	**Dinky Vans continued**	Rarity and Price Grading		
28l	1934-35	Delivery Van 'CRAWFORDS'	Red body, gold letters, *Crawfords Biscuits.* 83 mm. Type 1	£500	GV	☐
28m	1934-40	Delivery Van 'WAKEFIELD'	Green body, Red letters, *Wakefield Castrol Motor Oil.*			
			Type 1. 83 mm.	£500	GV	☐
			Type 2. 81 mm.	£250	GV	☐
			Type 3. 83 mm.	£175	GV	☐
28n (22d)	1934-35	Delivery Van 'MECCANO'	Yellow body, Red/Gold letters, *Meccano Engineering for Boys*			
			Type 1. 83 mm.	£500	GV	☐
			Type 2. 81 mm.	£250	GV	☐
28n	1935-41	Delivery Van 'ATCO'	Green body, Gold letters, *Atco Sales and Service* and *Motor Mowers.*			
			Type 2. 81 mm.	£250	GV	☐
			Type 3. 83 mm.	£175	GV	☐
28p	1935-36	Delivery Van 'CRAWFORDS'	Red body, Gold letters *Crawfords Biscuits.*			
			Type 2. 81 mm.	£250	GV	☐
			Type 3. 83 mm.	£175	GV	☐
28r	1936-41	Delivery Van 'SWANS'	Black body, Gold letters *Swans Pens.*			
			Type 2. 81 mm.	£250	GV	☐
			Type 3. 83 mm.	£175	GV	☐
28s	1936-41	Delivery Van 'FRYS'	Chocolate body, Gold letters *Frys Chocolate.*			
			Type 2. 81 mm.	£250	GV	☐
			Type 3. 83 mm.	£175	GV	☐
28t	1936-41	Delivery Van 'OVALTINE'	Red body, Gold letters *Drink Ovaltine for Health.*			
			Type 2. 81 mm.	£250	GV	☐
			Type 3. 83 mm.	£175	GV	☐
28w	1936-41	Delivery Van 'OSRAM'	Yellow body, Gold letters, *Osram Lamps A G.E.C. Product.*			
			Type 2. 81 mm.	£250	GV	☐
			Type 3. 83 mm.	£175	GV	☐
28x	1936-41	Delivery Van 'HOVIS'	White body *Hovis* in Gold.			
			Type 2. 81 mm.	£250	GV	☐
			Type 3. 83 mm.	£175	GV	☐
28y	1936-41	Delivery Van 'EXIDE'	Red body, Gold letters *Exide Batteries, Drydex Batteries.*			
			Type 2. 81 mm.	£250	GV	☐
			Type 3. 83 mm.	£175	GV	☐
			Further issues in this series were numbered 280 onwards as the alphabet ran out!			
280	1948-54	Delivery Van	Red or Blue body, Type 3, No RWD. 83 mm.	£24	NC	☐
280a	1937-41	Delivery Van 'VIYELLA'	Blue body, White/Black letters *Viyella for the Nursery.*			
			Type 2. 81 mm.	£250	GV	☐
			Type 3. 83 mm.	£175	GV	☐
280b	1937-41	Delivery Van 'LYONS'	Dark Blue body, Red/White letters *Lyons Tea Always the Best.* 81 mm.			
			Type 2. 81 mm.	£250	GV	☐
			Type 3. 83 mm.	£175	GV	☐
280b	1939-40	Delivery Van 'HARTLEYS'	Cream body, Red/Green letters, *Hartleys is Real Jam.*			
			Type 2. 81 mm.	£250	GV	☐
			Type 3. 83 mm.	£175	GV	☐
280c	1937-41	Delivery Van 'SHREDDED WHEAT'	Cream body, Red/Black letters, *Shredded Wheat.*			
			Type 2. 81 mm.	£250	GV	☐
			Type 3. 83 mm.	£175	GV	☐
280d	1937-38	Delivery Van 'BISTO'	Yellow body, MLCD letters/design *Ah Bisto.* Type 2. 81 mm.	£350	NVE	☐
280d	1938-41	Delivery Van 'BISTO'	Yellow body, MLCD letters/design *Bisto.*			
			Type 2. 81 mm.	£250	GV	☐
			Type 3. 83 mm.	£175	GV	☐
280e	1937-41	Delivery Van 'EKCO'	Green body, Gold letters *Ekco Radio.* Type 2. 81 mm.	£250	GV	☐
280e	1938-39	Delivery Van 'EVENING POST'	Cream body, Gold letters *Yorkshire Evening Post.*			
			Type 2. 81 mm.	£250	GV	☐
			Type 3. 83 mm.	£175	GV	☐

Ref. No.		Model Type	**Dinky Vans continued**	Rarity and Price Grading		
280f	1937-41	Delivery Van 'MACKINTOSH'S	Red body, gold letters *Mackintosh's Toffee* pro.			
			Type 2. 81 mm.	£250	GV	☐
			Type 3. 83 mm.	£175	GV	☐
280f	1939-40	Delivery Van 'BENTALL'S'	Green/Yellow body, Green letters *Bentalls Kingston on Thames* Phone Kin 1001, Type 2.		NGPP	☐
NB Normal numbering resumed						
30e	1935-40	Bedford Breakdown Van	Red, Green or Grey body, RWD in cab. 92 mm.	£30	GV	☐
30e	1946-47	Bedford Breakdown Van	Red, Green or Grey body, No RWD in cab. 92 mm.	£11-£15	MPR	☐
30v (491)	1949-54	Electric Dairy Van	Cream/Red body, *N.C.B.* 85 mm.	£28-£35	MPR	☐
30v (490)	1951-54	Electric Dairy Van	Grey/Blue body *Express Dairy*. 85 mm.	£22-£27	MPR	☐
30v	1953-4	Electric Dairy Van	Cream/Red, *Job's Dairy* pro. 85 mm.	£65	NC	☐
31	1935-40	Holland Coachcraft Van	Blue or Green *Holland Coachcraft Registered Design* in gild. 88 mm.	£250	NVE	☐
31a (450)	1951-54	Trojan 15 cwt Van	Red body, *Esso*. 85 mm.	£45	NC	☐
31b (451)	1952-54	Trojan 15 cwt Van	Red body, *Dunlop the Worlds Master Tyre*. 85 mm.	£50	NC	☐
31c (452)	1953-54	Trojan 15 cwt Van	Green body, *Chivers Jellies* and design. 85 mm.	£50	NC	☐
31d	1953-54	Trojan 15 cwt Van	Blue body, *Beefy Oxo* issued without box. 85 mm.	£100	GV	☐
33d	1936-38	Box Van Trailer and Tug	Green body, *Hornby Trains British and Guaranteed.* 70 mm.	£100	GV	☐
33d	1938-39	Box Van Trailer and Tug	Green body, *Meccano Engineering* for boys in Black etc. 70 mm.	£75	NVE	☐
33r	1935-40	Mechanical Horse L.N.E.R.	Blue/Black body, *L.N.E.R. 901.*	£35	GV	☐
33r	1935-40	Trailer Van and Horse 'L.N.E.R.'	Blue/Black body, *L.N.E.R., Express Parcels Traffic.*	£100	GV	☐
33r	1935-40	Mechanical Horse 'L.M.S.'	Brown/Black body, *L.M.S. 2246.*	£35	GV	☐
33r	1935-40	Trailer Van and Horse 'L.M.S.'	Brown/Black body, *L.M.S., Express Parcel Service.*	£100	GV	☐
33r	1935-40	Mechanical Horse 'G.W.R.'	Brown/Cream body, *G.W.R. 2742.*	£35	GV	☐
33r	1935-40	Trailer Van and Horse 'G.W.R.'	Brown/Cream body, *G.W.R., Express Cartage Service.*	£100	GV	☐
33r	1935-40	Mechanical Horse 'S.R.'	Green with Black or White roof *3016 M.*	£35	GV	☐
33r	1935-40	Trailer Van and Horse 'S.R.'	Green/Black *Southern Railway, Express Parcels Service.*	£100	GV	☐
34a	1935-38	'ROYAL AIR MAIL SERVICE' Car	Blue body. 83 mm.	£75	NVE	☐
34b	1938-40	'ROYAL MAIL' Van	Red/Black body, Rear WDS, *GR* and crown. 83 mm.	£45	NC	☐
34b	1948-52	'ROYAL MAIL' Van	Red/Black body, No rear WDS, *GR* and crest. 83 mm.	£24	NC	☐
34c (492)	1948-55	Loudspeaker Van	Brown body, Blk LS, OC/Type 3. 81 mm.	£14-£17	MPR	☐
260	1955-61	'ROYAL MAIL' Van	Red/Black body, crest. 78 mm.	£32	NC	☐
261	1956-61	'POST OFFICE TELEPHONES' Van	Green and Black body, crest. 73 mm.	£32	NC	☐
262	1956-59	VW Swiss Postal Van	Yellow Black body, *P.T.T./*crest. 90 mm.	£75	NC	☐
273	1965-70	'R.A.C.' Mini Minor Van	Blue body, *Road Service* CEM/SS/FS/OD. 78 mm.	£25	NC	☐
			LV Blue/White body	£20	NC	☐
274	1967-71	'A.A.' Mini Minor Van	Yellow body, *Patrol Service* CEM/SS/FS/OD. 78 mm.	£20	NC	☐
			LV Yellow/Black body	£16	NC	☐
275	1964-69	Brinks Armoured Car	Grey/blue body, *Brinks Security Since 1859,* 2D/LHD/SS/WDS/OD/IBC. 120 mm.	£30	NC	☐
			LV 1979 No bullion or drivers	£10-£14	MPR	☐
280	1948-54	Delivery Van	Red or Blue body, Type 3, No RWD. 83 mm.	£13-£16	MPR	☐
280	1967-68	Mobile Midland Bank	Sil/Cream/Blue body, *Midland Bank Ltd.* 124 mm.	£25	NC	☐

Ref. No.		Model Type	**Dinky Vans continued**	Rarity and Price Grading		
407	1966-69	Ford Transit Van	Blue White, *Kenwood* Pro. 129 mm.	£20	NC	☐
407	1970-71	Ford Transit Van	White body, *Colour TV, Telefusion* Pro. 129 mm.	£20	NC	☐
407	1970-73	Ford Transit Van	Yel body, *Hertz Truck Rentals* Pro. 129 mm.	£15	NC	☐
407	1970-73	Ford Transit Van	White body *Rediffusion Colour TV* Pro. 129 mm.	£15	NC	☐
407	1970-73	Ford Transit Van	Red body, *Avis Truck Rentals.* 129 mm.	£15	NC	☐
410	1972-76	Bedford Van	Black/Red, *Simpsons* and CEM. 90 mm.	£12	GV	☐
410	1974-75	Bedford Van	Blue body, *John Menzies.* 90 mm.	£8-£11	MPR	☐
410	1974-75	Bedford Van	Orange/Black body, *Belaco Brake and Clutch Parts.* 90 mm.	£12	GV	☐
410	1975-76	Bedford Van	White body *MJ Hire Service.* 90 mm.	£6-£8	MPR	☐
410	1975-77	Bedford Van	White body *Modellers World.* 90 mm.	£25	GV	☐
410	1975-77	Bedford Van	Red body *Marley Building* etc. 90 mm.	£12	NC	☐
410	1979	Bedford Van	White body *Collectors Gazette.* 90 mm.	£15	GV	☐
410	1972-80	Bedford 'ROYAL MAIL' Van	Red body *EIIR* PW. 90 mm.	£4-£6	MPR	☐
412	1974-80	Bedford 'AA SERVICE' Van	Yellow/Black body PW. 90 mm.	£4-£6	MPR	☐
416	1975-78	Ford Transit Van	Yellow body, *Motorway Services* SL/20D. 129 mm.	£7-£9	MPR	☐
417	1978-79	Ford Transit Van	Yellow body, *Motorway Services* SL/OD. 129 mm.	£4-£6	MPR	☐
450 (31a)	1955-57	Trojan Van 'ESSO'	Red/White body *Esso* decals. 85 mm.	£45	NC	☐
450	1965-70	Bedford TK Van	Metallic Green and White body, *Castrol The Masterpiece in Oils* OD. 143 mm.	£45	NC	☐
451 (31b)	1955-57	Trojan Van 'DUNLOP'	Red body *Dunlop The Worlds Master Tyre.* 85 mm.	£40	NC	☐
452 (31c)	1954-57	Trojan Van 'CHIVERS'	Green body *Chivers Jellies* and design. 85 mm.	£50	NC	☐
454	1957-59	Trojan Van 'CYDRAX'	Green body *Drink Cydrax* and design. 85 mm.	£50	NC	☐
455	1957-61	Trojan Van 'BROOKE BOND'	Red body *Brooke Bond Tea* and design. 85 mm.	£50	NC	☐
465	1957-59	Morris 10 cwt Van 'CAPSTAN'	Blue/Dark Blue body, cigarette design *Have a Capstan.* 78 mm.	£55	NC	☐
470	1954-56	Austin Van 'SHELL BP'	Red/Green body *Shell, BP* decals. 89 mm.	£35	NC	☐
471	1955-60	Austin Van 'NESTLÉS'	Red body *Nestlés* decals. 89 mm.	£35	NC	☐
472	1957-60	Austin Van 'RALEIGH CYCLES'	Green body *Raleigh Cycles* decals. 89 mm.	£38	NC	☐
480	1954-56	Bedford Van 'KODAK'	Yellow body, *Kodak Cameras and Films.* 83 mm.	£36	NC	☐
481	1955-60	Bedford Van 'OVALTINE'	Blue body *Ovaltine* decals. 83 mm.	£36	NC	☐
482	1956-60	Bedford Van 'DINKY TOYS'	Yellow body *Dinky Toys* decals. 83 mm.	£36	NC	☐
490 (30v)	1954-56	Electric Dairy Van	Grey/Blue or Cream/Red body *Express Dairy.* 85 mm.	£17-£21	MPR	☐
491 (30v)	1956-60	Electric Dairy Van	Cream/Red body *N.C.B.* on front. 85 mm.	£30	NC	☐
491	1960	Electric Dairy Van	Cream/Red body, *Jobs Dairy,* PRM. 85 mm.	£65	NC	☐
492 (34c)	1954-57	Loudspeaker Van	Brown body, Type 3, OC, Black LS. 81 mm.	£14-£17	MPR	☐
492	1964-65	Election Mini Van	White body *Vote for Somebody* Fig/OD. 78 mm.	£30	GV	☐

Ref. No.		Model Type	Dinky Vans continued	Rarity and Price Grading		
514	1949-52	Guy Van 'SLUMBERLAND'	Red *Slumberland Spring Interior Mattresses* and crest. 1st type ST/OD/SPW. 134 mm. NB At Phillips Auction 27th July 1983 a similar van fetched £80.	£75	NC	☐
514	1951-54	Guy Van 'LYONS'	Blue *Lyons Swiss Rolls* 1st type ST/OD/SPW. 134 mm.	£225	GV	☐
514	1952-54	Guy Van 'WEETABIX'	Yellow body 1st type ST/OD/SPW. 134 mm.	£250	GV	☐
514	1953-54	Guy Van 'SPRATTS'	Red/Cream body, 1st type *Bonio Ovals & Dog Cakes* ST/OD/SPW. 134 mm.	£175	GV	☐
561	1962-64	Citroen Delivery Van	Metallic Blue body, *Cibie* sliding doors. 90 mm.	£30	NC	☐
917	1955-56	Guy Van 'SPRATTS'	Red/Cream body — details as for 514. 134 mm.	£175	GV	☐
918	1955-58	Guy Van 'EVER READY'	Blue body, 2nd type ST/OD/SPW *Ever Ready Batteries for Life*. 134 mm. NB At Phillips Auction on 27th July 1983 an Ever Ready Van fetched £110.	£85	NC	☐
919	1957-58	Guy Van 'GOLDEN SHRED'	*Red body, 2nd type ST/OD/SPW Robertson's Golden Shred* plus CEM. 134 mm.	£225	NC	☐
920	1960-61	Guy Warrior Van 'HEINZ' Tomato Ketchup Bottle decal	Red and Yellow body, Warrior front *Heinz 57 Varieties* ST/OD/SPW. 137 mm.	£400	GV	☐
923	1955-58	Big Bedford Van 'HEINZ'	Red/Yellow body, *Heinz 57 Varieties* plus Baked Beans tin ST/SPW. 146 mm. NB At Phillips Auction June 1st 1983 a similar van fetched £60	£60	NC	☐
923	1958-59	Big Bedford Van 'HEINZ'	Red/Yellow body, *Heinz 57 Varieties* plus Tomato Ketchup bottle ST/SPW. 146 mm.	£175	NC	☐
930	1960-64	Bedford Pallet — Jekta Van	Orange/Yellow body, *Dinky Toys, Meccano* ST/OD/WPEM. 177 mm.	£60	NC	☐

Gift Sets Dinky Vans

28 Series	1934-40	28/1 Delivery Vans All 1st Type	Contains 28a Hornby, 28b Pickfords, 28c Manchester Guardian, 28d Oxo, 28e Ensign, 28f Palethorpes		NGPP	☐
28 Series	1934-40	28/2 Delivery Vans All 1st Type	28g Kodak, 28h Sharps, 28k Marsh's, 28l Crawfords, 28m Wakefield, 28n Meccano		NGPP	☐
28 Series		Revised Set 28/1 Delivery Vans	Contains 28a Hornby, 28b Pickfords, 28c Manchester Guardian, 28e Firestone, 28f Palethorpes, 28n Atco		NGPP	☐
28 Series		Revised Set 28/2 Delivery Vans	Contains 28d Oxo, 28g Kodak, 28h Dunlop Van, 28k Marsh's, 28m Wakefield, 28h Crawfords		NGPP	☐
28 Series	1936-40	28/3 Delivery Vans (2nd Type)	Contains 28r Swans, 28s Frys, 28t Ovaltine, 28w Osram, 28x Hovis, 28y Exide		NGPP	☐
280 Series	1936-40	280 Series Delivery Vans (2nd Type)	Contains 280a Viyella, 280b Lyons, 280c Shredded Wheat, 280d Bisto, 280e Ekco, 280f Mackintosh's		NGPP	☐
299	1958	Post Office Services	Contains 260, 261, plus Telephone Box Messenger and Postman	£55	GV	☐

1d Dinky Buses, Taxis & Trams

Ref. No.		Model Type	Model Features and Size	Rarity and Price Grading		
Note: For a description and diagrams of the different types of Buses turn to Section IV						
27	1934-38	'OVALTINE' Tram	Red/White, Blue/White or Or/White, WW *Drink Delicious Ovaltine Every Day.* 77 mm.	£150	NVE	☐
27	1934-38	'LIPTON'S TEA' Tram	Red and White body. 77 mm.		NGPP	☐
29	1934	Double Decker Bus 'MARMITE'	Blue, Green or Yel body, Wh roof, MW *Marmite Definately Does You Good.* 69 mm.	£150	NVE	☐
29b	1935-40	Streamline Bus	TT Green or Blue body open RWD. 88 mm.	£100	GV	☐
29b	1948-50	Streamline Bus	Cream and Red body, No rear window. 88 mm.	£35	NC	☐
29c	1938-40	Double Decker Bus 'DUNLOP TYRES'	Blue and Cream body, 1st type (A.E.C.) with stairs. 100 mm.	£150	GV	☐
29c	1947-48	Double Decker Bus	Green or Red body, Cream or Grey top, no stairs 1st type (AEC) No adverts. 100 mm.	£50	NC	☐
29c (290)	1948-54	Double Decker Bus 'DUNLOP TYRES'	Red/Cream or Green/Cream, 2nd type LV *Dunlop The Worlds Master Tyre.* 100 mm.	£40	NC	☐
29e	1948-52	Single Deck Bus	Cream/Blue, TT Blue or TT Green body. 113 mm.	£45	NC	☐
29f	1950-54	Observation Coach	Grey body, Red flashes. 112 mm.	£28-£34	MPR	☐
29g (281)	1951-54	Luxury Coach	Cream body, Orange flashes. 113 mm.	£28-£34	MPR	☐
29h (282)	1952-54	Duple Roadmaster Coach	Blue and Silver body. 119 mm.	£28-£34	MPR	☐
36g	1938-41	'TAXI' with Driver	Blue/Black, Green/Black or Yellow and Black body, with rear window *Taxi* cast on roof, Black/Silver HCLP. 72 mm.	£55	GV	☐
36g	1946-49	'TAXI' with Driver	Maroon/Black or Green/Black body, no rear window. 72 mm.	£35	NC	☐
40h (254)	1951-54	'TAXI'	Blue or Yellow body, *Taxi* CI roof. 94 mm.	£21-£26	MPR	☐
241	1977	'SILVER JUBILEE TAXI'	Silver body, 1977 IS/ODB. 112 mm.	£6-£8	MPR	☐
254 (40h)	1954-56	London 'TAXI'	Dark Blue or Yellow body. 94 mm.	£24	NC	☐
254	1956-62	London 'TAXI'	Green and Yellow body. 94 mm.	£18-£22	MPR	☐
265	1960-64	Plymouth U.S.A. Taxi	Yellow/Red *25c First 1/5 Mile 5c Additional* LHD/IS/WDS/A. 108 mm.	£16	NC	☐
266	1960-66	Canadian Plymouth Taxi	Yellow/Red *Taxi* and *450 Metro Cab.* 108 mm.	£16	NC	☐
268	1962-67	Renault Dauphine Mini Cab	Red body *Meccano, Kenwood* VADS. 90 mm.	£32	GV	☐
278	1978-79	Plymouth Yellow Cab	Yellow body, *Yellow Cab Co* PCH/PW/A. 134 mm.		MPR	☐
280 (29f)	1954-60	Observation Coach	Cream body Red flashes. 112 mm.	£24-£29	MPR	☐
281 (29g)	1954-60	Modern Coach	Fawn body, Orange flashes on Maroon body, Cream flashes.	£24-£29	MPR	☐
282 (29h)	1954-60	Duple Roadmaster Coach	Blue/Silver or Red/Silver body *Leyland Royal Tiger* on BP. 119 mm.	£23-£29	MPR	☐
282	1967-68	Austin 1800 T	Blue body, SL/FS/SS/ODB. 101 mm.	£10-£14	MPR	☐
283	1956-63	B.O.A.C. Coach	Blue body, White roof, *British Overseas Airways Corporation* and *B.O.A.C. 120 mm.*	£30-£35	MPR	☐
283	1971-77	'RED ARROW' Single Decker Bus	Red body, White band. ODB/Bell. 167 mm.	£19-£24	MPR	☐
284	1972-79	London 'TAXI'	Black body, D/PW/SWS *Taxi.* 112 mm.	£3-£5	MPR	☐

Ref. No.		Model Type	**Dinky Buses continued**	Rarity and Price Grading		
289	1964-79	London Routemaster Bus	Several issues. 121 mm.		MPR	☐
	1964-65	'TERN SHIRTS FOR CRISPNESS'	Red body, *London Transport*	£20	NC	☐
	1965-69	'SSSCHWEPPES'	Red body *London Transport*	£20	NC	☐
	1970?	'FESTIVAL OF LONDON STORES'	Rare Promotional	£55	NVE	☐
	1970-77	'ESSO SAFETY GRIP TYRES'	Red body, RT or PW, RT price only	£8-£11	MPR	☐
	1977-78	'VISIT MADAME TUSSAUD'S'	Red body, *London Transport*	£20	NC	☐
290 (29c)	1954-63	Double Decker Bus	Red/Cream body *Dunlop The Worlds Master Tyre* 2nd or 3rd Type. 103 mm.	£40	NC	☐
291	1959-63	Double Decker Bus 'EXIDE BATTERIES'	Red body, Yellow/Black decals, *73* DBD 3rd Type Radiator front. 103 mm.	£40	NC	☐
291	1974-77	Atlantean City Bus 'KENNING'	Orange MB, WH or Blue REC, *Kenning Car Van and Truck Hire* D/WDS. Leyland. 123 mm.	£9-£12	MPR	☐
292	1962-68	Atlantean Bus 'REGENT'	Red/White body, D/WDS *Regent for Peak Pulling Power* and *Corporation Transport. Leyland.* 121 mm.	£30	NC	☐
292	1962-66	Atlantean Bus 'RIBBLE'	Same model as 292 with *Ribble* replacing *Corporation Transport* D/WDS. Leyland. 121 mm.	£35	NC	☐
293	1963-68	Atlantean Bus 'BP'	Green/White body, *BP is the Key to Better Motoring and Corporation Transport* D/WDS. Leyland.	£30	NC	☐
293	1973-78	Swiss Postal Bus	Yellow/Cream body, *P.T.T.* crest BUP. 119 mm.	£5-£7	MPR	☐
295	1960-64	Atlas Kenebrake Bus	Light Blue/Grey body, SS/WDS. 86 mm.	£11-£14	MPR	☐
295	1973-74	Atlantean Bus 'YELLOW PAGES'	Yellow body, *Let Your Fingers Do the Walking,* YPRHBD. Leyland. 123 mm.	£25	NC	☐
295	1974-76	Atlantean 'YELLOW PAGES'	Deep Yellow type, YPCHBD. Leyland. 123 mm.	£12-£15	MPR	☐
			Pale Yellow type, YPCHBD. 123 mm.	£9-£12	MPR	☐
296	1972-75	Luxury Coach	Blue body, White/Cream interior	£8-£11	MPR	☐
297	1977	Silver Jubilee Bus	Silver/Black body Leyland Atlantean	£8-£11	MPR	☐
297	1977	Woolworths Silver Jubilee Bus	Silver body Leyland Atlantean	£18	NC	☐
306	1973-75	Luxury Viceroy Coach	Metallic Red body	£15	NC	☐
949	1961-64	Wayne 'SCHOOL BUS'	Yellow/Red body, ST/WDS. 195 mm.	£55	NC	☐
952	1964-71	Vega Major Luxury Coach	Grey/Maroon body, ST/SS/ODB/SL/WDS. 242 mm.	£30	NC	☐
953	1963-65	Continental Touring Coach	Blue/White body *Dinky Continental Tours* ST/WDS. 195 mm.	£85	GV	☐
954	1972-77	Vega Major Luxury Coach	White/Maroon body, SS/ODB/SL/WDS/BW. 242 mm.	£19-£24	MPR	☐
961	1973-77	Vega Major Coach	Yellow/Cream body, *P.T.T.* plus emblem. 242 mm.	£55	NC	☐

Gift Set

300	1978-80	London Scene Set	Contains 289 and 284	£5-£7	MPR	☐

1e Dinky Fire, Police and Ambulance Vehicles

Ref. No.		Model Type	Model Features and Size	Rarity and Price Grading		
Note: For description of the different chassis types see section IV						
24a	1934-38	Ambulance (No crosses)	Grey/Red or Cream/Red body, CCCH/PLR/ open windows. 102 mm.	£125	GV	☐
24a	1938-40	Ambulance (No crosses)	Green/Red or Grey/Red body, CCCH/RB/ open windows. 102 mm.	£100	GV	☐
25h	1936-40	Streamline Fire Engine	Red/Silver body, No CH/TPLD/bell/WT. 101 mm.	£125	GV	☐
25h (250)	1948-54	Streamline Fire Engine	Red/Silver body, No CH/TPLD/bell. 101 mm.	£19-£25	MPR	☐
25k	1938-40	Streamline Fire Engine	Red/Silver body, No CH/6 TP FM/TPLD/bell. 101 mm.	£150	GV	☐
30f	1935-38	Ambulance (Red crosses)	Red/Grey body, MCH/PLR/open WDS. 99 mm.	£125	GV	☐
30f	1938-40	Ambulance (Red crosses)	Black/Grey body, MCH/RB/open WDS. 99 mm.	£100	GV	☐
30f	1946-47	Ambulance (Red crosses)	Grey body, Black, MCH, open WDS. 99 mm.	£55	NC	☐
30f	1947-48	Ambulance (Red crosses)	Cream body, Black, MCH, No WDS. 99 mm.	£35	NC	☐
30h	1950-54	Daimler Ambulance	Cream body, Red crosses. 96 mm.	£20-£25	MPR	☐
195	1971-74	Fire Chiefs Land Rover	Red, *Fire Service,* FLL/OD/SWS/BUP. 109 mm.	£7-£9	MPR	☐
243	1978-79	Volvo Police Car	White/Red, *Police,* FLL/PCH/PW. 141 mm.	£3-£5	MPR	☐
244	1978-79	Plymouth Fury Police Car	Black/White body, *Police* FLL/PCH/PW/A. 134 mm.	£3-£5	MPR	☐
250 (25h)	1954-62	Fire Engine	Red/Silver body, TPL/bell. 99 mm.	£19-£25	MPR	☐
250	1968-74	Police Mini Cooper S	White *Police* cones/sign/FLL/TS. 75 mm.	£5-£7	MPR	☐
251	1971-74	U.S.A. 'POLICE' Car	White/Black body, D/FLL/SWS/A. 132 mm.	£7-£9	MPR	☐
252	1971-74	R.C.M.P. Chevrolet	Blue/White body, D/FLL/SWS/2A/crest. 132 mm.	£7-£9	MPR	☐
253 (30h)	1954-64	Daimler Ambulance	Cream body, Red crosses, some have WDS. 95 mm.	£11-£16	MPR	☐
254	1977-79	Police Range Rover	White body, *Police,* FLL/OD/SWS. 109 mm.	£3-£5	MPR	☐
255	1955-61	Mersey Tunnel Police	Red body, *Mersey Tunnel* and *Police* H. 77 mm.	£13-£17	MPR	☐
255	1968-71	Ford Zodiac Police Car	White body, *Police* D/FLL/ODB/SS/FS/A. '1st AGAIN! 4 OPENING DOORS'. 114 mm.	£9-£12	MPR	☐
256	1960-64	Humber Hawk Police Car	Black body, *Police* D/PM/SS/WDS/A.	£20	NVE	☐
256	1977-79	Police Mini Clubman	Blue/White body, *Police,* FLL/ODB/PW. 82 mm.	£3-£5	MPR	☐
257	1961-68	Canadian 'FIRE CHIEF'	Red body, ST/FLL/SS/WDS, Nash Rambler. 102 mm.	£11-£14	MPR	☐
258	1960-61	U.S.A. 'POLICE' Car	Black/White body, LHD/FLL/WDS, De Soto Fireflite. 114 mm.	£16-£20	MPR	☐
258	1961-62	U.S.A. 'POLICE' Car	Black body, LHD/A/WDS, Dodge Royal, Sedan. 111 mm.	£16-£20	MPR	☐
258	1962-67	U.S.A. 'POLICE' Car	Black/White body, LHD/FLL/FS/A, Ford Fairlane. 111 mm.	£13-£16	MPR	☐
258	1967-68	Cadillac	Black/White body *Police,* LHD/SS/FS/FLL/A. 111 mm.	£8-£11	MPR	☐
263	1962-68	Superior Criterion	Cream body *Ambulance* on WDS. 127 mm.	£10-£14	MPR	☐
263	1978-79	Fire Tender	Yellow body *Airport Rescue,* PL/FLL. 177 mm.	£5-£7	MPR	☐
264	1967-68	R.C.M.P. Cadillac	Blue/White body, SS/FS/FLL/A/crest. 111 mm.	£14-£17	MPR	☐
264	1978-79	Rover 3500	White/Yellow body *Police,* FLL/ODB. 131 mm.	£3-£5	MPR	☐
266	1977-79	E.R.F. Fire Tender	Red body *Fire Service,* white PLD. 223 mm.	£6-£8	MPR	☐
267	1978-79	Paramedic Truck	Red body, 5 yellow cylinders, PW. 119 mm.	£3-£5	MPR	☐
268	1974-77	Range Rover	White body *Ambulance,* FLL/OD/BUP/SR. 109 mm.	£5-£7	MPR	☐
269	1962-66	Jaguar 'POLICE' Car	White body, FLL/SS/FS/WDS/A/2PM. 95 mm.	£20	NVE	☐
269	1978-79	Ford Transit	White/Red body *Ambulance,* SR/PM etc. 129 mm.	£3-£5	MPR	☐
270	1971-74	Ford Panda	Blue/White body, *Police* SWS/BUP. 97 mm.	£4-£6	MPR	☐
271	1975-76	Ford Transit 'FIRE'	Red body, hose/axe/bells/PLD/BUP. 129 mm.	£5-£8	MPR	☐
272	1975-77	Police Accident Unit	White body, *Police* OD FLL/A/cones/signs. 129 mm.	£5-£8	MPR	☐
274	1978-79	Ford Transit Ambulance	White body, *Ambulance,* SR/FLL/RCS. 129 mm.	£3-£5	MPR	☐
276	1962-69	'AIRPORT FIRE CONTROL' Tender	Red body, FLL/SS/FS/WDS/bell. 117 mm.	£11-£16	MPR	☐
277	1962-68	Superior Criterion Ambulance	Blue/White/Red, D/LHD/SR/ODB/FLL. 127 mm.	£11-£16	MPR	☐
277	1977-79	Land Rover	Blue/White body *Police,* FLL. 110 mm.	£3-£5	MPR	☐

Ref. No.		Model Type	**Fire Police and Ambulance Vehicles continued**	Rarity and Price Grading		
278	1964-68	Vauxhall Victor	White body *Ambulance,* SR/SL/SS/FS/ODB. 87 mm.	£11-£15	MPR	☐
282	1974-79	Land Rover Appliance	Red body *Fire Service,* FLL/Metal LD/BUP.	£4-£6	MPR	☐
285	1970-79	Merryweather Marquis	Red/White body *Fire Service,* PL/FLL. 177 mm.	£6-£8	MPR	☐
286	1969-74	Ford Transit	Red body *Fire Service,* hose/FLL/BUP. 112 mm.	£6-£8	MPR	☐
287	1967-74	Police Accident Unit	Cream/Orange body *Police Accident Unit.* 122 mm.	£6-£8	MPR	☐
288	1974-79	Superior Cadillac	Red/White body *Ambulance,* SR/FLL. 152 mm.	£4-£7	MPR	☐
555	1952-69	Fire Engine	Red/Silver body, ST/ladder. 140 mm.	£18-£23	MPR	☐
956	1958-71	Turntable Fire Escape	Red body, small cab/ST LV. 200 mm.	£16-£21	MPR	☐
			LV *Berliot* large cab.	£9-£14	MPR	☐
2253	1974-76	Ford Capri Police Car	White/Red body *Police/Accident.* 175 mm.	£7-£9	MPR	☐

Gift Sets

Ref. No.		Model Type	Model Features and Size	Rarity and Price Grading		
294	1973-76	Police Vehicles Gift Set	Contains 250, 254, 287	£15	NC	☐
297	1967-72	Police Vehicles Gift Set	Contains 250, 255, 287	£18	NC	☐
298	1963-64	Emergency Services Set	Contains 258, 276, 263, 277 (9 figures)	£55	GV	☐
299	1963-66	Motorway Services Set	Contains 257, 276, 263, 277	£55	GV	☐
299	1978-79	Crash Squad Gift Set	Contains 244, 732 helicopter	£3-£5	MPR	☐
302	1978-79	Emergency Squad Gift Set	Contains Paramedic Truck and 288	£7-£9	MPR	☐
304	1978-79	Fire Rescue Gift Set	Contains 195, 282, 384	£9-£11	MPR	☐
957	1959-64	Fire Services Gift Set	Contains 257, 955, 956	£55	GV	☐

1f Dinky Road Making Equipment

Ref. No.		Model Type	Model Features and Size	Rarity and Price Grading		
25p (251)	1948-54	Aveling Barford Diesel Roller	Green/Red body, driver and hook. 110 mm.	£14-£19	MPR	☐
279	1967-79	Aveling Barford DRL	Orange/Green or Orange/Yellow body. 116 mm.	£3-£5	MPR	☐
430	1977-80	Johnson 2 ton Dumper	Orange/Yellow body, Blue driver. 166 mm.	£3-£5	MPR	☐
436	1963-69	'ATLAS COPCO' Lorry	Yellow MB, compressor, FS/OEC. 89 mm.	£11-£14	MPR	☐
437	1962-80	Muir Hill 2WL Loader	Yellow body, hook, BUP. 105 mm.	£5-£8	MPR	☐
561 (961)	1949-55	Blaw Knox Bulldozer	Red body, rubber tracks, driver, ST. 138 mm.	£9-£13	MPR	☐
562 (962)	1948-65	Muir Hill Dumper	Yellow body, rubber tyres, hook. 105 mm.	£5-£8	MPR	☐
563	1948-64	Blaw Knox Heavy Tractor	Red body, rubber tracks, hook, ST. 116 mm.	£8-£11	MPR	☐
924	1972-76	Aveling Barford 'CENTAUR'	Red/Yellow body, dump truck. 180 mm.	£7-£9	MPR	☐
959	1961-68	Foden DTR & Bulldozer	Red/Orange body, MN badge/ST/D/WDS. 165 mm.	£13-£16	MPR	☐
960	1960-68	Albion Lorry CMX	Orange/Yellow/Blue body, SPW/ST. 128 mm.	£13-£16	MPR	☐
961 (561)	1955-64	Blaw Knox Bulldozer	Red body, rubber tracks, driver, ST. 143 mm.	£9-£13	MPR	☐
962 (562)	1955-66	Muir Hill	Yellow body, hook, ST. 108 mm.	£5-£8	MPR	☐
963	1955-59	Blaw Knox Heavy Tractor	Red body, rubber tracks, hook, ST. 116 mm.	£8-£11	MPR	☐
963	1973-75	Road Grader	Yellow/Red/Silver body, BUP. 238 mm.	£6-£8	MPR	☐
965	1955-69	'EUCLID' Dump Truck	Yellow body, *Stone Ore Earth,* CEM. 142 mm.	£11-£14	MPR	☐
965	1969-70	'TEREX' Rear Dump Truck	Yellow body. 142 mm.	£12-£15	MPR	☐
966	1960-64	Marrel Multi Bucket Unit	Yellow body, Grey buckets, ST. 115 mm.	£14-£17	MPR	☐
967	1973-78	Muir Hill Loader/Trencher	Yellow/Red or Orange/Black body. 163 mm.	£3-£5	MPR	☐
973	1971-75	Eaton 'YALE' Tractor Shovel	Red/Silver/Yellow body, BUP. 178 mm.	£6-£8	MPR	☐
975	1963-67	Ruston Bucyrus Excavator	Yellow/Red/Grey body, rubber tracks. 190 mm.	£15-£18	MPR	☐
976	1968-76	'MICHIGAN' Tractor Dozer	Yellow/Red body, BUP, D/EC/DDC. 147 mm.	£6-£8	MPR	☐
977	1973-78	Shovel Dozer	Yellow/Red/Silver, BUP. 151 mm.	£6-£8	MPR	☐
984	1974-79	Atlas Digger	Red/Yellow, plastic tracks. 247 mm.	£7-£9	MPR	☐

Gift Set

900	1964-65	Building Site Set	Contains 437, 960, 961, 962, 965	£55	NVE	☐

1g Dinky Farm and Garden Models

Ref. No.		Model Type	Model Features and Size	Rarity and Price Grading		
22e	1933-40	Farm Tractor 'Modelled Miniature'	Yellow/Blue/Red body, metal wheels, SW cast in. 70 mm.	£250	NVE	☐
27a (300)	1948-54	Massey Harris Tractor	Red/Yellow body, D/SW/H. 89 mm.	£14-£17	MPR	☐
27ak (310)	1948-54	Tractor and Hay Rake	Red/Yellow body	£20-£25	MPR	☐
27b	1949-54	Halesowen Harvest Trailer	Brown/Red body. 121 mm.	£11-£14	MPR	☐
27c	1949-54	M.H. Manure Spreader	Red body, towbar, hook. 113 mm.	£8-£11	MPR	☐
279 (342)	1949-56	Moto-Cart	Brown/Green body. 110 mm.	£8-£11	MPR	☐

Ref. No.		Model Type	Farm and Garden Models continued	Rarity and Price Grading		
27m	1950-55	Land Rover Trailer	Orange/Green body, TB/H. 79 mm.	£8-£11	MPR	☐
27n (301)	1950-60	Field Marshall Tractor	Orange body, D/SW/H/FAS. 79 mm.	£30	NC	☐
30n	1950-60	Farm Produce Wagon	Green/Yellow or Blue/Red body, H. 107 mm.	£17-£21	MPR	☐
105a (381)	1949-54	Garden Roller	Green/Red body. 67 mm.	£5-£7	MPR	☐
105b (382)	1949-54	Wheelbarrow	Brown body. 82 mm.	£5-£7	MPR	☐
105c (383)	1949-54	4 Wheeled Hand Truck	Green body. 126 mm.	£2-£4	MPR	☐
105e (384)	1949-54	Grass Cutter	Red/Green/Yellow body. 73 mm.	£15	NC	☐
107a (385)	1949-54	Sack Truck	Blue body. 65 mm.	£11-£15	MPR	☐
300	1954-75	'MASSEY HARRIS' Tractor	Red body, driver, SW/H. 89 mm.	£14-£17	MPR	☐
300	1960-65	'MASSEY FERGUSON' Tractor	Red/Orange body, driver, SW/H. 89 mm.	£14-£17	MPR	☐
301 (27n)	1954-61	Field Marshall Tractor	Orange body, D/SW/H/FAS. 79 mm.	£25-£35	MPR	☐
301	1962-67	Field Marshall Tractor	Red body, D/SW/H. 76 mm.	£15-£20	MPR	☐
305	1965-70	'DAVID BROWN' Tractor	Red/Yellow body, detachable cab, D. 83 mm.	£12-£15	MPR	☐
305	1971-75	David Brown Tractor	White body, detachable cab, D/BUP. 83 mm.	£12-£15	MPR	☐
308	1971-75	'LEYLAND 384' Tractor	Met Red body, D/SW/H/BUP. 86 mm.	£12-15	MPR	☐
308	1976-79	'LEYLAND 384' Tractor	Blue body, D/SW/H/BUP. 86 mm.	£7-£9	MPR	☐
310	1954-60	Tractor with Hay Rake	Red/Yellow body. 157 mm.	£11-£14	MPR	☐
319	1961-68	Weeks Tipping Trailer	Red/Yellow body. 105 mm.	£3-£5	MPR	☐
320	1954-60	Halesowen Trailer	Red/Brown body, tow bar, hook. 120 mm.	£5-£7	MPR	☐
321	1954-60	Massey Harris Manure Spreader	Red/Silver body. 113 mm.	£4-£6	MPR	☐
322	1954-60	Disc Harrow	Red/Yellow body. 86 mm.	£4-£6	MPR	☐
323	1954-63	Triple Gang Mower	Red/Yellow/Green body. 114 mm.	£4-£6	MPR	☐
324	1954-64	Hayrake	Red/Yellow body. 77 mm.	£4-£6	MPR	☐
325	1967-73	'DAVID BROWN' Tractor	White/Red Body. 83 mm.	£15-£22	MPR	☐
342	1955-60	Moto-Cart	Green/Brown body. 110 mm.	£5-£7	MPR	☐
343	1954-64	Farm Produce Wagon	Green/Yellow (Dodge BP). 107 mm.	£12-£15	MPR	☐
			Red/Blue body	£15-£18	MPR	☐
381	1977-80	Convoy Farm Truck	Yellow/Black body. 110 mm.	£3-£5	MPR	☐
399	1969-75	Tractor and Trailer Set	Red/Orange body, *Massey Ferguson*. 188 mm.	£15-£18	MPR	☐
428	1967-71	Trailer	Red or Grey body. 105 mm.	£2-£4	MPR	☐

Gift Sets

1952-54	Set No 1	Contains 27a, b, c, g, h	£40	NVE	☐
1960-69	Set No 387	Contains 300, 320, 321, 322, 324	£35	NVE	☐

1h Dinky Military Models

Ref. No.		Model Type	Model Features and Size	Rarity and Price Grading		
22f	1933-40	Army tank	Green/Orange body turret rotates. 87 mm.	£85	GV	☐
30hm	1950-54	Daimler Ambulance	Green body, Red crosses, US issue. 96 mm.	£85	GV	☐
37c	1938-40	Signals Dispatch Rider	Khaki/Green body, Blue/White arms and WT. 46 mm.	£55	GV	☐
150a	1938-40	Royal Tank Corps Officer	Khaki, binoculars in hand	£7-£9	MPR	☐
150b	1938-40	Royal Tank Corps Private	Khaki uniform (sitting) DC	£3-£5	MPR	☐
150c	1938-40	Royal Tank Corps Private	Khaki uniform (standing) DC	£3-£5	MPR	☐
150d	1938-40	Army Driver	Khaki uniform DC (sitting)	£3-£5	MPR	☐
150e	1938-40	Royal Corps NCO	Khaki uniform DC (walking)	£3-£5	MPR	☐
151a	1937-40	Medium Tank	MG body White SQM/TRR/CHT/A. 92 mm.	£35	GV	☐
151b	1938-40	6 W Transport Wagon	MG body, SPW/H/holes/TP cover. 99 mm.	£35	GV	☐
151b	1946-48	6 W Transport Wagon	MG body, SPW/H/holes/TP cover. 99 mm.	£28	NC	☐
151c	1938-40	Cooker Trailer	MG (with stand). 60 mm.	£11-£13	MPR	☐
151c	1946-48	Cooker Trailer	MG (with stand). 60 mm.	£8-£10	MPR	☐
151d	1938-40	Water Tank Trailer	Military green. 52 mm.	£11-£13	MPR	☐
151d	1946-48	Water Tank Trailer	Military green. 52 mm.	£8-£10	MPR	☐
152a	1937-40	Light Tank	MG body, White, SQM/TRR/CHT/A. 68 mm.	£35	GV	☐
152a	1946-48	Light Tank	MG body, White, SQM/TRR/CHT/A. 68 mm.	£25	GV	☐
152b	1938-40	Reconnaissance Car	Military Green body, Green BP, 6 wheels. 89 mm.	£35	GV	☐
152b	1946-48	Reconnaissance Car	Military Green body, 6 wheels. 89 mm.	£20-£25	MPR	☐
			Brown version 6 wheels	£15-£20	MPR	☐
153a	1946-48	Jeep (U.S. Market)	MG body, White star, SW/LHD/SPW at rear. 69 mm.	£24	GV	☐
160a	1939-40	Royal Artillery NCO	Khaki uniform	£3-£5	MPR	☐
160b	1939-40	Royal Artillery Gunner	Khaki uniform (seated)	£3-£5	MPR	☐
160c	1939-40	Royal Artillery Gunlayer	Khaki uniform	£3-£5	MPR	☐
160d	1939-40	Royal Artillery Gunner	Khaki uniform (standing)	£3-£5	MPR	☐
161a	1939-40	Searchlight on Lorry	Military Green body. 99 mm.	£55	GV	☐
161b	1939-40	A.A. Gun on Trailer	MG body, H/gun elevates/holes/TB. 115 mm.	£35	GV	☐
161b	1946-48	A.A. Gun on Trailer	MG body, H/gun elevates/holes/TB. 115 mm.	£14-£20	MPR	☐
162a	1939-40	Light Dragon Tractor	MG body, chain track. 89 mm.	£35	GV	☐
162a	1946-48	Light Dragon Tractor	MG body, chain track/holes. 65 mm.	£25	NC	☐
162b	1939-40	Trailer	MG body towbar and hook. 43 mm.	£10	GV	☐
162b	1946-48	Trailer	MG body towbar and hook. 54 mm.	£4-£6	MPR	☐
162c	1939-40	18-pdr Gun	MG body towbar. 78 mm.	£5-£7	MPR	☐
162c	1946-48	18-pdr Gun	MG body towbar. 78 mm.	£5-£7	MPR	☐
170	1957-58	Ford Fordor	MG body, White star on nose. 102 mm.	£32	NVE	☐
601	1974-78	Austin Paramoke	MG/Grey body, PW/BUP. 76 mm.	£4-£6	MPR	☐
602	1977-80	Armoured Car Command	MG body, White star/fires sparks. 57 mm.	£7-£9	MPR	☐
603	1950-68	Army Private	Khaki (seated)	£1 each	MPR	☐
603a	1950-68	Army Personnel Set	Khaki 6 figures	£5	MPR	☐
604	1960-72	Army Personnel	Khaki 6 drivers	£5	MPR	☐
604	1976-79	Land Rover Bomb Disposal	MG/Orange body, *Explosive Disposal.* 110 mm.	£9-£11	MPR	☐
609	1976-79	105 mm with Crew	MG body, 3 soldiers, BUP. 160 mm.	£6-£8	MPR	☐
612	1976-79	Commando Jeep	MG/D/2 guns/A. 108 mm.	£5-£7	MPR	☐
612a	1974-79	Commando Jeep	MG or camouflage. 108 mm.	£4-£6	MPR	☐
615	1968-74	US Jeep and 105 mm	MG US Army markings/D. 199 mm.	£8-£11	MPR	☐
616	1968-78	AEC with Chieftain	MG *Army* AVTU/SQM/CN/PT/UJ. 318 mm.	£12-£15	MPR	☐
617	1969-78	VW KDF and 50 mm	German MG and crosses	£12-£15	MPR	☐
618	1976-78	AEC with Helicopter	MG body *Rescue* etc. AVTV/SQM/CN/UJ. 318 mm.	£9-£11	MPR	☐
619	1976-78	Bren Gun Carrier and Anti Tank Gun	MG, WS/D/PS/SQM/SPW/PT/A/H/SH/BUP. 125 mm. 159 mm.	£9-£12	MPR	☐
620	1967-71	Berliot Missile Launcher	MG Body, Black/White missile. 150 mm.	£20-£25	MPR	☐
621	1954-63	3 ton Army Tank	MG body, SQM/SPW/H. 113 mm.	£11-£15	MPR	☐

Ref. No.		Model Type	**Dinky Military Models continued**	Rarity and Price Grading		
622	1954-63	10 ton Army Truck	MG body, ST/D/SQM/SPW/holes/6 W. 137 mm.	£17-£25	MPR	☐
622	1975-78	Bren Gun Carrier	MG body, Star/D/PS/SQM/PT/SPW. 125 mm.	£7-£9	MPR	☐
623	1954-63	Army Covered Wagon	MG Body, D/SQM/SPW. 105 mm.	£11-£15	MPR	☐
624	1954-60	Daimler Ambulance	MG body, Red crosses (US market). 105 mm.	£25	GV	☐
625	1975-78	Six Pounder Gun	MG body. 159 mm.	£3-£5	MPR	☐
626	1956-62	Military Ambulance	MG Body, Red crosses, ODB/SPW. 110 mm.	£11-£15	MPR	☐
630	1973-78	Ferret Armoured Car	MG body. 80 mm.	£6-£8	MPR	☐
641	1954-62	Army 1 ton Cargo Truck	MG body, D/SQM/holes for PS. 79 mm.	£10-£13	MPR	☐
642	1957-62	R.A.F. Pressure Refueller	RAF Blue body, *roundel,* ST/D/H/6 W. 142 mm.	£16-£23	MPR	☐
643	1958-64	Army Water Tanker	MG body, D/SQM. 89 mm.	£9-£12	MPR	☐
651	1954-70	Centurian Tank	MG body, ST/SQM/rubber tracks. 149 mm.	£9-£12	MPR	☐
654	1974-76	155 mm Mobile Gun	MG body, star/PT/shells. 151 mm.	£4-£6	MPR	☐
656	1975-79	88 mm Gun	MG body. 218 mm.	£6-£8	MPR	☐
660	1956-64	Tank Transporter	MG body, 6×6 W/folding ramps/SPW. 335 mm.	£13-£16	MPR	☐
660a	1978-80	AA Gun with Crew	MG body, 3 soldiers, BUP. 218 mm.	£6-£8	MPR	☐
661	1957-64	Recovery Tractor	MG body, ST/D/SQM/CO. 134 mm.	£20-£25	MPR	☐
662	1975-77	88 mm Gun with Crew	MG body, 3 Germans/shells/BUP. 185 mm.	£7-£9	MPR	☐
665	1964-69	Honest John M.L.	MG, Black/White missile/10 W/SPW. 188 mm.	£28	NC	☐
666	1959-64	Missile Erector Vehicle and Corporal Missile	MG body, Black/White missile erector elevates, ST/D/WDS/SPW/H. 240 mm.	£50	NC	☐
667	1960-61	Missile Servicing P.V.	MG body, ST/WDS/SPW/platform lifts. 197 mm.	£50	NC	☐
668	1977-79	Foden Army Truck	MG body, SQM/WDS. 197 mm.	£9-£12	MPR	☐
669	1956-58	U.S.A. Universal Jeep	MG body, star (U.S. market issue). 83 mm.	£14-£17	MPR	☐
670	1954-64	Armoured Car	MG body, SQM/turret rotates. 73 mm.	£8-£11	MPR	☐
673	1953-61	Scout Car	MG body, holes/SQM. 68 mm.	£8-£11	MPR	☐
674	1954-62	Austin Champ	MG body, D/TPWS/SW/SPW. 69 mm.	£8-£11	MPR	☐
674	1958	'U.N.' Austin Champ	White body, D/TPWS/SW/SPW. 69 mm.	£60	NVE	☐
674	1965-71	Austin Champ	MG body, D/SPW. 70 mm.	£7-£9	MPR	☐
675	1966-67	Ford Fordor	MG body, star (U.S. market issue). 102 mm.	£35	NVE	☐
676	1955-62	Saracen A.P.C.	MG body, SQM/turret rotates. 82 mm.	£8-£11	MPR	☐
676a	1960-66	Daimler Armoured Car	MG body, rubber tracks. 72 mm.	£7-£9	MPR	☐
677	1973-76	Daimler Armoured Car	MG body, plastic wheels. 72 mm.	£3-£4	MPR	☐
677	1957-62	Armoured Command Vehicle	MG body, SQM/6 wheels. 134 mm.	£16-£21	MPR	☐
680	1972-75	Ferret Armoured Car	MG body, PW/BUP/SQM. 80 mm.	£2-£4	MPR	☐
681	1972-75	D.U.K.W.	MG or Blue body, PW/BUP. 127 mm.	£2-£4	MPR	☐
682	1972-77	Stalwart Load Carrier	MG body, PW/BUP. 103 mm.	£2-£4	MPR	☐
683	1972-79	Chieftain Tank	MG body, SQM/PT/shells/BUP. 117 mm.	£12-£15	MPR	☐
686	1978-79	Convoy Army Truck	Green/Black body. 110 mm.	£3-£5	MPR	☐
686	1957-67	25 pdr Field Gun	MG body. 90 mm.	£5-£7	MPR	☐
687	1957-67	25 pdr Trailer	MG body, towbar, hook. 58 mm.	£5-£7	MPR	☐
688	1957-70	Field Artillery Tractor	MG body, SQM/SPW. 79 mm.	£12-£15	MPR	☐
689	1957-66	Medium Artillery Tractor	MG body, ST/SQM/D/H/6 W. 140 mm.	£14-£17	MPR	☐
690	1975-79	Scorpion Tank	MG body, SQM/PT/2A/CN/BUP. 120 mm.	£8-£10	MPR	☐
691	1976-79	Striker Anti Tank	Camouflaged 5 firing rockets. 122 mm.	£5-£7	MPR	☐
692	1955-62	5.5 Medium Gun	MG body, towbar. 131 mm.	£7-£9	MPR	☐
692	1974-79	Leopard Tank	MG body, SQM/PT/2A/CN/BC/BUP. 198 mm.	£8-£10	MPR	☐
693	1958-67	7.2″ Howitzer Gun	MG body, gun elevates. 130 mm.	£6-£8	MPR	☐
694	1974-80	Hanomag Destroyer	MG body, SQM/PT/PW/BC/BUP. 171 mm.	£3-£5	MPR	☐
696	1976-78	Leopard Anti-Aircraft Tank	MG body, SQM/PT/2A/BC/BUP. 147 mm.	£9-£11	MPR	☐
697	1964-71	25 pdr Gun Set	Contains 686, 687, 688. 174 mm.	£14-£17	MPR	☐
699	1976-78	Leopard Recovery Tank	MG body, SQM/PT/A/jib/black cross/BUP. 147 mm.	£9-£11	MPR	☐
815	1962-64	Panhard Armoured Tank	Green body, French flag/FI. 104 mm.	£25	GV	☐
817	1962-64	AMX 13 ton Tank	Green body, French flag/FI. 107 mm.	£30	GV	☐
822	1962-64	Half Track M3	Green body, rubber tracks/FI. 121 mm.	£45	GV	☐
884	1962-64	Brockway Bridge Truck	Green body, pontoons/FI. 181 mm.	£85	GV	☐

Dinky Military Models Gift Sets

Ref. No.		Model Type	Model Features and Size	Rarity and Price Grading		
	1938-40	150 Series Royal Tank Corp Set	Contains 150a, 2xb, 2xc, 150d	£15-£20	MPR	☐
	1937-40	151 Series Royal Tank Corps Medium Tank Set	Contains 151a, b, c, d and 150d	£55	GV	☐
	1937-40	152 Series Light Tank Set	Contains 152a, b, c, d	£75	NVE	☐
	1939-40	156 Series Mechanised Army Set	Contains 151, 152, 161, 162		NGPP	☐
	1939-40	160 Series Royal Artillery Set	Contains 160, a, b, c, d	£15-£20	MPR	☐
	1939-40	161 Series Anti Aircraft Unit	Contains 161a, 161b	£55	GV	☐
	1939-40	162 Series Field Gun Set	Contains 162a, b, c	£35-£45	MPR	☐
	1956-67	Military Vehicles Set	Contains 621, 641, 674, 676	£45-£55	MPR	☐
303	1978-80	Commando Squad Set	Contains Truck/AC/HC	£8-£11	MPR	☐
695	1963-66	Howitzer/Tractor Set	Contains 689 and 693	£22-£27	MPR	☐
697	1963-66	25 pdr Field Gun Set	Contains 686, 687, 688	£14-£17	MPR	☐
698	1958-62	Tank Transporter Set	Contains 651 and 660	£15-£19	MPR	☐
281	1974-77	Military Helicopter	MG body, *Army* plus union jack. 139 mm.	£5-£7	MPR	☐

Collectors Notes

1i Dinky Aeroplanes

Ref. No.		Model Type	Model Features and Size	Rarity and Price Grading		
60a	1934-41	Imperial Airways Liner	Gold/Blue body, OC, 4×2, PB, DC/TP. 125 mm.	£55	NVE	☐
60a	1937-40	Imperial Airways Liner	Gold body, OC, DC/TP, 4×2 PB. 125 mm.	£55	NVE	☐
60b	1934-36	D. H. Leopard Moth	Blue body, Orange wing tips OC/DC, 1×2 PB. 75 mm.	£30	NVE	☐
60b	1936-40	D. H. Leopard Moth	Silver body, 1×2, PB. 75 mm.	£25	GV	☐
60c	1934-37	'Percival Gull'	White/Blue body, 1×2 PB. 75 mm.	£25	GV	☐
60c	1937-40	Percival Gull	White body, OC *G-ADZO*, 1×2 PB. 75 mm. Note for the purposes of continuity all the Percival Gull aircraft are together.			
60k	1936	Percival Gull (Amy Mollinson's)	Blue/Silver body, *G-ADZO* in blue, BX, 1×2 PB. 75 mm.	£35	NVE	☐
60k	1937-	Percival Gull (H. L. Brook's)	Blue/Silver body, 1×2 PB, *G-ADZO* in black, BX. 75 mm.	£35	NVE	☐
60k	1946-48	Percival Gull Light Tourer	Various single colours, 1×2 PB. 75 mm.	£11	GV	☐
60d	1934-36	Low Wing Monoplane	Red/Cream body, OC/no pilot, 1×2 PB. 75 mm.	£25	NVE	☐
60d	1936-40	Low Wing Monoplane	Orange body, 1×2 PB, OC/pilot *G-AVYP*. 75 mm.	£25	GV	☐
60e	1934-36	General Monospar Plane	Gold/Red body, 2×2 PB. 80 mm.	£30	NVE	☐
60e	1936-40	General Monospan Plane	Silver body 2×2 PB. 80 mm.	£30	NVE	☐
60f	1934-36	Cierva Autogiro	Gold/Blue no pilot, 3 vanes. 50 mm.	£40	NVE	☐
60f	1937-40	Cierva Autogiro	Gold/Blue with pilot, 3 vanes. 50 mm.	£30	NVE	☐
60g	1935-37	D. H. Comet	Red/Gold body, 2×2 PB. 85 mm.	£30	NVE	☐
	1937-40	D. H. Comet	Silver body, OC, 2×2 PB. 85 mm.	£20	NVE	☐
	1946-49	Light Racer (D. H. Comet)	Silver body, OC, *G-RACE* 2×2 PB. 85 mm.	£10	NC	☐
60h	1936-40	'Singapore' Flying Boat	Silver body, RAF RDLS, 2×2 PB. 125 mm.	£65	GV	☐
60m	1939-40	Four Engined Flying Boat	Silver body, OC/DRGN/BX/4×2 PRB. 125 mm.	£45	NVE	☐
60n	1937-39	Fairy 'Battle' Bomber	Silver body, RAF roundels 1×3 PB. 75 mm.	£15	GV	☐
60s	1939-40	Fairy 'Battle' Bomber	Camouflage body, 1×3 PB. 55 mm.	£15	GV	☐
60p	1936-40	Gloucester Gladiator	Silver body, RAF roundels, Red 1×2 PB. 45 mm.	£20	NVE	☐
60r	1937-40	Empire Flying Boat	Silver/Red body, 12 different types eg *Caledonia* Red 4×3 PB. 125 mm.	£40	NVE	☐
60t	1938-40	Douglas DC3	Silver/Black body, Red 2×3 PB. 130 mm.	£35	NVE	☐
60v	1937-40	Armstrong Whitworth Bomber	Silver body, RAF roundels, Red 2×3 PB. 86 mm.	£40	GV	☐
60w	1938-40	Flying Boat 'Clipper III'	Silver body, Red 4×3 PB. 125 mm.	£40	NVE	☐
60w	1946-48	Flying Boat	Silver body, with no markings 4×3 PB. 125 mm.	£25	NVE	☐
60x	1937-41	Atlantic Flying Boat	Blue/White body, Red 4×3 PB.	£30	NVE	☐
62a	1938-40	Vickers-Supermarine 'Spitfire'	Silver body, RAF roundels 1×3 PB. 80 mm.	£20	GV	☐
62b	1938-40	'Bristol' Blenheim	Silver body, RAF roundels Red 2×3 PB.	£20	NVE	☐
62c	No record of model with this number in Meccano Magazine.					
62d	1940-41	'Bristol Blenheim'	Camouflaged body, RAF RDLS, 2×3 PB. 75 mm.	£15	NVE	☐
62e	1940-41	Vickers Supermarine 'Spitfire'	Camouflaged body, RAF RDLS, 1×3 PB. 80 mm.	£15	GV	☐
62g	1939-41	Flying Fortress	Silver body, 4×3 PB.	£45	NVE	☐
62g	1945-48	'Long Range Bomber'	Silver body, Red 4×3 PB.	£20	NVE	☐
62h	1938-40	Hawker Hurricane	Camouflaged body, RAF RDLS, 1×2 PB.	£20	GV	☐
62k	1938-41	Kings Aeroplane	Silver/Red body, Red 2×2 PB. 125 mm.	£30	GV	☐
62m	1938-41	Airspeed Envoy Monoplane	Green/Silver body, Red 2×2 PB. 125 mm.	£30	GV	☐
62m	1946-48	Light Transport	Red or Silver body, *G-ATMH,* Red 2×2 PB. 125 mm.	£10-£14	MPR	☐
62n	1939-41	Junkers JU90 Air Liner	Silver/Red body, D-AALV etc. Red 4×3 PB. 125 mm.	£55	NVE	☐
62p	1938-41	Ensign Air Liner	Silver body, *Ensign* G-ADSR, Red 4×3 PB. 125 mm. Also issued in 5 other names and reg nos.	£25	GV	☐
62p	1946-49	Armstrong Whitworth Air Liner	Silver body, OC 4×3 PB. 86 mm.	£15	GV	☐

Ref. No.		Model Type	**Dinky Aeroplanes continued**	Rarity and Price Grading		
62r	1939-41	D. H. Albatross Mail Liner	Silver body, G-AEVV, Red 4×3 PB. 140 mm.	£25	GV	☐
62r	1946-49	Four Engined Liner	Blue body, G-ATPV OC and reg nos. Red 4×3 PB. 140 mm.	£15	GV	☐
62s	1939-41	Hawker Hurricane	Silver body RAF roundels 1×2 PB. 88 mm.	£15	GV	☐
62s	1946-49	Hawker Hurricane	Silver body RAF roundels 1×2 PB. 88 mm.	£11	GV	☐
62t	1939-41	Armstrong Whitworth Bomber	Camouflaged body RAF roundels 4×3 PB. 86 mm.	£40	GV	☐
62w	1939-41	'Frobisher' Clan Air Liner	Silver body *G-AFDI,* 4×3 PB.	£25	GV	☐
62x	1939-41	40 Seat Airliner	Two tone Green/G-AZCA/OC 4×3 PB. 140 mm.	£25	GV	☐
62y	1946-49	Giant High Speed Monoplane	Silver body, OC/G-ATBK 4×3 PB. 125 mm.	£16	GV	☐
63	1939-41	Mayo Composite Aircraft	Sil/Red body, *G-ADHJ/G-ADHK,* Red 2×4×3 PB. Models 63a and 63b combined PBF. 125 mm. 102 mm.	£75	GV	☐
63a	1939-41	Flying Boat 'MAIA'	Sil/Red body, *G-ADHK,* Red 4×3 PB. 125 mm.	£25	GV	☐
63b	1939-41	Seaplane 'MERCURY'	Sil/Red body, *G-ADHJ,* 4×3 PB. 102 mm.	£20	GV	☐
66a	1940-41	Heavy Bomber	Camouflaged body, RAF RDLS, 4×2 PB (60a). 125 mm.	£35	V	☐
66b	1940-41	Dive Bomber	Camouflaged body, RAF RDLS, 1×2 PB (60b). 75 mm.	£20	V	☐
66c	1940-41	Two Seater Fighter	Camouflaged body, RAF RDLS, 1×2 PB (60c). 75 mm.	£20	V	☐
66d	1940-41	Torpedo Dive Bomber	Camouflaged body, RAF, RDLS, 1×2 PB. 75 mm.	£20	V	☐
66e	1940-41	Medium Bomber	Camouflaged body, RAF RDLS, 2×2 PB (60e). 75 mm.	£20	V	☐
66f	1940-41	Army Co-operation Autogiro	Gold or Silver, 3 vanes, (60f).	£35	NVE	☐
67a	1940-41	Junkers Heavy Bomber JU89	Black/Blue body, swastikas, BX, 4×3 PB. 190 mm.	£100	GV	☐
68a	1940-41	'ENSIGN' Air Liner	Camouflaged body, RAF RDLS, 4×3 PB. 140 mm.	£30	GV	☐
68b	1940-41	'FROBISHER' Air Liner	Camouflaged body, RAF RDLS, 4×3 PB. 125 mm.	£30	GV	☐
70a (704)	1946-59	Auto York Airliner	Silver body, *G-A, GJC* Red 4×3 PB. 102 mm.	£12-£16	MPR	☐
70b (730)	1946-55	Tempest II Fighter	Silver body, RAF RDLS, Red 1×4 PB. 51 mm.	£11-£15	MPR	☐
70c (705)	1947-62	Viking Air Liner	Silver body, *G-A,GOL* Red 2×4 PB. 140 mm.	£15-£19	MPR	☐
70d (731)	1946-55	Twin Engined Fighter	Silver body, no markings, Red 2×3 PB. 51 mm.	£9-£11	MPR	☐
70e	1946-62	Gloster Meteor	Silver body, RAF roundels. 66 mm.	£9-£11	MPR	☐
70f	1947-62	Shooting Star	Silver body, US markings on wings. 60 mm.	£9-£11	MPR	☐
700 (63b)	1979	Spitfire Mark II	Plated body, Onyx stand, 1×3 PB *Diamond Jubilee of the RAF.* 135 mm.	£20-£25	MPR	☐
701	1947-49	Shetland Flying Boat	Silver body, G-AGVD, BX, Black 4×4 PB.	£75	GV	☐
702 (999)	1954-65	DH Comet Airliner	Silver body, *B.O.A.C.* decals. 184 mm.	£35	NC	☐
706	1956-57	Vickers Viscount Airliner	Sil/Red/White body, *Air France,* Red 4×4 PB. 150 mm.	£35	NC	☐
708	1957-65	Vickers Viscount Airliner	Silver/White/Red body, Red 4×4 PB *British European Airways.* 150 mm.	£25-£32	MPR	☐
710	1965-76	Beechcraft Bonanza S35	Red/White or Bronze/Yel body, 1×2 PB. 133 mm.	£7-£9	MPR	☐
712	1972-77	U.S. Army T.42A	Military Green body, 2×2 PB. 153 mm.	£7-£9	MPR	☐
715	1956-62	Bristol 173 Helicopter	Blue body/Red body, FL, G-AVXR 2×3 Red vanes. 127 mm.	£12-£15	MPR	☐
715	1968-76	Beechcraft C55 Baron	White or Red body, with Yellow 2×2 PB. 150 mm.	£7-£9	MPR	☐
716	1957-62	Westland Sikorsky HLC	Red/Cream/Silver body, 2×3 vanes. 89 mm.	£11-£14	MPR	☐
717	1970-75	Boeing 737 'LUFTHANSA'	White/Blue body, ARV a Dinky first. 152 mm.	£10-£13	MPR	☐

Ref. No.		Model Type	Dinky Aeroplanes continued	Rarity and Price Grading		
718	1972-75	Hawker Hurricane Mk II	Camouflaged body, RAF RDLS, 1×3 PB. 188 mm.	£7-£9	MPR	☐
719	1969-78	Spitfire Mk II	Camouflaged body, RAF RDLS, Black 1×3 PB. 173 mm.	£7-£9	MPR	☐
721	1969-80	Junkers JU876 Stuka	MG body, Black crosses, DCFB/1×3. 191 mm.	£7-£9	MPR	☐
722	1970-80	Hawker Harrier	Camouflaged body, RAF markings. 125 mm.	£7-£9	MPR	☐
723	1970-75	Hawker Siddeley HS 125	Yellow/White or Blue/White body. 133 mm.	£7-£9	MPR	☐
724	1971-79	Seaking Helicopter	White/Blue body, RAF RDLS, 5 vanes, BOF. 179 mm.	£7-£9	MPR	☐
725	1972-78	Royal Navy Phantom II	Dark Blue body, Black nose, RAF RDLS. 132 mm.	£7-£9	MPR	☐
726	1972-76	Messerschmitt BF 109E	Desert CM, BC, Brown 1×3 PB/A. 165 mm.	£9-£13	MPR	☐
727	1976-77	German Phantom II	TT Grey CM body, BC, RTW/FMS. 132 mm.	£9-£13	MPR	☐
727	1976-77	F-4K Phantom	CM body, US Air Force, RTW/FMS. 132 mm.	£9-£13	MPR	☐
728	1972-75	R.A.F. Dominic	Blue/Green body, CM body, RTW, RAF RDLS. 132 mm.	£7-£9	MPR	☐
729	1974-76	Multi-Role Aircraft	Camouflage Grey/Green RTW. 164 mm.	£9-£11	MPR	☐
730	1972-76	US 'NAVY' Phantom II	Grey/Red body, *USS Saratoga* RTW/FMS. 132 mm.	£9-£11	MPR	☐
731	1973-76	S.E.P.E.C.A.T.	Blue/Green body, CM body, Orange pilot, OCP, RTW. 106 mm.	£9-£11	MPR	☐
732	1974-80	Bell's Helicopter	Orange/Blue/White body, 2 vanes. 211 mm.	£3-£4	MPR	☐
734	1955-62	Supermarine Spitfire	Camouflaged body, RAF markings 1×3 PB. 51 mm.	£14-£17	MPR	☐
734	1975-78	P47 Thunderbolt	Metallic Silver body, Red 1×4 PB, RTW. 190 mm.	£7-£9	MPR	☐
735	1956-66	Gloster Javelin	Camouflaged body, RAF markings. 82 mm.	£11-£14	MPR	☐
736	1973-78	Bundesmarine Seaking HC	Grey body, Black crosses. 179 mm.	£3-£5	MPR	☐
736	1959-63	Hawker Hunter	Camouflaged body, RAF markings. 54 mm.	£12-£16	MPR	☐
737	1959-68	PIB Lightning Fighter	Silver body, RAF markings. 55 mm.	£7-£9	MPR	☐
738	1960-65	DH 110 Sea Vixen	Grey/White body, Black nose, RAF RDLS. 81 mm.	£7-£11	MPR	☐
739	1975-78	A6M5 Zero Sen	Metallic Green body, Japanese markings 1×3 PB. 184 mm.	£7-£9	MPR	☐
741	1978-80	Spitfire Mk II	Camouflaged body, RAF RDLS, RTW. 1×3PB. 173 mm.	£7-£9	MPR	☐
749 (992)	1955-56	Avro Vulcan Delta Wing Bomber	Silver body, RAF RDLS and tail markings, only 500 models made so —	£500	NVE	☐
997	1962-65	Caravelle SE 210	White/Blue/Sil body, *Air France*. 126 mm.	£35-£45	MPR	☐
998	1959-65	Bristol Britannia	White/Blue/Sil body, *Canadian Pacific*. 225 mm.	£35-£45	MPR	☐

Gift Sets

60	1935-41	Gift Set	Contains 60a, b, c, d, e, f	NGPP ☐
61	1937-41	R.A.F. Aeroplanes Set	Contains 60h, 60n×2, 60p×2	NGPP ☐
64	1939-41	Wartime Aircraft Set	Contains 60g, 62h, k, m, s, 63b	NGPP ☐
65	1939-41	Passenger Aircraft Set	Contains 60r, t, v, m, 62n, p, v, m	NGPP ☐
66	1940-41	Wartime Camouflage Set	Contains 66a, b, c, d, e	NGPP ☐
68	1940-41	Wartime Aircraft Set	Contains 60s×2, 62d×2, 62e×3, 62h×3, 62t, 68a, 68b	NGPP ☐

Not all wing span sizes are known to the compiler as the model listings indicate. Any supported information in this direction would be welcomed.

Dinky Aeroplanes

60h Singapore Flying Boat 1936-40
60v Armstrong Whitworth 1937-40
Whitley Bomber

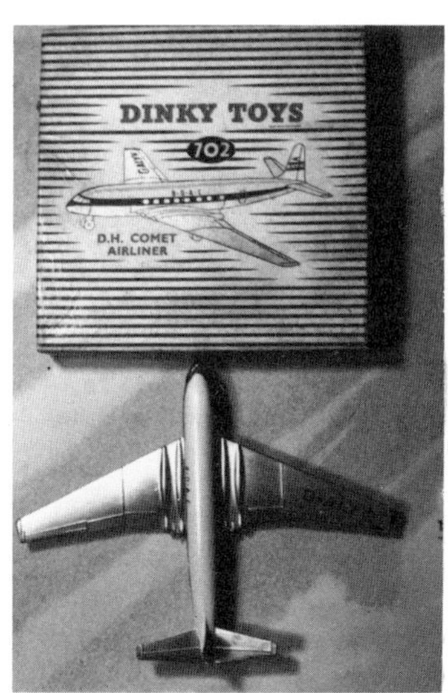

First Dinky aeroplane to have the full authentic company livery.

First aeroplane to have a retractable undercarriage.

Dinky Ships

Ref. No.		Model Type	Model Features and Size	Rarity and Price Grading		
50a	1934-40	Battle Cruiser 'Hood'	Battleship Grey UB	£10-£13	MPR	☐
50b	1934-40	Battleship 'Nelson'	Battleship Grey UB	£10-£13	MPR	☐
50c	1934-40	Cruiser 'Effingham'	Battleship Grey UB	£7-£10	MPR	☐
50d	1934-40	Cruiser 'York'	Battleship Grey UB	£7-£10	MPR	☐
50e	1934-40	Cruiser 'Delhi'	Battleship Grey UB	£7-£10	MPR	☐
50f	1934-40	Destroyer 'Broke' Class	Battleship Grey UB	£5-£7	MPR	☐
50g	1935-40	Submarine 'K' Class	Battleship Grey UB	£5-£7	MPR	☐
50h	1935-40	Destroyer 'X' Class	Battleship Grey UB	£5-£7	MPR	☐
51a	1936-38	'United States of America'	Black/White hull, Red/Black Funnell/BX	£8-£11	MPR	☐
51b	1934-40	'Europa'	Black/White hull, Brown Funnell	£8-£11	MPR	☐
51c	1934-40	'Rex'	Black/White hull, Red/Green Funnell/UB	£8-£11	MPR	☐
51d	1934-40	'Empress of Britain'	White hull, Cream Funnell	£30	GV	☐
51e	1935-40	'Strathaird'	White hull, Brown Funnell/UB	£10-£15	MPR	☐
51f	1934-40	'Queen of Bermuda'	Grey/White hull, Red/Black Funnell	£8-£11	MPR	☐
51g	1934-40	'Britannia'	Black/White/Brown hull, Black Funnell	£8-£11	MPR	☐
52	1934-35	Cunard-White Star Liner 'Queen Mary' '534'	Boxed without rollers, Black/White hull, Red Black Funnell	£35	GV	☐
52a/b	1935-40	'Queen Mary'	Same model boxed WW runers	£25	GV	☐
52m	1936-40	'Queen Mary'	Same model boxed without runners	£15	GV	☐
52a	1947-49	'Queen Mary'	Unboxed with brass runners	£9-£12	MPR	☐
52c	1935-40	'Nomandie'	Black/White/Blue hull, Red/Black FN/BX	£15	GV	☐
53az	1938-39	Battleship 'Dunkerque'	Battleship Grey, Black on funnel FI/B	£15	GV	☐
281	1973-76	Military Hovercraft	Green/Black *'Army'* UJ/gunner/A	£5-£7	MPR	☐
290	1970-76	SRN6 Hovercraft	Red/White/Yellow ODB/radar	£5-£7	MPR	☐
671	1976-78	Mk I Corvette	Grey/Brown/Black, fires rockets	£3-£5	MPR	☐
672	1976-77	OSA 2 Missile Boat	Grey, fires missiles	£3-£5	MPR	☐
673	1977-78	Submarine chaser	Grey, fires depth charges	£3-£5	MPR	☐
674	1977-78	Coastguard Missile Launch	Grey, fires missiles *Coastguard*	£3-£5	MPR	☐
675	1973-77	Motor Patrol Boat	Grey hull	£3-£5	MPR	☐
678	1974-77	Air Sea Rescue Launch	Grey hull, Orange dinghy, pilot/launch	£3-£5	MPR	☐
796	1960-62	Healey Sports Boat	Cream/Green 2 figures	£5-£7	MPR	☐

Gift Sets, Ships

Ref. No.		Model Type	Model Features and Size	Rarity and Price Grading		
50	1935-40	Warship Gift Set	Contains 50a, b × 2, c, d, e, f × 3, k		NGPP	☐
51	1935-40	Great Liners Set	Contains 51b, c, d, e, f, g		NGPP	☐

Dinky Trains and Trams Single and Gift Sets

Ref. No.		Model Type	Model Features and Size	Rarity and Price Grading		
16	1935-40	Silver Jubilee Set	Loco 2 coaches in Silver	£45	NVE	☐
16	1946-50	L.N.E.R. Set	*L.N.E.R.* livery	£40-£45	MPR	☐
16	1954-56	British Rail Set	*B.R.* livery	£40-£45	MPR	☐
17	1935-40	Passenger Train Set	Loco, tender, coach, guards van	£35	GV	☐
18	1935-40	Goods Train Set	Tank loco, 3 wagons	£35	GV	☐
19	1935-40	Mixed Goods Set	Loco, tanker, 2 wagons	£35	GV	☐
20	1935-40	Passenger Train Set	Loco, 2 coaches, guards van	£35	GV	☐
21	1935-40	Modelled Miniatures Set	Goods train	£35	GV	☐
26	1934-48	G.W.R. Rail Car	Red/Cream runs on bobbins. 106 mm.	£60	GV	☐
26z	1937-40	Diesel Rail Car	Cream/Orange runs on bobbins FI. 99 mm.	£120	GV	☐
				£150	GV	☐
784	1972-75	Goods Train Set	Various colours	£20	NC	☐
798	1954-59	Express Passenger Set	Various colours	£25	GV	☐

1j Novelty, Space and Film/TV Link Up Models

Ref. No.		Model Type	Model Features and Size	Rarity and Price Grading	
100	1967-75	Lady Penelope FAB 1	Pink, SS/SL/D/PS/fires rockets. 107 mm.	£24	NC ☐
101	1967-73	Thunderbird 2 and 4	Green with yellow Thunderbird 4. 143 mm.	£20	NC ☐
102	1969-74	Joe's Car	Green body/battery powered/D. 139 mm.	£20	NC ☐
103	1968-74	Spectrum Patrol Car	Met Red body, *Spectrum* badge A/SS. 121 mm.	£15	NC ☐
104	1968-74	Spectrum Pursuit	Met Blue body, *SPV* decal/badge/2A. 160 mm.	£11-£15	MPR ☐
105	1968-70	Maximum Security	White/Red body, Isotope crate SS/A. 137 mm.	£15-£20	MPR ☐
106	1967-70	'Prisoner' Mini Moke	White body, Red/White canopy. 73 mm.	£12	GV ☐
106	1974-79	Thunderbird 2 and 4	Blue body, Reissue of 101. 143 mm.	£8-£11	MPR ☐
107	1967-69	Stripey the Magic Mini	White body, Yellow Red/Blue stripes. 75 mm.	£15	NVE ☐
108	1969-71	Sam's Car	Red or Grey body, *Win* badge, keyless motor. 111 mm.	£20	NC ☐
109	1969-71	Gabriel Model T Ford	Yellow/Black body, *Gabriel* D/SW/SPW. 79 mm.	£15	NC ☐
111	1976-78	Cinderella's Coach	White/Gold/Pink body, D/PS/4 horses. 242 mm.	Current	MPR ☐
112	1978-80	Purdey's TR7	Yellow body, Silver decal *P* PW/PCH. 98 mm.	Current	MPR ☐
115	1977	United Biscuits UB TAXI	Blue/Black/Yellow (promotional). 86 mm.	£8-£11	MPR ☐
120	1976-78	Happy Cab	White/Blue/Yellow plus flowers. 86 mm.	£5-£7	MPR ☐
267	1978-79	Paramedic Truck	Red with Yellow cylinders. 119 mm.	£3-£5	MPR ☐
281	1968-70	'PATHE NEWS' Camera Car	Black body, camera and operator, OD.	£20	GV ☐
350	1970-71	Tiny's Mini Moke	Red body, White/Yellow striped canopy. 73 mm.	£15-£18	MPR ☐
351	1971-78	U.F.O. Interceptor	Met Green body *Shado* decal. 194 mm.	£5-£8	MPR ☐
352	1971-75	Ed Straker's Car	Red body, keyless motor, WDS. 124 mm.	£12	NC ☐
353	1971-79	Shado 2 Mobile	Met Green body, *Shado 2* decal. 145 mm.	£4-£6	MPR ☐
354	1972-79	Pink Panther	Pink body and panther. 175 mm.	£5-£7	MPR ☐
355	1972-75	Lunar Roving Vehicle	Met Blue, White PS, pivoting W. 114 mm.	£3-£5	MPR ☐
357	1977-79	Klinger Battle Cruiser	Met Blue/White, fires pellets. 220 mm.	£3-£5	MPR ☐
358	1976-80	'U.S.S. Enterprise'	White body, *NCC 1701* (from Star Trek). 234 mm.	£5-£7	MPR ☐
359	1975-79	Eagle Transporter	White, Metallic Green logo. 222 mm.	£5-£7	MPR ☐
360	1975-79	Eagle Freighter	White/Blue, Yellow drums cargo. 222 mm.	£5-£7	MPR ☐
361	1978-79	Galactic War Chariot	Metallic Green, White PS, rockets. 126 mm.	£4-£6	MPR ☐
362	1978-79	Trident Star Fighter	Black/Orange, fires rockets. 170 mm.	£3-£5	MPR ☐
363	1979	Zygon Patroller	Metallic Silver/Blue, 2 pilots. 210 mm.	£12	NC ☐
364	1979	Space Shuttle	White body, *United States* 5 U.S. flags. 186 mm.	£25	GV ☐
367	1979	Space Battle Cruiser	White/Red body, pilot, P. weapons. 187 mm.	£15	GV ☐
368	1979	Zygon Marauder	Red/White 4PS/*Z* decals	£11-£15	MPR ☐
368	1979	Cosmic Cruiser	Blue body, (Marks and Spencer issue)	£25	NVE ☐
370	1969-76	The Dragster	Yellow/Silver/Pink/White, large Wheel	£8-£11	MPR ☐
371	1979	U.S.S. Enterprise	White body, small scale, BUP	£5-£8	MPR ☐
372	1979	Klingon Cruiser	Blue body, small scale, BUP	£5-£8	MPR ☐
475	1964-66	Model T Ford	Blue/Black/Gold body, D/PS (female). 79 mm.	£15	GV ☐
476	1967-69	Morris Oxford (Bullnose)	Yellow body, Blue CH, Fawn head, D. 92 mm.	£15	GV ☐
477	1970-72	Parsley's Car	Green body, animal figure. 92 mm.	£12	GV ☐
485	1964-67	Santa Special Model T Ford	Red/White body, Santa Claus, Xmas decals, Xmas tree and toys. 79 mm.	£22	GV ☐
486	1965-69	Dinky Beats Morris Oxford (Bullnose)	White/Green/Gold body, *Dagear* etc 3 figures playing music. 92 mm.	£20	GV ☐
602	1976-79	Armoured Command Car	MG, D/WS/sparks gun. 160 mm.	£5-£8	MPR ☐
803	1978-79	U.S.S. Enterprise	White body, *NCC-1701* BUP/MV	£8-£11	MPR ☐
804	1978-79	Klingon	Blue, Bubble pack, MV	£8-£11	MPR ☐

Gift Sets

Ref. No.		Model Type	Model Features and Size	Rarity and Price Grading	
309	1978-80	Star Trek Gift Set	Contains 357 and 358	£18	NC ☐

1k Miscellaneous

(i) Dinky Dublo

Ref. No.		Model Type	Model Features and Size	Rarity and Price Grading		
061	1958-59	Ford Prefect	Fawn body. 58 mm.	£7-£10	MPR	☐
062	1958-60	Singer Roadster	Orange body, Red seats, OC. 50 mm.	£9-£11	MPR	☐
063	1958-60	Commer Van	Blue body. 53 mm.	£9-£11	MPR	☐
064	1957-62	Austin Lorry	Green body. 64 mm.	£10-£12	MPR	☐
065	1957-60	Morris Pick-up	Red body. 55 mm.	£6-£9	MPR	☐
066	1959-69	Bedford Flat Truck	Grey body. 116 mm.	£10-£12	MPR	☐
067	1959-64	Austin Taxi	Blue and Cream body. 59 mm.	£11-£14	MPR	☐
068	1959-64	Royal Mail Van	Red body *Royal Mail, EIIR,* WDS. 47 mm.	£11-£14	MPR	☐
069	1959-64	Massey Harris Tractor	Blue body, hole for driver. 36 mm.	£6-£8	MPR	☐
070	1959-64	A.E.C. Mercury Tanker	Green cab, Red tank, WDS *Shell Petroleum Products BP.* 91 mm.	£15	GV	☐
071	1960-64	Volkswagen Delivery Van	Yellow body, Red *Hornby Dublo* decal, WDS. 54 mm.	£15	GV	☐
072	1959-64	Bedford Articulated Truck	Yellow cab, Red trailer, WDS. 116 mm.	£12-£15	MPR	☐
073	1960-64	Landrover/Trailer/Horse	Green/Orange, with White horse, WDS. 103 mm.	£15	NC	☐
076	1960-64	Lansing Bagnall Tractor & Trailer	Maroon/Blue, D/H/TB. 75 mm.	£12	NC	☐
078	1960-64	Lansing Bagnall Trailer	Maroon body, H/towbar. 49 mm.	£4-£6	MPR	☐

(ii) Motor Cycles

Ref. No.		Model Type	Model Features and Size	Rarity and Price Grading		
37a	1938-40	Civilian Model	Black MC, Green or Brown rider, fine detail to paintwork, SWRW. 46 mm.	£20	GV	☐
37a	1946-48	Civilian Model	Black MC, Green or Brown rider, crude paintwork detail, SBRW. 45 mm.	£11-£14	MPR	☐
37b	1938-40	Police Motor Cyclist	Black MC, Blue rider, SWRW. 46 mm.	£24	GV	☐
37b	1946-48	Police Motor Cyclist	Black MC, Blue rider, SBRW. 45 mm.	£14-£17	MPR	☐
37c	1938-41	Signals Despatch Rider	Green MC, Khaki rider, SWRW or SBRW. 46 mm.	£22	GV	☐
42b	1935-40	Police MC Patrol	Blue MC, Green SC, Blue RDR/PS, SWRW. 47 mm.	£18	GV	☐
42b	1948-55	Police MC Patrol	Blue MC, Green SC, Blue RDR/PS, SBRW. 47 mm.	£11-£14	MPR	☐
43b	1936-40	R.A.C. MC Patrol	Black MC, Blue/Wh RDR, Red sash, SWRW. 46 mm.	£30	GV	☐
43b	1946-50	R.A.C. MC Patrol	Black MC, Blue rider, OC/SBRW. 45 mm.	£11-£14	MPR	☐
44b	1935-40	'AA' Motor Cycle Patrol	Black MC, Yel SC, Blue sash, SWRW. 46 mm.	£25	GV	☐
44b	1946-50	'AA' Motor Cycle Patrol	Black MC, Yellow SC, SBRW. 45 mm.	£11-£14	MPR	☐
270 (44b)	1959-62	'AA' Motor Cycle Patrol	Black MC, Yellow S with *AA*. 46 mm.	£11-£14	MPR	☐

Gift Set

	1938-40	Motor Cycles Set	Contains 37a, b, c.	£75	NVE	☐

(iii) Caravans

Ref. No.		Model Type	Model Features and Size	Rarity and Price Grading	
30g	1936-40	Caravan	Two Tone Green, 2W/H. 81 mm.	£25	GV ☐
30g	1948-50	Caravan	Orange/Cream *Caravan Club*, TB/H. 81 mm.	£35	GV ☐
117	1963-65	Four Berth Caravan	Blue/Cream, clear roof, SS/H/DI. 118 mm.	£9-£12	MPR ☐
188	1961-63	Four Berth Caravan	Green/Cream or Blue/Cream, OC/WDS/OD/DI/SS/H. 132 mm.	£15-£19	MPR ☐
190	1956-60	Caravan	Orange/Cream OC tow bar. 118 mm.	£11-£14	MPR ☐

(iv) Large Scale Models

Ref. No.		Model Type	Model Features and Size	Rarity and Price Grading	
2162	1974-76	Ford Capri	Met Blue, Black roof, SS/WDS/CP/NP. 175 mm.	£6-£8	MPR ☐
2214	1974-76	Ford Capri Rally Car	Red/Black body, *Shell*, SS/WDS/CP/WM/NP. 175 mm.	£6-£8	MPR ☐
2253	1974-76	Ford Capri Police Car	White/Orange body, SL/SS/WDS/CP/WM/NP. 175 mm.	£6-£8	MPR ☐

(v) Convoy Series

Ref. No.		Model Type	Model Features and Size	Rarity and Price Grading	
380	1977-78	Skip Wagon	Green cab, Orange skip. 112 mm.	Current	MPR ☐
381	1977-79	Farm Wagon	Blue cab, Yellow cattle carrier. 110 mm.	Current	MPR ☐
382	1978-79	Dumper Truck	Yellow cab, Orange tipper. 118 mm.	Current	MPR ☐
383	1978-79	Truck	Yellow body, *National Carriers*. 110 mm.	Current	MPR ☐
384	1977-79	Fire Rescue Truck	Red/White body, *Rescue*. 126 mm.	Current	MPR ☐
385	1977-79	Royal Mail Truck	Red body, *Royal Mail*. 112 mm.	Current	MPR ☐
399	1977-79	Convoy Gift Set	Contains 380, 381, 382	Current	MPR ☐
687	1978-79	Army Truck	Military Green body, *Army*. 110 mm.	Current	MPR ☐

(vi) Dinky Action Kits — All issued mid seventies

Ref. No.	Model Type	Model Features and Size	Rarity and Price Grading		
No model number on Base Plates etc.					
1001	RR Phantom V	Various colours	£7-£10	MPR	☐
1002	Volvo 1800 S Coupe	Yellow or Green	£7-£10	MPR	☐
1003	VW 1300	Red and White	£7-£10	MPR	☐
1004	Ford Escort Police Car	Blue and White	£5-£7	MPR	☐
1006	Ford Escort Mexico	Red	£5-£7	MPR	☐
1007	Jensen F.F.	Various colours	£5-£7	MPR	☐
1008	Mercedes Benz 600	Yellow or Green	£5-£7	MPR	☐
1009	Lotus F.1.	Red and Gold, OC	£5-£7	MPR	☐
1012	Ferrari 213-B2	Red	£5-£7	MPR	☐
1014	Beach Buggy	Blue	£4-£5	MPR	☐
1017	Routemaster Bus	Red body, *Esso* adverts	£10	NC	☐
1018	Leyland Atlantean Bus	Various colours and adverts	£25	GV	☐
1023	A.E.C. Single Decker Bus	Green body, *Greenline Bus*	£15	GV	☐
1025	Ford Transit Van	Red body, *Avis Truck Rental*	£7-£10	MPR	☐
1027	Lunar Rover Kit	Blue/White	£3-£5	MPR	☐
1029	Ford D800 Tipper Truck	Yellow, OC.	£5-£7	MPR	☐
1030	Land Rover Breakdown Truck	Red/White body	£5-£7	MPR	☐
1032	Army Land Rover	M.G. plus transfers	£4-£6	MPR	☐
1033	U.S.A. Army Jeep	M.G.	£5-£7	MPR	☐
1034	Mobile Gun	M.G.	£3-£4	MPR	☐
1035	Striker Anti-Tank Vehicle	M.G. plus transfer	£3-£4	MPR	☐
1036	Leopard Tank	M.G. plus transfers	£6-£8	MPR	☐
1037	Chieftain Tank	M.G. plus transfers	£6-£8	MPR	☐
1038	Scorpion Tank	M.G. plus transfers	£6-£8	MPR	☐
1039	Leopard Recovery Tank	M.G. plus transfers	£6-£8	MPR	☐
1040	Seaking Helicopter	Blue/White plus transfers	£5-£7	MPR	☐
1041	Hawker Hurricane	Camouflage RAF roundels	£5-£7	MPR	☐
1042	Spitfire Mk II	Camouflage RAF roundels	£5-£7	MPR	☐
1043	S.E.P.E.C.A.T. Plane	Blue/Green	£5-£7	MPR	☐
1044	Messerschmitt BF109E	Brown, Luftwaffe transfers	£6-£8	MPR	☐
1045	Multi-Role Combat Aircraft	Camouflage plus transfers	£5-£7	MPR	☐
1050	Motor Patrol Boat	Black/Blue/White	£4-£6	MPR	☐

(vii) Mini-Dinky Models

These were issued in 1968 and were made in Hong Kong and Holland.
The compiler has no value information and the list of models shown is almost certainly incomplete. It is also doubtful whether many of the models were actually issued. The compiler would welcome any further details concerning these models.

10 Ford Corsair
11 Jaguar 'E' Type
12 Corvette Stingray
13 Ferrari 250 LM
14 Chevrolet Chevy II
15 Rolls Royce Silver Shadow
16 Ford Mustang
17 Aston Martin DB6
18 Mercedes Benz 230 SL
19 MGB
20 Cadillac Coup de Ville
21 Fiat 2300 Station Wagon
22 Oldsmobile Tornado
23 Rover 2000
24 Ferrari Superfast
25 Ford Zephyr 6
26 Mercedes 250 SE
27 Buick Riviera
28 Ferrari F.I.
29 Ford F.I.
30 Volvo P. 1800
31 V.W. 1600 TL Fast Back
32 Vauxhall Cresta
33 Jaguar Mk X

(viii) Airfix Products Ltd Dinky Production

Ref. No.		Model Type	Model Features and Size	Rarity and Price Grading	
Made in France 1/43 scale					
500	1980	Citroen 2CV	Green or Red body, Yellow ducks. 88 mm.	Current	MPR ☐
501	1980	Fiat Strada	Blue/Yellow body	Current	MPR ☐
502	1980	BMW 530	Green body, Black decal	Current	MPR ☐
503	1980	Alfetta GTV	Met Yellow body, Green decal	Current	MPR ☐
504	1980	Citroen Visa	Met Red body. 84 mm.	Current	MPR ☐
505	1980	Peugeot 504	Met Gold body, Black decal	Current	MPR ☐
506	1980	Alfasud	White/Red flash (never seen)	Current	MPR ☐
507	1980	Renault 14	Met Red body (never seen)	Current	MPR ☐
508	1980	Ford Fiesta	Met Silver body (never seen)	Current	MPR ☐

Models made in Hong Kong in 1980 (approx) (Match box model size)

Ref. No.		Model Type	Model Features and Size	Rarity and Price Grading	
101		56 Corvette	White/Red flash, BUP. 68 mm.	Current	MPR ☐
103		Chevette Hatchback	Yellow body, *Turbo* decal, BUP. 68 mm.	Current	MPR ☐
104		Honda Accord	Lilac Orange flash, BUP. 68 mm.	Current	MPR ☐
105		Toyota Celica	Red body, BUP. 68 mm.	Current	MPR ☐
106		Datsun 2802	Brown body, BUP. 68 mm.	Current	MPR ☐
107		BMW Turbo	Orange body, Black and Yellow flash, BUP. 68 mm.	Current	MPR ☐
108		Alfa Romeo	Purple body, Yellow flash, BUP. 68 mm.	Current	MPR ☐
110		Stepride Pick up	Blue/Brown body, BUP. 68 mm.	Current	MPR ☐
111		Camper	Yellow/two tone Brown body. 68 mm.	Current	MPR ☐
113		Pick up	Red/Black body, *4×4* decal. 68 mm.	Current	MPR ☐
114		Firebird	Black body. 68 mm.	Current	MPR ☐
115		Camaro	Red RN 'Z28'. 68 mm.	Current	MPR ☐
116		63 Corvette	Metallic Blue body. 68 mm.	Current	MPR ☐
117		71 Corvette	Yellow body, *Vette* decal. 68 mm.	Current	MPR ☐
119		Ford Van	Blue body, Orange flash. 68 mm.	Current	MPR ☐
120		Renegade Jeep	Yellow body, Green flash	Current	MPR ☐
121		Chevy Blazer	Red body. 68 mm.	Current	MPR ☐
122		Sun Van	Orange body, *Sun Van* decal. 68 mm.	Current	MPR ☐
123		Yamaha 250 MX	Blue body, *Yamaha* decal. 82 mm.	Current	MPR ☐
124		Honda MT 250	Orange body, *Honda* decal. 82 mm.	Current	MPR ☐
125		Kawasaki F11250	Red body, *Kawasaki* decal. 82 mm.	Current	MPR ☐
126		Suzuki TM400	Yellow/Black body *CCI, Suzuki* decals. 82 mm.	Current	MPR ☐
129		T Bird Convertible	Red/White body. 68 mm.	Current	MPR ☐
130		Chevy Convertible	Met Blue/White body	Current	MPR ☐

Extremely doubtful whether all the models listed were in fact issued.

11 Accessories — Pre-War and Post-War

(i) Pre-War

Ref. No.		Model Type	Model Features and Size	Rarity and Price Grading	
1	1934-40	Station Staff (6)	Station Master, Guard, Ticket collector, Driver, Porter with bags, Porter, BX.	£20	GV ☐
2	1934-40	Farmyard Animals (6)	2 horses 2 cows pig sheep, BX	£15	GV ☐
3	1934-40	Passengers (6)	Woman and child, business man, male hiker, female hiker, newsboy, woman, BX	£2	GV ☐
4	1934-40	Engineering Staff (5)	2 Blue figures, 3 Brown figures, BX	£20	GV ☐
5	1934-40	Train & Hotel Staff (6)	A conductor, 2 waiters, 2 porters, BX	£20	GV ☐
6	1934-40	Shepherd Set (6)	Shepherd, sheepdog, 4 sheep, BX	£20	GV ☐
12a	1935-40	G.P.O. Pillar Box 'G.R.'	Red, with or without *Post Office* notice on top in Yel/Red, White panel. 50 mm.	£10	GV ☐
12b	1935-40	Air Mail Pillar Box	Blue body *Air Mail,* White panel. 50 mm.	£10	GV ☐
				£8	GV ☐
12c	1936-40	Telephone Box	Cream/Silver body. 62 mm.	£8	GV ☐
12d	1938-40	Telegraph Messenger	Blue body, Brown pouch. 35 mm.	£5	GV ☐
12e	1938-40	Postman	Blue body, Brown post bag and badge. 35 mm.	£5	GV ☐
13	1934-40	'HALLS DISTEMPER' Advert	Various colours	£45	GV ☐
15		Railway Signals Set		£15	GV ☐
42a	1936-40	Police Box	Blue body *Police* in Silver	£5	GV ☐
42c	1936-40	Point duty policeman	White coat. 42 mm.	£5	GV ☐
42d	1936-40	Point duty policeman	Blue *R.A.C.* badge. 40 mm.	£5	GV ☐
43a	1935-40	'R.A.C.' box	Blue with *R.A.C.* emblem. 81 mm.	£20	GV ☐
43b	1935-40	'R.A.C.' Motor Cycle Patrol	See Section on Motor Cycles		
43c	1935-40	'R.A.C.' Guide	Blue with Red sash. 37 mm.	£5	GV ☐
43d	1935-40	'R.A.C.' guide saluting	Blue with Red sash. 36 mm.	£5	GV ☐
44a	1935-40	'A.A. box'	Yellow *A.A.* badge and 3 signs. 81 mm.	£20	GV ☐
44b	1935-40	'A.A.' Motor Cycle Patrol	See Section on Motor Cycles		
44c	1935-40	'A.A.' Guide	Yellow body, Blue sash. 3 mm.	£5	GV ☐
44d	1935-40	'A.A.' Guide Saluting	Yellow body, Blue sash. 36 mm.	£5	GV ☐
45	1935-40	Garage	Tinplate, opening doors	£45	NVE ☐
46	1937-40	Pavement Set	Grey cardboard box	£5	NC ☐
47	1935-40	12 Road Signs	Black, Red and White, BX	£25	NC ☐
47a	1935-40	4 Face Traffic Lights	Black and White, Yellow beacon, White base	£3	NC ☐
47b	1935-40	3 Face Traffic Lights	Black and White, White base	£3	NC ☐
47c	1935-40	2 Face Traffic Lights	Black and White (back/back) White base	£3	NC ☐
47c	1935-40	2 Face Traffic Lights	Black/White (right angles) White base	£3	NC ☐
47d	1935-40	Belisha Beacon	Black/White/Orange, White base	£3	NC ☐
48	1935-40	Filling Station/Garage	*Filling and Service Station,* MLCD body, many ADS, TP	£45	NVE ☐
49a	1935-40	Bowser Petrol Pump	Green body, White rubber pipe. 46 mm.	£5	GV ☐
49b	1935-40	Wayne Petrol Pump	Blue body, White rubber pipe. 39 mm.	£5	GV ☐
49c	1935-40	Theo Petrol Pump	Brown body, White rubber pipe. 58 mm.	£5	GV ☐
49d	1935-40	'SHELL' Petrol Pump	Red body, White rubber pipe. 53 mm.	£5	GV ☐
49e	1935-40	'Pratts' Oil Bin	Yellow body, *Pratts Motor Oil.* 32 mm.	£5	GV ☐

Gift Sets — Accessories

	Model Type	Model Features and Size		
1938-40	12 Series Set	Contains 12a, b, c, d, e, 34b	£50	NVE ☐
1934-40	Railway Signals Set	Contains 15a, b, c, d, e, f	£30	NVE ☐
1936-40	42 Series Set	Contains 42a, b, c, d	£30	NVE ☐
1935-40	43 Series Set	Contains 43a, b, c, d	£65	NVE ☐
1935-40	44 Series Set	Contains 44a, b, c, d	£65	NVE ☐
1935-40	49 Series Set	Contains 49a, b, c, d, e	£20	NVE ☐

(ii) Post War

Ref. No.		Model Type	Model Features and Size	Rarity and Price Grading		
001	1960-	Station Staff	Blue, 5 figures. 35 mm.	£8	GV	☐
002	1960-	Farmyard Animals	Set of six various colours	£8	GV	☐
003	1960-	Passengers	Set of six, various colours. 35 mm.	£8	GV	☐
004	1960-	Engineering Staff	2 Blue, 3 Brown. 35 mm.	£8	GV	☐
005	1960-	Train and Hotel Staff	Set of 5, various colours. 35 mm.	£8	GV	☐
006	1960-	Shepherd Set	Set of 6, shepherd, dog, 4 sheep	£8	GV	☐
007	1960-68	Petrol Pump Attendants	White coats 1 male 1 female. 35 mm.	£5	GV	☐
008	1961-68	Fire Station Personnel Set	Blue uniforms, 6 plus hose. 35 mm.	£7	GV	☐
009	1962-68	Service Station Personnel Set	Various colours/stances, 8 in set. 35 mm.	£10	GV	☐
010	1962-68	Road Maintenance Personnel Set	6 workmen using pick, barrow, shovels, drill etc, hut, brazier, barrier, 4 lamps. 35 mm.	£10	GV	☐
011	1952-	Telegraph Messenger	Blue body. 35 mm.	£3	GV	☐
012	1952-	Postman	Blue body. 35 mm.	£3	GV	☐
051	1960-	Station Staff	Set of six. 35 mm.	£10	GV	☐
053	1960-	Passengers	Set of six 3 male 3 female. 35 mm.	£10	GV	☐
12c	1946-48	Telephone Box	Red/Silver body. 62 mm.	Current	MPR	☐
502	1961-63	Garage	Blue/Grey body, OD/FI/P. 272 mm.	£5	GV	☐
750	1960-74	Telephone Call Box	Red body. 58 mm.	Current	MPR	☐
751 (42a)	1954-60	Police Box	Blue. 66 mm.	Current	MPR	☐
752	1953-54	Goods yard crane	Blue/Yellow body. 100 mm. 195 mm.	£9-£12	MPR	☐
753		Police Crossing	Grey/Black/White body plus PM. 151 mm.	£4-£6	MPR	☐
754	1958-62	Pavement Set		£4-£6	MPR	☐
755	1960-64	Lamp Standard (Single)	Grey/Fawn/Orange body. 145 mm.	£3-£5	MPR	☐
756	1960-64	Lamp Standard (Double)	Grey/Fawn/Orange body. 145 mm.	£3-£5	MPR	☐
760	1954-60	Pillar Box	Red/Black body, *EIIR* decals. 42 mm.	£4-£6	MPR	☐
763	1959-64	Posters for Hoarding	Red/Black *EIIR* decals, different colours etc. 42 mm.	£5	GV	☐
764	1959-63	Posters for Hoarding	Different colours on six posters	£5	GV	☐
765	1959-64	Road Hoardings (6 Posters)	Green, *David Allen and Sons Ltd.*	£10	GV	☐
766	1959-64	British Road Signs Country Set	Signs of the times (6). 55 mm.	£12	GV	☐
767	1959-64	British Road Signs Country Set	Signs of the times (6)	£12	GV	☐
768	1959-64	British Road Signs Town Set	Signs of the times (6). 55 mm.	£12	GV	☐
769	1959-64	British Road Signs Town Set	Signs of the times (6). 55 mm.	£12	GV	☐
771	1953-65	International Road Signs	Various colours, 12 signs	£24	GV	☐
772	1959-65	British Road Signs	Various colours, 24 signs	£45	GV	☐
773	1959-63	Four Face Traffic Lights	Black/White, Black base. 62 mm.	£1-£2	MPR	☐
777	1959-63	Belisha Beacon	Black/White/Orange, Black base. 51 mm.	£1-£2	MPR	☐
778	1962-65	Road Repair Boards	Green and Red, 6 different. 30-40 mm.	£2-£3	MPR	☐
781	1955-62	'ESSO' Pump Station	*Esso* sign, kiosk, 2 pumps. 114 mm.	£4-£6	MPR	☐
782	1960-68	'SHELL' Pump Station	*Shell* sign, kiosk, 4 pumps. 203 mm.	£4-£6	MPR	☐
783	1960-63	'BP' Pump Station	*BP* sign, kiosk, 4 pumps. 203 mm.	£4-£6	MPR	☐
785	1960-66	'SERVICE STATION'	*BP* sign	£8-£11	MPR	☐
786	1960-66	Tyre rack with tyres	21 assorted tyres	£4-£6	MPR	☐
787	1960-66	Lighting Kit	Bulb and wire	£2-£3	MPR	☐
788	1960	Spare bucket for 966	Grey	£2-£3	MPR	☐
792	1960-64	Packing Cases (3)	White/Cream P. *Hornby Dublo*	£4-£6	MPR	☐
793	1960-64	Pallets	Orange for use in 930 van	£2-£3	MPR	☐
846	1961-	Oil Drums	French issue 6 drums	£2-£3	MPR	☐
847	1961-	Barrels	French issue 6 barrels	£2-£3	MPR	☐
849	1961-	Packing Cases	French issue 6 cases	£2-£3	MPR	☐
850	1961-	Crates of bottles	French issue 6 crates	£2-£3	MPR	☐
851	1961-	Sets of 846/7/9/50	Two of each	£4-£6	MPR	☐

8

Collectors Notes

~~Page 26 234 Ferrari Racing Car~~ ✓

Page 32 204 " 312P

" 209 "

" 216 " Dino

" 220 " P5

Page 33 226 Ferrari 312/B2

234 " RC

242 " R.C.

Collectors Notes

CHAPTER 2 SPOT ON MODELS

i) INTRODUCTION

Messrs Lines Bros Ltd who were already exporting their famous Triang Toys all over the world launched Spot On die-cast models in 1959.

They were determined to compete successfully against Dinky Toys and the newly established Corgi Toys so all of the models contained many features and were extraordinarily detailed for toys.

They were built in a large modern factory in Belfast, Northern Ireland, to the slightly larger scale of 1/42.

Each item in the range was 'SPOT-ON' to scale with all the other items and was issued to the correct colour specifications of their real life counterparts.

In addition all the early models also included in the box a coloured picture of the real model.

The range of models produced included the rarer quality cars such as the Bentley 4 door Sports Saloon, the Jensen 541 and the Armstrong Siddeley '236' Sapphire Saloon amongst others.

The commercial vehicles are extremely sought after today and command high prices. They are particularly noted for their attractive real life liveries and their detailed chassis.

The Mammoth Major 8 range of A.E.C. vehicles are extremely popular with collectors.

Probably the most sought after in this range is the 'SHELL-BP' Tanker which was produced in the perfect livery of its period and is today extremely hard to find.

One of the rarest of all the Spot On commercials was introduced in 1963 and was Model No 145 the 'Ovaltine' A.E.C. Routemaster Bus which is now among the rarest of all the Post War Buses sought by collectors.

Another rarity is the Gift Set number 806 'Royal Occasion'. This featured H.M. the Queen and H.R.H. Prince Philip seated in the rear of the Royal Rolls-Royce Phantom V Limousine. Again the model detail is exceptional for a toy.

Spot-on models were issued for about eight years and during this period produced over one hundred different designs.

An indication of the number of features incorporated into the first models may be gained from the following reprinted page taken from the Spot On Catalogue for 1959.

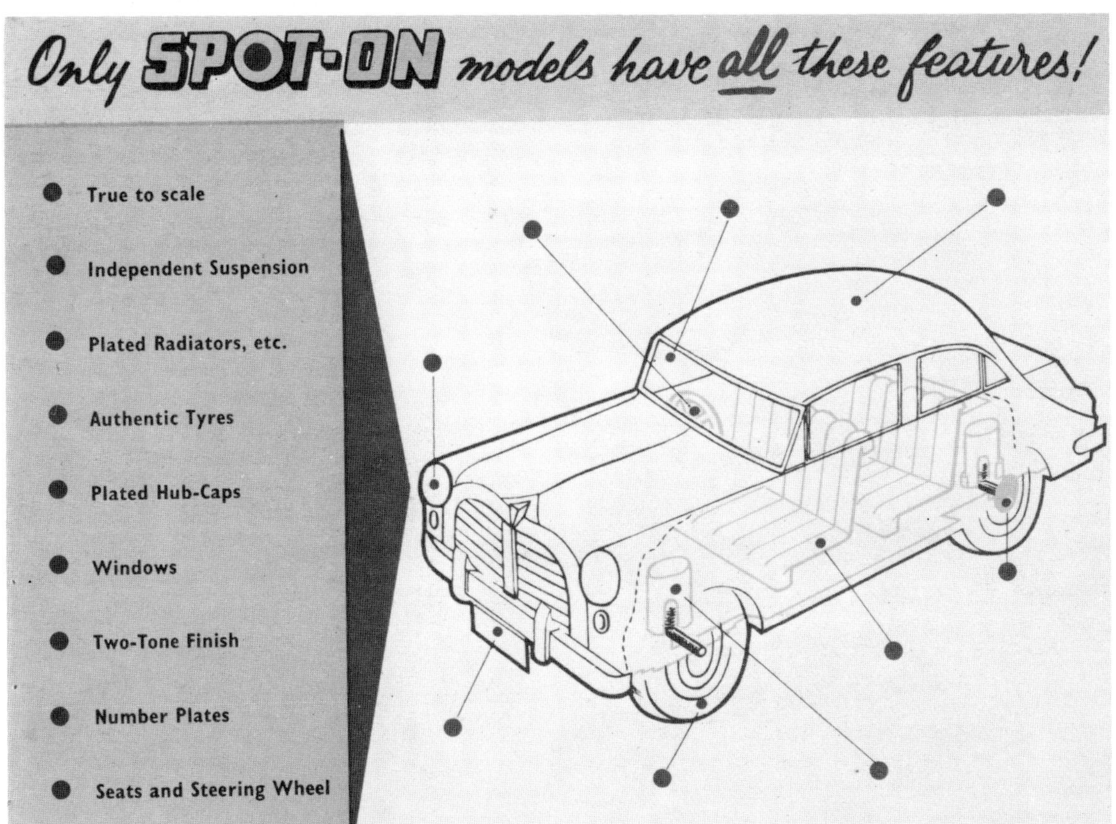

ii) PACKAGING AND MODELS

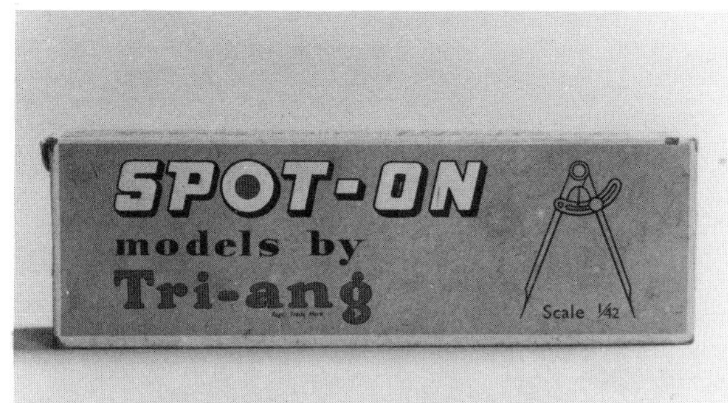

1st box design with the famous 'dividers'.

2nd all card box 157 SL Rover 3 litre with battery powered lights.

Special window box for 263, 4½ litre Bentley.

The last window box design.

No 191 Sunbeam Alpine Convertible.

No 118 BMW Isetta (bubble car).

iii) SPOT ON MODEL IDENTIFICATION

COMMON FEATURES

a Manufacturers Name and Trade Mark
All models have clearly stamped on their chassis 'SPOT-ON' and 'MODELS by Tri-ang'.

b. Model Types
All models indicate on their chassis their type:—
eg 'A.E.C. MAJOR 8'.

c Model Numbers
These are always shown on the boxes but NOT on the models themselves.

d Model Scale
All models have 1/42 scale stamped on the chassis.

e Wheel Hubs for Cars
All the wheels are assumed to have spun metal appearance with a raised hub cap in the centre unless otherwise described eg Cast In Spoked Wheels or Plastic Spoked Wheels.

f Wheel Hubs for Heavy Commercial Vehicles
All the heavy commercial vehicles are assumed to have the following sets of wheels.

At the Front — Four single wheels with a bulbous pattern showing six cast-in broad spokes.

At the Rear — Four double wheels with special double tyres. The wheels hubs are different from the front having a hollowed out appearance showing six cast in broad spokes.

In addition a single spare wheel (SPW) is suspended beneath the rear end of the chassis.

The exceptions to the foregoing such as the Model 158, Bedford 'S' Type Tanker and others have individual descriptions.

g Windscreens and Windows
All models have either plastic windows or windscreen.

h Chassis
All models assumed to have a detailed metal chassis unless otherwise indicated eg Plastic Chassis.

i Construction Materials
All models assumed to be constructed of die-cast metal unless otherwise described eg Plastic mudguards Plastic Running Boards.

j Length of Models
The length of the models shown should be approximately accurate as they are the nearest metric equivalent sizes to the 'inches' shown in the original catalogues.

k Number Plates
Assumed that all the standard issues of production models have number plates front and rear.

The only exceptions to this being the later issues which had plastic chassis such as Model 266 Bull Nose Morris (1923) and Model 279 MG PB Midget (1935).

l Tyres
All models assumed to have treaded rubber tyres.

m Seats, Suspension, Steering Wheels and Windows
All car models are fitted with these.

NB Model Values
NB. Because of the extreme rarity of many of the Spot On Models very little information has been produced by the survey in respect of several of the models as the rarity coding alongside the models clearly indicates.

In addition, in respect of those models about which reasonable quantities of comparative price information is available, very considerable differences were noticed in the asking prices for the same models.

Consequently the catalogue has endeavoured to take the middle course in respect of the estimated prices shown.

The Rarity and Price Grading system used by this catalogue is particularly apt for the Spot On Models and should be studied in conjunction with the figures shown.

iv) ABBREVIATIONS — EXAMPLE OF USE

110/3 A.E.C. Mammoth Major 8
British Road Services. 210 mm.

Red body, Blk cab roof, Sil CH and trim, 4 DW/4 SGW/SPW/DDTB/DPBA/FFS/CEMS

Red body, Black cab roof, Silver chassis and trim, 4 double wheels, 4 single wheels, spare wheel, drop down tailboard, detailed propshaft and back axle, flat float with sides, company emblems.

Spot On Models

2a Saloons Estates and Sports Cars

Ref. No.		Model Type	Model Features and Size	Rarity and Price Grading		
100	1959	Ford Zodiac	Red/Cream, Blue/Cream or Green body, OC. 107 mm.	£24-£30	MPR	☐
100L	1959	Ford Zodiac	Yellow/White body, BOWL/PP. 107 mm.	£30	NC	☐
101	1959	Armstrong Siddeley '236' Sapphire Saloon	Blue and Grey, Yellow and Black or Blue body, OC/PP/ORG. 108 mm.	£45	NC	☐
102	1959	Bentley 4 Door Sports Saloon	Met Green and Silver, Maroon and Silver or Grey and Silver body, ORG. 127 mm.	£50	GV	☐
103	1959	Rolls Royce Silver Wraith	Met Green and silver, Maroon and Silver or Met Blue and Silver body, ORG. 131 mm.	£50	GV	☐
104	1959	M.G.A. Sports Car	Red, Blue or White body, DI/ORG. 95 mm.	£32	GV	☐
105	1959	Austin Healey 100-SIX	Blue or Green, OC/DD/WS/SW/S/ORG. 89 mm.	£30	NC	☐
107	1960	Jaguar XKSS	Red or Green, WS/SW/S/NP/FHD/ORG. 91 mm.	£30	NC	☐
108	1960	Triumph TR '3'	Green or Blue body, WS/SW/S/NP/ORG. 88 mm.	£30	NC	☐
112	1960	Jensen 541	Green, Red or Yel/Black body, OC/ORG. 106 mm.	£25-30	MPR	☐
113	1960	Aston Martin DB3	Met Green, Blue or Yel body, OC/ORG. 104 mm.	£27-£32	MPR	☐
114	1960	Jaguar 3.4 Litre	Maroon or Grey, OC/ORG/PP. 106 mm.	£27-£32	MPR	☐
115	1960	Bristol 406	Met Green, Blue or Red body, OC/ORG. 116 mm.	£24-£30	MPR	☐
118	1960	BMW Isetta Bubble Car	Yellow, Green or Blue body, OC. 57 mm.	£16-£20	MPR	☐
119	1960	Meadows Frisky Sport	Orange/Grey or Green body, Grey HD, OC. 69 mm.	£10-£13	MPR	☐
120	1960	Fiat Multipla	Green or Red body, Silver trim, OC. 85 mm.	£10-£13	MPR	☐
131	1960	Goggomobile 'Super'	Green or Red body, OC/ORG. 70 mm.	£14-£17	MPR	☐
154	1960	Austin A40	Red/Black, Blue or Green body, OC/ORG. 88 mm.	£22-£28	MPR	☐
157		Rover 3 Litre	Grey or Blue body, OC/ORG/PP/SW. 107 mm.	£28-£33	MPR	☐
157SL		Rover 3 Litre	Same as previous with BOWL. 107 mm.	£35	NC	☐
165	1961	Vauxhall Cresta	Maroon, Blue or Green body, OC/ORG. 108 mm.	£19-£23	MPR	☐
166	1960	Renault Floride Convertible	Red or Yellow body, OC/BB/WS/SW. 101 mm.	£18-£21	MPR	☐
183	1963	Humber Super Snipe Estate Car	Blue or Green body, OC/RR/LG/PP/ORG. 113 mm.	£19-£23	MPR	☐
184	1963	Austin A60 with skis	Green, Red or Blue body, OC/RR/PP/ORG. 106 mm.	£24-£30	MPR	☐
185	1963	Fiat 500	Red or Blue body, WM/PP/ORG. 73 mm.	£14-£17	MPR	☐
191	1963	Sunbeam Alpine Convertible	Green or Blue body, OC/WS/ORG/PP. 95 mm.	£19-£24	MPR	☐
191	1963	Sunbeam Alpine Hardtop	Blue/White or Red/White body, OC/ORG/PP. 95 mm.	£21-£26	MPR	☐
193	1963	N.S.U. Prinz	Blue or Cream body, OC/ORG/PP. 84 mm.	£13-£15	MPR	☐
195	1963	Volkswagen Rally Car	Red or Blue body, OC, 2 flags, SL/RN/SPW. 110 mm.	£17-£20	MPR	☐
211	1963	Austin Baby Seven	Blue, Red or Yellow, OC/ORG/PP. 73 mm.	£14-£17	MPR	☐
212	1963	Car, Dinghy and Trailer Set	Blue body, RR/LG, Blue/White boat. 222 mm.	£25	NVE	☐
213	1963	Ford Anglia Saloon	Grey, Red or Blue body, OC/ORG/PP. 95 mm.	£15-£18	MPR	☐
215	1962	Daimler SP250 Dart	Blue, Red or Yellow, OC/PP/ORG/WS/SW/S. 97 mm.	£27	NC	☐
216	1963	Volvo 122S	Blue, Grey or Red body, OC/ORG. 108 mm.	£21-£26	MPR	☐
217	1962	'E' Type Jaguar	Red, Blue or Green body, OC/OBN/ORG. 106 mm.	£32	NC	☐
218	1963	Mk 10 Jaguar	Blue or Green body, OC/OBT/ORG/PP. 122 mm.	£32	NC	☐
219	1962	Austin Healey Sprite	Blue or Red body, D/WS/PP/ORG. 84 mm.	£17-£21	MPR	☐
259	1963	Ford Consul Classic	Red or Blue body, OC/PP/ORF/ORG/SW. 105 mm.	£18-£22	MPR	☐
260	1963	Rolls Royce Phantom V	Maroon body, Blue int, 2 flags on roof, DI/PP/ORG/S/SW/RB/NP. 143 mm.	£75	GV	☐
261	1963	Volvo P1800	Blue or Red body, OBN/PP/ORG/DI/NP. 106 mm.	£16-£19	MPR	☐
262	1965	Morris 1100 Saloon	Blue or Red body, OBN/PP/ORG/DE. 89 mm.	£14-£17	MPR	☐
263	1964	Vintage 4½ Litre Bentley (Supercharged)	Green body, Grey TN, RN '27', '11' or '15', Silver trim, D/FWS/FHD/UJ/SDB/ORG/PCH/PMG/SL/DEX/PC/SPW. 108 mm.	£30	NC	☐

Saloons Estates Sports Cars cont.

266	1965	Bull Nose Morris (1923) $^1/_{48}$ Scale)	Red/Black body, OC/DPHD/PCH/ODS/D/SPW/PP/ ORG/DCH/NP/SDL/WS	£25	NC	☐
267	1961	M.G. 1100 Saloon	Red/White or Blue/White, OBN/DE/ORG. 88 mm.	£22-£25	MPR	☐
269	1965	Ford Zephyr Six and Caravan	Red body, D/ORG/PP/SW/H/OD, Blue/White/Red CRV, Red VB, TB. 262 mm.	£28	NVE	☐
270	1965	Ford Zephyr Six	Blue or Red body, FDR/OD/PP/ORG/dog. 110 mm.	£17-£21	MPR	☐
274	1965	Morris 1100 and Canoe	Blue or Red body, Brown/Bl boat, OC/DRG. 88 mm.	£24	NC	☐
276	1964	Jaguar 'S' Type	Met Gold or Met Blue MB, D/PS/PP/ORG. 114 mm.	£24	NC	☐
278	1965	Mercedes Benz 230SL	Metallic Red, OC/FDR/PS/PP/ORG. 103 mm.	£18-£22	MPR	☐
279	1965	MG PB Midget (1935)	Red/Black, DD/PCH/WS/PP/CISPKW/ORG. 79 mm.	£24	NC	☐
286	1965	Austin 1800	Blue or Red body, D/PS/PP/ORG. 10 mm.	£20-£25	MPR	☐
287	1965	Hillman Minx	Green or Red, OC/RR/LG/PP/ORG/NP. 84 mm.	£19-£23	MPR	☐
289	1963	Morris Minor 1000	Blue or Met Green, OC/PP. 87 mm.	£36	NC	☐
306	1963	Humber Super Snipe Estate	Brown, Green or Blue, OC/RR/PP/ORG/LG. 113 mm.	£26-£32	MPR	☐
307	1965	Volkswagen Beetle 1200	Met Blue body, Blue interior, ORG. 89 mm.	£16-£19	MPR	☐
308	1965	Land Rover and Trailer	Green body, Brown roof and trailer. 170 mm.	£25	NC	☐
401	1966	Volkswagen Variant with Skis	Blue/White body, OC/ORD/RR/PP/ORG. 100 mm.	£25	NVE	☐
405	1966	B.E.A. Vauxhall Cresta	Dark Green body, Red *BEA* fig/PP/ORG. 110 mm.	£28	NC	☐
407	1966	Mercedes 230SL	Brown body, Red interior, LG/PP/ORG. 103 mm.	£25	NVE	☐
408	1966	Renault Caravelle	Red body, FDR/SL/TS/OD/PP. 101 mm.	£24	NVE	☐
410	1966	Austin 1800 and Rowboat	Olive Green car, Red boat, OBN/DE/ORG/PP. 100 mm.	£19-£24	MPR	☐

Collectors Notes

2b Spot On Commercial and Utility Vehicles. Lorries, Tankers, Mobile Cranes and Land Rovers

Ref. No.		Model Type	Model Features and Size	Rarity and Price Grading		
106A/1	1959	Austin Prime Mover with Flat Float with Sides	Red cab and float sides, Silver float bed, cab CH and trim, BRT/4DW/2SGW/AV. 234 mm.	£45	NC	☐
106A/1C	1960	Austin Prime Mover with Flat Float with Sides and Crate Load	Blue cab and float sides, Silver float bed, cab CH and trim, BRT/4DW/2SGW/AV. 234 mm.	£55	NVE	☐
106A/0C	1960	Austin Prime Mover with MGA Sports Car in Crate	Red cab and FFWS, Sil trim and CH, Cream crate, *British Motor Corporation Ltd,* on trailer and crate, BRT/4DW/2SGW/AV. 234 mm.		NGPP	☐
109/2	1960	E.R.F. with Flat Float	Turquoise body, Black cab roof, OC/DPBA/RB/4DW and 4SGW/SPW/SW/S. 210 mm.	£55	GV	☐
109/2P	1960	E.R.F. 68G with Flat Float without Sides with Planks	Turquoise body, Black cab roof, OC/DPBA/RB/4DW and 4SGW/SPW/SW/S. 210 mm.	£75	GV	☐
109/3	1960	E.R.F. 68G with Flat Float with Sides	Dark Blue cab, Pale Blue float, OC/DPBA/RB/4DW and 4SGW/SPW/SW/S. 210 mm.	£55	NC	☐
109/3B	1960	E.R.F. 68 with Flat Float and Barrel Load	Turquoise cab and float, Sil float bed, OC/RB/DPBA/ 4DW and 4SGW/SPW/SW/S. 210 mm.		NGPP	☐
110/2	1960	A.E.C. Mammoth Major 8 Flat Float without Sides	Red body, Silver chassis, DPBA/4DW/4SGW/SPW/ SW/S/ORG. 210 mm.	£60	GV	☐
110/2B	1960	A.E.C. Mammoth Major 8 'LONDON BRICK COMPANY LTD'	Red body, Black cab roof, Brown load, CEM/SW/S/ORG/DPBA/4DW/4SGW/SPW. 210 mm.	£65	GV	☐
110/3	1960	A.E.C. Mammoth Major 8 'BRITISH ROAD SERVICES'	Red body, Black roof, Sil CH and trim, 4DW/4SGW/SPW/DDTB/DPBA/FFA/CEMS. 210 mm.	£65	GV	☐
110/3D	1962	A.E.C. Mammoth Major 8 Oil Drums Load	Red body, Black roof, Sil CH and trim, FFS/DPBA/ DDTB/SW/S/4DW/4SGW/SPW. 210 mm.		NGPP	☐
110/4	1961	A.E.C. Mammoth Major 8 'SHELL-BP' Tanker	Green cab, Red tank, Black CH and CWK, Silver trim, DPBA/4DW/4SGW/SPW/CEMS. 210 mm.	£200	GV	☐
110/4	1963	A.E.C. Mammoth Major 8 'SHELL-BP' Tanker	Yellow cab, White/Yel tank, Silver CH and CWK, DPBA/4DW/4SGW/SPW/CEMS. 210 mm.	£200	GV	☐
111A/1	1959	Ford Thames Trader 'BRITISH RAILWAYS'	Mrn and White body, AV/4DW/2SGW/SPW/FFS, *4884 BG M* and *M1741GT6* on cab/TRL. 219 mm.	£75	NC	☐
111A/1S	1960	Ford Thames Trader with Sack Load	Dark Blue cab, Pale Blue float, Blk CH, OC/FFS/SW/ S/ORG/AV/4DW/2SGW/SPW. 219 mm.		NGPP	☐
111A/30T	1961	Ford Thames Trader with Log Load	TT Blue cab and float, Silver CH, OC/FF/SW/S/ ORG/AV/4DW/2SGW/SPW. 219 mm.	£125	GV	☐
111A/30G	1962	Ford Thames Trader with Garage Kit	Orange cab and float, Silver CH and trim, FFS/S/ SW/ORG/AV/4DW/4SGW/SPW/CPL. 219 mm.	£135	GV	☐
117	1963	'JONES' Mobile Crane	Red/Black/White body, WCJ/4DW/2SGW. 289 mm.	£55	GV	☐
158A/2	1961	Bedford 'S' Type 2000 Gal 'SHELL-BP' Tanker	Green cab, Red tank, Black CH, Sil trim, AV/4DW/ 2SGW/ORG/CEMS, *P33A37.* 199 mm.	£200	GV	☐
158A/2	1962	Bedford 'S' Type 2000 Gal 'SHELL-BP' Tanker	Yellow cab, White tank, Silver trim, AV/4DW/ 2SGW/ORG/CEMS, *P33A37.* 202 mm.	£200	GV	☐
158A/3C	1961	Bedford Low Loader with Cable Drum	Red cab and loader, Blue wheels, AV Silver trim. In cat but not seen. 270 mm.		NGPP	☐
161	1961	Land Rover with L.W.B.	Grey body, White roof, SPW. 108 mm.	£24	NC	☐
258	1963	'R.A.C.' Land Rover	Blue body, *Radio Rescue* SPW/ORG/A. 108 mm.	£36	GV	☐
308	1965	Land Rover and Trailer	Green body, Beige HD, Brown TRL. 170 mm.	£28	NC	☐
402	1966	Crash Service Land Rover	Orange body, WCJ/H *Motorways Crash Service* in Blue. 125 mm.	£28	NC	☐

2c Vans

Ref. No.		Model Type	Model Features and Size	Rarity and Price Grading		
122	1961	'UNITED DAIRIES' Milk Float Van	Red/White body and crest, chains, *Lada the New Yoghourt,* CEMS. 98 mm.	£35	GV	☐
210	1961	Morris Mini Minor Van	Bright Yellow, S/SW/NP/SS. 79 mm.	£24	NVE	☐
210/1	1962	Morris Mini Minor Van 'ROYAL MAIL'	Red body, Post Office crest, S/SW/NP/SS *EIIR.* 79 mm.	£24	NVE	☐
265	1964	'TONIBELL DAIRY ICE CREAM' Van	Blue body, Red flash, OWD, attendant, *Soft Ice Cream.* 107 mm.	£45	GV	☐
271	1965	'EXPRESS DAIRIES' Milk Float Van	Blue/White body, RC/RCH/3W/D, *Lada the New Yoghourt,* CEMS. 98 mm.	£30	GV	☐
273	1965	'SECURITY EXPRESS LTD' Commer Van	Green/Gold, CEMS/OD/PP/NP/SS/ORG, driver and seated guard. 126 mm.	£45	NC	☐
315	1965	'GLASS & HOLMES' Commer Van	Blue/Yellow, OD/LD/2 figs/ORG/PP, *Window Cleaning Company Est 1891.* 126 mm.	£35	NC	☐
404	1966	Morris Mini Minor Van 'SHELL'	Yellow body with Silver trim, CEM/SS/S/SW/LD/fig. 79 mm.	£27	NVE	☐

2d Bus, Coach and Taxi Cab

Ref. No.		Model Type	Model Features and Size	Rarity and Price Grading		
145	1963	Routemaster Bus 'LONDON TRANSPORT'	Red/Black body, DI/2DW/2SGW/ORG *Ovaltine the Worlds Best Nightcap.* 198 mm.	£150	GV	☐
155	1961	Austin F×4 Taxicab	Black body, Red seats *Taxi,* ORG. 117 mm.	£24	NC	☐
156	1961	Mulliner Luxury Coach (Guy Warrior)	Pale Blue/Grey body, Red flash, OC *Triang Tours.* 213 mm.	£75	GV	☐

2e Emergency Services Fire, Police and Ambulances (Civilian)

Ref. No.		Model Type	Model Features and Size	Rarity and Price Grading		
207	1964	Wadham 'AMBULANCE'	Cream/Blue or White, RCS/ST/D/PS/ORD. 115 mm.	£45	NVE	☐
256	1966	Mk 10 Jaguar 'POLICE' Car	Blue body, roof sign, S/SW/SS/ORG/PP. 106 mm.		NVP	☐
309	1965	BBC 'Z' Car (Ford Zephyr)	White body, A/OD/SS/SW/S/2PM/ORG. 110 mm.	£35	NVE	☐
316	1966	'FIRE DEPT' Land Rover	Red body, Brown HD, RC/SS/S/2FM. 112 mm.	£30	NC	☐
409	1966	'LEYLAND' Black Maria	Blue body, *Police,* ORD/SS/SL/PM/robber. 114 mm.		NVP	☐

2f Military and R.A.F. Models

Ref. No.		Model Type	Model Features and Size	Rarity and Price Grading		
415	1965	R.A.F. Land Rover	Blue/Grey body, R.A.F. EM, hose/FP/AM. 111 mm.	£28-£35	MPR	☐
416	1965	'LEYLAND' Military 'AMBULANCE'	Olive Green body, RCS/SQM/SS/PP/3SLDS. 114 mm.		NVP	☐
417	1965	Military 'FIELD KITCHEN'	MG, Olive Green body, SQM/OW/SS/3LDS/MNP. 108 mm	£32-£40	MPR	☐
418	1965	'LEYLAND' Military Bus	MG, Olive Green body, *Army Personnel,* SQM/MNP/3SLDS. 114 mm.		NVP	☐

2g Roadmaking Equipment and Tractors

Ref. No.		Model Type	Model Features and Size	Rarity and Price Grading		
116	1959	Caterpillar Tractor D9	Brown/Silver body, White RTR. 153 mm.	£40	NVE	☐
123	1959	Bamford Excavator	Red/Yellow body, J.C.B. 272 mm.		NVP	☐
137	1962	'MASSEY HARRIS' Tractor	Red/Silver/Blue body, driver/SW. 79 mm.	£34	NVE	☐

2h Caravans and Boats

Ref. No.		Model Type	Model Features and Size	Rarity and Price Grading		
135	1964	14ft GP Sailing Dinghy	Brown or Yellow boat on BR TRL. 128 mm.	£8-£10	MPR	☐
139	1960	Eccles E. 16 Caravan	Blue body, White roof, TB. 146 mm.		NVP	☐
264	1962	Tourist Caravan	Blue body, White roof, TB. 152 mm.	£9-£12	MPR	☐

2i Presentation and Gift Sets

Ref. No.	Model Type	Model Features and Size	Rarity and Price Grading
1960	No 0 Presentation Set	Contains 106A/1, 100, 103, 104 and 113	NGPP ☐
1960	No 1 Presentation Set	Contains 100, 101, 103 and 104	NGPP ☐
1960	No 2 Presentation Set	Contains 109/3, 101, 102 and 105	NGPP ☐
1960	No 3 Presentation Set	Contains 111A/1, 101, 104, 108, 112, 113, 114	NGPP ☐
1960	No 4 Presentation Set	Contains 106A/1, 109/3, 100, 107, 112	NGPP ☐
1963	No 4 Presentation Set	Contains 104, 105 and 108	NGPP ☐
	No 5 Presentation Set	Contains 118, 119 and 131	NGPP ☐
	No 6 Presentation Set	Contains 131, 185, 193 and 211	NGPP ☐
	No 7 Presentation Set	Contains 166, 191, 211, 213, 215, 217	NGPP ☐
	No 8 Presentation Set	Contains 157, 191, 213, 216, 258	NGPP ☐
	No 9 Presentation Set	Contains 122, 145, 193, 207, 211, 256	NGPP ☐
	No 10 Presentation Set	Contains 122, 145, 157, 158A/2, 165, 166, 185, 211, 215 and 262	NGPP ☐
	Gift Set 702	Contains Zephyr Six, 274 Morris 1100 and canoe, 286 Austin 1800, and 135	£75 GV ☐

Tommy Spot Gift Set Series

Ref. No.	Model Type	Model Features and Size	Rarity and Price Grading
801	Home with Tommy Spot	Hillman Minx with Mr Spot, Ford Zephyr Six with driver, BK/TSP	£45 GV ☐
802	Cops 'n Robbers with Tommy Spot	BBC 'Z' car with driver and robber, Jaguar 'S' with driver, BK/TSP	£55 GV ☐
803	Superville Garage Service with Tommy Spot	Austin 1800 with Driver, Austin Healey Sprite with Driver, 2 garage workers, BK/TSP	£45 NVE ☐
804	Sailing with Tommy Spot	Vauxhall Cresta and sailing dinghy with Mr Spot, BK/TSP	£35 GV ☐
805	Fire with Tommy Spot	Land Rover and trailer (both Red) two firemen, BK/TSP	£40 GV ☐
806	Royal occasion with Tommy Spot	Royal Rolls Royce with D/PS/BOL 6 guardsmen, BK/TSP	£135 NVE ☐
807	Pit stop with Tommy Spot	Mercedes 230 SL and Jaguar 'S', 2RD/BK/TSP	£55 NVE ☐
808	Motorway Rescue with Tommy Spot	Crash service Land Rover and mechanic, A.A. van/A.A. man, BK/TSP	£75 NVE ☐

Collectors Notes

CHAPTER 3 MATCHBOX TOYS

i) INTRODUCTION

The first 1-75 Series toys were produced by Lesney Products Ltd in 1953.

They were packaged and marketed by the Moko Company who specialized in the distribution of toy manufacturers products. Consequently the early boxes reflected this arrangement by displaying the name 'MOKO LESNEY'. This partnership lasted until the late fifties, when Lesney began distributing their products themselves and issued the first catalogue which depicted just 42 models.

Lesney Products had in fact been formed just after the war, when the unrelated Leslie and Rodney Smith set up their factory and linked their names to form 'Lesney' Products Ltd. They were soon joined by Jack O'dell who was a recognised die-casting expert.

Various Products were made prior to the launch of the 1-75 Series, probably the most well known of which was the 1953 Coronation Coach and horses.

Since those early days the number of models issued in the 1-75 Series has topped well over five hundred. This large range therefore provides collectors with many opportunities for collecting specific types of models whether they be buses or racing cars. With new low cost models continually being issued each year, this is an ideal collecting area for the younger generation.

For the specialist collector the early models are greatly sought after and most importantly the price levels are still within the reach of most people. Furthermore reasonable quantities are available for building up a collection.

Matchbox have been known to produce the staggering figure of over 5 million models a week to satisfy the demands made by collectors in 140 different countries, particularly in the USA. Many of todays adult collectors were probably unwittingly hooked at an early age by the little models they could buy at the corner shop for just a few coppers of their pocket money. Today no doubt many of them collect 'The Models of Yesteryear' Series but thats another story!

It is to be hoped that the Matchbox Toys 1-75 Series models continues to bring joy to many more generations of school children.

The "Matchbox" Story

IT ALL BEGAN IN 1953, with a miniature diecast model of the Coronation Coach with its team of eight horses. In Coronation Year over a million were sold and this tremendous success was followed by the introduction of the first miniature vehicle models packed in matchboxes. And so the famous "Matchbox" Series was born.

At the very beginning it was decided to make the whole "Matchbox" Series sell at one price and this new range was numbered from 1, until 75 different models were produced by 1960. Models were then regularly withdrawn and replaced by new models which included many of the now-famous "Matchbox" features such as windows, opening doors, suspension, engines, etc. Thus, the "Matchbox" Series is ever-changing, making it the most modern and exciting of its kind in the world.

Some of the early models were perhaps simple compared with the super "Matchboxes" of today, but even so they have now become collectors pieces and often change hands for much more than their original price.

The tremendous success of this new range was soon followed by the introduction of the "Models of Yesteryear", "Matchbox" Major Packs and "Matchbox" King Size. A similar demand for these has grown, and today "Matchbox" models are enjoyed in just about every country in the world.

From the tiny Coronation Coach of the Queen of England to the world's largest makers of model vehicles—that is the miniature success story of "Matchbox".

2

Extract from the 1966 catalogue.

MODELS AVAILABLE AT TOYFAIRS AND COLLECTORS SHOPS

2a Atlantic Tractor
14a Ambulance
10a Mechanical Horse

56a London Trolley Bus
17b London Austin Taxi

37b Coca Cola Lorry (Even Load)
42a Bedford 'EVENING NEWS' Van

4c Triumph Motorcycle and side car
66b Harley Davidson Motorcycle and side car

74c 'ESSO' Daimler Bus
74e 'BEEFEATER GIN' Promotional

17f Londoner Buses

74a Mobile Canteen

ii) PACKAGING

1953-54 (Approx)

1954-55 (Approx)

1955-56 (Approx)

1956-57 (Approx)

1957-58 (Approx)

1958-59 (Approx)

Matchbox Packaging continued

1959-63 (Approx)

1962-64 (Approx)

1971 (Approx)

1973 (Approx)

1981 The Bubble Pack

1983 The new type Window Box

Other Box designs will also be found

iii) MODEL IDENTIFICATION

Many models have common identifying features and these are shown below to avoid unnecessary repetition.

i) Model Number

With the exception of the very first models which did not have model numbers all the remainder have the number of the model either cast on the model itself or on the base plate or chassis.
The only exceptions to this rule are models from the TP Series where no model numbers are shown.

ii) 'Lesney'

It has been assumed that all models issued between 1953 and 1982 had the word 'LESNEY' either cast on the model itself or on the base plate or chassis.

iii) Model Name

It has been assumed that all models issued after 1957 had the model name stamped on the base plate or chassis. The only exceptions to this rule being those models issued without a base plate e.g. No 24 Hydraulic Excavator.

iv) 'Matchbox' or 'Matchbox Series'

Assumed that all models after 1965 had 'MATCHBOX' stamped onto the baseplate or chassis.

v) Suspension

Assumed that all Saloon Cars issued after 1965 were fitted with suspension.

vi) Windscreeens

All assumed to be Plastic.

vii) Interior fittings — seats and steering wheels

All assumed to be Plastic.

viii) Windows

Assumed to be plastic and fitted to all saloon cars after 1961 onwards.

ix) Lengths of Models

The figures given have either been taken from original Matchbox catalogues, or from the models themselves. Fortunately the measurements were shown in both mm and inches in the first Lesney issued catalogue in 1958. Models 1-42 were included in this issue.

x) Construction Materials

All models assumed to be constructed at least in part of a die-cast alloy.

xi) Base plates

Assumed that all Base plates were of metal construction until the late seventies when plastic became increasingly used.

xii)

Wheels All the early models had metal wheels which were gradually changed to a Grey Silver or Black Plastic construction before Superfast wheels were introduced in the late sixties.

Axles All the early axles had crimped ends which gradually changed to round ended axles prior to the Superfast wheels.

xiii) Model Names

The catalogue has tried to give the original catalogue description in respect of each of the model names listed.
However the manufacturers catalogue listings are known to be inaccurate concerning the colour range depicted. This is because the model photos shown are taken from mock-ups produced many months before production commences.

xiv) Rolamatics

Some models issued in the seventies had built in working parts which operated when the model was pushed. They have been indicated in the model listings by the abbreviation RLM.

iv) Abbreviations — Examples of Use

MATCHBOX 1-75 SERIES EXAMPLE

Model
54b 1968 Mercury Police Car 77 mm.

Abbreviations
White MB, Red/Bl PCR, SL/ASM/2PS/BPW/SF

Non Abbreviated Form
White main body, Red and Blue Police crest special light (eg flashing roof light) auto steer mechanism, 2 passengers, Black plastic wheels OR Superfast wheels.

Wheel Abbreviations

Wheel abbreviations such as GSBPW (Grey, Silver or Black Plastic Wheels) indicate that the first models were fitted with Grey Plastic wheels the second with Silver and the third with Black etc.

Collectors Notes

3A Matchbox 1-75 Series and Junior Models

Ref. No.		Model Type	Model Features and Size	Rarity and Price Grading		
No 1						
1a	1953	Diesel Road Roller	Light or Dark Green, Red MRW, Gold trim, Tan D, No number, crimped axles, tow hook. 49 mm.	£14	GV	☐
1b	1955	Diesel Road Roller	Pale Green MB, Red MRW, Lt or Dk Tan D, high peaked canopy, CA/NN/H. 55 mm.	£9	NC	☐
1c	1958	Diesel Road Roller	Lt or Dk Green MB and driver, Red MRW number cast in, CRA/HPC/H. 64 mm.	£7	NC	☐
1d	1962	Diesel Road Roller	Green MB, and driver, Red PRW, MIECI/HPC/H. 67 mm.	£4-£6	MPR	☐
1e	1968	Mercedes Truck	Green or Gold MB, Orange or Yellow CNP, BP/SF/H. 76 mm.	£2-£3	MPR	☐
1f	1972	Mod Rod	Yellow MB, Silver ERE, cat LB, TW/SF. 73 mm.	Current	MPR	☐
1g	1976	Dodge Challenger	Red body, White roof, Silver trim, CW/SF. 74 mm.	Current	MPR	☐
	1982	Customised Dodge Challenger	Blue or Orange MB, *Revin Rebel,* CW/SF. 74 mm.		MPR	☐
	1983	Customised Dodge Challenger	Yellow MB, Black roof, *Toyman,* CW/SF	Current	MPR	☐
No 2						
2a	1953	Dumper Truck	Green MB, Red DMP, Gold TR, PN/UPN MW, NN/CA. 40 mm.	£5-£7	MPR	☐
2b	1957	Dumper Truck	Colours SAPM, Tan D, CA/NCI/MW/GPW. 49 mm.	£5-£7	MPR	☐
2c	1962	(Muir Hill) Dumper Truck	Red MB, Green DMP, *Laing,* BPW. 54 mm.	£3-£4	MPR	☐
2d	1968	Mercedes Trailer	Green body, Yellow canopy, BPW/SF/H. 90 mm.	Current	MPR	☐
	1970	Colour change	Gold body, Orange canopy	Current	MPR	☐
2e	1972	Jeep Hot Rod	Red or Pink MB, Silver EE, Cream S, SF. 58 mm.	Current	MPR	☐
2f	1977	Rescue Hovercraft	Green/Fawn MB, *Rescue* SF. 77 mm.	Current	MPR	☐
2g	1981	S-2 Jet	Black/Yellow MB, four wheels, FWT/TCC. 76 mm.	Current	MPR	☐
	1982	Colour change	Blue/White MB, Red flash, *Viper*	Current	MPR	☐
No 3						
3a	1953	Cement Mixer	Blue MB, Orange MW or GPW, NN/CA with or without 4 mixers in barrel. 45 mm.	£7	NC	☐
3b	1961	Bedford Tipper Truck	Grey cab, Bright Red or Maroon tipper, opening tailboard, GPW/BPW. 64 mm.	£4-£5	MPR	☐
3c	1968	Mercedes Benz — Binz Ambulance	White MB, Red X decals, STR/BPW/SF/OTG. 73 mm..	£3-£4	MPR	☐
3d	1973-	Monteverdi Hai	Red MB, Blue TW, Sil trim, RN '3', OD/SF. 74 mm.	Current	MPR	☐
3e	1979	Porsche Turbo	Brown or Silver MB, OD/SF. 74 mm.	Current	MPR	☐
	1981	Colour change	Green MB, Yellow interior, OD/SF	Current	MPR	☐
	1982	Colour change	Red MB, Tan driver, 4 spoke FMW, SRMW/NN. 40 mm.	Current	MPR	☐
No 4						
4a	1954-	Tractor	Red MB, Tan driver 4 spoke FMW, SRMW/NN. 40 mm.	£7	NC	☐
4b	1957-	Tractor	SAPM with solid FMW/hollow RMW/NCI. 45 mm.	£6	NC	☐
4c	1960-	Triumph Motor Cycle and Side-car	Steel Blue MB, Silver SPKW, BPT. 57 mm.	£12	NC	☐
4d	1967	(Dodge) Stake Truck	Yellow cab and CH, Green SB, BPW/SF/H. 73 mm.	£2-£3	MPR	☐
4e	1972	Gruesome Twosome	Gold MB, Pink TW/RF, Silver EE, SF. 73 mm.	Current	MPR	☐
4f	1976-	Pontiac Firebird	Met Blue MB, Silver trim, Orange TW, SF. 73 mm.	Current	MPR	☐
4g	1981-	'57' Chevy	Met Mauve MB, Silver trim and E, OD, SF. 75 mm.	Current	MPR	☐
	1982	Colour change	All Red MB, *Cherry Bomb,* labels, SF. 75 mm.	Current	MPR	☐
	1983	Colour change	Black/Red/Yellow, 'on fire effect' MB, SF. 75 mm.	Current	MPR	☐

Matchbox 1-75 Series and Junior Models cont.

No 5

5a	1954	London Bus 'BUY MATCHBOX SERIES'	Red MB, Gold grille, No '5' CI, front and rear, Yellow and Green decal, MW/CA/DD. 50 mm.	£12	NC ☐
5b	1956	London Bus 'PLAYERS PLEASE'	Red MB, Gold or Silver grille, No '5' CI, *Players Please* or *Buy Matchbox Series* decals, MW or LSM, GPW, CRA/DD. 58 mm.	£12	NC ☐
5c	1961	London Bus 'PLAYERS PLEASE'	Red MB, Silver grille, GPW/BPW/DD. 67 mm.	£12	NC ☐
5c	1961	London (Routemaster) Bus	Red MB, Silver grille, *Drink Peardrax* or *BP Viscostatic*. DD. 67 mm.	£8	NC ☐
5d	1966	London (Routemaster) Bus	Red MB, Red grille, White S, BPW/DD *BP Longlife* or *BP Viscostatic*. 71 mm.	£5-£7	MPR ☐
5e	1969	Lotus Europa	Met Blue or Pink MB, Silver trim, OD/SF/H. 71 mm.	£2-£3	MPR ☐
5f	1976	Seafire Motor Boat	Blue/White MB, Yellow D, *Seafire*. 75 mm.	Current	MPR ☐
5g	1980	U.S. Mail Truck	Blue MB, White roof, *U.S. Mail,* SF. 59 mm.	Current	MPR ☐
5h	1982-	4×4 Jeep	Bronze MB, large wheels, black ARBB. 74 mm.	Current	MPR ☐

No 6

6a	1954	Quarry Truck	Orange MB, Grey DMP, 6 ribs, 6MGPW/CA/NN. 55 mm.	£7	NC ☐
6b	1958	Quarry Truck	Yellow MB and DMP 4 ribs, 6GBPW/DCS/CRA. 64 mm.	£5-£6	MPR ☐
6c	1963	Quarry Truck	Yellow MB and DMP, A or B, CI/6BPW/CRA. 67 mm.	£3-£4	MPR ☐
6d	1969	Ford Pick Up	Red MB, White DCV, ASM/BPW/SF. 75 mm.	£2-£3	MPR ☐
6e	1974-	Mercedes 350SL	Orange MB, Black CV top, Yel int, SF. 75 mm.	Current	MPR ☐
	1980	Colour change	Met Silver MB, Black hood, White seats, *Rennservice,* Issued in G15 Gift Set		MPR ☐
	1981	Colour change	Red MB, White CV top, SF. 75 mm.	Current	MPR ☐
6f	1982	Mercedes 350 Convertible	Blue MB, White seats, Silver trim, SF. 75 mm.	Current	MPR ☐

No 7

7a	1954	Horse Drawn Milk Float	Orange MB, Brown horse, White mane and D, MSPKW or GPW, Gold trim, CRA. 55 mm.	£25	GV ☐
7b	1961	Ford Anglia	Lt Blue MB, Green TW, GBPW, WW 1. 67 mm.	£4-£5	MPR ☐
7c	1968	Ford Refuse Truck	Orange or Red MB, Silver DMP, TW/BPT/SF. 76 mm.	£2-£3	MPR ☐
7d	1973	Hairy Hustler	Orange MB, Yellow seats, RN '5'. 72 mm.	Current	MPR ☐
7e	1977-	Volkswagen Golf	Green MB, Yellow TW, 2 Black SB, SF/H. 72 mm.	Current	MPR ☐
	1981	Colour change	Yellow MB, Red seats, BB/SF/H	Current	MPR ☐
	1982	Colour change	Silver MB, Green flash *Golf,* SF	Current	MPR ☐
7f	1983	IMSA Mazda	Blue MB, orange/white flash, *Mazda*. 76 mm.	Current	MPR ☐

No 8

8a	1955	Caterpillar Tractor	Yellow MB, Gold trim, MRW/RT/CA/NN Black or Yellow driver's hat. 40 mm.	£8	NC ☐
8b	1959	Caterpillar Tractor	Yellow MB and D, NCI (8), MRW/RT/CA. 43 mm.	£8	NC ☐
8c	1961	Caterpillar Tractor	Yellow MB and D, NCI (18), MRW or PRW, RT. 48 mm.	£5-£6	MPR ☐
8d	1964	Caterpillar Tractor	Yellow MB, No D, SBPRW, Green RT, NCI (8). 51 mm.	£4-£5	MPR ☐
8e	1966	Ford Mustang Fastback	White MB, Red seats, BPT or SF, CW/H. 74 mm.	£3-£4	MPR ☐
	1970	Colour change	Red MB, Yellow seats, SF. 74 mm.	£2-£3	MPR ☐
8f	1970	Wildcat Dragster	Orange MB, Black Wild Cat decal, SF/TW. 74 mm.	Current	MPR ☐
8g	1975	De Tomaso Pantera	White or Blue MB, Red seats, RN '8' and *Panther*. 77 mm.	Current	MPR ☐
8h	1981	Rover 3500	Red MB, Cream seats SF, Black base. 73 mm.	Current	MPR ☐
8i	1983-	Rover 3500 'POLICE' Car	White MB, Yellow/Black decal, 2 Blue FL. 73 mm.	Current	MPR ☐

Matchbox 1-75 Series and Junior Models cont.

No 9

9a	1955	Fire Escape	Red MB, WW Gold trim, NFB/CA/NN/MW. 55 mm.	£10	NC ☐
9b	1958	Fire Escape	Red MB, Gold trim, CA/NCI/MW/FB. 59 mm.	£10	NC ☐
9c	1959	Fire Engine	Red MB, GD, Sil or Tan LD, 17/18 RG, GBPW. 67 mm.	£4-£6	MPR ☐
9d	1966	Boat and Trailer	Blue deck, White hull, Blue TRL, BPW. 89 mm.	£3-£4	MPR ☐
	1970	Colour change	White deck, Blue hull and TRL. 89 mm.	£2-£3	MPR ☐
9e	1972	AMX Javelin	Met Lime Green MB, Yel seats, TW, SF, OD. 77 mm.	Current	MPR ☐
	1983	Colour change	Met Silver, Red/Black labels, RN '9'. 77 mm.	Current	MPR ☐
9f	1978	Ford Escort	White MB, *Shell* and *Ford* decals, SF. 74 mm.	Current	MPR ☐
	1981	Colour change	Met Green, White grille, *Seagull,* SF. 74 mm.	Current	MPR ☐

No 10

10a	1955	Mechanical Horse and Trailer	Red cab, Grey SMB, TRL, Gold TR, 5MW/NN/CA. 55 mm.	£10	NC ☐
10b	1957	Mechanical Horse and Trailer	Red Cab, Grey RBDB, TRL, Gold TR, 5MW/NN/CA	£9	NC ☐
10c	1961	'TATE & LYLE' Sugar Truck	Blue MB, Yel decal with crown, GBPW. 67 mm.	£12	NVE ☐
	1962	Decal changed	Crown removed from decal	£9	NC ☐
10d	1966	Pipe Truck	Red or Orange MB, Grey plastic pipes, TW/BPT. 74 mm.	£3-£4	MPR ☐
10e	1973	Piston Popper	Met Blue MB, Silver EE, SF/RLM/OC. 75 mm.	Current	MPR ☐
10f	1979-	Plymouth Gran Fury	White/Black MB, 2FL/SF *Police* decals. 75 mm.	Current	MPR ☐

No 11

11a	1955	'ESSO' Road Tanker	Green or Red body, Gold trim, ERF cast in, LSM decal, NN/MW/CA. 50 mm.	£10	NC ☐
	1957	Colour change	Yellow body, ERF CI, Silver trim, MW/CA/NN	£10	NC ☐
11b	1958	'ESSO' Petrol Tanker	Red MB, Silver trim, ERF CI, MGSBPW/NCI. 64 mm.	£10	NC ☐
11c	1965	Jumbo Crane	Yellow MB, Red HL, Red or Yel box, BPW. 76 mm.	£2-£3	MPR ☐
11d	1969	Scaffolding Truck	Silver MB, Yellow SCF, Green TW, BPW *Builders Direct Supply*. 76 mm.	£2-£3	MPR ☐
11e	1973	Flying Bug	Red/Yellow body, Silver DH, SF. 73 mm.	Current	MPR ☐
11f	1978	Car Transporter	Red/Cream MB, Black grille, 3 cars, SF. 75 mm.	Current	MPR ☐
	1983	Colour change	Red/White MB, Silver grille	Current	MPR ☐

No 12

12a	1955	Land Rover	Green MB, WW Sil trim, Tan D, CA/NN/MW. 42 mm.	£7	NC ☐
12b	1959	Land Rover	Green MB, WW Sil trim, No D, BB/GBPW/CRA. 60 mm.	£4-£5	MPR ☐
12c	1966-	Safari Land Rover	Green or Blue MB, Tan LG/CW/BPW/H. 72 mm.	£3-£4	MPR ☐
	1970	Colour change	Metallic Gold, BPW/SF. 72 mm.	£3-£4	MPR ☐
12d	1970	Setra Coach	Gold, Yellow or Magenta MB, White roof, Red lights, CW/SF. 76 mm.	£2-£3	MPR ☐
12e	1975	Big Bull	Orange MB, Green DB, Red wheels, SF. 63 mm.	Current	MPR ☐
12f	1980-	Citroen CX	Met Blue MB, Yel S, Sil base, OTG/SF/H. 77 mm.	Current	MPR ☐
	1982	Colour change	Yellow MB, *Matchbox* decal	Current	MPR ☐
	1983	Colour change 'AMBULANCE'	White MB, Red DCS, Blk/Wh cross, SF	Current	MPR ☐

Matchbox 1-75 Series and Junior Models cont.

No 13

13a	1955	Wreck Truck	Tan MB, Red crane and hook, MW/CA. 50 mm.	£8	NC	☐
13b	1958	Wreck Truck	Tan MB, Red crane and H, 13 CI, GPW/CRA. 55 mm.	£8	NC	☐
13c	1960	Thames Trader Wreck Truck 'MATCHBOX GARAGES'	Red MB, Silver trim, Red or Silver hook, Yellow decal, MLCD letters, GPW/WWCLW. 64 mm.	£7	NC	☐
13d	1965	(Dodge) Wreck Truck	Green/Yellow MB, *BP,* Red P hook, BPT. 76 mm.	£3-£4	MPR	☐
13e	1972	Baja Buggy	Green MB, Black/Red trim, Silver E, SF. 66 mm.	Current	MPR	☐
13f	1977	Snorkel Fire Engine	Red MB, Yellow hoist and FM, Sil trim, SF. 78 mm.	Current	MPR	☐
	1983	Colour change 'METRO FIRE DEPT SNORKEL No 1'	Red MB, White hoist and FM, early models had small square hole next to *Fire,* SF (Basically a re-issue of 35e). 78 mm.	Current	MPR	☐

No 14

14a	1956	Ambulance	Cream MB, Silver trim, WW RCS, CRA, *Ambulance* cast onto sides, MGPW/NN. 50 mm.	£9	NC	☐
14b	1958	Ambulance	Cream MB, Red cross on roof, CRA, 14CI, *Ambulance* cast onto sides, GPW. 59 mm.	£6-£8	MPR	☐
14c	1962	Ambulance	White MB, *LCC Ambulance* and Red cross on sides, ORD/GPW/RA. 67 mm.	£4-£5	MPR	☐
14d	1968	Iso Grifo	Blue MB (many shades) BPT/SF/H/CW. 76 mm.	£2-£3	MPR	☐
14e	1977	Mini-Ha-Ha	Red MB, Blue seats, Silver trim, driver. 60 mm.	Current	MPR	☐
14f	1982	(Leyland) Petrol Tanker	Red MB, White tank, *Elf,* PLP, SF. 77 mm.	Current	MPR	☐

No 15

15a	1956	Prime Mover	Yellow or Orange MB, 6 MW or 10 GPW, NN/H/SPWBC. 55 mm.	£7	NC	☐
15b	1959	Atlantic Tractor	Orange MB, SPWBC, Silver trim, H/GBPW. 67 mm.	£6-£7	MPR	☐
15c	1963	Refuse Truck	Blue MB and CH, Grey DMP with OD, *Cleansing Service* logo, 6 BPW. 64 mm.	£5-£6	MPR	☐
15d	1968	Volkswagen 1500 Saloon	Off white MB, Silver trim, CW/BPT/SF/H. 72 mm.	£2-£3	MPR	☐
	1970	Colour change	Red MB. 72 mm.	£2-£3	MPR	☐
15e	1973	Fork Lift Truck	Red MB, Yel forks, *Lansing Bagnall.* 70 mm.	Current	MPR	☐
	1982	Colour change	Red MB, White forks. 70 mm.	Current	MPR	☐

No 16

16a	1956	Transporter Trailer	Tan MB, rear ramp moves, TB/6MW/OC. 77 mm.	£7-£8	MPR	☐
16b	1960	Atlantic Trailer	Orange or Tan MB, 8 GBPW, towbar. 79 mm.	£6-£7	MPR	☐
16c	1963	'Mountaineer' Dump Truck with Snowplough	Grey cab and chassis, Orange tipper Red/White dozer blade, 6 GBPW. 76 mm.	£4-£5	MPR	☐
16d	1969	Case Bull-Dozer	Red/Yellow MB and DB, Black PR, DCNP/H. 64 mm.	£2-£3	MPR	☐
16e	1974	Badger Truck	Bright Red MB, White Radar, 6 BPW/RLM/TW. 68 mm.	Current	MPR	☐
16f	1981	Pontiac	Gold MB, Red seats, eagle decal, SF. 77 mm.	Current	MPR	☐
	1982	Colour change	White MB, Blue flash, *Firebird*	Current	MPR	☐
	1983	Colour change	Black MB, Red seats, *Turbo*	Current	MPR	☐

Matchbox 1-75 Series and Junior Models cont.

No 17

17a		Bedford Removals Van 'MATCHBOX REMOVALS SERVICE'	Blue, MRN, Lt or Dk Green body, WW Black border to GRN versions, logo. 55 mm.		MPR ☐
17b	1960	Austin Taxi	Maroon or Red MB, Silver trim, GPW. 61 mm.	£8	NC ☐
17c	1964	'HOVERINGHAM' Tipper Truck	Red cab and CH, Orange tipper, 8 BPW. 76 mm.	£4-£5	MPR ☐
17d	1969	Horse Box	Red or Orange cab, Cream or Green box, 2 White horses, BPW or SF, H. 74 mm.	£3-£4	MPR ☐
17e	1972	Londoner Bus Issues 1st Type	Unless otherwise shown each has a Red body, White seats, Black metal or PBP. One door opening, two open rear windows, DD/SF. 78 mm.		MPR ☐
		i) 'SWINGING LONDON — CARNABY STREET'	Yellow Red Blue and Black decal, Metal BP.	£2-£3	MPR ☐
		ii) 'BERGER PAINTS'	Purple/Blk/Orange decals with either round or square corners. Model exists with Paintbrush facing to the right or left. Metal or PBP.	Current	MPR ☐
		iii) 'TYPHOO PUTS THE T IN BRITAIN'	White and Black decals. Metal BP.	£10	NVE ☐
		iv) 'CHAMBOURCEY YOGURTS' 'VIVE LE DIFFERENCE'	Multicoloured decal with countryside scene and yogurt carton. Metal BP.	£5	GV ☐
		v) 'ESSO EXTRA PETROL'	Red, White and Blue decals. Metal BP.	£10	NVE ☐
		vi) 'AIM BUILDING FUND 1976'	Black and White decal. Metal BP.		NVPP ☐
		vii) 'JACOBS BISCUITS'	Orange MB, Black and White decals, Metal BP.	£3-£4	MPR ☐
		viii) 'SILVER JUBILEE'	Silver MB, Blue and Gold decals, Metal BP.	£3-£4	MPR ☐
		ix) 'MATCHBOX 1953-78'	Red/Yellow/Orange/Black decals, Metal BP.	£3-£4	MPR ☐
		x) 'THE BISTO BUS'	Green, Yellow and White decal, PBP.	£2-£3	MPR ☐
	1982	Londoner Bus Issues 2nd Type	Unless otherwise shown the body is Red. Two door openings, three open rear windows, DD/SF.		MPR ☐
		i) 'LAKER SKY TRAIN'	Red, White and Blue decals, PBP.	Current	MPR ☐
		ii) 'CHESTERFIELD' ANNIVERSARY	Green MB, Green and White decal, PBP.	Current	MPR ☐

NB Many Code III promotional models have been produced using the Londoner Bus types, eg Bryant & May, Double Diamond, Redifusion, Highland Park Whisky, Findus Travel our way.

No18

18a	1956	Bulldozer	Yellow MB and D, Red DB, MRW/RT, NN. 45 mm.	£9	NC ☐
18b	1958	Bulldozer	Orange or Yel MB, MRW, Green RT, driver, No 18 cast in. 50 mm.	£7	NC ☐
18c	1960	Bulldozer	Yellow MB, Black PRL/RT, No D. 58 mm.	£5 £6	MPR ☐
18d	1964	Caterpillar Crawler Bulldozer	Yellow MB, no driver, Black PRL/RT. 62 mm.	£4-£5	MPR ☐
18e	1969	Field Car	Yellow MB, Tan roof, ASM/H/BPW/SF/SPW. 58 mm.	£2-£3	MPR ☐
18f	1975	Hondarora	Red MB, Black seat, Sil Trim, *Honda,* SPKW. 63 mm.	Current	MPR ☐
	1981	Colour change	Red MB, Black seat and front forks	Current	MPR ☐
	1982	Colour change	Yellow MB, Black seat and front forks	Current	MPR ☐

Matchbox 1-75 Series and Junior Models cont.

No 19					
19a	1956	M.G. Sports Car	Cream or White MB, Red S, Tan D, SPW/NN. 50 mm.	£14	NC ☐
19b	1958	M.G.A. Sports Car	Cream MB, Tan D, Sil trim MW or GPW. 55 mm.	£10	NC ☐
19c	1961	Aston Martin Racing Car	Met Green MB, Grey or White RCD, various RN, eg 5, 19, 52, Sil MSPKW. 64 mm.	£5-£7	MPR ☐
19d	1965	Lotus Racing Car	Green or Orange MB, White RF, BPW. 70 mm.	£4-£5	MPR ☐
	1970	Colour change	Purple MB	£4-£5	MPR ☐
19e	1971	Road Dragster	Red MB, Silver EE, CW/SF. 76 mm.	Current	MPR ☐
19f	1976	Cement Truck	Red MB, Yellow barrel with Red stripes. 75 mm.	Current	MPR ☐
19g	1982	Peterbilt Cement Truck	Met Green/Orange/Blk body, RVD/TW/D Silver trim and BP, *Big Pete.* 77 mm.	Current	MPR ☐
No 20					
20a	1956	Heavy Lorry	Dark Red MB, Silver trim MW or GPW/NN. 55 mm.	£6-£7	MPR ☐
20b	1959	Heavy Lorry 'EVER READY FOR LIFE'	Dark Blue MB, Silver trim, 8 metal or plastic wheels. 70 mm.	£8	NC ☐
20c	1965	Taxi Cab	Orange/Yellow MB, *Taxi* GBPW, Red Int. 76 mm.	£3-£4	MPR ☐
20d	1969	Lamborghini Marzal	Met Dark Red, White seats, Sil TR, SF. 70 mm.	Current	MPR ☐
20e	1975	Police Range Rover	White MB, Orange flash *Police,* FL. 82 mm.	Current	MPR ☐
	1981	Colour change	White MB, Red/Yel/Blk flash	Current	MPR ☐
	1983	Colour change	Gold, *Securite Rallye Paris Dakar 83*	Current	MPR ☐
No 21					
21a	1956	Long Distance Coach 'LONDON TO GLASGOW'	Lt Green MB, Sil trim, Red/Yel decal, NN/BB, metal wheels. 55 mm.	£15	GV ☐
21b	1958	Long Distance Coach 'LONDON TO GLASGOW'	Green MB, Silver trim, Red/Yel decal, number, metal wheels. 69 mm.	£15	GV ☐
21c	1961	Milk Delivery Truck 'DRINK MORE MILK'	Pale Green MB, Cream load, CTW, Red cow or bottle decal on doors. Black plastic wheels. 57 mm.	£5-£6	MPR ☐
21d	1968	Foden Concrete Truck	Orange/Yellow MB, Orange RVD, BPW or SF. 76 mm.	£2-£3	MPR ☐
21e	1973	Road Roller	Yellow MB, Red seats, Black PRL. 70 mm.	Current	MPR ☐
21f	1978	Renault 5TL	Blue MB, Silver trim, Tan seats, SF. 65 mm.	Current	MPR ☐
	1980	Colour change	Yellow MB, *Le Car* decals, OTG	Current	MPR ☐
	1981	Colour change	Silver MB, Orange flash *Le Car,* OTG	Current	MPR ☐
	1982	Colour change	White MB, Green labels, *Michelin* decals etc	Current	MPR ☐
No 22					
22a	1956	Vauxhall Cresta	Dark Red MB, Cream roof, CA/MW/NN/BB/H. 64 mm.	£6-£7	MPR ☐
22b	1958	Vauxhall Cresta	Cream, Pink, Bronze or TQ MB, GSPW/BB. 66 mm.	£5-£6	MPR ☐
22c	1964	Pontiac Grand Prix	Orange or Purple MB, BPW/SF/OD/BB. 76 mm.	£2-£3	MPR ☐
22d	1971	Freeman Inter City Commuter	Mauve MB, White seats, *Arrow* Motif, SF. 76 mm.	Current	MPR ☐
22e	1976	Blaze Buster	Red MB, *Fire* on rear, Yellow LD, SF. 77 mm.	Current	MPR ☐

Matchbox 1-75 Series and Junior Models cont.

No 23					
23a	1956	(Berkeley Cavalier) Caravan	Blue or Green MB, *On Tow MB23*, TB/MW/CA. 64 mm.	£6-£7	MPR ☐
23b	1961	(Bluebird Dauphine) Caravan	Green or brown body, *On Tow MB23* TB/MGPW/RA. 64 mm.		MPR ☐
23c	1965	Trailer Caravan	Yel/White or Pink/White MB, DRF/GPW. 76 mm.	£3-£4	MPR ☐
23d	1970	Volkswagen Camper	Blue or Orange MB, Orange or White Int, OC/EM/NP/SF. 67 mm.	£2-£3	MPR ☐
23e	1976	Atlas Truck	Metallic Blue Cab and CH, Orange, DMP/SF. 71 mm.	Current	MPR ☐
	1981	Colour change	Red cab and chassis, Silver dumper, SF	Current	MPR ☐
23f	1983	Tipper Truck	Yellow MB, Grey DMP, Sil trim, *Dirty,* SF. 76 mm.	Current	MPR ☐
No 24					
24a	1956	'WEATHERILL' Hydraulic Excavator	Orange or Yel MB, Silver trim, NCI/MW/CA. 55 mm.	£6-£7	MPR ☐
24b	1959	'WEATHERILL' Hydraulic Excavator	Yellow MB, *Lesney* cast in, GPW. 67 mm.	£5-£6	MPR ☐
24c	1967	Rolls Royce Silver Shadow	Met Red or Gold MB, Ivory Int, Silver, BPW or SF wheels, Black, Green, Pink or Grey base plate, OBT/CW.	£3-£4	MPR ☐
24d	1973	Team 'MATCHBOX'	Yellow, Red, Green or Blue MB, RN '8' in Blk, D/SF. 75 mm.	Current	MPR ☐
24e	1979	Diesel Shunter	Green or Yellow MB, *Railfreight* or *D1496RF.* 72.5 mm.	Current	MPR ☐
24f	1983	Datsun 280 ZX	Black MB, Gold flashes, OD/SF/CW. 74 mm.	Current	MPR ☐
No 25					
25a	1956	Bedford 12 cwt Van 'DUNLOP'	Dark Blue MB, Silver grille, BB/MW/GPW, decal in Orange or Yellow. 53 mm.	£8-10	MPR ☐
25b	1960	Volkswagen Sedan	Silver Blue MB, OREC/EE, TW/GSPW. 60 mm.	£5-£6	MPR ☐
25c	1964	'BP' Tanker	Yel cab, Grn CH, Wh tank, *BP* crest, BPW/SF. 76 mm.	£4-£5	MPR ☐
25cc	1964	'ARAL' Tanker	Blue cab (German issue). 76 mm.	£10	GV ☐
25d	1968	Ford Cortina G.T.	Brown MB, White int, OD/BPW/SF. 67 mm.	£2-£3	MPR ☐
			Colour Change, Metallic Blue MB.	£2-£3	MPR ☐
25e	1972	Mod Tractor	Purple or Red MB, Silver engine, SF. 57 mm.	Current	MPR ☐
25f	1979	Flat Car and Container	Black CH, Red/Beige CNT, *NYK* and *USL.* 72.5 mm.	Current	MPR ☐
25g	1982	'AUDI SPORT' QUATTRO	White MB, Brown/Red panels, RN '20'. 76 mm.	Current	MPR ☐
No 26					
26a	1956	(E.R.F.) Ready Mixed Cement Lorry	Orange MB and RTB Silver or Gold TR, MW/PW. 45 mm.	£7	NC ☐
26b	1961	(Foden) Ready Mixed Cement Lorry	Orange MB and PRTB, Gold trim, GPW. 64 mm.	£5-£6	MPR ☐
26c	1968	G.M.C. Tipper Truck	Red cab, Green CH, TW/OTE/BPT/SF. 66 mm.	£3-£4	MPR ☐
26d	1972	'BIG BANGER'	Red MB, Silver EE and trim, SF. 76 mm.	Current	MPR ☐
26e	1976	Site Dumper	Yellow MB, Black base, SF. 64 mm.	Current	MPR ☐
	1981	Colour change	Red MB, Silver dumper, SF. 64 mm.	Current	MPR ☐
26f	1982	Cable Truck	Yellow MB, Blk/Grey cable drums, TW/SF. 77 mm.	Current	MPR ☐

No 27

27a	1956	Bedford Low Loader	Light Blue cab, Dark Blue TRL, 6MW or Light Green cab, Light Brown TRL. 77 mm.	£7	NC ☐
27b	1959	Bedford Low Loader	Light Green cab, Dark Tan TRL, or Dark Green cab, Light Tan TRL. 95 mm.	£15	NC ☐
27c	1960	Cadillac Sedan	Mauve/Pink or Grn/White MB, GSBPW. 70 mm.	£4-£5	MPR ☐
27d	1966	Mercedes 230SL	White MB, Red seats, Silver TR, OD/BPT/SF. 71 mm.	£2-£3	MPR ☐
	1970	Colour change	Yellow MB, Red or Black seats, BPW/SF	£2-£3	MPR ☐
27e	1973	Lamborghini Countach	Yellow or Orange/Red MB, RN '3', TW/SF. 74 mm.	Current	MPR ☐
27f	1981	Swing Wing 'JET'	Red/White MB, TW/BPW, RTT wings. 76 mm.	Current	MPR ☐

No 28

28a	1956	Bedford Compressor Truck	Yellow or Orange MB, Silver trim, CA/MW. 45 mm.	£7-£8	MPR ☐
28b	1959	Ford Thames Compressor Truck	Yellow MB, Silver trim, BPW/CRA. 60 mm.	£4-£5	MPR ☐
28c	1964	Mark Ten Jaguar	Metallic Brown MB, White seats, GBPW. 70 mm.	£3-£4	MPR ☐
28d	1969	Mack Dump Truck	Orange or Light Green MB, BP. 67 mm.	£1-£2	MPR ☐
28e	1974	Stoat	All Gold MB, driver rotates, SF/RLM. 67 mm.	Current	MPR ☐
28f	1979	Lincoln Continental	Red MB, White roof, Tan seats SF. 72 mm.	Current	MPR ☐
28g	1982	Formula Racing Car 'CHAMPION'	Gold and Black, RN '8', White D, SF. 75 mm.	Current	MPR ☐
	1983	Colour change	Met Green and Black MB	Current	MPR ☐

No 29

29a	1956	Bedford Milk Delivery Van	Tan MB, White bottles, Sil trim, CA/MW. 55 mm.	£6-£7	MPR ☐
29b	1961	Austin Cambridge	Two tone Green MB, Silver trim, GSBPW. 70 mm.	£3-£4	MPR ☐
29c	1966	Fire Pumper	Red MB, White EQ, *Denver* BPW. 76 mm.	£3-£4	MPR ☐
29d	1971	Racing Mini	Dark Orange or Red MB, RN '29' SF. 57 mm.	Current	MPR ☐
29e	1977	Shovel Nose Tractor	Yellow MB, Red shovel, Black trim. 72 mm.	Current	MPR ☐
	1981	Colour change	Orange MB, Black shovel, Grey trim	Current	MPR ☐
	1982	Colour change	Yellow MB, Black shovel	Current	MPR ☐

No 30

30a	1956	Ford Prefect	Lt Blue or Lt Brown, WWPTL/MW/CRA/TB. 60 mm.	£7-£8	MPR ☐
30b	1961	6 Wheel Crane Lorry	Silver MB, Orange jib, metal H, GSBPW. 67 mm.	£4-£5	MPR ☐
30c	1965	8 Wheel Crane Lorry	Green MB, Orange or Gold jib, P hook, BPW/SF. 76 mm.	£3-£4	MPR ☐
30d	1970	Beach Buggy	Met Mauve or Yellow MB, *Clover* motif SF. 65 mm.	Current	MPR ☐
30e	1976	'SWAMP RAT'	Olive Green body, superfast. 77 mm.	Current	MPR ☐
30f	1981	Articulated Truck	Blue cab, Sil TRL, *Leyland* on front, SF. 77 mm.	Current	MPR ☐
30g	1983	Colour change	Blue cab, Yel TRL, *International*	Current	MPR ☐

Matchbox 1-75 Series and Junior Models cont.

No 31

31a	1957	American Ford Station Wagon	Yellow MB, WWPTL/BB/MW/GPW/H. 67 mm.	£7-£8	MPR ☐
31b	1960	Ford Station Wagon	All Yellow MB or Pink/Green MB, GBSPW/H. 70 mm.	£3-£4	MPR ☐
31c	1964	Lincoln Continental	Blue, Green or Lime Grn MB, OBT/BPW/SF. 76 mm.	£2-£3	MPR ☐
31d	1972	Volks-dragon	Red body, Silver EE, eyes decal. 66 mm.	Current	MPR ☐
31e	1977	Caravan	White MB, Orange door and WDS, OD. 70 mm.	Current	MPR ☐
	1981	Colour change	White MB, Blue door, Orange TW	Current	MPR ☐
31f	1983	'MAZDA RX7'	Met Gold and Black, Red seats, OD/SF. 76 mm.	Current	MPR ☐

No 32

32a	1957	Jaguar XK140 fixed head coupe	Cream, Red or White body, MW/GPW/WWPTL. 60 mm.	£9	NC ☐
32b	1962	'E' Type Jaguar	Met Red MB, Cream int, MSPKW/BGPW/CW or TW. 67 mm.	£5-£7	MPR ☐
32c	1968	Leyland Petrol Tanker 'BP'	Dark Green MB, White tank, Yellow logo, BPW/SF. 76 mm.	£2-£3	MPR ☐
		Leyland Petrol Tanker 'ARAL'	Blue MB, White tank, Blue logo	£11	GV ☐
32d	1972	Maserati Bora	Met Pink MB, Yel int, RN '8', OD/SF. 76 mm.	Current	MPR ☐
32e	1977	Field Gun and Diorama	Military Green and Black, 2 figs, 4 shells. 77 mm.	Current	MPR ☐
32f	1981	Excavator	Orange cab, Black base and grab, cab SMV. 80 mm.	Current	MPR ☐
	1982	Colour change	Yellow cab, Black base and grab	Current	MPR ☐

No 33

33a	1957	Ford Zodiac	Blue, Light or Dark Green MB, MGPW, H. 67 mm.	£6-£7	MPR ☐
	1961	Colour change	Brown/Orange MB, WITH windows, GPW	£5-£6	MPR ☐
33b	1963	Ford Zephyr	Green MB issued in VS, CW/H/GB PW. 64 mm.	£3-£4	MPR ☐
33c	1969	Lamborghini Miura	Yellow MB Red seats, opening doors, SF. 77 mm.	Current	MPR ☐
	1971	Colour change	Met Gold MB, Cream seats, SF	Current	MPR ☐
33e	1973	Datsun 126X	Yellow MB, Orange BP, Silver E, TW/OREC. 76 mm.	Current	MPR ☐
33f	1977	POLICE Motor Cycle	All White MB, Silver E, Blue rider. 74 mm.	Current	MPR ☐
	1982	Colour change	White and Black MB	Current	MPR ☐

No 34

34a	1957	Volkswagen Microvan 'MATCHBOX INTERNATIONAL EXPRESS'	Blue MB, Metal or BGSPW, Yellow lettering. 55 mm.	£9	NC ☐
34b	1961	Volkswagen Camping Car	Light Green MB, Dark Green int, OD/GBPW. 65 mm.	£5-£6	MPR ☐
34c	1967	Volkswagen Camper	Silver MB, Orange int, TW/BPW. 65 mm.	£3-£4	MPR ☐
34d	1971	Formula 1 Racing Car	Met Pink, Orange, Blue or Yellow MB, RN '15' or '16', White D, SF. 73 mm.	Current	MPR ☐
34e	1976	Vantastic	Orange MB, White BP and int, EE/TW/SF or without EE, RN '34'. 74 mm.	Current	MPR ☐
				Current	MPR ☐
34f	1981	Chevy Pro-Stocker	White and Blue MB, RN '34', *Lightning,* SF. 76 mm.	Current	MPR ☐
34g	1983	Chevy Stock Car	Yellow MB, Orange/Blk ST, RN '4' *Chevy.* 76 mm.	Current	MPR ☐

Matchbox 1-75 Series and Junior Models cont.

No 35

35a	1957	(E.R.F.) Marshall Horse Box MK 7	Red MB and CH, Brown box, DDR, MW/CA. 53 mm.	£8	NC ☐
35b	1964	Snowtrac Tractor	Dark Red MB, White RT, *Sno-Trac,* or *Sno-Trac* CI, TW. 56 mm.	£5-£6	MPR ☐
35c	1969	Merryweather Marquis Fire Engine	Met Red MB, White DLD, plastic BP, SF *London Fire Service.* 76 mm.	£2-£3	MPR ☐
35d	1975	Fandango	White or Red MB, RN '35', SF. 75 mm.	Current	MPR ☐
35e	1982	Zoo Truck	Red MB, Blue cage, Yel lions, TW/SF. 77 mm.	Current	MPR ☐

No 36

36a	1957	Austin A50	Pale Turquoise MB, Silver trim, MGPW/WWPTL/H. 60 mm.	£7-£8	MPR ☐
36b	1960	Lambretta TV175 Scooter and Sidecar	Lt or Dk Met Green MC and SC, BPW. 57 mm.	£12	NC ☐
36c	1966	Opel Diplomat	Gold body, White seats, OBN/SF. 70 mm.	£2-£3	MPR ☐
36d	1970	Hot Rod Draguar	Met Red or Pink body, Silver E, *Draguar* SF. 72 mm.	Current	MPR ☐
36e	1976	Formula 5000	Orange body, Blue D, RN '3' *Formula 5000* or Red body with *Marlboro, Texaco* and *Good Year* decals, Sil EE, SF. 74 mm.	Current	MPR ☐
36f	1980	Refuse Truck	Met Red and Yellow body, PLP, Sil BP, SF/OTE *Collectomatic, Metre D.P.W. 66.* 77 mm.	Current	MPR ☐
	1982	Colour change	Blue and Orange body, PLP	Current	MPR ☐
	1983	Colour change	Blue and Cream body, PLP	Current	MPR ☐

No 37

37a	1956	(Karrier Bantam) 'COCA-COLA' Lorry	Dark Yellow body, UNEVEN crates, Red and White decal side and rear, MGPW. 55 mm.	£9	NC ☐
37b	1958	(KB) 'COCA-COLA' Lorry	Dark Yellow body, EVEN crates, MGPW. 55 mm.	£7	NC ☐
37c	1960	(KB) 'COCA-COLA' Lorry	Larger model with EVEN load. 61 mm.	£7	NC ☐
37d	1966	(Dodge) Cattle Truck	Yel/Grey body, BPW/SF/DDR/2AN/TW. 65 mm.	£2-£3	MPR ☐
37e	1973	Soopa Coopa	Met Blue or Purple, flower decal, SF. 74 mm.	Current	MPR ☐
37f	1977	Skip Truck	Red Cab and CH, Yel skip, Silver trim. 69 mm.	Current	MPR ☐
	1981	Colour change	Blue cab and chassis	Current	MPR ☐
37g	1982	Matra Rancho	Yel/Orange/Blk body, Black S, H/OTG/SF. 74 mm.	Current	MPR ☐

No 38

38a	1957	(Karrier Bantam) Refuse Wagon	Dark or Light Grey MB, MW/CA *Cleansing Department* decal. 53 mm.	£6-£8	MPR ☐
38b	1963	Vauxhall Victor Estate	Yellow body, White seats, OTG, GSBPW/H. 64 mm.	£3-£4	MPR ☐
38c	1967	Honda Motor Cycle with Trailer	Met Green MC, Orange or Yellow TRL, *Honda,* BPW/SF. 76 mm.	Current	MPR ☐
	1970	Colour Change	Blue or Pink MC, Orange TRL.	Current	MPR ☐
38d	1973	Stingeroo	Met Purple body, Cream HS, Sil TR, SF. 78 mm.	Current	MPR ☐
38c	1976	Armoured Jeep	Green body, White star, Black gun. 61 mm.	Current	MPR ☐
38f	1981	Camper	Red and Cream body, TW/SF. 76 mm.	Current	MPR ☐
38g	1982	Ford Model A	Blue body, White RF, Black chassis, *Champion Spark Plugs,* SF. 76 mm.	Current	MPR ☐

Matchbox 1-75 Series and Junior Models cont.

No	Year	Model	Description	Price		
No 39						
39a	1957	Zodiac Convertible	Pink body, Blue seats, Tan D, MW/GPW/WWPTL. 67 mm.	£6-£7	MPR	☐
39b	1962	Pontiac Convertible	Met Lilac body, GSBPW/H. 70 mm.	£6-£7	MPR	☐
			Yellow body version	£4-£5	MPR	☐
39c	1967	Ford Tractor	Blue and Yellow body and wheels, or Orange body version, BPW. 54 mm.	£2-£3	MPR	☐
39d	1973	Clipper	Met Pink, Yellow interior, OD/RLM. 77 mm.	Current	MPR	☐
39e	1979	Rolls Royce Silver Shadow Mk II	Met Silver body, Red seats, OD/SF. 75 mm.	Current	MPR	☐
	1981	Colour change	Metallic Red body, Cream seats	Current	MPR	☐
	1982	Colour change	Metallic Gold body, White seats	Current	MPR	☐
No 40						
40a	1957	Bedford 7 Ton Tipper	Red cab and CH, Brown tipper, OTB, MGPW/WWPTL. 53 mm.	£8	NC	☐
40b	1961	Long Distance Bus	Met Grey body, Green WDS, GSBPW. 76 mm.	£3-£4	MPR	☐
40c	1968	Hay Trailer	Blue body, Yellow sides and wheels, OC. 86 mm.	Current	MPR	☐
40d	1972	Guildsman	Pink or Red MB, Green WDS, Cream seats, RN '40', SF. 76 mm.	£1-£2	MPR	☐
40e	1976	Horse Box	Orange and Cream MB, Tan DDR, 2 WHS/SF. 72 mm.	Current	MPR	☐
	1981	Colour change	Green and Cream body, Brown DDR	Current	MPR	☐
	1983	Colour change	Orange and Brown body, White DDR	Current	MPR	☐
No 41						
41a	1957	'D' Type Jaguar	Dark Green MB, Tan D, RN '41' FR, MGPW/CA. 55 mm.	£6-£8	MPR	☐
41b	1960	'D' Type Jaguar	Dark Green MB, Tan D, RN '41' FR, GSBPW. 62 mm.	£6-£8	MPR	☐
41c	1965	Ford GT	Yellow or White MB, Red S, Blue stripe, Yel or Red wheels, RN '6', BPW/SF/CW/H. 67 mm.	£2-£3	MPR	☐
	1970	Colour Change	Metallic Red MB, Blue band, RN '6', Yellow, Green or Black BP, SF.		MPR	☐
41d	1973	Siva Spyder	Met Red MB and Silver band, OC and decals, SF. 77 mm.	Current	MPR	☐
41e	1979	'AMBULANCE'	White MB, Red/Yel/Blk decal, RC/ORD/SF. 75 mm.	Current	MPR	☐
	1981	Colour change	White MB, Blue/Yellow decal	Current	MPR	☐
41f	1983	Racing Porsche	TT Blue MB, *Team Porsche, Elf* etc SF	Current	MPR	☐
No 42						
42a	1957	Bedford 'EVENING NEWS' Van	Yellow MB, Red and White decals, news board, *First With The News* CRA/MGPW. 55 mm.	£8-£9	MPR	☐
42b	1965	Studebaker Station Wagon	Blue MB, White int, ORF/PHD/CW/H/BPW. 76 mm.	£3-£4	MPR	☐
42c	1969	Iron Fairy Crane	Red MB, Yellow or Green boom and H, OC/BPW/SF. 76 mm.	£2-£3	MPR	☐
42d	1972	Tyre Fryer	Met Blue or Orange MB, Yel int, Sil TR, BB/SF. 76 mm.	Current	MPR	☐
42e	1978	Mercedes Container Truck 'SEALAND'	Red MB, Red/Cream *Sealand* or *OCL* decals, ORD/SF. 77 mm.	Current	MPR	☐
	1981	'MATCHBOX' livery	Red MB, Red/Yellow decal	Current	MPR	☐
	1982	'MAYFLOWER' livery	Red MB, Green/Yellow/Red decal, TW.	Current	MPR	☐
42f	1983	'57 T-Bird	Red and White MB, Red seats, Sil trim, SF. 76 mm.	Current	MPR	☐

Matchbox 1-75 Series and Junior Models cont.

No	Year	Model	Description	Price		
No 43						
43a	1958	Hillman Minx	Pale Green or TQ/WH, WWPTL/MGPW/H/CRA. 67 mm.	£6-£7	MPR	□
43b	1962	Aveling Barford Tractor Shovel	Yellow MB, Red or Yellow trim, BPW	£3-£4	MPR	□
43c	1968	Pony Trailer	Yellow MB, Grey DDR, BPW/SF/2WHS or Tan MB, Dark Brown DDR. 67 mm.	Current	MPR	□
43d	1973	'DRAGON WHEELS'	Green MB, Red decal, Sil E, LOB/SF/TW. 72 mm.	Current	MPR	□
43e	1979	Steam Locomotive	Red/Black body, Yel '4345', 0-4-0, H. 68 mm.	Current	MPR	□
No 44						
44a	1958	Rolls Royce Silver Cloud	Met Blue MB, No WDS, BB/CRA/MGPW/WWPTL. 70 mm.	£6-£7	MPR	□
44b	1964	Rolls Royce Phantom V	Met Grey or Pink, Cream S, OBT/GBPW/CW. 72 mm.	£3-£4	MPR	□
44c	1967	Refrigerator Truck	Red and Green body, Grey ORD, GPW/SF. 77 mm.	£2-£3	MPR	□
	1971	Colour change	Yellow and Red body	£2-£3	MPR	□
44d	1972	Boss Mustang	Yellow body, Black OBN, EE, SF. 75 mm.	Current	MPR	□
44e	1979	Passenger Coach	Red/CR/Blk body, Green TW, *431-432.* 73 mm.	Current	MPR	□
44f	1983	Citroen 15	Black body, Tan seats, Silver trim, SF	Current	MPR	□
No 45						
45a	1958	Vauxhall Victor	Yellow MB, WW GRN TW, CRA/MGBSPW/WWPTL. 60 mm.	£5-£6	MPR	□
45b	1965	Ford Corsair with Boat	Yellow MB, Green boat, Red S and H, BGPW. 67 mm.	£3-£4	MPR	□
45c	1970	Ford Group Six	Met Green body, Cream S, RN '7', CW, SF. 75 mm.	£1-£2	MPR	□
	1973	Colour change	Lime Green body, TW, RN '45'	Current	MPR	□
	1974	Colour change	Red body RN '45', TW	Current	MPR	□
45d	1976	B.M.W. 3.0 CSL	Red body, Yellow int, *BMW,* SF/OD. 74 mm.	Current	MPR	□
	1979	Colour change	Orange body, *BMW*	Current	MPR	□
45e	1982	Kenworth	White/Blue body, Amber TW, SF. 71 mm.	Current	MPR	□
No 46						
46a	1958	Morris Minor 1000	Dark Green MB, No WDS, WWPTL, CA/MW. 51 mm.	£12	GV	□
46b	1960	'PICKFORDS' Long Distance Removal Truck	Dark Blue or Green MB, White ORD, *Removals & Storage, Branches in all Large Towns* in White, GSBPW. 67 mm.	£8	NC	□
46c	1968	Mercedes 300 SE	Met Blue MB, Cream S, OD/OBT/BPW. 73 mm.	£3-£4	MPR	□
	1969	Colour change	Green body, SAPM, BPW	£2-£3	MPR	□
	1970	Colour change	Gold body, SAPM, SF	£1-£2	MPR	□
46d	1973	Stretcha Fetcha	White MB, Red BP/Cross, Blue TW and 2FL. 70 mm.	Current	MPR	□
46e	1979	Ford Tractor and Harrow	Blue MB, Silver E, Yel harrow and S, H. 52 mm.	Current	MPR	□

Matchbox 1-75 Series and Junior Models cont.

No	Year	Model	Description	Price		
No 47						
47a	1958	Trojan Van 'BROOKE BOND TEA'	Red MB, No WDS, Green leaf decal, logo lettering in White, BB/CRA/MW. 57 mm.	£9	NC	☐
47b	1963	'LYONS MAID' Ice Cream Mobile Shop	Met Blue body, MLCD decals, White interior with attendant, CW/GBPW. 64 mm.	£10	NC	☐
	1967	Colour change	Cream body	£8	NC	☐
47c	1969	DAF Tipper Container Truck	Silver/Yellow/Grey body, TW/SF. 77 mm.	£2-£3	MPR	☐
	1972	Colour change	Silver/Orange/Grey body	£2-£3	MPR	☐
47a	1974	Beach Hopper	Met Blue MB, Yel D and EM, Or S, SF/RLM. 66 mm.	Current	MPR	☐
47e	1980	'G.W.R.' Pannier Locomotive	Green/Black body, gold decals, 0-6-0, H. 77 mm.	Current	MPR	☐
47f	1982	Jaguar SS100	Red body, Silver trim, Beige S/SW, SF. 76 mm.	Current	MPR	☐
No 48						
48a	1958	Meteor Sports Boat on Trailer	Blue/Cream boat, Black trailer, MGPW. 66 mm.	£5-£6	MPR	☐
48b	1962	Sports Boat and Trailer	Red/White boat, Gold OB, Black TRL. 75 mm.	£4-£5	MPR	☐
48c	1967	Dodge Dumper Truck	All Red body, Silver trim, BPW/SF. 76 mm.	£2-£3	MPR	☐
	1970	Colour change	Blue cab and CH, Yellow tipper	£2-£3	MPR	☐
48d	1973	Pie Eyed Piper	Met Blue MB, Silver EE, MLCD decal, SF/TW. 75 mm.	Current	MPR	☐
48e	1978	Sambron Jacklift	Yel forklift and MB, Blk CH, arms adjust. 78 mm.	Current	MPR	☐
48f	1983	(Mercedes) Unimog	Yel/White/Blk MB, Red *Rescue,* SNP/SF. 64 mm.	Current	MPR	☐
No 49						
49a	1958	Army Halftrack	MG body, White star, Grey tracks, MGBPW	£4-£5	MPR	☐
49b	1967	(Mercedes) Unimog	Tan MB, Green CH and TW/H/SPW/BPW. 62 mm.	£2-£3	MPR	☐
	1968	Colour change	Blue MB, Red chassis	£1-£2	MPR	☐
49c	1973	Chop Suey	Met Red body, Silver E and handlebars. 72 mm.	Current	MPR	☐
	1974	Colour change	Met Red body, Red handlebars	Current	MPR	☐
49d	1977	Crane Truck	All Yel MB, Grn TW, Blk STB, Red PH. 76 mm.	Current	MPR	☐
	1981	Colour change	Yellow body, Black jib	Current	MPR	☐
49e	1983	'SAND DIGGER'	Grn MB, Sil EE, White S, Yel logo, BPW	Current	MPR	☐
No 50						
50a	1958	Commer Pick Up	All Tan body, No WDS, MGPW/CRA. 67 mm.	£5-£6	MPR	☐
	1962	Colour change	Red/White body, GBPW/RA	£5-£6	MPR	☐
50b	1964	John Deere Lanz Tractor	Green MB, Silver/Yellow trim, GBPW/H. 54 mm.	£3-£4	MPR	☐
50c	1969	Kennel Truck	Met Green body in VS, ASM/4WPD/BPW/SF. 70 mm.	£2-£3	MPR	☐
50d	1974	Articulated Truck	Yellow cab, Blue TRL, WW Yel FL, SF/TW. 78 mm.	Current	MPR	☐
50e	1981	Harley Davidson Motor Cycle	Met Brown MB, Silver E, Black S and HB. 70 mm.	Current	MPR	☐
	1982	Colour change	Met Plum MB, Brown rider	Current	MPR	☐

Matchbox 1-75 Series and Junior Models cont.

No 51

51a	1958	Albion 'PORTLAND CEMENT' Lorry ('BLUE CIRCLE')	Yellow body, Beige cement bag load, Blue logo and EM on cab doors, MGSBPW. 65 mm.	£8	NC ☐
51b	1964	Tipping Trailer	Green MB, 3 Brown barrels, Yel W, GBPW. 67 mm.	£2-£3	MPR ☐
51c	1969	8 Wheel Tipper 'DOUGLAS'	Orange, cab and CH, Silver tipper, Orange and White decal, BPW/SF/TW. 76 mm.	£3-£4	MPR ☐
	1970	Colour and Decal Change 'POINTER'	Yellow cab and CH, Silver Green and Yellow decal with dog	£2-£3	MPR ☐
51d	1973	Citroen SM	Met Red MB, Cream seats, OD/CW/SF. 78 mm.	Current	MPR ☐
	1977	Colour change	Blue MB, Red flash RN '8'	Current	MPR ☐
51e	1978	Combine Harvester	Red body, Yellow moving parts. Non SF or SF PW. 72 mm.	Current	MPR ☐
51f	1983	Pontiac 'FIREBIRD'	Red body, White decals, Tan seats, SF. 76 mm.	Current	MPR ☐

No 52

52a	1958	Maserati 4 CLT	Red or Yellow MB, White or Cream D, Black RN '5' '41' or '52', BPT/SPKW. 63 mm.	£6-£7	MPR ☐
52b	1965	B.R.M. Racing Car	Blue or Red body, RN '5', Yel W, BPT. 70 mm.	£3-£4	MPR ☐
52c	1970	Dodge Charger Mk III	Red MB, Blk/Yel FL, LMS/SF. 76 mm.	Current	MPR ☐
	1973	Colour change	Purple MB, no decal	Current	MPR ☐
	1974	Colour change	Green MB, no decal	Current	MPR ☐
52d	1977	'POLICE' Launch	Blue and White boat, Blue TW, 2 PM. 77 mm.	Current	MPR ☐
52e	1981	BMW MI	Silver MB, Black RN '52', Red S, SF. 75 mm.	Current	MPR ☐
	1983	Colour change	White MB, Black RN '52', Red *BMW MI* SF	Current	MPR ☐

No 53

53a	1958	Aston Martin	Met Green or Red MB, WWPTL, MWGPW. 66 mm.	£6-£8	MPR ☐
53b	1963	Mercedes Benz 220S	Maroon or Red MB, Cream S, BB/GSPW/OD. 70 mm.	£3-£4	MPR ☐
53c	1968	Ford Zodiac Mk IV	Met Blue MB, Cream S, OBN/SPW/BPW. 70 mm.	£3-£4	MPR ☐
	1970	Colour change	Met Green MB, S	£2-£3	MPR ☐
53d	1973	Tanzara	Orange MB, Clover leaf decal, TW/SF. 76 mm.	Current	MPR ☐
	1976	Colour change	White MB, Blue/Red stripes, RN '53', SF	Current	MPR ☐
53e	1977	CJ6 Jeep	Red MB, Fawn seats and roof, SF. 75 mm.	Current	MPR ☐
	1981	Colour change	Green MB, Yellow seats, Fawn roof	Current	MPR ☐
53f	1982	Flareside Pick-Up	Blue MB, White S, *Baja Bouncer, 326,* SF. 76 mm.	Current	MPR ☐
	1983	Colour change	Red MB	Current	MPR ☐

No 54

54a	1958	Army Saracen Carrier	Olive Green MB, RGT, 6 Black PW, CRA/RTR. 56 mm.	£4-£5	MPR ☐
54b	1965	Cadillac Ambulance	White MB, Red cross and SL, White S, BPW/SF/TW. 73 mm.	£3-£4	MPR ☐
54c	1971	Ford Capri	Red MB, Black OBN, White seats, SF. 77 mm.	Current	MPR ☐
	1974	Colour change	Met Purple MB, White seats	Current	MPR ☐
54d	1977	Personnel Carrier	Green MB, Brown figures and RGT, SF. 76 mm.	Current	MPR ☐
	1980	Mobile Home	Green MB, Orange interior, Brown OD, SF. 76 mm.	Current	MPR ☐
54e	1982	'NASA' Tracking Vehicle	White MB, Blue/Red decal, WW *Space Shuttle Command Center,* SOD/SF. 76 mm.	Current	MPR ☐

Matchbox 1-75 Series and Junior Models cont.

No	Year	Model	Description	Price		
No 55						
55a	1958	D.U.K.W. Amphibian	Olive Green body, MGPW. 70 mm.	£4-£5	MPR	☐
55b	1963	'POLICE' Car	Blue MB, Red/Wh/Blue PCR, SL/BB/GBPW. 67 mm.	£3-£4	MPR	☐
55c	1966	'POLICE' Car	White MB, Red/Blue PCR, SL, BPW. 73 mm.	£3-£4	MPR	☐
55d	1968	Mercury 'POLICE' Car	White MB, Red/Bl PCR, SL/ASM/2PS/BPW/SF. 77 mm.	£2-£3	MPR	☐
55e	1971	Mercury 'POLICE' Estate Car	White MB, WW, PCR, 2SL/No PS/SF. 77 mm.	£2-£3	MPR	☐
55f	1976	Hell Raiser	White MB, Silver EE, Red seats. 75 mm.	Current	MPR	☐
	1978	Colour change	Met Blue MB, stars and stripes decal	Current	MPR	☐
55g	1980	Ford Cortina 1600 GL	Met Green MB, Red seats OD/SF. 75 mm.	Current	MPR	☐
	1981	Colour change	Met Red MB, Yel seats, OD/SF	Current	MPR	☐
	1982	Colour change	Met Bronze and White MB, Yellow seats	Current	MPR	☐
55h	1983	Ford Sierra XR41	Met Silver and Black MB, Red seats, SF. 76 mm.	Current	MPR	☐
No 56						
56a	1958	Trolley Bus 'DRINK PEARDRAX'	Red MB, 2 Red or Black roof poles. Decal in Red/White/Black, MGPW/CRA. 66 mm.	£15	NC	☐
56b	1966	Fiat 1500	Green or Red MB, Red seats, Brown LG, BPW/H. 67 mm.		MPR	☐
56c	1969	B.M.C. 1800 Pininfarina	Gold MB, White seats, OD/BPT. 70 mm.	£2-£3	MPR	☐
	1970	Colour change	Orange MB, White S, WDW/SF	Current	MPR	☐
	1971	Colour change	Bronze MB, White seats, SF	Current	MPR	☐
	1973	Colour change	Orange MB, THW/SF	Current	MPR	☐
56d	1975	Hi-Trailer 'TEAM MATCHBOX'	White MB, Blue or Orange Driver, Sil E, Red/Yel/Bl stripes, RN '5' and 'MB' in Black, SF. 75 mm.	Current	MPR	☐
56e	1980	Mercedes 450 SEL	Met Blue MB, White seats, OD/H/SF. Also issued with *Martini Racing* decals with RN '7'. 75 mm.	Current	MPR	☐
	1981	Taxi version	Cream MB, Red *Taxi* on roof	Current	MPR	☐
	1983	Policecar version	Green and White MB, *Polizei,* 2 Blue SL, SF	Current	MPR	☐
No 57						
57a	1958	Wolseley 1500	Pale Green MB, WWPTL/CRA/GPW/BB/OC. 55 mm.	£6-£7	MPR	☐
57b	1961	Chevrolet Impala	TT Blue MB, WW Red TL, TW, GBPW/H. 70 mm.	£4-£5	MPR	☐
57c	1966	Land Rover Fire Truck 'KENT FIRE BRIGADE'	Red MB, Yellow decals and crest, White plastic ladder, TW/SL/BPW/SF. 67 mm.	£4-£5	MPR	☐
57d	1970	Eccles Caravan	Pale Yel MB, Orange RF, Mrn stripe, SF. 75 mm.	Current	MPR	☐
	1971	Colour change	Off White MB, flower decal	Current	MPR	☐
	1973	Colour change	Cream MB, flower decal	Current	MPR	☐
57e	1974	Wild Life Truck	Yellow MB *Ranger* decal, RLM, CPC. 70 mm.	Current	MPR	☐
	1981	Colour change	White MB, Black stripes	Current	MPR	☐
57f	1982	Carmichael 'POLICE' Vehicle	White MB, Black roof, *Police Rescue* PLD SF/6W/2SL.77 mm.	Current	MPR	☐
57g	1983	Carmichael 'FIRE' Vehicle	Red/White MB, Black PLD SF/6W/2SL	Current	MPR	☐

Matchbox 1-75 Series and Junior Models cont.

No 58

58a	1958	'BRITISH EUROPEAN AIRWAYS' Coach	Blue body of VS, White logo, GSBPW. 65 mm.	£10	NC ☐
	1959	Colour and decal change	Red panel with *BEA* added to logo	£10	NC ☐
58b	1962	Drott Excavator	Red or Orange MB, BPW, Green RT, OC. 67 mm.	£3-£4	MPR ☐
58c	1968	DAF Girder Truck	Cream MB, Red girders, TW/BPW/ST. 76 mm.	£2-£3	MPR ☐
58d	1973	Woosh-N-Push	Yellow or Met Pink MB, RN '2' or '8' SF. 77 mm.	Current	MPR ☐
58e	1977	Faun Dumper	Yellow MB in VS, Black CH, *Cat* SF. 71 mm.	Current	MPR ☐
58f	1983	'RUFF TREK' (Pick Up)	Gold/Brown MB, Red trim, Blk load, SPW. 74 mm.	Current	MPR ☐

No 59

59a	1958	Ford 'SINGER' Van	Green MB in VS, Red Seats and logo, GSPW. 57 mm.	£10	NC ☐
59b	1963	'FIRE CHIEF' Car	Red MB, Yel logo, SL on roof, BPW. 65 mm.	£5-£6	MPR ☐
59c	1966	'FIRE CHIEF' Car	Red MB, Yel logo, Blue SL, BPW/SF/H/D. 73 mm.	£3-£4	MPR ☐
59d	1971	'FIRE CHIEF' Car	Red MB, Yel logo, D and PS, Blue SL, SF. 73 mm.	£2-£3	MPR ☐
59e	1976	Planet Scout	TT Green MB, TW, Silver trim, 2SL. 70 mm.	Current	MPR ☐
	1979	Colour change	Red MB, Cream chassis	Current	MPR ☐
59f	1980	Porsche 928	Met Brown MB, *Porsche,* OD/SF. 75 mm.	Current	MPR ☐
	1981	Colour change	Blue MB	Current	MPR ☐
	1982	Colour change	Black MB, White stripes, crest on BN	Current	MPR ☐

No 60

60a	1958	Morris Pick Up Truck 'BUILDERS DIRECT SUPPLY'	Light Blue MB, Red and Black logo, WW cab rear window, GSBPW. 57 mm.	£5-£6	MPR ☐
60b	1966	Truck with Site Office	Blue MB in VS, Yel/Green office, BPW/SF. 65 mm.	£2-£3	MPR ☐
60c	1972	Lotus Super Seven	Light Brown MB, Black seats, BPW. 74 mm.	Current	MPR ☐
	1976	Colour change	Yellow MB, Red stripes RN '60'	Current	MPR ☐
60d	1977	Holden Pick-Up	Red or Blue MB, 2 Yel MC, *500* decal, SF. 77 mm.	Current	MPR ☐
	1981	Colour change	White MB, 2 Red MC, *Superbike*	Current	MPR ☐
60e	1983	'TOYOTA RACING' Supra	White MB, Black OHB, RN '41' in Red SF. 76 mm.	Current	MPR ☐

No 61

61a	1959	Military Scout Car	Olive Green MB, Tan driver, SPW/BPW. 57 mm.	£3-£4	MPR ☐
61b	1966	Alvis Stalwart 'BP EXPLORATION'	White MB, Yellow DTC, Green hubs, Yellow and Green logo, BPT. 66 mm.	£3-£5	MPR ☐
			Yellow hubs version	£6	GV ☐
61c	1972	Blue Shark	Met Blue MB, White D, Sil EE, RN '86' SF. 77 mm.	Current	MPR ☐
61d	1978	Wreck Truck	Red MB, 2 White jibs, 2 Red H and SL, SF. 76 mm.	Current	MPR ☐
	1981	Colour change	Yellow MB, 2 Red jibs, 2 Black hooks	Current	MPR ☐
61e	1982	Wreck Truck	Red MB, 2 Blk jibs, *Eddies Wrecker* SF/6W. 77 mm.	Current	MPR ☐
	1983	Colour and decal change	White MB, 2 Blk jibs, *9* and *Dial 911,* SF	Current	MPR ☐

Matchbox 1-75 Series and Junior Models cont.

No 62

62a	1959	General Service Lorry	Olive Green MB, tow hook, 6BPW. 68 mm.	£4-£5	MPR	☐
62b	1963	TV Service Van 'RENTASET'	Cream MB Red logo, plastic ladder, TV aerial and 3 TV's, White ORS, BPW. 64 mm.	£7	NC	☐
62c	1969	Mercury Cougar	Met Green MB, Red int, OD/ASM/BPW/SF. 76 mm.	£1-£2	MPR	☐
62d	1970	'RAT ROD' Dragster	Lime Green MB, Red decal, Sil EE, SF. 76 mm.	Current	MPR	☐
62e	1974	Renault 17 TL	Red MB, White seats, Blue TW, RN '9', SF. 76 mm.	Current	MPR	☐
62f	1980	Chevrolet Corvette	Met Red MB, White flashes and int, SF. 74 mm.	Current	MPR	☐
	1983	Colour change	White MB, Orange/Black stripes, RN '09'	Current	MPR	☐

No 63

63a	1959	Service Ambulance	Olive Green MB, Red crosses, BPW. 67 mm.	£4-£5	MPR	☐
63b	1964	Fire Fighting Crash Tender	Red MB, Gold trim, White PLD and *Airport Crash Tender,* BPW. 61 mm.	£3-£4	MPR	☐
63c	1969	Dodge Crane Truck	Yellow MB, Rotating Crane Jib, Red hook, BPW/SF. 76 mm.	£1-£2	MPR	☐
63d	1973	Freeway Gas Tanker Series	Red cab, White/Red tank			
		i) 'BURMAH'	Black logo Red/Blue company motif TW/AV/SF. 78 mm.	Current	MPR	☐
		ii) 'ARAL' (German issue)	Blue cab, Blue and White logo, SF	£2-£3	MPR	☐
		iii) 'SHELL'	White/Yellow body, Red logo, SF	Current	MPR	☐
		iv) 'CHEVRON'	Red cab, Red/White/Blue logo, SF	Current	MPR	☐
		v) 'BP SUPER'	White cab, White/Grn tank, Yel logo, SF	Current	MPR	☐
63e	1982	4×4 Pick-Up	Yellow MB, Orange panels RN '24', HLPW. 71 mm.	Current	MPR	☐

No 64

64a	1959	Scammell Breakdown Truck	Olive Green MB, metal or P hook, BPW. 67 mm.	£5-£6	MPR	☐
64b	1966	MG 1100	Green MB, White seats, BPW/D/dog. 66 mm.	£3-£4	MPR	☐
	1970	Colour change	Metallic Blue MB	£1-£2	MPR	☐
64c	1972	Slingshot Dragster	Pink MB, Silver/Black EE, RN '9' D/SF. 76 mm.	£1-£2	MPR	☐
	1974	Colour change	Green MB, Silver/Red exposed engine	£1-£2	MPR	☐
	1975	Colour change	Blue MB, Silver/Red exposed engine	£1-£2	MPR	☐
64d	1976	Fire Chief Car	Red MB, Yel/Blk *Fire,* Blue TW. 77 mm.	Current	MPR	☐
64e	1982	Bulldozer	Black/Yellow/Silver body Blk PT, H	Current	MPR	☐

No 65

65a	1959	Jaguar 3.4	Blue body, WW PTL/CRA/GPW/BB. 61 mm.	£6-£7	MPR	☐
65b	1962	Jaguar 3.8 Sedan	Red body, Silver trim and E, OBN/GBPW/H	£5-£6	MPR	☐
65c	1968	Combine Harvester	Red MB, Yellow RCB and wheels, BPT. 76 mm.	£1-£2	MPR	☐
65d	1973	Saab Sonnet	Met Blue MB, Orange seats and TW, OTG/SF. 73 mm.	£1-£2	MPR	☐
65e	1978	Airport Coach (Series)	Met Blue and White body, Amber TW, Red/White/Blue			
		i) 'BRITISH AIRWAYS'	logo, Silver trim, SF. 78 mm.	Current	MPR	☐
		ii) 'AMERICAN AIRWAYS'	Red/White/Blue logo. 78 mm.	£1-£2	MPR	☐
		iii) 'LUFTHANSA'	Orange/White/Black/Blue logo. 78 mm.	£1-£2	MPR	☐
		iv) 'QUANTAS'	Met Red and White MB, White logo. 78 mm.	£1-£2	MPR	☐
		v) 'TWA'	Met Red and White MB, Red logo. 78 mm.	£1-£2	MPR	☐

Matchbox 1-75 Series & Junior Models Cont.

No 66

66a	1959	Citroen DS 19	Yellow MB, Silver trim, GPW. 64 mm.	£5-£6	MPR ☐
66b	1962	Harley Davidson Motorcycle and Sidecar	Met Bronze body, 3 SPKW, BPT. 67 mm.	£15	NC ☐
66c	1967	'GREYHOUND' Bus	Silver MB, Grn/Wh decal, BPW/SF. 76 mm.	£3-£4	MPR ☐
66d	1972	'Mazda' RX500	Orange MB, White BP, TW, OREC/SF. 74 mm.	Current	MPR ☐
	1976	Colour change	Red MB, White BP	Current	MPR ☐
66e	1978	Ford Transit	Red MB, 2 Dark Brown crates *Fragile,* SF. 71 mm.	Current	MPR ☐
	1980	Colour change	Yellow in VS, 2 Light Brown crates SF etc	Current	MPR ☐
66f	1983	Tyrone Malone 'SUPERBOSS'	White MB, Red Blue bands and decals, SF/TW. 77 mm.	Current	MPR ☐

No 67

67a	1959	Saladin Armoured Car	Olive Green MB, RGT/6BPW. 57 mm.	£4-£5	MPR ☐
67b	1968	Volkswagen 1600 TL	Red MB White seats, opening doors, BPT. 68 mm.	£2-£3	MPR ☐
	1970	Colour change	Metallic Purple MB, SF	£2-£3	MPR ☐
67c	1974	Hot Rocker	Met Green MB, Sil EE, White S, SF/RLM. 77 mm.	£1-£2	MPR ☐
	1976	Colour change	Red MB	£1-£2	MPR ☐
67d	1979	Datsun 260 Z	Met Pink, Yellow interior, H/SF. 75 mm.	Current	MPR ☐
	1981	Colour change	Met Silver MB, Red interior, SF	Current	MPR ☐
	1982	Colour change	SAPM plus Red/Blk flashes *Datsun 2+2*	Current	MPR ☐
	1983	IMSA 'FORD MUSTANG'	Black MB, Red/White/Blue stripes TW/SF	Current	MPR ☐

No 68

68a	1959	Austin Military Radio Truck Mk II	Olive Green MB, Black plastic wheels, CRA. 64 mm.	£4-£5	MPR ☐
68b	1965	Mercedes Coach	Green or Orange metal MB, White PUS and int, BPW. 73 mm.	£2-£3	MPR ☐
68c	1970	Porsche 910	Metallic Red, White seats RN '68', SF/TW. 76 mm.	£1-£2	MPR ☐
68d	1976	Cosmobile	Metallic Blue and Yellow MB, Silver trim TW. 73 mm.	Current	MPR ☐
	1979	Colour change	Metallic Red and Brown MB	Current	MPR ☐
68e	1980	Chevrolet Van	Orange MB, Red and Blue flashes SF. 77 mm.	Current	MPR ☐
	1981	Colour change	Green MB, Orange flash, *Chevvy* SF	Current	MPR ☐
	1982	Colour change	Sil MB, Blk/Bl/Red flashes *Vanpire* SF	Current	MPR ☐
	1983	Colour Change	White MB, Orange Flashes, *Matchbox Racing* and *BF Goodrich* decals, HLPW		MPR ☐

No 69

69a	1959	Commer 'NESTLES' Van	Maroon or Red MB, Yellow logo, PSD/D/GPW. 57 mm.	£9	NC ☐
69b	1965	Hatra Tractor Shovel	Orange MB, BPT, shovel lifts. 80 mm.	£3-£4	MPR ☐
	1967	Colour change	Yellow MB, Black plastic tyres	£2-£3	MPR ☐
69c	1970	Rolls Royce Silver Shadow	Met Blue MB, Red S, Tan HD, OBT/TW/SF BP in VS. 76 mm.	£1-£2	MPR ☐
	1973	Colour change	Met Gold MB, White seats, Black hood, BP in VS	£1-£2	MPR ☐
69d	1974	Turbo Fury	Red MB, MLCD FL, RN '69', White D, SF/RLM. 76 mm.	Current	MPR ☐
69e	1979	'WELLS FARGO' Security Truck	Red MB, White RF and logo, TW/SL/SF. 73 mm.	Current	MPR ☐

Matchbox 1-75 Series and Junior Models Cont.

No 70

70a	1959	Ford Thames Estate Car	Green and Yellow body, GSBPW/WWWDS. 54 mm.	£4-£5	MPR ☐
70b	1966	Ford Grit Spreader	Red and Yellow body, OH/BB/TW/BPT. 67 mm.	£3-£4	MPR ☐
70c	1972	Dodge Dragster	Pink MB, snake decal, LOB/EE/SF. 78 mm.	Current	MPR ☐
70d	1977	SP Gun	Olive Green MB, Black gun, Tan tracks. 68 mm.	Current	MPR ☐
70e	1981	Ferrari 308 GTB	Red MB, Black flash, Black int, SF. 75 mm.	Current	MPR ☐
	1982	Colour change	Same colours with *Ferrari* de SF	Current	MPR ☐
	1983	Colour change	Red MB, White chassis, SF	Current	MPR ☐

No 71

71a	1959	200 Gallon Water Truck	Olive Green MB, BPW/MCB/SPW. 60 mm.	£4-£5	MPR ☐
71b	1964	Jeep Gladiator Pick-UP	Red MB, White interior, OD/BPW. 67 mm.	£2-£3	MPR ☐
71c	1969	Ford 'ESSO' Wreck Truck	Red/White MB, Green SL, Red PH, 6 BPW/SF. 76 mm.	£2-£3	MPR ☐
71d	1973	Jumbo Jet Motor Cycle	Met Blue MB, Silver exhaust. 70 mm.	Current	MPR ☐
71e	1977	Dodge Cattle Truck	Red and Yellow MB, 2 Black P cows, SF. 74 mm.	Current	MPR ☐
	1979	Colour change	Bronze and Yel MB, 2 Black P cows	Current	MPR ☐
	1981	Colour change	Green and Yel MB, 2 Brown P cows, SF	Current	MPR ☐
	1983	Colour change	Green and White MB, 2 Brown P cows, SF	Current	MPR ☐

No 72

72a	1959	Fordson Tractor	Blue MB, Orange PW, Silver trim, BPT. 49 mm.	£4-£5	MPR ☐
72b	1967	Standard Jeep	Yellow MB, Red seats, SPW/BPT/H. 61 mm.	£2-£3	MPR ☐
72c	1972	'SRN6' Hovercraft	White/Red/Black body, union jack. 77 mm.	Current	MPR ☐
72d	1979	B omag (Road Roller)	Yellow MB, Red engine and interior, SF. 71 mm.	Current	MPR ☐
72e	1982	Dodge 'PEPSI' Delivery Truck	Red and White MB, Red/Wh/Blue decal, SF. 72 mm.	Current	MPR ☐

No 73

73a	1960	R.A.F. 10 ton Pressure Refueller	Blue body, R.A.F. roundel, GPW. 65 mm.	£5-£6	MPR ☐
73b	1963	Ferrari Racing Car	Red MB, Sil trim, White D, RN '73', SPKW. 67 mm.	£3-£4	MPR ☐
73c	1969	Mercury Commuter	Grn MB, White seats, 2WPD/ASM/BPT/SF. 76 mm.	£1-£2	MPR ☐
	1972	Colour change	Red MB, White seats	Current	MPR ☐
73d	1974	Weasel	Met Green MB, Black RGT/SF/RLM. 72 mm.	Current	MPR ☐
73e	1980	Model A Ford Series	Cream MB, Green CH/TW, WW SPW and WDS, SF. 71 mm.	Current	MPR ☐
	1981	Colour change	TT Green MB and CH, WW SPW and WDS, TW/SF		MPR ☐
	1982	Colour change	Cream/Blk MB, Brown CH, Orange TW, SF		MPR ☐

Matchbox 1-75 Series & Junior Models cont.

No 74

No	Year	Model	Description	Price	
74a	1960	Mobile 'REFRESHMENTS' Bar 'COFFEE TEA SNACKS'	Cream MB, Blue int, opening hatch, GPW/H. 67 mm.	£12	NC ☐
	1963	Colour change	Silver MB, Green interior, SPW	£7-£8	MPR ☐
74b	1966	Daimler Bus 'ESSO EXTRA PETROL'	Cream MB, Red/White/Blue decals White interior, BPW or SF. 76 mm.	£6-£7	MPR ☐
	1968	Colour change	Green MB, same decals etc	£4-£5	MPR ☐
	1969	Colour change	Red MB, same decals etc	£4-£5	MPR ☐
			N.B. SF models £1-£2 less	£4-£5	MPR ☐
74c	1973	Toe Joe Breakdown Truck	Met Green MB, 2 Red PH, 2 SL, SF. 75 mm.	Current	MPR ☐
74d	1979	Cougar Villager	Met Green MB, Yel seats, OTG/SF. 78 mm.	Current	MPR ☐
74c	1982	'FIAT' Abarth	White MB, Red S, *M'box Toys,* RN '45', SF. 76 mm.	Current	MPR ☐

No 75

No	Year	Model	Description	Price	
75a	1960	Ford Thunderbird	Pink and White MB, Green TW, GBSPW. 66 mm.	£4-£5	MPR ☐
75b	1965	Ferrari Berlinetta	Green MB, White S, Sil trim, SPKW/BPW. 73 mm.	£2-£3	MPR ☐
	1970	Colour change	Red MB, White seats, BPW	£2-£3	MPR ☐
75c	1971	Alfa Carabo	Met Pink MB, Yellow BP, SF. 76 mm.	£1-£2	MPR ☐
75d	1977	Seasprite Helicopter	Red and White MB, *Rescue* Blk Rotors. 74 mm.	Current	MPR ☐
75e	1982	'MB TV NEWS' Helicopter	Orange/White MB, TW. 76 mm.	Current	MPR ☐
75f	1983	'POLICE' Helicopter	Black/White MB, Black rotors	Current	MPR ☐

Collectors Notes

Matchbox 1-75 Series and Junior Models Gift Sets

Ref. No.		Model Type	Model Features and Size	Rarity and Price Grading		

Information relating to the very early gift sets would be welcomed by the compiler.

Ref. No.		Model Type	Model Features and Size	Rarity and Price Grading		
G1	1963	Gift Set No 1	Contains 5c *Visco-Static,* 10c, 12b, 13c, 14c, 21c, 46b, 74a	£80	GV	☐
G2	1963	Gift Set No 2	Contains 25b, 30b, 31b, 39b, 48b, 65b, Accessory Pack No 2	£60	GV	☐
G4	1963	Gift Set No 4	Contains 13c, 14b, 19c, 41b, 47b, 52a, 32b, 73b, Major Pack No 1b.	£45	GV	☐
G5	1963	Army Gift Set	Contains 54a, 62a, 63a, 67a, 68a, 64a, Major Pack No 3	£38	GV	☐
G10	1963	Service Station Set	Contains Service Station, 13c, 25b, 31b, and Accessory Pack No 1		MPR	☐
G1	1967	Service Station Set	Contains Service Station, 13d, 31c, 64b, and Accessory Pack No 1	£18	NC	☐
G2	1967	Car Transporter Set	Contains 22c, 28c, 36c, 75b, Major Pack 8b	£22	NC	☐
G3	1967	Vacation Set	Contains 12c, 23c, 27d, 42b, 45b, 56b, 68b, and Sports Boat on Trailer	£24	NC	☐
G4	1967	Racetrack Set	Contains 13d, 19d Green, 19d Orange, 41c White, 41c Yellow, 52b Blue, 52b Red, 54b, Major Pack M6 29c	£27	NC	☐
G5	1967	Fire Station Set	Contains Fire Station, 29c, 54b, 59c	£18	NC	☐
G6	1967	Commercial Trucks Set	Contains 16c, 17c, 25c, 26b, 30c, 69b, 70b, 71b	£40	NC	☐
G1	1969	Service Station Set	Contains Service Station, 32c, 13d, 64b	£12	NC	☐
G2	1969	Transporter Set	Contains Transporter, 14d, 24c, 31c, 53c	£15	NC	☐
G3	1969	Farm Set	Contains 12c, 37d, 40c, 43c, 65c, 72b, 47c, 39c	£15	NC	☐
G4	1969	Race 'N Rally Set	Contains 19d Orange, 19d Green, 52b Blue, 52b Red, 29d, 3c, 41c, 67b, 25d, 8e	£20	NC	☐
G6	1969	Truck Set	Contains 1e, 10d, 21d, 30c, 60b, 70b, 49b, 26c	£20	NC	☐
G1	1971	Service Station Set	Contains 13e, 32d, 15e and Service Station	£9	NC	☐
G2	1971	Transporter Set	Contains Transporter and 5 SF models	£11	NC	☐
G3	1971	Racing Specials Set	Contains 5e, 20d, 45c, 56c, 52c, 68c	£8	NC	☐
G4	1971	Truck Superset	Contains 47c, 63d, 58d, 49c, 16d, 21e, 11d, 51d	£12	NC	☐
G2	1973	Transporter Set	Contains Transporter and 5 SF Cars	£5	NC	☐
G3	1973	'WILD ONES' Set	Contains 5 Superfast Cars	£5	NC	☐
G4	1973	Team Matchbox Set	Contains Racing Car Transporter and 4 Racing Cars	£8	NC	☐
G6	1973	Drag Race Set	Contains 6 Superfast Cars	£5	NC	☐
G7	1973	Ferry Boat	Contains Plastic Boat and 4 SF Cars	Current	MPR	☐
G11	1978	Strike Force Set	Contains 6 Army Vehicles	Current	MPR	☐
G12	1978	Rescue Set	Contains 6 Rescue Vehicles	Current	MPR	☐
G13	1978	Construction Set	Contains 6 Construction Vehicles	Current	MPR	☐
G14	1978	Grand Prix Set	Contains Transporter and 4 Racing Cars	Current	MPR	☐
G15	1978	Transporter Set	Contains Transporter and 5 SF Cars	Current	MPR	☐
G7	1978	Car Ferry Set	Contains 3 Cars and Sports Boat	Current	MPR	☐
G1	1981	Transporter Set	Contains Transporter and 5 SF Cars	Current	MPR	☐
G2	1981	Railway Set	Contains 43f, 2×4 4f, 25g	Current	MPR	☐
G3	1981	Racing Car Set	Contains Transporter and 4 Racing Cars	Current	MPR	☐
G4	1981	Military Assault	Contains, Landing Craft and 6 Models	Current	MPR	☐
G5	1981	Construction Set	Contains 5 Construction Models	Current	MPR	☐
G6	1981	Farm Set	Contains 6 Farming Models	Current	MPR	☐
G7	1981	Emergency Set	Contains 5 Rescue Models	Current	MPR	☐

UK MATCHBOX CLUB

Whilst much information of a general nature has been given in this catalogue relating to the major identifying features of each Matchbox model, it has not been the intention to describe all the technical variations which exist. For example Model 69c Rolls Royce Silver Cloud, has at least twenty different variations in respect of the colours used for its baseplate and the types of wheels used etc.

The UK Matchbox Club founded some seven years ago by Ray Bush the Editor of its bi-monthly Magazine, can fill this gap for collectors. The Magazine is full of useful information about past, present and future issues and is well worth the small annual membership charge.

On occasions UK Matchbox Club members have the opportunity to obtain special promotional models such as the Y13 1918 Crossley R.A.F. Tender produced in an attractive red and yellow livery and carrying the Club logo plus "800 members Xmas 1979". Today club membership approaches 3000.

Ray Bush is always happy to answer Club members queries so why not drop him a line at the address below and find out how club membership can help build your collection.

UK MATCHBOX CLUB
1 Torr Road,
Hartley,
Plymouth,
Devon
PL 35 TD, England

Matchbox Toys

3B Major Series Models

Ref. No.		Model Type	Model Features and Size	Rarity and Price Grading		
M1 a)	1960	Caterpillar Excavator	Yellow MB, Silver MW, BPT. 99 mm.	£6-£8	MPR	☐
b)	1963	'BP' Petrol Tanker	Green/Yellow/White MB, CEM, BPW/TW. 102 mm.	£7-£9	MPR	☐
M2 a)	1960	Bedford Articulated Truck 'WALLS ICE CREAM'	Light Blue cab, Cream box TRL, Red and Blue logo, MW or GPW, No WDS, BB. 101 mm.	£15	GV	☐
b)	1963	'YORK FREIGHTMASTER' Trailer 'DAVIES TYRES THE BEST FOR MILES'	Red cab, Grey box TRL, Silver trim, Yel/Black/Red decals, AV/10BPW/WDS/ORD. 117 mm.	£10	NC	☐
c)	1966	'YORK FREIGHTMASTER' Trailer 'LEP INTERNATIONAL TRANSPORT'	Silver cab, Maroon box trailer, Yel/Black/Red decals, AV/10BPW/WDS/ORD. 117 mm.	£8-£10	MPR	☐
M3	1960	Centurion Tank with Transporter	Olive Green TRPT and tank, BPW and Green RTR, MRW, DDR AV/10 wheels. 155 mm.	£12	NC	☐
M4 a)	1960	'RUSTON BUCYRUS'	Brown/Yel MB and jib, Green RTR, PRW. 99 mm.	£6-£8	MPR	☐
b)	1966	'FREUHOF' Hopper Train	Maroon TRL, 2 Sil hoppers, Red W, BPT. 286 mm.	£9-£11	MPR	☐
M5	1966	'MASSEY FERGUSON' Combine	Red MB, Tan D, Yel blades, 2BPT/2SBPW. 117 mm.	£7-£9	MPR	☐
M6 a)	1960	'PICKFORDS' 200 Ton Transporter	Blue tractor (6W), Red/Blue TRL (12W), BPW. 279 mm.	£15	GV	☐
b)	1966	'BP RACING TRANSPORTER'	Green MB, Yel/Grn decal, Red hubs, BPT. 127 mm.	£6-£7	MPR	☐
M7	1960	'Jennings' Cattle Truck	Red tractor, Tan trailer, GBPW, DDR. 121 mm.	£6-£8	MPR	☐
M8 a)	1960	'MOBILGAS' Petrol Tanker	Red MB, Silver trim, Blk/Wh decal, GBPW. 99 mm.	£15	GV	☐
M8 b)	1964	Car Transporter 'FARNBOROUGH MEASHAM'	Blue cab, Orange TRL, Silver trim, DDR *Car Auction Collection* Orange hubs, GPT. 209 mm.	£6-£8	MPR	☐
M9	1963	Dinkum Rear Dumper	Yellow MB and Dumper *DD70* Red hubs, BPT. 108 mm.	£4-£6	MPR	☐
M10	1962	'COOPER JARRETT' Freighter	Blue tractor, 2 TRL, 34 BPW, Yel/Blk, DCS. 289 mm.	£15	GV	☐

Gift Set

G9	1963	Major Series Set	Contains Major Packs 1, 2, 4, 6	£50	GV	☐

3C Early Accessory Packs

Ref. No.		Model Type	Model Features and Size	Rarity and Price Grading		
1a	1957	'ESSO' Petrol Pump Set	Red pumps, White figure	£3-£4	MPR	☐
b	1963	'BP' Petrol Pump Set	White pumps, Yel/White decal	£3-£4	MPR	☐
2	1957	'MATCHBOX CAR TRANSPORTER'	All blue body, Silver trim, GMW	£6-£8	MPR	☐
3	1957	Garage	Yellow/Green/Red, opening doors, all metal	£3-£4	MPR	☐
4	1960	Road Signs Set	Eight Red/White/Black signs *Lesney* on BP	£3-£4	MPR	☐
5	1960	'HOME STORES'	Food shop with window display, OD	£5-£6	MPR	☐

N.B. In 1959 the first of a continuing series of 'MATCHBOX GARAGES' was issued (MG1A). In 1963 a 'MATCHBOX FIRE STATION' was issued (MF1A). Models made of Plastic £9 GV.

MAJOR SERIES & ACCESSORIES BOXES

1st design

2nd design

The last design

Accessory Pack design

3D 'MODELS OF YESTERYEAR'

i) INTRODUCTION

These delightful models have become amongst the most sought after of all die-cast models.

Few could have realised back in 1956 when Lesney Products Ltd issued the first model which was a 1925 Allchin Steam Tractor, just how popular this series of models was to become.

Today it is estimated that there are probably in excess of one hundred thousand collectors world wide with their numbers apparently growing all the time. As the listing shows there are a large number of different models and variations available for collection. Amongst the most popular of these are the first and second series models in their most attractive all card boxes. Of these a delightful 2nd series model, the Y-4(B) Shand Mason Horsedrawn Fire Engine, is an outstanding example of the high degree of detailed workmanship which has gone into the production of these models.

The first Yesteryear catalogue appeared in 1958 and featured the nine models available at the time. Since those early days regular issues of new models have been made although when sales were slow in the early seventies there were no new issues for a two year period. However 1973 saw the introduction of new models including the superb Y-11c Lagonda Coupe plus the reissue of older models in new colours.

With the introduction in 1979 of the Y-5 1927 Talbot Van series followed in 1981 by the Y-12 Ford Model 'T' Van series, the Yesteryear range has been greatly enhanced by their highly attractive colours and decals.

The 'Models of Yesteryear' series therefore has much to offer collectors be they new or established and it's not surprising that they are so popular around the world.

ii) THE 'YESTERYEAR' CODING SYSTEM

The models listed in the catalogue are in respect of all those models manufactured and labelled by the Matchbox factory and generally released for sale, albeit on occasions, in very small numbers indeed.

In so doing, we hope that the catalogue will help collectors to avoid any confusion which might be caused by the present day large scale issue of models not totally produced by Matchbox.

A coding system has been introduced for use when describing a models' origins and is now increasingly to be found on mail order lists.

The Code is as follows:—

Code 1. Models of Yesteryear which have been manufactured and labelled by the Matchbox factory.

N.B. Only code 1 models have been included in the official listings in this catalogue.

Code 2. Models of Yesteryear manufactured by Matchbox but not on general release or they have been labelled by others WITH Matchbox permission.

Code 3. Yesteryears manufactured by Matchbox but labelled WITHOUT their permission normally to commemorate an event or special occasion — providing a sticker is on the box stating that it is not an official Matchbox Issue — this is allowed.

Code 2 models which are produced for specific promotional purposes are not always on sale to the general public. Nevertheless they are sought after by collectors and can fetch high prices. If a collector is interested in buying one of these models he should be wary of the forgeries that we understand are beginning to be produced of the more valuable issues.

The code 3 models have proved to be very popular with collectors. Usually a specific limited number are produced, each with its own numbered certificate.

N.B. Whilst the above system has been referred to as the 'Yesteryear' coding system it also equally applies to other manufacturers models.

MODELS OF YESTERYEAR

iii) PACKAGING

1956-61
The earliest had just the
model number on the end flaps.

1962-65
All card with
coloured picture of model.

1963
All card with coloured
model and background picture

4th design
Purple/Yellow or Pink/Yellow
1st window-type box

1972-78
'Woodgrain' box

1978-
Current 'All Cream' box

N.B. It should be understood that variants exist in respect of the above examples.

MODELS OF YESTERYEAR CONT.

iv) MODEL IDENTIFICATION

a) Model Listings

The listing of models and their colours have been taken from an official Matchbox Toys Listing, which was originally prepared for the Company by Ray Bush of the U.K. Matchbox Club.

The only exceptions to this being firstly the inclusion of the extremely rare Y4(D) White, Yellow and Red Duesenberg. Whilst this model was not included on the above official list 2000 models were apparently released for general issue and today it has become highly sought after, so details have been included.

The other exceptions to the Matchbox Company listings are those models issued since 1982 and not included in the official Listing.

b) Common Features

Many models have common identifying features and these are shown below to avoid unnecessary repetition in the Features Column.

i) Models of Yesteryear
and Made in England by Lesney

All models issued prior to the end of 1982 have the above stamped onto their base-plates/chassis.

ii) Wheels

All the wheels prior to 1970 were of metal construction.

From 1972 approximately plastic wheels were used on all models. Nevertheless the models issued at this changeover period are to be found with either metal or plastic wheels. The varieties of wheels are:—

MSPKW	Metal Spoke Wheels
MPSPKW	Metal or Plastic Spoke Wheels
PBHD	Plastic Bolt Head Wheels
PSPKW	Plastic Spoke Wheels
SSPKW	Solid Spoke Wheels

The number of spokes in a particular wheel has been indicated by a figure in brackets following the wheel abbreviation e.g. (12) in plated form mounted on items such as cigarette boxes. Models with these holes have been identified in the features column by:— e.g. 2 BPHS (two base plate holes on some).

x) Scale Sizes

These are not all made to the same scale ranging from 34:1 to 130:1. The sizes are shown with the boxes which makes for easy reference.

xi) Purchasing Check

Always ensure that the model bought is the correct model for its box, i.e. it has been known for a last issue model to be 'accidentally' put into a first issue box!

c) Catalogue Listings

Do not place too much reliance on the model colours shown in catalogues. Very often the pictures shown are from mock-ups in colours never actually issued. E.g. the 1969 catalogue showed a picture of a Blue Y-5 (c) Peugeot when it was issued in Yellow. Similarly the 1973 catalogue showed a Silver Hispano Suiza when it was issued in Red.

iii) Model Number and Name

It has been assumed that all models have both shown on the baseplate or chassis.

iv) Bumpers, Dashboards, Headlights,
Radiator Shells and Windscreens

All assumed to be of metal construction prior to approx. 1974 after which time plastic was increasingly used.

v) Base Plate and Chassis

All assumed to be of metal construction.

vi) Tyres

All assumed to be treaded Black Plastic unless otherwise indicated.

vii) Seats

All assumed to be of plastic construction unless otherwise indicated.

viii) Die Cast Construction

All models assumed to be constructed at least in part of a die-cast alloy.

ix) Base Plate Holes

Some models produced from the mid sixties onwards display 2 holes in their base plate. This is because they were also sold

V) ABBREVIATIONS — EXAMPLE OF USE

Y-1A 1925 Allchin 7 NHP Steam Traction Engine

Abbreviations
Green MB, Red MSPKW (2 × 18/12), Gold or Silver trim, Black flywheel, UNP RWTS/CF, CRA/SDWT/MCBV.

Non Abbreviated Form
Green main body, Red metal spoke wheels, two with 18 spokes and two with 12 spokes, Gold or Silver trim, Black flywheel, unpainted rear wheel treads and cab floor, crimped or riveted axles, straight or diagonal wheel tread, minor colour and body variations.

Collectors Notes

MODELS OF YESTERYEAR

VI) INDEX TO MODEL TYPES AND LOGO

1st Issues

Y-1(A) 1925 Allchin 7NHP Steam Traction Engine
Y-2(A) 1911 'B' Type Bus, 'GENERAL'
Y-3(A) 1907 'LONDON TRANSPORT' 'E' Class Tram
Y-4(A) Sentinel Steam Wagon
Y-5(A) 1929 Le Mans Bentley
Y-6(A) 1916 A.E.C. 'Y' Type Lorry
Y-7(A) 4 ton Leyland Lorry 'W & R JABOB & CO LTD'
Y-8(A) Morris Cowley 1926 'BULLNOSE'
Y-9(A) 1924 Fowler 'BIG LION' Showman's Engine
Y-10(A) 1908 'GRAND PRIX' Mercedes
Y-11(A) Aveling & Porter 1920 Steam Roller
Y-12(A) 1899 Horse Drawn Bus
Y-13(A) 1862 USA 'SANTE FE' Locomotive 'GENERAL'
Y-14(A) 1903 'DUKE OF CONNAUGHT' GWR Locomotive
Y-15(A) 1907 Rolls Royce Silver Ghost
Y-16(A) 1904 Spyker Veteran Automobile
Y-17(A) 1938 Hispano Suiza
Y-18(A) 1937 Cord 812
Y-19(A) 1933 Auburn Speedster
Y-20(A) 1937 Mercedes 540K
Y-21(A) 1930 Ford Model 'A' Wagon
  i) Woody Wagon
  ii) 'A & J BOX GENERAL STORES'
Y-22(A) 1930 Ford Model 'A' Van
  i) 'OXO'
  ii) 'MAGGI SOUPS'
Y-23(A) 1922 A.E.C. 'GENERAL' 'S' Type Omnibus
Y-24(A) 1927 Bugatti T44
Y-25(A) 1910 Renault Type AG 'PERRIER'

2nd Issues

Y-1(B) 1911 Model 'T' Ford car
Y-2(B) 1911 Renault Two Seater
Y-3(B) 1910 Benz Limousine
Y-4(B) Shand Mason Horse Drawn Fire Engine
  i) Kent Fire Brigade
  ii) London Fire Brigade
Y-5(B) 1929 4½ Litre 'BLOWER' Bentley
Y-6(B) 1923 Type 35 Bugatti
Y-7(B) 1913 Mercer Raceabout
Y-8(B) 1914 Sunbeam Motorcycle & Sidecar
Y-9(B) 1912 Simplex
Y-10(B) 1928 Mercedes Benz 36/220
Y-11(B) 1912 Packard Landaulet
Y-12(B) 1909 Thomas Flyabout
Y-13(B) 1911 Daimler
Y-14(B) 1911 Maxwell Roadster
Y-15(B) 1930 Packard Victoria
Y-16(B) 1928 Mercedes Benz Coupe

* Awaiting release

Models of Yesteryear cont.

3rd Issues

Y-1(C) 1936 SS100 Jaguar
Y-2(C) 1914 Prince Henry Vauxhall
Y-3(C) 1934 Riley MPH
Y-4(C) 1909 Opel Coupe
Y-5(C) 1907 Peugot
Y-6(C) 1913 Cadillac
Y-7(C) 1912 Rolls Royce
Y-8(C) 1914 Stutz
Y-9(C) No model issued as yet.
Y-10(C) 1906 Rolls Royce 'SILVER GHOST'
Y-11(C) 1938 Lagonda Drophead Coupe
Y-12(C) 1912 Ford Model 'T' Van
- i) 'COLMANS MUSTARD'
- ii) 'ENJOY COCA COLA
- iii) 'SUZE A LA GENTIANE'
- iv) Silver Jubilee 'MODELS OF YESTERYEAR'
- v) 'SMITHS POTATO CRISPS'
- vi) 'ARNOTTS BISCUITS'
- vii) 'BIRDS' Custard Powder
- viii) 'CEREBOS TABLE SALT'
- ix) 'HARRODS EXPRESS DELIVERY
- x) 'SUNLIGHT SEIFFE'
- xi) 'ROYAL MAIL'
- xii) 'CAPTAIN MORGAN BLACK LABEL RUM'
- xiii) 'HOOVER IT BEATS AS IT SWEEPS AS IT CLEANS'

Y-13(C) 1918 Crossley Wagon
- i) 'R.A.F.' Tender
- ii) 'EVANS BROS COAL AND COKE' Coal Wagon
- iii) 'CARLSBERG' Beer Wagon

Y-14(C) 1931 Stutz Bearcat

4th issues

Y-1(D) No issue as yet
Y-2(D) No issue as yet
Y-3(D) 1912 Ford Model 'T' Tanker
- i) 'BRITISH PETROLEUM COMPANY LTD'
- ii) 'ZEROLENE'
- iii) 'EXPRESS DAIRY'

Y-4(D) 1930 Duesenberg Model 'J' Town Car
Y-5(D) 1927 Talbot Van
- i) 'LIPTONS TEA BY APPOINTMENT' (Royal Crest)
- ii) 'CHOCOLATE MENIER'
- iii) 'LIPTONS TEA CITY ROAD LONDON' (Simulated Crest)
- iv) 'TAYSTEE OLD FASHIONED ENRICHED BREAD'
- v) 'MERITA OLD FASHIONED ENRICHED BREAD'
- vi) 'LANGENDORF OLD FASHIONED ENRICHED BREAD'
- vii) 'NESTLES MILK THE RICHEST IN CREAM'
- viii) 'CHIVERS & SONS LTD JAMS JELLIES & MARMALADES'
- ix) 'WRIGHTS ORIGINAL COAL TAR SOAP'
- x) 'EVER READY BATTERIES FOR LIFE'

Y-6(D) 1920 Rolls Royce Fire Engine
Y-7(D) No issue as yet.
Y-8(D) 1945 MG TC.

MODELS OF YESTERYEAR

Y 9(A) Fowler 'BIG LION'
Showman's Engine

Y-7(A) W&R Jacob & Co Ltd
Y-6(A) 'OSRAM LAMPS' (Light Grey)

Y-1(A) 1925 Allchin 7NHP
Traction Engine
Y-11(A) 1920 Aveling & Porter
Steam Roller

Y-5(B) 1929 4½ litre
(S) Bentley

Y-4(B) Shand Mason Fire Engine
i) 1960 White horses 'KENT' decal
ii) 1962 Black horses 'LONDON' decal

Model 'T' Commercials
Y-3 (D) Tanker
Y-12(C) Van

Models of Yesteryear

1st Issues

Ref. No.		Model Type	Model Features and Size	Rarity and Price Grading	
Y-1 (A)	1956	1925 Allchin 7 NHP Steam Traction Engine	Green MB, Red MSPKW (2×18/12) Gold or Silver trim, Black flywheel, CRA/SDWT/MCBV, unpainted RWTS. 67 mm.	£35	NC ☐
			Painted rear wheel treads	£40	NC ☐
Y-2 (A)	1956	1911 'B' Type Bus 'GENERAL'	Red MB, Silver Radiator, Grey or Black MSPKW (2×16/8), 4 lower WDS & 8 USDW, Blue Driver, DBD - *Putney Common,* DR-*Pears, Dewars, Oakeys, Nestles,* MCBV. 68 mm.	£40	NC ☐
			Variation 4 lower WDS and 4 USDW	£48	GV ☐
Y-3 (A)	1956	1907 'LONDON TRANSPORT' 'E' Class Tram Car.	Red MB, Cream or White roof, Silver or Gold trim, Grey LFB, GM or BPW, OCATD DBD — *City, DR-Buy Lesney Toys, News of the World, World Record Sale,* MCBV. 79 mm.	£28	NC ☐
Y-4 (A)	1956	Sentinel Steam Wagon	Blue MB, Black CH, GMW/CRA/MCBV *Sand and Gravel Supplies* in Yellow. 69 mm.	£35	NC ☐
			Last issue Black plastic wheels		NGPP ☐
Y-5 (A)	1958	1929 Le Mans Bentley	Green MB, Red Seats, Silver or Gold trim, Silver or Green grille, RN'5' in Black, Solid MSPKW with BPT, CRA/MCBV. 80 mm.	£35	NC ☐
Y-6 (A)	1957	1916 A.E.C. 'Y' Type Lorry 'OSRAM LAMPS'	Pale Grey body, driver and SW, GMW/CRA *Osram Lamps G.E.C. London,* MCBV. 69 mm.	£35	NC ☐
	1959	Colour change	Dark Grey body	£40	GV ☐
Y-7 (A)	1957	4 ton Leyland Lorry 'W & R JACOB & CO LTD'	Brown MB, Cream or White roof, *By Royal Appt. to H.M. The King Biscuit Manufacturers,* GMW/BPW (R). 69 mm.	£40	NC ☐
Y-8 (A)	1958	Morris Cowley 1926 'BULLNOSE'	LT or DK Tan MB, DK Brown CH/MDG, Silver or Gold MSPKW (10), BPT/CRA/SPW/ODS/MCBV. 65 mm.	£32	NC ☐

Models of Yesteryear cont.

No.	Year	Model	Description	Price	Rarity
Y-9 (A)	1958	1924 Fowler 'BIG LION' Showmans Engine 'LESNEYS MODERN AMUSEMENTS'	Maroon MB, Cream roof, Silver or Gold trim, Silver or Gold (R) Canopy Support, Yellow MSPKW (2×18/12) RA/MCBV. 83 mm.	£40	GV ☐
	1961	Colour change	Bright Red main body, White roof	£45	NC ☐
Y-10 (A)	1958	1908 'GRAND PRIX' Mercedes	White MB, Green seats, 2SPW/CRA/MCBV Silver Gold or UNP MSPKW (12) and trim. 75 mm.	£35	NC ☐
Y-11 (A)	1958	Aveling and Porter. 1920 Steam Roller.	Green MB, Black Canopy Supports, Red Roller Wheel, Red MSPKW (14), UNP treads, Black FWL, Gold trim on SR and SF MCBV. 79 mm.	£35	NC ☐
	1962	Colour change	Green MB, Green canopy supports	£40	GV ☐
Y-12 (A)	1959	1899 Horse Drawn Bus 'LONDON GENERAL OMNIBUS COMPANY LTD	Red MB, Tan driver and top deck, Black MSPKW (16) and driver's hat, 2 Brown horses, DBD *Victoria — Kings Cross* and *Picadilly,* DR- *Liptons Tea, Hudsons, Sanitas, Colmans, Horlicks,* and *Heinz,* MCBV. 83 mm.	£40	NC ☐
Y-13 (A)	1959	1862 USA 'SANTE FE' locomotive 'GENERAL'	Dark Green and Maroon MB and CH, Black base plate and MSPKW (4×12), 8 WDS, silver HL, Gold trim, Yellow logo MCBV. 84 mm.	£28	NC ☐
	1964	Colour change	Pale Green and Maroon MB and CH	£33	NVE ☐
Y-14 (A)	1959	1903 'DUKE OF CONNAUGHT' G.W.R. locomotive	Green and Brown MB and Chassis, Gold trim, Brown MSPKW (12), Yellow and Red decal. 76 mm.	£35	NC
Y-15 (A)	1960	1907 Rolls Royce Silver Ghost	Green (many shades) MB, Black seats, Gold trim, Gold or Silver MSPKW (12) MCBV, BPHS. 83 mm. Black tyres	£8-£10	MPR ☐
			Grey tyres	£25	NC ☐
Y-16 (A)	1961	1904 Spyker Veteran automobile	Pale Yellow MB and RS, Gold MSPKW (12) and Trim, Green S, BGPT, BPHS, SPW, MCBV. 83 mm.	£14	NC ☐
	1968	Colour change	Dark yellow MB and radiator shell	£10-£12	MPR ☐

Models of Yesteryear cont.

No.	Year	Model	Description	Price		
Y-17 (A)	1974	1938 Hispano Suiza	Red MB, Black CH and HD, Sil MSPKW (24). 112 mm.	£5-£7	MPR	☐
	1979	1st colour change	Steel Blue/Pale Blue MB and wings PBHW	Current	MPR	☐
	1980	2nd colour change	SAPM but with Black wings PBHW	Current	MPR	☐
Y-18 (A)	1981	1937 Cord 812	Red MB, White HD/S, Sil TR, PBHW/WWT. 120 mm.	Current	MPR	☐
	1983	Colour change	Maroon MB, White hood.	Current	MPR	☐
Y-19 (A)	1980	1936 Auburn Speedster	Coffee and Beige MB, Dark Brown chassis, Red seats, Red PBHW, Silver TR, WWT/DD. 116 mm.	Current	MPR	☐
	1982	1st colour change	Off White MB, Black chassis	Current	MPR	☐
	1983	2nd colour change	All Cream MB, Black chassis	Current	MPR	☐
Y-20 (A)	1981	1938 Mercedes 540K	Met Silver MB, Black CH, Red S, LHD, Silver PSPKW (24) and TR, ODS/SPW/WWT. 124 mm.	Current	MPR	☐
Y-21 (A)		Ford Model 'A' Wagon				
i)	1981	Woody Wagon	Yellow MB, Brown Chassis, Wood PNB. 100 mm.	Current	MPR	☐
	1982	colour change	Yellow MB, Black chassis.	Current	MPR	☐
ii)	1983	'A & J BOX GENERAL STORES'	Copper MB, Black wings, Wood PNB. 100 mm.	Current	MPR	☐
Y-22 (A)		1930 Ford Model 'A' Van				
i)	1982	'OXO ITS MEAT AND DRINK TO YOU'	Red MB, Black CH and roof, Silver trim and PSPKW (24), Black/White/Blue logo, WWT. 102 mm.	Current	MPR	☐
*ii)	1983	'MAGGI SOUPS'	Red body, Yellow roof (Expected colours)	Current	MPR	☐
Y-23 (A)	1983	1922 AEC 'GENERAL' 'S' Type Omnibus.	Red MB, Black chassis, Light or Dark (R) Tan seats, Red PSPKW (12), smooth Black plastic tyres, Silver R, Black G, DBD/PLP, DR — *Hudsons, Oxo, Cerebos, Schweppes Tonic Water* in Red on White Label. 102 mm.	£20	NC	☐
	1983	1st Colour Change.	Schweppes logo in Black on White Label.	Current	MPR	☐
	1983	2nd Colour Change.	Schweppes logo in White on Yellow Label.	Current	MPR	☐
Y-24 (A)	1983	1927 Bugatti T44.	Black and Yellow MB, Tan Roof, Silver Trim, PSPKW (24), 2 SPW, WDS.	Current	MPR	☐
Y-25 (A)	1983	1910 Renault Type AG "PERRIER"	Dark Green bonnet, cab floor and CH, Light Green Van Sides, cast in rear doors, White roof, seats and TL. SPW, Gold PSPKW (12), HLS, White logo, *Mise en bouteille a la source Vergeze (Gard) France.*	Current	MPR	☐

* Release awaited

Models of Yesteryear
2nd Issues

Ref. No.		Model Type	Model Features and Size	Rarity and Price Grading	
Y-1 (B)	1964	1911 Model 'T' Ford.	Red MB, Black Roof, Seats and Grille, Gold Trim and MSPKW (12), VNS/BPHS/MCBV. 76 mm.	£10-£13	MPR ☐
	1974	1st Colour Change.	White main body, Red Roof	£8-£11	MPR ☐
	1976	2nd Colour Change. US Issue shown.	Black main body, Black Roof, Gold Trim, only 1000 produced and sold to Matchbox Club members in the United States.		MPR ☐
Y-2 (B)	1963	1911 Renault Two Seater.	Green (many shades) MB and SW, Red Seats, Gold or Silver, MSPKW (12) and TR, SPW/BPT. 76 mm.	£10-£13	MPR ☐
Y-3 (B)	1966	1910 Benz Limousine.	Cream MB and SW, Green Roof, S and G, Gold MSPKW (12) and Trim, BPT/SPW/MCBV. 83 mm.	£13	NC ☐
	1968	1st Colour Change.	Pale Green MB, Lemon (Chartreuse) roof	£11	NC ☐
	1970	2nd Colour Change.	Pale or Dark Green MB, Black Roof.	£8-£10	MPR ☐
Y-4 (B)	1960	Shand Mason Horse Drawn Fire Engine 'KENT FIRE BRIGADE'	Red MB, White Horses, grey mane and tail, Gold Boiler and Pump, 3 Black/Gold Firemen, Black MSPKW (2×25/13), Yellow logo. 89 mm.	£88	GV ☐
	1983	Colour and logo change 'LONDON FIRE BRIGADE 72'.	Red MB, Black Horses, white mane and tail, Yellow/ Gold/Black decals.	£85	GV ☐
Y-5 (B)	1962	1929 4½ Litre Bentley.	Metallic Pale or Dark Green MB and TN, Gold or Silver R, SW and MSPKW (24) BPT/UJ. Silver or Green G, Green BP, BPHS, MCBV. 89 mm.	£17	NC ☐
	1962	Early Rare Colour.	Metallic Apple Green, Green Tonneau.	£120	GV ☐
	1965	Colour Change.	British Racing Green. Green or Red Tonneau.	£17	NC ☐
Y-6 (B)	1961	1923 Type 35 Bugatti.	Blue MB, Gold MSPKW (8) and Trim, Red DB, Black CH and S, White Circle, Red RN '6'. 79 mm.	£16	NC ☐
	1964	Colour Change.	Red Main Body.	£14	NC ☐
Y-7 (B)	1957	1913 Mercer Raceabout.	Lilac MB, Black Seats, Gold or Silver MSPKW (12), Gold Trim, BPHS, MCBV. 83 mm.	£12-£15	MPR ☐
	1965	Colour Change.	Yellow main body, Black Seats	£8-£10	MPR ☐
Y-8 (B)	1962	1914 Sunbeam Motorcycle and Milford Sidecar.	All Chrome Plated MB, Black MC Seat, MSPKW (12), Green Sidecar Seat. 67 mm.	£14-£17	MPR ☐
			Black Sidecar Seat version		NGPP ☐

Models of Yesteryear cont.

No.	Year	Model	Description	Price	Status
Y-9 (B)	1968	1912 Simplex.	Yellow Green MB and CH, Red S, Tan RF, BPT/BPHS, Gold MSPKW (12) and TR, SPW 96 mm.	£11	NC □
	1969	1st Colour Change.	Green MB and CH, Red seats, Tan roof.	£10	NC □
	1971	2nd Colour Change.	Gold main body, Red seats and chassis, Silver PSPKW (12), Black roof.	£7-£9	MPR □
	1974	3rd Colour Change.	Red main body and chassis, Yellow seats, Black roof, Red PSPKW (12).	£5-£7	MPR □
	1979	4th Colour Change.	Red main body, Yellow seats and roof, Black chassis, Red PSPKW (12)	Current	MPR □
Y-10 (B)	1963	1928 Mercedes Benz 36/220.	White MB, Red seats, Tan DB, Silver MSPKW (12), BPT, BPHS, 2 spare tyres. 96 mm.	£16	NC □
			One Spare Tyre	£12-£14	MPR □
Y-11 (B)	1964	1912 Packard Landaulet.	Dark Red MB, Black seats, Gold or Silver MSPKW (12), SPW/BPT/SHOD/BPHS. 80 mm.	£9-£11	MPR □
Y-12 (B)	1967	1909 Thomas Flyabout.	Blue MB, Yellow seats, Tan roof, Gold or Silver MSPKW (12) and trim, Red grille, BPT/SPW/BPHS/MCBV. 99 mm.	NGPP	GV □
	1967	1st Colour Change.	Blue MB, Dark Red seats, Tan roof.	£6-£8	MPR □
	1974	2nd Colour Change.	Red MB, White seats, Black roof, Silver PSPKW (12).	£5-£7	MPR □
Y-13 (B)	1966	1911 Daimler.	Yellow MB, Black chassis and seats, Gold MSPKW (26) and trim BPT/SPW/BPHS/MCBV. 84 mm.	£10-£12	MPR □
	1967	Colour Change.	Yellow MB, Black CH, Dark Red seats.	£8-£10	MPR □
Y-14 (B)	1965	1911 Maxwell Roadster.	Turquoise MB, Black roof, Red seats, Gold or Silver MSPKW (12) and trim, BPT/BPHS/MCBV. 82 mm.	£8-£10	MPR □
Y-15 (B)	1969	1930 Packard Victoria.	Brownish Gold MB, Dark Red roof, Dark Brown CH, Red G, Gold or Silver MSPKW (24), Grey (R) or Black Tyres. 109 mm.	£9-£12	MPR □
	1974	1st Colour Change.	Greenish-Gold MB, Black roof, Silver PSPKW (24).	£5-£7	MPR □
	1979	2nd Colour Change.	Black and Red MB, White roof, Black CH, Silver PBHW (12), WWT.	Current	MPR □
Y-16 (B)	1972	1928 Mercedes Benz SS Coupe.	Silver Grey MB, Red CH, Black RF and S, Gold MSPKW (24) and trim, BPT/2SPW. 107 mm.	£10	NC □
	1974	1st Colour Change.	Green MB, Very Dark Green chassis, Black roof, Silver PSPKW (24), (CH Colour identical to Y-14(C) CH).	£39	GV □
	1974	2nd Colour Change.	Green MB and chassis, Black roof.	£7-£9	MPR □
	1976	3rd Colour Change.	Green MB, chassis and roof.	£5-£7	MPR □
	1979	4th Colour Change.	White MB and chassis, Black roof.	Current	MPR □
	1981	5th Colour Change.	Blue bonnet and CH, Grey Sides, Black roof.	Current	MPR □
	1983	6th Colour Change.	Blue Bonnet and CH. Cream Sides, Black roof.		NGPP □
	1983	7th Colour Change.	Dark Blue Bonnet and CH, Eggshell Blue Sides, Black roof.		NGPP □

N.B. Both the 1983 models have been issued in limited quantities.

Models of YesterYear

3rd Issues

Ref. No.		Model Type	Model Features and Size	Rarity and Price Grading		
Y-1 (C)	1977	1936 SS 100 Jaguar.	White MB and BP, Black seats, tonneau and int, Silver PSPKW (24) and trim, FWS, SPW. 101 mm.	£5-£7	MPR	☐
	1979	Colour change	Steel-Blue MB, Black Seats.	£4-£6	MPR	☐
	1981	Colour change	Green MB, Black Seats, WWT.	Current	MPR	☐
Y-2 (C)	1970	1914 Prince Henry Vauxhall.	Silver bonnet, Red body and CH, White seats, Gold, MSPKW (26) and TR, BPT/SPW. 90 mm.	£6-£8	MPR	☐
			Rare Red seat version		NGPP	☐
	1974	1st Colour Change.	Silver BN and PSPKW, Blue MB and CH.	£5-£7	MPR	☐
	1979	2nd Colour Change.	Silver bonnet, Red body, Black chassis.	Current	MPR	☐
Y-3 (C)	1974	1934 Riley MPH.	Red MB, White seats, Silver PSPKW (24). 101 mm.	£4-£6	MPR	☐
	1979	Colour Change.	Blue main body, White seats.	Current	MPR	☐
Y-4 (C)	1966	1909 Opel Coupe.	White MB, Tan roof, Red seats and grille, Gold MSPKW (12) and trim, BPT, BPHS. 81 mm.	£9-£11	MPR	☐
	1974	Colour Change.	Orange MB, Black roof, Silver PSPKW (12).	£14	NC	☐
Y-5 (C)	1969	1907 Peugeot.	Yellow MB, Black roof and CH, Red S, Gold MSPKW (12) and trim, BPT, SPW, TW. 90 mm.	£10-£12	MPR	☐
	1974	Colour Change.	Orange/Gold MB and RF, Silver PSPKW (12).	£9-£11	MPR	☐
Y-6 (C)	1967	1913 Cadillac.	Gold MB, Dark Red roof, Red seats, Gold MSPKW (12), BPT, BPHS, SPW. 86 mm.	£7-£9	MPR	☐
	1974	Colour Change.	Green MB, Black roof, Silver PSPKW (12).	£5-£7	MPR	☐
Y-7 (C)	1968	1912 Rolls Royce.	Silver MB, Red smooth roof, Red CH, Gold MSPKW (12), BPT, BPHS, SPW, BPSW. 98 mm.	£12-£15	MPR	☐
	1969	1st Colour Change.	Silver MB, Grey smooth roof.	£12-£15	MPR	☐
	1970	2nd Colour Change.	Silver MB, Grey roof, ribbed at rear.	£50	GV	☐
	1970	3rd Colour Change.	Silver MB, Red roof, ribbed at rear.	£9-£11	MPR	☐
	1974	4th Colour Change.	Gold MB, Red roof ribbed at rear. Silver PSPKW (12).	£5-£7	MPR	☐
	1979	5th Colour Change.	Yellow MB, Black roof, ribbed at rear, Red PSPKW (12).	Current	MPR	☐
Y-8 (C)	1969	1914 Stutz.	Red MB, Tan roof, Green seats and grille, Gold MSPKW (12), BPT, SPW. 89 mm.	£8-£10	MPR	☐
	1974	Colour Change.	Blue MB, Black roof, Silver PSPKW (12).	£5-£7	MPR	☐
Y-9 (C)		No model issued yet.				

Models of Yesteryear cont.

No.	Year	Model	Description	Price		
Y-10 (C)	1969	1906 Rolls Royce "Silver Ghost".	Goldish Green MB, Dark Red seats and grille, Gold MSPKW (12) and trim, BPHS/BPT/SPW. 92 mm.	£11-£13	MPR	☐
	1974	1st Colour Change.	White MB Black S and G, Silver PSPKW (12).	£6-£8	MPR	☐
	1979	2nd Colour Change.	Silver MB, Dark Red S, Red PSPKW (12).	Current	MPR	☐
	1979	3rd Colour Change.	Silver MB, Yellow S, Red PSPKW (12).	Current	MPR	☐
Y-11 (C)	1972	1938 Lagonda Drophead Coupe.	Gold MB, Purple chassis, Black seats, Gold MSPKW (24) and trim, FHD/BPT. 92 mm.	£20	NC	☐
	1972	1st Colour Change.	Gold MB, Bright Red chassis (known as the Strawberry Red).	£200	GV	☐
	1972	2nd Colour Change.	Gold MB, Dark Red chassis.	£15-£18	MPR	☐
	1972	3rd Colour Change.	Gold MB, Maroon chassis.	£15-£18	MPR	☐
	1974	4th Colour Change.	Orange-Red MB, Gold CH, PSPKW (24).	£8-£10	MPR	☐
	1979	5th Colour Change.	Dark Beige MB, Black CH, Silver PBHW (12).	Current	MPR	☐
	1979	6th Colour Change.	Dark Beige MB, Black CH, Red seats.	Current	MPR	☐
Y-12 (C)		1912 Ford Model 'T' Van. The following issues are all based on this model and have the same reference number.	Unless otherwise described each model has Gold trim, Black seats, Red PSPKW (12), LHD/HRR, 2 SDW/2RWDS/NP/HSL/BPT/PBSW/RPR. 91 mm.			
(i)	1979	'COLMANS MUSTARD' Livery.	Yellow MB, Black CH and roof, Red and Black decals, RDD-1st SGL, 2nd DL.	Current	MPR	☐
ii)	1979	'ENJOY COCA COLA' Livery (USA Issue).	White MB, Black CH and roof, Red and Black decals. SGLRDD.	£25	NC	☐
iii)	1980	'SUZE A LA GENTIANE' Livery.	Yellow MB, Black CH and roof, Black and Red decals, RDD-1st SGL, 2nd DL.	Current	MPR	☐
iv)	1981	'SILVER JUBILEE' EDITION '25 YEARS MAY 1956-1981'.	Two Tone Green MB and CH, Grey roof, WWT Yellow wheels, Silver trim and decals, DLRDD.	Current	MPR	☐
v)	1981	'SMITHS POTATO CRISPS' Livery.	Blue MB, White RF, Black CH, Black (R) or Tan seats, Red wheels, Red and White logo, Silver or Gold trim.	£6-£8	MPR	☐
vi)	1982	'ARNOTTS BISCUITS' Livery. (Australian Issue).	Red MB, Black roof and chassis, Gold wheels, White/Gold logo, MLCD decal.	£45	NC	☐
vii)	1982	'BIRDS' 'CUSTARD POWDER' Livery.	Blue MB, Yellow RF, Black CH, Red wheels, WWT, Silver TR, Red/WH decals. Rear door design — 1st DL, 2nd Cast In. Tan seats.	Current £4-6	MPR MPR	☐ ☐

Models of Yesteryear cont.

viii)	1982	'CEREBOS' 'TABLE SALT' Livery.	Blue MB, White RF, Black chassis, Gold wheels, White/Gold decals.	Current	MPR ☐
ix)	1982	'HARRODS EXPRESS DELIVERY' 'MOTOR ACCESSORIES' Livery.	Cream and Green MB, Tan RF, Black CH, Gold Trim, 1st RDD (Double Line).	£11-£13	MPR ☐
			2nd RDD (Cast In). Black Seats	£7-£9	MPR ☐
			3rd Issue Tan Seats	£6-£8	MPR ☐
x)	1982	'SUNLIGHT SEIFFE' Livery. German Issue.	Yellow MB, Black roof and chassis, Red wheels, multicoloured decal.	£25	NC ☐
xi)	1983	'ROYAL MAIL' Livery. 'GR'.	Red MB, Black roof and chassis, Red wheels, Black and Gold decals.	Current	MPR ☐
xii)	1983	'CAPTAIN MORGAN' 'BLACK LABEL RUM'	Brown MB, White roof, Black CH, Gold wheels, multicoloured decals. 1st issue has 2 separate lables, 2nd issue just one.	Current	MPR ☐
xiii)	1983	'HOOVER' 'IT BEATS AS IT SWEEPS AS IT CLEANS'.	Orange MB, Black roof, Black chassis, Black PSPKW. N.B. Hoover started in 1908 which was the same year that the Model 'T' Ford was introduced.	Current	MPR ☐
Y-13 (C)		1918 Crossley Wagon			
i)	1974	R.A.F. Tender.	Grey-Blue MB, Tan CNP, Silver PSPKW (12), Gold trim, White S, R.A.F. RDLS, RCS/SAW. 96 mm.	£12-£15	MPR ☐
	1976	Colour Change.	Grey-Blue MB, Olive canopy.	£45	NC ☐
ii)	1979	'EVANS BROS COAL AND COKE' Coal Wagon.	Red MB, Black roof, S and CH, Gold trim, Red PSPKW (12), BPT/SPW/BPCL/HLS.	Current	MPR ☐
iii)	1983	'CARLSBERG' Beer Wagon.	White MB, Green roof and CNP, Red seats, Gold trim, Black chassis, HLS/SPW.	Current	MPR ☐
			Silver Trim issue	£5-7	MPR ☐
Y-14 (C)	1974	1931 Stutz Bearcat.	Two tone Green MB, Red seats and grille, LHD, Silver PSPKW (24), Gold TR, 2SPW. 110 mm.	£5-£7	MPR ☐
	1979	1st Colour Change.	Red and Pale Cream MB, Red seats.	£6-£8	MPR ☐
	1979	1st Colour Change.	Red and Pale Cream MB, Black seats.	Current	MPR ☐
	1981	3rd Colour Change.	Cream MB, Green chassis, Black seats.	Current	MPR ☐

Models of Yesteryear

4th Issues

Ref. No.		Model Type	Model Features and Size	Rarity and Price Grading	
Y-1 (D)		No Model as yet.			
Y-2 (D)		No Model as yet.			
Y-3 (D)		1912 Ford Model 'T' Tanker. 99 mm.			
i)	1981	'BRITISH PETROLEUM COMPANY LTD' Tanker. 'MOTOR 'BP' SPIRIT'.	Green MB, Red tank, White RF, Black CH and seats, Red PSPKW (12), Gold and White logo with/without SE to "BP".	Current	MPR ☐
			Gold wheels version.	£10	NC ☐
ii)	1982	'ZEROLENE' 'STANDARD OIL COMPANY' Tanker.	Green MB and tank, White roof, Gold PSPKW (12), Black CH and S, White logo.	£25	NC ☐
			Red PSPKW version.	£30	NC ☐
iii)	1983	'EXPRESS DAIRY' Milk Tanker.	Dark Blue MB, White roof, Black CH and seats, Gold PSPKW (12) White logo.	Current	MPR ☐
Y-4 (D)	1976	1930 Duesenberg Model 'J' Town Car.	* White MB, Yellow hood and seats, Red wings and CH, Silver PSPKW (24), 2SPW, BPSW, only 2000 models were issued.		NGPP ☐
	1976	1st Colour Change.	All Red MB, Black hood, seats and CH, Silver PSPKW (24), 2SPW, BPSW.	£5-£7	MPR ☐
	1979	2nd Colour Change.	Green MB, Pale Green sides, Dark Green roof, Silver PBHW (12), 2SPW.	Current	MPR ☐
	1982	3rd Colour Change.	Green MB, Pale Green sides, Black roof and seats, Silver PBHW (12), WWT, 2SPW.	Current	MPR ☐
	1983	4th Colour Change.	Dark Brown MB, Beige sides, Light (R) or Dark Beige hood.	Current	MPR ☐

* Possibly not recognised as a code 1 model.

Models of Yesteryear cont.

Y-5 (D)		1927 Talbot Van. The following issues are all based on this model and have the same reference number.	Unless otherwise described each model has Black seats, Plastic 12 spoke wheels, Gold BCV, Silver trim, RHD/ORD/2RWDS/2SDW/RPR/SPWR/BRB/HSL/PSW/BPT. 95 mm.		
i)	1978	'LIPTON'S TEA' 'BY APPOINTMENT' Livery.	Green MB, Black roof and CH, Green wheels, Gold decal and Royal Crest.	£11-£14	MPR ☐
ii)	1978	'CHOCOLATE MENIER' Livery.	Blue MB, Black roof and CH, Yellow logo.	Current	MPR ☐
iii)	1980	'LIPTONS TEA' 'CITY ROAD, LONDON EC1' Livery.	Green MB, Black roof and CH, Green wheels, Yellow logo and simulated crest.	Current	MPR ☐
iv)	1980	'TAYSTEE OLD FASHIONED ENRICHED BREAD' Livery.	Yellow MB and CH, Black RF, Red wheels, WWT, Red and Black decals.	Current	MPR ☐
	1981	Colour Change.	Black Base Version.	£4-£6	MPR ☐
v)	1980	'MERITA OLD FASHIONED ENRICHED BREAD' US Issue.	Yellow MB and CH, Black RF, Red wheels, WWT, Red and Black decals.	£20	GV ☐
vi)	1980	'LANGENDORF OLD FASHIONED ENRICHED BREAD' US Issue.	Yellow MB and CH, Black RF, Red wheels, WWT, Red and Black decals.	£20	GV ☐
vii)	1981	'NESTLES MILK' 'THE RICHEST IN CREAM' Livery.	Blue MB, Black CH and RF, Red wheels, WWT, Blue/Gold/Red decals, White letters.	£8-10	MPR ☐
			Light Grey roof (Australian Issue)	£15	GV ☐
viii)	1982	'CHIVERS & SONS LTD JAMS, JELLIES AND MARMALADES' Livery.	Cream MB and RF, Green CH, Red wheels, WWT, Green decal, Black "EST 1873".	Current	MPR ☐
ix)	1982	'WRIGHTS ORIGINAL COAL TAR SOAP' Livery.	Dark Brown MB, Beige chassis, RF and RD, Dark Brown and Cream decal. Gold (R) or Silver wheels.	Current	MPR ☐
x)	1983	'EVER READY BATTERIES FOR LIFE' Livery.	Dark Blue MB, White roof/Black CH, WWT, Orange/Blue/White decal. 1st issue Tan Seats 2nd issue Black Seats	Current	MPR ☐

Models of Yesteryear cont.

Y-6 (D)	1977	1920 Rolls Royce Fire Engine 'BOROUGH GREEN AND DISTRICT'.	Red MB, Black seats, Gold trim, Brown PLD, Gold PSPKW (12), Yellow LTS.	Current	MPR ☐
	1982	1st Colour Change.	Red MB with Red seats.	Current	MPR ☐
	1983	2nd Colour Change.	Red MB, Black seats, White PLD.	Current	MPR ☐
Y-7 (D)		No issue as yet.			
Y-8 (D)	1978	1945 MG TC.	Dark Green MB, Tan RF, Red S, Silver PSPKW (24), WH circle RN '3' in Black, SPW. 99 mm.	£7-£9	MPR ☐
	1979	1st Colour Change.	Dark Green MB, Beige roof and seats.	£5-£6	MPR ☐
	1981	2nd Colour Change.	Red MB, Red Rust roof, Black seats.	£6-£8	MPR ☐
	1982	3rd Colour Change.	Red MB, Dark Brown roof, Black seats.	Current	MPR ☐
	1983	4th Colour Change.	Blue MB. Black or Tan seats.	Current	MPR ☐

Models of Yesteryear
Gift Sets

Ref. No.			Contents	Rarity and Price Grading	
	1956-60	1st Gift Sets	These were issued in sets of 5 models made up from the first ten models to be issued (Y1(A)-Y10(A)) in mixed lots.	£225	GV □
G7	1961-63	Gift Set	Contains Y-2A 'B' Type Bus, Y-6A *Osram* Lorry, Y-10A Mercedes, Y-15A Rolls, Y-16A Spyker Pale Yellow.	£165	GV □
G6	1961-63	Gift Set.	Contains Y-6B Bugatti, Y-7B Mercer Raceabout, Y-15B Packard Victoria, Y-16A Spyker, Y-5B 4½ litre Bentley.	£85	GV □
G7	1961-63	Gift Set.	Contains Y-3A Tram, Y-4B Shand Mason Fire Engine, Y-11A Steam Roller, Y-12A Horse Bus, Y-13A *Santa Fe* Loco.	£250	GV □
G7	1963-66	Gift Set.	Contains Y-1B Model T Ford, Y-3 Benz, Y-11B Packard, Y-14B Maxwell.	£35-£45	MPR □
G5	1968	Gift Set.	Contains Y-4C Opel White, Y-6C Cadillac, Y-9B Simplex Yellow Green, Y-9B Simplex Green.	£28-£32	MPR □
G5	1970-72	Gift Set.	Contains Y-8C Stutz Red, Y-14 Maxwell, Y-16A Spyker (Dark Yellow), Y-7C Rolls Royce Silver and Red.	£22-27	MPR □
Y-50	1982	Gift Set.	Contains Y-3 BP Tanker, Y-5 Chivers, Y-10 Rolls Royce, Y-12 Model T, Y-13 Crossley Coal.	Current	MPR □

COLLECTORS NOTES

Page 102 70E. FERRARI 308 GTB.

1981 ✓
1982 ✓
1983

73B FERRARI Racing Cars

Page 103

75B " BERLINETTA.

COLLECTORS NOTES

CHAPTER 4

CORGI TOYS

i) INTRODUCTION

'THE ONES WITH WINDOWS'

Corgi gained its name and trade mark from the Welsh breed of dog because its manufacturers, Playcraft Toys Ltd, were situated in Swansea, South Wales, as were the Mettoy Company with whom they were to ultimately merge. Ever since the launch of the first Corgi Toys, all of which contained windows, the marketing strategy has been to produce superior models with unique and exciting features.

The following extract from the 1961 Catalogue illustrates the number of features first introduced by Corgi.

—the precision die-cast scale models with the all-star finish

The diagram shows many of the features which appear in Corgi Toys—not all of them, of course, in any one particular model. Those features marked with a star were first introduced by Corgi.

1 Jewelled head lights
2 Plated grille and bumpers
3 Opening bonnet revealing detailed engine
4 Steering wheel
5 Windows
6 Seats and internal panelling
7 Venetian blind
8 Opening boot revealing rear engine
9 Opening boot revealing spare wheel
10 Ruby rear lights
11 Self-adhesive accessories
12 Engine under automatically opening bonnet
13 Castored steering —self-centring
14 Glidamatic spring suspension
15 Two-tone colouring

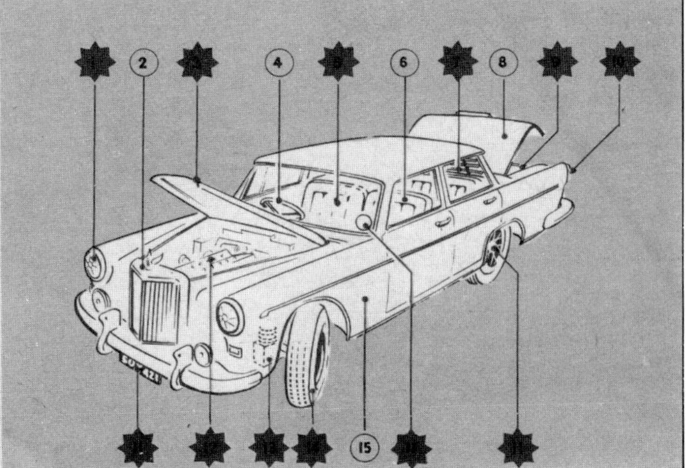

THE MODEL RANGE AND FEATURES

Apart from windows some of the early models were issued with a mechanical friction motor. Independent suspension was introduced from 1959 and was quickly followed in 1960 by the first die-cast model to have an opening bonnet.

The first production models were all based on real cars of the period. Similarly, with the launch of 'Corgi Major Toys' in 1959, models of real commercial vehicles were available; no doubt issued as Corgi's answer to the Dinky 'Supertoys' range.

During the sixties Corgi produced many very successful film and TV link up models. Probably the best remembered and most successful of these being the 'James Bond' Aston Martin which sold in huge quantities in the autumn of 1965. Indeed such was the popularity of the model that a version is still available at the time of publication.

It was also in 1965 that the superb 'Corgi Classics' range was introduced and what little beauties they were, incorporating a great range of real life features in perfect miniature.

Many heavy commercial vehicles were produced in the sixties and seventies again containing enormous detail and often working parts as well.

One particularly attractive model of the early sixties, which apparently did not sell well at the time, was the Midland Red Motorway Express Coach. The detailed interior even incorporated a toilet! Needless to say good examples of this model are highly sought after today by the bus collectors.

Similarly the 'Chipperfields Circus' collection of models were beautifully produced and are highly prized today.

As mentioned earlier Corgi Toys are famous for their innovations and in the late sixties they introduced 'Golden Jacks' which was a built-in jacking system which enabled models to have 'Take Off' wheels.

A further exciting feature was the introduction of 'Trans-O-Lite' whereby light rays were captured and fed through glass tubes to illuminate the headlights.

The seventies saw 'WHIZZWHEELS' and the slightly larger scale of $^1/_{42}$ being introduced.

No commentary on the Corgi range would be complete without talking about a market strategy unique to Corgi — launching a replica model car simultaneously with the real car.

To date simultaneous launches have occurred with Austin Metro, Ford Escort, Triumph Acclaim, Ford Sierra and the MG Maestro 1600, which is a unique record. Corgi were the first die-cast manufacturers to introduce the dimensions of light, sound and movement into their models by using the micro-chip in their 'Corgitronic' range. The models 'come alive', for example by just pushing down on the rear axle or, in the case of the Road Repair Unit, by pressing the workman to activate the pneumatic drill sound. Some models such as the Sonic Corgi Truck Set are activated by a remote controlled handset which controls the movements of forward, stop, reverse and swinging round.

1983 has seen the introduction of the most-advanced electronic features so far — the new MG Maestro 1600 with working headlights and brake lights.

The most exciting category in the current range is the 'Corgi Cars of the 50's' series. These superbly engineered models contain unusual and detailed features combined with all the nostalgia associated with the elegant models of the fifties and are highly collectable.

Bus collectors have not been forgotten either for the early eighties has seen the Corgi range greatly enhanced by the issue of an attractive range of Routemaster Buses.

Corgi have come a long way since they were launched 'WITH WINDOWS'. The advent of the micro chip and its introduction into the Corgi range is very much in keeping with the Company's marketing strategy of producing superior models.

STOP PRESS 31st OCTOBER 1983

Announcement made that the Mettoy Company plc had asked its bankers to call in the receivers. The business would continue for a few months in the hope that a buyer could be found.

ii) PACKAGING

1

1st Small model design 1958

2

1st 'Major' Box design 1960 approx.

3

Special Window Box for 'Bertie Wooster'

4

Normal 'Classic Series' Box

5

Later All Card 'Major' Box

6

1969-71 (approx)

7

The coloured line window box of the seventies

8

The latest design

'CORGI' models available at Toyfairs

Corgi Classics 1965-69
9002 Bentley 1927 Tourer.

No. 273. Rolls Royce Silver Shadow
with 'Golden Jacks' — 1970 only.

No. 321. 1966 Monte Carlo Rally Mini-Cooper.
No. 227. BMC Morris Mini-Cooper competition car, 1962-65.

No. 441. Volkswagen Van
'Trans 'O' Lite' opening on roof.

No. 302. Hillman Hunter.
One of many excellent Corgi Rally Cars.

No. 1142. The highly detailed 'Holmes Wrecker'.

Gift Set 37.
Lotus Racing Team Set, 1967-69.

No. 469. Routemaster.
Promotional Issue — one of the first of many.

iii) MODEL IDENTIFICATION

The compiler has endeavoured to show the major identifying features in respect of each model.

Common Features

Many models have common features and these are shown below to avoid unnecessary repitition.

a. Base Plates

The early base plates were mostly all of the tinplate variety until about 1960 when they changed to a more realistic diecast type of chassis which became increasingly detailed. The later plastic chassis are indicated where applicable as (PCH).

b. Wheel Hubs

Prior to about 1961 wheel hubs were plain and smooth. After this date they became contoured and more realistic in appearance.

c. Mechanical

All the early Corgi Toys were produced in either the normal form or there was a mechanical friction type flywheel version. The only exceptions being the sports cars and trucks which could not be converted to take the flywheel. The mechanical versions were not all that popular and were phased out in 1959.

d. Model Number and Name

It has been assumed that all models have the name of the model on the base plate or chassis. Unlike Dinky Toys the model numbers are not shown on all models which can make unboxed models a little difficult to categorize at times.

e. Windows

It goes without saying that all vehicles are assumed to have windows.

f. Construction Materials

All models assumed to be comprised at least in part of a diecast alloy.

g. Corgi Toys

All models have the name shown on the body.

iv) ABBREVIATIONS — EXAMPLE OF USE

CARS OF THE 50's SERIES MODEL

C803 1983 1952 Jaguar XK 120 124 mm.
'Coupes Des Alpes'

Abbreviations

Cream body, Grey/Black tonneau. RN 56 in Blue Black on BN and doors. CF/PP/BS/WS/OBB/DI/SS/RE/SPKW.

Non Abbreviated Form

Cream Body, Grey and Black Tonneau, Rally Number 56 in Blue Black on Bonnet and Doors. Competition Finish, Plated Parts, Bonnet Strap, Windscreen, Opening Bonnet and Boot, Detailed Interior, Suspension, Rally Emblems, Spoke Wheels.

Collectors Notes

Corgi Toys
4a i) Saloons Estates and Sports Cars

Ref. No.		Model Type	Model Features and Size	Rarity and Price Grading		
200	1956-61	Ford Consul	Cream or two tone Green body, OC. 90 mm.	£15	NC	☐
200 M	1956-59	Ford Consul	Blue or Green body, FWM. 90 mm.	£18	NC	☐
C200	1976-78	B.L.M. Mini 1000	Blue/Silver body, Red and White arrow. 85 mm.	Current	MPR	☐
201	1956-63	Austin Cambridge	Blue or Cream body, OC/SDL/RB. 90 mm.	£15	NC	☐
201 M	1956-59	Austin Cambridge	Cream or Grey body, FWM. 90 mm.	£18	NC	☐
202	1956-60	Morris Cowley	Cream or Green body. 91 mm.	£15	NC	☐
202 M	1956-59	Morris Cowley	Cream/Green/Grey body, FWM. 91 mm.	£18	NC	☐
202	1970-72	Renault R16	Blue/Silver body. 91 mm.	Current	MPR	☐
203	1956-60	Vauxhall Velox	Red or Cream or Red/Cream. 91 mm.	£18	NC	☐
203 M	1956-59	Vauxhall Velox	Red or Yellow body, FWM. 91 mm.	£21	NC	☐
203	1971-72	De Tomaso Mangusta	Green/Gold body, WZW. 99 mm.	Current	MPR	☐
204	1956-60	Rover 90	White or Bronze body. 97 mm.	£18	NC	☐
204 M	1956-59	Rover 90	Green or Grey body, FWM. 97 mm.	£22	NC	☐
204	1972-74	Morris Mini Minor	Dark Blue or Orange body, WZW. 73 mm.	Current	MPR	☐
205	1956-61	Riley Pathfinder	Red or Blue body. 97 mm.	£19	NC	☐
205 M	1956-59	Riley Pathfinder	Red or Blue body, FWM. 97 mm.	£22	NVE	☐
206	1956-60	Hillman Husky Estate	Tan or Blue/Silver body. 86 mm.	£15	NC	☐
206 M	1956-59	Hillman Husky Estate	Cream or Blue body, FWM. 86 mm.	£17	NC	☐
207	1957-62	Standard Vanguard III	White/Red or Green/Red body. 95 mm.	£15	NC	☐
207 M	1957-59	Standard Vanguard III	Yellow or Green/Red body, FWM. 95 mm.	£18	NC	☐
208	1957-60	Jaguar 2.4 litre. 95 mm.	White body, S/SW/No SS/WS. 95 mm.	£15	NC	☐
208 M	1957-59	Jaguar 2.4 litre	Dark Blue body, S/SW/No SS/WS/FWM. 95 mm.	£18	NVE	☐
208S	1960-62	Jaguar 2.4 litre	Blue or White body, S/SW/SS/WS. 95 mm.	£15	NC	☐
210	1957-60	Citroen DS19	Red/Yellow body, LHD/No SS/SW/S. 97 mm.	£15	NC	☐
210S	1960-65	Citroen DS19	Green/Black body, LHD/SS/SW/S. 97 mm.	£7-£9	MPR	☐
211	1958-60	Studebaker Golden Hawk	Blue/Gold body, LHD/No SS. 104 mm.	£15	NC	☐
211 M	1958-59	Studebaker Golden Hawk	White/Gold body, LHD/No SS. 104 mm.	£18	NC	☐
211S	1960-65	Studebaker Golden Hawk	Blue/Gold body, LHD/SS. 104 mm.	£8-£10	MPR	☐
214	1959-62	Ford Thunderbird	Green/Cream body, LHD/No SS. 102 mm.	£15	NC	☐
214 M	1959 only	Ford Thunderbird	Pink/Black body, LHD/No SS. 102 mm.	£19	NVE	☐
214 S	1962-65	Ford Thunderbird	Green/Cream body, LHD/SS. 102 mm.	£8-£10	MPR	☐
215	1959-62	Thunderbird Open Sports	White body, LHD/No SS. 102 mm.	£14	NC	☐
215S	1962-65	Thunderbird Open Sports	White body, LHD/SS. 102 mm.	£11	MPR	☐
216	1959-62	Austin A40	Two tone Blue body. 86 mm.	£15	NC	☐
216 M	1959 only	Austin A40	Two tone Blue body. 86 mm.	£19	NVE	☐
217	1960-63	Fiat 1800 Saloon	Two tone Blue/Silver body. 95 mm.	£5-£7	MPR	☐
218	1960-62	Aston Martin DB4	Red or Yellow body, OBN/SS/DE. 95 mm.	£8-£10	MPR	☐
219	1959-62	Plymouth Suburban	Brown/Cream body, LHD/S/SW. 104 mm.	£9-£12	MPR	☐
220	1960-62	Chevrolet Impala	Pink or Blue body, LHD/SS/S/SW. 108 mm.	£9-£12	MPR	☐
222	1959-60	Renault Floride	Dark Red body, S/SW/WDS/No SS. 91 mm.	£9-£12	MPR	☐
222	1960-65	Renault Floride	Blue or Green body, OC/S/SW/SS. 91 mm.	£4-£6	MPR	☐
224	1961-66	Bentley Continental	Blue/Silver body, OC/PP/SL/DSPW/SCS/S/OBT. 108 mm.	£11-£14	MPR	☐
225	1961-66	Austin 7 Saloon	Red body, WDS/SS/S/SW. 73 mm.	Current	MPR	☐
226	1960-71	Morris Mini Minor	Blue or Maroon body, SS/S/SW. 73 mm.	Current	MPR	☐
228	1962-66	Volvo P 1800	Gold or Red body, LHD/SL/SW/SS. 95 mm.	Current	MPR	☐

Saloons, Estates and Sports Cars cont.

229	1961-66	Chevrolet Corvair	Blue or Gold body, LHD/OEC/SS/SW. 97 mm.	Current	MPR
230	1962-64	M-Benz 220 SE Coupe	Red body, SS/OBT/SPW. 102 mm.	£7-£9	MPR
231	1961-65	Triumph Herald	Blue/White body, SS/SW/OBT/DE. 90 mm.	£5-£7	MPR
232	1961-65	Fiat 2100	Red/Yellow body, OC/SS/SL/VB/S/SW. 95 mm.	£6-£8	MPR
233	1962-72	Heinkel Trojan	Yellow, Blue or Red body, S/SW/SS. 64 mm.	£4-£6	MPR
234	1961-64	Ford Consul Classic	Brown/Pink body, S/SW/SS/OBN/DE. 95 mm.	£5-£7	MPR
235	1962-66	Oldsmobile Super 88	Steel Blue/White body, S/SW/SS. 108 mm.	£4-£6	MPR
236	1964-69	'CORGI DSC' Austin A60	Blue body D/PS/SS/STC/DI. 95 mm.	£7-£9	MPR
238	1962-67	Mk 10 Jaguar	Blue or GRN body, DE/OBB/LG/BOFL. 108 mm.	£8-£11	MPR
239	1963-68	VW 1500 Karmann Ghia	Red body, OBT/SS/LG/SPW. 91 mm.	£3-£5	MPR
240	1963-65	Fiat 600 Jolly	Blue body, DRF/SS/D/PS/WS/PP/SW. 79 mm.	£3-£5	MPR
241	1963-69	Chrysler Ghia L64	Green body, OC/DE/TS/SS/OBT/DD/RVM/PP. 108 mm.	£5-£7	MPR
242	1965-66	Fiat 600 Jolly	Yellow body, SS/D/PS no canopy. 79 mm.	£4-£6	MPR
245	1964-68	Buick Riviera	Gold or Blue body, OC/TOL/PP/SS/SPKW. 108 mm.	£7-£9	MPR
246	1965-68	Chrysler Imperial	Red body, OC D/PS golf clubs ODBB/SPKW. 108 mm.	£4-£6	MPR
247	1964-69	Mercedes Benz Pullman	Met Maroon body, WSW/OWD/DD/PP/SS. 121 mm.	£5-£7	MPR
248	1965-67	Chevrolet Impala	Brown/White body, LHD/SS/PP. 108 mm.	£4-£6	MPR
249	1965-68	Morris Mini-Cooper	Black/Red body, Wickerwork panels. 73 mm.	£4-£6	MPR
251	1963-66	Hillman Imp	Blue or Bronze body, OWD/LG. 83 mm.	£4-£6	MPR
252	1963-66	Rover 2000	Blue or Maroon body, SS/SL. 95 mm.	£6-£8	MPR
253	1964-68	Mercedes 220 SE Coupe	Met Maroon or Blue body, SS/OBT/LG/SPW. 121 mm.	£4-£6	MPR
255	1964-68	Motor School A60	Same as 236 only LHD	£6-£8	MPR
259	1966-69	Citroën 'LE DANDY'	Blue or Maroon body, ODBN/SL/TS/SPKW. 102 mm.	£5-£7	MPR
260	1969	Renault 16 TS	Met Maroon body, OBNHB/SPW/AS. 91 mm.	£5-£7	MPR
262	1967-69	Lincoln Continental	Gold/Black body, ODBB/BOCTV/SL/IS/CPT. 149 mm.	£22	GV
263	1966-69	Marlin Rambler Sports	Red/Black body, OD/SS/SPKW/H. 102 mm.	£6-£8	MPR
264	1966-69	Oldsmobile Toronado	Blue body, SL/PP/SPKW. 108 mm.	£4-£6	MPR
271	1969	Ghia 500 Mangusta	Blue/White/Yellow body, LOB/WZW. 97 mm.	£4-£6	MPR
273	1970	Rolls Royce Silver Shadow	Silver/Blue body, GJ/TOW/SPW/PP. 120 mm.	£30	NVE
274	1970-72	Bentley T Series	Red body, ODBN/SL/DD/DE/PP/WZW. 120 mm.	£10	NC
275	1968-70	Rover 2000 TC	Green body, TP roof/GJ/TOW/SPW opens. 95 mm.	£4-£6	MPR
C275	1981-	Mini Metro	Red body, Yellow interior OC/ODHB. 94 mm.	Current	MPR
C276	1982-	Triumph Acclaim	Metallic Blue body, STC. 120 mm.	Current	MPR
276	1968-70	Oldsmobile Toronada	Plum or Gold body, GJ/TOW/SL. 108 mm.	£4-£6	MPR
C278	1982-	Triumph Acclaim DSC	Yellow/Black body, STC. 118 mm.	Current	MPR
C279	1979-	Rolls Royce Corniche	Met Maroon or Yellow body, DE/ODBB/TS. 144 mm.	Current	MPR
C280	1970-78	Rolls Royce Silver Shadow	Gold body, ODBB/SL/DD/DE/PP/WZW. 120 mm.	Current	MPR
281	1971-73	Rover 2000 TC	Met Purple/Silver body, clear roof/WZW. 95 mm.	£3-£5	MPR
283	1971-74	'DAF CITY' car	Brown/Black body, WZW/SL/ODBN/TS. 73 mm.	Current	MPR
C284	1970-76	Citroen S.M.	Lilac or Yellow body, PP/ODT/WZW. 112 mm.	Current	MPR
C285	1975-81	Mercedes-Benz 240 D	Silver or Met Blue body, WZW/H. 127 mm.	Current	MPR
C286	1975-79	Jaguar XJC V-12	Blue/Black or Red/Black, ODBT/WZW/H. 127 mm.	Current	MPR
C287	1975-78	Citroen Dyane	Green/Black body, ORD/WZW/duck decal. 115 mm.	Current	MPR
C288	1975-79	Minissima	Green and Cream body, ODBN. 63 mm.	Current	MPR
C289	1977-81	Volkswagen Polo	Green body, ODHB. 97 mm.	Current	MPR
291	1977-78	AMC Pacer	Met Maroon body, LHD/ODHB. 118 mm.	Current	MPR
C293	1977	Renault 5TS	Yellow body, Black trim, ODHB. 97 mm.	Current	MPR
C294	1980	Renault 5TS Alpine	Black body, White stripe, ODHB. 97 mm.	Current	MPR
C299	1982	Ford Sierra 2.3 Ghia	Met Blue body, White int., ODHB/HPS. 124 mm.	Current	MPR
300	1956-63	Austin Healey 100-4	Red/Cream body, PWS/SWCI/DI. 86 mm.	£11-£14	MPR
300	1970-72	Corvette Stingray	Maroon/Black body, OC/SPW/LG/VD/GJ/TOW. 102 mm.	£4-£6	MPR
301	1956-59	Triumph TR2	Cream or Green body, PWS/SWCI/DI. 86 mm.	£15	NC
301	1970-73	Iso Grifo 7 litre	Blue/Black body, ODBN/WZW/SL. 102 mm.	Current	MPR
302	1957-64	MG 'A'	Red/Cream or Green/Cream body, WS/DI/SW. 90 mm.	£12	NC
303	1958-60	M-Benz 300 SL Open	Blue/White body, OC/LHD/PWS/No SS/SW. 95 mm.	£8-£10	MPR
303 S	1961-66	M-Benz 300 SL Open	Blue/White body, OC/LHD/PWS/SS/SW. 95 mm.	£7-£9	MPR
304	1959-61	M-Benz 300 SL Hard Top	Yellow or Yellow/Red body, No SS/SPKW.	£8-£11	MPR
304	1971-73	Chevrolet Camaro	Green/Black or Blue/White body, DRF/SL. 102 mm.	£4-£5	MPR

Saloons, Estates and Sports Cars cont.

305	1960-62	Triumph TR3	Light Green or Cream body, PWS/No SS. 86 mm.	£20	GV	☐
305S	1962-64	Triumph TR3	Light Green or Cream body, PWS/SS. 86 mm.	£17	NC	☐
306	1971-73	Morris Marina 1.8 Coupe	Maroon or Green, ODBN/WZW. 98 mm.	Current	MPR	☐
307	1962-64	'E' Type Jaguar	Red or Met Grey body, Red RHT. 95 mm.	£16	NC	☐
310	1963-68	Chevrolet Stingray	Red or Silver body, SL/SS/PP/SPKW. 90 mm.	£5-£7	MPR	☐
C311	1970-72	Ford Capri V6	Red/Black body, OD/SS/WZW. 102 mm.	£4-£5	MPR	☐
312	1971-73	Marcos Mantis	Met Plum body, OC/OD/SPKW. 110 mm.	Current	MPR	☐
313	1970-73	Ford Cortina GXL	Blue/Black body, OD, Graham Hill fig. 102 mm.	£4-£6	MPR	☐
C314	1976-79	Fiat X1-9	Green or Silver body, OEC/SS/H. 110 mm.	Current	MPR	☐
C314	1982-	Supercat Jaguar XJS-HE	Black body, Red interior, OD. 118 mm.	Current	MPR	☐
C315	1976-78	Lotus Elite	Red/Black body, OD/SS. 120 mm.	Current	MPR	☐
316	1963-66	NSU Sport Prinz	Plum body, S/SW/SS. 86 mm.	£5-£7	MPR	☐
318	1965-68	Lotus Elan	Blue or Green/Yellow body, TS/SS/OBN/OWDS. 90 mm.	£5-£7	MPR	☐
319	1978-82	Jaguar XJS	Met Plum/Black body, OD/SS. 128 mm	Current	MPR	☐
320	1965-67	Ford Mustang Fastback	Met Blue or Green body, OD/SL/SS/CP/OWDS. 95 mm.	£5-£7	MPR	☐
321	1978-82	Porsche 924 Saloon.	Green or Red body, *Porsche* ODHB/H. 118 mm.	Current	MPR	☐
324	1966-69	Marcos Volvo 1800GT.	White/Green body, OD/DE/SPKW/SS. 91 mm.	£5-£7	MPR	☐
325	1981-	Chevrolet Caprice.	Met Gold body ODBT/WWT. 150 mm.	Current	MPR	☐
327	1967-68	MGB GT.	Red body OBT/TS/SPKW. 90 mm.	£11-£14	MPR	☐
329	1980-	Opel Senator.	Purple or Gold body, OD. 142 mm.	Current	MPR	☐
332	1967-69	Lancia Fulvia Sports.	Met Blue, OC/ODBN/TS/SS/DE. 91 mm.	£5-£7	MPR	☐
334	1968-70	Mini Magnifique.	Green or Blue body, Red RF/ODBN/PLE. 73 mm.	£4-£6	MPR	☐
C334	1981-	Ford Escort 1.3GL.	Steel Blue or Red body, OD/SS. 112 mm.	Current	MPR	☐
335	1968-69	Jaguar 4.2 litre.	Blue body TS/SPKW/PP/ODBNHB. 108 mm.	£7-£9	MPR	☐
338	1968-70	Chevrolet SS350.	Yellow/Black body, RHT/SS/WS/GJ/TOW. 102 mm.	£5-£7	MPR	☐
C338	1980-	Rover 3500.	Blue/Silver body, ODBNHB/WDS/SS.	Current	MPR	☐
341	1968-70	Mini Marcos GT850.	Maroon body, ODBNHB/HLS/GJ/TOW. 86 mm.	£4-£6	MPR	☐
342	1969-72	Lamborghini Muira.	Red body, RWS/OEC/WW or GJ/TOW/OBN. 95 mm.	£5-£7	MPR	☐
343	1969-73	Pontiac Firebird.	Silver/Black body, OD/TS/PP/GJ/TOW. 102 mm.	£4-£6	MPR	☐
343	1980-	Ford Capri 3 litre.	Yellow/Black body, 'S' Stripe ODHB. 124 mm.	Current	MPR	☐
C345	1981-	Honda Prelude.	Met Blue/Black body, ORF/OD/SR. 114 mm.	Current	MPR	☐
C346	1982-	Citroen 2CV.	Yellow or Maroon/Black body, OBN/SR. 108 mm.	Current	MPR	☐
347	1969-74	Chevrolet Astro.	Blue or Gold body, WS/WZW/2PS. 102 mm.	Current	MPR	☐
372	1970-72	Lancia Fulvia.	Red/Black body, ODBN/WZW/SS. 91 mm.	Current	MPR	☐
C373	1981-	Peugeot 505.	Metallic Gold body, SS/OD. 127 mm.	Current	MPR	☐
374	1970-76	Jaguar 'E' Type.	Red or Yellow body, TTEC/WZW. 108 mm.	£7-£9	MPR	☐
375	1970-72	Toyota 2000GT.	Blue or Purple body, A/WS/WZW. 102 mm.	Current	MPR	☐
377	1970-73	Marcos 3 litre.	Yellow/Black body, OEC/DE/SS/WZW. 91 mm.	Current	MPR	☐
378	1970-72	MGC GT.	Red/Black body, ODHB/WZW. 90 mm.	£12-£15	MPR	☐
C378	1982-	Ferrari 308GTS.	Red body, pop up HL/OEC. 115 mm.	Current	MPR	☐
380	1970-74	Alfa Romeo P33.	White/Black body, AF/WZW. 95 mm.	Current	MPR	☐
381	1970-74	VW Beach Buggy.	Yellow/MRN body, 2SKIS/WZW/DR. 95 mm.	Current	MPR	☐
382	1970-75	Porsche Targa 911S.	Met Blue or GRN, BLK RF/WZW. 95 mm.	Current	MPR	☐
C382	1981-	Lotus Elite 2.2.	Blue body, *Elite 22* OD/NP. 120 mm.	Current	MPR	☐
383	1971-73	Bertone Barchetta.	Yellow body, Black interior. AF/WZW. 83 mm.	Current	MPR	☐
384	1970-73	Adams Brothers Probe.	Met Maroon body, OC/WZW/TTWDS/OD. 97 mm.	Current	MPR	☐
386	1971-73	Bertone Barchetta.	Yellow body, Black interior and trim, AF/WZW. 83 mm.	Current	MPR	☐
387	1970-73	Chevrolet Corvette.	Red/Blue body, OC/RHL/DR/OBN/WZW. 102 mm.	Current	MPR	☐
388	1970-74	M-Benz C111.	Orange/Black body, WZW. 104 mm.	Current	MPR	☐
389	1971-74	Reliant Bond Bug 700ES.	Green *Bug* raised HL/body lifts. 67 mm.	£5-£7	MPR	☐
391	1971-73	Ford Mustang Mach 1.	Red/Black body, OD/PP/WZW. 113 mm.	Current	MPR	☐
392	1973-74	Bertone Shake Buggy.	Yellow body, OC/DE/PP/flag. 89 mm.	Current	MPR	☐
C393	1972-79	M-Benz 350SL.	Metallic Blue body, ODBN/SPKW/PP. 102 mm.	Current	MPR	☐
394	1973-76	Datsun 240Z.	Red/Black body, non rally version. 102 mm.	Current	MPR	☐
C400	1975-77	VW 1200DSC.	Blue body, STC, *Corgi MSC.* 92 mm.	Current	MPR	☐
424	1961-65	Ford Zephyr Estate.	Two Tone Blue, SS/WDS/MLG. 97 mm.	£8-£11	MPR	☐
440	1966-67	Ford Cortina Estate.	Blue/Brown, SL/OTG/SS/2 figs/Golf EQ. 95 mm.	£7-£9	MPR	☐
485	1966-69	Mini Countryman.	Blue, 2 Red Surfboards/RR/fig. 79 mm.	£4-£6	MPR	☐
491	1967-69	Ford Cortina Estate.	Red or Blue, a revised 440. 95 mm.	£5-£7	MPR	☐

Saloons, Estates and Sports Cars cont.

Gift Sets

Ref. No.		Model Type	Model Features and Size	Rarity and Price Grading		
1	1957-62	Carrimore Transporter and 4 Cars.	Contained 4 British Cars plus 1101 in 1957 and 4 U.S. in 1959. 4 various in 1962.	£65	NC	☐
C1	1983	Ford Sierra Set.	(299) Blue body with Blue/Cream Caravan.	Current	MPR	☐
10	1968-69	Camping Gift Set.	263 with RR/2 Canoes and 109.	£11-£14	MPR	☐
C12	1981-	Glider and TRL Set.	345 plus TRL and glider.	Current	MPR	☐
13	1969-72	Renault 16 Film Unit.	WH/BLK, *Tour De France* cyclist.	£11-£14	MPR	☐
C13	1981	Tour De France Set.	373 plus 3 figs, 4 bikes.	Current	MPR	☐
20	1961	Golden Guinea Set.	Contains Gold plated 224, 229, 234.	£40	GV	☐
20	1970-72	Transporter and 6 Cars.	Contains 1146 plus 6 cars.	£25-£32	MPR	☐
24	1976-	Mercedes and Caravan Set.	Contains 285 and 490 with colour change 1980.	Current	MPR	☐
25	1963-66	BP or Shell Garage Set.	Contains Garage, 5 various cars plus figs and ACCS.	£55	GV	☐
26	1971-75	Beach Buggy Set.	381 plus Sailing Boat.	£4-£6	MPR	☐
28	1963-66	Transporter and 4 Cars.	Contains 1105, 222, 230, 232, 234.	£35	NC	☐
31	1965-68	Buick Boat Set.	Contains (245) plus TRL and boat.	£9-£12	MPR	☐
36	1967-70	Marlin Rambler Set.	Contains (263) plus boat.	£8-£11	MPR	☐
36	1967-70	Oldsmobile Set.	Contains (276) plus boat/TRL/3 figs.	£10-£12	MPR	☐
37	1979-82	Fiat X19 Set.	Fiat X19 plus boat *Carlsberg*.	Current	MPR	☐
38	1977-78	Mini Camping Set.	Mini plus 2 figs/tent/barbecue.	Current	MPR	☐
C38	1980-	Jaguar XJS Set.	319 plus powerboat or TRL.	Current	MPR	☐
48	1966-69	Transporter and 6 Cars.	1138 plus 6 various cars.	£33	NC	☐

COLLECTORS NOTES

Page 140 C378 Ferrari 308 GTS

CORGI

4aii) CARS OF THE 50's SERIES

The appeal of this range is based on several factors. Firstly the parents of today remember with nostalgia the famous cars of their childhood and the toy company which brought them models "with windows". Combine these factors with the selection of elegant models with unusual features, engineered superbly in detail and construction and you have the most exciting category in the present Corgi range. All the four new models issued in 1983 appear in a new brown box designed to emphasise the elegance of the models inside.

No. 801. Ford Thunderbird with pre "Cars of the 50's" packaging.
No. 802. Mercedes 300SL also similarly issued in Red prior to becoming one of the set in Silver. Both the cars re-numbered to 810 and 811 respectively, in the "Cars of the 50's" Series.

"Cars of the 50's" Set, plus at the top 'Dan Tanner' of 'Vegas' in his special issue Ford Thunderbird box. Notice the special boxes used for this series and the Gull wing doors on the Mercedes 300SL.

C801	1982	1957 Ford Thunderbird.	White body with Tan hood, PP/SPW/LHD/WWT/OBB/TW/WS/SS. 132 mm.	Current	MPR ☐
C802	1982	1954 Mercedes 300SL.	Burgundy body, OD/SS/DI/PP. 126 mm.	Current	MPR ☐
C803	1983	1952 Jaguar XK120 Soft Top Sports	Red body, Black hood, PP/SPKW/OBB/SS/DI. 124 mm.	Current	MPR ☐
C804	1983	1952 Jaguar XK120. 'Coupes Des Alpes'.	Cream body, Grey/Black tonneau, RN '56' in Blue/Black on BN and doors, CF/PP/BS/WS/OBB/DI/SS/RE/SPKW. 124 mm.	Current	MPR ☐
C805	1983	1956 Mercedes 300SC Cabriolet.	Black body, Tan hood, PP/SS/WDS/OBB.	Current	MPR ☐
C806	1983	1956 Mercedes 300SL Open Roadster.	Black body, Grey/Black folded hood, SS/OBB/PP.	Current	MPR ☐
C810	1983	1957 Ford Thunderbird.	Yellow body, Black hood, SPW/LHD/WWT/OBB/TW/SS. 132 mm.	Current	MPR ☐
C811	1982	1954 Mercedes SL.	All Silver body, ODBN/PP/SS/DI/LHD. 127 mm.	Current	MPR ☐

4b Racing, Rally and Speed Cars

Ref. No.		Model Type	Model Features and Size	Rarity and Price Grading		
150	1957-61	Vanwell Racing Car.	Green body, RN '25' No SS/WS/No D. 91 mm.	£14-£16	MPR	☐
150S	1961-65	Vanwell Racing Car.	Green body, RN '25' D/WS/SS. 91 mm.	£9-£11	MPR	☐
150	1972-74	Surtees TS9 Formula 1.	Blue body, RN '16' BL/WH/ DH. 116 mm.	£4-£6	MPR	☐
151	1958-60	Lotus XI Racing Car.	White body, RN '3' WS/No D/No SS. 83 mm.	£11-£14	MPR	☐
151S	1961-63	Lotus XI Racing Car.	Blue body, RN '3' WS/D/SS. 83 mm.	£11-£14	MPR	☐
C151	1974-76	'YARDLEY' Mclaren M19A.	White body, RN '55', Red/White DH. 112 mm.	Current	MPR	☐
152	1958-61	BRM Racing Car.	Green body, RN '3' No SS/WS. 91 mm.	£13-£16	MPR	☐
152S	1961-65	BRM Racing Car.	Green body, RN '3' SS/WS. 91 mm.	£13-£16	MPR	☐
C152	1974-76	Ferrari 312B2	Red body, RN '5' Blue/White DH. 104 mm.	Current	MPR	☐
153	1960-62	Bluebird Record Car.	Blue body, GB/US flags on nose, MW. 127 mm.	£17	NC	☐
153A	1961-65	Bluebird Record Car.	Blue body, GB/US flags on nose, PW. 127 mm.	£14	NC	☐
153	1963-65	Team Surtees TS9B.	Red/Black/White body, RN '26' WS. 112 mm.	£4-£6	MPR	☐
154	1963-72	Ferrari Formula 1.	Red/Silver body, RN '36' D/WS. 91 mm.	Current	MPR	☐
C154	1974-78	'JOHN PLAYER SPECIAL' Lotus.	Black/Gold body, RN '1', *Firestone.* 130 mm.	Current	MPR	☐
C154	1979-82	'TEXACO' Special Lotus.	Black/Gold body, RN '1', *Goodyear.* 130 mm.	Current	MPR	☐
155	1965-68	Lotus Climax Racing Car.	Green Yellow body, RN '4' RCD/DS/RUM/SS/EX/PP. 90 mm.	£5-£6	MPR	☐
C155	1974-76	'SHADOW' F1 Racing Car.	Black body, RN '17' D/WS. 90 mm.	Current	MPR	☐
156	1967-69	Cooper Maserati Racing Car.	Blue body, RN '7' White D/WS. 90 mm.	£4-£5	MPR	☐
C156	1974-76	Graham Hill's Shadow.	White/Red body, RN '12' RCD, *Embassy Racing.* 132 mm.	Current	MPR	☐
158	1969-72	Lotus Climax Racing Car.	Red/White body, RN '8' RCD/WS/SS. 90 mm.	£3-£4	MPR	☐
C158	1975-77	Elf Tyrrell Ford F1.	Blue body, RN '1', *Elf,* RCD. 110 mm.	Current	MPR	☐
159	1969-72	Cooper Maserati.	Yellow/White body, RN '3' RCD/DCST. 90 mm.	£3-£4	MPR	☐
C159	1974-76	Indianapolis Racing Car.	Red body, RN '20', Racing Driver. 130 mm.	Current	MPR	☐
C160	1976-78	Hesketh 308 F1.	WH/Red/Blue, RN '24', Blue DH. 130 mm.	Current	MPR	☐
161	1971-73	Santa Pod 'COMMUTER' Dragster.	Red/Silver body, RN '2' VJ/SS/PP/SPKW/WZW. 123 mm.	Current	MPR	☐
161	1977	'ELF-TYRRELL — Project 34	Blue/White body, RN '3' AF/RCD, *Good Year.* 113 mm.	Current	MPR	☐
162	1971-72	'QUARTERMASTER' Dragster.	Green and White body, AF/RCD/PW. 146 mm.	Current	MPR	☐
C163	1971-76	Santa Pod 'GLO-WORM' Dragster.	White/Blue body, LOB/VADS/RCD/PW. 113 mm.	Current	MPR	☐
164	1972-75	Ison Bros 'WILD HONEY' Dragster.	Yellow/Red body, *Jaguar,* WZW. 171 mm.	Current	MPR	☐
165	1974-76	Adams Brothers Dragster.	Orange/Yellow body, 4E/32EX/RCD/WZW. 113 mm.	Current	MPR	☐
166	1971-74	Ford Mustang 'ORGAN GRINDER'.	Yellow/Green body, RN '39' TW/RCD. 102 mm.	Current	MPR	☐
C167	1973-74	U.S.A. Racing Buggy.	White/Red body, RN '7' RCD/PS/SPW/U.S. flag. 95 mm.	£3-£4	MPR	☐
C169	1974-76	Starfighter Jet Dragster.	Blue/Silver/Red body, *Firestone.* 155 mm.	Current	MPR	☐
C170	1974-76	John Woolfe's 208 Dragster.	Blue/Yellow body, *Radio Luxembourg,* RCD. 146 mm.	Current	MPR	☐
190	1974-76	'JOHN PLAYER SPECIAL' Lotus.	Black/Gold body, RN '1', *Texaco,* AF/RCD/TOW. 270 mm.	Current	MPR	☐
191	1974-77	'TEXACO MARLBORO' Mclaren.	White/Red body, RN '5', VADS/AF/TOW. 245 mm.	Current	MPR	☐

Racing, Rally and Speed Cars cont.

No.	Years	Model	Description	Price	
C201	1979-82	Mini 1000 'TEAM CORGI'.	Metallic Silver body, RN '8', VADS. 85 mm.	Current	MPR ☐
227	1962-63	Mini Cooper Rally.	Blue/White body, OC, RN '3', 2 flags. 73 mm.	£5-£7	MPR ☐
256	1971-74	VW Safari Rally.	Red body, RN '18', STC/ODBN/rhino. 91 mm.	£9-£12	MPR ☐
C281	1982-	'DATAPOST' Metro.	Blue/White body, RN '77', VADS/ODHB. 94 mm.	Current	MPR ☐
282	1971-74	Mini Cooper Rally.	White/Black body, RN '177', WZW/ODBN/SL. 73 mm.	£3-£4	MPR ☐
C291	1982	M-Benz 'EURO RALLY' 240.	Cream/Black body, SPW/RR/HG/SP/ODBT. 127 mm.	Current	MPR ☐
C300	1979-82	Ferrari 'DAYTONA'.	Green with MLCD flash, RN '5', OD. 120 mm.	Current	MPR ☐
C301	1979-82	Lotus Elite Racing Car.	Yellow/Red body, *Ferodo*. 120 mm.	Current	MPR ☐
302	1964-70	Hillman Hunter Rally.	Blue/Black, GJ/TOW/HG/2DSPW/VADS/TB/K. 104 mm.	£6-£7	MPR ☐
C302	1979-82	VW Polo.	Met Brown/Red, RN '4', VADS/OHB. 97 mm.	Current	MPR ☐
303	1970-72	Roger Clarks Capri.	White, RN '73', OD/WZW/VADS. 102 mm.	£3-£4	MPR ☐
C303	1980-	Porsche 924 Racer.	Yellow/Black, RN '2', *Firelli,* ODHB. 118 mm.	Current	MPR ☐
304S	1961-66	M-Benz 300SL Hard Top.	Yellow/Red or Silver/Red, RN '3', SPKW. 95 mm.	£6-£8	MPR ☐
305	1972-73	Mini Marcos GT850.	White/Red body, Blue/White stripes, RN '7'. 86 mm.	£3-£4	MPR ☐
C306	1980-	Fiat X19 Racer.	Blue with Red/Yellow bands, RN '3'. 110 mm.	Current	MPR ☐
307	1981-	Renault Turbo.	Yellow/Red body, RN '8', *Cibie,* ODHB/VADS. 100 mm.	Current	MPR ☐
C308	1972-76	Mini Cooper S.	Yellow body, RN '177', 2RE/RR/2SPW. 73 mm.	£3-£4	MPR ☐
C308	1982-	BMW M1.	Yellow body, RN '25', *Goodyear,* OHB/DE. 129 mm.	Current	MPR ☐
309	1962-65	Aston Martin DB4.	Green/White body, RN '1', SS/SL/OBN/DE/SPKW. 95 mm.	£6-£8	MPR ☐
C309	1982-	VW 'TURBO'.	White/Brown body, RN '14', VADS/OHB. 97 mm.	Current	MPR ☐
C310	1982-	'PORSCHE' 924 Turbo.	Black/Gold, ODHB, *Goodyear.* 124 mm.	Current	MPR ☐
312	1964-68	'E' Type Jaguar.	Chrome/Gold, RN '2', RCD/DI/SS/SPKW. 95 mm.	£8-£11	MPR ☐
C312	1983-	Ford Capri 'S'.	White body, RN '6', VADS/HPS/ODB/OHB. 97 mm.	Current	MPR ☐
314	1965-71	Ferrari Berlinetta 250LM.	Red, RN '4', RE/DE/SS. 95 mm.	£4-£5	MPR ☐
315	1964-66	Simca 1000.	Chrome/Black, RN '8', SS/WDS. 90 mm.	£5-£6	MPR ☐
316	1971-73	Ford GT70.	Met Green body, RN '3', VADS/REC/WZW/SS. 92 mm.	£4-£5	MPR ☐
317	1964	MTC 1964 Mini Cooper S.	Red/White body, RE '1964', RN '37', SL/SS. 73 mm.	£4-£5	MPR ☐
318	1965	MTC 1965 Mini Cooper S.	Red/White body RE '1965', RN '37', SL/SS. 73 mm.	£4-£5	MPR ☐
C318	1983-	'MOTUL' Jaguar XJS.	Black/Red/White body, RN '4', *Jaguar.* 118 mm.	Current	MPR ☐
319	1967-68	Lotus Elan Hard Top.	Blue/White or Green/Yellow body, RN '6', LOB. 90 mm.	£4-£5	MPR ☐
C319	1974-75	Lamborghini Miura.	Silver/Purple/Yellow body, RN '7', WZW/OD/OEC. 95 mm.	Current	MPR ☐
321	1965-67	MTC Mini Cooper S.	Red/White body, RN '52', SL/SS/WDS/SW. 73 mm.	£5-£6	MPR ☐
322	1965-66	Monte-Carlo Rover 2000.	Plum/White body, RN '136', RE/SS/WDS. 95 mm.	£9	NC ☐
323	1965-66	Monte-Carlo Citroen DS19.	Blue/White body, RN '75' RE/SS/SW/WDS. 97 mm.	£9	NC ☐
C323	1974-78	Ferrari Daytona 365 GTB/4.	White/Red/Blue body, RN '81', OD/TG. 122 mm.	Current	MPR ☐
324	1974	Ferrari Daytona Le Mans.	Yellow, RN '33', RE/VADS, *A. Bamford.* 122 mm.	£4-£6	MPR ☐
325	1966-69	Ford Mustang.	White or Silver with Red stripes, RN '6'. 95 mm.	£5-£7	MPR ☐
328	1966-67	Monte-Carlo Hillman Imp.	Blue/White body, RN '107', RE/SL/SS. 83 mm.	£5-£7	MPR ☐
329	1973-76	Ford Mustang.	Green/White body, RN '69', OD/SS. 113 mm.	Current	MPR ☐
330	1967-69	Porsche Carrera 6.	Red/White body, RN '60', RE/RD/RW/SS. 97 mm.	£5-£6	MPR ☐
331	1974-76	Ford 'TEXACO' Capri GT.	White/Black body, RN '5'. 102 mm.	Current	MPR ☐

Racing, Rally and Speed Cars cont.

333	1966	Mini Cooper S.	Red/White body, RN '21', *RAC,* decals. 73 mm.	£6-£8	MPR ☐
337	1967-69	Chevrolet Stock Car.	Yellow body, PP/SS/WDS, RN '2'. 95 mm.	£5-£7	MPR ☐
339	1967-72	MTC 1967 Mini Cooper S.	Red/White body, RN '177', RR/2SPW/PP. 73 mm.	£4-£5	MPR ☐
340	1967-68	MTC Sunbeam Imp.	Blue/White body, RN '77', RE '1967', SL/SS. 83 mm.	£6-£8	MPR ☐
C340	1981	Rover 'TRIPLEX'.	White/Red/Blue, ODHB/HPS, RN '1'. 140 mm.	Current	MPR ☐
C341	1981-	Chevrolet Caprice.	Red/White/Blue body, ODBN, RN '43', *STP,* 150 mm.	Current	MPR ☐
344	1969-73	Ferrari Dino Sports.	Yellow or Red body, RN '23', AF/WZW. 104 mm.	Current	MPR ☐
345	1968-69	MGB GT.	Yellow/Black body, RN '11', OC/OD/SL/TS. 90 mm.	£11-£14	MPR ☐
370	1982	Ford Cobra Mustang.	Yellow/Black, *Mustang,* OBNHB/SR. 135 mm.	Current	MPR ☐
371	1970-73	Porsche Carrera 6.	White/Red, RN '60', TTEC/WZW. 97 mm.	Current	MPR ☐
376	1970-72	Corvette Stock Car.	Silver, RN '13', *Go-Go-Go,* WZW. 95 mm.	Current	MPR ☐
C380	1983-	BASF BMW M1.	Red/White body, RN '80', AF/OEC/PP. 129 mm.	Current	MPR ☐
C381	1983-	'ELF' Renault Turbo.	Red/White/Blue, RN '5', ODHB/VADS, *Facom.* 100 mm.	Current	MPR ☐
385	1970-76	Porsche 917.	Blue or Red body, RN '3', WZW/OBT/TW. 108 mm.	Current	MPR ☐
394	1973-76	Datsun 240Z.	Red, RN '11', *East African Safari.* 97 mm.	£4-£5	MPR ☐
396	1974-76	Datsun 240Z.	Red/White body, RN '46', SPKW/OD. 97 mm.	Current	MPR ☐
397	1974-78	Porsche-Audi 917-10.	White or Orange, RN '6', *Corgi,* RCD. 120 mm.	Current	MPR ☐
C447	1983-	4×4 'RENEGADE' Jeep.	Blue/White body, RN '5', SW/SPW/ARB. 100 mm.	Current	MPR ☐

Gift Sets

Ref. No.		Model Type	Model Features and Size	Rarity and Price Grading	
5	1959-63	Racing Car Set.	Contains 150, 151 and 152.	£40	GV ☐
6	1968-69	Racing Car Set.	Contains 156 and Trailer.	£9-£11	MPR ☐
12	1968-72	Grand Prix Racing Set.	Contains 155, 156, Tender/TRL/EQ.	£36	GV ☐
15	1961-65	Silverstone Set.	Contains 150, 151, 152, 215, 304, 309, 417 plus 3 Buildings.	£100	GV ☐
16	1961-66	Ecurie Ecosse TPTR.	Contains 1126, 150, 151A, 152S.	£70	GV ☐
17	1963-67	Ferrari and Land Rover Set.	Contains 438, 154 and TRL.	£9-£12	MPR ☐
25	1969-71	Racing Car and Tender Set.	Contains 159 plus VW Tender.	£9-£12	MPR ☐
C26	1981-	F1 Racing Car Set.	Contains C26 plus F1 Racer on TRL.	Current	MPR ☐
29	1975-76	Ferrari Racing Set.	Contains 323 and 150.	£7-£9	MPR ☐
C29	1982-	Lotus Racing Set.	Black/Gold C301, C154 on TRL.	Current	MPR ☐
32	1976	Lotus Racing Team Set.	Green/Yellow 318 and 319, 490 and TRL.	£5-£7	MPR ☐
38	1965-67	Monte Carlo Rally Set.	Contains 321, 322, 323.	£19-£24	MPR ☐
45	1966	All Winners Set.	Exported to France only.		
46	1966-69	All Winners Set.	264 or 310, 261, 310, 314, 324, 325.	£35	NVE ☐

Major Packs

Ref. No.	Model Type	Model Features and Size	Rarity and Price Grading	
1126	Ecurie Ecosse TPTR.	Dark or Light Blue, SS/OD/SW. 197 mm.	£19-£24	MPR ☐

4c Commercial Vehicles and Vans Single Models

Ref. No.		Model Type	Model Features and Size	Rarity and Price Grading	
403	1956-61	Bedford 15 Cwt Van	Blue/Silver body *Daily Express* 83 mm	£25	NC ☐
403	1956-59	Bedford 15 Cwt Van	Red/Silver body *K.L.G. Plugs,* FWM. 83mm.	£28	GV ☐
404	1956-62	Bedford Dormobile	Green, Maroon, Yel or Blue body. 83 mm	£14-£17	MPR ☐
404M	1956-59	Bedford Dormobile	Red or Blue body FWM. 83 mm	£18	NC ☐
C405	1982	Ford Transit Milk Float	Blue/White body, *Lotta Bottle* OD. 143mm.	Current	MPR ☐
407	1957-61	Smiths Karrier Bantam Mobile Grocery Shop	Red & White body. *Home Services Hygenic Mobile Shop.* 95 mm	£18	NC ☐
408	1957-62	Bedford 15 cwt (Automobile Association)	Yellow/Black body, *Road Service* on roof and sides with *AA* emblems. 83mm.	£22	NC ☐
411	1958-62	Karrier Bantam Van "LUCOZADE'	Yellow/Grey body, *Lucozade Replaces Loss Energy* OD. 102 mm.	£25	NC ☐
413	1957-62	Karrier Bantam Mobile Butchers Shop	White/Blue body, *Home Services Hygenic Mobile Shop* Meaty Decals. 93 mm.	£24	NC ☐
421	1960-62	Bedford 12 Cwt Van 'EVENING STANDARD'	Black/Sil/Red body, Newsboards on doors *Evening Standard.* 83 mm.	£28	NC ☐
422	1960-62	Bedford 12 Cwt Van 'CORGI TOYS'	Blue/Yellow body, Corgi Livery *Corgi Toys* and Corgi dog decal. 83 mm.	£30	NC ☐
C423	1978	'ROUGH RIDER' Chevvy Van	Yellow body, *Rough Rider* MC decal. 122 mm.	£6-£8	MPR ☐
C424	1977-79	Security Van	Black/Yel/White body, *Security* WDS with grille. 100 mm.	Current	MPR ☐
426	1962-64	Karrier Bantam Van Circus Booking Office	Red/Blue body, circus and office staff (2) decals, *Booking Office.* 91 mm.	£35	NC ☐
C426	1978-81	Chevrolet Booking Office Van	Yel/Red/Blue body, 2 loudspeakers, *Pinder-Jean Richard*	Current	MPR ☐
428	1963-66	Karrier Bantam Van	Blue/White body, DCH salesman swivels. *Mr Softee Ice Cream* Vans. 91 mm	£18	NC ☐
C431	1978-80	*'VANATIC'* Chevvy Van	White, body, RF. WDS, *Vanatic* TW. 122 mm.	Current	MPR ☐
C433	1978	*'VAN-ISHING POINT'* Chevvy Van	Gold body, In the 1978 Cat but not issued. 122 mm.		NVP ☐
433	1962-64	Volkswagen Delivery Van	Red/White body, *VW* on R/S/SW/IS. 91 mm.	£7-£9	MPR ☐

Commercial Vehicles and Vans cont.

435	1962-63	Karrier Bantam Dairy Produce Van	Blue/White/Yellow body, DCH/OD *Drive Safely on Milk*	£15	NC ☐
C437	1978-82	*'COCA COLA'* Chevvy Van	Red/White body, *Enjoy Coca-Cola.* 122 mm.	Current	MPR ☐
441	1963-67	Volkswagen Van 'TOBLERONE'	Blue body, Trans-o-lite headlights, *Chocolate Toblerone.* 91 mm.	£14	NC ☐
443	1963-65	Plymouth Suburban U.S. Mail Car	Blue/White official postal livery *Address Your Mail Carefully.* 104 mm.	£13-£16	MPR ☐
447	1964-67	Ford Thames 'WALLS ICE CREAM'	Blue/Cream body, Salesman and boy, OH. 90 mm.	£14	NC ☐
450	1964-67	Austin Mini Van	Green body ODB/OW/IS. 79 mm.	£5-£6	MPR ☐
452	1956-63	Commer Dropside Lorry	Red/Fawn/Silver body, TBD drops. 120 mm.	£8-£10	MPR ☐
453	1956-60	Commer Refrigerated Van *'WALLS ICE CREAM'*	Cab dark Blue, Box body cream. *More Than a Treat a Food*	£20	GV ☐
454	1957-62	Commer Platform Lorry	Yel/Grey or Blue/Grey. 120 mm	£7-£9	MPR ☐
455	1957-61	Karrier Bantam 2 tonner	Blue Cab, Red platform. 102 mm	£7-£9	MPR ☐
456	1960-63	E.R.F 449 Dropside. Lorry.	Yellow Cab. 120 mm.	£7-£9	MPR ☐
457	1957-62	E.R.F. 449 Platform Lorry.	Two Tone Blue body. 120 mm.	£7-£9	MPR ☐
459	1958-60	E.R.F. 449 Van 'MOORHOUSE'.	Yel/Red, *Moorhouses Lemon Cheese* and *Moorhouses Jam.* 117 mm.	£32	GV ☐
462	1970	Commer 'CO-OP' Van	White/Blue body, *Co-op,* PRM. 90 mm.	£11	NC ☐
462	1971	Commer 'HAMMONDS' Van.	Green/Yel/Brown body, *Hammond.* PRM. 90 mm.	£11	NC ☐
471	1965-66	Karrier Bantam Van.	Blue/White body, *Joe's Diner,* OH. 95 mm.	£10	NC ☐
474	1965-67	Musical 'WALLS' Ice Cream Van.	447 again, with chimes/no figs. 90 mm.	£15	NC ☐
479	1968-71	Commer Mobile Camera Van	Dark Blue White body, Camera/Operator on roof, *Samuelson Film Company Ltd.* 90 mm.	£12	NC ☐
484	1967-71	Dodge Livestock Transporter	Beige/Green body, *Kew Fargo,* 5 figs. 140 mm.	£5-£7	MPR ☐

Commercial Vehicles and Vans cont.

	1983	Ford Escort 55 Van Series	All have Orange SL and TL, Silver trim. ORD/PCH/PW. 118 mm.		
496		'ROYAL EIIR MAIL'	All Red body, Gold letters and crown.	Current	MPR ☐
497		'RADIO RENTALS' TV and Radio	White body, Green/White decals. MLCD stripe, *Radio Rentals* on roof. *RR* on doors.	Current	MPR ☐
498		'BRITISH GAS'	Blue roof, White/Blue sides, 2 Light Blue stripes and *Gas* decal.	Current	MPR ☐
499		'BRITISH TELECOM'	All Yellow body, Blue letters, Black PLD on roof.	Current	MPR ☐

Gift Sets

Ref. No.		Model Type	Model Features and Size	Rarity and Price Grading	
11	1960-64	E.R.F. Dropside and TRL.	456 and 101 with cement and planks.	£16-£19	MPR ☐
21	1962-66	E.R.F. Dropside and TRL.	456 and 101 plus milk churns and SAA.	£16-£19	MPR ☐
24	1963-68	Commer ¾ ton vehicle constructor set.	2 cab and chassis units plus 4 interchangeable bodies, TOL.	£17	NC ☐

Major Packs and Large Size Models

Ref. No.		Model Type	Model Features and Size	Rarity and Price Grading		
1100	1958-63	Bedford Carrimore Low Loader.	Red/Blue body, OC/AV/DDTG/WO. 220 mm.	£18	NC	☐
1100	1971-73	Mack Container Truck and TRL.	White/Yel body, *Trans Continental.* 257 mm.	£8-£11	MPR	☐
1101	1957-62	Bedford Carrimore Car Transporter.	TT Blue body, *Corgi Car TPTR,* AV/DDR. 263 mm.	£16	NC	☐
1104	1958-62	Bedford Carrimore Machinery Low Loader.	Red/Grey body, AV/DDR/WO/DRAXW. 220 mm.	£16	NC	☐
1104	1974-77	Bedford TK Horse Transporter.	Green/Orange body, *Newmarket,* 4 horses, boy, 3DDR, AV. 256 mm.	£15	NC	☐
C 1105	1977-81	Berliet Horse Box.	Brown/White body, *National,* 4 horses, AV, 3DDR. 280 mm.	Current	MPR	☐
1106	1971-77	Mack Container Truck.	Yel/Black/White body, *A.C.L.,* AV/2PC. 290 mm.	£7-£10	MPR	☐
C 1107	1979-	Berliet 'US LINES' Truck.	Never Issued? 290 mm.		NVP	☐
C 1109	1979-	'MICHELIN' Container Truck.	Blue/Yel body, AV/TV/2CNT. 243 mm.	Current	MPR	☐
1110	1959-65	Bedford 'MOBIL' Tanker.	Red/White body, *Mobil Gas,* AV/DDC. 191 mm.	£38	GV	☐
1129	1962-65	Bedford 'MILK' Tanker.	Blue/White body, AV/DDC.	£38	GV	☐
C 1129	1983	Mercedes Container Truck.	MLCD body, *Corgi,* AV/CS/OD.		MPR	☐
1130	1983	'CORGI CHEMCO' Tanker.	Yellow/Black/Silver body, AV/DDT/TW. 188 mm.	Current	MPR	☐
1131	1963-66	Bedford Carrimore 'TK' Machinery Low Loader.	Blue/Yel body, AV/2SPW/RVM/SS/DRAXW/DDR/DDC. 241 mm.	£17	NC	☐
C 1131	1983	CHRISTIAN SALVESON Truck.	White/Black/Blue, CS/OD/TW/CNT/AV. 243 mm.	Current	MPR	☐
1132	1963-65	Bedford Carrimore 'TK' Low Loader.	Yel/Red body, AV/2SPW/RVM/SS/DDR/DDC. 241 mm.	£15	NC	☐

Major Packs and Large Size Models cont.

C 1132	1983-	Scania Container Truck.	Yel/Black body, *Danzas,* DCNT/CS/OD/TW. 138 mm.	Current	MPR ☐
C 1133	1983-	Scania Giant Tipper.	Green/Sil body, Tipping Action. 145 mm.	Current	MPR ☐
C 1134	1983-	Scania 'KOHLER' Silo Truck.	Red/White body, *Made in Germany,* OH/LD. 145 mm.	Current	MPR ☐
1137	1966-69	Ford H Series, 'EXPRESS SERVICES'.	Blue/Sil/Red body, AV/DDC/TCB/OD. 235 mm.	£12	NC ☐
1138	1966-69	Bedford Carrimore Car Transporter.	Red/Blue body, *Corgi Cars,* AV/CTS/TCB/DDC. 273 mm.	£16	NC ☐
1140	1966-67	Bedford TK Petrol Tanker.	Red/Sil/White body, *Mobil Gas,* AV/DDC/RVM. 191 mm.	£35	GV ☐
1141	1966-67	Bedford TK Milk Tanker.	Blue/White body, *Milk,* AV/DDC/KVM. 191 mm.	£35	GV ☐
C 1144	1983	Mercedes 'ROYAL MAIL' Truck.	Red/Gold body, *Parcels,* EIIR Crest, AV/TU, 205 mm.	Current	MPR ☐
C 1145	1983-	Mercedes 'YORKIE' Truck.	Blue/Yel body, *Yorkie Chocolate,* AV/TU, 205 mm.	Current	MPR ☐
1146	1970-73	Scammell Car Transporter	White/Yel/Blue body, AV/3CTS/DDC. 290 mm.	£20	NC ☐
C 1146	1983-	'DUNLOP' Truck.	Model details unknown. 205 mm.	Current	MPR ☐
C 1146	1983-	Scania Container Truck.	White/Blue/Black body, *Corgi,* AV/OD. 138 mm.	Current	MPR ☐
1147	1970-72	Scammell 'FERRYMASTERS' Container Truck.	Yel/White body, *International Hauliers,* AV/DDC. 235 mm.	£15	GV ☐
C 1147	1983-	Scania Container Truck.	Yel/Black body, *Ryder Truck Rentals* AV/OD. 138 mm.	Current	MPR ☐
C 1148	1983-	Scania Container Truck.	Blue/White body, *Securicor Parcels* AV/OD. 138 mm.	Current	MPR ☐
C 1149	1983-	Scania Container Truck.	White/Red/Blue body, *BRS Truck Rentals* AV/OD. 138 mm.	Current	MPR ☐
C 1150	1983-	'BRITISH SUGAR' Silo Truck.	Blue/White body, *Silver Spoon,* OH. 145 mm.	Current	MPR ☐

Major Packs and Large Size Models cont.

No.	Years	Model	Details	Price		
C 1151	1983-	'SPILLERS' Silo Truck.	Orange/White body, *Graded Grains,* OH. 145 mm.	Current	MPR	☐
1152	1971-75	Mack 'ESSO' Tanker.	White/Red/Blue body, AV/TCB/DDC/JW. 278 mm.	£10	NC	☐
C 1152	1983-	'BARRATT' Tipper Truck.	Green/White body, Tips. 145 mm.	Current	MPR	☐
C 1153	1983-	'WIMPEY' Tipper Truck.	Green/Silver body, Tips. 145 mm.	Current	MPR	☐
C 1154	1983-	'BLOCK CONSTRUCTION' Truck.	No details as yet	Current	MPR	☐
C 1157	1976-81	Ford 'ESSO' Tanker.	White/Red body, AV/TCB/DDC/OH/JW. 270 mm.	£7-£9	MPR	☐
1159	1976-79	Ford Car Transporter.	Green/White body, AV/TCB/DDR/CTS/JW. 360 mm.	£10	NC	☐
C 1160	1976-76	Ford 'GULF' Tanker.	White/Orange body, AV/TCB /DDC/OH. 270 mm.	£10	NC	☐
C 1161	1979-80	Ford 'ARAL' Tanker.	Blue/White/Black body, AV/TCB/DDC/OH. 270 mm.	£10	NC	☐
•C 1166	1983	Mercedes Benz Truck.	Brown body, *Guinness,* AV. 188 mm.	Current	MPR	☐
C 1167	1983	Mercedes '7 UP' Truck.	Green/White body, *The Difference Is Clear.* 205 mm.	Current	MPR	☐
C 1167	1983	Mercedes 'DUCKHAMS' Tanker.	Yellow Cab and Tank, Dark Blue CH, Blue/White/ Yellow Labels, Black filler hatch, 8W/TU.	Current	MPR	☐
C 1169	1982	Ford 'GUINNESS' Tanker.	Cream/Brown/Black body, AV/TCB/DDC/OH. 270 mm.	Current	MPR	☐
C 1170	1982	Ford Car Transporter.	Red/White/Yel body, AV/TCB/DDC/JW. 360 mm.	Current	MPR	☐
C 1175	1983	Mercedes 'TI RALEIGH' Truck	Dark Blue Cab and CNT, Yellow CH, White TI Logo, Logo on CNT and CS in Yellow/Red, AV/TU/8W	Current	MPR	☐
C 1176	1983	Mercedes 'ZANUSSI' Truck	Black/Yellow Cab and CNT. *The Applicance of Science* Logo on CNT. *Zanussi* on CS. AV/TU/8W.	Current	MPR	☐
C 1177	1983	Mercedes 'WEETABIX' Truck	Yellow Cab and CNT, Red CH, Logo in Blue on CNT and on Red CS, AV/TU/8W	Current	MPR	☐
C 1178	1983	Mercedes 'MAYNARDS' Truck	White Cab and CNT, Black CH *Original Wine Gums* in Red. MLCD Stripes and Sweet bag. AV/TU/8W	Current	MPR	☐

4d Public Transport i) Buses and Coaches

All the following Double Decker Bus Models are based on the famous Routemaster Type.

Ref. No.		Model Type	Model Features and Size	Rarity and Price Grading		
467	1977-81	'HAMLEYS' 'LONDON TRANSPORT'	Red DD, PCH/WZW, Supplied to *Hamleys* of Regent St. 123 mm	£7-£9	MPR	☐
467	1977-81	'SELFRIDGES' 'LONDON TRANSPORT'	Red DD, PCH/WZW RT '12' *There's no place like Selfridges.* 123 mm.	£7-£9	MPR	☐
468	1964-74	'CORGI TOYS' 'LONDON TRANSPORT'	Red DD, D/CDS/DI/SL/SS/DBD This was the 1st normal bus issue. 114 mm	£20	NC	☐
468	1964	'CORGI TOYS' NEW 'SOUTH WALES ANNIVERSARY'	Green Roof, Cream Middle Section. Chocolate Brown Lower body and CH. Also has *Corgi Classics* decal D/CDS/DI/SS/DBD. 114 mm.	£125	GV	☐
468	1964-74	'OUTSPAN' 'LONDON TRANSPORT'	Red DD, D/CDS/DI/SL/SS/DBD *Outspan oranges are refreshing.* 114 mm.	£12	NC	☐
468	1965-74	'GAMAGES' RM 'LONDON TRANSPORT'	Red DD, D/CDS/DI/SL/SS/DBD Supplied to *Gamages.* 114 mm.	£15	NC	☐
468	1965-74	'DESIGN CENTRE' 'LONDON TRANSPORT'	Red DD, D/CDS/DI/SC/SS/DBD Supplied to *Design Centre.* 114 mm.	£12	NC	☐
468	1965-74	'MADAME TUSSARDS' 'LONDON TRANSPORT'	Red DD, D/CDS/DI/SL/SS/DBD available at *Madame Tussards.* 114 mm	£15	NC	☐
C469	1975	'BTA' 'LONDON TRANSPORT'	Red DD, RT '11', WZW/PCH *BTA Welcome to Britain.* 123 mm.	Current	MPR	☐
C469	1979-81	'LEEDS' 'OMNIBUS'	Dark Green and Yellow DD, WZW/PCH *Say the Leeds and You're Smiling George Shillibeer 1829 London Transport 1979.* 123 mm.	£14	NC	☐
C469	1974-80	'SWAN & EDGAR''LONDON TRANSPORT'	Red Double Decker, PCH/WZW *Swan Edgar — Picadilly Circus.* 123 mm.	£7-£9	MPR	☐
C469	1979	'CADBURYS'	All Orange Double Decker PCH/WZW *Cadburys Double Decker.* 123 mm.	£8	NC	☐
C469	1983	'GAMLEYS'	Red Double Decker. PCH/WZW *Toyshop of the South. Got to go to Gamleys.* 123 mm.	Current	MPR	☐
C469	1983	'WORLD AIRWAYS'	Brown and Cream DD, RT '14' PCH/WZW *I Wish I was Flying to the USA.* 123 mm.	Current	MPR	☐
C469 /10	1983	'OLD HOLBORN' Open Top Bus	All Orange body, RT '14', PCH/WZW. 123 mm	Current	MPR	☐

Buses and Coaches cont.

Ref	Year	Model	Description	Price	
C469 /11	1983	'REDGATES'	Cream and Brown DD, PCH/WZW. 123 mm		NGPP ☐
C469 /16	1983	'LONDON TRANSPORT' GOLDEN JUBILEE	Red/White and Silver DD, PCH/WZW Supplied to the Routemaster Club. 123 mm.	£17	GV ☐
C469 /17	1983	'BLACKPOOL TRANSPORT' Bus	Cream and Green DD, PCH/WZW Supplied to Brookes Gift Stores. *Britain's No 1 Tourist Attraction Blackpool Pleasure Beach.* 123 mm	£12	GV ☐
C469 /18	1983	'BLACKPOOL TRANSPORT' Open Top Bus.	Cream & Green, PCH/WZW Supplied to Brookes Gift Stores. *Britain's No 1 Tourist Attraction Blackpool Pleasure Beach.* 123 mm	£12	GV ☐
C469 /19	1983	'NORBROOK MOTORS'	Blue DD, PCH/WZW Supplied to Norbrook Motors. 123 mm	£9	GV ☐
C469 /20	1983	'JOLLY GIANT TOY SUPERSTORE'	Green/Yellow DD, PCH/WZW, Supplied to Jolly Giant.		NGPP ☐
C469 /19	1983	'GLOUCESTER TRAIN AND TOY SALE'	Black Double Decker, PCH/WZW Supplied to Model Centre. *It's Britains Top of the Swaps. No 1. 25 Leisure Centre.* Second small label states *to commemorate the Gloucester Train and Toy Sale 12th July 1975.* 25 15th October 1983. 123 mm.	£5-£7	MPR ☐
C469 /22	1983	'ARMY AND NAVY STORES'	Red Double Decker PCH/WZW Supplied to the Army and Navy Stores. 123 mm.	Current	MPR ☐
C469 /23	1983	'MANCHESTER UNITED' Open Top Bus	Red Body PCH/WZW *Man Utd 83' Cup Winners.* 123 mm	Current	MPR ☐
C469 /24	1983	'LLANDRINDOD WELLS VICTORIAN FESTIVAL'	Green and White DD, PCH WZW Brian Evans Models, Church Stretton. 123 mm	£5-£7	MPR ☐
C469 /60D	1983	'DION'	Dark Blue body, South African Issue. *Dion Saves You More,* Orange/White/Blue Label.	£20	GV ☐
C469 /26	1983	'TROWBRIDGE TOYS' and MODELS!	Sky Blue and Dark Blue DD, PCH/WZW Supplied — Trowbridge Toys, Trowbridge. *I'm on my way to — Where are you going.* 123 mm	Current	MPR ☐
C469 /27	1983	'LONDON MARRIOTT' Hotels	Red Double Decker, PCH/WZW Labelled by *Marriott Hotels.* 123mm.		NGPP ☐
C469 /28	1983*	'MANCHESTER LIONS CLUB'	Cream Double Decker, PCH/WZW Supplied to the *Lions Club.* 123 mm.		NGPP ☐
C469 /30	1983	'BOURNEMOUTH' Open Top Bus	Orange or Yellow body, PCH/WZW. *Old Holborn* decals. 123 mm.	Current	MPR ☐
C469 /31	1983	Trans Clyde	Yellow and Green DD, PCH/WZW *Buy Before You Fly.* 123mm.	Current	MPR ☐

Buses and Coaches cont.

C469 /32	1983	Tayside 'BARRATT HOMES'.	Two tone Blue DD, PCH/WZW *Building Houses to Make Homes In.* 123 mm.	Current	MPR ☐
C469 /33	1983	South Yorkshire Bus 'WORLD AIRLINES'	Cream and Brown DD. 123 mm.	Current	MPR ☐
C469 /50	1982	'LION BAR'	All Green DD, RT 'ref', WZW/PCH *Watch this Bus Roar Bus.* 123 mm.	Current	MPR ☐
c469 /60	1982	'AERO BAR'	Cream DD, RT '14' WZW/PCH *Unforgettabubble* 123 mm	Current	MPR ☐
C469 /70	1982	'TDK' Cassettes	All Red DD, RT '14' WZW/PCH *The Great Name in Tape Cassettes.* 123 mm.	Current	MPR ☐
C469 /80	1982	'OXO'	Brown and Cream body, RT '14' WZW/PCH *Oxo Make it Again and Again.* 123 mm.	Current	MPR ☐
C470	1983	London Country 'PENTEL'	Green Double Decker, WZW/PCH *Click On The Draw.* 123 mm.	Current	MPR ☐
471	1977	QUEENS SILVER JUBILEE.	All Silver body, *London Celebrations* and *See more London* in Red.	£10-£13	MPR ☐
C475	1983	'BRISTOL AIRPORT'	Blue Double Decker, WZW/PCH. *Take off From Bristol . . . It's so Easy!.* 123 mm	Current	MPR ☐
C476	1983	'BRITISH TELECOM'	Yellow Double Decker, WZW/PCH. *Dial a Date Tonight, Off Peak Dialling Saves Money, 'Dial Your Chicks After 6'.* 123 mm.	Current	MPR ☐
C477	*1983	'BUZBY'	2 tone Blue DD, *'International Dialling'.* 123 mm.		NGPP ☐
C478	*1983	'SUNDEKKER' Open Top	Orange and White body PCH/WZW. 123 mm *SUNTREKKER*		NGPP ☐
C479	*1983	'LONDON CRUSADER'	Green/White Double Decker, PCH/WZW. 123 mm.		NGPP ☐
C480	*1983	A.E.C. Renown Bus	Blue & Primrose body, Replica of A.E.C. East Yorkshire *Renown* Bus.	Current	NGPP ☐
508	1974-78	Commer Mini Bus 'HOLIDAY CAMP SPECIAL'	Red & White body, with roof rack and luggage and opening doors. 90 mm.	£12	NC ☐

* This indicates a proposed 1983 issue not available at the time of publication.

FOOTNOTES

a. Because the labels are easily interchangeable on many of the Buses beware of non listed items.
b. A few Red Routemaster buses with the TDK side were supplied to TDK themselves for internal promotional activities.
c. A limited number of Black buses but without labels applied were supplied to John Gaye models.
d. A small quantity of Routemasters were sold to the Brunnings advertising agency with front and rear (Kelly Girl) destination boards only.
e. Approximately 150 Red Routemasters were supplied to the distributors of the James Bond Octopussy film with an Octopussy paper label overstruck the normal BTA on one side only.
f. The high asking prices shown for very recent models reflects the demand for models issued in strictly limited quantities.

Buses and Coaches cont.

Major Models

Ref	Year	Model	Description	Price	Grading
1120	1961-78	'MIDLAND RED' Motorway Express Coach	Red body, Black roof, DCH/D11T, *Birmingham-London Motorway Express*	£38	*GV* ☐
C1168	1983	'NATIONAL EXPRESS' Single Deck Coach	White, Red and Blue body, *Greyhound and Americruiser* TW. 169 mm.	£8-£10	MPR ☐
C1168		'MOTORWAY EXPRESS' Single Deck Coach	All White body, Brown/Yellow/Red Labels, CW	Current	MPR ☐

COLLECTORS NOTES

Page 144

C300 Ferrari Daytona

~~C314 Ferrari Berlinetta~~

~~C323 " Daytona 365 GTB/4~~

C344 (C440) " Dino Sports

C324 " Daytona Le Mans

Page 143

~~C152 Ferrari 312 B2~~ ✓

~~C154 " Formula I~~

4d (ii) Taxis

Ref. No.		Model Type	Model Features and Size	Rarity and Price Grading		
221	1960-63	Chevrolet Impala Cas	Yellow, *Taxi* LHD/A *Yellow Taxis.* 108 mm.	£20	GV	☐
c327	1980	Chevrolet Caprice Taxi	Yellow, *Think TWA,* fare on door. 90 mm.	Current	MPR	☐
c411	1976-80	Mercedes Benz 240D	Orange/Black, *Taxi* on roof. 127 mm.	Current	MPR	☐
418	1971-74	Austin Taxi	Black body, Orange sign, SS (1963). 97 mm.	£7-£9	MPR	☐
c425	1978	London Taxi	Black, *Taxi,* whizz wheels. 121 mm.	£4-£6	MPR	☐
430	1962-64	Ford Bermuda 'TAXI'	WH/GR/Red DC/LHD/D *Bermuda.* 102mm.	£18	NVE	☐
480	1965-66	Chevrolet Impala Taxi	Yellow/Red *Taxi* fares on door. 108 mm.	£9-£11	MPR	☐
507	1969	Chrysler Bermuda Taxi	Shown in catalogue — not issued			

Gift Sets

11	1971-75	London Gift Set	468 *Outspan,* 418 and 226 Mini	£17	NC	☐
C11	1980	London Gift Set	Contains C469 *B.T.A., C425 and PM*	*Current*	*MPR*	☐
35	1965-68	London Gift Set	Contains 648 *Corgi Toys,* 418 Taxi and PM	£35	GV	☐

COLLECTORS NOTES

4e Military Models
Single Models

Ref. No.		Model Type	Model Features and Size	Rarity and Price Grading	
350	1958-62	Thunderbird GMS on Loading Trolley.	Red/White Missile, R.A.F. Blue, LTRL. 140 mm.	£9-£12	MPR ☐
351	1958-62	R.A.F. Land Rover.	Blue/Silver, R.A.F. roundel, SPW/WDS. 95 mm.	£14-£17	MPR ☐
352	1958-62	R.A.F. Vanguard Staff Car.	Blue/Silver, R.A.F. roundel, WDS. 95 mm.	£16-£19	MPR ☐
353	1959-61	Decca Radar Scanner.	Blue/Orange, scanner rotates. 83 mm.		MPR ☐
354	1964-66	Commer Military Ambulance.	MG, Red Crosses, S/SW/SS/AD. 90 mm.	£7-£9	MPR ☐
355	1964-65	Commer 'MILITARY POLICE' Van.	MG, AD/BOFL/S/SW/SS. 90 mm.	£7-£9	MPR ☐
356	1964-66	Commer Personnel Carrier.	MG, AD/S/SW/SS/WHS, *US Personnel.* 91 mm.	£7-£9	MPR ☐
357	1964-66	Land Rover Weapons Carrier.	MG, S/SW/SS/DC/A/Star. 95 mm.	£7-£9	MPR ☐
358	1964-68	1961 Oldsmobile Staff Car.	MG, S/SW/SS/AD/3PS/A/Star. 108 mm.	£7-£9	MPR ☐
359	1964-66	Commer Army 'FIELD KITCHEN'.	MG, S/SW/SS/DI/OWD, Attendant. 91 mm.	£7-£9	MPR ☐
414	1961-64	Bedford Military Ambulance.	Military Green, Red Crosses, WDS. 83 mm.	£8-£10	MPR ☐
500	1963-64	US Army Land Rover.	MG, Rare version of 357. 95 mm.	£12-£15	MPR ☐
C900	1974-78	German Tiger MKI Tank.	Brown/Green, FSH (12)/RTR/A, '144'. 103 mm.	£3-£4	MPR ☐
C901	1974-78	Centurion MK Tank.	MGC, FSH(12)/RTR/A/UJ. 121 mm.	£3-£4	MPR ☐
C902	1974-80	American M60 A1 Tank.	MGC, FSH(12)/RTR. 115 mm.	£2-£3	MPR ☐
C903	1974-80	British Chieftain Tank.	MG, FSH(12)/RTR. 125 mm.	£3-£4	MPR ☐
C904	1974-78	German King Tiger Tank.	MGC, FSH(12)/RTR, 'B 34', BC. 120 mm.	£3-£4	MPR ☐
C905	1975-76	Russian SU100 Tank Destroyer.	Grey, FSH(12), EG/OH/AD/Red Star. 112 mm.	£4-£6	MPR ☐
C906	1975-76	Saladin Armoured Car.	MG, FSH(12), EG. 108 mm.	£3-£4	MPR ☐
C907	1976-80	German Half Track Rocket Launcher.	Steel Blue/Red, FRK(12)/DAT/BC. 167 mm.	Current	MPR ☐
C908	1977-80	French AMX Recovery Tank.	MG, CR/LDB/SL/EQ, 3 figures. 127 mm.	£3-£4	MPR ☐
C909	1977-80	British Tractor, Gun and Trailer.	Sandy, Gun and TRL, DT, FSH(12). 280 mm.	£4-£6	MPR ☐
C920	1977-80	Bell Army Helicopter.	MGC, FRK(12), *US Army.* 130 mm.	Current	MPR ☐
C923	1977-80	Sikorsky Sky Crane, Helicopter.	MG, Red Cross, *Army.* 160 mm.	Current	MPR ☐

Major and Large Size Models

Ref. No.		Model Type	Model Features and Size	Rarity and Price Grading		
1106	1959-61	Karrier Decca Radar Van.	Cream Orange, RTT Scanner, A. 134 mm.	£20-£25	MPR	☐
1108	1958-61	Bristol Bloodhound, GMS on Launching Ramp.	MG, LRP/LM, Yel/Red/WH, GMS, R:A.F. MK. 178 mm.	£14-£17	MPR	☐
1109	1959-62	Bristol Bloodhound, GMS on Loading Trolley.	MG, LTRL/SPW, Yel/Red/WH, GMS, R.A.F. MK. 228 mm.	£11-£15	MPR	☐
1112	1959-62	Corporal GMS on LRP.	MG, LRP/LM, WH/Red GMS, PH/EDI. 330 mm.	£8-£11	MPR	☐
1113	1959-62	Corporal GMS and Erector Vehicle.	MG, V/SPW/BM/LM, GMS/PH/EDI. 292 mm.	£16-£21	MPR	☐
1115	1958-62	Bristol Ferranti Bloodhound GMS.	Yellow/Red/White with R.A.F. MK.	£6-£8	MPR	☐
1116	1959-62	Bristol Ferranti Bloodhound Launching Ramp.	Military Green, rotates/LM.	£5-£7	MPR	☐
1117	1959-62	Bristol Ferranti Bloodhound Loading Trolley.	Military Green, SPW/TB pivots.	£5-£7	MPR	☐
1118	1958-62	International 6×6 Army Truck.	Military Green, six wheels, WDS. 140 mm.	£14-£18	MPR	☐
1124	1959-62	Corporal GMS, Launching Ramp.	Military Green, LM/AFT.	£5-£7	MPR	☐
1133	1965-66	Troop Transporter.	MG, 'US 7811332', 6W/DC. 140 mm.	£13-£16	MPR	☐
1134	1965-66	'US ARMY' Fuel Tanker.	MG, US Star, AV/DDC, *'No Smoking'*. 191 mm.	£35	NVE	☐
1135	1965	'US ARMY' Heavy EQ, TPTR.	MG, US Star, D/AV/DDR/RVM/DRAXW/2SPW. 241 mm.	£25	NVE	☐

Gift Sets

Ref. No.		Model Type	Model Features and Size	Rarity and Price Grading		
3	1959-62	Land Rover with Thunderbird GMS Set.	Contains 350 and 351.	£20	GV	☐
4	1959-62	Bristol Ferranti Bloodhound GMS Set.	Contains 351, 1115, 1116, 1117.	£25	GV	☐
6	1959-62	Guided Missiles Set.	Contains 350, 351, 352, 353, 1106, 1108, 1117.	£55	GV	☐
9	1959-62	Corporal GMS Set.	Contains 1112, 1113, 1118.	£55	GV	☐
10	1974-78	Centurion Tank and Transporter Set.	Contains 901 and TPTR/DRAXW/AV.	£7-£9	MPR	☐
17	1976-81	Military Set.	Contains 900, 906, 920.	£5-£7	MPR	☐

4f Novelty, Film and TV Tie-In Models Single Models

Ref. No.		Model Type	Model Features and Size	Rarity and Price Grading		
104	1965-66	Dolphin 20 Cabin Cruiser.	Blue/White boat, Red TRL, helmsman. 136 mm.	£5-£7	MPR	☐
C107	1967-70	Batboat on Trailer.	Black/Red body, many decals. 140 mm.	£3-£4	MPR	☐
201	1970-72	The Saint's Volvo P1800.	White/Red, Saint design. No D/WZW. 90 mm.	£4-£6	MPR	☐
258	1965-69	The Saint's Volvo P1800.	White/Red, D/SL/SS, Saint design. 90 mm.	£5-£7	MPR	☐
C259	1979-	Penguinmobile.	White, D under Red/Yel parasol. 95 mm.	Current	MPR	☐
C260	1981-	Superman Police Car.	Blue, *City of Metropolis.* 150 mm.	Current	MPR	☐
261	1965-68	James Bonds DB5 Aston Martin.	Gold body, RTT gun, ejector seat, bullet shield, D/PS. 97 mm.	£7-£9	MPR	☐
C261	1979-82	Spiderbuggy.	Red/Blue body, 2 figures. 150 mm.		MPR	☐
C262	1979-82	Captain Marvel's Porsche.	White with flames and stars. D. 120 mm.	£3-£4	MPR	☐
C263	1979-82	Captain America's Jetmobile.	Red/White/Blue body with Blue D. 155 mm.	£2-£3	MPR	☐
C264	1979-82	Incredible Hulk Van.	Hulk in cage on Mazda pick-up. 120 mm.	£3-£4	MPR	☐
C265	1981-82	Supermobile.	Blue/Red/Silver body, pilot/RL. 148 mm.	£3-£4	MPR	☐
266	1968-72	Chitty Chitty Bang Bang.	Silver body, Yel/White RTT, wings, D/3PS, SL/DI/HBR/CL/horn/SPW/SW/WS. 162 mm.	£35	NC	☐
C266	1979-	Spider Bike.	Red/Black MC, Red/Black figure, RL. 115 mm.	Current	MPR	☐
C267	1966	Batmobile.	Black/Red body, RL, Batman/Robin. 127 mm.	£5-£6	MPR	☐
268	1967-70	Green Hornet.	Black body, driver and gunman. RL. 127 mm.	£5-£7	MPR	☐
C268	1978-	Batmans Bat Bike.	Black/Red M/C with Batman. RL. 110 mm.	Current	MPR	☐
C269	1977-81	James Bond's Lotus Esprit.	White body, hydroplanes. 120 mm.	£3-£4	MPR	☐
270	1968-76	J.B's Aston Martin.	Silver body, ejector seat and passenger. 102 mm.	£6-£8	MPR	☐
C271	1978-	J.B's Aston Martin.	Silver body, ejector seat and passenger. 130 mm.	Current	MPR	☐
C272	1982-	J.B's Citroen 2CV.	Yellow body, ORF/ODB/LHD. 108 mm.	Current	MPR	☐
277	1968-70	The Monkeemobile	Red/White body, DE, 4 *Monkees.* 127 mm.	£8-£10	MPR	☐
C278	1981-	Dan Dare Car.	Red/Yel body, retractable wings. 132 mm.	Current	MPR	☐
C290	1976-81	Kojak Buick.	Bronze body, ODB/SL, badge, 2 figures. 150 mm.		MPR	☐
C292	1978-81	Starsky and Hutch Ford Torino.	Red/White body, 3 figures. 153 mm.	Current	MPR	☐
C298	1983-	Magnum PI Ferrari.	Red/Tan body, WS/LHD. 115 mm.	Current	MPR	☐
C320	1978-81	The Saints Jaguar XJS.	White body, OD, Saint logo on BN. 128 mm.	Current	MPR	☐
336	1967-69	James Bond's Toyota 2000.	White body, D/PS/A, SS/RL in boat. 102 mm.	£7-£9	MPR	☐
C342	1980-82	'PROFESSIONALS' Ford Capri.	Sil/Black body, TW/OD, 3 figures. 124 mm.	Current	MPR	☐
C348	1980-	Vegas Thunderbird.	Red body with Dan Tanner. 124 mm.	Current	MPR	☐
395	1972-73	Fire Bug.	Orange body, Yellow LD, *Firebug.* 83 mm.	Current	MPR	☐
426	1962-63	Circus Booking Office.	Red/Blue body, *Booking Office.* 93 mm.	£35	NC	☐
C426	1978-82	Circus Booking Office.	Yellow/Red body, *Jean Richard Pinder.* 122 mm.	Current	MPR	☐
C434	1978-82	'CHARLIE'S ANGELS' Van.	Pink body, DI/TW. 122 mm.	Current	MPR	☐
C435	1980-	'SUPERVAN'.	Grey body, OD, laboratory. 122 mm.	Current	MPR	☐
C436	1980-	'SPIDER-VAN'.	Blue body, OD, laboratory. 122 mm.	Current	MPR	☐
436	1963-65	Citroen 'WILDLIFE' Safari ID19.	Yellow body, D/PS/OT/BEM/HRS/DI/SS. 108 mm.	£8-£11	MPR	☐
472	1964-66	Land Rover LS Vehicle.	Green/Brown/Yel body, *Vote For Corgi.* 91 mm.	£12	NC	☐
475	1964 only	Citroen Safari Olympic Winter Sports.	White/Yel, *1964,* HRS/OT/BEM/RR/Skier/Skis. 108 mm.	£11-£14	MPR	☐
475	1965-66	Citroen Safari.	White/Yellow body, *Corgi Ski Club,* HRS/OT/BEM/RR/Skier/Skis. 108 mm.	£11-£14	MPR	☐
486	1967-69	'KENNEL CLUB TRUCK.'	Red/White body, trainer and 4 dogs. 108 mm.	£8-£11	MPR	☐
487	1966-69	'CHIPPERFIELDS PARADE VEHICLE'.	Red body, animal figures, *Circus Is Here.* 91 mm.	£18	NC	☐

Novelty, Film and TV Tie-In Models, cont.

No.	Year	Model	Description	Price		
497	1966-69	Man from U.N.C.L.E.	Blue, 2PS plus *Waverley* ring. 108 mm.	£7-£10	MPR	☐
499	1968-69	Citroen 1968 'GRENOBLE' Olympic Winter Sports.	White/Blue/Red, 2 figures, HRS/OT/BEM/RR/Sled/ Skis. 108 mm.	£8-£11	MPR	☐
503	1966-72	Giraffe TPTR.	Red/Blue body, 2 giraffes, *Chipperfields Circus.* 97 mm.	£13	NC	☐
510	1970-72	Citroen DS19 Team Managers Car.	Red, *Tour De France,* fig/LSP, *Paramount,* LHD/D/4 wheels/A. 108 mm.	£11-£14	MPR	☐
511	1970-72	Circus Poodles Truck.	Red/Blue livery, 6 dogs and trainer, *Performing Poodles.* 108 mm.	£14	NC	☐
513	1970-72	Citroen Safari Alpine Rescue Car.	White/Red/Yel, *Alpine Rescue,* HRS/OT/RR/dog/sled/ male fig. 108 mm.	£9-£12	MPR	☐
607	1962-68	Elephant Cage.	Brown/Yellow/Blue body, *Chipperfields Circus.* 76 mm.	£5-£7	MPR	☐
C647	1981	Buck Rogers Starfighter.	Yel/White/Blue, RTT wings, 2 figs. 150 mm.	Current	MPR	☐
C648	1980	NASA Space Shuttle.	White body, *U.S.A. Satellite,* OH. 156 mm.	Current	MPR	☐
C649	1980	J.B's Space Shuttle.	Same as C648 with *Moonraker.* 156 mm.	Current	MPR	☐
801	1969-75	Noddy's Car.	Yel/Red/Sil, 3 Noddy figures. 95 mm.	£11-£14	MPR	☐
802	1970-72	Popeye's Paddle Wagon.	MLCD, Popeye, Olive, Sweet Pea, Bluto, Wimpey, all HP. 127 mm.	£65	NC	☐
803	1969-70	The Beatles Submarine.	Yel/Wh, 2 OH, 4 periscopes, 4 Beatles. 133 mm.	£65	NVE	☐
805	1970	Hardy Boys Rolls Royce.	Red/Yellow, RR, 5 figures. 118 mm.	£20	NC	☐
806	1970-72	Lunar Bug.	Red/White/Blue, *Lunar Bug,* WDS/DDR. 127 mm.	£3-£5	MPR	☐
807	1972	Magic Roundabout Car.	MLCD, Dougal, Dylan and Brian, all HP. 118 mm.	£17	NC	☐
807	1974	Dougals Car.	MLCD, Brian, Dougal and Dylan. 118 mm.	£15	NC	☐
808	1972	Basil Brush's Car.	Red/Yellow, HP, Basil and laugh tapes. 95 mm.	£15	NC	☐
809	1974	Dick Dastardly's Car.	MLCD plus Dick and Muttley. 128 mm.	£15	NC	☐
811	1972-73	James Bond's Moon Buggy.	White/Blue/Yel, with Red gear, U.S. flag. 113 mm.	£9	NC	☐
851	1973-74	Magic Roundabout Train.	MLCD, Dougal, Mr Rusty, Basil, Rosalie and Paul, Loco and 2 carriages. 311 mm.	£22	NC	☐
852	1973-74	Musical Carousel.	MLCD, Dylan plus the children. 200 mm.	£25	NC	☐
853	1973-74	Magic Playground.	Contains 851, 852, 860/1/2, 868 and kids. 820 mm.	£100	GV	☐
859	1973-74	Mr McHenrys Trike.	MLCD, Mr McHenry and Zebedee. 117 mm.	£14	GV	☐
		Models 860-868 Individual Magic Roundabout Figures.	860 Dougal, 861 Florence, 862 Zebedee, 863 Mr Rusty 864 Brian Snail, 865 Basil, 866 Ermintrude the Cow 868 Dylan the Rabbit.	£1-£2	MPR	☐
C925	1981	Batcopter.	Black/Red body, *Batman* winch. 143 mm.	Current	MPR	☐
C928	1981	Spidercopter.	Blue/Red body, RTT tongue. 142 mm.	Current	MPR	☐
C929	1981	'DAILY PLANET' Jetcopter.	Red/White body, RL. 156 mm.	Current	MPR	☐
C930	1980	Drax Helicopter.	White/Yel, *Drax Airlines,* RL. 156 mm.	Current	MPR	☐

Major Packs

Ref. No.		Model Type	Model Features and Size	Rarity and Price Grading		
1119	1960-62	H.D.L. Hovercraft.	Green, Blue and White body, *SR-N1*. 120 mm.	£9-£12	MPR	☐
1121	1960-68	Circus Crane Truck.	Red/Grey/Yel, *Chip Circus* in Blue H. 200 mm.	£15	NC	☐
1123	1961-63	'Chipperfields' Circus Cage.	Red and Blue body, 2AN/TB/H. 127 mm.	£10-£13	MPR	☐
1130	1962-72	Circus Horse TPTR.	Red and Blue body, CHS/AV/DDR, *Chipperfields Circus*. 260 mm.	£15-£19	MPR	☐
1139	1969-72	Scammell Handyman Circus Transporter.	Red and Blue body, 3 cages, 4 animals, *Chip Circus Menagerie*. 232 mm.	£30	NC	☐
1144	1970-72	Circus Crane and Cage.	Red and Blue body, plastic cage with rhino, *Chipperfields*. 200 mm.	£30	NC	☐
C 1163	1978-82	Circus Cannon Truck.	Red and Blue body, *Marvo* figure. 130 mm.	Current	MPR	☐
C 1164	1980-83	Dolphinarium Truck.	Blue body, P tank, girl and dolphin. 290 mm.	Current	MPR	☐

Gift Sets

Ref. No.		Model Type	Model Features and Size	Rarity and Price Grading		
C3	1981	Batmobile and Batboat.	267 and Batboat.	Current	MPR	☐
7	1968-75	'DAKTARI' Gift Set.	Land Rover, tiger, lions, figures.	£7-£9	MPR	☐
8	1960-74	'LIONS OF LONGLEAT' Set.	Land Rover, keeper, 3 lions, dens and meals.	£7-£9	MPR	☐
12	1961-66	Circus Gift Set.	Contains 1121 and 1123.	£55	NC	☐
14	1969-73	Giant 'DAKTARI' Set.	Contains 484, 503, Land Rover.	£20	NC	☐
19	1962-68	'CHIPPERFIELDS' Circus Cage Set.	Contains 438, 607 and elephant.	£15	NC	☐
21	1969-71	Circus Gift Set, 'CHIPPERFIELDS'	Contains 1144 and 1139.	£55	NC	☐
C21	1980-82	Superman Set.	Contains 260, 265 and 925.	Current	MPR	☐
C22	1980-82	James Bond Set.	Contains 269, 271 and 649.	Current	MPR	☐
23	1963-66	Circus Gift Set. 'CHIPPERFIELDS'.	Contains 101, 406, 426, 607, 1121, 2×1123.	£75	GV	☐
C23	1980-82	Spiderman Set.	Contains 261, 266 and 928.	Current	MPR	☐
C30	1978-80	Circus Gift Set.	Land Rover and Trailer.	Current	MPR	☐
C31	1977-80	Safari LR and TRL.	White with black Zebra stripes.	Current	MPR	☐
C36	1977-78	Tarzan Set.	LR, TRL, dinghy and animals.	£5-£7	MPR	☐
40	1967-69	The Avengers Set.	Steed's Bentley plus Emma Peel and her Lotus Elan Convertible.	£35	GV	☐
C40	1977-80	Batman's Gift Set.	Contains 107, 267, 925.	Current	MPR	☐
C41	1977-81	Silver Jubilee Set.	State London with their Majesty's.	Current	MPR	☐
C48	1978-81	Circus Set. 'JEAN RICHARD PINDER'.	Contains C426, C1163, C30, ringmaster, artists, animals.	Current	MPR	☐

4g Roadmaking Vehicles, Crane and Hoists
Single Models

Ref. No.		Model Type	Model Features and Size	Rarity and Price Grading	
54	1974-	Massey Ferguson Tractor Shovel	Yellow Red or Red White body. 150 mm.	Current	MPR ☐
109	1968-69	'PENNYBURN' Trailer	Blue cabinet, Yellow chassis. 76 mm.	Current	MPR ☐
403	1974-79	Thwaites Skip Dumper	Yellow/Green body, DMP tips, Driver. 83 mm.	Current	MPR ☐
406	1971-75	Mercedes Benz Unimog	Yel/Grn body, DRF/SL/RUM/SS/H. 91 mm.	Current	MPR ☐
409	1971-75	Unimog Dumper	White/Red body, SL/RUM/SS/H. 104 mm	Current	MPR ☐
C409	1981	'ALLIS CHALMERS' Forklift	Yellow body, pallets/load/D. 112 mm.	Current	MPR ☐
458	1958-66	E.R.F. Earth Dumper	Red and Yellow body. E.R.F. Cast in. 95 mm	£5-£7	MPR ☐
459	1974-78	Raygu Rascal Roller	Yellow/Green body, *Road Roller*. 125 mm.	Current	MPR ☐
460	1959-63	E.R.F. Cement Tipper	Yellow/Grey body, (Neville) E.R.F. CI. 95 mm.	£5-£7	MPR ☐
483	1968-72	Dodge Tipper Truck	Yellow Black body, *Kew Fargo*. 136 mm	Current	MPR ☐
494	1967-72	Bedford Tipper	Red/Yellow body, RVM. 102 mm.	Current	MPR ☐

Major Packs

C1101	1976-81	Mobile Crane	Yellow/Blue body, *Warner & Swasey*. 150 mm.	Current	MPR ☐
1102	1958-62	EUCLID TC 12 TRC	Green/Sil/Blk body, on tracks. 159 mm.	£5-£7	MPR ☐
C1102	1976-77	'BERLIET' Bottom Dumper	Yel and Black body, *Road Construction*. 287 mm.	Current	MPR ☐
1103	1960-63	'EUCLID' Crawler TRC	Yel/Green/White body, No D, on tracks. 111 mm.	£8-£11	MPR ☐
1107	1963-66	'EUCLID' with Dozer	Yel/Green body, Driver, on Tracks. 159 mm.	£8-£11	MRP ☐
1110	1976-80	J.C.B. Crawler	Yellow and White body, Driver. 115 mm.	Current	MPR ☐
C1113	1981-	'HYSTER' Container Handler	Yellow or Bl/Wh MB *US Lines* HST. 212 mm.	Current	MPR ☐
1128	1963-76	'PRIESTMAN' cub Shovel	Red/Yellow body, Driver. 165 mm	£5-£7	MPR ☐
1145	1970-76	Unimog Goose Dumper	Yel/Red body '406'. 171 mm.	Current	MPR ☐
1153	1973-74	'PRIESTMAN' Crane	Red/Orange body *Higrab*. 230 mm.	£8-£11	MPR ☐
1154	1974-76	PRIESTMAN Crane Truck	Yel/Red body, Silver boom H. 240 mm	£8-£11	MPR ☐
C1155	1975-79	'SKYSCRAPER' Tower Crane	Yellow/Red body, Black Tracks. 340 mm.	£5-£7	MPR ☐
1156	1977-	Volvo Concrete Mixer	Yellow/Red, *Block Construction*	Current	MPR ☐

Gift Sets

2	1971-73	Unimog Dumper and Shovel	Contains 1128 and 1145	£8-£11	MPR ☐
C2	1980	Construction Site Set	Contains 440 and 54.	Current	MPR ☐
27	1963-72	Priestman 9ft Set	Contains 1128 and 1131 Bedford TPTR	Current	MPR ☐
14	1961-65	Tower Wagon Set	Contains Jeep FC 150, and fig/EQ	£8-£11	MPR ☐

4h Ambulance, Fire, Police and Rescue Vehicles

Ref. No.		Model Type	Model Features and Size	Rarity and Price Grading		
209	1958-61	Riley Police Car	Black & Silver MB, *Police* Bell. 97mm.	£16	GV	☐
213	1959-61	Jaguar Fire Service Car	Red body, *Fire* EM/A/bell. 95 mm.	£16	GV	☐
213S	1961-62	Jaguar Fire Service Car	Red body, *Fire* EM/SS/A/bell. 95 mm.	£16	GV	☐
223	1959-61	Chevrolet State Police Car	Black/Yel/White body, *State Patrol* A. 108 mm.	£12	GV	☐
237	1962-66	Oldsmobile Sheriffs Car	White/Black body *County Sheriff* SL/SS. 108 mm.	£8-£10	MPR	☐
C326	1980-81	Chevrolet Caprice Police Car	Black/White body, *Police.* ODB/SS. 150 mm.	Current	MPR	☐
C332	1980-81	Opel Doctors Car	White/Red body, *Notartz* OD. 142 mm.	Current	MPR	☐
C339	1980	Rover Police Car.	White and Red body, EM, *Police.* 140 mm.	Current	MPR	☐
373	1970-76	VW 1200 Police Car.	Black/White/Blue body, *Police.* 91 mm.	£3-£4	MPR	☐
402	1974-77	Ford Cortina Police Car.	White/Red body, *Police,* SL/OD. 102 mm.	£3-£4	MPR	☐
405	1956-60	Bedford Fire Tender.	Green body, Sil Ladder, A.F.S. in Yel. 83 mm.	£30	GV	☐
405M	1956-59	Bedford Fire Tender.	Red body, Sil Ladder, *Fire Dept,* in Yel. 83 mm.	£30	GV	☐
C405	1978-80	Chevrolet 'AMBULANCE'.	White/Orange, OD/STR/AM/SL. 119 mm.	Current	MPR	☐
C406	1980-81	Mercedes 'AMBULANCE'.	White/Red body, OD/STR/2AM/SL. 150 mm.	Current	MPR	☐
412	1957-60	Bedford 15 CWT Ambulance.	Cream body, *Ambulance.* 83 mm.	£20	GV	☐
C412	1976-78	Mercedes Police Car.	Green/White body, *Polizei,* OD/SL. 108 mm.	£3-£4	MPR	☐
414	1976-77	Coastguard Jaguar XJ12C.	White/Blue body, *Coastguard,* OL.	£3-£4	MPR	☐
416	1958-62	R.A.C. Land Rover.	Blue body, *Radio Rescue,* A/No SS. 95 mm.	£12	NC	☐
416	1962-64	R.A.C. Land Rover.	Blue body, *Radio Rescue,* A/SS. 95 mm.	£10	NC	☐
C416	1977-79	Buick Police Car.	Met Blue body, *Police,* 2PM. 150 mm.	Current	MPR	☐
419	1960-63	Ford Zephyr Motorway Patrol.	White/Blue body, *Police.* 97 mm.	£12-£15	MPR	☐
421	1977-79	'FOREST WARDEN'S FIRE' Land Rover.	Red/White body, SPW/RR/SL/OD. 135 mm.	Current	MPR	☐
422	1977-80	Riot Police Wagon.	Red/White body, *6 Riot Police.* 95 mm.	Current	MPR	☐
423	1960-62	Bedford Fire Tender.	Red body, Blk/LD, *Fire Dept.* 82 mm.	£12-£15	MPR	☐
C428	1978-79	Renault Police Car.	Black/White body, *Police,* ODHB/SL/A. 97 mm.	Current	MPR	☐
C429	1978-80	Police Jaguar XJ12C.	White/Red/Blue body, *Police,* ODB/SL/A. 127 mm.	Current	MPR	☐
C430	1978-80	Porsche 924 Police Car.	Black/White body, *Police,* ODHB/SL/A. 118 mm.	Current	MPR	☐
437	1962-68	Superior Cadillac.	Blue/White body, plain or battery versions. 114 mm.	£7-£9	MPR	☐
439	1963-65	Chevrolet Fire Chiefs Car.	Red/White body, *Fire Chief,* SL/A/2FM. 108 mm.	£7-£9	MPR	☐
448	1964-69	Police Mini Van.	Blue body, *Police,* dog and PM/SL/OD. 79 mm.	£7-£10	MPR	☐
461	1971-79	Range Rover Police Vehicle.	White/Red/Blue body, PM/FB/9BLS/3WNS. 108 mm.	Current	MPR	☐
463	1964-66	Commer 'AMBULANCE'.	Cream body, Blue TW/SL. 90 mm.	£5-£7	MPR	☐
464	1963-68	Commer 15 cwt Police Van.	Blue body, *County Police* or *Police,* BOFL. 90 mm.	£5-£7	MPR	☐
481	1965-69	Chevrolet Police Car.	White/Blk body, *Police Patrol,* SL/2PM/A. 108 mm.	£5-£7	MPR	☐
482	1966-69	Chevrolet Fire Chief.	White/Red body, *Fire Chief,* PP/Badge. 108 mm.	£6-£8	MPR	☐
482	1974-77	Range Rover Ambulance.	White/Red/Blue body, *Ambulance,* SL/STR/2PM. 100 mm.	Current	MPR	☐
C482	1978-80	AMC Racer 'RESCUE'.	White/Orange/Black body, RN '35', OHB/SL. 118 mm.	Current	MPR	☐
C489	1980	VW Polo 'POLICE' Car.	White/Green body, *Polizei,* ODHB/SL. 97 mm.	Current	MPR	☐
492	1966-69	Volkswagen Police Car.	Green/White body, *Polizei,* SVRMSL. 91 mm.	£6-£8	MPR	☐
506	1968-71	Sunbeam Imp Panda Car.	Blue/White body, *Police,* TS/SL/FS. 83 mm.	£4-£6	MPR	☐
509	1970-72	Porsche Targa Police Car.	White/Red body, *Polizei,* siren/SL. 95 mm.	£3-£4	MPR	☐
513	1970-72	Citroen ID19 'ALPINE RESCUE'.	White/Red body, Roof Rack/fig/dog/sled/skis/poles. 108 mm.	£10-£12	MPR	☐
700	1974-79	Motorway 'AMBULANCE'.	White/Red body, *Accident,* Red Cross. 98 mm.	Current	MPR	☐
703	1976-78	Hi-Speed Fire Engine.	Red body, Yellow ladder, SL. 115 mm.	Current	MPR	☐
921	1975-81	Hughes OH-6A Police Helicopter.	White/Red, *Police, Rescue,* SL. 143 mm.	Current	MPR	☐
924	1977-81	Air Sea Rescue HLC.	Orange/Yel/Black body, *Rescue,* 150 mm.	Current	MPR	☐
927	1978-79	Surf Rescue HLC.	Blue/White body, *Surf Rescue.* 156 mm.	Current	MPR	☐

Major Packs and Large Size Models

Ref. No.		Model Type	Model Features and Size	Rarity and Price Grading		
C1001	1981-	HC8 Angus Firestreak.	Red/White/Sil, *Rescue,* 2FM/LD/EQ. 165 mm.	Current	MPR	□
1103	1976-81	'PATHFINDER AIRPORT CRASH TRUCK'.	Red/Sil, *Airport Fire Brigade,* OWP. 240 mm.	£5-£7	MPR	□
1126	1977-81	'SIMON SNORKEL' Fire Engine.	Red/White/Yel, TUT/EBMS/LD/RSJ/2SL/6FM. 265 mm.	£5-£7	MPR	□
1127	1964-74	'SIMON SNORKEL' Fire Engine.	Red/Yel/Sil, TUT/EBMS/RSJ/6FM/2SL. 252 mm.	£7-£9	MPR	□
C1143	1969	'AMERICAN LA FRANCE' Fire Engine.	Red/White/Yel, TUT/RCTLD/4ELD/5FM. 285 mm.	Current	MPR	□
			Early Box Type only	£12-£16		

Gift Sets

Ref. No.		Model Type	Model Features and Size	Rarity and Price Grading		
18	1976-77	Emergency Gift Set.	Contains 402, 482, C921.	Current	MPR	□
C19	1979-82	Emergency Gift Set.	Contains C339 and C921	Current	MPR	□
C20	1978-80	Emergency Gift Set.	Contains C429, C482, C921.	Current	MPR	□
C35	1978-79	'CHOPPER SQUAD' Surf Boat.	Contains 927, 419, TRL, Rescue Boat.	Current	MPR	□
C44	1978-80	Metropolitan Police Land Rover and Horsebox.	Contains LR, HSB, HP, HS and PM.	Current	MPR	□
C45	1978-80	Royal Canadian Mounted Police Land Rover and horsebox.	Contains LR, HSB, HP, HS and PM.	Current	MPR	□

4i Agricultural Models
Single Models

Ref. No.		Model Type	Model Features and Size	Rarity and Price Grading		
50	1959-66	Massey Ferguson '65' Tractor.	Red/Beige body. 79 mm.	£6-£8	MPR	☐
C50	1974-77	Massey Ferguson '50B' Tractor.	Yellow/Black/Red body, WDS. 138 mm.	Current	MPR	☐
51	1959-69	Massey Ferguson Tipper Trailer.	Red/Brown body. 102 mm.	Current	MPR	☐
53	1960-66	Massey Ferguson Tractor with Shovel.	Red/Brown tractor, Grey/Blue shovel. 124 mm.	£3-£5	MPR	☐
54	1974	Massey Ferguson Tractor with Shovel.	Yellow/Red or White/Red body. 150 mm.	Current	MPR	☐
54	1958-62	Fordson Half Track Tractor.	Blue/Brown/Silver body, rubber tracks. 91 mm.	£5-£7	MPR	☐
55	1961-63	Fordson Major Tractor.	Blue/Grey/Red body. 83 mm.	£5-£7	MPR	☐
55	1977	David Brown Tractor.	Black/Red/White body. SW. 105 mm.	Current	MPR	☐
56	1961-63	Four Furrow Plough.	Red/Brown/Yellow body. 90 mm.	Current	MPR	☐
56	1977	Farm Tipper Trailer.	Red/Yel or Red/Wh body, DDTBD. 130 mm.	Current	MPR	☐
57	1963-65	Massey Ferguson Tractor with stock.	Red/Silver/Green body, D/SW. 127 mm.	£4-£6	MPR	☐
58	1965-72	Beast Carrier.	Red, Cream and Blue body, 4 calves. 112 mm.	Current	MPR	☐
60	1964-66	Fordson Power Major Tractor.	Blue body, Plough lifts. 83 mm.	£4-£6	MPR	☐
61	1964-70	Four Furrow Plough.	Blue/Silver body. 90 mm.	Current	MPR	☐
62	1965-70	Ford Tipper Trailer.	Red/Yellow body. 144 mm.	Current	MPR	☐
64	1965-69	Conveyor on Jeep.	Red body, Yel/White, CVB, farmland. 197 mm.	£6-£8	MPR	☐
66	1966-72	Massey Ferguson '165' Tractor.	Red/Blue/White body, engine sound. 76 mm.	£4-£6	MPR	☐
67	1967-72	Ford Super Major Tractor.	Blue/White/Sil body, *Ford 5000.* 90 mm.	£4-£5	MPR	☐
69	1967-70	Massey Ferguson '165' Tractor and Shovel.	Red/Blue body, Sil Shovel, fig. 127 mm.	£4-£5	MPR	☐
71	1967-72	Fordson Disc Harrow.	Yellow/Red/Silver body. 90 mm.	Current	MPR	☐
72	1971-73	Ford '5000' Tractor and Towbar.	Model 67, frame/bucket/pipes. 90 mm.	£4-£5	MPR	☐
73	1970-72	Massey Ferguson Tractor and Saw.	Model 66 plus Yel rotating saw. 90 mm.	£4-£5	MPR	☐
74	1969-72	Ford '5000' Tractor and Scoop.	Model 67 plus Yellow/Silver Scoop. 90 mm.	£4-£5	MPR	☐
100	1957-61	Dropside Trailer.	Yellow/Red/Grey body. 108 mm.	Current	MPR	☐
101	1958-61	Platform Trailer.	Yellow/Grey body.	Current	MPR	☐
102	1957-65	Rice's Pony Trailer.	Red body, Brown pony, 2DDR. 86 mm.	£4-£6	MPR	☐

Major Packs and Large Size Models

Ref. No.		Model Type	Model Features and Size	Rarity and Price Grading		
1111	1959-62	Massey Ferguson Combine Harvester.	Red/Yellow body, metal tines. 172 mm.	£15	GV	☐
1111	1968-72	Massey Ferguson Combine Harvester.	Same as 1111 with plastic tines. 172 mm.	£7-£9	MPR	☐
C1112	1977-78	David Brown Combine Harvester.	Contains C55 plus Red/Wh/Blk CHVR. 220 mm.	£3-£4	MPR	☐

Agricultural Models cont.

Gift Sets

Ref. No.		Model Type	Model Features and Size	Rarity and Price Grading	
1	1968-72	Tractor and Beast Carrier Set.	Tractor (67) and Beast Carrier (58).	£10-£12	MPR ☐
2	1958-66	Land Rover and Pony Trailer Set.	Land Rover (438), Pony Trailer (102).	£8-£11	MPR ☐
4	1974-75	Country Farm Set.	Contains 50, 62, and EQ.	£5-£7	MPR ☐
5	1968-72	Agricultural Set.	Contains 484, 438, 71, 69, 62, D/EQ.	£14-£17	MPR ☐
7	1959-63	Tractor and Trailer Set.	Contains 50 and 51.	£11-£14	MPR ☐
8	1959-61	Combine, Tractor and Trailer Set.	Contains 1111, 50, 51.	£14-£17	MPR ☐
9	1968-72	Trailer, Tractor and Shovel Set.	Contains 66, 69 and 62.	£7-£9	MPR ☐
13	1964-67	Fordson Tractor and Plough Set.	Contains 60 and 61.	£7-£9	MPR ☐
15	1968-76	Land Rover and Horse Box.	Contains 438, Brown, pre 70, Met Blue post, 112, mare and foal. 197 mm.	£3-£5	MPR ☐
18	1961-63	Ford Tractor and Plough Set.	Contains 55 and 56.	£8-£10	MPR ☐
22	1963-66	Agricultural Set.	Contains 1111, 50, 438, 100, 55, 61, skip and milk churns.	£30-£35	MPR ☐
29	1963-64	Massey Ferguson Tractor and Trailer.	Contains 50, 51, Driver.	£7-£9	MPR ☐
C29	1981	'CORGI' Ponyclub.	Contains 441 and accessories.	Current	MPR ☐
32	1965-68	Tractor, Shovel and Trailer Set.	Contains 54, 62.	£7-£9	MPR ☐
33	1965-68	Tractor and Beast Carrier.	Contains 55, 58.	£7-£9	MPR ☐
34	1977-79	Tractor and Tipping Trailer.	Contains 55, 56 (Trailer).	Current	MPR ☐
C42	1979-80	Agricultural Set.	Contains C34, C43, Silo/Elevator.	Current	MPR ☐
C43	1979-80	Silo and Conveyor Set.	Silo and Elevator, *Corgi Harvesting Company Ltd.*	Current	MPR ☐
47	1966-69	Ford Tractor and Conveyor Set.	Model 67, TRL with CVB/D/fig/ACCS.	£8-£11	MPR ☐
C47	1978-80	Pony Club Set.	Brown/White Land Rover, Brown Trailer, girl, horse.	Current	MPR ☐

4j Corgi Classics

A factory fire ended production in 1969

Ref. No.		Model Type	Model Features and Size	Rarity and Price Grading	
9001	1964-69	1927 3 Litre Bentley. Le Mans Winner.	Dark Green body, RN '3', DTH/SPKW/SPW/RCD/ HBR/SDB/DCH/WS/SW/AR. 102 mm.	£20	NC ☐
9002	1964-68	1927 3 Litre Bentley.	Red body, CD/No RN, then as 9001. 102 mm.	£20	NC ☐
9004	1967-69	The 'WORLD OF WOOSTER' Bentley.	Model 9001 again in Green or Red. Jeeves and Wooster figures. 102 mm.	£17	NC ☐
9011	1964-68	1915 Model T Ford.	Black, SPKW/BRR/SPW/CL/FHD/WS/D and PS. 86 mm.	£18	NC ☐
9012	1965-68	1915 Model T Ford.	Yellow body, SAPM 9011. 86 mm.	£18	NC ☐
9013	1964-69	1915 Model T Ford.	Red/Black body, LHD/DTH/SPW/D cranks. 83 mm.	£18	NC ☐
9014	—	1915 'LYONS TEA' Van.	In 67/68 Cat but not issued.		NVP ☐
9021	1964-69	1910 38 h.p. Daimler.	Red body, SPKW/FHD/SPW/DCH/AR/D and 3 PS. 108 mm.	£20	NC ☐
9022	—	1910 38 h.p. Daimler.	In 1966 Cat but not issued.		NVP ☐
9031	1965-68	1910 Renault 12/16.	Lavender/Black body, CL/SPKW/LHD. 102 mm.	£16	NC ☐
9032	1965-69	1910 Renault 12/16.	Primrose/Black body, CL/SPKW/LHD. 102 mm.	£16	NC ☐
9041	1966-70	1912 Rolls Royce Silver Ghost.	Silver/Black body, SPKW/CL/SPW/SW/AR. 118 mm.	£18	NC ☐

Note. The boxed models should contain a picture of the model.

4k Corgitronics and Corgimatics

Ref. No.		Model Type	Model Features and Size	Rarity and Price Grading	
C 1001	1982	HCB Angus Firestreak.	Red/Yel/White, *Rescue,* BOMCA/ELS/2FB/OOS. 165 mm.	Current	MPR ☐
C 1002	1981	Sonic Corgi Truck Set with two interchangeable bodies.	Yel/White/Black/Red, *Shell Super Oil, BP Oil,* Tanker, AV/BOMCA/FW/RV/RCC. 228 mm.	Current	MPR ☐
C 1002	1981	'YORKIE' Truck Set.	White/Yel/Blue/Orange, *Milk Chocolate Yorkie,* AV/CS/BOMCA/FW/RV/RCC. 228 mm.	Current	MPR ☐
C 1003	1981	Ford Road Hog.	Black with Yel/Wh twirls, 2A/PDS/BOMCA/two tone horn. 150 mm.	Current	MPR ☐
C 1004	1981	Beep Beep Bus.	Red body, *BTA Welcome To Britain,* PDS/BOMCA/two tone horn. 123 mm.	Current	MPR ☐
C 1004 /01	1983	Beep Beep Bus.	Red, *Welcome To Hamleys'.* Available at the Regent St, London, shop.	Current	MPR ☐
C 1005	1982	Police Land Rover.	White/Red/Blue, *Police,* PDS/BOMCA/ELS/FB. 132 mm.	Current	MPR ☐
C 1006	1982	'RADIO WEST' Roadshow.	Yel, Red and Blue, *Your Local Radio 605,* OOS/ BOMCA/AM Radio/3LS/OD. 123 mm.	Current	MPR ☐
C 1006	1982	'RADIO LUXEMBOURG' Roadshow.	Red/White body, 'RTL 208', OOS/BOMCA/AM Radio/3LS/OD. 123 mm.	Current	MPR ☐
C 1007	1982	Road Repair Unit. Land Rover TRL and FIG.	Yel/Red/Sil, *Roadworks,* SPW/drill/BOMCA/Road Drill Sound/PDS. 264 mm.	Current	MPR ☐
C 1008	1982	Fire Chief's Car.	Red/White/Yel/Sil, *Fire Department,* PDS/BOMCA/ ELS/FB. 150 mm.	Current	MPR ☐
C 1009	1983	MG Maestro 1600.	Yellow/Black, PDS/BOMCA/WHL/WRL. 118 mm.	Current	MPR ☐
C 1024	1983	Beep Beep Bus.	Red, *BTA,* Supplied to Mothercare exclusively.	Current	MPR ☐

41 Miscellaneous
Jeeps, Land Rovers, Pick-ups, Breakdown Trucks, Caravans, Motor Cycles, Go-Karts and Trailers

Ref. No.		Model Type	Model Features and Size	Rarity and Price Grading	
C46	1983-	Super Karts.	Blue or Orange body, Red/Sil RCD.	Current	MPR ☐
100	1957-61	Dropside Trailer.	All Yel or Red body, TB. 108 mm.	Current	MPR ☐
101	1958-61	Platform Trailer.	Grey/Yel body, axle swivels, TB. 108 mm.	Current	MPR ☐
C171	1982-	Street Bike.	Red, Silver and Black body, MLCD, swirl.	Current	MPR ☐
C172	1982-	'POLICE' Bike.	White, Black and Silver body.	Current	MPR ☐
C173	1982-	Cafe Racer.	Silver and Black, RN '26', *750cc Class.*	Current	MPR ☐
406	1957-63	Land Rover Pick-up.	Yel/Black body, OC/SPW/TBD. 95 mm.	£5-£7	MPR ☐
409	1959-63	Forward Control Jeep.	Blue body, Red R grille, TBD/SWP. 91 mm.	£5-£7	MPR ☐
C415	1976-78	Mazda Camper PV.	Red body, DDTBD plus White caravan. 140 mm.	Current	MPR ☐
417	1963-65	Land Rover 'BREAKDOWN SERVICE'.	Red/Yel/Sil, SPW/H/WKW, SS in 63. 114 mm.	£5-£7	MPR ☐
C419	1978-79	Covered Jeep CJ5.	Green with White plastic top. 100 mm.	Current	MPR ☐
420	1962-66	Ford Thames 'AIRBORNE' Caravan.	White/Green body, OC/ODB/DI/S/VB. 95 mm.	£7-£9	MPR ☐
C421	1977-79	Land Rover.	Gold/Black body, RR/LD/SPW/SDW(3)/ODB. 114 mm.	Current	MPR ☐
431	1964-66	Volkswagen Pick-up.	Yellow/Red, S/SW/SS/DC. 91 mm.	£4-£6	MPR ☐
434	1963-66	Volkswagen Kumbe MB.	Two Tone Green, Yellow S/IS. 91 mm.	£6-£8	MPR ☐
438	1963-77	Land Rover with SPWB.	Early models — Red or Green body. 95 mm.	£4-£6	MPR ☐
C440	1979-	Mazda Custom Pick-up.	Orange/Yel/Red, US flag, MLCD. 120 mm.	Current	MPR ☐
C441	1979-82	'GOLDEN EAGLE' Jeep CJ5.	Brown/Tan or Gold/Wh, DRF/SPWS. 100 mm.	Current	MPR ☐
C448	1983-	4×4 Renegade Jeep.	Yel/Red, *Renegade,* SPWS/LHD. 104 mm.	Current	MPR ☐
C457	1981-	Talbot Matra R.	Red/Black or Green/Black, ODB/OT/TS. 120 mm.	Current	MPR ☐
465	1963-66	Commer Pick-up Truck.	Red/Orange, S/SW/SS/TOL. 90 mm.	£4-£6	MPR ☐
470	1965-72	Forward Control Jeep.	Blue/Grey, OC/DC/SS/LHD. 91 mm.	Current	MPR ☐
477	1966-67	Land Rover 'BREAKDOWN SERVICE'.	Red/Yel/Sil, SPWS/WKW/H. 114 mm.	Current	MPR ☐
478	1965-69	Jeep Tower Wagon.	Green, Yellow and Silver body, figure. 129 mm.	£4-£6	MPR ☐
C490	1967-70	Volkswagen Breakdown Van.	Beige/Red, Tool Box, 2SPW. 102 mm.	£4-£6	MPR ☐
C490	1976-79	Touring Caravan.	White and Blue body, OD/TB. 125 mm.	Current	MPR ☐
C493	1976-78	Mazda B 1600 Pick-up.	Blue body, DDTB. 120 mm.	Current	MPR ☐
C495	1983-	4×4 Mazda 'OB TRUCK'.	Blue/Black, *Corgi Cruiser,* DDTB. 121 mm.	Current	MPR ☐
702	1975-79	Breakdown Truck.	Red/Black, single BM/H. 100 mm.	Current	MPR ☐

Miscellaneous Models cont.

Major Models

Ref. No.		Model Type	Model Features and Size	Rarity and Price Grading	
C 1116	1979	Refuse Collector.	Orange/Silver body, *City Sanitation*. 151 mm.	Current	MPR ☐
C 1117	1980	Streetsweeper.	Orange/Yel body, Red/White stripes, *Faun* fig. 135 mm.	Current	MPR ☐
C 1140	1982	Ford Transit Wrecker.	White/Red, *24 Hour Service,* WO/H. 131 mm.	Current	MPR ☐
1142	1967-74	'HOLMES WRECKER' Recovery Vehicle.	Red/White/Blue, TC/2SPW/LD/SL/2WD/2H. 114 mm.	£13-£16	MPR ☐
1144	1975-78	Berliet Wrecker Recovery Vehicle.	Red/Grey body, 2 hoists and hooks. 130 mm.	£8-£11	MPR ☐
1150	1974-77	Unimog with Snow Plough.	Yel/Brown body, Sil Blade, 2 flags. 155 mm.	£4-£6	MPR ☐

Gift Sets

Ref. No.		Model Type	Model Features and Size	Rarity and Price Grading	
17	1963-67	Land Rover and Ferrari Set.	(438) LR plus (154) Ferrari on TRL.	£8-£11	MPR ☐
19	1973-77	'CORGI FLYING CLUB' Set.	Green/Brown LR, Yel/Red AC.	£7-£9	MPR ☐
28	1963-66	Mazda Dinghy Set.	Mazda (493) plus dinghy and TRL.	£5-£7	MPR ☐
C49	1978-80	'CORGI FLYING CLUB' Set.	Green/White Jeep, Blue/White AC.	£5-£7	MPR ☐
64	1965-69	Forward Control Jeep 150 and Conveyor Belt.	Jeep (409), Yel/Wh CVB.	£7-£9	MPR ☐

Chapter 5
Models of Days Gone by Lledo (London) Ltd

A new Toy Company formed by Jack Odell one of the founders of Matchbox Toys. First Toys issued in the Summer of 1983.

Ref. No.		Model Type	Model Features and Size	Rarity and Price Grading	
DG1	1983	London Open Sided 'WESTMINSTER' Horse Tram.	Bright Green chassis, Grey roof, Orange seats, 2 Gold 'Bells' on roof, Gold shafts, Green/Red decals, White crests front and rear ends, White plastic rollers, Brown plastic horse. Set of 5 White UPF. 120 mm.	Current	MPR ☐
DG1a	1983	U.S. Variant 'MAIN STREET' Horse Tram.	Dark Brown chassis, Deep Cream roof, Orange seats, Green/Red decals, White crests front and rear ends, White plastic rollers, Brown plastic horse. Set of 5 White UPF. 120 mm.	Current	MPR ☐
DG2	1983	'EXPRESS DAIRY' Milk Float.	Dark Blue body, Light Blue chassis and shafts, White plastic roof, Gold 12 spoke wheels, Black plastic tyres and horse, 4 White UPF, White letters. 94 mm.	Current	MPR ☐
DG3	1983	'WINDMILL BAKERY' Bread Float.	Yellow body, Cream chassis and shafts, Brown plastic roof and horse, Gold 12 spoke wheels, Brown/White decals, Black plastic tyres, 3 White UPF. 94 mm.	Current	MPR ☐
DG4	1983	Horse Bus, 'LIPTON'S TEAS' 'LARGEST SALES IN THE WORLD'.	Red body and swivelling shafts, Green plastic seats, 2 Brown plastic horses, 2 small and 2 large Black metal wheels (12 and 16 spokes), Yellow *London General Omnibus Company, Victoria and Kings Cross,* decals with Light (R) or Dark Green background. 5 White UPF. 107 mm.	Current	MPR ☐
DG4a	1983	US Variant 'BOWERY-BROADWAY' Horse-Bus	Green body and swivelling shafts, Light Brown plastic seats, Brown metal wheels *Fifth Avenue Coach Company* decal in Yellow plus the same *Liptons Tea* decal in Dark Green. 5 White UPF.	Current	MPR ☐
DG5	1983	Shandmason Fire Engine 'LONDON FIRE BRIGADE'.	Red body and shafts, Gold boiler and pump, 2 small and 2 large metal wheels (12 and 16 spokes), 2 Black plastic horses, 3 Blue UPF. 105 mm.	Current	MPR ☐
DG5a	1983	U.S. Variant 'CHICAGO FIRE BRIGADE'.	Red body and shafts, Gold boiler and pump, 2 small and 2 large metal wheels (12 and 16 spokes), 2 Black plastic horse, 3 Blue UPF. 105 mm.	Current	MPR ☐
		Model T Ford Van Issues			
DG6	1983	'OVALTINE'.	Orange body, Gold trim, Dark Brown chassis, Light Brown plastic roof, metal 12 spoke wheels, Black plastic tyres, Blue/Cream/Orange decal, 3 Blue UPF, 2 SDW and 2 RWDS, cast in rear doors, BPT. 70 mm.	Current	MPR ☐
DG6 YP	1983	'YORKSHIRE POST'	Dark Blue body, Black roof and chassis. Gold trim, *12 mph* and *Twixt Trent & Tweed* in Yellow, metal 12 spoke wheels, Black plastic tyres, 3 Blue UPF, 2 SDW and 2 RWDS, cast in rear doors, BPT. 70 mm.	Current	MPR ☐
DG6 CCC	1983	'COOKIE COACH COMPANY'	Orange body, Black roof and chassis, Decals in yellow with gold letters, Black headboard with White letters, metal 12 spoke wheels, Black plastic tyres, 3 Blue UPF, 2 SDW and 2 RWDS, cast in rear doors, BPT. 70 mm.	Current	MPR ☐
DG6 BM	1983	'BRITISH MEAT'	White body, Brown roof and chassis, Decals in Red/White/Blue with Blue lines, White letters on headboard, metal 12 spoke wheels, Black plastic tyres, 3 Blue UPF, 2 SDW and 2 RWDS, cast in rear doors, BPT. 70 mm.	Current	MPR ☐

MODELS OF DAYS GONE

Model No. 1.

The Box Design.

An early Lledo variation — Dark and Light Green backgrounds to the 'LIPTON'S TEA' decal. The Light Green is the rare one.

CATALOGUE OMISSIONS

Accurate birth records do not exist in respect of all the diecast models issued. Therefore whilst every effort has been made to provide comprehensive information it is inevitable that collectors will have knowledge of models which have not been included. Consequently the compiler will be pleased to receive details of these models in order that they be included in any future editions. Naturally supporting evidence regarding authenticity will be required.

CATALOGUE ADVICE SERVICE

The Catalogue compiler is always pleased to try and advise collectors on any topics connected with diecast model collecting. However it will be appreciated that obtaining the correct answers can often take considerable time and involve the expense of long distance telephone calls and postage. Consequently it is regrettably necessary for collectors to enclose £2 (or its overseas equivalent) when requesting technical information. Please submit all enquiries in writing in the first instance.

FORMATION OF THE SWAPMEET COLLECTORS CLUB

The main objective of the Club will be to provide a regular link between all who are interested in the buying and selling of toys and models.

This will be achieved by issuing to Club members bi-monthly lists of toys for sale.

Any club member, Collector's shop, Toy Auctioneer or Mail Order dealer may advertise on the lists.

Club membership will enable collectors to have access to a wide range of models for sale and to keep up to date about new issues and current price levels. Collectors unable to regularly visit a collectors shop or Toy Fair should find membership to be very helpful.

Collectors Shops and Mail Order dealers should find that advertising to Club Members will be an economic and effective method of reaching additional buyers.

For further details of Club Membership and/or Trade terms please complete the attached slip.

. . . .

To SWAPMEET TOYS AND MODELS LTD
LIONS LODGE, 10 HIGH ROAD WEST, FELIXSTOWE, SUFFOLK, ENGLAND IP11 9JB

I am interested in joining the SWAPMEET COLLECTORS CLUB. Please send me further details completely without any obligation.
or
I am interested in further details of the trade terms available.

Name ____

Address ____

LATE AMENDMENTS TO THE CATALOGUE LISTINGS

DINKY COMMERCIAL AND UTILITY VEHICLES

i) Text should now read:—

959 Foden Dump Truck with Bulldozer Blade, Red body, Silver blade. £16-21 MPR

ii) Rarity and Price Grading to read:—

977 Servicing Platform Vehicle. £85 GV

DINKY VANS

i) Text should now read:—

410 Bedford Van with *Modellers World* decals. Only 200 issued. NGPP

ii) Include additional model:—

410 Bedford Van with *Wimpey* decals. Black letters, Orange body, 90 mm. NGPP

DINKY BUSES, TAXIS AND TRAMS

Text should now read:—

283 'RED ARROW' Single Decker Bus. The first issue was Non Metallic Red with Black BP, White doors and labels, Yellow interior. 2 OD/RT/Bell, *Pay as you enter* and *Red Bus Rovers* decals. £9-12 MPR
Second Issue had Metallic Red body, White BP, Blue interior. £25 GV

DINKY MODELS ISSUED IN DENMARK

The following models were issued with the Danish 'FALCK' labels. Insufficient information is available to give price guidance.

271 Ford Transit Fire Appliance
282 Land Rover Fire Appliance
285 Merryweather Marquis Fire Engine
286 Ford Transit Fire Appliance
288 Superior Cadillac Ambulance
410 Danish Post Office Bedford Van
442 Land Rover Breakdown Crane
956 Berliet Fire Escape

DINKY GERMAN ISSUES

260 Deutsche Bundesposte Volkswagen
261 Ford Taunus *Polizei*
F-4K Phantom Der Bundesluftwaffe

DINKY BELGIUM ISSUES

271 T.S. Motor Cycle Patrol (Special Issue of 270 A.A. Patrol)

DINKY MISCELLANEOUS GIFT SET

1978-80 DINKY WAY SET Contains 207, 256, 412 and Dumper Truck, Roadway and Signs, £15 GV

MATCHBOX 1-75 SERIES GIFT SET

i) G-1 Commercial Motor Set contains:—
  5b 'PLAYERS PLEASE' GPW, 57 mm
  47a 'BROOKE BOND' Van, GPW
  69a 'NESTLÉS' Van GPW
  60a 'BUILDERS SUPPLY COMPANY' Pick Up, RWDS/GPW
  37a 'COCA COLA' Lorry, Even Load, GPW
  59a Ford 'SINGER' Van GPW
  20a 'EVER READY' Truck, GPW
  51a Albion 'PORTLAND CEMENT' Lorry, GPW. £125 GV

ii) **MATCHBOX 1-75 SERIES 1983 NEW ISSUES**
  The base plates have been modified to show 'MADE IN MACAU'

MODELS OF YESTERYEAR SERIES

Model Variant

Y-3(D) 'ZEROLENE' Ford Model 'T' Tanker Red PSPKW £30 GV

MODELS OF YESTERYEAR 1984 ISSUES

Y-3 Model T Tanker, 'CARNATION FARM PRODUCTS' Livery
Y-6 Rolls Royce Fire Engine, a colour change
Y-8 MG TC, a colour change
Y-12 Model T Ford Van, 'PEPSI COLA' Livery
Y-15 Packard Victoria, a colour change
Y-22 Ford Model A Van, 'PALM TOFFEE' Livery
Y-26 Crossley Delivery Truck, 'LOWENBRAU' Livery
Y-27 Foden Steam Wagon, 'PICK FORDS' Livery
Y-28 'UNIC' Taxi, a new model

MATCHBOX CLUBS IN THE U.S.A.

American International Matchbox
Collectors and Exchange Club
72 Belleaire Avenue
Lynn, Massachusetts 01904

'MATCHBOX' U.S.A.
Rural Route 3 Box 216
Saw Mill Road
Durham
Connecticut 06422

ABBREVIATIONS

The Wheel abbreviations SF (Superfast) and RT (Rubber Ty res) also appear in the Features abbreviations where they represent Steam Funnel and Route respectively.

COLLECTORS NOTES

ADDENDUM

i.) N.B. Copyright holder is John Ramsay and not John Ramsey as shown in the copyright notice.
ii.) Page 11 MRP should read MPR — Market Price Range.
iii.) Page 79 The "BEEFEATER GIN" Bus should read 74c not 74e.

Above: The Oberon class submarine HMS *Opossum* under way in March 1984 after being refitted with the new Type 2051 bow sonar.

Above: The broad beam of this Soviet Oscar class submarine houses 12 SS-N-19 cruise missile tubes on each side of the sail.

MODERN SUBMARINE WARFARE

David Miller • John Jordan

TIGER BOOKS INTERNATIONAL
LONDON

Credits

This edition published in 1991 by
Tiger Books International PLC, London.

ISBN 1 85501 167 0

All correspondence concerning the content of this volume should be addressed to Salamander Books Ltd., 129-137 York Way, London N7 9LG.

Editor: Bernard Fitzsimons

Designers: Mark Holt, Nigel Duffield

Colour artwork: Tony Gibbons, Terry Hadler, Janos Marffy, Maltings Partnership, Stephen Seymour, TIGA

Diagrams: TIGA

Filmset by Rapidset & Design Ltd.

Colour reproduction by Melbourne Graphics

Printed in Singapore

Acknowledgements: The publishers wish to thank wholeheartedly the many organizations and individuals in the defence and naval construction industries, and the armed forces of various nations, who have supplied photographs and information used in the compilation of this book. Sources of individual photographs are credited individually at the end of the book, but particular thanks are due to David Foxwell of *Naval Forces*. The diagrams appearing on pages 46-49 are based on information in *General Oceanography* by G. Dietrich and K. Kalle (Willey-Interscience, New York); *Fundamentals of Ocean Acoustics* by L. Brekhovskikh and Yu. Lysanov (Springer, Berlin, 1982); *Sound Propagation in the Sea* by Robert J. Urick (DARPA/US Government Printing Office); and *Underwater Acoustics Handbook II* by Vernon M. Albers (Pennsylvania State University, 1965).

The Authors

Below: The Trafalgar class nuclear powered attack submarine HMS *Tireless* caught by the camera while running on the surface in November 1985.

David Miller is a serving officer in the British Army, a career which has taken him to Singapore, Malaysia, Germany and the Falkland Islands and which has included service in the Royal Corps of Signals, several staff jobs at Army headquarters and the command of a regiment in the UK. He has contributed numerous articles to technical defence journals on subjects ranging from guerilla warfare to missile strategy and is the author of *An Illustrated Guide to Modern Submarines* (1982) and *An Illustrated Guide to Modern Subhunters* (1984), co-author of *Modern Naval Combat* (1986) and a contributor to *The Vietnam War* (1979), *The Balance of Military Power* (1981) and *The Intelligence War* (1983), all published by Salamander Books.

John Jordan is well known for his contributions on modern ships and submarines to journals such as *Navy International*, *Warship*, *Defence* and *Jane's Defence Weekly*. His work for Salamander includes authorship of the Illustrated Guides to *The Modern US Navy*, *The Modern Soviet Navy*, *Modern Naval Aviation*, *Battleships and Battlecruisers* and *Modern Destroyers*, and he was contributor to *The Balance of Military Power*.

Contents

Below: The Swedish submarine *Sjöormen*, name ship of a class of five 1,125-ton diesel-electric Albacore-hulled submarines launched in the late 1960s.

Foreword

For the first fifty years of its existence the submarine was a vessel which travelled and fought primarily on the surface, retiring under water only to hide or when under attack. Even when it submerged it did not go deep; indeed, it was not until the mid-1940s that submarines could dive to a depth greater than their own length. Sonar was an imprecise instrument and anti-submarine weapons were fairly ineffective, but a major problem for the submarine was the considerable speed advantage held by surface ships. During World War II the development of ship and aircraft radar forced submariners to spend longer below the surface, and while the invention of the schnorkel tube gave them a means of recharging their batteries at periscope depth their mast heads were still detectable, both visually and by radar. World War II also saw the appearance of the specialised anti-submarine aircraft as a particularly dangerous foe for the submarine, whether submerged or on the surface.

Freedom from regular forays to the surface for life support and propulsion came with the nuclear-powered steam plant, which gave endurance effectively limited only by human psychological and physiological factors and produced a truly underwater weapon system, capable of world-wide deployment and able to operate at fleet speeds with surface task groups. It also enabled submarines to travel submerged at speeds at least equal to those of attacking surface vessels.

Until the 1950s submarines' primary strategic role was against surface warships and seaborne logistic traffic. In both World Wars Germany brought the United Kingdom to the brink of starvation by attacking the supply routes across the Atlantic and in the second the US Navy won a great underwater victory against the Japanese, sinking millions of tons of shipping. The role still exists, but the evolution of submarine-launched ballistic missiles and, later, cruise missiles has brought a further and even more important strategic role, that of striking at targets in the enemy's homeland. Indeed, no spot on Earth is now beyond the reach of a submarine-launched weapon.

The USSR, while developing ballistic missile submarines like those of other nations, has also paid great attention to cruise-missile submarines intended primarily to counter US Navy carrier groups. The Americans, on the other hand, have avoided the need for such specialised boats by developing missiles – Tomahawk and Sub-Harpoon – which can be launched from either standard 21in torpedo tubes or from vertical launch tubes mounted between the submarine's outer casing and its pressure hull.

Top: The Los Angeles class nuclear-powered attack submarine USS *Birmingham* (SSN 695) surfaces in spectacular fashion. Nuclear propulsion has freed submarines which make use of it from the need to surface.

Above: There continues to be a big demand for conventional diesel-electric submarines: among the latest is the Indian Navy's HDW Type 1500, of which S45, seen here on builder's trials, is the second to be delivered.

Finally, the conventional diesel-electric submarine continues to thrive, and many hundreds are operational with 39 navies. Very few countries can afford the increasingly expensive nuclear powered boats; for Japan, the political implications of nuclear power are insuperable; and only the French and US navies have opted for all-nuclear underwater fleets.

Although submerged submarines are difficult to locate, all underwater craft give both acoustic and non-acoustic indications of their presence and there is no such thing as an undetectable submarine. Many countries are conducting expensive research programmes aimed at making detection of their submarines more difficult. Here NATO has long possessed a definite advantage since Soviet submarines are inherently noisier, so NATO forces should be able to detect and identify the enemy first. Early confrontations of a possible future conflict are secretly rehearsed every day: Soviet hunter-killers endeavour to track Western ballistic missile boats, NATO surface task groups practise anti-submarine techniques against tracking Soviet submarines and, as the incident of the Soviet Whiskey class submarine grounding off the Swedish Karlskrona naval base in November 1981 showed, clandestine reconnaissance missions do take place, though their frequency can only be guessed at.

The value and importance of the modern submarine was underlined during the South Atlantic War of 1982: after HMS *Conqueror* became the first nuclear-powered submarine to sink a surface warship when she attacked and sank the Argentinian cruiser *General Belgrano* the threat from the British submarines was so powerful that no further surface unit of the Argentinian Navy left coastal waters to threaten the British fleet. The Argentinian Navy, however, had submarines of its own and its West German-designed Type 209 diesel-electric submarines were a major threat to the Task Force throughout the campaign, especially to the aircraft carriers.

The modern submarine is difficult to find, identify and sink. It has a global capability, and in its current role the ballistic missile submarine is the ultimate deterrent, for its missiles threaten the enemy's cities and population in a counter-value role, while its inherent survivability gives it a virtually guaranteed second-strike role. The oceans of the world are now designated 'Inner Space', being so vast and unexplored and of ever greater economic value. It could well be that the military battle for control of this difficult and alien environment is only just beginning, and that the real age of the submarine is only now beginning to dawn.

Left: The bow and fin of a Soviet Tango class submarine. The Tangos are diesel-electric counterparts of the Victor class, the first Soviet nuclear-powered attack submarines, and are equipped with a large bow sonar and six or eight torpedo tubes able to fire torpedoes or SS-N-15 antisubmarine missiles. The 19 Tangos built before production was terminated in favour of the Kilo are stationed with the Northern and Black Sea Fleets.

Above: The first use of submarines as carriers of strategic nuclear weapons involved a couple of American World War II diesel electric submarines converted to launch Regulus cruise missiles. The only nuclear-powered cruise missile carrier built for the US Navy was USS *Halibut* (SSGN 587), completed in 1960 and seen here launching the RGM-6 training version of Regulus I. The Regulus II programme was cancelled in 1959.

Modern Submarine

Technology

David Miller

Below: Subdued lighting aids the hushed concentration of technicians monitoring the sonar console of the Los Angeles class attack submarine USS *La Jolla*.

Introduction

The remarkable range of submarine designs currently at sea is displayed in the central section of this book: the range of sizes, and the number of variations on a fundamentally cylindrical shape, is a reflection of the different roles for which they have been designed and the technological and economic resources available to the customer navies for which they were built. This section of the book describes and illustrates the various factors which bear on modern submarine design, and explains the characteristics that determine the modes of employment outlined in the final section.

As the brief historical survey with which the section opens shows, the relatively short history of the modern submarine has encompassed many strands of development, but the overall thrust remains clear. To survive a submarine depends on stealth, and as the performance of acoustic and other sensors improves, the ability to remain under water as long as possible, and the need to make as little noise as possible while there, are paramount. The latest developments in such areas as water-jet propulsion are highly classified, like many aspects of submarine design and operations, but the constraints of security still permit a reasonable survey of current technology.

In terms of construction there have been few dramatically new developments since the appearance of the teardrop-hulled *Albacore* in the early 1950s, though variations such as multiple pressure hulls and improvements such as anechoic hull coatings continue to crop up. The same is true of propulsion, with nuclear propulsion having conferred a startling increase in operational flexibility on those navies in a position to make use of it, but the rest having to be content with enhancements to the time-honoured combination of electric batteries charged by diesel generators for underwater propulsion. However, Swedish experiments with the closed-cycle Stirling propulsion system, which involves transferring the heat from burning fuel to helium enclosed in a working cycle of pistons and cylinders, separated by heater, regenerator and coding units continue to hold out hopes of advances in this area.

Weaponry is a different matter. Microprocessors have had an enormous impact on the capabilities of all modern weapons and their associated fire control systems, and not only has the traditional weapon of the submarine, the torpedo, been given entirely new autonomous homing capabilities, but whole new classes of weapon have become available, so that the modern attack submarine, exemplified by the Los Angeles class, has the ability to launch attacks with a range of missiles against land as well as the traditional surface and sub-surface targets at ranges far beyond those of the most advanced torpedo. And in the strategic arena submarines have become the repositories of the ultimate deterrent, since they would expect to survive a nuclear first strike that would attempt to neutralise land-based ballistic missiles and air-launched strategic weapons.

THE WORLD'S SUBMARINE FLEETS – JANUARY 1987

Country	SSBN		SSGN		SSB		SSN		SS			Totals	Remarks
	S	B	S	B	S	B	S	B	S	B	R		
Albania									3			3	Soviet Whiskey (3)
Alberia									2			2	Soviet Romeo (2)
Arbentina									4	2		4	West German Type 209 (2), Type 1400 (2+2)
Australia									6			6	UK Oberon (6)
Brazil									7	3		7	UK Oberon (3), US Guppy (4), West German Type 1400 (3 on order)
Canada									3			3	UK Oberon (3)
Chile									4			4	West German Type 1300 (2), UK Oberon (2)
China	2	2			1		3	1	102		6	108	Most SS of Soviet design but all others of Chinese design
Colombia									2			2	West German Type 209 (2)
Cuba									3			3	Soviet Foxtrot (3)
Denmark									4			4	West German Type 205 (2), Danish Delfinen (2); 3 Type 207 may be bought from Norway
Ecuador									2			2	West German Type 209 (2)
Egypt									7			7	Soviet/Chinese Romeo (8), Soviet Whiskey (3)
France	6	1			1		2	3	13			22	All of French design and construction. No more non-nuclear submarines to be built
West Germany									24	12		24	Type 206 (18), Type 205 (5); 12 Type 211 on order
Greece									10			10	West German Type 209 (8), US Guppy (2)
India									8	7		8	Soviet Foxtrot (8); 4 West German Type 1500, 3 Soviet Kresta on order
Indonesia									3			3	West German Type 209 (2), Soviet Whiskey (1); order for third Type 209 postponed
Israel									3			3	West German Type 206 built in UK by Vickers (3)
Italy									10	2		10	Nazario Sauro (4+2) Enrico Toti (4), US Tang (2)
Japan									14	4		14	Yuushio (6+4), Uzushio (7), Asashio (1); all of Japanese design and construction
North Korea									21			21	Soviet Romeo (17), Soviet Whiskey (4); 18 midget submarines also in use as special forces transports
Libya									6			6	Soviet Foxtrot (6). Six Yugoslav midget submarines also in use as special forces transports
Netherlands									7	3		7	Zeele (2+3), Zwaardvis (2), Dolfijn (3); all of Dutch design and construction
Norway									14	6		14	West German Type 207 (14); 6 West German Type 210 on order
Pakistan									6	2		6	French Agosta (2+2), Daphne (4); also 2 midget submarines
Peru									12			12	West German Type 209 (6), US-built Dos de Mayo (4), US Guppy (2)
Poland									3			3	Soviet Whiskey (3)
Portugal									3			3	French Daphné (3)
South Africa									3			3	French Daphné (3)
Spain									8			8	Agosta (4), Daphné (4); Spanish-built to French designs. Next class may be nuclear-powered.
Sweden									12	4		12	Näcken (3), Sjöormen (5), Draken (4); 4 Vastergötland on order; all Swedish designed and built
Taiwan									2	2		2	US Guppy (2); 2 modified Dutch Zwaardvis on order
Turkey									17	7		17	West German Type 209 (5+7), US Guppy (10), US Tang (2); 7 Type 209 building in Turkey
USSR	64	4	49 +16 SSG		15		81	?	147	?		372	See separate table
United Kingdom	4	4					14	5	15	1		33	See separate table
USA	36	6					96	19	4			134	See separate table
Venezuela									3			3	West German Type 209 (2), US Guppy (1)
Totals	112	17	65		17		196	28+	517	51+	6	907+	

S = in service; B = building; R = reserve

MAJOR SUBMARINE FLEETS

	USSR	S	B	USA	S	B	UK	S	B
SSBN	Typhoon	4	?	Ohio	6	6	Resolution	4	
	Delta IV	1	3	Lafayette	30		Vanguard		4
	Delta III	14							
	Delta II	4							
	Delta I	18							
	Yankee II	1							
	Yankee I	21							
	Hotel III	1							
	Totals	64	?		36	6		4	4
SSB	Golf V	1							
	Golf III	1							
	Golf II	13							
	Total	15							
SSGN	Oscar	2	?						
	Papa	1							
	Charlie II	6							
	Charlie I	11							
	Yankee	1							
	Echo II	8							
	Totals	49	?						
SSS	Juliett	16							
	Total	16							
SSN	Akula	1	?	Los Angeles	33	(+19)	Trafalgar	3	5
	Sierra	1	?	Lipscomb	1		Swiftsure	6	
	Mike	1	?	Bturgeon	37		Valiant	5	
	Alfa	6		Narwhal	1				
	Victor III	21		Parmit	13				
	Victor II	7		Tullibee	1				
	Victor I	16		Ethan Allen	2				
	Yankee	1	10	Shipjack	5				
	Echo	5		Skate	2				
	Hotel	1	4						
	November	12							
	Totals	72	?		95	(+19)		14	5
SS	Kilo	6	?	Barbel	3		Upholder	0	1
	Tango	19		Darter	1		Oberon	15	
	Foxtrot	58							
	Golf	3							
	Romeo	6							
	Zulu IV	2							
	Whiskey	55							
	Totals	162	?		4			15	1

Along with improvements to armament have come impressive enhancements to sensor and communications facilities – again largely based on the power of modern computers to process and display quantities of data that human being simply could not handle otherwise in any time frame that would enable tactical use to be made of it.

The consequence of all these improvements to the capabilities of modern submarines is that the resources devoted to antisubmarine warfare have also increased, and with naval weapon systems and platforms of every variety ranged against them, today's submariners must conduct their peacetime operations at a higher state of readiness than that applied in almost any other area of military activity. The day-to-day gathering of data on the performance and acoustic characteristics of hostile submarines is a fundamental part of the preparation for war in which navies are constantly engaged, which is why they are so reluctant to release more than the barest details of their performance and capabilities.

Finally, the hazards to which the crews of submarines are subjected cannot be overlooked by any navy which seeks to recruit personnel of suitable calibre and maintain a healthy level of morale, and the section concludes with a look at the modern rescue systems that would help crews survive in the event of an underwater accident, as well as some of the postwar disasters which have occurred.

Right: Submarines operate in three dimensions, and the forces ranged against them involve aircraft and surface ships as well as hostile submarines. This French Atlantic maritime patrol aircraft has flushed its target submarine to the surface.

Below: Computer-aided design is as important in the construction of modern submarines as electronic processing is in the operation of sensor and weapon systems. This design engineer is using a Kockums 3D CAD system to investigate mast arrangements.

Submarine Types

The submarine became a major factor in naval warfare during World War I, when Imperial Germany demonstrated its full potential for the first time after a long process of development by a variety of inventors and enthusiasts. A Dutchman, Cornelius van Drebel, is usually credited with building the first practicable submarine in 1620; he demonstrated his oar-powered craft in the Thames in London and even, so it is said, persuaded King James I to take a trip.

By the early eighteenth century numerous ideas for underwater craft had been patented, and during the American Revolutionary War the *Turtle*, a one-man submersible designed by David Bushnell, was used to attack the British man-of-war HMS *Eagle* in New York harbour. It was intended to attach a gunpowder charge to the ship's bottom with screws and explode it with a time fuze, but the attempt was unsuccessful. Robert Fulton designed a craft, the *Nautilus*, which he offered to France, Britain and the United States in 1801, but without any response.

Several more submersibles appeared during the American Civil War and on February 17, 1864, a Confederate vessel, the CSS *Hunley*, sank the Federal Navy corvette USS *Housatonic* outside Charleston harbour. *Hunley* was driven by a screw propeller, turned by a hand-crank operated by a crew of eight men, and used a torpedo suspended ahead of her bow. As with the development of aircraft, which ran roughly parallel with that of the submarine, the problem of the submarine was not really soluble until a suitable means of propulsion was available. An English clergyman, the Reverend Barrett, successfully operated a steam-driven submarine, as did the Swede Nordenfeldt, but it was the electric motor which finally cracked the problem.

Credit for the first really effective submarine must go to J.P. Holland, of New Jersey, whose first boat was launched in 1875: many of his ideas are still in use today, notably the use of water ballast to submerge the vessel and of horizontal rudders to dive. The *Holland*, launched on May 17, 1897, was 54ft (16.45m) long and was propelled by a gasoline engine on the surface and by electric motors run from storage batteries when submerged. Despite successful trials, a cautious US Navy did not accept such a revolutionary device into service until April 11, 1900, and she was subsequently commissioned on October 12, 1900, Lieutenant Harry H Caldwell, USN, commanding. The company which produced this boat, the Holland Submarine Torpedo Boat Company, was reorganised in 1900 to become the Electric Boat Company and is still producing submarines today as the Electric Boat Division of the General Dynamics Corporation at Groton, Connecticut.

Above: USS *Holland*, the US Navy's first submarine, accepted April 11, 1900. Armed with three torpedoes, 53ft 10in (16.4m) long and capable of 8kt surfaced, 2kt submerged, she had a crew of six.

Right: Commissioned in 1903, the Royal Navy's *Holland 5* was the last of her class. Vickers-built and virtually identical to the US Navy's Hollands she lies aground at Fort Blockhouse, Portsmouth.

Below: The first of a long line of Royal Navy submariners, the crew of *Holland 1* adopt a stern and resolute mien for the camera. Presumably the seventh crew member took the photograph.

Above: The Royal Navy's *Holland 3* in pristine condition and with a very smart crew. Displacement was 104 tons surfaced, 150 tons submerged. These boats had one 14in (551mm) bow torpedo tube.

Left: The first British-designed boats, the A class (4 built), were succeeded by the 11-strong B class, built 1905-06. The latter were the first to be fitted with fore hydroplanes.

Below: The Royal Navy's fourth class of submarine, the 38-strong C class, had a displacement of 290 tons surfaced, 320 submerged, and two bow-mounted 18in (457mm) torpedo tubes.

The French had long been interested in submarines, and a craft built in the 1860s, *Le Plongeur*, incorporated many excellent ideas. She was driven by an 80hp engine powered by compressed air stored in large steel bottles; the air was also used to blow the ballast tanks and to provide fresh air for the crew. Unfortunately *Le Plongeur* was very unstable and the French Navy failed to solve the problems of this very promising boat. A series of submersibles designed by Goubet were followed by the *Narval*, completed in 1899, which had steam and electric propulsion and good performance both on the surface and when submerged.

Once the feasibility of the submarine boat had been demonstrated by the Americans and the French, many navies became interested in the idea. The British Admiralty had watched progress with a mixture of scepticism and disdain, but by 1900 it felt compelled to become involved: development started with five Holland boats built in England by Vickers who, like Electric Boat, are still producing submarines today. *Holland 1* displaced 104 tons surfaced and 122 tons dived and had a crew of seven men; its speed was eight knots surfaced and five submerged. The five *Hollands* were followed by 13 A class (completed 1903-05), 11 B class (1905-10), 38 C class (1906-08) and eight D class (1908-11) boats, and the first of the very successful E class were just joining the fleet by August 1914, when World War I started: the Royal Navy had by far the largest submarine fleet in the world, some 74 boats strong.

World War I saw submarines being used from the very start, with Kapitän-Leutnant Wedigen of the Imperial German Navy scoring an astonishing success on September 22, 1914, when he torpedoed and sank three British heavy cruisers. British submarines were very successful throughout the war, but it was the Germans who first used the submarine as a strategic rather than a tactical weapon. In attempting to seal off the transatlantic trade routes they sank a huge tonnage of Allied shipping, almost succeeding in their aim.

The submarines in use at the end of World War I were essentially bigger versions of those in service at the start of the conflict. Armed with torpedoes, plus guns for

Above: HM Submarine *H.2* in Mudros Harbour in May 1916, during the ill-fated Dardanelles campaign. The first 20 were built in the USA to the American Holland class design and another 25 were constructed in the UK during the years 1915-19. The first boats to be armed with the 21in (533mm) torpedo tubes, they saw service in both World Wars, the last two being scrapped in 1945.

Above: Electric welding for hull construction was first used in the US Navy's two-boat Cachalot class – this is USS *Cuttlefish* (SS 171) – built 1931-34. This saved weight, added strength and solved the long-standing problem of oil-fuel leakage, which not only reduced range but also left a tell-tale oil slick on the surface.

Below: The Royal Navy's HMS *M.1* was armed with a 12in gun and four bow-mounted 18in (457mm) torpedo tubes. The gun had to be loaded on the surface, then the muzzle was blanked off before diving; when a target came in range she broached until the muzzle was clear of the water before opening fire.

Above: Steam turbine-powered for a surface speed of 24 knots, the British K-class was designed to work with the fleet. *K.26*, a bigger boat than her sisters, completed a round trip to Ceylon in 1924.

Right: The British *M.2*, originally identical to the M.1 (opposite), had her gun removed and was converted to a submersible seaplane carrier. She sank in 1932 when the hangar was left open.

Below: A major step in diesel-electric submarine design was the snorkel tube, which enables boats to travel with just the head of the tube exposed while diesels are run to recharge the batteries. This diagram shows the system used on postwar US Guppy boats.

Snorkel induction system

1. Snorkel induction head valve (21in)
2. Snorkel induction mast (15in)
3. Moisture separator
4. Snorkel induction valve (aft battery compartment)
5. Main induction valve (aft battery compartment)
6. Ship's ventilation hull valve (forward engine room)
7. Forward engine room induction hull valve
8. Aft engine room induction hull valve
9. Water drain to negative tank
10. Water drain to pump room
11. Compressed air supply (225psi)

surface action, they were capable of limited forays under water and were propelled by diesel-electric power. The Germans were already planning to take the war to the coasts of the USA and were building large 'cruiser' submarines as the war ended: *U-135*, for example, had a displacement of 1,175 tons surfaced and 1,534 tons submerged, and was armed with a 150mm gun and six 20in torpedo tubes; with a crew of 46 men she had a speed of 17.5 knots on the surface and 8.1 knots submerged.

The inter-war years saw slow but steady development of the patrol types. The German Type IXA of 1940 had a displacement of 1,032 tons surfaced and 1,153 tons submerged, and was armed with six 21in torpedo tubes and a 104mm gun. With a speed of 18.3 knots on the surface and 7.7 knots submerged she offered little additional capability and performance over the *U-135* of 22 years previously, although reliability and habitability were obviously much better.

The years 1918-39 had also seen some unusual submarine developments, though the vast majority proved worthless. The use of guns appeared to offer some advantages over torpedoes and the British developed a series of submarines (K, M and X classes) in which guns were the principal weapons, while the French produced the mighty *Surcouf* (4,304 tons submerged) with two 8in guns in an immense turret forward of the conning tower. Experiments were also conducted with aircraft-carrying submarines by the British, French and Japanese navies but with very limited success.

World War II saw two great submarine campaigns, the first in the Atlantic, where German submarines again tried to cut off the United Kingdom from North America and again failed, and the second in the Pacific, where the US Navy set out to destroy the Japanese merchant fleet and succeeded. Much new equipment for submarines was introduced, notably radar, sonar, electronic warfare devices such as radio direction finding, and the snorkel. Speed, meanwhile, increased remarkably little: the US Navy's Balao class of 1943 had an underwater speed of just 8.7 knots, only marginally better than that of World War I submarines.

There were, however, three very significant breakthroughs, the first being the German discovery that by streamlining the hull, doing away with all unecessary protuberances and increasing battery power, much greater speeds and endurance could be achieved. These refinements, coupled with that of the snorkel, resulted in the first boats to be more at home under the surface than above it and led to a programme of new boats or radical changes to old ones in virtually every navy.

The second great development was that of the tear-drop hull, pioneered by the US Navy's experimental submarine USS *Albacore*, which made submarines capable of much greater underwater speeds and solved the control problems, besides giving much greater internal space. The third was the perfection of nuclear propulsion, which – for the navies that could afford it – made submarines totally free of the surface for protracted periods.

THE OCEAN

Submarines must operate in a three-dimensional environment with a nature and properties all its own, one which we are only now beginning to understand. The ocean is fundamentally hostile to human beings, who can only exist there if they carry with them a part of their normal atmosphere, and has a behaviour pattern of its own, which is so far as unpredictable as atmospheric weather was before the advent of satellites.

The nature of the oceans pervades every aspect of submarine and anti-submarine warfare and leads to some very curious situations. A surface warship, for example, may detect a submarine some 30 miles away only to be sunk by a submarine just one mile away whose presence its sensors had been totally unable to detect. And just as sound behaves in an odd way, so too do explosions.

One example of the latter phenomenon occurred during World War II, when some British midget submarines were being towed across the North Sea to attack the German battleship *Tirpitz*. One of them, *X-8*, sprang a leak in her starboard detachable side-cargo (which contained the explosives), and this was jettisoned, exploding a few minutes later whilst still comparatively close; it did no damage to either *X-8* or the towing submarine. Some time later the port side-cargo developed a similar problem and was also released, but this time the fuze was set for a two-hour delay: the fuze worked perfectly 120 minutes later, but the explosion caused such severe damage to X-8 that she had to be

German Type IXB U-boat

Origin: Germany
Type: Patrol submarine, diesel-electric powered
Displacement: 1,051 tons surfaced; 1,178 tons submerged
Dimensions: Length 251ft (76.5m); beam 22ft (6.8m); draught 15.7ft (4.7m)
Propulsion: Two 2,000hp MAN diesel engines, two 500hp electric motors for 18.2 knots surfaced; 7.3 knots submerged; 8,700nm at 12 knots surfaced; 64nm at 4 knots submerged; design diving depth 492ft (150m)
Complement: 48
Background: The Types I and II were training boats and were followed by the two types which bore the brunt of the U-boat war: the Types VII and IX. The Type IX was derived from the Type I, which itself had been derived from the U-81 series of 1916. Intended for distant water operations the Type IX had longer range, greater displacement and much better habitability than the Type VII: a double hull design was used and part of the 154 tons fuel load and all the ballast tanks were located between the hulls. Surface range was 10,500nm at 10 knots.

The Type IXB had a 165-ton fuel load, giving a range of 12,000nm, while the Type IXC and C-40, built in larger numbers than any other version, utilised yet more space between the hulls to house even more fuel (208 tons and 214 tons respectively) giving still greater range (12,000 and 12,300nm).

The D series boats were a major redesign, being 36ft (10m) longer and with yet further increases in range and speed. Two boats of Type IX-D1 were built, each having six high-speed 1,500hp diesels of a type normally fitted in motor-torpedo boats, giving a maximum surface speed of 21.8 knots. This installation, however, proved to be dangerous and unpleasant for the crew, and the idea was dropped after one operational cruise. The original engines were replaced by two of the usual MAN U-boat diesels, the torpedo tubes removed and they were then used as transport and refuelling boats, carrying 252 tons of fuel (in addition to their own 203 tons).

Types IX D2 and D-42 were designed for operations in the South Atlantic and Indian Oceans and their maximum fuel load of 441 tons gave them an incredible surface range of 31,500nm at 10 knots, and a maximum surface speed of 19.2 knots. Many D2s carried Focke-Achgelis FA-330 single-seat autogyros, which could be towed by the submarine at a height of some 300ft (100m) to enhance surface surveillance capability. They had a surface range of 23,700nm at 12 knots. Some IXD boats were used for importing vital stores from Japan and some were used as submarine tankers, most of which were lost. 29 Type D2 were built and two Type D-42, but it was then decided to switch production to the Type XXI.

Many Type IX boats were fitted with snorkel tubes from 1943 onward, and radar and DF antennas were also fitted. As a result top weight increased, as did crash-diving time, which had originally been 35 seconds. Part of the weather deck was removed from some boats, which reduced the number of spare torpedoes.

Below: The Type IXA mounted two periscopes, but all later models were fitted with three. Electronic sensor devices were fitted in increasing numbers as the war progressed. The threat from ever more effective, radar equipped Allied ASW aircraft was countered by a succession of detectors, including, the FuMB29 (Bali), which was later replaced by the FuMB10, a more capable, wide-band set. U-boats were also fitted with their own radars, including FuM029 and FuM030. U-862, one of the boats which went to Malaya, was fitted with FuMG200 'Hohentwiel', a set developed from a Luftwaffe ship-detection set.

Left: The 1915 Admiralty Submarine Development Committee proposed several disastrous concepts, among which was the idea for this X-class 'cruiser'. X.1, the only example built, weighed 3,585 tons submerged and was armed with four 5.2in guns in two turrets plus six 21in (533mm) torpedo tubes. She was laid up in 1930.

Right: The Soviet Hotel class nuclear-powered ballistic missile submarines, of which nine were built before construction was terminated in 1960, were the first SSBNs in service. This example is seen off Newfoundland after an accident in 1972.

abandoned. The charges were identical, but the detonation of one at a few hundred yards did no damage at all, while that at a distance of a little over three miles caused a great deal of damage, entirely because of the curious nature of the sea.

BALLISTIC MISSILE SUBMARINES

The first true ballistic missile submarines were those of the Soviet Navy's diesel-engined Golf class, with three SS-N-4 missiles mounted vertically in the fin. The subsequent Hotel class also had fin-mounted missiles, and it was not until the appearance of the Yankee class in 1966 that the Soviets had a purpose-built SSBN equivalent to those in the West. Even so, the Yankee I had the SS-N-6 missile with a comparatively short range, which meant that the boats had to deploy close to the US mainland to obtain

Above and left: The Type IXB had a single 105mm gun on the foredeck, one 37mm anti-aircraft gun on the afterdeck and one 20mm AA gun mounted on a platform at the rear of the conning tower. From 1944 the 105mm and 20mm weapons were replaced by two twin 20mm. All versions had six 21in (533mm) torpedo tubes, four bow-mounted and two stern-mounted, with 16 reloads; the standard torpedo carried was the G7E.

Ballistic missile submarines in service

Golf (USSR, 1959)

Hotel (USSR, 1960)

Lafayette (USA, 1963)

Yankee (USSR, 1967)

Resolution (UK, 1967)

Le Redoutable (France, 1971)

Delta I (USSR, 1972)

Delta II (USSR, 1974)

Delta III (USSR, 1978)

Ohio (USA, 1981)

Typhoon (USSR, 1981)

Xia (China, 1985)

Delta IV (USSR, 1985)

Above: SSBN classes currently in service, shown by the date of completion of the first example. The earliest Soviet boats, the Golf and Hotel classes, have their missiles mounted vertically in the sail, but all the rest carry their primary armament in the hull abaft the sail, except for the Typhoon, in which the tubes are forward. The inexorable growth in submarine size is clear.

Above: A Soviet Delta takes a buffeting while running on the surface in the North Atlantic. The size of the missile compartment is dictated by the length of the SS-N-8 missiles.

Right: The Ethan Allen class were designed as SSBNs from the outset; this is USS *John Marshall* (SSBN 611). The earlier George Washingtons were lengthened versions of the Shipjack class.

good coverage of targets such as SAC bases.

Yankee numbers are declining as boats are converted to other roles to keep within the SALT II limits, and the sole Yankee II carries the experimental SS-NX-17, but the next class, the Delta, is now in its fourth major modification – Delta I had 12 SS-N-8, Delta II 16 SS-N-8, Delta III 16 SS-N-18 and Delta IV 16 SS-N-23 – having grown in the process from 10,000 tons submerged (Delta I) to 13,600 tons (Delta IV). The latest Typhoon class (29,000 tons) boats carry 20 SS-N-20 missiles ahead of the fin.

Soviet SSBN design tended to lag behind that of the West for some years, with much evidence of very hasty conversions in the early types. Even in the recent Deltas the ungainly whaleback necessary to accommodate the large missiles is very poorly matched to the fin, which will undoubtedly give rise to much underwater noise at any speed. The Typhoon is an interesting design which has been discussed at length in the West: the consensus view is that it is constructed of two parallel hulls joined together and surrounded by an elliptical outer hull – it is even suggested that the hulls may simply be two Yankee or Delta hulls suitably modified – which should make for a very spacious interior which could be used for extra crew, longer patrols, additional equipment or an esoteric propulsion system.

The Typhoons appear to have been designed specifically for

Above: Artist's impression of the British Vanguard class SSBN designed for the Trident missile, the first of which was laid down at the Vickers Yard in Barrow. A major national debate has raged within the UK about the wisdom of adopting the Trident system, with each of the major political parties taking a different stance on the issue. Four are planned and a fifth is unlikely.

under-ice deployment, and one example has demonstrated an ability to launch at least four ballistic missiles simultaneously, whereas all other ballistic missile submarines fire their missiles in a 'ripple', which could take as much as 15 minutes in the case of the older types, and during which they are very vulnerable; thus, to fire salvos is a major change. One interesting note is that the first commanding officer of the first Typhoon was awarded a very high decoration at the end of his tour of command – so high and rare, indeed, that he was the first recipient since World War II.

The US Navy has just three classes of SSBN in service: 31 of the virtually identical Lafayette and Franklin classes, of which 12 have 16 Trident I missiles while the remainder retain their 16 Poseidons, and an increasing number of the Ohio class, which mount 24 Trident missiles abaft the fin. Unlike previous classes, the Ohios are powered by the S5G natural-circulation nuclear-reactor system, developed from that tested in the *Narwhal*.

British and French SSBNs, like the Lafayette and Franklin classes, carry 16 missiles abaft the fin and are of similar size. The French have now produced six SSBNs, with a gradual improvement in each case, while the Royal Navy has not built any since the last of the four Resolutions was finished in the late 1960s. There will, therefore, inevitably be substantial changes in design in the four new British Trident boats, which will obviously incorporate the lessons learned from the SSN programme. Finally, China is building an SSBN fleet, with two boats of the Xia class operational by the end of 1986 and a further four to follow.

In design and operational terms the Yankee, Delta, Lafayette, Franklin, Resolution and Le Redoutable classes have a lot in common, and it is only with the advent of the Typhoon and Ohio classes that there has been a divergence. The Typhoon is huge and there seems no reason why next-generation Soviet SSBNs should not be even bigger if all they are required to do is to cover the relatively short distance to the Arctic ice-cap. The Ohio is a less radical design than the Typhoon and is, in effect, a logical progression of the Lafayette and Franklin classes – bigger, longer, quieter and with more missiles. Perhaps the most interesting developments are the Chinese boats and the new, much smaller nuclear reactor fitted in the French Rubis class SSNs, and it will be interesting to see the effect of the latter on the design of the next generation of SSBNs.

CRUISE MISSILE SUBMARINES

The Soviet Navy's submarine-launched cruise missile programme originated in the 1950s as a response to the threat posed by

Nuclear-powered attack submarines in service

Skate (USA, 1957)

Skipjack (USA, 1959)

Permit (USA, 1961)

Valiant (UK, 1966)

Sturgeon (USA, 1967)

Victor (USSR, 1968)

Alfa (USSR, 1972)

Swiftsure (UK, 1973)

Glenard P Lipscomb (USA, 1974)

Los Angeles (USA, 1976)

Rubis (France, 1982)

Trafalgar (UK, 1983)

Sierra (USSR, 1984)

Mike (USSR, 1984)

Akula (USSR, 1986)

Above: Nuclear-powered attack submarines (SSN) currently in service, arranged by date of completion of the first unit of the class and shown to the same scale as the ballistic missile submarine profiles on page 20 for comparison. Only the USSR can afford the resources to maintain two classes, Mike and Akula, in production. Mike is thought to serve as a propulsion testbed; Akula is similar to Victor III and Sierra classes. Insufficient data was available on the Chinese Han and Ming classes.

Above: The need to increase the range of submarines' weapons continued from the British *M.1* and *X.1* to this first missile boat, USS *Carbonero* (SS 337). The conversion was carried out under the Loon programme in the late 1940s, and involved the installation of a launch ramp for copied German V1 missiles. *Carbonero* was subsequently refitted for Regulus trials.

the US Navy's aircraft carrier task groups. Some crude conversions of Whiskey class patrol submarines were followed by the first purpose-designed classes, the nuclear-powered Echo class and the diesel-electric Juliett class. Twenty-nine Echo IIs, each armed with eight SS-N-12s, and 16 Julietts armed with four SS-N-3As each were still in service in mid-1987.

In both classes the missiles are mounted in bins stowed flush with the hull casings, and the bins are raised prior to launching on the surface. There are prominent indentations behind each launcher to act as blast deflectors, which generate a lot of underwater noise. The missiles are fired from ranges of about 200 miles, well beyond the normal ASW screen, but such ranges necessitate external assistance to achieve over-the-horizon targeting; initially this was provided by two Bear-D reconnaissance aircraft, but the difficulty of achieving coordination and the vulnerability of the aircraft made this a relatively ineffective system and it is believed that satellites are now used. A large radar is also needed on the launch submarine, the antenna for which – Front Door or Front Piece – is mounted at the forward end of the fin.

The first Charlie class SSGN appeared in 1968: smaller, quieter, faster and with much greater hydrodynamic efficiency than the Echo class, it fires its SS-N-7 missiles under water and does not need an aircraft in the control loop. Also, the missile bins are all mounted forward of the fin and flush with the hull. The later Charlie class boats have a lengthened bow section, suggesting that they may be fitted with the SS-N-15 ASW missile.

Next to appear was the Oscar class (18,000 tons), armed with 24

Below: Some US submarines were converted for cruise missiles, but USS *Halibut* (SSGN 587) was designed specifically for the task. The missile facilities were removed in the late 1960s and *Halibut* was used for DSRV trials.

Right: Soviet Navy Juliett class SSG, armed with four SS-N-3A cruise missiles. Sixteen of these boats were commissioned in the early 1960s and all still serve, six in the Baltic, the rest in the Atlantic and Mediterranean.

Chinese Type ES5G

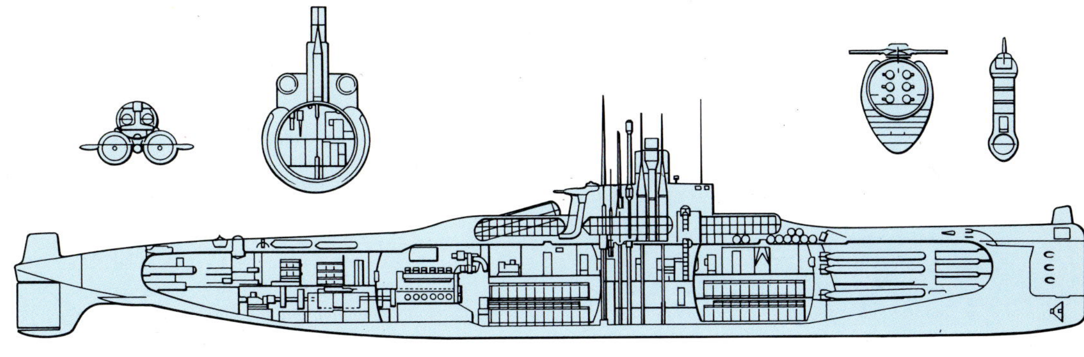

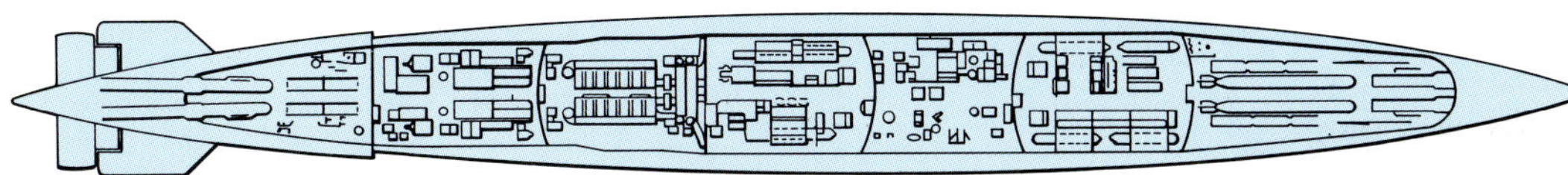

Right: The Chinese export submarine Type ES5G is armed with six missile launchers mounted in pairs beside the sail. It also has six forward and two after torpedo tubes.

SS-N-19 missiles, huge submarines with the exceptionally wide beam of 60ft (18.3m). The missile bins are in the casing, but the great girth is probably due to the use of double hulls, making this design, like the Typhoons, very difficult indeed to destroy.

The Soviet Navy has developed an SLCM similar to Harpoon, which is launched from a standard 21in (533mm) torpedo tube and which will obviously be deployed on SSNs, but it would appear that they still intend to continue SSGN development. However, there appears to be no intention in any Western navy to produce a such a specialised type.

NUCLEAR POWERED ATTACK SUBMARINES

The oldest SSNs in US Navy service are the five Skipjacks, which are small and handy but lack advanced sonar systems. The Permit and Sturgeon classes which followed are larger, carry more sophisticated sonar outfits and fire Subroc, but with no increase in power the speed of these classes fell to 28 knots. The latest type of SSN in service with the US Navy is the Los Angeles class, which showed a 50 per cent increase in displacement over their predecessors. These boats are fitted with more advanced sensors and fire control equipment – both of which are now being retrofitted to the 14 Permit class and 37 Sturgeon class boats – but, in addition, the Los Angeles class restored the speed levels of the Skipjack class.

Soviet Navy operating procedures have in the past made it unlikely that there would be surface task groups against which US SSNs could concentrate, though with the advent of the Kiev and Kremlin class aircraft carriers and the Kirov class battlecruisers the Soviets seem to be generating such targets. US SSNs are therefore designed for three primary roles: anti-submarine hunter-killer, particularly in defence of ballistic missile boats; independent forward area attack and reconnaissance; and the protection of surface task groups and convoys.

Nuclear propulsion is a relatively noisy way of powering a submarine, particularly at high speeds, but successive US designs have shown a steady improvement in this respect. In the Los Angeles class particular attention has been paid to quiet operation, and the large hull makes it easier to cushion the machinery. The increase in speed also reflects the increasing tactical requirement for the defence of carrier task groups against Soviet SSGNs, and all US SSNs except the Skipjacks are being fitted with Harpoon missiles to give them a new capability against surface units.

The Soviet Navy still retains a number of elderly and unreliable November class SSNs in service, but its principal current type is the second-generation Victor, which has a much improved hull form, greater diving depth, a much quieter propulsion system and a submerged speed of about 30 knots. The 16 Victor Is were followed by six Victor IIs, 15.4ft (4.7m) longer and capable of carrying the SS-N-15. Then came the Victor III, longer still and with an unusual cylindrical object on top of its fin, which may be associated either with a towed array or an advanced propulsion system.

Finally, there are no fewer than three new types of Soviet SSN, the Mike, Sierra and Akula classes. The Sierra appears to be a logical development of the Victor III and the Akula seems to be yet a further development of that line, but the Mike has a somewhat different hull

Above: HMS *Dreadnought*, the first British SSN, was powered by a US S5W reactor while the first British powerplant was developed and tested at Dounreay. The boat was listed for disposal in 1982.

Below: The Chinese ES5E export model diesel-electric submarine is derived from the Soviet Romeo, produced in Chinese yards for many years. As with the ES5G (overleaf) this boat has two stern torpedo tubes in addition to the six bow tubes. When submerged the ES5E displaces 2,113 tons and has a maximum speed of 18 knots and an endurance on batteries of 330nm at 4 knots.

Chinese Type ES5E

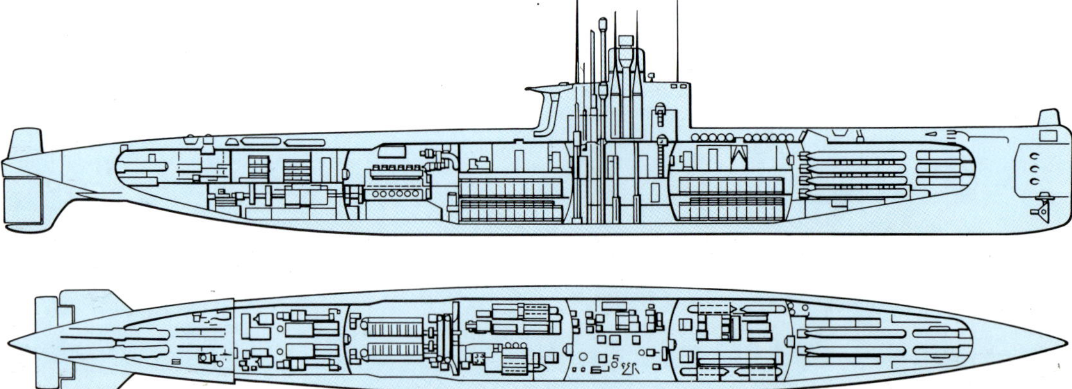

and fin shape and lacks the large bullet found on the vertical rudders of both the Sierra and the Akula classes.

The Royal Navy has produced a series of highly effective SSNs; *Dreadnought*, first of the line, has been retired, but all the others remain in service. The British SSNs are similar to the American types, but by no means identical: their main design features are that the hulls tend to be fuller and to taper at a greater angle at the stern than those of the US boats, and the forward hydroplanes are mounted at the bow rather than on the fin. A conformal sonar array is installed at the bow, rather than the US sphere, which allows the torpedo tubes to remain at the bow. The drive system on the latest Trafalgar class employs hydrojets rather than propellers to cut down on cavitation noises.

The French Rubis class SSNs are much smaller than other SSNs, which must be a result of a new type of small nuclear reactor, and there has been much speculation, but no confirmation, that such a size reduction has been achieved by the use of liquid-metal cooling. The actual design of the boat is not unusual, however, being basically a modified version of the Agosta conventional submarine design.

CONVENTIONAL SUBMARINES

Conventional submarines fall into three main categories, the first being the coastal or shallow-water submarine of 400-600 tons, epitomised by the German Type 205 and 206 and Italian Toti classes. These have proved effective little boats, but obviously suffer from limitations in range, torpedo reloads and sensor capacity.

The 900-1,300-ton bracket includes the German Type 209, Yugoslavian Sava and Swedish Näcken and Sjörmen classes. These, too, are limited in endurance and carrying capacity and are to be found in the smaller navies with medium-range roles. It is, however, of interest that the Swedish Näcken class is one of the finalists in the Australian submarine competition. The majority of current types are of 1,600 tons or more and include the British Type 2400, Dutch Walrus and Soviet Foxtrot, Kilo and Tango, the last being the largest non-nuclear submarine at 3,700 tons.

In design terms there is no one design or nation that stands out as being significantly different from the rest, and clearly the operational requirements are remarkably similar in many respects. Of the three latest designs in the West, for example, the Japanese Yuushio is 249.25ft (76m) long with a surface displacement of 2,200 tons, while the figures for the British Type 2400 are 2,125 tons and 230.5ft (70.25m) and the Dutch Walrus 2,350 tons and 220ft (67m). All three types are armed with six 21in torpedo tubes and all have submerged speeds in the vicinity of 20 knots.

The number of countries capable of producing their own submarines is growing rapidly. The traditional manufacturers have been the UK, USA, USSR, France, Germany, Italy and Sweden, but these have been joined in recent years by Argentina, Turkey, Yugoslavia, Denmark, Spain, China and North Korea. And it is interesting that this is one area where the USA has no capability whatsoever. The last operational diesel-electric submarine built in a US shipyard

Above: One of the major naval developments of recent years is the rapid spread in submarine manufacturing capability from the few countries to which it was formerly confined. Typical is this West German Type 209 design being built at the Golcuk Yard in Turkey. The cleanness of the hull, a major factor in the Type 209's exceptional quietness, is visible under the scaffolding.

Below: US Navy research sub *Dolphin* (AGSS 555), used in many experiments since 1969. Her pressure hull is a perfect cylinder, closed at each end by hemispherical bulkheads.

was the *Bonefish*, launched on November 22, 1958, and when there was a brief spate of interest in another conventional class in the late 1970s it was a West German yard that made the offer.

Conventional submarine development is currently at a very interesting stage, with many existing boats in several navies becoming due for replacement, notably the ex-US Balao, Tench and Guppy types, the British Porpoises and Oberons, the French Daphnes and the Soviet Whiskeys and Romeos. Available designs include the British Type 2400, French Agosta, Italian Sauro, Dutch Walrus, Swedish Näcken, and West German IKL and Thyssen designs, while further designs are in production but unlikely to be offered for sale abroad, including the Japanese Yuushio and Soviet Kilo and Tango classes.

OTHER SUBMARINE TYPES

Some navies have submarines for other purposes. Both the US and Soviet navies have submarines designated 'troop carriers,' which are clearly used for special forces – SEALs in the US case and Spetznaz in the Soviet. The US examples are two former Ethan Allen class SSBNs deactivated under the SALT II agreement, while the Soviet boats of this type are the newly completed first unit of the Uniform class and a converted Echo II. The USSR also has numerous small submersibles, at least some of which are tracked bottom-crawlers, used for Spetsnaz operations. Yugoslavia builds Mala class two-man midget submarines, of which they operate two themselves while Libya has six, and North Korea has 18 indigenously built midget submarines.

There are also a number of research submarines. The US Navy has the purpose-built *Dolphin* and nuclear-powered *NR-1* as well as using older submarines for research from time to time. The USSR follows the same pattern with at least one research boat of the Lima class, and a number of former front-line combat submarines of the Foxtrot, Zulu, Whiskey and Romeo classes used for various types of research.

Although submarines are now much safer and accidents much rarer than formerly, there is nevertheless a need for specialised rescue craft. The US Navy uses two Deep Sea Rescue Vehicles which are air transportable in C-141 Starlifter aircraft, and can be ferried to the scene of an accident by various US and British submarines. The Swedish Navy has a similar Swedish-designed vehicle, the URF, and the Italian Navy has its own Usel. As is to be expected, the USSR has a large variety of such vehicles, including two varieties which are transported in the deck wells on purpose-built India class submarine mother-ships.

Milestones

This book is not a historical survey of the submarine, but it is necessary for a proper understanding of present-day submarine technology to know a little about its development, examined here in terms of six submarines which are considered to be milestones in submarine design.

The British E class submarines were in service throughout World War I and were the immediate descendants of the original naval submarines, in turn developed from the Holland boats which were the first submarines to be true weapons of war. They are, therefore, taken to be archetypical of the first generation of true combat boats.

During the years between the world wars the development of the submarine proceeded at a slow, steady and unspectacular way, leading to the boats used by the navies in World War II, but there was a great deal of experimentation, mainly due to the disparity of views on the employment of the submarine in war. Having seen that a great deal of successful action by submarines had taken place on the surface using guns, there was a strong school which argued that large calibre guns should be carried and another that advocated the carriage of aircraft to provide the means for reconnaissance and gun spotting. Various heavy gun and aircraft-carrying submarines were constructed, but the only one to combine both features was the French Surcouf, the biggest submarine of its day.

Many excellent submarines were constructed by the navies involved in World War II, and there was steady development in many fields, particularly in diving ability and sensors. The US Navy's Gato class boats, which served primarily in the Pacific, are a good example of the culmination of the original line of slow, shallow-diving boats, still totally dependent on regular exposure on the surface to recharge the batteries – the last of the submersibles.

All the World War II developmental lines came together in the Type XXI, which had a streamlined hull and fin, schnorkel tube, much reduced gun armament and greatly increased propulsive power and was the first of a totally new generation of true submarines and one which had a dramatic effect on post-war development.

Dramatic as they were, the improvements made by the Type XXI were all evolutionary, and two more fundamental developments were to come. The first was the new hull form introduced by the USS *Albacore*, a diesel-electric powered experimental submarine capable of 33 knots submerged speed. The second great step forward was the successful development of nuclear propulsion which, in conjunction with the carbon-dioxide scrubber, finally made the submarine independent of the surface.

Above: *A.1*, the first British designed submarine. The A class, developed from the Holland, had a higher conning tower, a short periscope and a crew of 14. After a late start, by 1914 the RN had the world's largest submarine fleet.

Above right: The D class, built 1908-1911, were the first British boats with diesel engines, twin screws, saddle tanks and radios. *D.4* was also first to mount a gun, although *D.8*, here entering Portsmouth harbour, had none.

Right: An unusual line-up representing the first five classes of British submarine; from the right, *A.5*, *B.1*, *C.35*, *D.2* and *E.1*. They clearly show the gradual increase in size and displacement from the 207 tons (submerged) of the A class to the 800 tons of the E class.

E Class

Origin: UK, first unit completed 1913
Type: Patrol submarine, diesel-electric powered
Displacement: 667 tons surfaced; 807 tons submerged
Dimensions: Length 181ft (55.2m); beam 22.5ft (6.9m); draught 12ft (3.7m)
Propulsion: (E.1 type) one petrol engine; one electric motor; 150bhp on one shaft; (E.7 and E.21 types) two Vickers 8-cylinder diesel engines, each 800bhp; two electric motors, each 420bhp; two shafts; (all) 16kt surfaced, 10kt submerged, 2,600nm at 10kt surfaced, 99nm at 3kt submerged; design diving depth 150ft (45.7m), crushing depth 350ft (106m)
Complement: 3 officers, 28 ratings
Background: The British E class, probably the first truly formidable and reliable submarines, were the outcome of a progressive development programme going back to the turn of the century. In the early days of submarine development the Royal Navy had monitored foreign progress closely and in 1900 negotiations were started for the successful Holland design that had just been tested in the USA. By 1914 Britain had the largest submarine fleet in the world, with 74 boats built, 31 under construction and a further 14 either projected or on order.

In 1900 the Royal Navy entered into a contract with Vickers to build submarines for the Royal Navy until 1906, later extended to 1912. The first boats, *Holland 1-5*, were similar to the American A class, but they were difficult to control both on and below the surface, and a modified and enlarged version was ordered. The first, *A.1*, was a great improvement, although the hull form was not particularly efficient and was improved in later members of the class, giving increased speed. Although more

Above: HM Submarine *E.2* on her return from a World War I patrol against Turkish targets on the Sea of Marmara. The E class boats had a distinguished war record, though they paid a heavy price for their success, 25 being lost and one interned.

Right: *E.14* leaves for the Sea of Marmara, where she was to sink three Turkish ships, in April 1915. Note the high-frequency radio antenna stretching from the bow to the top of the radio mast. E boats were the RN's major submarines during the war.

controllable than the *Hollands* they were still prone to dive without warning, and *A.8* was lost with all her crew after such an incident. Also, the use of petrol engines meant that vapour built up in the enclosed space of the hull, which led to several explosions. *A.13* was built with a Hornsby-Ackroyd heavy-oil engine; she was launched in 1905, but tests delayed her completion until 1908.

The A class was followed by the larger B and C class boats, both of which types had a surface displacement of 280 tons and the same armament as the A class, but with two sets of hydroplanes to improve controllability and more powerful machinery giving improved performance, while both habitability and range were improved. Ten B class and 37 C class boats were built. *D.1*, the first of eight D class boats, had a surface displacement of 550 tons and was fitted with Vickers machinery and

Above: HM Submarine *E.31*, one of two E class boats built by Scotts. Armament of the E class varied. *E.1-E.6* had four 18in (457mm) torpedo tubes, two in the bow and one on each beam, while the E.7 and E.21 types had an additional stern torpedo tube. Torpedoes were Mk 8s, with a maximum range of 6,000 yards (5,486m), although effective range was more like 3,000 yards (2,783m). All E class boats had a mounting for a gun; 6-pounder, 12-pounder and 4in weapons were fitted, though it appears to have been up to the captain whether or not one was actually carried. Shown here is the 12-pounder. Six boats were completed as minelayers with the two beam torpedo tubes replaced by mine tubes with a capacity of 20 mines.

Left: *E.47* clearly shows her shape, particularly the saddle tanks. A gun is mounted abaft the conning tower and the stern torpedo can just be seen above the men scrubbing the hydroplane.

twin screws. She also had much greater reserve buoyancy and an armament of three 18in torpedo tubes and a 12-pounder gun, but did not have the size and habitability for long-range work.

Design: The E class were enlarged Ds, being some 30ft (9.1m) longer and approximately 15in (38cm) wider, and were divided into three groups: the E.1 type (*E.1* to *E.6*, *AE.1* and *AE.2*), the E.7 type (*E.7* to *E.20*) and the E.21 type (*E.21* to *E.56*, less *E.28*, which was cancelled). The E class boats were built to an excellent design, and with their stronger hull and transverse bulkheads achieved new standards of integrity. They were the first British boats to have water-tight bulkheads, the early boats having two bulkheads, dividing the hull into three main compartments – fore-ends; control room and beam torpedo space; and engine-room, motor room and stern space – while later examples had three. All had 10-ton drop keels, which could be jettisoned from the control room in an emergency.

Like all early British submarines they could dive quickly, though they also exhibited a tendency to dive suddenly at high speed on the surface. Their Vickers solid-injection eight-cylinder diesel engines, though less sophisticated than contemporary German diesels, were extremely reliable for the time, and electric power for the two motors was provided by two 112-cell Exide batteries, each cell weighing 865lb (392kg). The batteries generated 220 volts/600 amps and could be connected into four 56-cell groups either in parallel at 110 volts or in series at 220 volts.

The E class was to have been succeeded by the G class, with a surface displacement of 700 tons, but the latter took longer to build and on the outbreak of war a further 20 E class were ordered to build up British submarine forces as quickly as possible. *E.1* to *E.18* had taken between 20 and 30 months each to build, but *E.19*, ordered in November 1914, took just eight months to build, fit out and hand over to the navy. Another two boats, *AE.1* and *AE.2* were built for the Royal Australian Navy.

E.22 was converted in 1916 to carry two Sopwith Schneider floatplanes, which were intended to bomb German Zeppelin sheds at Cuxhaven and Tondern and to shoot down Zeppelins on their way to bomb targets in England. Unlike later aircraft-carrying submarines, (such as the *M.2* and *Surcouf*) the aircraft were mounted in the open on rails on the afterdeck; there was no watertight container and so there was no question of the submarine submerging with the aircraft in position. Also, there was no crane and the aircraft were floated off and recovered by trimming down aft. This particular experiment appears not to have been a success, although a number of aircraft-carrying submarines were to appear in the 1920s and 1930s.

The E class boats had a distinguished war record in the North Sea, the Baltic and, particularly, the Dardanelles, where several broke through into the Sea of Marmara. The class was worked very hard throughout the war and the captains were nothing if not aggressive, winning a number of Victoria Crosses in the process. As a result 25 were lost during the war and one was interned in Denmark in 1915. All the remaining boats were paid off in 1921-22.

The E class was typical of World War I submarines, with an armament of one gun and a number of torpedo tubes. Indeed, no succeeding class until the arrival of the Type XXI was different in concept or in overall performance, the only increases being in size and range.

Armament: All E class submarines had either one six-pounder or one 4in gun and were the first Royal Navy production class to be so fitted. The original E.1 type had four 18in torpedo tubes, two in the bow and two in the beam (one on each side), spanning the bulged lateral tanks. The E.7 and E.21 types had an additional 18in (457mm) torpedo tube mounted in the stern, but the six boats completed as minelayers (*E.24*, *E.34*, *E.41*, *E.45*, *E.46*, *E.51*) had the two beam tubes replaced by mine tubes for 20 mines. The torpedoes were Mk 8s, which had a maximum range of 6,000 yards (5,486m), but by the time they had travelled that far their speed was down to about 29 knots. Running speed out to 3,000 yards (2,783m) was about 41 knots.

Construction: 57 E Class boats were built between 1913 and 1917, 55 for the Royal Navy and two (*AE.1* and *AE.2*) for the Royal Australian Navy. They were the first major class to be built in yards other than those of Vickers: Chatham Dockyard (6); Vickers (20); Beardmore (6); Yarrow (1); Armstrong Whitworth (4); Scotts (2); White (1); Thornycroft (2); John Brown (3); Fairfield (2); Cammell Laird (4); Swan Hunter (3); and Denny (3)

Surcouf

Origin: France, completed 1929
Type: Cruiser submarine, diesel-electric powered
Displacement: 3,252 tons surfaced; 4,304 tons submerged
Dimensions: Length 361ft (110m); beam 29.5ft (9m); draught 23.7ft (7.3m)
Propulsion: Diesel-electric drive on two shafts; two Sulzer diesel engines; two electric motors; 3,400shp for 18.5kt surfaced, 10kt submerged, 10,000nm at 10kt surfaced, 70nm at 4.5kt submerged; design diving depth 400ft (122m)
Complement: 118
Background: The search for a weapon with greater range and flexibility than the torpedo has continued almost since the inception of the submarine. For a long time attention concentrated on the only available alternative, the gun, and it was not until the 1960s that a really effective weapon, the submarine-launched cruise-missile, became available. The last, and arguably the epitome, of the gun-armed cruiser submarines, was the *Surcouf*.

Up to the beginning of World War I submarines had very limited capabilities, but as the war progressed there were great improvements in design and performance, until it appeared possible that submarines could become capable of more than just lying in wait for merchant ships and warships and attacking them with short-range guns or torpedoes. Obviously, a bigger gun would enable the submarine to attack surface targets at much greater ranges, but it was very difficult to acquire targets and estimate ranges from the relatively low conning tower, so several navies experimented with submarines equipped to operate aircraft.

The British built 18 of the K class so-called 'fleet' submarines between 1916 and 1918; they had a submerged displacement of 2,600 tons and were armed with two 4in guns. The next step was the M class which had 12in guns in large turrets forward of the conning tower: of the three built, *M-1* was lost with all hands in 1925, *M-2* was converted into a seaplane carrier and sank when the hangar door was inadvertently left open during a dive, and *M-3* was converted into a minelayer. Another type, the *X-1* (3,585 tons submerged), mounted four 5.2in guns in two twin turrets. None of these classes was at all satisfactory and after the *X-1* the Royal Navy abandoned this particular line of development.

At this point the French came on the scene with the *Surcouf*. Designed under the 1926 naval programme, the *Surcouf* was, in her time, the biggest submarine in the world, her enormous dimensions being necessary to carry all the items considered necessary for her role of world-wide commerce-raiding. The twin 8in turret was forward of the conning tower and was controlled by a director and a 40ft (12m) rangefinder. Abaft the conning tower was an aircraft hangar, with AA guns mounted on its roof. A 16ft (4.9m) motor cutter was also carried to take the boarding party to its prizes, and a compartment was provided for 40 prisoners.

The 8in guns had a range of

Above: *Surcouf* in a Scottish loch during World War II. Designed for an anti-shipping role, she proved difficult to employ as there was so little Axis shipping at sea. She carried out Atlantic patrols and also led the seizure of St Pierre-et-Miquelon by Gaullist forces.

Above: The Besson MB 411 floatplane was developed for use on the *Surcouf*. It could be dismantled in 10 minutes and was stored in a large hangar at the after end of the bridge structure. The aircraft was withdrawn from active service just before the start of World War II and the concept was never tested in combat.

around 15 miles (24,000m), which in theory enabled the *Surcouf* to deal with armed merchant cruisers and other lightly armed convoy escorts from well outside their guns' maximum range. However, the visual horizon of the director could have been little more than 12,000 yards (11,265m) and it was presumably to extend this range that the seaplane was carried. However, the aircraft – a Besson MB floatplane – was apparently not a success and had been removed by the outbreak of war in 1939, the hangar being used thereafter for stores.

Having taken some seven years to build, *Surcouf* was commissioned in 1935 and made several lengthy cruises up to the start of World War II. In 1939-40 she served as a convoy escort on several occasions, but was forced to leave Brest on June 18, 1940, to avoid capture by the Germans. She lay at Plymouth, England, for some weeks before being seized by the Royal Navy on July 3; three Britons and one Frenchmen were killed and two men wounded during the incident. Thereafter *Surcouf* served with a French crew under British operational control. There was much discussion as to the best use for this odd submarine: she was used as convoy escort and for anti-surface raider patrols in the Caribbean, and was also used – under French control – in the operation to bring the islands of St Pierre and Miquelon under Free French control in December 1941. It was then decided to send her to the Pacific where she would be employed in the defence of the Free French Pacific Islands, but she was rammed and sunk with all hands on February 18, 1942, while en route from Bermuda to the Panama Canal. Ironically, having been built to sink merchantmen it was by a US merchant ship, the *Thomas Lykes*, that the *Surcouf* was sunk.

Surcouf was the last attempt to use guns as an alternative to torpedoes for major actions by submarines against surface ships, and apart from being an inherently unlucky boat she spent most of her career in search of a proper role. However, the basic operational concept was not totally unsound and it was the technology that was deficient.

Armament: *Surcouf*'s main armament was two 8in/50 guns, for which 600 rounds were carried. Secondary armament comprised two 37mm guns with 1,000 rounds and two twin Hotchkiss 13.2mm machine guns with 16,000 rounds. No fewer than 12 torpedo tubes were fitted, eight 550mm – four in the bows and four externally aft – with 14 torpedoes and four 400mm tubes internally aft with eight torpedoes.

Sensors: Like all submarines of her generation, *Surcouf* had just two periscopes. A large stereoscopic range-finder with a 13.1ft (4m) base was mounted on the superstructure just forward of the bridge, and she had a good communications fit of HF radios, with two large masts on the port side.

Aircraft: The aircraft, a Besson MB floatplane developed specifically for this application, was withdrawn from use just before the start of World War II. With a span of 32.3ft (9.85m), a length of 22.96ft (7m) and a height of 7.87ft (2.40m) the aircraft was small enough to be placed in a container 13.1ft (4m) square and 22.96ft (9m) long and could be dismantled in 10 minutes. It was powered by a 120hp Salmson air-cooled radial engine.

Construction: *Surcouf* was launched on October 18, 1929, at Cherbourg.

Above: The French concept was not original, as evidenced by this picture of the US submarine *S-1* (SS 105), taken on October 24, 1923. The Martin MS-1 floatplane, one of a dozen examples built, could be dismantled and stowed in the cylindrical hangar.

Left and above: Almost everything about Surcouf's armament was unique. Her main armament of two 8in guns was housed in a watertight turret at the forward end of the bridge structure (above). Maximum range of these guns was 30,000 yards (27,500m) at an elevation of 30°, but effective range was 13,128 yards (12,000m); 600 rounds were carried and a 13ft (4m) rangefinder was mounted just behind the turret. *Surcouf's* torpedo armament consisted of eight 21in (533mm) and four 15.75in (400mm) tubes. The four bow tubes were all of 21in diameter and the rest were installed in two traversing mounts (opposite), each containing two 21in and two 15.75in tubes. Also clear from the number of antennas is the comprehensive radio fit for her intended role of attacking enemy ships in distant waters.

Gato Class

Origin: USA
Type: Patrol submarine, diesel-electric-powered
Displacement: 1,816 tons surfaced; 2,424 tons submerged
Dimensions: Length 311.75ft (95.2m); beam 27.25ft (8.3m); draught 15.25ft (4.7m)
Propulsion: Diesel electric drive on two shafts; four Fairbanks, Morse/General Motors/Hooven, Owens, Rentschler diesel engines; two General Electric/Elliot Motor/Allis-Chalmers electric motors; 2,740shp for 20.25 knots surfaced, 8.75 knots submerged, 10,000-13,000nm at 14 knots, design diving depth 300ft (91m).
Complement: 80-85
Background: Geography dictates that virtually all US Navy warships must operate at considerable distances from the continental USA. Apart from purely coastal vessels, therefore, the majority of its warships, and particularly the submarines, need long range and a good cruising speed to reach their operational areas in a reasonable time. During World War I the enemy was Imperial Germany and Japan was an ally, but the possibility of a confrontation with the ever more powerful Japanese was increasingly important to US Navy planners from the early 1920s onwards. The ranges of operations involved in such a conflict were beyond anything then being considered by other leading navies, and in the major strategic plan – Plan Orange – it was expected that the principal operational base in a war against Japan would be the US west coast, the Philippines and the mid-Pacific islands being presumed lost in the early stages.
Design: The US Navy had long followed a policy of gradual improvement, producing submarines which without excelling in any single aspect of their performance were, nevertheless, extremely reliable, with long range, good habitability

Above: USS *Gato* (SS212) as she appeared in August 1942, at the time of her return from her second operational patrol. Weapon and sensor fits and fin shapes changed constantly throughout the war on all US submarines as experience was gained and new equipment became available. At this stage *Gato*'s principal surface weapon was a 3in/50 gun (above), while a water-cooled 0.50in AA machine gun (top) was mounted abaft the fin. The 21in (533mm) Mk XIV torpedo (right), in use up to 1944, had a range of 4,500yd (4,115m) at 46kt or 9,000yd (8,230m) at 31.5kt. Notoriously unreliable, it was in such short supply that some submarines went out on patrol armed only with mines.

and large numbers of reload torpedoes, all essential attributes in boats operating for protracted periods at great distances from base. Particular emphasis was placed on propulsion, and the US Navy was so determined to have a guaranteed source of really reliable and economical diesel engines that it even assisted in the dieselisation of the US railroads, a policy which resulted in the perfection of four types of high-speed diesel. In addition, it had also experimented in the inter-war years with a composite drive on the S class and direct drive on the Ts and Gs, but for the Gato class it returned to the proven diesel-electric drive.

There had been constant debate in the US Navy about the gun armament for submarines, and so strongly did the naval staff feel about preventing submarine captains from becoming involved in surface actions that they deliberately restricted the armament to one Mk 21 Mod 1 3in/50 anti-aircraft gun. This weapon's inadequacy was proved beyond doubt in the early war years, and US submarines underwent constant up-gunning throughout the war, as did those of most other navies, until the revolution in submarine design led to the elimination of all gun armament. The replacement for the 3in/50 on the Gato class was the Mk 17 5in/25, a 'wet' gun produced from non-corrosive materials, which enabled the muzzle and breech covers to be eliminated. In design terms the Gato class was a progressive development of the Porpoise class, and the Gatos' high surface speed of just over 20 knots proved invaluable in reaching patrol areas and achieving good firing positions for torpedoes.

The all-welded construction faciliated production, which was confined to four yards, the most unusual being that at Maniwotoc on Lake Michigan, some 1,000 miles (1,610km) inland. Not only did the boats have to be launched sideways into the river, but they then had to travel down the Mississippi to reach the sea.

This highly successful class show the soundness of the American policy of developing reliable hull and engine designs over a long period. The US Navy's task was, however, somewhat simplified by having no real requirement for smaller, more manoeuvrable and shorter ranged submarines.

During World War II US submarines, normally operating at considerable distances from their bases, sank over nine-tenths of Japan's major vessels, an achievement in which code-breaking played a considerable part, but to which successful submarine design also contributed. Most of the later fighting was done by the 73-strong Gato class, and by the 132 Balaos and 31 Tenches that were developed from them. Eighteen of the Gato class were sunk by enemy action and one was a constructive total loss.

Above: US Navy prewar policy was one of progressive development, with a series of large boats being produced for operations against Japanese battleships and aircraft carriers. The few US bases were far apart so the boats had long ranges and were more self-sufficient than those of other nations: average range was 10,000nm with stores for 60 days. USS *Swordfish* (SS 193), seen here, belonged to the Salmon/ Sargo class, which, with the T class, were the Gatos' immediate predecessors. Swordfish sank the first Japanese merchant ship of the war on December 15, 1942.

The Gato class is one of those which bridged the gap between the last of the submersibles and the first of the true submarines. In its original form the Gato epitomised the US Navy's long-range attack submarine and operated with great success and distinction against the Japanese, and with the other similar classes, the Gatos played a significant part in bringing Imperial Japan to the verge of surrender by devastating its merchant fleet. However, the Gato class boats were slow under water: their maximum submerged speed was 8.75 knots, and even this could not be sustained for any great period without draining the batteries. Also, as with virtually all their contemporaries, the designed operating depth of 300ft (91m) was a trifle less than the overall length of 311.75ft (95.2m), which imposed considerable constraints on manoeuvrability.

The next class of US submarine – the 132-strong Balao class – was virtually identical with the Gato, but had a strengthened hull, enabling the members of the class to dive to 400ft (122m), and earning them the name 'thick-skinned Gatos'. The Tench class was also based on the Gato, but only 31 had been built when the war ended and production ceased.

Electronics: The Gato class boats were among the first to have a comprehensive electronics fit, eventually comprising a full range of radar, sonar, communications and electronic warfare equipment. The actual fit was in a constant state of change as new equipment became available and as boats could be spared to have it installed, and masts and antennas proliferated with little effort at reducing drag until by the war's end there was a veritable forest atop every submarine's fin.

The first air search radar small enough to install in a submarine, the SD, became available at the end of 1941, and its small bar antenna was usually mounted at the head of the HF communications rod antenna. The SD gave no directional information, had a maximum range of only 10 miles (16km) and was easily detected by enemy RDF; nevertheless, it met the submariners' urgent need for early warning of the approach of an aircraft, and by mid-1942 all US submarines were fitted with SD, while the SJ, which gave both range and bearing, was starting to enter service. Although difficult to calibrate and somewhat unreliable, the SJ gave submariners a totally new capability, and when the circular plan position indicator display replaced the earlier horizontal line display great confidence was placed in the system. The SJ antenna was ovoid, originally solid but later a lattice, and unlike the SD it had a mast of its own. The last wartime set was the SS.

Sonars, too, were being constantly improved, and by 1945 most US submarines had the active

Above: USS *Perch* (SS 313) of the Balao class. The Balaos were virtually identical to the Gatos, but design changes to facilitate rapid building resulted in greater structural strength and an increase in diving depth from 300ft (91m) to 400ft (122m). This photograph shows clearly the many protrusions on a typical World War II submarine. As well as creating considerable underwater drag, leading to low speed and limited endurance, they were a source of considerable noise, making them readily detectable.

Right: USS *Cubera* (SS 347), a postwar GUPPY-2 (Greater Underwater Propulsive Power) conversion of a World War II Balao class boat. Comparison with the original configuration (above) shows the streamlining and the way external fittings have been either removed or made retractable. These measures, allied to more powerful batteries, led to great increases in underwater performance.

Above: As the GUPPY conversion was relatively expensive ($2.5 million each at 1950 prices) 19 boats were given a simpler 'Fleet Snorkel' modernisation, involving the removal of deck armament and streamlining the fin. This is USS *Sabalo* (SS 302) in the mid-1960s; she was stricken in 1971.

WFA system, which combined echo-ranging, listening and sounding using a retractable keel-mounted dome. The latter feature prevented the sonar from being used when the submarine was lying on the bottom, and a passive listening device was therefore mounted topside. Initially the JP, a converted surface patrol craft set, was used; like the later JT it enabled the submarine to detect surface ship propeller noise at ranges of up to 20,000 yards (18,288m) and was also used to detect self-noise. The JP was manually rotated but the later JT was powered and consisted of a 5ft (1.53m) line hydrophone with a 22° beam scanning at 4rpm. It covered the sonic (100Hz-12kHz) and, with a converter, supersonic (up to 65kHz) frequencies. A new and highly specialised type of sonar came into use late in the war: the FM, later redesignated QLA-1, was a precision mine-evasion sonar which was so effective that US submarines were able to work in Japanese home waters with relative confidence.

Other sensors included the usual two periscopes, Number 1 for search and Number 2 for attack, and there was a variety of radio masts, whip antennas and stubs, the actual fit changing with bewildering rapidity. Electronic warfare equipment also began to be fitted, one external indication being a large direction-finding loop. Finally, for surface actions with the gun, there were two target bearing transmitters mounted on the bridge.

Armament: As built, the Gatos were armed with one 3in/50 gun in line with the prewar policy of ensuring that a submarine captain would not be given a gun which might encourage him to fight it out on the surface. However, weapons were progressively added throughout the war and by 1945 armament normally comprised one 5in/25 gun and two 40mm and two twin 20mm cannon. By 1950, however, the Guppy conversion programme (described below) had eliminated the guns.

There were ten 21in torpedo tubes, six forward and four aft, with 24 reloads, and while the boats themselves were very reliable the torpedoes were far less so. Certainly, the Mk 14 torpedo with its Mk VI magnetic exploder used from 1941 to 1943 was notoriously unreliable; the torpedo ran much deeper than designed and left a prominent wake, while the exploder frequently failed to detonate and the back-up contact exploder only seemed to work when hitting the target a glancing blow. Later in the war the Mk 18 torpedo, a direct copy of a captured German G7e, was widely used, and was credited with sinking a million tons of Japanese shipping.

Construction: The 73 boats of the Gato class were launched between 1941 and 1943, construction being shared between Electric Boat, Groton (41), Portsmouth Navy Yard (14), Mare Island Navy Yard (4) and Maniwotoc, Wisconsin (14). Of the 54 that survived the war, most were converted to Guppy 1 (Greater Underwater Propulsive Power) standard: all guns and other external protuberances were removed, the sail was streamlined, a schnorkel was fitted and new, lighter and much more powerful batteries were fitted. This conversion, based on the lessons of the German Type XXI, had a dramatic effect on performance, with considerable increases in underwater speed and range. Of the remaining boats six were transferred abroad and seven converted to hunter-killer submarines with more powerful batteries for a higher underwater speed. Another six were converted to radar pickets in 1951-52, with an extra 31ft (8.3m) portion added to their hulls. *Tunny* (SS-282) was converted into a Regulus I missile launching submarine and was then again altered to a troop-carrying submarine in 1964.

Left: The first US strategic deterrent submarines carried Regulus, a cruise missile only launched from the surface. Final preparations for launch took place on deck outside the hangar; a further hazard was that if the hangar accidentally flooded the boat would turn turtle. USS *Tunny* (SSG 282), built in 1941 as a Gato class fleet boat, was one of the first operational conversions.

Left: USS *Tunny* (SSG 282) launches a Regulus I missile in the 1950s; two missiles were carried in the portly hangar. Regulus I was a turbojet-powered remote-controlled aircraft, which flew at a speed of about Mach 0.9 and had a range of some 400nm. It cruised at a height of over 30,000ft (9,144m) until near its target, guided by radio signals from submarines at periscope depth whose position was known from Loran. Its warhead was a 120kT W-5 nuclear device, and the system was designed to be used only against large fixed targets.

Type XXI

Origin: Germany, first unit completed 1944
Type: Patrol submarine, diesel-electric powered
Displacement: 1,621 tons surfaced; 1,819 tons submerged
Dimensions: Length 251.6ft (76.7m); beam 21.7ft (6.6m); draught 20.7ft (6.3m)
Propulsion: Diesel-electric drive on two shafts; two MAN M6V 40/46 diesel engines, each 1,000bhp at 522rpm; two SSW or AEG GU 365/30 electric motors for normal running, each 2,500hp; two SSW GW323/38 electric motors for silent running, each 83kW; 15.6kt surfaced, 17.2kt submerged (5kt in silent mode), 11,150nm at 12kt surfaced, 285nm at 6kt submerged; design diving depth 435ft (133m)
Complement: 57
Background: By the middle of 1943 German submarine losses were reaching unacceptable levels as a result of Allied improvements in anti-submarine equipment and techniques, and it appeared to Admiral Dönitz that sonar and radar, together with the ever more effective use of ships and aircraft, were proving too much for his captains. To a large extent he was correct, although he was not to know that electronic warfare, and in particular the breaking of the Enigma code, was having a major influence in enabling Allied ships and aircraft to be in the right place at the right time. What was required, in the German view, was a true submersible, which would be able to operate for protracted periods under water and to avoid detection by radar or sonar. It would also improve survivability if the boats could operate at considerably higher speeds and so would be able to outrun surface hunters.

Professor Walther had been experimenting for some years with both streamlining and propulsion. His hydrogen peroxide powerplants proved too unreliable for operational use, although a number of boats with such units were built, and the only alternative at the time was to streamline the outer casing and to vastly increase the battery power of diesel-electric boats. Accordingly, new hull forms were adopted which made possible higher speeds under water than those achieved on the surface, while the adoption of the snorkel, which had been invented by a Dutch naval officer in the late 1930s, enabled the resulting Type XXI to travel at periscope depth using its diesels rather than its batteries.

The new boat's performance was remarkable: periscope depth could be reached in 10 seconds and 100ft (30.5m) in 40 seconds – much faster than anything else then in service – but the numerous flooding and ventilation openings involved added considerably to drag and the number of apertures was reduced, adding some 15

Right: The after anti-aircraft turret, mounting two 20mm cannon. Despite the intention to make the Type XXI a true submarine and the deletion of the deck gun, the designers still kept anti-aircraft cannon, presumably as a result of the experiences of the older U-boats. In fact, of the nine Type XXIs actually sunk on patrol, three were mined and the remaining six were lost during attack from aircraft.

Above: A Type XXI immediately after launching at the AG Weser yard at Bremen, probably in 1944. The guard rails were only fitted for the launch and fitting-out, and were then removed. Note the anti-aircraft cannon in the streamlined mounting at the forward end of the sail; there is another twin mount at the after end.

seconds to the diving time.

Safe operating depth was 435ft (132.6m), but with a safety factor of 2.5 it could operate down to approximately 700ft (213m), beyond the Allied sonar's effective range of approximately 400ft (122m). Underwater speed and endurance put it in a totally new class: the maximum underwater speed of 16.7 knots could be sustained for 72 minutes, while 12 knots could be kept up for 5 hours and endurance at its 'silent' speed of 5.2 knots was around 72 hours, compared with the Type VIIC's endurance of just 45 minutes at five or six knots. The snorkel enabled the Type XXI to cruise almost indefinitely below the surface and was virtually undetectable by the contemporary airborne radars, especially in anything over Sea State 2. The streamlining of hull and fin also led to a significantly smaller sonar cross-section, and the effect was reinforced by the use in some cases of anti-radar and anti-sonar coatings.

The Type XXIs were designed for easy fabrication and no fewer than 131 were completed. However, the chaotic state of Germany in the final stages of the war and Dönitz' decision to order the type straight into production without any prototypes meant that very few attained operational status. Those that did overcome their teething troubles and actually carry out operational patrols found that the revolutionary design did indeed confer undreamt-of improvements, and a number of successes were achieved. Fortunately for the Allies, however, the boats were too late to

Below: The exceptional lines of a Type XXI make a fascinating contrast with boats such as the Type IX. *U-2502* was the second Type XXI to be completed: note the active sonar in the forward edge of the fin and the passive array under the bow. Like other early Type XXIs she is armed with four 20mm AA cannon; later boats had 30mm cannon, which, having longer range, were more effective.

Below: *U-793*, a Walter Type XVII (Wa201) boat, following completion by Blohm und Voss, Hamburg, in April 1944. During official tests this boat achieved a speed of 20.3 knots on her Walther hydrogen-peroxide (H_2O_2) plant, and it was hoped to reach 26 knots eventually.

Above: The original Type XXI had six bow torpedo tubes, although it was planned to fit additional sets of side tubes in later models. The G7e torpedoes shown here were 21in (533mm) in diameter and 23.5ft (7.163m) in length. There were two models; the first (codename Geier) had acoustic homing, while the second (codename Lerche) was wire-guided, using acoustic information passed back along the wires.

make a major impact; 120 were sunk or scuttled and 11 surrendered.

The US, British, French and Soviet navies all used their captured Type XXIs for experimental and development purposes in the early postwar period. The US Navy developed a new class, based on many of the features of the Type XXI; the Tang (SS-564) class, of which only six were built, improved on the performance of the Type XXI, most notably in operating depth, safe depth being 700ft (213.4m) and collapse depth 1,100ft (335.3m). With the prospect of nuclear submarines on the horizon, however, the US Navy did not want to produce a large class of new diesel-electric boats, instead converting many of its excellent and relatively new Gato, Balao and Tench class submarines to the new Guppy standard.

The Soviets made the staff at the Schichau yard in Danzig (Gdansk) finish the five Type XXIs which had been laid down as *U-3538* to *U-3542* and then produced a further unknown number in the USSR; they were followed by the Whiskey class, which was produced in vast numbers. The British carried out a number of experiments on the Walther hydrogen-peroxide system in the

Above right: *U-3008* at the US Portsmouth Navy Yard, August 30, 1946, with periscopes and radar masts raised. Several Type XXIs were examined and tested with great interest by the Allies, who had nothing comparable.

Right: Following tests of the captured German Type XXIs the Americans built the Tang class in the early 1950s. This is USS *Gudgeon* (SS 567), still serving the Turkish Navy as *Hizir Reis*.

Below: Name-ship of her class, USS *Tang* (SS 563), off Hawaii in 1964, her descent from the Type XXI clear from her lines. Like *Gudgeon* she serves on with the Turkish Navy as *Piri Reis*.

late 1940s and 1950s, and even built two boats using this system, HMS *Explorer* and *Excalibur*, but concluded – to the great relief of their crews – that this was not the way ahead. Instead, the Royal Navy, like the US Navy, modernised a number of its World War II boats, but then built the very successful Porpoise and Oberon classes, whose design was based on the lessons of the Type XXI but which, like the Tangs, did not use the German figure-8; they also achieved significantly better diving depths.

The French used the Type XXI as the basis for their Narval class, of which six were built in the years 1951-54. The West German Bundesmarine also recovered a Type XXI which had been scuttled in 1945, and used it for many years as an experimental submarine under the new name *Wilhelm Bauer*.

The Type XXI thus had its main impact in the first decade of the postwar era, when it formed the basis of all diesel-electric submarine development. The next stage, which took submarine evolution a further great leap forward, was the US Navy's *Albacore*.

Armament: The Type XXI was the first World War II submarine type to reverse the trend of increasing surface armament, weaponry being confined to four 20mm or 30mm AA cannon in twin streamlined turrets at either end of the fin. There were six 21in (533mm) bow-mounted tubes with 23 torpedoes carried. Part of the torpedo load could be replaced by mines.

Sensors: Too many U-boats had been attacked on the surface by aircraft, due to Allied advances in aircraft radars. The Germans, therefore, developed a series of radar detectors designated Funkmess Beobachtungsgerät (FuMB), with individual models being named after islands. The Type XXI normally carried an FuMB-29 Bali I detector, with the antenna mounted on top of the schnorkel mast, although later this was replaced by the FuMB-37 Leros in many boats. A DF loop was also installed at the forward end of the fin.

U-boats were fitted with active air- and surface-search radars during the course of the war, like their Allied counterparts, the sets being designated Funkmess-Ortungsgerät (FuMO), and Type XXI boats used the FuMO-61 Hohentwiel-Drauf model, with a rectangular antenna array on a short mast.

Radio antennas included a UHF antenna mounted beside the bridge and an HF rod antenna on its own extending mast. Surprisingly, despite the requirement for silent operation, two long-wire HF radio antennas were mounted fore and aft; such devices always have a tendency to vibrate at speed.

The usual very effective German sonars were used. A Schallortung-Gerät, or active sonar set, located in the forward edge of the fin structure provided bearings of ±100° with a directional accuracy of ±0.5°.

A Balkon (balcony, or gondola) array was built in under the bow to provide passive detection out to ranges at least as good as those being obtained by Allied sonars, though its location prevented this device from covering the angled segment aft of 150°-210° and it was, therefore, intended to install a Schallortung-Passiv Anlage (passive listening device) on later Type XXIs; SPA consisted of a swivelling bar with two passive receiver elements mounted under a streamlined, hooded fairing on the after casing.

Construction: One hundred and thirty-one Type XXI boats were completed between 1944 and the end of the war. The yards involved were Blohm und Voss, Hamburg, Weser, Bremen, and Schichau, Danzig (Gdansk). The last yard also completed at least five more boats at the behest of the Soviets.

Right: HMS *Excalibur* had Type 187 sonar dome and short sail, a submerged displacement of 1,000 tons and a length of 225ft (68.6m) she had a diving depth of 550ft (167m). She and her sister were developed from the Type XVII, one scuttled example of which *U-1407* – was raised and recommissioned as HMS *Meteorite*.

Below: HMS *Explorer* at sea in 1956. The Royal Navy saw the Walther propulsion process as a cheaper alternative to nuclear power, but controlling the hydrogen peroxide proved too difficult, despite the presence of Helmut Walther and five colleagues at the Vickers yard at Barrow from 1946 to 1949.

Albacore

Origin: USA, completed 1953
Type: Experimental submarine, diesel-electric powered (AGSS)
Displacement: 1,500 tons surfaced; 1,850 tons submerged
Dimensions: Length as built 203.75ft (62.1m), length after Phase III modification 210.5ft (64.2m); beam 27.5ft (8.4m); draught 18.5ft (5.64m)
Propulsion: Diesel-electric drive on one shaft; two General Motors radial diesels; one Westinghouse electric motor; 15,000shp for 25kt surfaced, 33kt for short periods submerged
Complement: 52
Background: From World War I onward the submarine hull form was essentially long and narrow; even the Type XXI and the still later USS *Nautilus*, the first nuclear-powered attack submarine, were of this shape. It had been discovered, however, that the Type XXIs and their derivatives tended to pitch at high underwater speeds to the point where, under certain conditions, control could be lost. The US Navy in a postwar programme developed a new hull form based on that of an airship and an experimental diesel-electric submarine, USS *Albacore*, was built to test this new shape. Initially conceived as a high-speed underwater target for surface ASW forces and financed by the cancellation of a destroyer conversion programme, *Albacore* was to prove one of the great milestones in submarine development.
Design: *Albacore*'s hull form was a body-of-revolution, that is to say, like a torpedo, symmetrical around its long axis. The results showed that the new shorter, fatter hull was very much more manoeuvrable, being capable of turning at 3.2°/sec compared to 2.5°/sec or less for the more traditional hull. Indeed, the *Albacore* proved that a submarine could be 'flown' in three dimensions like an aircraft, making tight banked turns and even, it is rumoured, looping. The new hull was also dynamically stable at all speeds and could be driven faster for a given power; the boat needed only 136hp to sustain seven knots, and with her full 15,000shp could travel for brief periods at over 33 knots, a hitherto undreamt-of underwater speed. Moreover, the single propeller was not only much more efficient, but also much quieter, so helping to avoid detection by hostile anti-submarine forces. There were internal benefits, too, since the fatter hull could accommodate a multi-deck layout, providing greater storage space and better habitability.

The *Albacore* was used to test a variety of features. In her original state she could travel at 26 knots submerged, but with silver-zinc batteries and contra-rotating propellers – both fitted later in Phase IV of the programme – she

Above: This 1960 photograph of USS *Blueback* (SS 581), one of the three members of the last conventionally powered submarine class to be built for the US Navy, shows her teardrop-shaped hull. These Barbels were built with bow-mounted hydroplanes as shown, but these were eventually moved back to the fin.

could achieve an amazing 33 knots. Another feature was an aircraft-type dive brake abaft the fin to control inadvertent dives. Although German World War II research had shown that at underwater speeds above 12 knots bow planes tended to destabilise the submarine in a vertical plane, the *Albacore* was built with bow hydroplanes; these were apparently very successful, but were not adopted for subsequent production classes, which all had fin-mounted planes. She originally had cross-shaped after control surfaces but was later modified (Phase III) to test an X-configured stern empennage. Although this has certain advantages, and has since found favour with the navies of Sweden and the Netherlands, it has not been pursued further by the US Navy.

As a result of the dramatic demonstrations by the *Albacore* the hull forms of the next class of US Navy nuclear powered attack submarine, the Skipjack class, and the last class of US diesel-electric submarines, the Barbel class, were altered, with great benefits to their performance. The details were also made available to the United States' allies, as a result of which a number of designs, among them the Japanese Uzushio and Yuushio and the Dutch Walrus and Zwaardvis classes, make use of what became known as the 'Albacore hull'.

Armament: Albacore carried no weapons.

Electronics: As an experimental submarine *Albacore* was used to test various sonar and other sensor fits. One such was a bow-mounted BQR-2 with digital multi-beam steering (DIMUS), which enabled a submarine to listen in all directions and to detect weak signals which might otherwise be lost in the background noise. It was estimated that DIMUS, as applied to the BQR-2, increased detection range by a quiet submarine against a schnorkelling submarine from 50 to 70nm (93 to 130km). DIMUS also considerably enhanced multi-target tracking capability.

Construction: One unit only was constructed at Portsmouth Naval Yard. Laid down on March 15, 1952, launched on August 8, 1953, and commissioned on December 5, 1953, she was withdrawn from active service in 1972 and stricken on May 1, 1980.

Left: USS *Albacore* (AGSS 569), one of the truly great milestones in submarine history. Her hull was designed as a body of revolution – that is, symmetrical about the horizontal axis – and based on airship practice. This shape gave dynamic stability at all speeds, resulted in truly outstanding manoeuvrability, and permitted a substantial increase in internal volume, which in turn enhanced crew comfort. *Albacore* tested various devices; completed in the configuration shown here, with a cruciform tail empennage, she later tasked X-shaped control surfaces, a feature not adopted by the US Navy but currently used by some others.

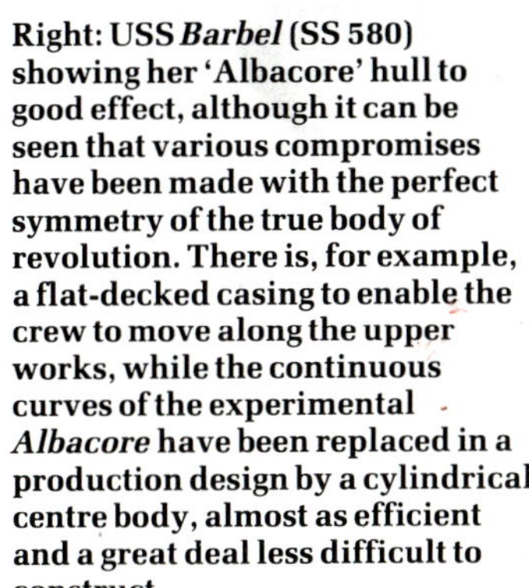

Right: USS *Barbel* (SS 580) showing her 'Albacore' hull to good effect, although it can be seen that various compromises have been made with the perfect symmetry of the true body of revolution. There is, for example, a flat-decked casing to enable the crew to move along the upper works, while the continuous curves of the experimental *Albacore* have been replaced in a production design by a cylindrical centre body, almost as efficient and a great deal less difficult to construct.

Nautilus

Origin: USA, launched 1954
Type: Attack submarine, nuclear-powered
Displacement: 3,764 tons surfaced; 4,040 tons submerged
Dimensions: Length 319.4ft (97.4m); beam 27.6ft (8.4m); draught 22ft (6.7m)
Propulsion: One S2W Westinghouse pressurized water-cooled reactor on two shafts; 15,000shp for 20+kt surfaced, 22.5kt submerged
Complement: 105
Background: The one insurmountable problem with diesel-electric submarines is that they must periodically approach the surface to run their diesel engines and recharge their batteries and to replenish life support systems, and even when just the head of a snorkel is exposed there is a great danger of detection. Following the experiences of both sides in World War II a major search started in the mid-1940s to find an answer to this problem: by chance the technological answer was at hand, having been developed for an entirely different purpose. It had been appreciated from early on in the US nuclear weapons programme that a controlled nuclear reaction could produce enough heat to generate the steam to power conventional steam turbines. Such a concept offered particular advantages for submarine propulsion in that the reaction required no oxygen whatsoever and would give great range between core renewals. Accordingly, in 1949 the US Chief of Naval Operations issued a formal requirement for a nuclear-powered submarine with an in-service date of January 1955.
Design: Research and development into a submarine reactor had started in the USA at the Argonne National Laboratory as early as 1948 and was subsequently transferred to Westinghouse at the Bettis Atomic Power Laboratory. The Submarine Thermal Reactor Mark II which resulted from this work was later redesignated the S2W and was installed in the new hull of the *Nautilus*. The S2W initially had a core enriched by only some 18-20 per cent, but her second and subsequent cores were enriched by over 40 per cent, giving a much higher energy density. This improvement is reflected in the core lives: the first core drove Nautilus 62,562nm (100,681km), the second 91,324nm (146,968km) and the third 150,000nm (240,000km).

A key factor in this programme was the appointment of one of the outstanding submarine officers in history, Captain (later Admiral) Hyman G. Rickover, USN. USS *Nautilus* (SSN-571) was commissioned on September 30, 1954, and on January 17, 1955, she was able to make the historic signal, 'Under way on nuclear power', thus giving the US Navy a lead of three or four years over its Soviet counterpart. *Nautilus* was by far the largest submarine to have been built at that time and designed with a conventional hull based on Type XXI and Guppy

Above: Like the contemporary Nautilus, *Sea Wolf* (SSN 575) had a traditional, pre-Albacore hull. *Sea Wolf*'s liquid sodium reactor proved very troublesome and was replaced after two years.

Above: USS *Nautilus* (SSN 571) achieved man's dream of true and protracted underwater operations. But while the propulsion system was revolutionary, her hull form was the traditional long, thin design with twin propellers. Her submerged speed was 22.5kt and it was only when nuclear power was married to the Albacore hull in the Skipjack class that the full potential of these new developments was realised.

technology rather than an Albacore hull, presumably to avoid risking too many revolutionary advances in one project. (Indeed, it was some time before the US Navy adopted the new hull form, and the next five SSNs – *Sea Wolf*, and the four-boat Skate class – all had the old type of hull.) *Nautilus* had two shafts, driving two small, outward-rotating high-speed propellers on which she could achieve a sustained 22.5 knots submerged, considerably better than any other submarine then in service. A diesel engine was fitted as a stand-by, together with a snorkel and emergency batteries. She was armed with six bow-mounted 21in torpedo tubes, but unlike most of her contemporaries in the early 1950s did not have any stern tubes.

A similar hull was used for the second nuclear-powered submarine, USS *Sea Wolf* (SSN-575), used to test the S2G liquid sodium-cooled reactor which was thought to offer potential advantages over the pressurized water-cooled system. Known as the Submarine Intermediate Reactor (SIR) and developed by Westinghouse at the Knolls Atomic Power Laboratory, the S2W finally powered *Sea Wolf* on January 21, 1957, just over two years after *Nautilus*' success. Liquid sodium cooling had looked attractive as it offered much greater operating temperatures, giving more efficient heat transfer, but it had numerous drawbacks, including the fact that the working fluid had to be kept liquid at all times or it would freeze in the pipes and ruin them. Altogether, the S2G gave a great deal of trouble, including a superheater leak, and in December 1958 it was replaced by a pressurized water-cooled S2Wa reactor similar to that installed in *Nautilus*. Reports of liquid-metal cooled reactors have appeared from time to time since the *Sea Wolf*, notably as power plants for the Soviet Alfa class and the French *Rubis*, but none has been confirmed.

During her service the *Nautilus* made numerous historic voyages. By 1958 the US Navy had sufficient confidence in her capabilities to send her on the first submarine polar transit, starting in Hawaii and finishing in Portland, England, after passing under the North Pole on August 3, 1958. Her first refuelling took place in 1957, the second in 1959 and the third in 1964.

Armament: *Nautilus* was armed with six 21in bow-mounted torpedo tubes.

Electronics: *Nautilus* was equipped with conventional 1950s electronics and communications equipment. Primary sonar was the BQS-4 and the BQR-2C, the former comprising seven vertically-stacked transducers inside a BQR-2C and operated in listening, single-ping and automatic echo-ranging modes with a typical range of 600-8,000 yards (549-7,315m). The BQR-2C was a passive sonar with 48 3ft (0.9m) vertical elements in a 6ft (1.82m) circular array. Performance was claimed to be excellent, with auto target following on a noisy submarine with an accuracy of 0.25° at 12,000 yards (10,973m).

Construction: Constructed at the Electric Boat Company yard at Groton, Connecticut, *Nautilus* was laid down on June 14, 1952, launched on January 21, 1954, and commissioned on September 30, 1954. She was subsequently used as a research craft, before being decommissioned in the early 1980s. She is now on display at a museum.

Right: A significant advance achieved by the nuclear boats was their ability to travel under the Polar ice-cap. The first such trip was made by *Nautilus* in August 1958; here USS *Skate* (SSN 578), name-ship of the production class that followed *Nautilus*, surfaces through the Arctic ice in 1961.

The Oceans

It seems to be generally assumed that submarines, almost since their inception, have roamed at will in an underwater world of which they are the masters, moving in the depths of the oceans among the hills and canyons of the ocean bed. Nothing could be further from the truth: even today the most modern submarines penetrate only marginally into the ocean's depth, and during World War I they barely even left the surface. The submarines of 1915 had operating depths of around 180ft (55m), those of 1945 could reach 400ft (122m) or so, and even today's Los Angeles class can scarcely exceed 1,500ft (450m), although the Soviet Alfa class is reputed to have an operating depth of around 2,500ft (700m).

Even the Alfa's performance seems poor when it is considered that the abyssal plains, which form the floor of most of the underwater world, lie at an average depth of some 12,000ft (3,700m), and the deepest trenches extend down beyond 30,000ft (9,100m). The most sophisticated and specialised underwater vehicles are required to penetrate to such depths: for example, the US research submersible *Alvin* can operate down to 13,500ft (4,000m) and the bathyscaphe *Trieste* reached 35,600ft (4,500m) in the Challenger Deep in the Marianas Trench, where the pressure exceeds one ton per square inch.

Combat submarines have no current need to operate at such depths, but even so the world in which they must live and fight is quite different from that experienced on land. Over 70 per cent of the earth's surface is covered by oceans, a vast and still relatively unexplored part of the world whose topography, geology and specific nature are only imperfectly understood. Indeed, in many ways we know more about the Moon and the nearer planets than we do about our own oceans, which have been described as the last frontier but one, with only outer space being a greater challenge. It is essential to have some understanding of this different environment in order to appreciate both how submarines survive and operate, and also how the primary means of detecting submarines – sound – is affected.

Ocean depth profile and typical submarine operating depths

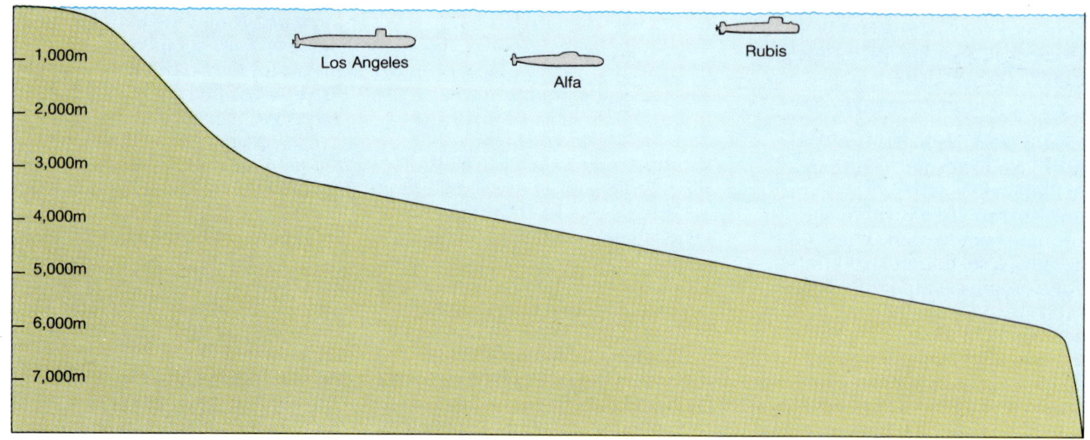

Above: Typical diving depths of current submarines compared with the average ocean depth distribution. Submarines do not dive as deep as is popularly assumed. Los Angeles SSNs operate at 1,500ft (450m) and titanium-hulled Soviet Alfas at 2,500ft (700m), but the French Rubis class are limited to 300m (980ft).

Below: Continental shelves (orange) extend from the coastlines reaching a depth of about 400ft (130m) before the continental break and a rapid increase in depth.

Continental shelves

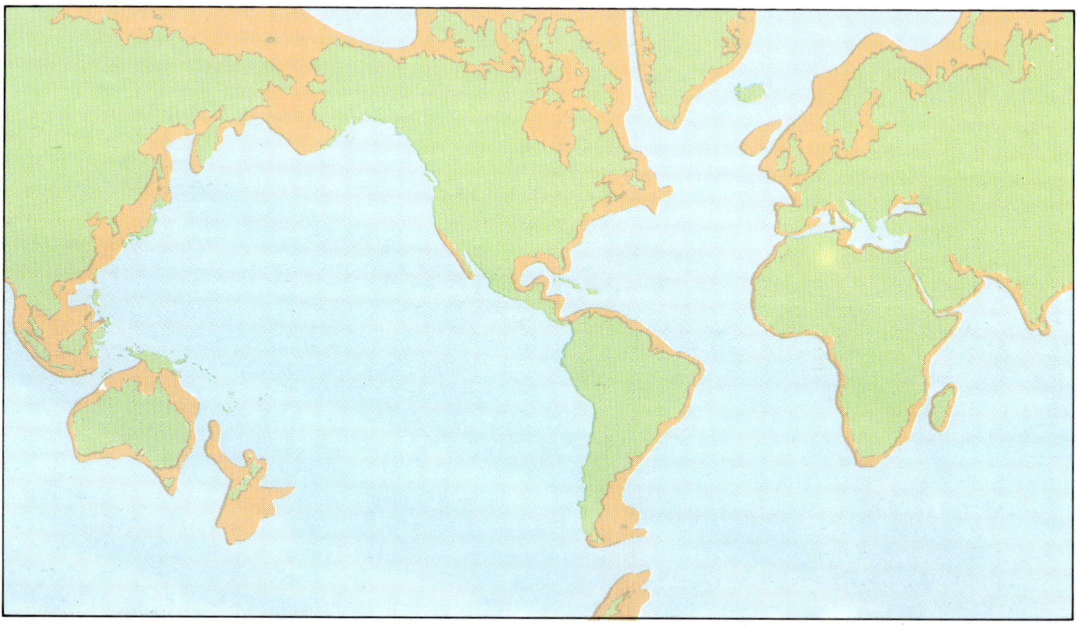

THE OCEANS	
Total surface area	139,400,000sq miles/361,000,000km^2
Overall average depth	12,450ft/3,795m
Pacific average depth	13,215ft/4,082m
Atlantic average depth	10,932ft/3,332m
Indian average depth	12,785ft/3,897m
Mean temperature	39.02°F/3.90°C
Mean density	64lb/cu ft/1.03gm/cm^3
Earth surface area	197,000,000sq miles/510,000,000km^2
Land surface area	57,500,000sq miles/149,000,000km^2

OCEANIC TOPOGRAPHY

The oceans can be physically divided into three main elements, the continental shelf, the abyssal plains and the deep ocean trenches. The shallow, sloping continental shelves account for some 24 million square miles, or 12.5 per cent of the Earth's surface, extending from the coast out to sea, often for several tens of miles and normally at an angle of about one degree below the horizontal and ending abruptly at the shelf-break, which is usually found at a depth of about 400ft (130m). From there the slope steepens to angles varying from a few degrees to the almost vertical until the abyssal plains are reached.

The abyssal plains lie at an average depth of 12,000ft (3,700m), although some are much deeper. They have their own mountain ranges, plains and basins, with the mountains breaking the surface in places to form chains of volcanic islands such as Hawaii and Iceland. In the Atlantic there is a mountain chain running from Spitzbergen in the North almost as far south as Antarctica, with extensive plains lying either side at depths of over 16,000ft (4,900m). The largest of the latter is the Argentine Plain, with an area roughly equal to that of the continental USA, while the North American basin, the Vatteras Plain off Florida and the Sohm Plain south of Newfoundland are only slightly smaller.

There is no similar central spine in the Pacific. The East Pacific Rise runs south of Australia to swing northward parallel to South America as far as Mexico, enclosing the basins of the South Pacific, Chile and Peru. To the west are a series of wide basins containing the mountain-like Christmas Island and the Hawaiian chain. The ocean floor becomes even more complex near Japan, where huge island arcs form volcanic mountains interspersed by deep trenches, and in the area of the Marianas, Fiji and Kermadec-Tonga it is more complex than the Rockies and the Himalayas combined. A further feature of the abyssal plains are guyots, truncated, flat-topped volcanoes, of which at least 2,000 exist in the Pacific, with many more elsewhere.

Plunging to three times the depth of the abyssal plains are the deep ocean trenches which form the hadal zone (from the Greek hades, or the underworld). Reaching depths of more than 21,000ft (6,400m) and up to 6,000 miles (10,000km) long, these are among the most extreme

Right: USS *Mendel Rivers* (SSN 686) of the Los Angeles class can operate at depths of 1,500ft (450m), but even this prevents her from penetrating more than a small proportion of the oceans.

Above: Ocean-bed imagery taken from the SEASAT satellite. Average depth of the Tonga-Kermadec Trench to the northeast of New Zealand is 35,702ft (10,882m); it is 34 miles (55km) wide and 870 miles (1,400km) long. We have more detailed knowledge of the Moon's surface than of the depths of our own planet.

PACIFIC TRENCH DIMENSIONS

Trench	Depth	Width (approx)	Length (approx)
Aleutian	26,585ft/8,100m	43.5 miles/70km	1,429 miles/2,300km
Kurile	34,587ft/10,542m	74.6 miles/120km	1,367 miles/2,200km
Japan	32,185ft/9,810m	62.1 miles/100km	559 miles/900km
Mariana	36,200ft/11,034m	43.5 miles/70km	1,584 miles/2,550km
Tonga	35,702ft/10,882m	34.2 miles/55km	870 miles/1,400km
Peru-Chile	26,427ft/8,055m	43.5 miles/70km	3,666 miles/5,900km

environments on earth. Most occur around the edges of the Pacific, but there are others in the Indian and Atlantic Oceans.

PHYSICAL CHARACTERISTICS

The complexity of the ocean environment is exacerbated by its dynamic nature, equivalent in many ways to that of weather in the atmosphere. Its phenomena are difficult to predict or characterise, particularly because only a few of them, such as surface-wave activity, ice, tidal effects and local weather, can be observed by the human eye.

Among the better known characteristics of the oceans are that they contain many dissolved chemicals, including, of course, salt (sodium chloride), and that

MAJOR CONSTITUENTS OF SEAWATER

Substance	Symbol	Per cent
Sodium	Na	30.62
Magnesium	Mg	3.68
Calcium	Ca	1.18
Potassium	K	1.10
Strontium	Sr	0.02
Chloride	Cl	55.07
Sulphate	SO_4	7.72
Bicarbonate	HCO_3	0.40
Bromide	Br	0.19
Borate	H_2BO_3	0.01
Fluoride	F	0.01

Per cent = typical % by weight of major constituents

Atlantic temperature profile

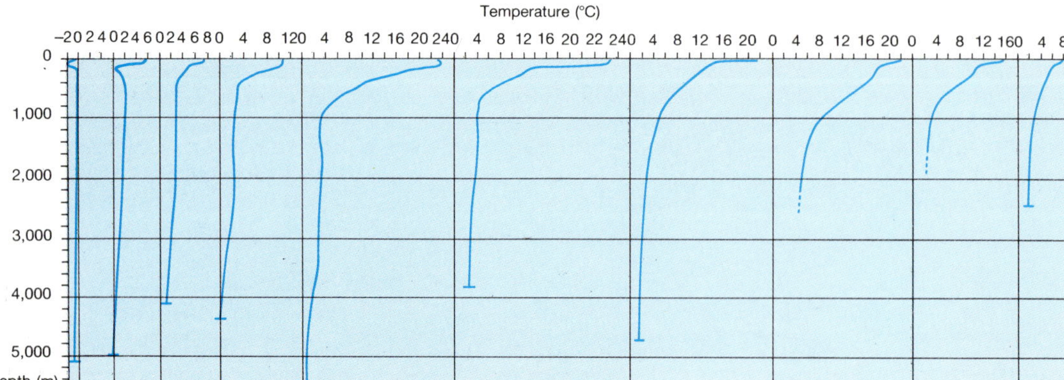

Above: Vertical temperature distribution at stations along an Atlantic meridian. A surface layer of widely varying depth is heated by solar radiation. Below this layer the temperature falls with depth, in layers sometimes only 2in (5cm) wide, before the thermocline, where it falls rapidly with depth until it stabilises and decreases evenly to the bottom.

Above: Knowledge of sound velocity is essential to an ASW tactician and this Expendable Sound Velocimeter (XSV) is used by surface ships to measure such velocities to an accuracy of ±0.82ft/sec (0.25m/sec) down to a depth of 6,560ft (2,000m). Data is read directly into an on-board computer for storage, processing and analysis.

pressure increases with depth. There are, however, many variations in salinity (haloclines) and temperature (thermoclines), sub-surface currents, counter-currents and waves, the topography and nature of the ocean floor, and the existence of macro- and micro-organisms. Finally, man-made noises such as those caused by other ships, oil drilling and harbour activity affect the acoustical and optical properties of the waters that constitute the ocean environment.

The ocean is virtually opaque to most forms of radiant energy, but one exception is acoustic energy, which can travel great distances under water. The exact speed of sound in water depends upon the precise combination of temperature, pressure and salinity, but an average speed is about 4,757ft/sec (1,450m/sec), some four times faster than the speed of sound in air. Underwater sound transmissions are reflected by any solid object and a sensitive receiver can detect any echoes. Unfortunately, the science of sonar is by no means a simple one and the detection of an echo is just the start in a laborious process of trying to decide just where the reflecting body is and what it might be.

TEMPERATURE STRUCTURE

One of the principal factors governing the behaviour of the ocean is its temperature structure. Solar radiation heats the surface layer, the depth of which varies from tens of metres near the Equator to more than 100 metres in the high latitudes; below that the temperature then falls with depth in layers as little as two inches (5cm) thick to a layer where it falls fairly sharply with depth (the thermocline) and then decreases at a more gradual and even rate to the bottom. The depth at which the permanent thermocline is found varies from 984-1,312ft (300-400m) in equatorial areas to 1,640-3,280ft (500-1,000m) in sub-tropical areas. There is also a seasonal thermocline above the permanent thermocline and even, in some areas, a diurnal thermocline known more prosaically as the afternoon effect from the time of day it occurs.

Atlantic surface temperatures

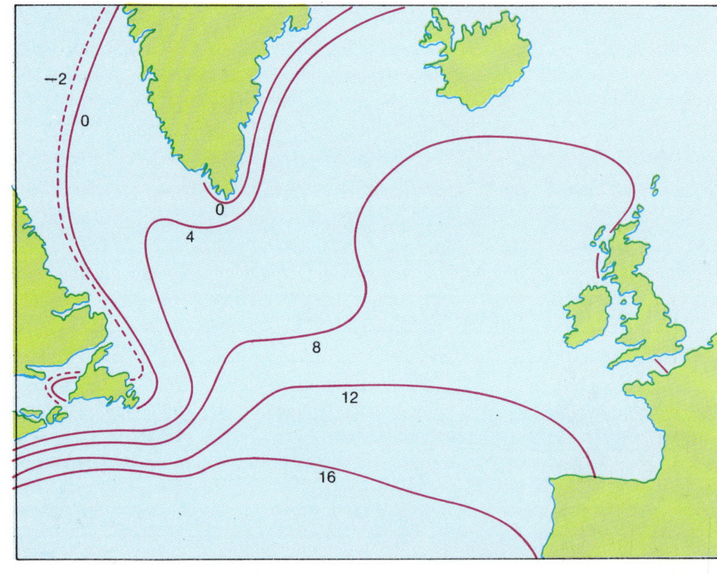

Below: Surface temperature variations in the North Atlantic. A chart like this would be of limited value to a submariner, who needs up-to-date knowledge on the precise conditions in which he is operating. He must have detailed local information on variable factors such as temperature and salinity to enable him to fight his submarine effectively.

Left: The oceans appear at first sight to be a simple, homogeneous mass of water; in fact they form a very complex environment requiring as least as much study as atmospheric meteorology.

The thermoclines separate waters of slightly different densities, and a variety of organic and inorganic particulates tend to concentrate in them since they lack the energy to fall further. Inorganic substances include the material deposited either deliberately or naturally from the land, products of erosion of both the land and the ocean bed, and general debris. Organic objects in the thermoclines are mainly planktonic organisms which attract fish and shrimps in large numbers.

SALINITY

The normal saline concentration in the open ocean varies between 32 and 37 parts per thousand (ppt). The variations are the consequence of a number of competing processes, including concentrating effects such as evaporation and ice-floe formation, and diluting effects such as rainfall, river run-off and melting ice.

Variations in salinity have considerable operational significance for submariners, since submarines ballasted and trimmed for salt-water operations will ride deeper in fresh water, which is not as dense, and when diving will submerge before the main ballast tanks are totally full. Thus, operations off major estuaries or in fjords, where the water is much less saline, have to be planned with particular care. Conversely, some seas are much more saline, for example, the Baltic, and thus much denser.

A major submarine hazard occurs where sharp salinity gradients are associated with sharp

Surface slainity

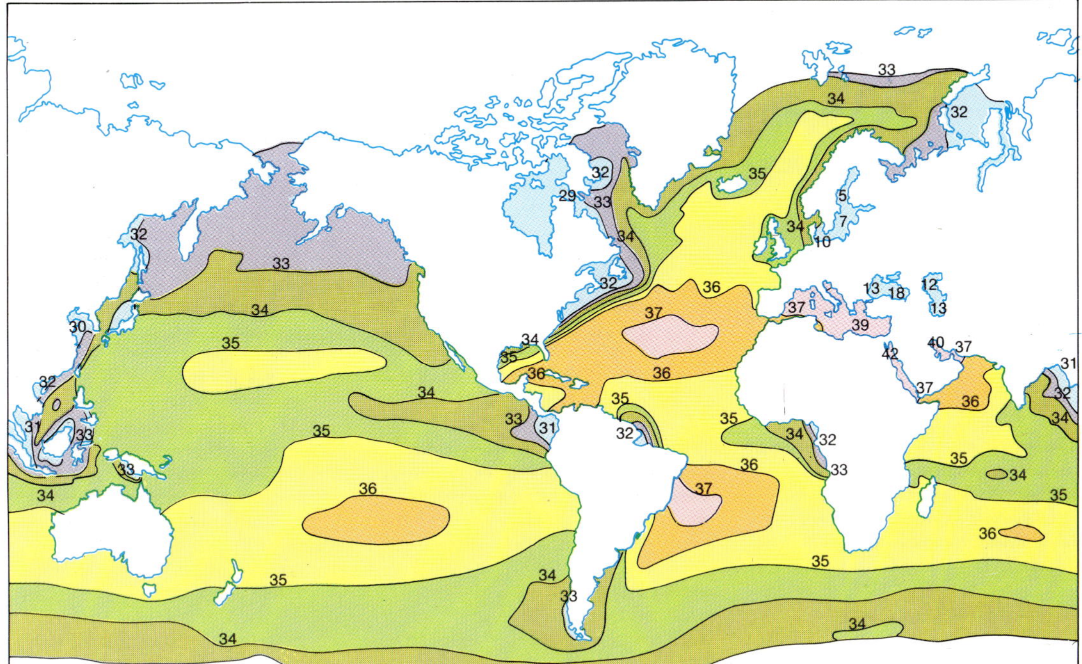

Above: Salinity variations have operational significance for submariners and are the consequence of factors such as evaporation and ice-flow formations which increase salinity, and rainfall, river run-off and melting ice which reduce it.

temperature gradients as this combination can produce severe underwater turbulence. It is thought that such an effect was at least partially responsible for the loss of the USS *Thresher*, which went to sea on post-overhaul trials in April 1963 and was about 220 miles (354km) east of Cape Cod when she was driven down to a depth where catastrophic hull failure occurred. In August 1963 the bathyscaphe *Trieste* found the wreck at a depth of 8,500ft (2,590m) and was able to photograph compressed elements of the ill-fated submarine.

Salinity is one of the less significant factors affecting sound propagation, its velocity being changed by 4.3ft/sec (1.31m per second) per 1ppt change. However, in the turbulent areas mentioned above, where sharp salinity gradients are coupled with sharp temperature changes, there is also a marked refraction of sound energy.

PRESSURE EFFECTS

Pressure increases with depth in a simple relationship and at a rate determined by the salinity. In seawater pressure increases by 44.45lb/sq in (3.13kg/cm^2) for every 100ft of depth, but the increase is 43.5lb/sq in (3.06kg/cm^2) in fresh water.

Right: Warm tropical water drifts towards the poles and in return cool polar water flows towards the equator. The cold water currents start as surface flows but gradually sink to the bottom.

Below: Salinity varies from 32 to 37 parts per thousand (ppt), but can fall to 23ppt in fjords. The diagram shows the speed of sound in seawater for a salinity level of 35ppt; at 3,228ft (948m) and 5°C, for example, sound velocity is 4,904ft/sec (1,494m/sec).

Below: Salinity levels vary: the diagram shows the correction factors. If the salinity level is actually 30ppt, the speed of sound is 4,904ft/sec (1,494m/sec) minus 26ft/sec (7.9m/sec), giving an actual speed of 4,878ft/sec (1,486m/sec).

Sound propagation

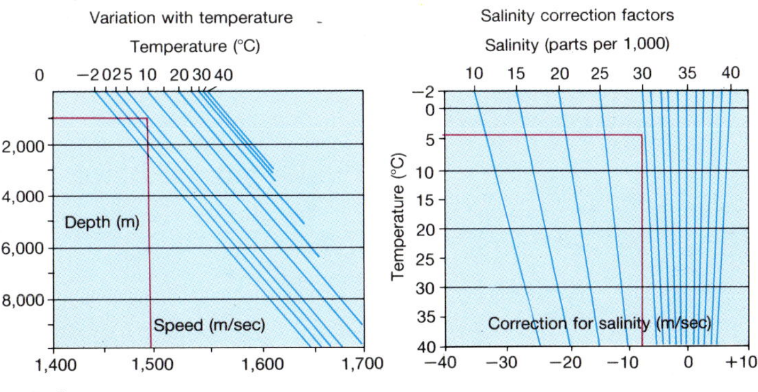

Major currents

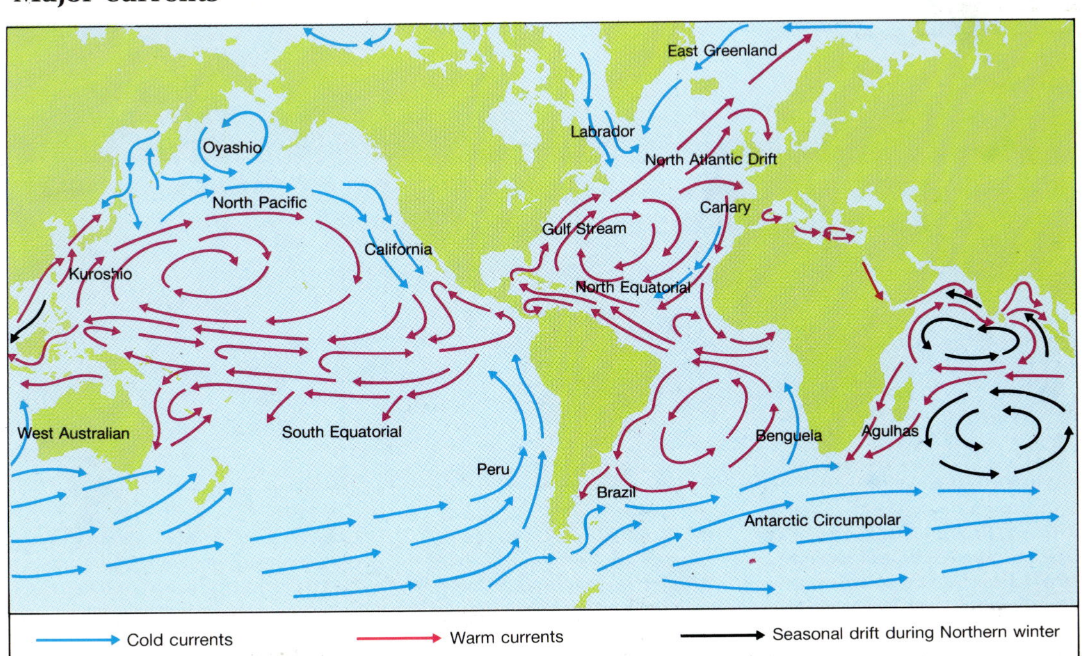

BATHYMETRIC EFFECTS

The bottom of the ocean can have two serious effects on anti-submarine warfare. If the bottom topography is irregular and rocky the complexity of the echoes returned may enable a submarine hugging the bottom to escape detection. This effect is known as reverberation.

Where the ocean bottom irregularities are sufficiently marked a submarine can shelter in the shadow of hills, an illustration of the fact that the more is known about the ocean bed from oceanographic survey the more successfully will submarines be able to make use of the effect.

For the submariner a knowledge of the ocean bed means more than just being able to take advantage of it to hide from the enemy's sonar. For him a knowledge of the continental shelf is vital as he must climb over the slope and the shelf proper on his return from a deep ocean patrol. Ballistic missile submarines patrol either the open ocean or under the ice cap and are unlikely to need detailed bathymetric information of such areas, but attack submarines need both such information and that for the bottom topography in operational areas such as the 1,000-fathom (1,820m) choke-points.

SURFACE EFFECTS

The main effect of surface currents is on sonobuoys, which will be dispersed from the impact point with resultant distortion of the accuracy of fixes on a target. Further, under certain conditions sonbuoys moving with a current will give the impression that a stationary target is moving in the reverse direction to that of the current.

Surface waves have a variety of effects, and really severe

conditions may prevent the launching or recovery of helicopters and variable-depth and towed sonar arrays. Similarly, waves can degrade the performance of air-dropped sonobuoys, which suffer a 75 per cent transmission loss in 10ft (3.04m) waves and a total loss in 15ft (4.57m) waves. In addition, high sea states can cause a mixing of water on either side of the thermocline, giving a relatively thick layer of isothermal water which increases the noise problem for the sonar systems. Finally, breaking waves add to the ambient noise level, again compounding the sonar problem.

Weather also has its effects. Thunder, rain on the surface and associated wave activity all add to the ambient noise level over a very considerable area, decreasing the signal:noise ratio at receivers and thus reducing target discrimination.

SOUND WAVES

The result of the layering of the oceans and the continuous variations of velocity with depth is that the paths of sound waves in the ocean are never straight lines, but are arcs of circles in accordance with Snell's Law, which was discovered in relation to light rays but is equally applicable to sound waves in water. The consequence of Snell's Law is that where a sound wave travels from one density layer to another its path is bent towards the normal when it enters a layer of greater density and away from it if the density is lower. Further, where density is altered gradually the sound wave will be bent, or refracted, similarly. In addition, sound waves are scattered by the barriers of the oceanic medium at the surface and the bottom, so that the circular arc trajectories converge, leaving large volumes of the ocean simply impenetrable by sound from a given source. This phenomenon, known as the convergence zone, is quite independent of the power intensity of the sound wave. A submarine in such a zone will not be detected even when it is very close to the sonar transmitter and a number of warships were lost during World War II because of the convergence effect.

If the acoustic transmitter is depressed below the horizontal and the water column is more than 2,000 fathoms (3,650m) deep the propagation path will bottom-out in the deep sound duct and be refracted, returning to the surface some distance away. This convergence zone phenomenon occurs at about 38nm (70km) in tropical waters and about 22nm (40km) in northern waters and the Mediterranean, and the width of the zones is about 5-10 per cent of the range. Increases in sound intensity of 15-20dB in the convergence zone are common.

The transmission profile and the length of the convergence zone are also influenced by the depth of the water column and of the acoustic source and receiver. In shallower waters the type of bottom and its topography can affect the quality of the signal, with a smooth rocky bottom giving good reflection but mud, slime or sand causing considerable attenuation.

The ocean itself is inherently noisy because of the abundance of marine life, seismic disturbances from underwater volcanoes and the crashing of waves. In addition, there is a growing amount of man-made noise from merchant ship activities and third-nation naval vessels, as well as the increasing use of seismic exploration methods and offshore drilling on the sea floor. The problem for the anti-submarine sonar operator is to recognise and screen out all those unwanted noise sources, whereas the submarine commander uses them for his own benefit.

The deep scattering layer is usually composed of a thick layer and three sub-layers consisting of microscopic photoplankton and zooplankton which reflect and scatter sound waves. The composition of the layer, its thickness and the depths at which it occurs vary from area to area, and also by the time of day. Sound waves projected at or near the vertical will generally penetrate the layer, but if projected at or near the horizontal to the layer they will be scattered and diffracted. The effects of the deep scattering layer can be overcome by optimising the relationship of frequency, pulse length and power output, but often the sonar operator will have little choice but to revert to passive methods.

The thermocline has a major influence on ASW as it affects the velocity of sound and in the permanent thermocline the velocity reaches a minimum. This layer of minimum velocity, known as the deep sound channel, has a

Sound propagation

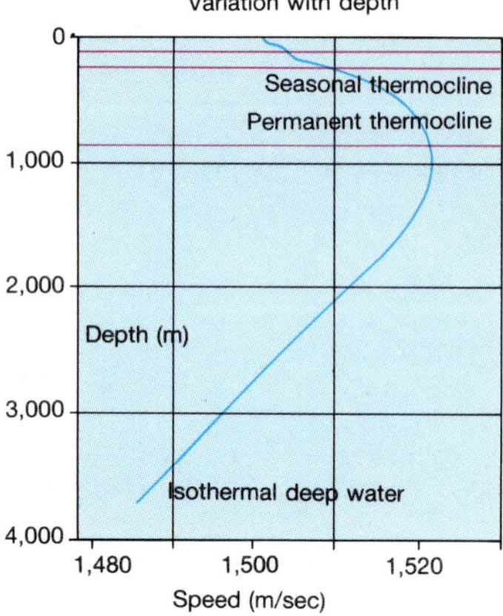

Above: This graph shows a typical variation in the speed of sound with depth in a temperate area. The layer of minimum velocity is designated the deep sound channel.

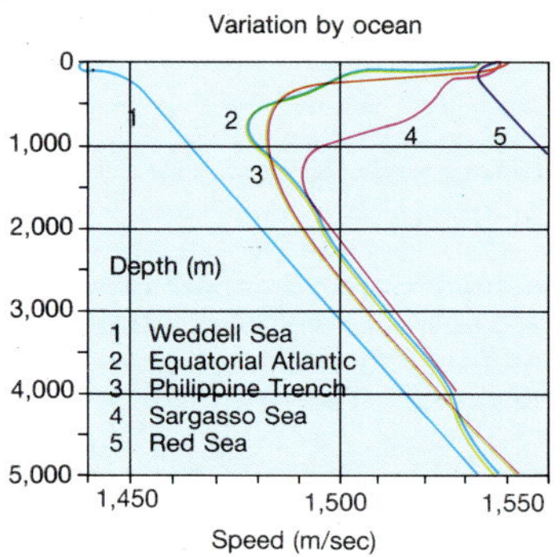

Above: The different acoustic characteristics of the world's oceans. Note how close to the surface is the level of minimum sound velocity in the Weddel Sea.

Choke points: Baltic exits

Above: The Soviet Baltic Fleet's operations in its home sea would be of value, but it would be bottled up unless the USSR were able to gain control of the sound between the Danish Island of Zealand and the Swedish coast, and of the Skagerrak. The importance of Sweden is clear, and recent Soviet submarine operations in Swedish territorial waters suggest there are plans to use them in war.

Choke points: Black Sea and Mediterranean

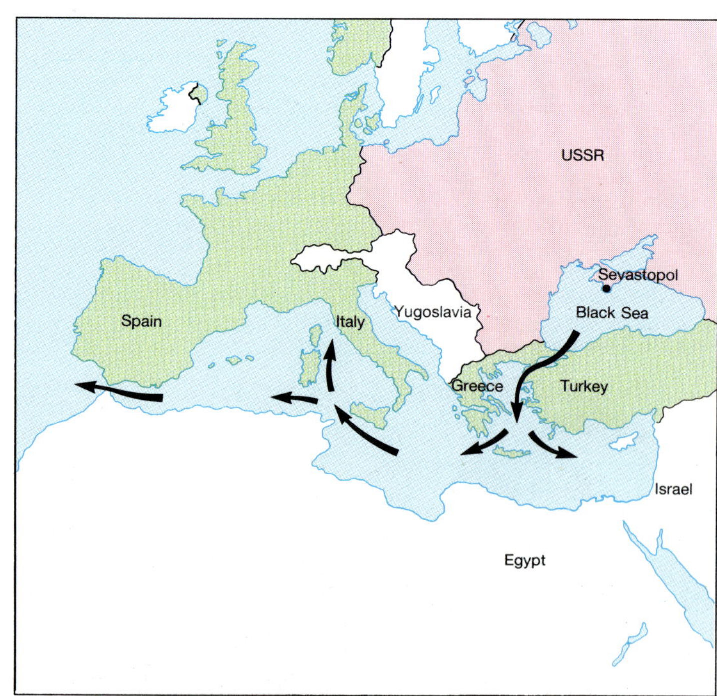

Above: The Mediterranean poses severe problems for the Soviets, with choke points in the Bosphorus, around the Aegean islands, in the Aegean Straits of Kithera and Karpathos, in the Sicilian Channel and in the Straits of Gibraltar. The Soviet Mediterranean squadron normally includes up to eight submarines, which would be primary targets for NATO ASW forces.

Surface duct

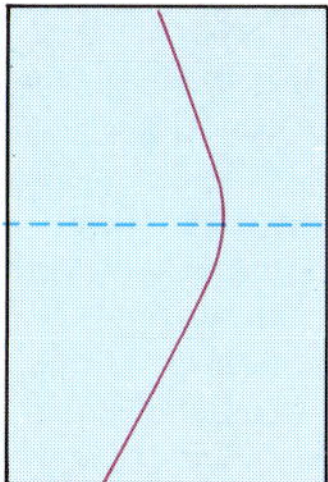
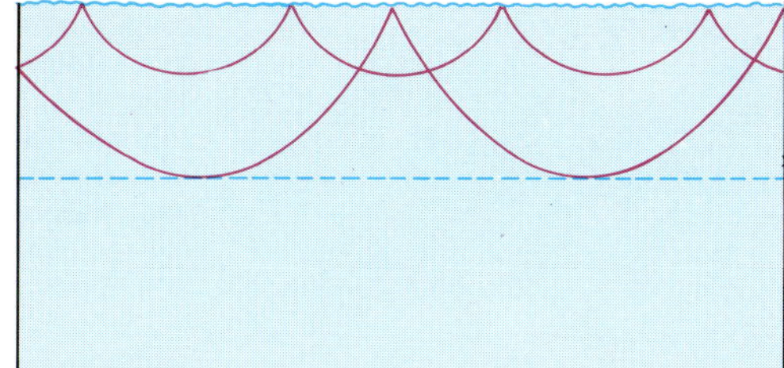

Convergence zones

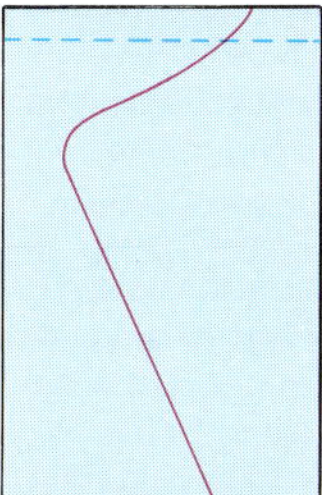
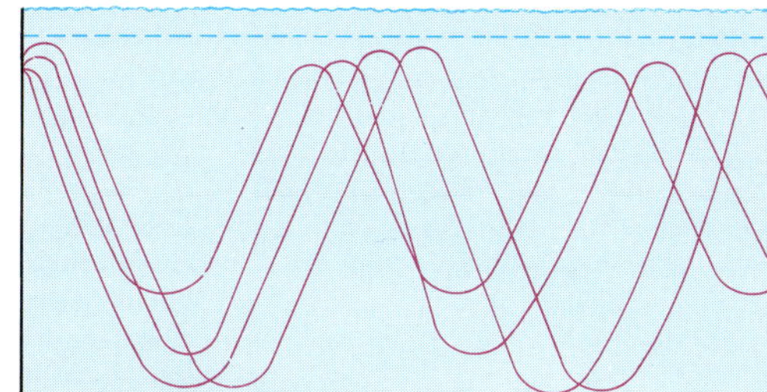

Underwater sound channel

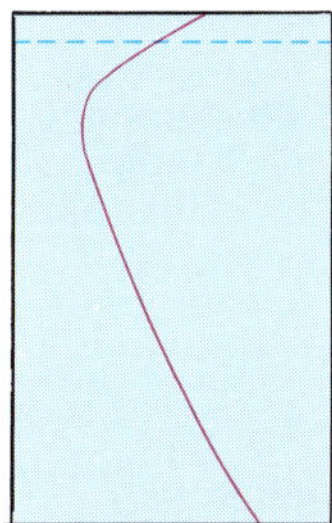
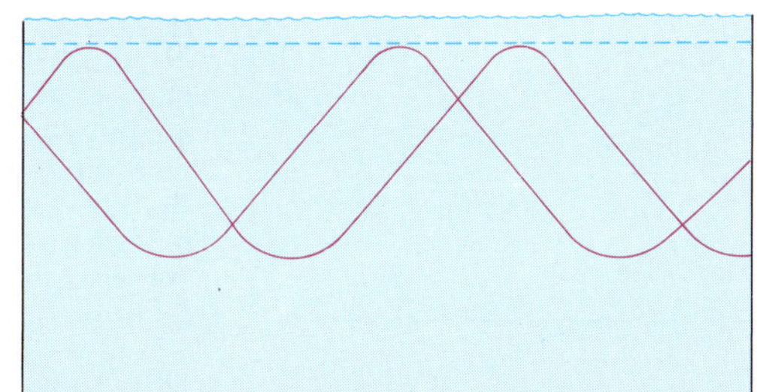

Above: Profiles on the left show how sound velocity varies with depth; ray diagrams are on the right. The surface duct is formed by reflection from the surface and the thermodine. Convergence zones widen with distance (centre) and shadow zones narrow. Underwater sound channel is formed by sound velocity increasing with temperature above it and hydrostatic pressure below.

Surface duct energy loss

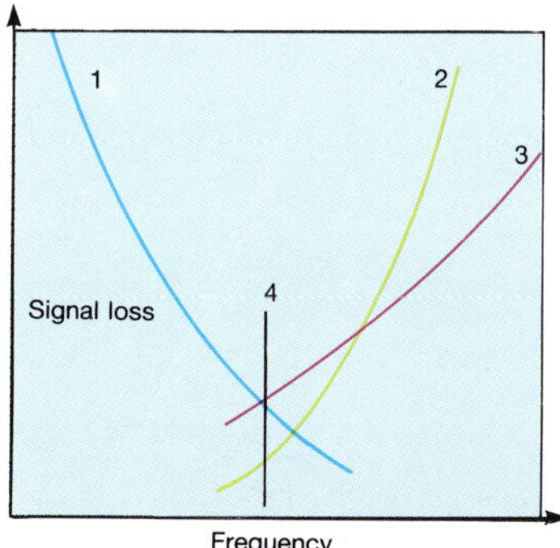

Left: Of the three major causes of signal attenuation, the first (1), the diffracting effect of the seawater medium, reduces as frequency increases; absorbtion loss (2), due to the sound wave transferring a certain amount of energy to the water, and rises with frequency. Scattering losses due to the sound wave striking and being reflected by foreign bodies in the water rise with frequency, the optimum frequency (4) being that at which the average loss is lowest.

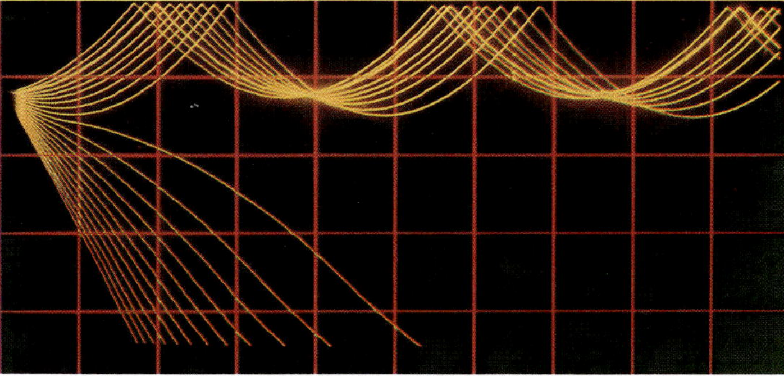

Above: The fact that sound waves do not travel in straight lines in seawater is shown clearly by this typical sound propagation trace, illustrating how sound energy transmitted at various angles from an active sonar transducer spreads through the ocean. As well as areas where a target will be hit by the radiated energy, there are extensive zones where it will be safe from detection.

variety of effects, one of which is that a sound signal can travel in it for more than 620 miles (1,000km) and still have one per cent of the energy it had 6.2 miles (10km) from the source. It is at least theoretically possible that a submarine could operate in this deep sound channel, exploiting this effect to achieve very long range detection.

Above the surface is an atmospheric duct as much as 600ft (183m) thick which can affect the electro-magnetic performance of ASW aircraft. If both transmitter and receiver are within the duct communications are unlikely to be affected; indeed, range and detection may well be enhanced. If, however, the aircraft is above the duct not only may its radar fail to detect targets on the surface – periscope, sail or snorkel – but its receivers could also fail to pick up signals from sonobuoys.

OCEANOGRAPHIC RESEARCH

The oceans of the world are vast and imperfectly understood; they are also of vital strategic importance. Consequently, many navies devote resources to oceanographic research and intelligence gathering, although the actual number of ships is surprisingly small in view of the size of the task. The Soviet Union has some 56 oceanographic research ships (24 of which are civilian crewed), 130 surveying ships (including 35 civilian) and an unknown number of deep-diving craft, four of which are known to be associated with the two India class submarines. Against this US naval resources include 14 oceanographic research ships, nine surveying ships and seven deep submergence vehicles, although other in-service ships are used in research activities from time to time. Some aircraft are also used and there are a further four oceanographic and hydrographic survey ships in the National Oceanographic and Atmospheric Administration. The world's third strongest navy – the Royal Navy – has a meagre four ocean-going, five coastal and one inshore surveying vessels, although a new and unusual ship, HMS *Challenger*, was commissioned in 1985. Described as a Seabed Operations Tender, the *Challenger* has a full-load displacement of 7,185 tons and is crewed by the Royal Navy, as opposed to the Royal Fleet Auxiliary. There can be no doubt that much greater resources need to be devoted to underwater research, not only to increase our knowledge of the oceans but also, from a military standpoint, to enable submarine operations to be conducted more effectively and with better safety margins.

Below: The fundamentally alien nature of the underwater environment is illustrated clearly by this picture of a diver undertaking a relatively simple photographic task. What would be a very straightforward assignment above water has become very complicated below the surface, requiring breathing apparatus for the diver and special protection for both man and equipment.

Design and Construction

As with any weapon system the design of a submarine starts with the naval staff requirement, which must state what role the vessel is designed to fulfil, its weapons and sensor fit and the performance parameters it must meet. Until the mid-1960s the primary strategic role of the submarine was to attack hostile naval surface vessels and maritime logistic traffic. This role still exists, but the evolution of submarine-launched ballistic and cruise missiles has brought a further strategic role, that of striking directly at targets in the enemy's homeland.

The modern submarine's third main role is to attack other submarines and surface shipping. While nuclear-powered attack submarines (SSNs) are most effective in this role, the conventionally powered diesel-electric submarine still has a major role and many hundreds are operational with some 39 navies, employed on attack missions, general patrol duties and clandestine special operations.

As nuclear-powered submarines are so expensive in capital cost and in their requirement for specialised manpower the majority of the world's navies will continue to operate non-nuclear submarines for the foreseeable future. All submarines, however, no matter what their propulsion system or role, have many design constraints in common.

DESIGN

Just as important as the advent of nuclear propulsion has been the revolution in submarine hull design pioneered in the 1950s by USS *Albacore* (AGSS-569). The long, narrow, highly streamlined hulls introduced by the German Type XXI of World War II proved unable to cope with the increased power becoming available and in certain circumstances, particularly at speeds of over 12 knots, control could be lost altogether. USS *Nautilus* (SSN-571) for example, despite her nuclear powerplant, could not exceed 23.3 knots under water, but the diesel-electric powered *Albacore*, with a teardrop hull shape based on airship practice, cruciform tail empennage and single propeller, achieved a sustained underwater speed of 26 knots in her original form and later, with contra-rotating propellers and silver-zinc batteries, became capable of an astonishing 33 knots. Not surprisingly, she has set the pattern for the majority of subsequent Western hull designs. Contemporary pressure hull designs are, however, less fat than that of the *Albacore*, because a parallel mid-body is almost as efficient if the forward and after ends are properly designed, and a tubular body is much easier and cheaper to construct.

The design of any weapon system is inevitably the result of a number of compromises, but that of submarines involves a number

Surfaced and submerged displacement

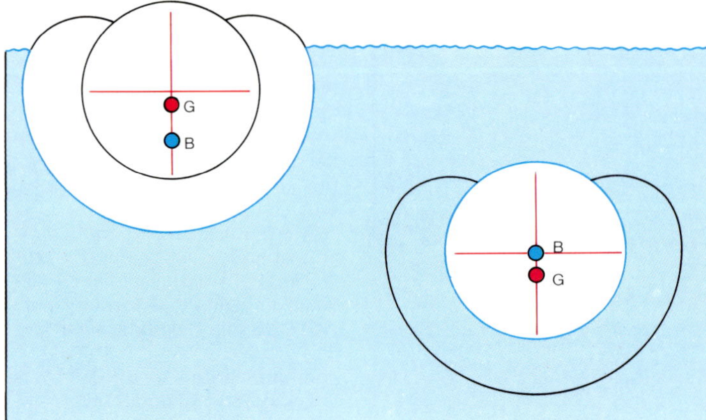

Left: A submarine's buoyancy depends on the volume of displaced water and is controlled by varying the volume of displacement. On the surface (left) the main ballast tanks are filled with air so the displaced water – the area within the heavy line – equals the weight of the submarine. When it is submerged (right) the main ballast tanks are filled with water; the submarine's weight is the same, but the volume of displaced water, again represented by the area within the heavy line, has been reduced, while the centre of buoyancy (B), the geometric centre of the volume of displaced water, has moved from below to above the centre of gravity (G).

Surface ship stability

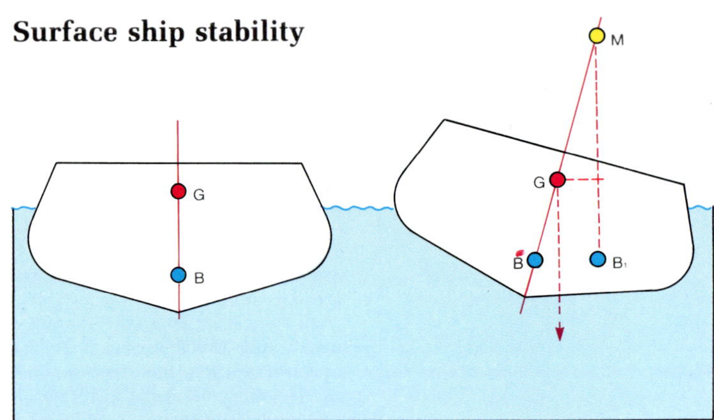

Left: When a surface ship lists (right) the centre of buoyancy, being at the centre of gravity of the displaced water, moves to B1, because the volume of displaced water to the left of G has decreased, while that to the right of G has increased. A vertical line through B1 now intersects the original line BG at M; the distance GM being termed the metacentric height. When M is above G the metacentric height is positive and the moment arm (horizontal broken line) tends to return the vessel to its original position, so the vessel is stable.

Surfaced submarine stability

Left: A surfaced submarine presents much the same situation as a surface ship. However, the three points B, G and M, although in the same relative positions, are much closer together; further, since the shape of a submarine is for practical purposes cylindrical there is no resistance to the motion. Submarines therefore have a tendency to roll, making their motion on the surface uncomfortable.

Effect of submergence

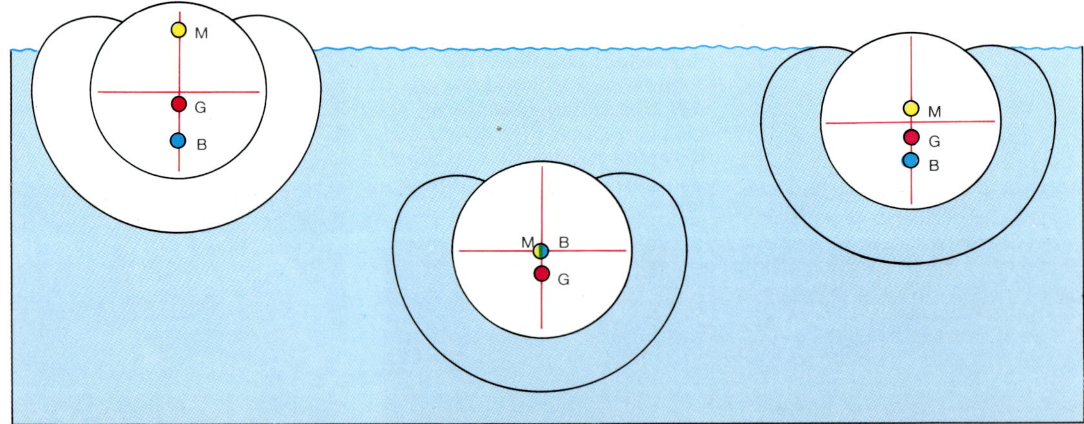

Above: When a surface ship lists its centre of buoyancy (B) shifts because of the different shape of the volume below the waterline. This does not happen in a submerged submarine because its entire volume is below the surface. For stability underwater it is necessary that the centre of gravity (G) be below the centre of buoyancy. As shown here, when the submarine is on the surface (left) B is below G, which is at a fixed point slightly below the centreline of the vessel, while M is well above. Then, as the submarine submerges (right), B and M approach each other until they meet on the centreline (centre). During this process the position of least stability is at the point when B and G coincide. This is not too serious during descent, but when surfacing the water ballast is ejected comparatively slowly by compressed air and the metacentric height (GM) may become negative and a list may occur. Most submarines have lever-operated, list-control valves which can restrict air to the high side and increase it to the low side.

G Centre of gravity
B Centre of buoyancy
M Metacentre

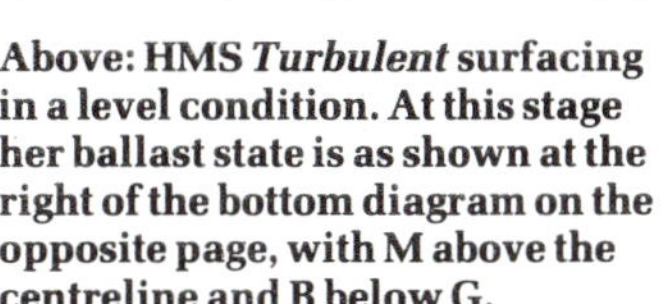

Above: HMS *Turbulent* surfacing in a level condition. At this stage her ballast state is as shown at the right of the bottom diagram on the opposite page, with M above the centreline and B below G.

Above right: HMS *Turbulent* running on the surface. In this state a submarine's stability depends on the position of her centre of gravity and her shape, above and below the waterline.

of particularly difficult problems. The most basic of these is that a submerged submarine must have neutral buoyancy and a centre of gravity lying below its centre of buoyancy, and every element in the craft affects their locations. The naval staff requirement must state the extremes in which the submarine must be able to operate, in particular the density of the seawater likely to be encountered. The distribution of weight within the submarine is crucial to its stability and the expenditure of items such as fuel, stores, weapons and provisions must be taken into account. The compressibility of the hull is a further factor, since in a deep-diving submarine this could result in a loss of buoyancy of several tons at depth.

Diving depth is obviously a crucial tactical consideration, because depth provides shelter, especially if the submarine can go deep enough to exploit the acoustic properties of the sea to thwart detection devices. Depth also gives a safety margin in high speed manoueuvres. Actual details are highly classified, but open source figures for some representative nuclear-powered attack submarines give a general indication of normal operating depths for comparative purposes: USS *Los Angeles* 1,475ft (450m); the Soviet Victor III 1,300ft (400m); and the French *Rubis* 980ft (300m). Depth performance is becoming more important as the anti-submarine threat increases and has stimulated extensive research and development into materials.

A lot of research is devoted to the subject of hydrodynamic efficiency. The total drag of a submerged submarine has three elements: skin friction, form drag and appendage drag. As was so successfully demonstrated by the *Albacore*, a solid-of-revolution form, and especially one without a parallel mid-body, has the minimum skin friction, although in practical terms a cylindrical mid-body provides a satisfactory compromise. As with an aircraft, skin friction is directly proportional to surface, or wetted area – in other words, the bigger the hull the greater the drag.

Form drag is usually only between two and four per cent of the total for a solid-of-revolution, but roughness of the hull can significantly affect resistance, and a badly finished hull or one with poorly designed or positioned flood openings will have significantly greater drag than one with a good finish, as well as making much more underwater

Right: The Tench class diesel-electric submarine USS *Pickerel* (SS 524), surfaces at a 48° angle from a depth of 150ft (46m) during a test programme off the Pacific island of Oahu on March 1, 1952.

Longitudinal stability

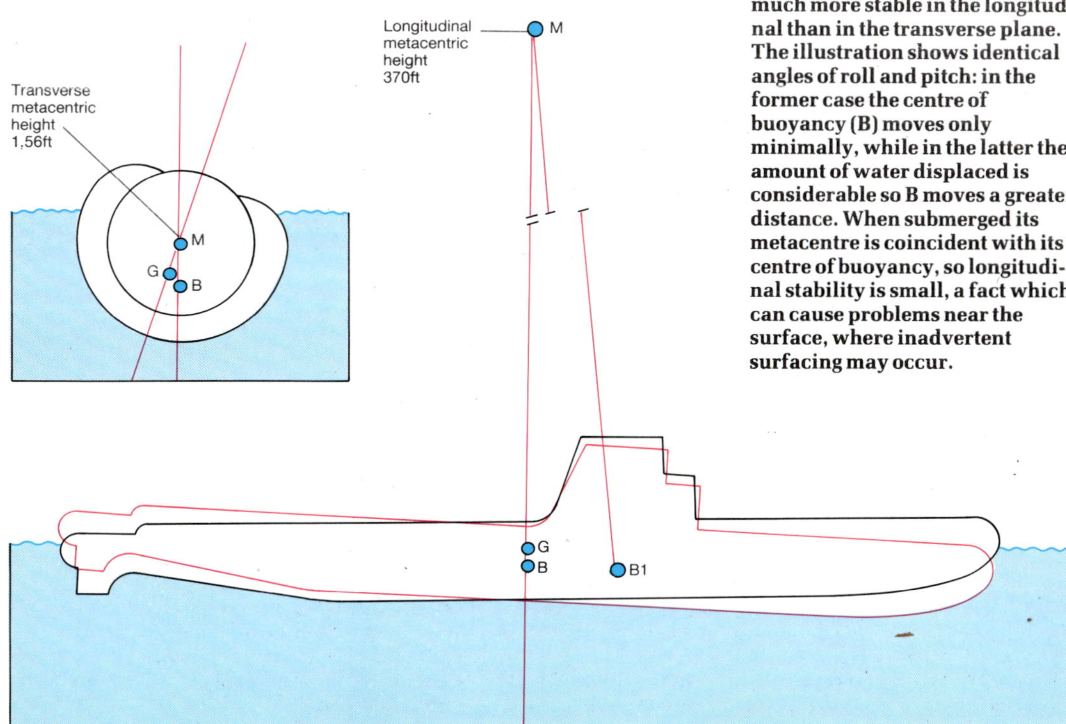

Left: A surfaced submarine is much more stable in the longitudinal than in the transverse plane. The illustration shows identical angles of roll and pitch: in the former case the centre of buoyancy (B) moves only minimally, while in the latter the amount of water displaced is considerable so B moves a greater distance. When submerged its metacentre is coincident with its centre of buoyancy, so longitudinal stability is small, a fact which can cause problems near the surface, where inadvertent surfacing may occur.

noise and so being easier to detect. Finally, appendages always add drag, no matter how well they are designed, sometimes equivalent to more than half the total bare hull resistance. Laminar flow has been tried, but while it offers apparent drag reductions of over 50 per cent putting the theories into practice has been thwarted so far by the impurities of seawater.

Streamlining has been the rule since the wartime Type XXI boats, but great attention is now being paid to the nature of the hull surface: special paints can reduce friction and thus either increase speed or reduce the amount of power required for a given speed. Releasing polymers around the hull is also used to increase speed for short periods, and it has been reported that the exteriors of Soviet submarines are coated with a compliant covering, derived from research into marine animals such as dolphins and killer whales, which combines suction and boundary-layer pressure equalisation.

Further development based on the same research may lead to devices to modify shapes to match the boat's speed by, for example, progressively retracting the hydroplanes or changing the shape of the fin as speed increases. And findings from such studies may account for the very interesting shape of the latest Soviet submarines, which have bulbous bows, similar in shape to the front end of a whale, and sails which are smaller than those on Western submarines and less angular in shape, merging rather more smoothly into the hull; they appear more akin to the fin of marine animals than do those on Westerm submarines.

Manoeuvrability is obviously of great importance to a submarine and again the *Albacore* had a great effect upon all subsequent designs. Her short hull gave substantially improved manoeuvrability over the then current long, narrow designs, and during trials she was able to turn at 3°/sec, much faster than conventional submarines of the time but a rate probably comfortably exceeded by current types.

High speed and efficient control systems enable modern submarines to be manoeuvred in three dimensions, like aircraft. A turn within four times the submarine's length is feasible and ascents and descents at rates of several hundred feet per minute are possible. Indeed, such aerodynamic problems as sideslip in turns have become important and the size and shape of the fin is a critical factor.

The major control surfaces are the hydroplanes. The original Holland submarines did not have forward hydroplanes; these were added later in order to maintain an even keel during a dive, but with the disappearance of such a requirement they have been retained for diving control and trimming, particularly at periscope depth. IKL-designed submarines have extendable scythe-shaped bow hydroplanes, set at a fixed angle: the control force required is achieved by varying the amount of area exposed, and the two planes are set at opposing angles, one being used for descent and the other for ascent. Other submarines are fitted with bow-mounted retractable or foldable hydroplanes which pivot to achieve upward or downward motion.

Some navies, such as those of the USA, Japan and France, use fin-mounted planes. While these may offer advantages in terms of manoeuvrability, they need to be capable of rotation to the vertical for breaking through ice if it is necessary to operate in the Arctic. Those on the Los Angeles class boats cannot do so, which is a serious tactical limitation now that under-ice operations have become so necessary to counter the growing Soviet use of the Arctic, and in 1985 US Secretary of Defense Weinberger announced that the planes would be moved to the bows on future members of the Los Angeles class.

Below: The apparently smooth exterior of a modern submarine actually houses dozens of hatches, connections, cleats and other items, compounding the underwater noise problem.

Right: USS *Richard B. Russell* (SSN 687), a Sturgeon class attack submarine which is identical to the USS Tautog, whose external installations are identified and described below.

Sturgeon class *Tautog* (SSN 639) external installations

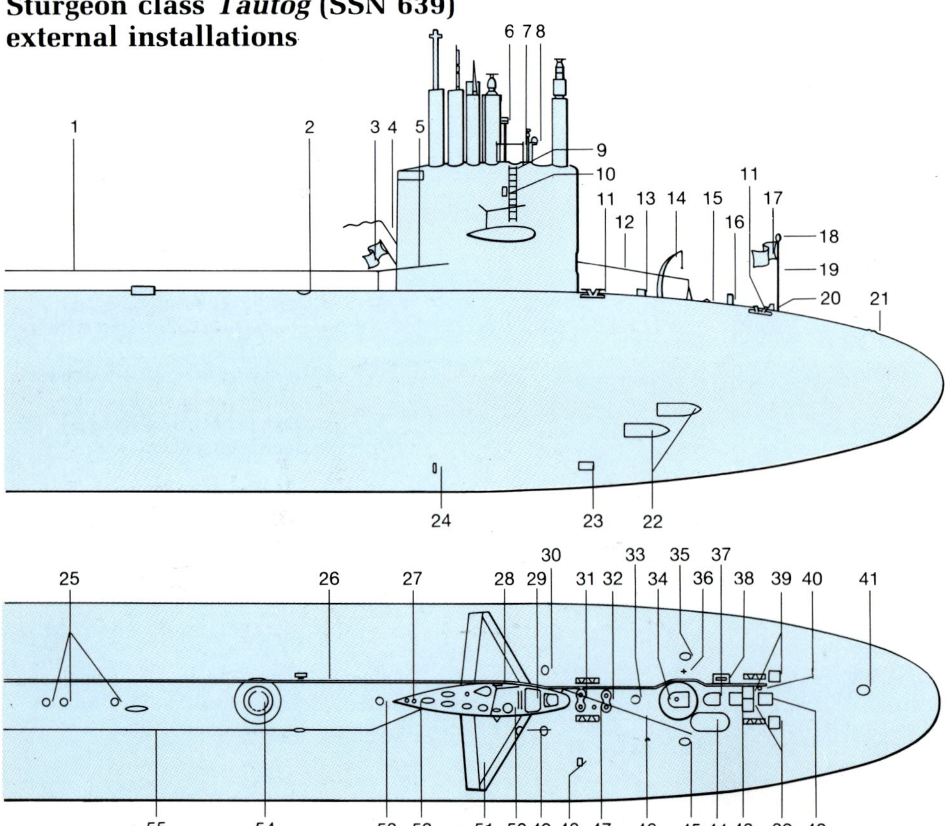

1 Portable emergency lifeline
2 Portable cleats (port and starboard)
3 Ensign No 11
4 No 7 commissioning pennant
5 HP air external charging connection
6 Identification beacon light
7 Portable lifeline
8 Masthead light
9 Portable ladder (P&S)
10 Sidelight (P&S)
11 Hinged cleat (P&S)
12 Portable emergency lifeline
13 Retractable capstan
14 Portable davit
15 Towing eye
16 Underwater log
17 No 7 union jack
18 Forward anchor light
19 Portable jackstaff
20 Hinged cleat (P&S)
21 Sonar sphere access
22 Torpedo tube shutters (P&S)
23 Torpedo ejection pump shutter (P&S)
24 Underwater log
25 Salvage air connections
26 Safety track
27 Ventilation exhaust
28 Sidelight (P&S)
29 Bridge
30 Access hatch
31 Main vent valves Nos 3A and 3B
32 Main vent valves Nos 2A and 2B
33 Retractable capstan
34 Escape trunk
35 Main vent valve No 1B
36 Capstan control
37 Escape hatch
38 Underwater log
39 Line locker access hatches
40 Salvage air connection
41 Sonar sphere access
42 Hinged towing fairlead
43 Access hatch
44 Messenger buoy
45 Main vent valve No 1A
46 Diesel lubricating oil fill connection
47 Salvage air connection
48 Signal ejector
49 Access hatches
50 Lookout station
51 Portable lifeline
52 Diesel exhaust
53 Salvage air connection
54 Weapons shipping hatch
55 Portable emergency lifeline

Right: This latest Soviet Akula class nuclear-powered attack submarine shows the smaller, less angular and more streamlined shape of Soviet sails, believed to be derived from research on marine animals such as dolphins.

The design of the after end of the submarine and the correlation of hull shape, propeller and control surfaces is also important. At one stage in the mid-1940s the after control surfaces were placed astern of the propeller and this was the original layout in the *Albacore*, but the majority of modern submarines have cruciform stern empennages, with horizontal and vertical control surfaces forward of the propeller. In the American Los Angeles and Ohio classes the after horizontal hydroplanes are fitted with vertical endplates, both to improve control and also to serve as housings for hydrophones.

The latest Swedish Näcken and Dutch Walrus classes, on the other hand, have indexed, X-shaped empennages. This concept was first tested on the *Albacore* in 1961 and proved far superior to any of the previous designs. The X-shape is 42 per cent more efficient in all major operating directions than a

Right: The Sturgeon class USS *Spadefish* (SSN 688) with her fin-mounted forward hydroplanes rotated to the vertical to penetrate ice. Such manoeuvres are not possible with Los Angeles boats.

Below: Soviet Oscar class SSGN showing the tiles which cover her hull; some are missing. These are believed to have both acoustic absorbing and boundary-layer pressure equalisation effects.

Guppy type submarine tank arrangements

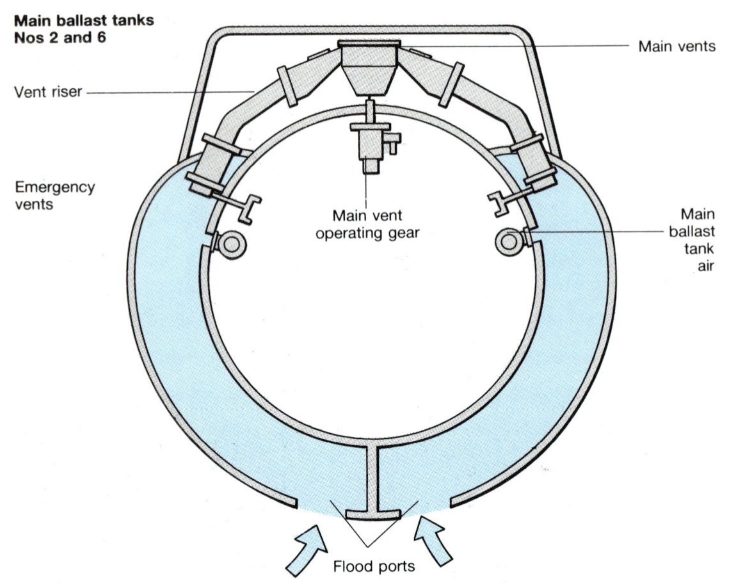

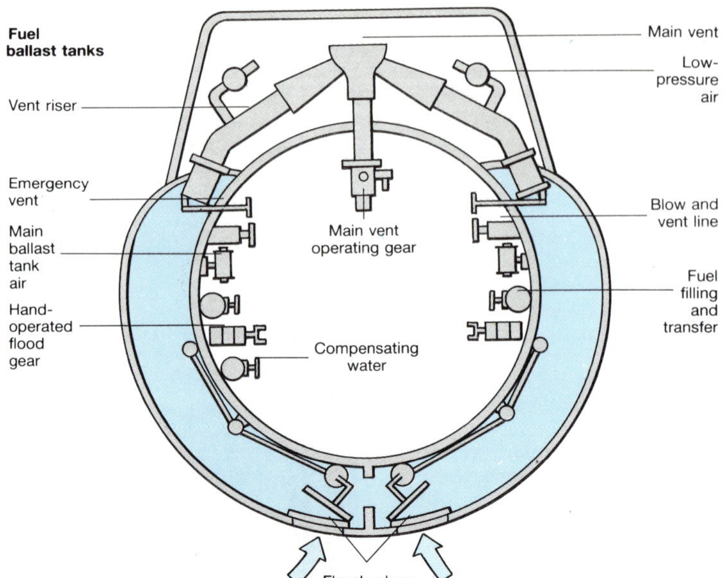

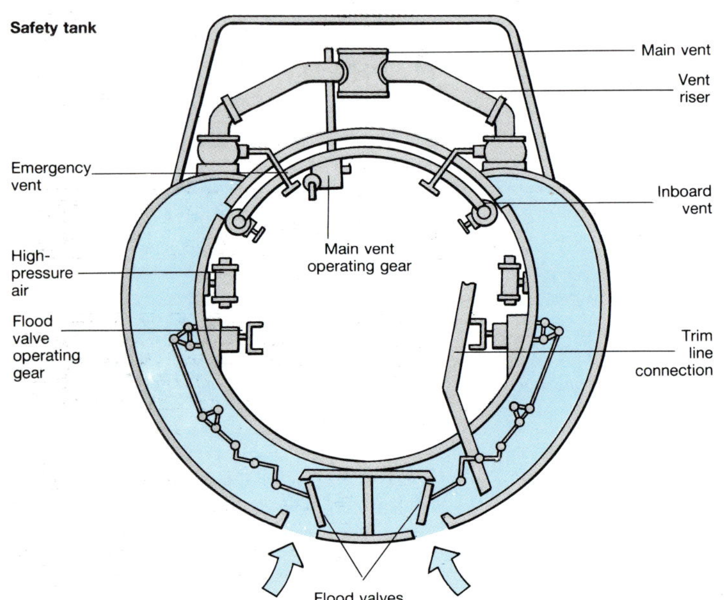

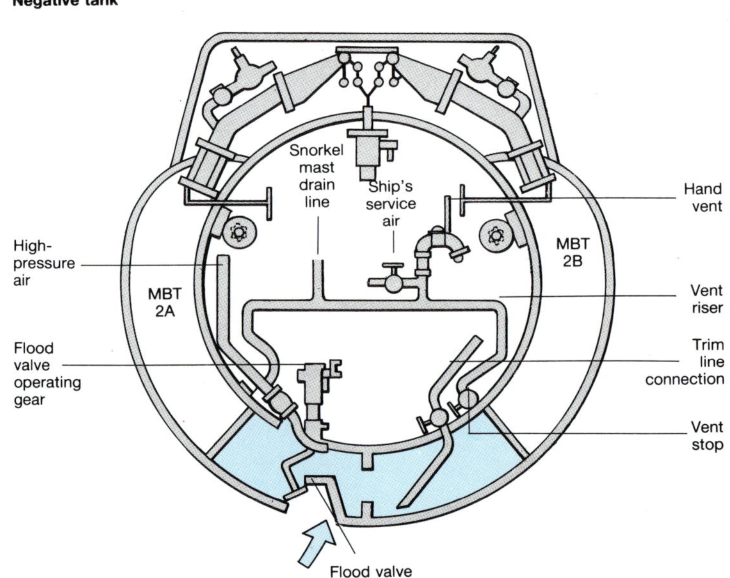

Top: To dive a submarine involves opening the vents, allowing seawater to enter through flood ports. The water is expelled by compressed air to surface.

Above: Blowing the safety tank when submerged restores positive buoyancy quickly. It is located amidships to minimise the effect on fore-and-aft trim.

Top: Fuel ballast tanks must be full before submerging. When fuel is expended seawater is admitted, and allowed to flow between the tanks by limber holes.

Above: Quick diving can be achieved by flooding the negative buoyancy tank, which is also used to drain the snorkel mast during preparations for snorkelling.

- Main ballast tanks
- Variable ballast tanks
- Special ballast tanks
- Fuel ballast tanks
- Fuel oil tanks
- Lubricating oil
- Main engine sump
- Fresh water
- Sanitary tanks

1 Bow buoyancy tank (capacity 18 tons of seawater)
2 Main ballast tank No 1 (44.35t)
3 Sanitary tank No 1 (2.06t/537gallons)
4 Fresh water tanks Nos 1 and 2 (1,000g each)
5 Normal fuel oil tank No 1 (11,401g)
6 Normal fuel oil tank No 2 (13,122g)
7 Main ballast tank No 2A (32.98t)
8 Main ballast tank No 2C (32.98t)
9 Fuel ballast tank No 3A (37.37t/9,521g)
10 Fresh water tanks Nos 3 and 4 (1,000g each)
11 Auxiliary ballast tank No 1 (31t)
12 Fuel ballast tank No 4a (47.12t/12,045g)
13 Sanitary tank No 2 (2.57t/673g)
14 Fuel ballast tank No 5A (38.12t/9,729g)
15 Main ballast tank No 6A (35.4t)
16 Main engine sump No 1 (450g)
17 Main engine sump No 2 (450g)
18 Main ballast tank No 6C (35.4t)
19 Clean fuel oil tank No 1 (611g)
20 Collecting tank (2,993g)
21 Main engine sump

1 2 3 4 5 6 7 8 9 10 11 12

29 30 31 32 33 34

Forward torpedo room — Forward battery compartment — Control room — Aft batte cruciform arrangement, and is also quieter and safer. In addition, the X-shape can be made more efficient hydrodynamically if individual blades are of a longer, narrower shape and, because they extend beyond the boundary layer into undisturbed water, of a smaller area. Finally, it is necessary that controls should not extend beyond the keel or the maximum horizontal breadth of the submarine and with the X-shape this can be achieved with ease. However, because of the complex relationship between steering and diving functions, such surfaces require computer-aided operation.

The submarine captain's greatest enemy is sonar and, apart from tactical methods of avoiding sonar detection, there are some passive measures which can be implemented at the design stage. The first is to make the submarine smaller and so a more difficult target, but it is difficult to fit the mass of weapons and sensors now considered essential into a small hull. Another technique is to shape the contours of the hull in such a way that the sonar beams are diffused. Finally, anechoic (sound absorbing) tiles can be used to coat the most critical parts of the submarine. These are already in use on Royal Navy submarines and on the latest Soviet submarines – one type of Soviet tile has the NATO designation Cluster Guard – and will be introduced on the next generation of US attack submarines.

CONSTRUCTION

There are four main types of hull arrangement: single-hull, saddle-tank, double-hull and multi-hull. Single-hull submarines have their main ballast tanks mounted either externally at either end of the pressure hull, as in the US Navy's Los Angeles class, or within the hull itself. Saddle-tank submarines have their main ballast tanks mounted externally as streamlined additions to the pressure hull, as in the British Oberon class, with free-flooding holes at the bottom and vents at the top. Such main ballast tanks are sometimes used as additional fuel tanks with the fuel floating on top of the seawater, which extends the range considerably but reduces the reserve of buoyancy, an acceptable risk in time of war. A double-hull submarine has a complete or almost complete outer hull surrounding the pressure hull over most of its length. The space between the two hulls is used for main ballast tanks and external fuel stowage, the distance between them being dictated mainly by construction and access considerations.

The final possibility is to have two or even three pressure-hulls. The Dutch Dolfijn class submarines have three separate, interconnected hulls in a treble-bubble arrangement. The large upper hull contains the crew and most of the equipment, while below it and alongside each other are two smaller hulls, each containing machinery and stores. The advantage of this layout is that it gives great strength and the Dolfijn class boats can dive to 980ft (300m).

Such a submarine is difficult and expensive to construct and the Dutch did not pursue this idea in their later classes. The Soviet Navy, however, appears to have adopted a double-hull arrangement in its Typhoon class ballistic missile submarines and it is the consensus view in the West that these gigantic vessels have two complete, interconnected pressure hulls, each containing crew quarters and propulsion machinery, with a third, smaller pressurized section above and between them and directly under the sail for the command and control centre. The space for the missiles is between the two lower hulls and, most unusually, before instead of abaft the sail. Apart from spaciousness and habitability, such a submarine will have great survivability.

Typhoon class internal arrangement (conjectural)

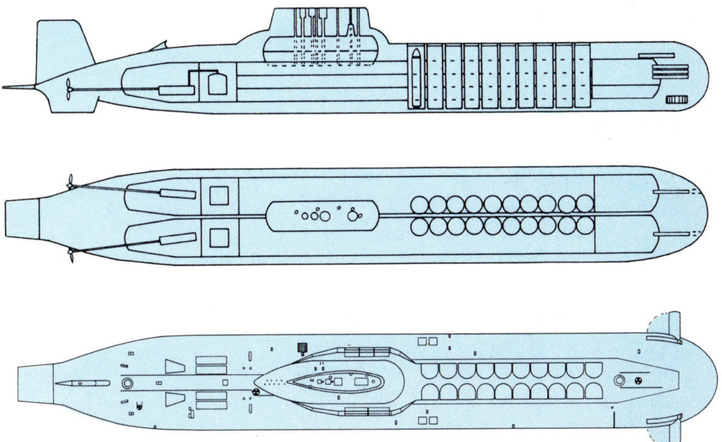

Top: The sheer size of the Soviet Typhoon SSBN took the West by surprise. One explanation of its considerable beam is that there may be two internal hulls.

Above: A possible interior layout of the Typhoon showing the side-by-side hulls containing missiles and a nuclear reactor, with a control centre above.

No 3 (450g)
22 Main engine sump No 4 (450g)
23 Normal fuel oil tank No 6 (15,201g)
24 Clean fuel oil tank No 2 (618g)
25 Normal fuel oil tank No 7 (10,599g)
26 Sanitary tank No 3 (0.87t/206g)
27 After water round torpedo tank (5t)
28 After trim tank (20t)
29 Forward trim tank (24t)
30 Water round torpedo tank (5t)
31 Main ballast tank No 2B (32.98t)
32 Negative tank (12t)
33 Main ballast tank No 2D (32.98t)
34 Fuel ballast tank No 3B (37.37t/9,521g)
35 Safety tank (23t)
36 Auxiliary ballast tank No 2 (31t)
37 Fuel ballast tank No 4B (47.12t/ 12,045g)
38 Fuel ballast tank No 5B (38.12t/9,729g)
39 Reserve lubrication oil tank (1,201g)
40 Main ballast tank No 6B (35.4t)
41 Main ballast tank No 6D (35.4t)
42 Normal lubrication oil tank No 1 (1,457g)
43 Expansion tank (2,993g)
44 Normal fuel oil tank No 6 (15,201g)
45 Normal lubrication oil tank No 2 (924g)
46 Main motor sump (200g)
47 Normal lubrication oil tank No 3 (1,040g)

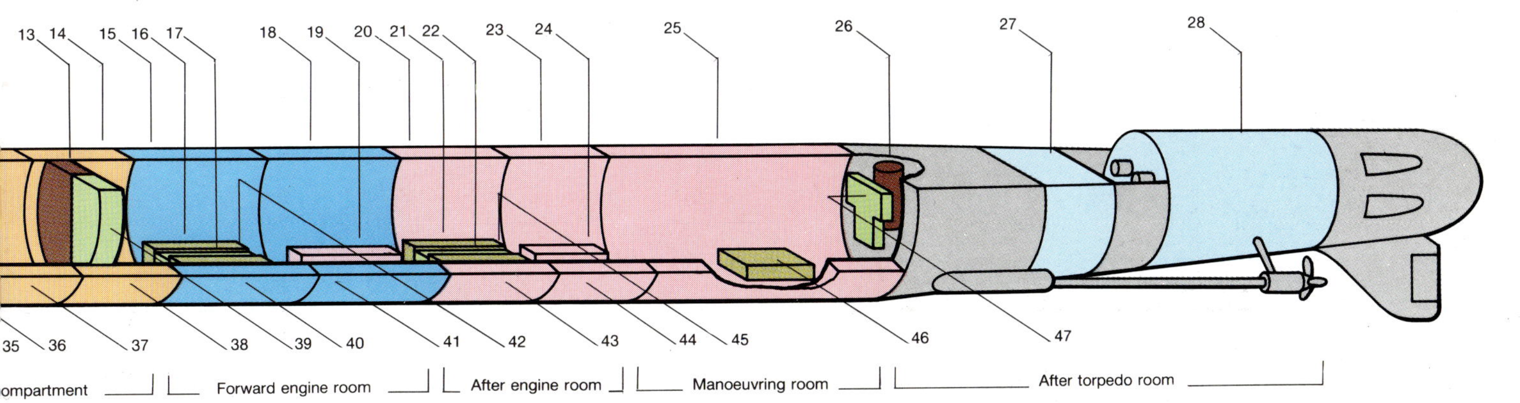

Upholder class cutaway

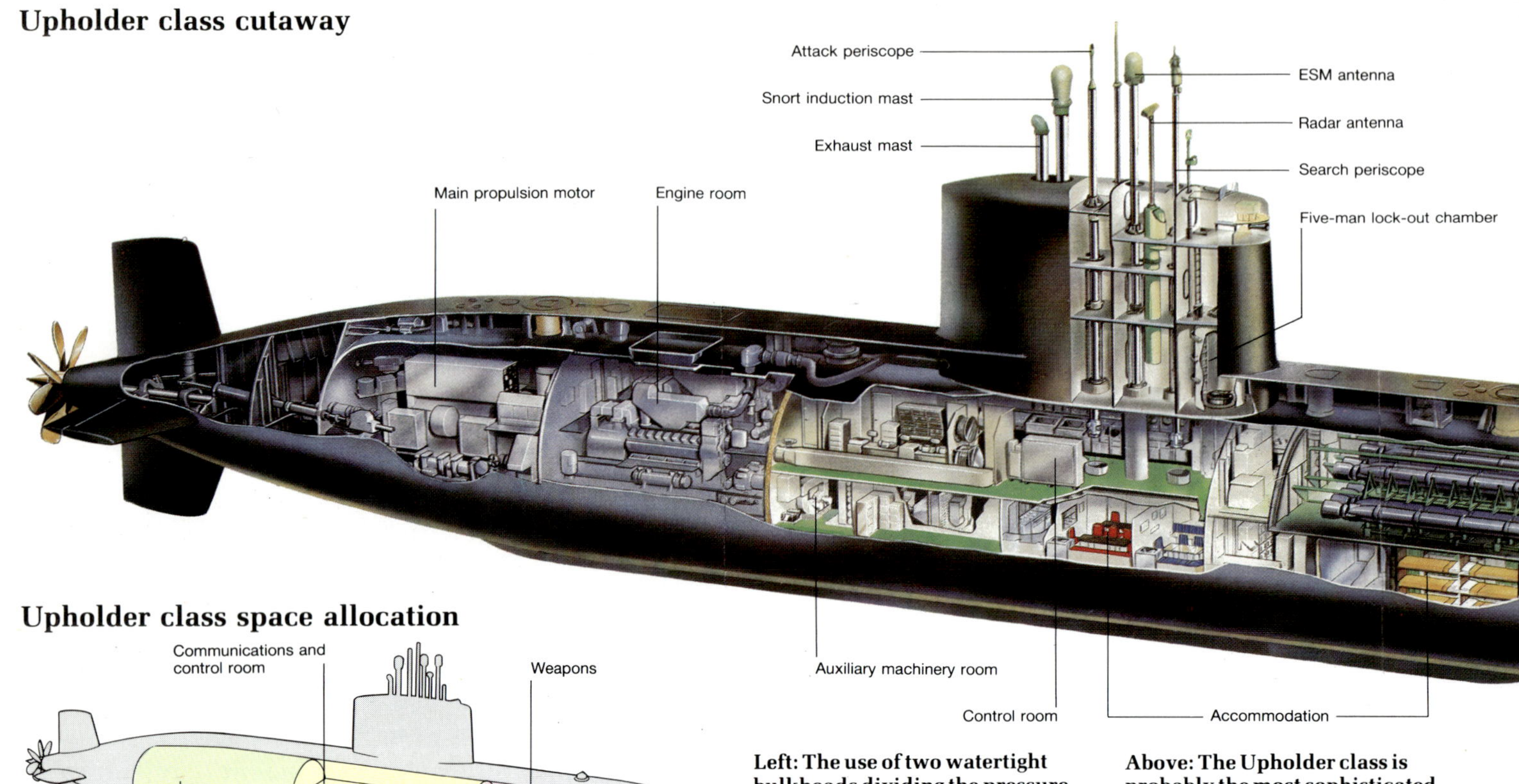

Upholder class space allocation

Left: The use of two watertight bulkheads dividing the pressure hull space into three main watertight compartments is now unusual. The aft compartment is divided by an acoustic bulkhead, with the propulsion motor room aft of the engine room.

Above: The Upholder class is probably the most sophisticated conventional design available. The cylindrical pressure hull is capped forward and aft by domed bulkheads and constructed of high tensile steel to permit diving depths in excess of 656ft (200m).

All hulls have ballast keels. In the double- and multi-hull configuration the keel is mounted within the outer hull; in the others it is mounted externally. Double- and multi-hull and saddle-tank arrangements have an additional and most valuable advantage in that weapon warheads exploding against the outer plates have a certain amount of their explosive impact absorbed, thus reducing the effect on the pressure hull.

The US Navy has used a series of high-yield (HY) steels for submarine construction, but all classes since the Thresher have been made of HY80. (The number gives the yield stress in lb/sq in; thus, HY80 has a yield stress of 80lb/sq in, or 5.624kg/cm^2). At one time it was planned to build the Los Angeles class boats of HY130, although in the event HY80 was used, and it is now hoped to develop HY130 to an acceptable standard in time for use in the later units of the US Navy's next class of attack submarines.

In other nations there is also much research and development aimed at producing ever stronger materials: titanium, aluminium and even glass have been considered. The Japanese use NS-90 in their Yuushio class, while the French Marel, a new high-tension steel claimed to give a 50 per cent increase in diving depth, is being used in the latest French and Dutch submarines. The USSR has continued to use steel for the majority of its submarines, but at least two classes, Alfa and Mike, are known to be built of titanium. The Alfas are not only the world's fastest submarines, capable of better than 42 knots (75km/h) but also the deepest diving, with estimates of their depth capability varying from 2,000ft (607m) to 3,000ft (914m).

Titanium is a very difficult material to weld, although the Soviets – long world leaders in metallurgy – seem to have overcome the problems. Only six Alfas were built, but their successors of the Mike class now entering service are also constructed of titanium. Titanium has, of course, an invaluable further advantage in that it is non-magnetic and thus undetectable by devices such as airborne MAD and bottom-laid coils. Some years ago the West Germans attempted to achieve similar results by using

Below: The cylindrical form of USS *Ohio* (SSBN 726) is shown as she is rolled out from the giant assembly hall at General Dynamics Electric Boat Division for final completion and testing.

Right: This view of the launch of USS *Phoenix* (SSN 702) includes a revealing glimpse of the missile tubes in USS *Michigan* (SSBN 727) fitting out on the pier. The tubes are located amidships to minimise changes to the trim of the boat as the missiles are fired.

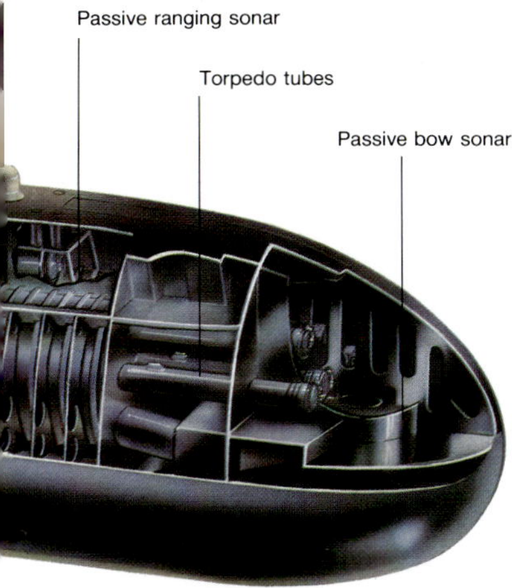

non-magnetic steel for their Type 205, 206, and 207 submarines, which were intended primarily for service in the shallow waters of the Baltic. Early corrosion problems have long since been resolved but the idea has not been extended to larger designs.

The essential body of the submarine is the long, relatively thin, cylindrical pressure hull, stiffened by internal or external ring frames and supported by transverse bulkheads. The pressure hull diameter varies, small changes being achieved by conical sections and large changes by steep torospherical cones, with bulkheads or stiffeners located at the smaller diameter transition point. The two extremities of the pressure hull are closed by domed end-closures, usually hemispherical in shape.

Obviously, the critical factor is the strength and integrity in the hull, which must be enough to enable the submarine to operate at depths specified in the operational requirement. Overall collapse due to insufficiently strong frames in relation to compartment length is a relatively unlikely event, but interframe shell buckling and shell yielding are of greater consequence. The designer endeavours to take all the possibilities of weakness into account, such as variations in material characteristics, residual stresses, deviation in circularity, stress concentrations, etc, in a factor of safety which is normally set between 1.5 and 2.0. This is used in the calculation: collapse depth (design depth) = factor of safety × operational depth. Thus, in a boat with a safety factor of 1.74 (a typical figure) and an operating depth of 300ft (91.4m), collapse depth would be 522ft (159m).

It should be noted that the majority of modern Western deep-diving submarines do not have very strong internal bulkheads, so that penetration of

Shock response spectra

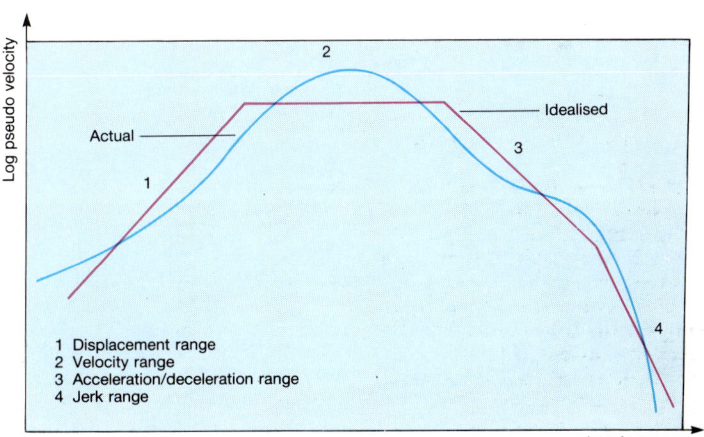

Above: The relationship between velocity and frequency in an underwater attack on a submarine, used in designing shock protection mounts for submarine equipment.

Below: Increasing resources are devoted to trials and research in underwater warfare. Here the former Royal Navy submarine HMS *Porpoise* undergoes conversion to a range target.

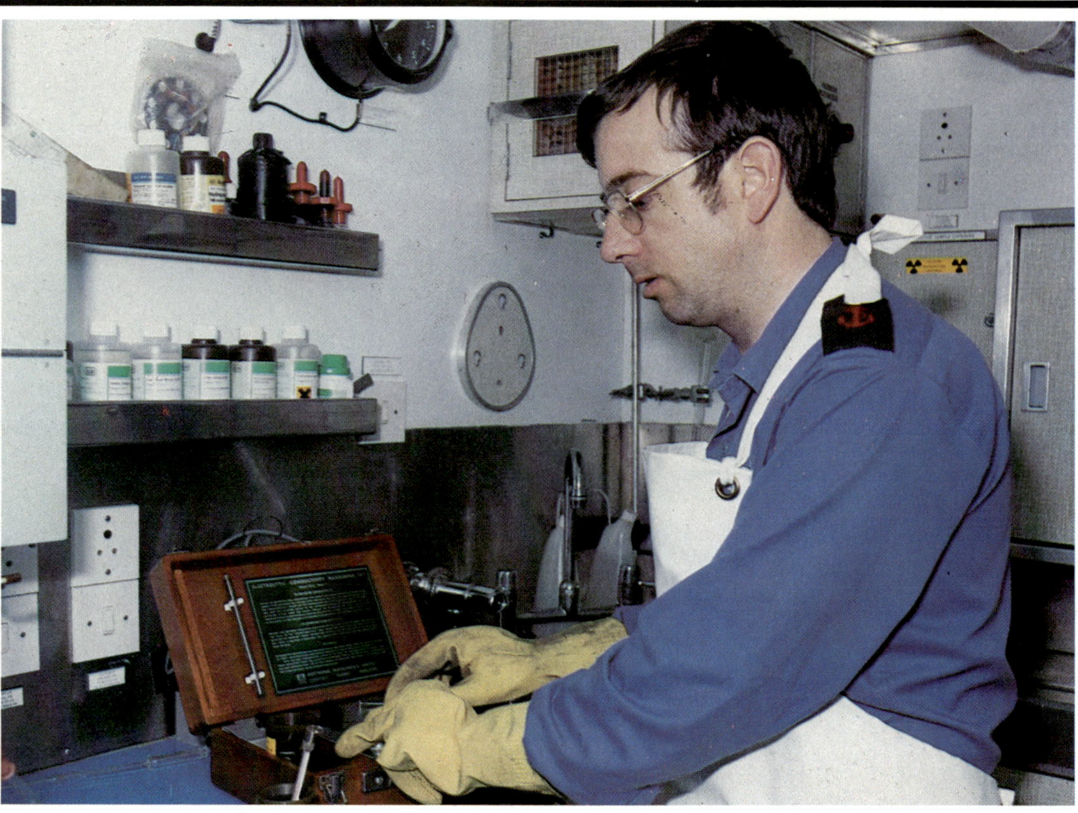
Right: A medical orderly on the British nuclear-powered hunter-killer submarine HMS *Trafalgar*. Such boats may be away from contact with land or other ships for months at a time and must be totally self-sufficient.

the pressure hull is likely to be disastrous and escape improbable. Most Soviet submarines, and the West German IKL-designs, do, however, have such bulkheads.

HABITABILITY

An important factor, as submarines require ever more highly trained crews and cruises become longer, is habitability. To a certain extent this problem can be solved by increasing size, but this is undesirable on grounds of expense and detectability, and all navies are aiming for increased automation to enable crews to be

Below: HMS *Trafalgar*'s mess-room, showing the increased space available for social activities aboard modern submarines, easing the strain during long cruises in confined spaces.

Above: The officers' wardroom in HMS *Trafalgar*. Submarine officers of all nations require lengthy training and carry considerable responsibilities, and many Western navies suffer a retention problem.

Left: Even in the large hulls of the latest SSNs – this is USS *La Jolla* (SSN 701) of the Los Angeles class – space is at a premium and the living quarters are located wherever room is available. Some of the crew must share their sleeping space with Mk48 torpedoes.

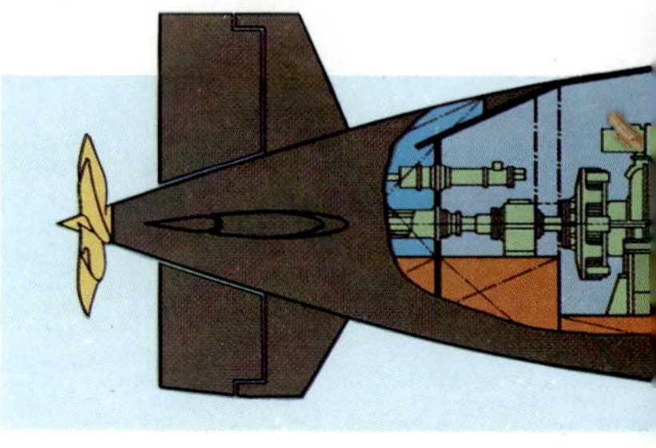

Right: In *Trafalgar*'s torpedo stowage space every inch is used for weaponry or equipment. Larger submarines merely contain more equipment and it is rare for additional room to be made available for crew comfort.

reduced dramatically. The Swedish Navy's Vastergötland class, for example, with a submerged displacement of 1,125 tons, will have a crew of just 5 officers and 19 men; the Peruvian Dos de Mayo class, similar in size but built in the 1950s, need a crew of 40. Neither type is likely to undertake particularly long cruises, but modern deep sea boats also have lower manpower requirement: the Dutch Walrus class (2,800 tons submerged), for example, will have a crew of 7 officers and 43 men, whereas the US Tang class (2,600 tons submerged) of the 1940s needed 11 officers and 75 men.

THE FUTURE

Perhaps the overriding factor in future submarine design is that of cost. Even conventional diesel-electric submarines, apart from those designed for restricted waters such as the Baltic, are growing in size and cost, and while many resolutions are made to produce smaller, cheaper designs, they somehow seldom seem to materialise. The major research efforts are now concentrating on making submarines quieter, faster and deeper diving. The emphasis on quietness does not necessarily make a submarine undetectable, but it does make the searcher work much harder, probably to the extent of using active sonar and thus giving himself away.

Possibly the greater potential breakthrough would be to find a propulsion system which would free the non-nuclear submarine from the surface. It seems unlikely that there will be any major advances in battery design, although continual refinement will obviously take place, and while closed-cycle engines and fuel cells both have possibilities a practical system in either field has yet to appear. Nevertheless, there does seem to be a reasonable prospect of viable fuel cells for submarines by the mid-1990s. Nothing is known of Soviet developments in this area, but in view of their huge investments in submarine technology there is no reason to think that they will be behind the West in this field.

Above: Visualisation of the US Navy's new Seawolf (SSN 21) class SSN. Of particular interest is the relocation of the forward hydroplanes from sail to bow to facilitate operations under the polar ice.

Below: Interior layout of the Thyssen TR-1700 submarines currently under construction for Argentina. Great endurance and long deployment times were met by large fuel and weapon storage capacity, but a high

standard of accommodation for the crew was also considered important. The design was also optimised for a high average transit speed, with substantial battery provision and charging capacity to match.

Propulsion

The greatest single advance in post-World War II submarine technology is the advent of nuclear propulsion. Nuclear power has released submarines using it from the need for regular forays to the surface to recharge their batteries and has virtually abolished range limitations.

PRESSURISED-WATER REACTORS

All British and American nuclear-powered submarines use pressurized-water reactors (PWRs) in which water acts as both coolant and moderator, a tried and tested technique which has proved exceptionally reliable in service. In such a system water passes round the primary circuit, several times through the nuclear reactor and thence to a steam generator. The cooling water in the primary circuit has to be kept at a high pressure to prevent it boiling and turning to steam, achieved by including a pressurizer in the primary circuit; steam at the top of the pressurizer is used to compensate for changes in coolant volume as the reactor inlet and outlet temperatures vary.

The heat energy is transferred in the steam generator from the water in the primary circuit to unpressurized water in the secondary circuit which then becomes steam and passes through the secondary circuit to the turbine; having driven the turbine it goes into a series of condensers, becoming water once again and returning in liquid form to the steam generator to continue the cycle. PWR condensers use seawater as a heat sink and require a constant throughput, provided either by the forward motion of the submarine or, at slow speeds, by the use of pumps.

The operation of a PWR requires considerable auxiliary power, mainly to operate the circulation pumps in the primary circuit and the electrical heater elements in the pressuriser. The system can be designed to utilise natural circulation resulting from the thermal gradient set up by the nuclear reaction, but at higher power levels the pumps still have to be switched in. Some systems, in an effort to minimise noise and vibration, use several pumps which can be selectively activated according to the power level. Whatever the system, however, all these pumps create noise which is detectable by suitable sensors.

LIQUID METAL-COOLED REACTORS

Various alternative coolants have been tried. The USS *Seawolf* (SSN-575), launched in 1955, was fitted with an S2G liquid sodium-cooled reactor, which gave a much more efficient heat transfer but was very troublesome in service. There were two particular problems: the more intractable was that the sodium had to be kept molten at all times,

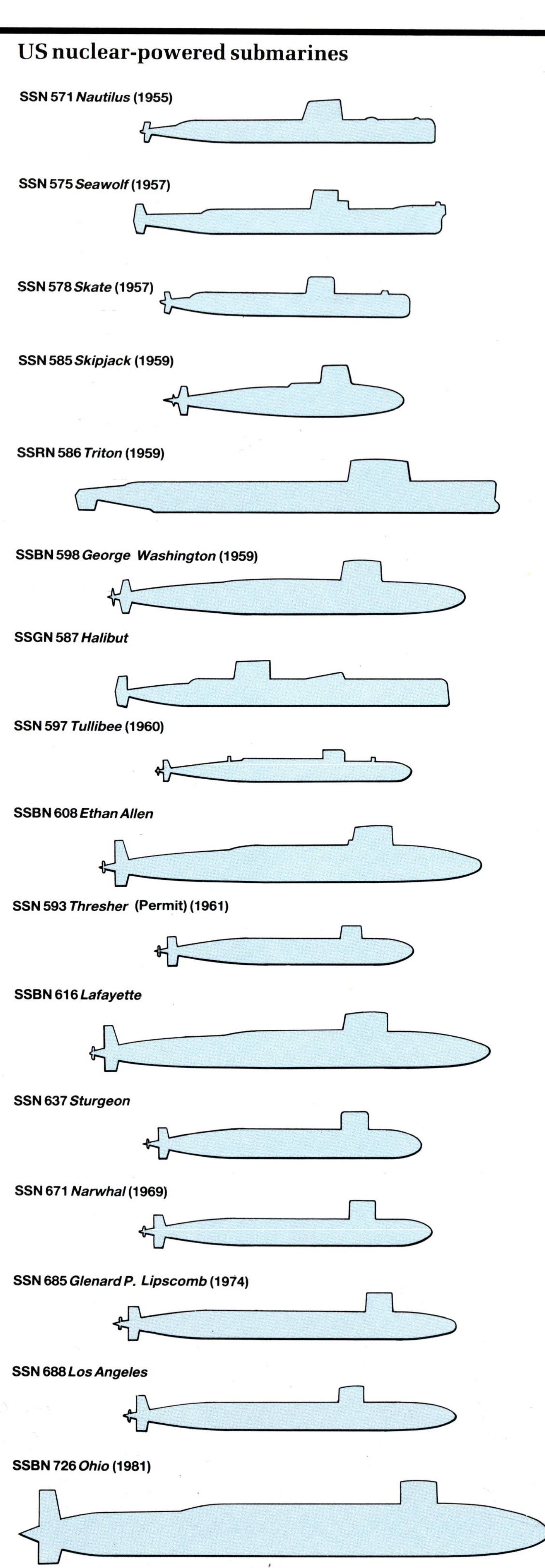

Left: Development of US nuclear-powered submarines has been one of logical progression, but there have been aberrations as alternative ideas have been tried. The US Navy's – and the world's – first nuclear-powered boat, *Nautilus*, was powered by an S2W pressurised-water reactor; the alternative S2G liquid-sodium reactor tried in the *Seawolf* was a failure and was replaced by an S2WA reactor.

The first production SSNs, the four Skates, were similar to *Nautilus* but slightly smaller. The six boats of the Skipjack class were the first SSNs to have Albacore hulls: indeed, as these comparative profiles clearly show, their hull is the nearest to the ideal of any American SSN. The original leader of the Permit class, *Thresher* (SSN-593), was lost in 1963, but the rest of the class has proved successful in service. The 37-strong Sturgeon class has also proved very successful in service, and led via the turbo-electric driven *Glenard P Lipscomb*, an attempt to produce a truly silent SSN, to the Los Angeles class. The last, with 58 examples already ordered, is probably one of the most expensive but effective defence programmes ever.

The first SSBN type, the George Washington class, was developed quickly by inserting an extra section in a Skipjack hull, and the subsequent Ethan Allen and Lafayette classes have been logical refinements of the design, all carrying 16 ballistic missiles, but the latest Ohio class boats have 24 missiles.

***Tullibee* was the first SSN with a spherical bow sonar dome and midships outward angled torpedo tubes and the last with deck casing. The huge *Triton*, a fleet radar picket, was the only US SSN ever designed to be faster on the surface than submerged, while *Halibut*, the only US nuclear cruise-missile submarine, was armed with five Rugulus Is.**

Right: A submarine pressurized-water reactor (PWR) comprises two circuits: the primary circuit transfers heat from the radioactive core to a water-filled secondary circuit in a heat-exchanger. The PWR's main competitor, the liquid metal reactor, has been dropped by the US Navy, although it is used in at least one Soviet Navy class.

PWRs need auxiliary power to operate the primary circuit circulation pumps, which must be kept running to remove the heat from the pressure vessel; also, the pressurizer needs electrical power to maintain steam. These pumps and generators produce noise, which is one of the main means of detecting nuclear-powered submarines. With proper design natural circulation can be sufficient at low power and the circulation pumps can be switched off, as in the US Narwhal and Ohio designs.

otherwise it solidified and ruined the primary circuit pipes; the second was that the plant was plagued by high-pressure steam leaks. After two years the S2G was replaced by an S2Wa pressurised water-cooled nuclear reactor, virtually identical to that installed in the *Nautilus*. Liquid metal cooling seems to be the only way to obtain smaller, lighter plants, and the Soviet Navy's Alfa class is generally agreed to have a liquid-metal cooled reactor in a fully automatic, unmanned engine room, leading to considerable savings in reactor shielding.

NOISE

A particular problem for nuclear-powered boats is that of noise from gearing and rotating machinery such as pumps which, as described above, must be kept running, especially in PWR systems. In most Western boats machinery is mounted on rafts in an effort to isolate the vibrations from the hull, but turbo-electric drive has been tried in USS *Lipscomb* (SSN-685); the *Lipscomb* is still in service with this system, but it has not been repeated in other boats. Direct drive with twin contra-rotating propellers of different sizes was utilised in USS *Jack* (SSN-605), but was unsuccessful and was removed. Free circulation is used in USS *Narwhal* (SSN-671) and has apparently been a success as it is now used in the S8G reactor that powers the Ohio class ballistic missile boats.

Above: British nuclear submarine propulsion system prototype at the Admiralty Reactor Test Establishment, Dounreay, Scotland. Work on the prototype started in 1957.

Above: The unusually compact nuclear reactor core vessel is installed in a French Navy SSBN (SNLE). The French nuclear submarine programme has been remarkably successful.

DIESEL-ELECTRIC PROPULSION

The diesel-electric submarine is far cheaper to build than a nuclear submarine, is far less complicated to operate and does not invite the political problems associated with nuclear power. However, it has an inherent problem in that it must go to the surface to run its diesels to recharge its batteries, a process which requires about 3.5lb (1.58kg) of oxygen for every 1lb (0.45kg) of fuel oil. In very few submarines are the diesels connected directly to the propeller shafts; rather, the propellers are normally run off the batteries at all times, even on the surface while the diesels recharge the batteries.

Batteries are heavy and space-consuming. Lead-acid batteries are cheap, simple to produce and relatively easy to maintain, while silver-zinc and silver-cadmium batteries are lighter, smaller and more efficient,

Pressurised-water nuclear propulsion system layout

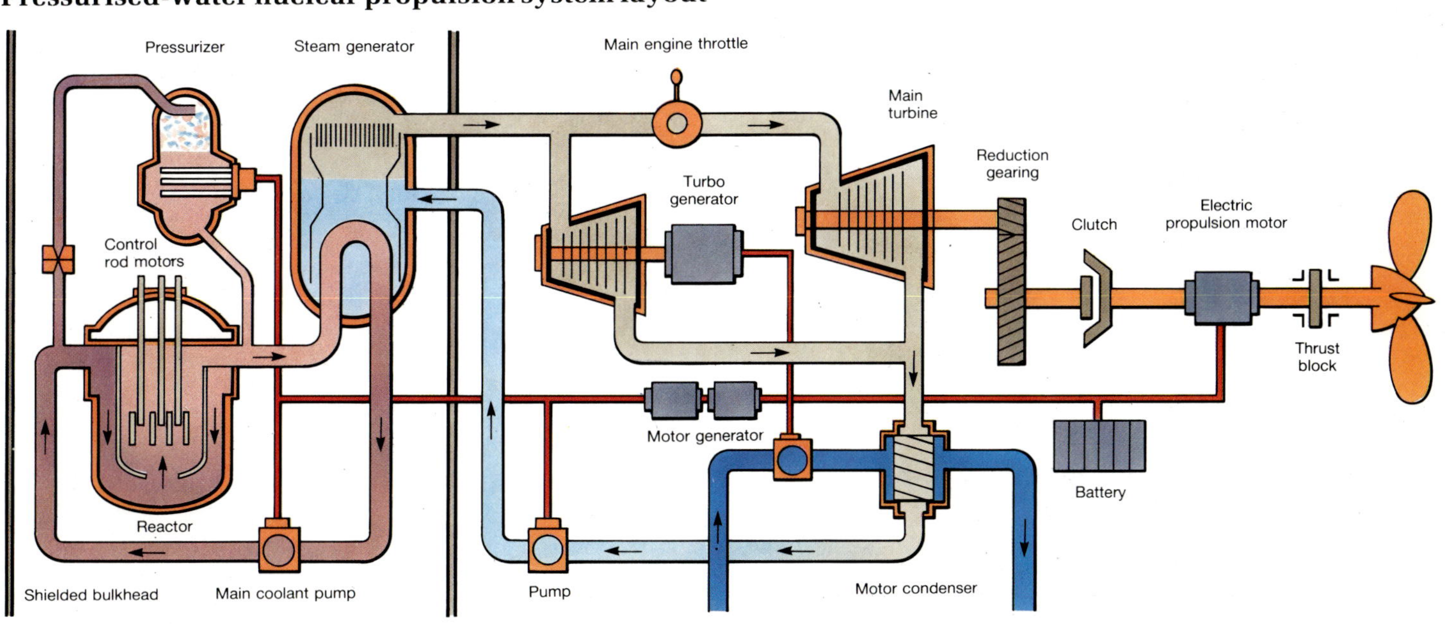

but are much more expensive and need more careful handling. Apart from constant research into new types of battery, much development effort is being put into improving the performance of lead-acid batteries, for example by changing the electrolyte under water to get rid of poisoned electrolyte.

PROPELLERS

The final item in the drive-train is the propeller, which is one of the major causes of noise and one of the most readily identifiable features of an individual submarine. Modern submarine propellers have up to seven blades, usually scythe-shaped, and are designed to be run at very low revolutions. The British Trafalgar class submarines are reported to use pump-jets, in which a ducted, multi-bladed rotor turns against stator vanes, thus virtually eliminating cavitation noise, although rotating noises will probably still exist.

OTHER PROPULSION SYSTEMS

The Soviet Navy is reported to be examining a variety of alternative means of propulsion, and is claimed in *Jane's Fighting Ships 1984-85* to be using both magnetohydrodynamic (MHD) generators and electrodynamic thrust (EMT). The former involves the use of an open tube filled with seawater and surrounded by a ferro-liquid in a sealed sleeve: a pulsating magnetic field causes sympathetic vibrations in the ferro-liquid, setting up a travelling wave which results in the water in the open tube being pumped out at the rear to impart forward thrust to the submarine.

This system, which has similarities with the electro-osmosis process, requires a great deal of electrical power and would probably be capable of moving the submarine only at low speeds. Nevertheless, if a ballistic missile boat was to use normal propeller drive for the relatively rapid transit to and from its patrol area, once there MHD could be very valuable for virtually undetectable low-speed cruise.

One theory concerning the enormous size of the Soviet Navy's Typhoon class SSBN is that there are two parallel pressure hulls within the outer casing, one of which contains a large nuclear plant to generate the enormous power necessary for MHD propulsion.

EMT employs a different technique. A line of electro-magnets is set up on the centreline of the vessel and banks of electrodes are mounted on either side: electric current is passed through the electrodes, setting up a magnetic field, and the action

Above: Three of these Brons O-RUB 215x12 1,400kW diesel units are installed in each of the Taiwanese Navy's Seadragon class submarines. At the right is the Holec AC generator with its built-in rectifier and air/water heat exchanger.

Below: Paxman Valenta 16RP 200SZ 16-cylinder diesel (for British Upholders). With a power output of 2,035 hp, this unit has a dry weight of some 8.89 tons (9,000kg), Total weight with the associated electrical generator is 23.4 tons (23,800kg).

Above: The GEC 4MW double-armature non-compensated DC main propulsion motor of the Upholder class. The unit's 85-ton weight and torque loadings are transferred to the submarine's structure by feet extending over its complete footprint.

Below: Stirling-cycle engines burn fuel and oxygen continuously in a combustion chamber, the heat being transferred by conduction to a gas of high thermal conductivity confined in a heater/regenerator/cooling circuit, achieving air-independent power.

between the two magnetic fields results in forward motion. The Soviet Union and Japan are both reported to be experimenting with this system. Both MHD and EMT produce thrust without the use of a propeller, so there is no cavitation noise, no mechanical noise and less wake turbulence.

Other systems have also been tried. Professor Helmuth Walther proposed a closed-cycle system using high-test hydrogen peroxide (HTP), and four Type XVIIA and three Type XVIIB boats had been completed by the end of World War II. All the latter were scuttled,

Above: The manoevring control console of a Swedish Näcken. The Saab Instruments console allows one man to control the submarine: here the operator is controlling the boat with his right hand while adjusting the speed of the motor with his left.

but two were recovered, *U-1407*, going to the Royal Navy and *U-1406* to the US Navy.

U-1407 was refurbished and, commissioned as HMS *Meteorite*, was used to develop the Walther system in 1947-48, with enough success for the Royal Navy to order two more submarines using the Walther cycle, HMS *Explorer* and *Excalibur*. Of 1,200 tons submerged displacement, these boats were purely experimental; they had no torpedo tubes or radar, mounted only one periscope and had diesel engines to recharge the batteries and to power them on the surface. Using HTP propulsion underwater speeds of 26.5 knots were attained for periods of up to three hours, or 12 knots for 15 hours on one turbine. They proved very hazardous in service, however, to the extent that *Explorer* was known to her crew as HMS Exploder, and they were, in any case, overtaken by the nuclear-powered submarine.

Closed-cycle systems continue to be studied. The Brayton cycle, using inert gases such as argon, helium or xenon as working fluids, was an unsuccessful competitor to power the US Navy's Advanced Lightweight Torpedo, while the Stirling piston engine was under serious consideration for the Royal Swedish Navy's Vastergötland class but was eventually rejected. It should be noted that in any of these systems a fundamental consideration is that if they should give off a gaseous exhaust its disposal is a problem, especially at depth.

Fuel cells have an apparent potential for use in submarines. In such devices two chemicals are combined in the presence of a catalyst, the reaction, which is usually fairly violent, being used for the direct production of electricity. Efficiency is high – up to 70 or 80 per cent in some cases – there are no severe heat dissipation problems, and in many cases, such as lithium/peroxide cells, the product is pure, potable water. No practicable submarine propulsion system has yet been produced using fuel cells, but they are generally considered to be the most likely way forward.

Weapons

After World War II guns were abandoned and for a decade the only weapons available to attack and patrol submarines were torpedoes which had little better performance than those of World War II; indeed, in many cases they *were* World War II torpedoes. HMS *Conqueror*, for example, sank the Argentinian cruiser *General Belgrano* in 1982 with a Mk 8 torpedo, a model which first went to sea in the late 1930s. The torpedo has had an extraordinary history in recent years, with vast sums being expended by many nations but, until recently, little overall advance in performance or reliability.

Since World War II, however, a whole new range of weapons has given submarines entirely new capabilities – in particular, the ability to carry out nuclear or conventional strikes against targets far inland. The submarine-launched ballistic missile (SLBM) has, for some 20 years, given the submarine the ability to strike at targets anywhere in the world in a counter-value role, and it may now be on the verge of attaining a dangerously destabilising counter-force role as well.

The submarine-launched cruise missile (SLCM) has been around for a similar period and the Soviet Navy has long had specialised boats to carry them. The US Navy also developed some specialised cruise-missile submarines in the late 1940s and 1950s but then decided to produce weapons which could be launched from standard torpedo tubes, the Sub-Harpoon anti-ship missile and the Tomahawk anti-ship (T-ASM) and land attack (T-LAM) missiles. However, after vast expenditure on the Tomahawk programme, it has been realised that the missile will take up too much valuable space in the torpedo rooms and it has been decided to fit them in vertically mounted tubes inside the upper casing between the bow sonar and the forward end of the pressure hull.

The only other submarine-launched anti-ship missile is the French SM39 Exocet, a new version of the very successful missile which achieved such a reputation in the 1982 South Atlantic war. Launched from a standard torpedo tube, the SM 39 has a range of over 312 miles (500km).

BALLISTIC MISSILES

At the end of World War II naval forces were primarily concerned, as they had been for centuries, with combat on the high seas. Heavy guns could be fired at inshore targets up to ranges of about 25 miles (40km) and carrier-based aircraft were capable of strikes even further inland, although seldom more than 100 miles (160km) – but there it ended. By the 1950s, however, the US Navy had developed a land-attack capability with its strike carriers equipped with the North American AJ-1 Savage, which was capable of carrying the Mk 5 atomic bomb whose yield was well in excess of the 20kT of the weapons used in the Nagasaki and Hiroshima attacks. This carrier-based capability, which improved rapidly through the 1950s and 1960s, caused major concern in the Soviet Union and helped spark off its major attack and cruise-missile submarine building programmes.

The next phase in the expansion of navies' traditional roles came with the ballistic missile-armed submarine. Apart from shore bombardment with their relatively small deck gun, submarines had never had a land attack role: the

Above: First launch of Trident I, January 18, 1977. The aerospike deployed on the nose gives the same streamlining effect as a long pointed nose without reducing the vehicle's internal volume.

Below: Test firing of an unidentified Soviet Navy SLBM. The weapon's ratio of diameter to length appears markedly different from that of the Western missiles such as Trident.

Below: Trident I SLBM launched from USS *James Madison* (SSBN 627), one of 12 units of the Lafayette and Franklin classes which have been converted to take Trident I.

Germans had given serious consideration in 1944-45 to methods of transporting V-2 rockets across the Atlantic by submarine to points where they could be launched against the USA, but the war ended before the plan could be implemented. The essence of the idea was sound, however, and both the Soviet and US navies began to pursue the idea in the Cold War era. The first ballistic missile submarines, those of the Soviet Navy's diesel-engined Golf class armed with three fin-mounted SS-N-3 missiles, came into service in 1958, but they were crude systems and the missiles could only be launched from the surface.

Above: Poseidon C-3 SLBM has only been deployed in the Lafayette/Franklin class SSBNs, twelve of which have been converted to take Trident leaving 18 with Poseidon.

Above: Royal Navy-launched Polaris A-3 SLBM. The RN is the only user of this elderly missile, which has been updated by the fitting of new rocket motors and the all-British Chevaline MRV.

Below: Despite renewed interest in nuclear-powered attack submarines by navies such as those of Spain and Canada, nobody is planning to join the extremely expensive SSBN club whose five present members will find that current moves to limit air- and land-based tactical and strategic nuclear weapons will increase the significance of their sea-based deterrent.

SUBMARINE-LAUNCHED BALLISTIC MISSILES (SLBM)

Country	Missle Type	Range		cep		Warhead			Guidance System	10G	Submarine Type	Number of SSBNs on 1 Jan 87	Number of Missiles per SSBN
		nm	km	nm	m	Type	Number per Missile	Yield (MT)					
USA	Trident C-4	4350	8056	0·25	463	MIRV	8	0·1	Inertial	1979	Ohio	8	24
											Lafayette/Franklin	12	16
	Poseidon C-3	2500	4630	0·25	463	MIRV	14	0·1	Inertial	1971	Lafayette/Franklin	16	16
UK	Polaris A-3	2500	4630	0·5	926	MRV	3	0·2	Inertial	1967	Resolution	4	16
France	MSBS M-20	1860	3445	0·54	1000	Single	1	1	Inertial	1976	Le Redoutable	5	16
	MSBS M-4	2160	4000	0·5	926	MRV	6	0·15	Inertial	1985	L'Inflexible	1	16
USSR	SS-N-6 Mod 2	1300	3000	1	1856	Single	1	1	Inertial	1967	Yankee-I	18	16
											Golf-III*	1	6
	SS-N-8 Mod 2	4800	9100	0·84	1560	Single	1	0·8	Stellar-Inertial	1974	Hotel-III*	1	6
											Delta-I	18	12
											Delta-II	4	16
	SS-N-17	2100	3900	0·75	1410	Single	1	1	Inertial	1977	Yankee-II	1	12
	SS-N-18 Mod 3	3300	6500	0·74	1370	MIRV	7	0·2	Stellar-Inertial	1976	Delta-III	14	16
	SS-N-20	4800	8900	0·35	640	MIRV	9	0·5	Stellar-Inertial	1982	Typhoon	4	20
	SS-N-23	4800	8900	0·35	640	MIRV	10		Stellar-Inertial	1985	Delta-IV	2	16
China	CSS-N-4	2150	3000	n.a.	n.a.	Single	1	2	Inertial	1983	Xia	2	12

* Missiles count towards SALT totals (12) but submarine hulls do not.

After a short-lived consideration of a system involving six solid-fuel Jupiter-S missiles in 8,500-ton submarines, the US Navy settled on the Polaris project. Few weapon systems in history have combined more dramatic technological innovations than this bold concept for a submarine-launched ballistic missile system, which was formulated by Admiral W.F. Rayborn, USN, and a team from Lockheed. The two most fundamental decisions, taken right at the very start, were to use solid propellant and to expel the missiles from vertical launch tubes while the submarine remained submerged, but the project also introduced many other novel technologies: lightweight ablative reentry vehicles, miniaturised inertial guidance, miniaturised nuclear and thermonuclear warheads, cold-gas launch techniques, submarine inertial navigation systems and submarine noise reduction to name but a few. When Polaris reached operational status in November 1960 it changed the nature of strategic warfare and, in particular, of deterrence, and improvement programmes have taken the US Navy from Polaris to Poseidon and now to Trident I (C-4) and Trident II (D-5).

The Soviet Navy ballistic missile programme started with the SS-N-4, a missile so large that it could only just be fitted into a Zulu V class submarine between the keel and the top of the fin. Liquid-fuelled and surface-launched, it was of limited value and was quickly succeeded by the SS-N-5, which, although still mounted in the fin, could at least be launched while the submarine was submerged.

The next Soviet missile, SS-N-6, was small enough for 16 to be installed within the hull of the first Soviet nuclear-powered ballistic missile submarine type – the Yankee class – thus matching the capability of the Western boats for the first time. A further advance was made with the SS-N-8, whose range of 4,800nm (8,890km) far exceeded that of any other SLBM at that time. Then came the SS-N-9 Mod 3, which at last gave the Soviet Navy a MIRV capability.

The SS-N-18, which was the next operational missile, has virtually all the capabilities of the American Trident II, but attained them a decade earlier, and its range of 4,300nm (7,964km) is such that it can threaten the USA from almost any part of any ocean in the world. The latest operational missiles, the SS-N-20 and SS-N-23, each have a range of 4,800nm (8,883km) and are now at sea in the

THE USA/USSR SLBM STRATEGIC BALANCE: (a)

Country	Missile	Submarine Type	Submarine Number in Fleet	Missiles per SSBN	Total missiles	Re-Entry Vehicles (RV): RVs per missile (c)	Total number of RVs	Effective Megatons (b): Yield per RV (MT) (d)	EMT
USA	Trident C-4	Ohio	8	24	192	8	1536	0·1	486
		Lafayette/ Franklin	12	16	192	8	1536	0·1	486
	Poseidon C-3	Lafayette/ Franklin	16	16	256	10	2560	0·04	512
Total			36		640		5632		1484
USSR	SS-N-6	Yankee-I	18	16	288	1	288	1	288
	SS-N-8	Golf-III	1	6	292	1	292	0·8	261
		Hotel-III	1	6					
		Delta-I	18	12					
		Delta-II	4	16					
	SS-N-17	Yankee-II	1	12	12	1	12	1	12
	SS-N-18	Delta-III	14	16	224	5	1120	0·2	501
	SS-N-20	Typhoon	4	20	80	6	480	0·1	152
	SS-N-23	Delta-IV	2	16	32	10	320	0·5	226
Total			63		928		2512		1440

Notes: (a) Figures given are for inventory totals of submarines, ie, the total number of submarines in the fleet, as of January 1, 1987; numbers actually available are many fewer. The US Navy has 66 per cent of Ohio SSBNs and 50 per cent of Lafayette/Franklin SSBNs at sea at any one time. The USSR, historically, has an average of just 13 SSBNs at sea.
(b) Effective Megatons (EMT) reflects the damage against soft point targets or area targets such as cities. The effect at a specific point distant from Ground Zero is proportional to the cube-root of the yield, while the area affected is proportional to the square of the distance. Thus:
$EMT = (Yield)^{2/3}$ BUT, where Yield $\geq$ 1MT then $EMT = (Yield)^{1/2}$
(c) Where missiles carry MIRVs the average load has been taken.
(d) Yield = Raw Yield per RV.

Above: The strategic balance between US and Soviet submarine-launched ballistic missiles was agreed in the SALT-II talks; although never ratified by the US Congress the constraints have been observed by both sides.

Above: A US Navy lieutenant mans *Ohio*'s missile compartment control and monitoring panel station. His submarine is armed with 24 Trident I missiles, each with 8 MIRVs – a total of 192 warheads with a combined raw yield of 19,200kT. Trident I is not sufficiently accurate to undertake counter-force strikes.

Below: Although the scale is different a missile launch tube has to be cleaned in much the same way as a rifle barrel. Here men work on one of the tubes on board USS *James Madison* at the time she was fitted with Polaris A-3.

Typhoon and Delta IV class submarines respectively.

The current ballistic missile systems in all navies are basically similar, differing only in detail and comprising five basic subsystems: the submarine, the navigational system, the fire control system, the missile and the launch system. The submarine is essentially a sea-mobile launch pad providing the missiles with transport and protection from the elements and hostile action up to the moment of launch. As part of this function it provides the other subsystems with electrical, hydraulic and pneumatic power, together with temperature and environmental control and overall systems monitoring.

The navigation subsystem is responsible for determining the precise position, velocity and attitude of the submarine, and for transmitting this data in a continuous update to the fire-control subsystem. The principal means of achieving this is the ship's inertial navigation system (SINS), which records every movement of the submarine with reference to a stable platform

Above left: USS *Ohio* (SSBN 726) alongside a wharf while a Trident I missile tube is lowered in by crane. Such operations are carried out quite openly so that orbiting Soviet satellites can observe and record the operation.

Left: With each missile measuring 44ft (13.4m) in length and 83in (210.8cm) in diameter and weighing nearly 60 tons, the *Ohio* had to be a huge vessel to accommodate 24 Trident IIs.

Below: A comparison of fleet ballistic missiles shows that Soviet missiles are larger than their US counterparts, providing greater payload range but requiring bigger submarines.

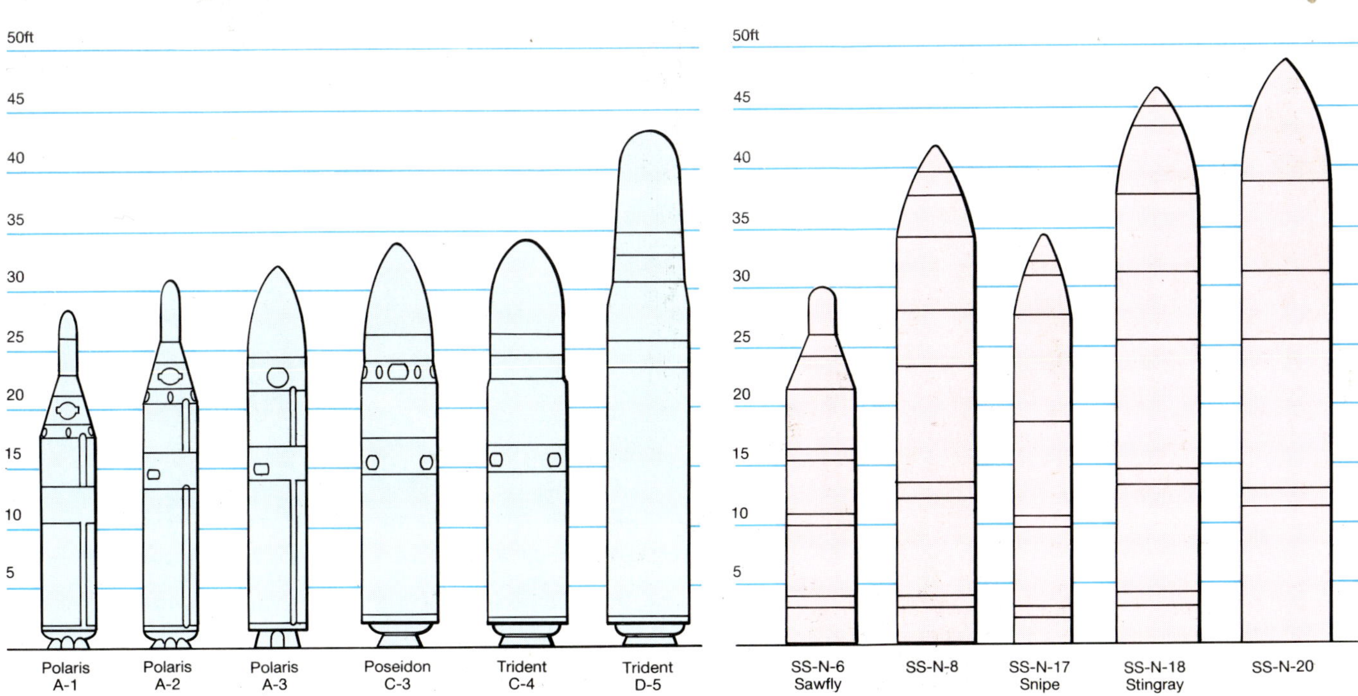

French SLBM installations

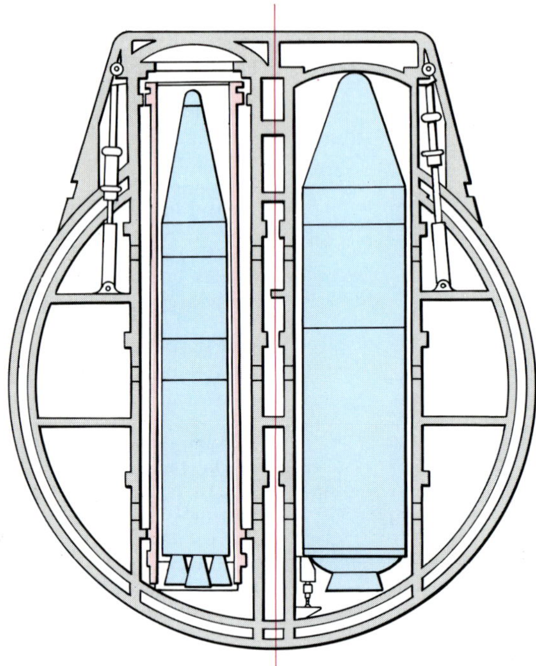

Above: The French Navy has developed its own strategic missiles with minimal help from other countries. This diagram compares the current MSBS (Mer-Sol Balistique Stratégique) M-20 with the new M-4 (same length but nearly 30 per cent greater diameter). The M-4 will be retrofitted in four of the five boats built to take M-20; the fifth, *Le Redoubtable*, is too old.

Above: A Missile Technician First Class (Submarines) sitting at the control room console during a simulated missile launch, part of the precommissioning activities aboard USS *Ohio* (SSBN 726). The control panel facing him was one bank of indicators and controls for each of the 24 missiles, but the actual launch must be authorised by two separate officers, each with his own key.

and which can be updated by external inputs such as optical and LORAN observations.

The fire-control subsystem is designed to prepare and fire the submarine's missiles in the shortest possible time. Its essential functions are to set up the missile guidance system inertial platform, to determine true launch bearing, to store and compute target data and to pass data to the missile guidance computer.

The launch subsystem is designed to store, protect and eject the missiles. The missiles are enclosed in capsules stowed inside shock-protected, watertight launch tubes. In some systems high-pressure air is used to eject the missile, while others have a steam generator; either method permits a flameless ejection from the submarine's launch tubes.

The missile is ejected with some force, but approximately 90ft (27.43m) clear of the tube the first-stage motor ignites to propel the missile through the surface, into the atmosphere and up into space. When the first stage has been expended it separates and falls away, and the second-stage motor ignites and propels the missile on its way; a third stage is also fitted to the latest missiles such as the Trident, SS-N-20 and SS-N-23.

During the second and third stages the missile's navigation subsystem is continuously measuring linear accelerations on the basis of its inertial system and altering the missile's trajectory to counteract any unwanted accelerations caused by outside forces. When at the correct

Left: The French MSBS M-4 is a three-stage missile fitted with six TN-70 150kT MRV warheads with a total area coverage (foot-print) of 81x189nm (150x350km) at a range of 2,162nm (4,000km).

Above: The computer suite on board USS *James Madison* (SSBN 627). Early-generation computer technology meant massive data banks were needed to store navigation, test and launch data.

Below: The internal systems of the three-stage Trident II D-5, which makes an interesting comparison with the MSBS M-4 opposite. The MIRVs are mounted on a circular bus in the third stage.

Below: MIRVs from a Trident missile heading toward the US testing area near Kwajalein Island. MIRVs enable one missile to attack a number of separate targets; accuracy is improving.

velocity, position and altitude for the assigned targets, the bus carrying the reentry vehicles (RVs) separates from the final stage of the main body of the missile and continues its flight, dropping individual RVs according to predetermined instructions fed to the missile computer just prior to launch. In the terminal phase the warheads reenter the atmosphere at steep angles, the ablative material with which they are coated absorbing the heat of reentry. Penetration aids such as decoys are released at the same time in order to deceive any anti-missile systems.

All SLBMs initially had just one reentry vehicle. However, as the technology developed it became possible to place multiple reentry vehicles (MRVs) on each missile, which were all aimed at the same target but, like shotgun pellets, improved the probability of actually hitting it. The next refinement was multiple independently targetable reentry vehicles (MIRVs) which, as their name implies, could be directed at different targets by being released from the bus at different points. The latest device is the manoeuvrable reentry vehicle (MARV), which contains a device to steer it precisely onto its target, so that its accuracy is independent of the launch accuracy or the precision of the deployment operation in space.

Warhead accuracy is assessed in terms of circular area probable (cep), being the radius in nautical miles of a notional circle centred on the point of aim into which 50 per cent of all warheads launched can be expected to fall. In early SLBM systems the missile navigation system could not be any more accurate than the submarine's SINS, on whose inputs it depended, so early single and multiple RVs were relatively inaccurate and had poor ceps, but the situation improved as both SINS and missile systems developed. Thus, Polaris had a cep of 0.5nm (926m), whereas Poseidon RVs have a cep of 0.3nm (550m), and those of Trident I one of 0.25nm (458m). Soviet RVs were originally even less accurate than those of the USA, but they have caught up: the cep of SS-N-20, for example, is 0.34nm (640m).

As long as the warheads remained fundamentally inaccurate they could only be used in a counter-value role – that is, targeted on cities and other area targets. The imminent advent of MARVs, with accuracies measured in tens of feet, will completely change the situation and there is a strong possibility that SLBMs will,

Trident II D-5

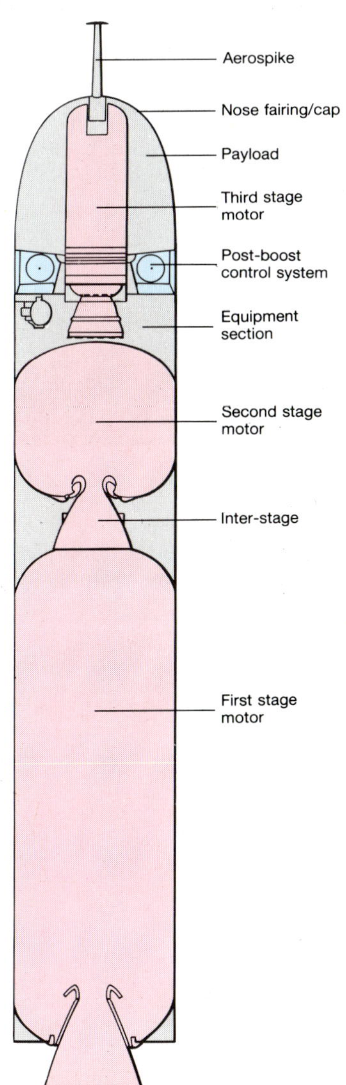

Left: **Sub-Harpoon is launched in a buoyant capsule which is jetisonned when the missile broaches the surface. Here the cap is seen being thrown upward prior to the booster ignition that will expel the missile from the tube.**

within the next few years, assume a counter-force as opposed to a counter-value role. It is estimated, for example, that the Mk 600 MARV to be fitted to Trident 2 will have a cep of 0.07nm (122m). This is a development with deeply significant implications for the balance of power.

The UGM-93A Trident I missile design requirement emphasised range. The fitting of an aerospike which extends after launch created the same aerodynamic effect as a sharp, slender nose, reducing drag by some 50 per cent, thus enhancing range; with a third-stage motor and improved fuel the missile has a range of 4,350nm (8,056km), compared to Poseidon's 2,500nm (4,630km). To overcome the inherent inaccuracies of the submarine's inertial system the Trident I's Mk 5 navigation system incorporates a stellar sensor which takes a star sight during the post-boost phase, enabling it to correct the missile's trajectory. The eight Mk 4 RVs, whose W-76 warheads each have a 100kT yield, have a reported cep of 0.25nm (457m), which may be reduced to 0.12nm (229m) in future. Their range is 4,230nm (7,833km) with a full eight RVs, or more with a reduced payload.

Trident I was designed to have similar payload and accuracy to

Above: Propelled by its booster the Sub-Harpoon missile accelerates away, with the cap still spinning through the air above it and the jetisonned capsule hidden by the cloud of propellant smoke.

Below: Sub-Harpoon's role is to deliver a 500lb (230kg) penetration/blast warhead over ranges of up to 60nm against surface ship targets. It is propelled by a solid rocket booster and a turbojet sustainer, and after reaching a maximum altitude of 5,000ft (1,500m) it cruises at high subsonic speed and low-level to minimise detection and the effect of countermeasures.

Above: The damage caused to a surface warship target by a Sub-Harpoon. The missile's warhead is constructed of steel and is designed to remain intact after penetration.

Sub-Harpoon launch and trajectory profile

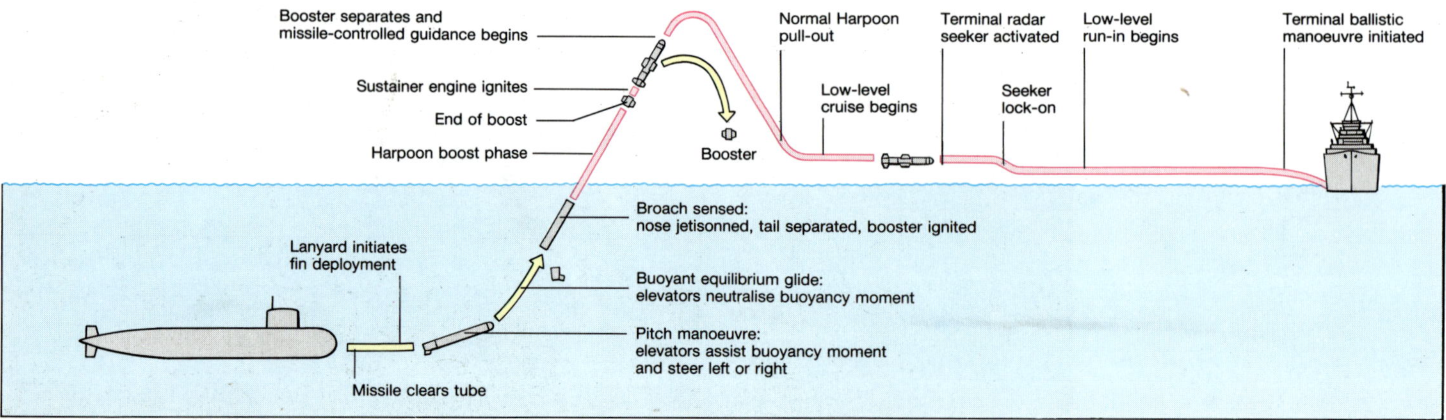

Above: A Tomahawk cruise missile launched from a submerged submarine off California approaches its target on San Clemente Island more than 400 miles (640km) away.

Below: Moments later the 1,000lb (450kg) warhead has detonated, totally destroying the aircraft target. Such a land-attack capability is new for submarines.

those of Poseidon but much greater range to allow the use of larger patrol areas. Trident II, however, is designed for greater accuracy; the resulting D-5 missile is longer – 45.8ft (13.96m) compared to 34.08ft (10.4m) – but only marginally greater in diameter, and is capable of carrying 14 RVs, though the SALT II agreement imposes a limit of ten.

The Mk 5 RV has a yield of 475kT and a cep of 0.19nm (122m), but the Mk 600 MARV may be carried in due course. The Mark 5 RV is reportedly designed to take different warheads tailored to the target assignment. Trident II is scheduled to equip 20 Ohio class SSBNs and four new British SSBNs. Each US boat will have 20 missiles, each with 10 RVs, for a total war load of 200 RVs, but the British government has stated that its Trident IIs will carry no more warheads in total than would have been carried by Trident I, which implies longer ranges and much greater flexibility in the Royal Navy's choice of patrol areas.

The Soviet Navy has recently introduced two new SLBMs, the SS-N-20 on the Typhoon class and the SS-N-23 on the Delta IV. The former is a three-stage solid-fuel missile with a design range of some 4,800nm (8,890km) carrying between six and nine RVs, and on October 21, 1982, the first Typhoon class SSBN conducted a simultaneous launch of four SS-N-20s; cep is 0.35nm (640m). Little is known of SS-N-23 except that, somewhat surprisingly, it is liquid-fuelled, and that it has greater throw-weight and accuracy than the SS-N-18 fitted to the Delta IIIs. It carries up to seven MIRVs.

The other nations currently possessing submarine-launched ballistic missile systems are the United Kingdom, France and China. The current British missile is the Polaris A-3, which was remotored in the early 1980s, and given a brand new front end of entirely UK origin and the designation Chevaline. Each missile is reported to carry six MRVs with a nominal yield of 40kT each, plus decoys. The older French SSBNs carry the M-20 missile, but the latest boats to join the fleet carry the new M-4 missile with six 150kT MIRVs. The Chinese SSBNs, of which two are believed to be in service with at least two more building, are armed with the two-stage solid propellant CSS-N-3. The first submerged launch of this missile took place on October 12, 1982, from the Chinese Golf class trials submarine, and its range is believed to be of the order of 1,500nm (2,795km). No other nations are known to be contemplating joining this very exclusive and extremely expensive club.

CRUISE MISSILES

The original naval strategic missile was the US Navy's Regulus, a cruise missile designed for use by both surface ships and submarines which was deployed with the US fleet in the 1950s and 1960s before being superseded by Polaris. The Soviet Navy has had tactical cruise missiles for many years, but in the 1970s the US Navy began development of a strategic SLCM which had the attraction of not being covered by existing arms limitation agreements: the BGM-109 Tomahawk is now in wide service with the US fleet and a similar missile, designated SS-N-21 by the US, is in service with the Soviet Navy.

Tomahawk was designed from the start to be fired by either surface ships from armoured box launchers or from standard submarines torpedo tubes. This target was achieved and Tomahawk is now being deployed in numerous surface warships as well as most Los Angeles class attack submarines. The earlier boats use Tomahawk in the torpedo tube mode with 12 missiles per boat, but a reappraisal by the US Navy concluded that this reduces their torpedo capacity. (Considering the vast expense that was incurred in ensuring that

Below: The French equivalent of Sub-Harpoon is the SM 39 version of the successful Exocet anti-ship missile. This picture shows the moment at which the booster rocket separates from the missile.

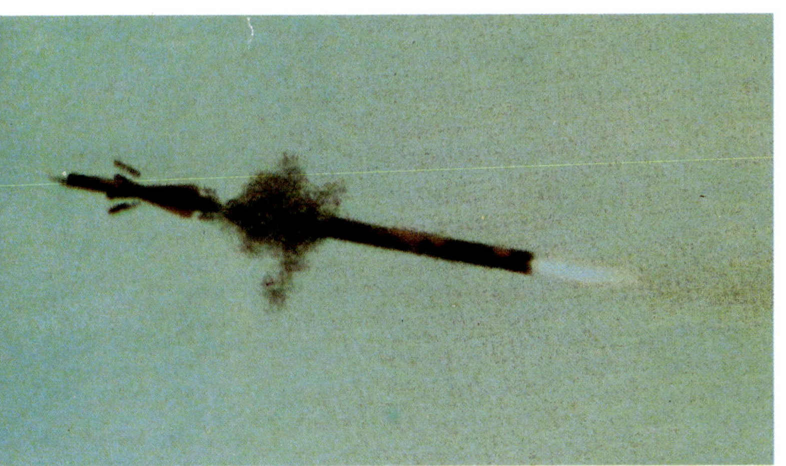

Right: This US DoD official drawing shows a Soviet Yankee class which has been converted from its previous role as an SSBN to test the new SS-NX-24 submarine-launched cruise missile.

Tomahawk would fit a standard torpedo tube, it seems extraordinary that nobody thought of this earlier.) As a result it has now been decided that SSN-721 and subsequent boats will have 15 vertical Tomahawk launch tubes in the bow casing between the outer and inner hulls, an installation which can be achieved without detriment to other on-board systems.

When fired from a submarine torpedo tube the Tomahawk missile is expelled hydraulically and a lanyard 33ft (10m) long runs taut then fires a rocket boost motor which burns for about seven seconds to drive the missile upwards in a 50° climb, through the surface and into the atmosphere. Once clear of the water the wings and tail extend and the gas turbine is started up; the missile then noses over to avoid radar detection and starts its cruise toward the target, travelling at very low level at about Mach 0.7 (550mph). The land attack version (T-LAM) is fitted with the Tercom-Aided Inertial Navigation System (TAINS) and when land is reached the Terrain Comparison (TERCOM) system starts to compare the ground beneath the missile with data stored on magnetic tape, which has been fed in from the submarine immediately prior to launch. TERCOM does not operate continuously, as that would alert the defences and attract countermeasures, but switches on when crossing the coast and at other selected reference points to update the inertial system, which remains in command throughout. The missile can be programmed to approach the target from any direction to confuse defences and its accuracy is incredible, a cep of approximately 33 yards (30m). The missile is dual-capable – that is, it can be fitted with either a high-explosive or a nuclear warhead, the nuclear warhead being the W-80, which has a 200-250kT yield. Range is 1,367 miles (2,200km).

There is also a ship-attack version (T-ASM). The main problem with T-ASM is that to exploit its capabilities fully it needs external target information; a system known as Outlaw Shark is being deployed to provide this, but two-way communication with submarines is notoriously difficult. T-ASM has a range of 250 miles (400km).

The UGM-84 Sub-Harpoon is an all-weather anti-ship cruise missile; the standard Harpoon missile has a diameter of 13.5in (0.343m), but the submarine version is fitted with a shroud to enable it to fit a standard 21in torpedo tube. As with Tomahawk a rocket booster drives the missile up through the water until, once airborne, the turbojet starts up. The warhead weighs 500lb (227kg) and the missile can attack ships up to 60 miles (97km) away. Sub-Harpoon is being purchased by various Western Navies,

Right: Many Western navies are equipped with the obsolescent Mk 37 torpedo but find modern replacements too expensive. Honeywell markets an upgrade kit to produce the NT 37E (New Technology Mk 37). The improvements are designed to make existing torpedoes 40 per cent faster and more than double their range, as well as improving reliability and tactical flexibility. Key to performance gains is the replacement of the electric drive by an Otto-fuel propulsion system.

Honeywell NT 37E modernisation kit

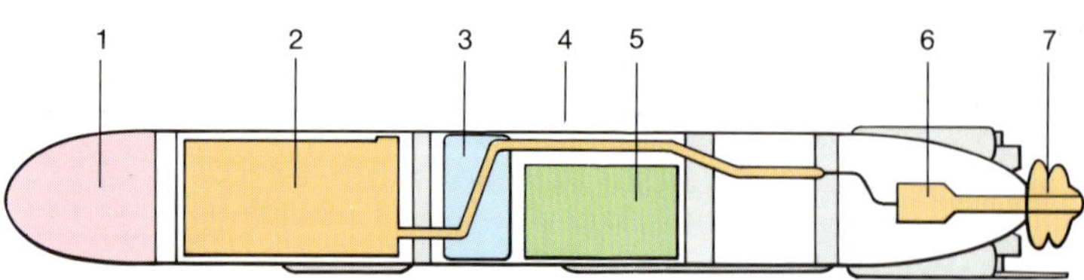

1 Self-noise reducing nose assembly
2 Fuel cell
3 Solid-state acoustic panel
4 Fuel lines
5 Software-programmable guidance and control system
6 Thermo-chemical Otto-fuel rotary piston cam engine
7 Contra-rotating propellers

Late-1940s electric torpedo

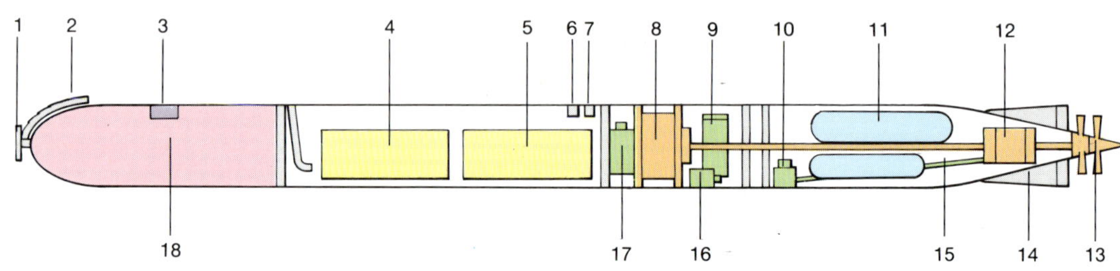

Above: A 21in submarine-launched, electric-powered torpedo, circa 1946. With a length of 18ft 11in (5.76m) and a weight of some 3,100lb (1,406kg), it had a speed of 30 knots and a range of 5,000 yards (4,572m).

1 Whisker
2 Net cutter
3 Detonator and firing pistol
4 Fore battery
5 After battery
6 Starting switch
7 Heating plug
8 Electric motor
9 Depth control gear
10 Hydrostatic valve
11 Compressed air bottle for driving gyro
12 Gearbox
13 Twin contra-rotating two-bladed propellers
14 Fin and rudder
15 Shafts to rudders
16 Gyro
17 Range-setting group
18 Warhead

Above: The torpedo stowage compartment on board the Royal Navy Polaris submarine *Resolution*. An SSBN would be most unlikely to use its torpedoes except in the direct emergency; it depends on stealth for survival. This picture fails to reveal the type of torpedo in use, though it is probably the old Mk 8. The Royal Navy, like many other navies, has spent vast sums on torpedo development since World War II, but only in the mid-1980s did these programmes start to bear fruit.

Krupp MaK weapons embarkation and loading system

Below: Loading torpedoes into submarines is inevitably a difficult task – the US Mk 48, for example, is 19ft (5.84m) long, 21in (533mm) in diameter and weighs 3,600lb (1,633kg). This diagram shows how the feat is achieved in the HDW Type 209/1400 and Thyssen TR-1700 export submarines. The torpedoes are mounted on tilting racks on the upper deck and then one at a time is lowered through a special tube until it rests at an angle on its tail empennage, with its nose just clear of the tube. It is then lowered by a block and tackle to rest in a rack, ready to be loaded into the tube.

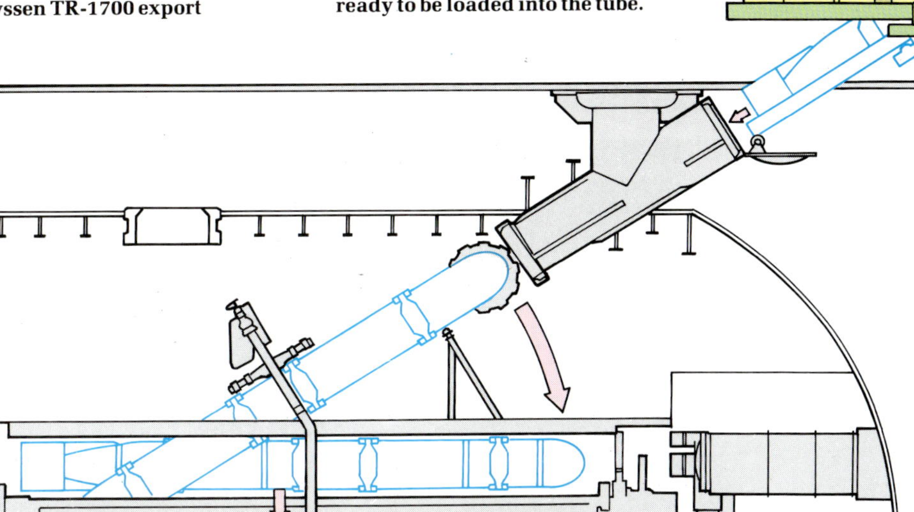

Below: Loader's eye view of one of the eight torpedo tubes in a Type 209 submarine, showing the guidance rails. The standard diameter of 21in (533mm) is universally accepted.

Above: A mine is loaded into a French Daphné class submarine. Although smaller than torpedoes these are still awkward to load – this French mine weighs around 1,875lb (850kg).

Above: The standard eight-tube assembly installed in HDW Type 209 export submarines. This is the heaviest battery of tubes in any submarines: most contemporary types have six or fewer tubes.

Below: RN submariner working on a Sub-Harpoon missile canister. This missile is fired from a standard 21in (533mm) torpedo tube and for every missile carried the torpedo load is reduced by one.

including those of the UK and Japan.

The Soviet Navy is producing similar systems. The smallest is the SS-N-21 which, like Tomahawk, has been designed to be fired from standard torpedo tubes. Possible applications for this missile include recent attack submarines such as those of the Victor III, Akula, Mike and Sierra classes, as well as the former Yankee class attack conversions of ballistic missile boats. According to data released so far, the SS-N-21 is a little larger than Tomahawk, with a range of the order of 1,620nm (3,000km).

However, the second Soviet naval SLCM, SS-NX-24, is much larger, with a length of around 40ft (12m) and a diameter of 4.1ft (1.25m); the highly swept wings have a span of 19.5ft (5.94m). Another Yankee class boat has been converted to be the trials platform for this new missile, which will probably become

Left and below: The decommissioned Royal Navy Type 12 frigate *Berwick* was the target in an October 1986 'Sinkex' to test the Marconi Tigerfish Mod 2 wire-guided torpedo. The torpedo was launched at long range from nuclear-powered attack submarine HMS *Tireless* in Sea State 5 and broke the back of the target, which then became a total loss. Tigerfish entered service in 1979 but was plagued by unreliability problems; these now appear to have been resolved.

Krupp MaK TR-1700 torpedo discharge system

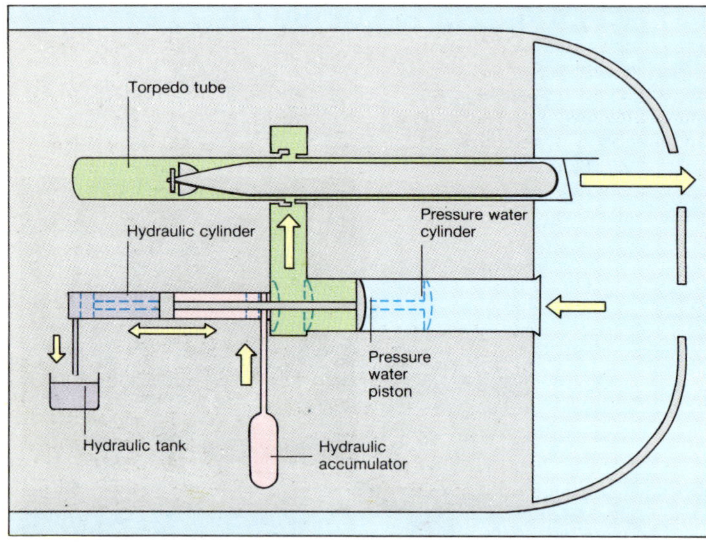

Above: The new Krupp MaK hydraulic system for ejecting torpedoes from their tubes. Such a technique is needed both for safety reasons with the new monopropellant fuels, and to enable torpedoes to be launched against the high water flow encountered when a submarine is travelling at high underwater speeds. Using compressed air would make life uncomfortable for the crew if a salvo of torpedoes were launched in quick succession, as the air would have to be vented into the submarine.

operational in 1987-88. Both systems are likely to be as accurate as their US counterparts, and presumably could also have either nuclear or conventional warheads.

TORPEDOES

Torpedoes have been the subject of some extremely expensive – and often abortive – development programmes. Current models have top speeds which are now being equalled or even surpassed by those of their quarry; the US Mk 46, for example, has a speed of 40 knots, exactly that of the Soviet Alfa class, so a stern chase is out of the question. The problem of lack of speed and range in torpedoes has been partly answered for surface ships by the use of helicopters and stand-off delivery systems such as Asroc and Ikara and, in the case of submarines, by Subroc, but there is still a need for a much faster torpedo. In the US this has led to the Advanced Capability (ADCAP) programme for the Mk 48 torpedo, which will raise its speed to 55 knots (63mph); the British Tigerfish is reported to be capable of a similar speed.

Most modern torpedoes have complicated guidance systems, typically including an

Whitehead A.184 submarine system

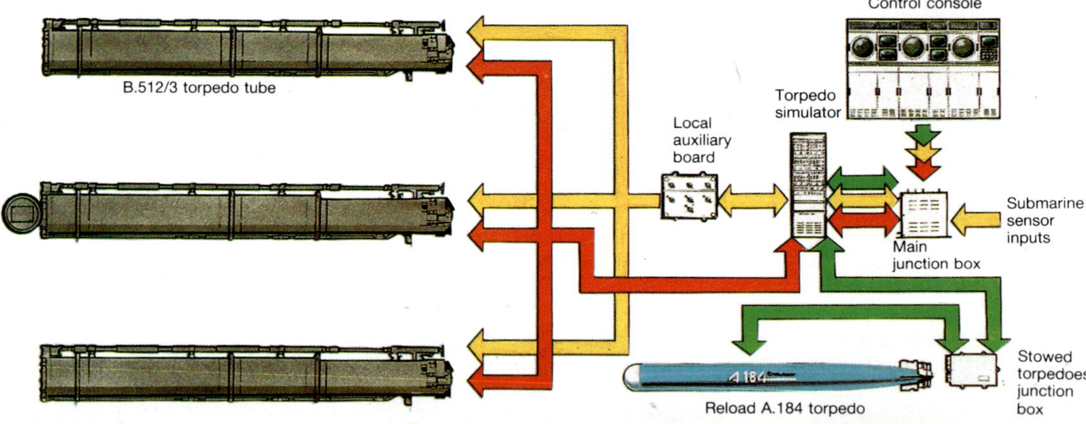

Above: The components of the Whitehead A.184 submarine torpedo system. The control console and main junction box are located in the control room, with the other units in the torpedo room. The optional torpedo simulator is used for attack team training and to check that the system is functioning properly. Right: The A.184 is 19ft 8in (6m) long and weighs 2,790lb (1,265kg). It combines wire guidance and acoustic homing and delivers a 550lb (250kg) warhead against surface or submarine targets.

FFV TP 617 torpedo

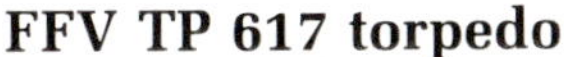

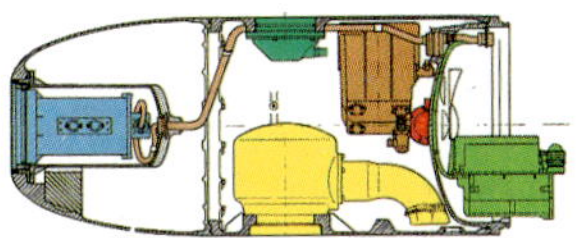

Above: The Swedish FFV Ordnance TP 617 21in (533mm) torpedo is an export version of the Swedish Navy's Type 613 long-range torpedo. Combining wire guidance and acoustic homing it weighs 4,078lb (1,850kg) and is 22ft 11½in (7m) in length. Designed for use against surface targets by surface ships and submarines, it can also be launched from shore-based submerged torpedo tubes by coastal defence units and has a thermal propulsion system which uses hydrogen peroxide alcohol and water as propellants. The TP 617 system is designed around a programmable digital computer which controls the homing system, communications between torpedo and launch vessel and the torpedo navigation system. The use of wire guidance enables the launch vessel to transmit orders to the torpedo, controlling its speed, depth, course and target data, while the torpedo is able to report its position, speed, course and depth, homing system parameters and target noise. Should communications be disrupted the computer automatically calculates the target's expected position and then guides the torpedo to the predicted point.

FFV TP 43X0 torpedo

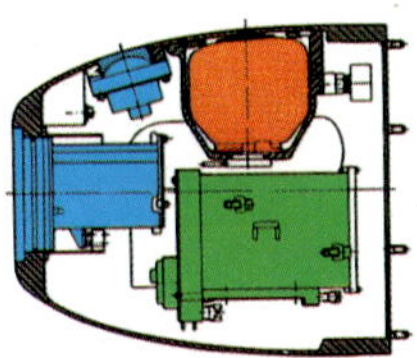

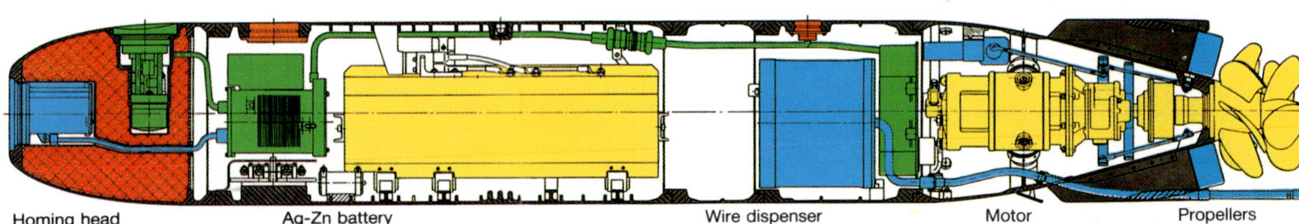

Above: The TP 43XO is intended for use by surface ships, submarines and helicopters against surface or submarine targets. Designed around a multi-processor computer system, it features a homing system optimised for use against very quiet submarines in shallow water and combines wire guidance with passive acoustic homing to give a high hit probability, even at long ranges. Speed, depth, course and target data commands can all be transmitted via the guidance wire, while the torpedo reports its position, speed, course, depth, homing system parameters and target noise all of which are stored in a computer.

active/passive sonar transducer working initially in the passive mode and changing to active automatically once the target indicates that it has become aware of the attack. Guidance wires linking the torpedo to the launching submarine are used to pass commands to the torpedo and sonar information back to the submarine's system.

Warhead design is also becoming more important as submarine hulls become ever stronger, the most difficult target being the enormous double-hulled Soviet Typhoon class SSBN. Some form of directed-energy (hollow-charge) warhead is necessary in such circumstances.

In general terms, however, the capabilities of current torpedoes lag behind those of the sonars that support them: they are slow, lacking in range and very noisy. Reports from the South Atlantic War of 1982, for example, abound with stories of both the Royal Navy and the Argentinian Navy suffering from malfunctioning torpedoes. The USSR and some other nations are experimenting with electric motors, but so far these have proved quiet but slow and lacking in range. Increases in either can only be obtained by more battery power, which means bigger torpedoes or smaller warheads. Torpedo sonar, too, needs to be improved and the US Defense Advanced Research Projects Agency is working on this, possibly heading towards a torpedo with on-board signal processing, coupled with an interactive fibre optic link with the parent submarine.

Krupp MaK mine-laying system

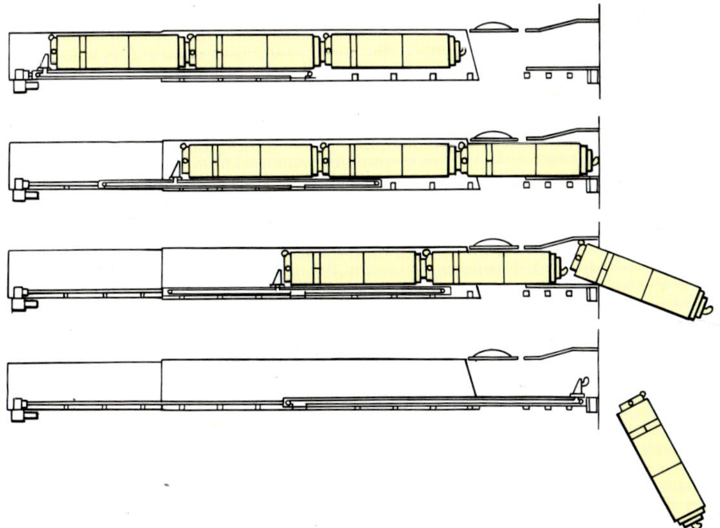

Above: The Krupp MaK mine-laying system employed with the torpedo tubes of the TR-1700 is typical of a number of such systems in use: three mines are carried in each tube, and a continuous belt on its mounting is pushed forward by a hydraulically operated piston, revolving as it moves, to expel each mine in turn. The forward part of the tube is designed to allow the mine to assume the correct angle prior to its final expulsion. Submarine-laid antisubmarine mines represent a major threat, particularly when laid in choke points or along known submarine routes. A submarine is unlikely to carry a complete load of mines but might use two tubes for this.

MINES

Mines are very effective antisubmarine weapons. Modern antisubmarine mines operate on one or more of a submarine's acoustic, magnetic or electrical signatures, and can be difficult to counter. Particularly effective is the US Captor (enCAPsulated TORpedo), a bottom-lying mine that fires a torpedo.

Most modern submarines can carry and deliver mines, launching them from their torpedo tubes. This results in precise, clandestine placement of the mines, but they can only be carried at the expense of the normal load of torpedoes. The West German Type 206 submarine, however, has an external mine-belt which enables it to carry 24 mines in addition to its torpedoes.

Sensors

Once submerged, the submarine is totally dependent upon its sensors, the most important of which is sonar. Most submarines have a large sonar mounted in the bow and many, such as American SSNs and SSBNs, are also fitted with conformal arrays. Hydrophones are also carried, usually with arrays near the bow, amidships and near the stern to give all-round coverage. One important submarine sensor is that for listening to its own noises: most navies use a surface ship to inspect their submarines as they leave harbour for noise emissions, but it is vital to continue such monitoring throughout the patrol to ensure that any new noise is detected and removed; otherwise it will act as a beacon for ASW forces.

Just as important as the sensors themselves is the ability to assimilate and process their outputs, and in this field modern technology is making a major contribution. Not only are modern processors able to handle vast amounts of information but they are much smaller and easier to use.

ACTIVE SONAR

Active sonar devices transmit acoustic pulses in the audio frequency band (approximately 5-20kHz) with pulse rates variable between 12.5 and 700 milliseconds. Such variations in frequency and pulse repetition rates are necessary to enable adjustments to be made to suit the prevailing oceanic conditions. Active sonars are used in submarines, surface vessels and air-deployed sonobuoys. They are also fitted in torpedoes, using somewhat higher frequencies – typically 20-35kHz – where shorter range is offset by improved spatial resolution.

One characteristic of all underwater transducers is self-noise, which is generated by the relative movement between the acoustic transmitter-receiver and the water surrounding it. A further complication is that transmission power is limited by the cavitiation effect of gaseous bubbles forming on the emitting surface. But the greatest difficulty for sonar is the complex variation in the prevailing conditions of the ocean described above, and to maximise a submarine's sonar capabilities it is frequently necessary to carry a variety of sonar sets, optimised for different regimes. And the major drawback of active sonar has always been that, by its very nature, an active system reveals its presence, enabling the target to detect it and take evasive action.

Active sonar systems comprise large numbers of transducers mounted in arrays. Cylindrical arrays are normally used in the bows of submarines, with beams formed electronically to give directional resolution, while Doppler shift in the return signal gives moving target indication, though a very slow moving target with a low Doppler in a noisy or high reverberation environment, such as a patrolling SSBN, is notoriously difficult to detect, even for another submarine.

The most effective current submarine active sonars are the US Navy's BQQ-5 installed in the Los Angeles class boats and the British Type 2020 now being installed in the Trafalgar class. The BQQ-5 has a bow-mounted spherical array which, using the Submarine Active Detection System (SADS) upgrade, is integrated with other onboard systems such as the Mine Detection and Avoidance Sonar (MIDAS), under-ice systems and the forward-mounted conformal array.

As with surface warships' sonars, further developments in submarine active sonar centre on maximising its excellent detection capabilities while trying to reduce its characteristic and revealing signature. Spread-spectrum transmission, in which the signal energy is spread over a wide range of frequencies in a pattern known only to the transmitter and receiver, may enable the signal to be lost in the general oceanic noise. It also increases the probability of overcoming fluctuations in the acoustic path inherent in the oceanic environment.

Parametric sonar depends on the mixing of two high frequencies to produce a different frequency (higher minus lower) which is then selected for transmission. Careful selection of the original frequencies will generate a suitable sonar signal (100-1,000Hz) with a narrow band-width, giving much better spatial resolution than can be obtained using a normal low-frequency beam. Although used in navigation, parametric sonar has been limited by problems over electronic scanning and in reducing transducers to a reasonable size.

PASSIVE SONAR

Of much greater importance to submarines is passive sonar, which involves no transmissions and so avoids giving away the submarine's position. The detector is the hydrophone, a very sensitive listening device optimised for submarine noises which can be assembled in a variety of arrays according to the particular task, although the only substantial

Los Angeles class combat systems

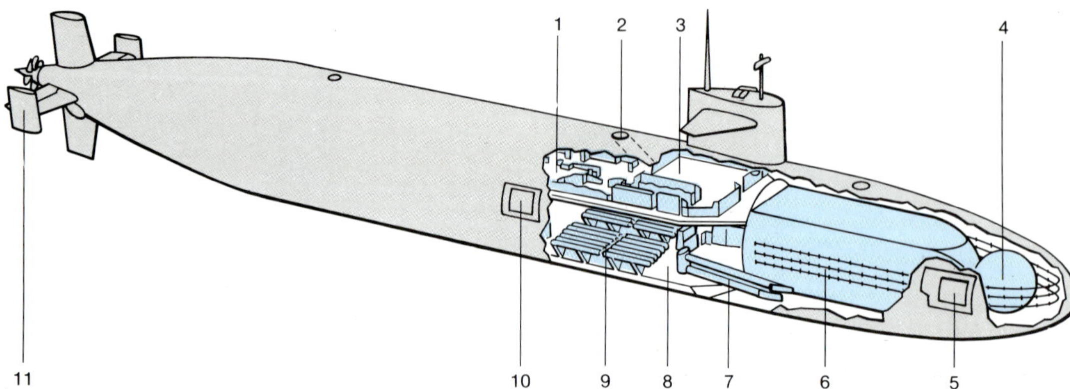

Above: The three hydrophone arrays on each side are for the passive underwater fire control system; not shown is the BQR-15 towed array.

1 Sonar control centre
2 Torpedo hatch
3 Attack control centre
4 BQQ-5 spherical sonar transducer
5 Bow hydrophone array
6 Conformal sonar
7 Torpedo tubes
8 Weapon control centre
9 Torpedo stowage
10 Midships hydrophone array
11 Aft hydrophone array

Below: A Soviet-built Foxtrot class submarine of the Indian Navy shows the sound-transparent, unpainted windows for the passive Herkules (bow) and active Feniks sonars.

Above: This cylindrical sonar bow array of 196 transducers is part of the Plessey Triton system. The array is stationary, the sonar beam steered electronically.

Krupp Atlas Elektronik CSU 83 sonar system

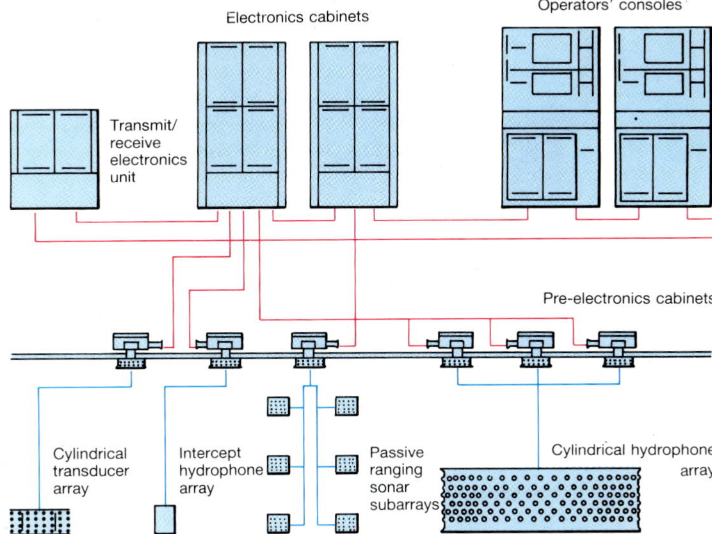

Right: Typical installation for small subs—passive panoramic, ranging and intercept sonars; active operating sonar; data handling system; and operator displays.

differences lie in the signal processing techniques. Narrow-band processing is an extremely sophisticated technique which requires spectrum analysers and great computer power to produce its information, although the current revolution in microprocessors is easing this problem. The USA is clearly ahead of the world, and especially of the USSR, in this area, which is of crucial importance in detecting and analysing slow-moving targets.

Broad-band processing looks at the full spectrum of incoming signals and separates constant noises such as submarine flow noise from random noises. It therefore tends to be used for the initial detection of a submarine target and for analysing the movement of the target relative to the searcher. It is most valuable where the noises emitted by the target exceed the ambient noise level when it makes possible rapid target detection as well as providing relatively accurate target bearings. New techniques such as transient acoustic processing – the detection and analysis of sudden brief noises such as a weapon launch or random machine noises – are adding to the effectiveness of

Left: HMS *Onslaught* with the somewhat elderly bow-mounted Type 2007 sonar. This class is also fitted with the Type 186 conformal array and the Type 197 sonar intercept/DF set atop the sail.

Below: HMS *Opossum*, one of nine Oberon class submarines being modernised by the fitting of the Type 2051 Triton sonar, which includes a clip-on towed array and new streamlined bow dome.

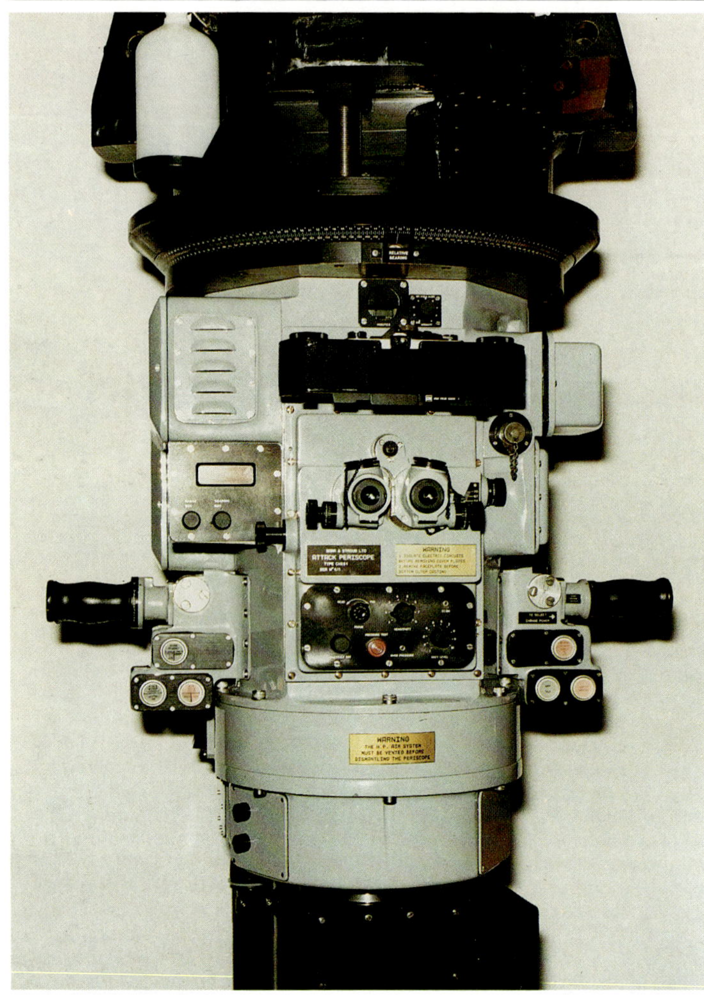

Above: Barr & Stroud 254mm attack periscope. Primary quantities in periscopes are size of lens and tube length; the former determines light gathering capability, the latter periscope depth.

Above: Barr & Stroud 254mm search periscope. Such modern periscopes can incorporate image intensifier, thermal imager, low-light TV camera, still camera and laser ranging.

broad-band processing.

Passive hull-borne sonars normally use the same arrays as the active systems and with a spherical submarine array using digital steering a coverage of some 270° horizontally and 50° vertically can be obtained. Towed arrays now being used by submarines comprise large numbers of hydrophones – several hundred in some cases. The BQQ-25 system used by the US Navy's Los Angeles class SSNs, for example, has a cable 2,624ft (800m) long and 0.37in (9.5mm) in diameter, which is tapered at both ends to reduce drag. The array contains the hydrophones and electronics, which include a multiplexer to reduce the wiring running through the towing cable. The manoeuvrability of the towing submarine is limited, as the array needs to be straight to obtain a coherent signal, and speed is also restricted since arrays oscillate above a certain speed, generating false readings and giving out signals detectable by other hunters. One particular advantage of towed arrays for submarines is that they provide a rearward-looking capability not available by any other means.

For submarines, the problem of stowing towed arrays is a serious one. Many classes have the cable clipped on by specially-trained divers as they leave harbour on patrol and removed as they return: although an apparently slow and clumsy method, this is a simple solution which has the added benefit of reducing the number of arrays needed, as they can be transferred from one submarine to another. The Los Angeles class boats, however, stow their BQR-23A STASS (Submarine Towed Array Sonar System) arrays in long tubes installed between the pressure hull and the outer casing, with the winch in the forward ballast tank.

Above: An RN photographer fits a camera to a periscope. Polaroid or 35mm cameras can be used for intelligence gathering; time and bearing data are injected automatically into each frame.

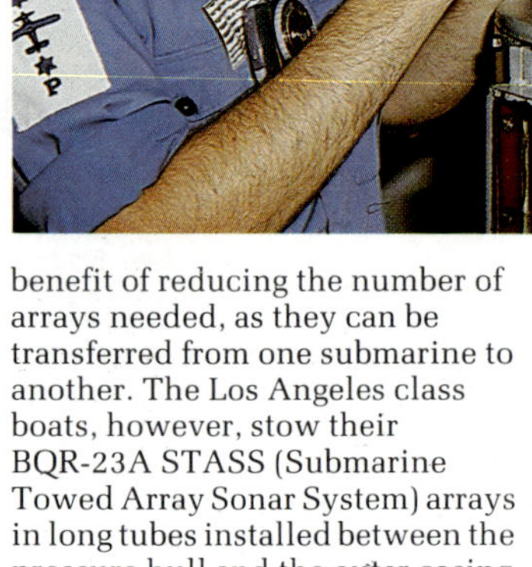

The Soviet Navy also uses towed arrays, and has developed a series of installations. In one, a large pod containing the array and winch is mounted atop the vertical rudder on submarines such as those of the Victor III and Sierra classes. This pod will undoubtedly generate both noise and hydrodynamic drag, and another type of fitting consists of an array dispensed from a comparatively narrow tube on top of the vertical rudder, with the storage drum and winch clearly inside the hull itself. This device has only been seen so far on the latest unit of the Oscar class SSGN.

PERISCOPES

All submarines are fitted with periscopes, which in the early days were the only means by which a submerged boat could sense its surroundings. Normally two periscopes are fitted, one for general use and a second, much smaller device for attacking surface ships. Periscopes create two problems for submariners. The first is that in use the head of the periscope is obviously above the surface of the sea and either the tube itself or the wake it generates is detectable both visually and by radar. The second is that in order to use the periscope the submarine must be close to the surface, which makes it more vulnerable than it is at depth, and great care and efficient control surfaces are needed to maintain the boat at the correct depth: it requires only a very minor miscalculation or a sudden change in trim as the result of a torpedo launch for the fin or even part of the hull to break the surface.

The tube, like any long device moving through a liquid, vibrates. Vibration normally starts at about 10 knots depending on the exposed length, rigidity and supporting structure of the tube. A submarine

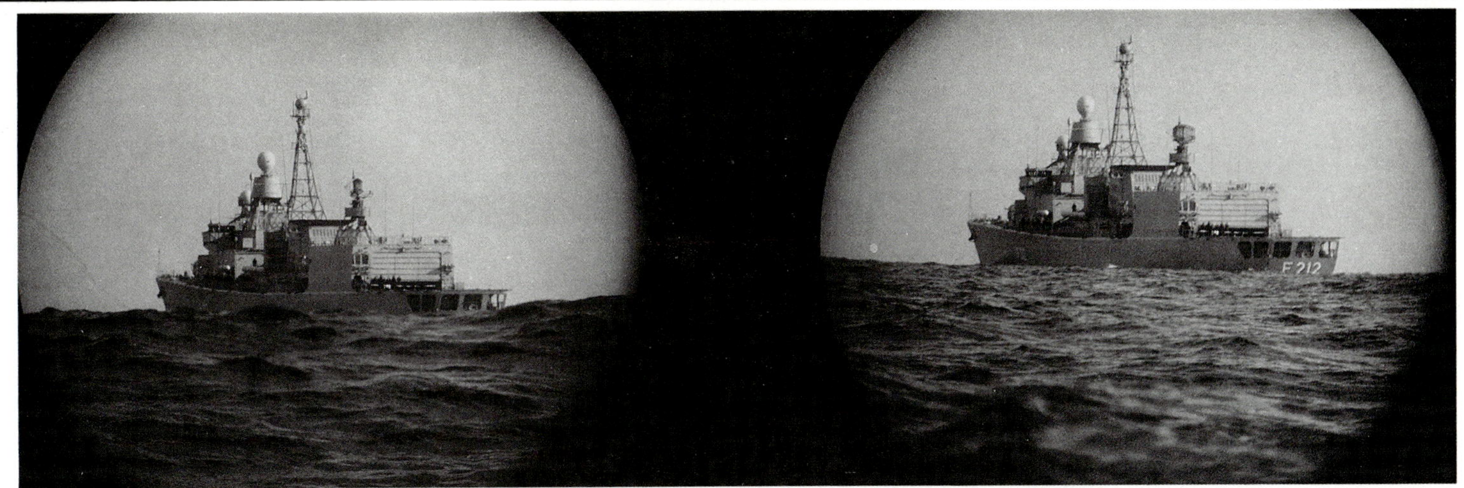

Above: Two photographs taken through HMS *Oberon*'s periscope of the West German Bremen class guided missile frigate *Karlsruhe*. The photographs have exceptional clarity.

Right: Sail of a Soviet Kilo class, diesel-electric submarine. The forward mast is the search periscope, while the after mast carries an ESM device. The cage antenna is for direction-finding.

Below: The comprehensive fit of antennas and sensors mounted in the sail of a USN Sturgeon class SSN. The relative heights of the masts and length of fairwater are not in true perspective.

Sturgeon class antennas and masts

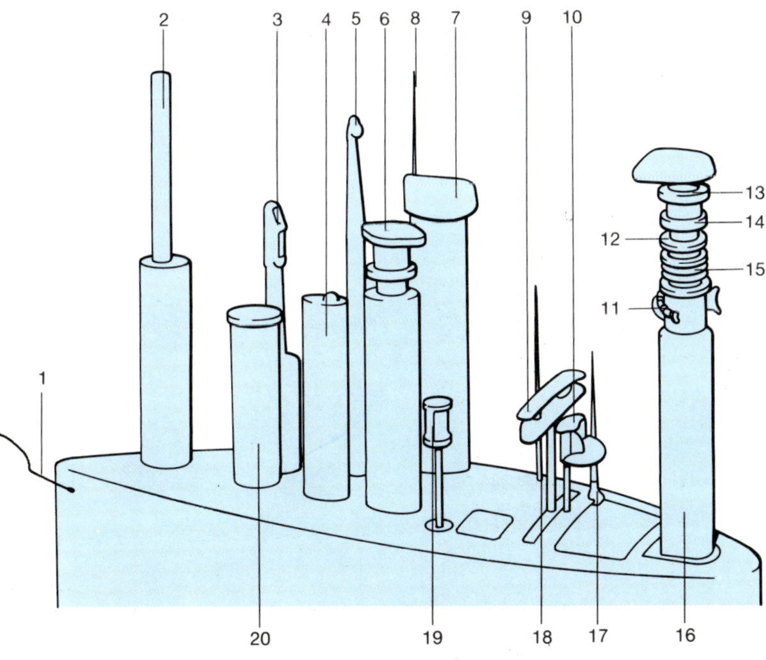

1 AS-1554/BRM(20) floating wire antenna
2 AS-1792/BRA-21 helical antenna
3 Observation periscope
4 AS-1201/BPX IFF/UHF antenna
5 Attack periscope
6 AS-1907/BRD-6 direction-finding antenna
7 Snorkel induction mast
8 AT-497/BRC snorkel whip antenna
9 AS-1640A/BPS-14 surface search radar antenna
10 Masthead light
11 AS-994/BLR directional antenna
12 AS-1584/BLR omni-directional antenna
13 AS-1071A/BLR directional antenna
14 AS-1649/0 omni-directional antenna
15 AS-962/BLR directional antenna
16 ECM/DF antenna mast
17 AT-774A/UR portable emergency whip antenna
18 AT-441/MRC portable emergency whip antenna
19 Identification beacon
20 AT-317F/BRR loop antenna

commander will frequently find himself torn between the wish for a long tube to enable him to keep the submarine at greater depth and a short tube which will not vibrate until higher speeds are reached, so that he does not need to slow down if he wishes to make observations during an attack run. The periscope lens is like that in a camera: the larger the diameter the better the field of view and the more limited the precision, and vice-versa, while the greater is the diameter of the periscope tube the greater are the turbulence and surface wake it will generate.

Like so much defence equipment these once straightforward devices are now highly sophisticated. The optical systems normally include split eyepieces to give a quasi-optical effect to reduce eyestrain, while bearing and range are estimated by a microprocessor and fed automatically into the fire control system. Various displays and data are injected into the eyepiece, and a laser rangefinder is frequently included in the attack periscope system, giving an accuracy of ±3ft (1m). Search periscopes can include artifical horizon sextants designed to take extremely rapid sights to update the boat's inertial navigation system, sensors to give warning of electronic threats, and either thermal imagers or image intensifiers to give bad-weather and night capabilities. A TV camera can also be installed to enable more than just one operator to see what is being observed.

ELECTRONIC SENSORS

Modern submarines carry a considerable range of sensors and other devices mounted on extendible tubes in addition to the traditional periscopes, schnorkel and diesel exhausts. The fin array can include radio antennas matched to various frequency bands, radio direction finding antennas, and surface- and air-search radars. The fins of the Los Angeles class boats, for example, contain no fewer than 12 masts of various lengths and diameters. Soviet submarines have similarly comprehensive arrays.

Air- and surface-search radars, essential for submarines running on or near the surface, use small rotating antennas mounted on masts. A widely used example is the French Thompson-CSF Calypso III, an I-band set with an output power of 70kW and a claimed range of 20nm against a $1m^2$ airborne target. Performance against surface targets is limited somewhat by the lack of height of the antenna.

Such masts have always been capable of withdrawal into the fin. The traditional practice of leaving the top of the fin exposed, however, results in considerable turbulence and consequent noise so modern submarines have remotely controlled hatches which cover the recesses when the various masts are not in use. This is particularly noticeable on Soviet submarines.

Communications

Communication with submerged submarines has been a problem since the earliest days. Initially there was none at all, but since they depended on stealth for success and survival this suited submariners well. There has, however, always been a need for the fleet commander to pass orders, to update intelligence and to receive information in return. Unfortunately, the unique nature of the oceans, which creates difficulties in other spheres such as detection, also impedes communications.

The general nature of the technical problem is quite simply stated: the oceans attenuate radio waves and the higher their frequency the greater the loss in strength. In addition, radio waves are refracted and diffracted in the same way as sound waves, so the best form of communication to a submerged submarine is a radio signal of very low frequency, but an immutable law of communications is that the lower the frequency the lower are the information content and the speed of transmission. It follows that the most reliable communications are achieved when the submarine is on or very near the surface, but this lays the submarine open to detection by nearby surface units, by satellite or by radio direction-finding.

VERY LOW FREQUENCY RADIO

The VLF band lies between 3kHz and 30kHz and can be received at depths of up to 50ft (15m). Submarines are normally fitted with two types of antenna systems to receive VLF transmissions. The first is a long trailing wire antenna; in the US Navy uses wires some 1,673ft (510m) long. The second is a loop antenna mounted in a plastic buoy, which is unreeled by a slow-moving submarine at its operating depth. Although this reduces the submarine's chances of being detected, such an antenna system is itself vulnerable, because the wire vibrates as it moves through the water, emitting acoustic signals which are detectable by sonar, while the buoy, if very close to the surface of particularly clear water, may be detected visually from the air.

Shore-based VLF transmitting antennas are big, vulnerable and expensive. According to published information, the US has seven major VLF transmitting stations, while the USSR has ten, of which five have transmitting power greater than 100kW, plus 16 smaller stations. NATO has two VLF transmitters and the British one 15kHz station at Rugby. The US Navy also has the TACAMO airborne ELF system described below.

EXTREMELY LOW FREQUENCY RADIO

The ELF band covers the range 300Hz to 3kHz and has been received by submarines at depths of up to 328ft (100m), although it is claimed that depths of up to 1,300ft (400m) are feasible using advanced reception equipment and antennas. ELF is also relatively invulnerable to jamming and nuclear explosion effects, which makes it eminently suitable for communicating with second-strike SSBNs. There are, however, two major problems, the first being that the information transmission rate is very low. The US Navy Seafarer system proposed in the 1970s would have had a transmission rate of only about 10 bits per minute, while the later Austere ELF system is said to require 15 minutes to transmit a three-letter group. It is claimed, however, that by using highly compressed codes some 17,500 different messages can be communicated using three-character groups.

In some of the earliest US trials, in 1963, USS *Sea Wolf* used a

Above: The US Navy's extremely low frequency (ELF) test facility at Clam Lake in Wisconsin. ELF is highly survivable, but it takes 15 minutes to transmit a three-letter group; even so, some 17,500 different messages can be sent using highly compressed codes.

Right: The first flight of the prototype Boeing E-6A TACAMO on February 19, 1987, was a 30-minute ferry trip from Renton to Seattle. The E-6 is scheduled to replace the EC-130A/Q aircraft, some of which have been in service for many years.

Below: A US Navy crew tests the facilities in a mock-up of the E-6A's very spacious communications centre. The TACAMO system provides communications links between the National Command Authority and the Poseidon and Trident SSBN fleet.

1,000ft (304.8m) trailing wire antenna to detect test signals at 250Hz, 156Hz, 125Hz and 78Hz. With the antenna at a depth of some 30ft (9m) reception was achieved at a range of 1,720nm (3,200km), but the range dropped to some 500nm (850km) when the antenna was taken deeper.

The second problem is that the land-based antennas cover such a large area that their positioning becomes a major difficulty, particularly in the West. The US Navy's Sanguine system, designed in the 1960s, would have had an antenna array covering an area of some 6,564 square miles (17,000km^3), while the much less ambitious Seafarer system would have covered some 3,088 square miles (8,000km^2).

In the 1970s the US Navy set up a test facility at Clam Lake, Wisconsin, which used telephone poles to carry an X-shaped centre-driven antenna, each arm of the cross being seven miles (11.25km) long, with a transmission power of only two watts. In 1976 a submarine travelling at a speed of 16 knots at a depth of 427ft (130m) under 33ft (10m) of Arctic sea-ice received signals from Wisconsin. This test facility is already used for operational message traffic and is to be used in combination with a second site at K.I. Sawyer AFB, Michigan, to provide a full operational system by FY88. This is far short of what the US Navy wants, but is a distinct improvement on what exists now.

TACAMO

The US Navy's operational TACAMO (Take Charge and Move Out) system, its primary current means of communication with submerged submarines, especially SSBNs, is regarded as being far more survivable than any other. The system is based on Lockheed EC-130A/Q Hercules aircraft deployed in two squadrons, one responsible for the Pacific and the other for the Atlantic. The aircraft act as airborne radio relays between the National Command Authorities and the submarines, using various transmission means in the VLF, LH, HF and UHF bands. VLF transmissions are achieved using a 200kW transmitter and a trailing-wire antenna some 6.2 miles (10km) long, with a drogue parachute at the end. When it becomes necessary to transmit the aircraft is flown in a continuous tight circle, which results in over 70 per cent of the wire hanging straight down and acting as a relatively efficient vertical antenna. One aircraft is airborne over each ocean at any time, with another at 15 minutes' notice on the ground. Missions last around 10 or 11 hours, of which about seven are spent loitering on station, and make random use of suitable airfields.

The TACAMO fleet currently comprises a few EC-130A aircraft and rather more EC-130Qs, a total of around 20 airframes. A new airframe, the E-6, based on the well-proven and widely used C-135 is under development and will enter service in 1989. This aircraft will fly at 25,000-30,000ft (7,620-9,144m) and its VLF antenna will be 26,000ft (7,925m) long. Fifteen aircraft are to be procured at a system cost of some $2,000 million.

COMMUNICATIONS BUOYS

Various types of buoy are used to communicate with submarines. One example is the SSQ-86 (XN-1) down-link communication (DLC) buoy, which is used to transmit a programmed message to a submerged submarine without the

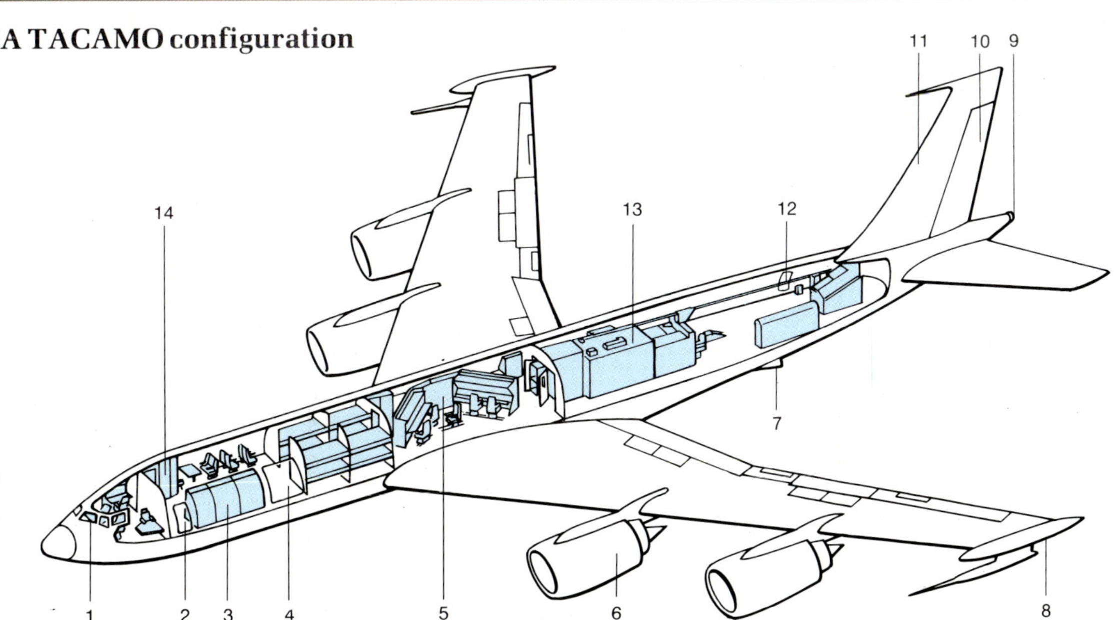

1 E-4B-type electro-magnetic pulse (EMP) resistant windshields
2 E-3A escape chute and spoiler have been deleted
3 VHF/UHF and HF radios; altitude alert, windshear and other systems
4 EMP-hardened 707-320 cargo door
5 Operators' stations
6 CFM-56 engines with 72-hour engine oil tanks
7 Long-wire drogue nest
8 Wingtip satellite antenna
9 Short-wire drogue nest in tail cone
10 Improved rudder boost
11 HF2 shunt antenna
12 Door modified for bailout
13 TACAMO mission equipment installed in place of E-3A equipment
14 Electronic support measures display added at navigator's station display

Above: The Boeing E-6A is yet another version of the ubiquitous Boeing C-135, the military progenitor of the civil 707 airliner. Total cost of the 15-strong force will be $1,600 million, and eight aircraft are earmarked for the Pacific and seven for the Atlantic fleets. The AWACS airframe is utilised, but without the rotodome and pylon. Generating plant gives radiated powers of some 200kW and a 2.5-mile (4km) trailing-wire antenna is deployed from a drum in the tail.

Above: Aircraft can communicate with submarines using buoys such as this Sippican SUS Mk 84, which is 15in (38cm) long, 3in (7.62cm) in diameter and weighs 6.5lb (2.95kg). Pulsed 3.5kHz and 2.95kHz tones pass messages such as: "emergency, stay down", "unknown submarine: surface to be identified" and "establish communications".

Right: The XSTAT expendable tactical transceiver enables submarines to establish two-way communications with aircraft on a 350MHz UHF-AM frequency over ranges, depending on the aircraft's altitude, of up to 100nm. The system uses a buoy launched from a standard tube in the submarine: a lifting body tethered to the submarine hull contains a reel of wire attached to the buoy, which rises to the surface; the buoy also has spooled wire, the two spools giving torsionless pay-out. Once on the surface the buoy provides up to one hour of two-way voice communications.

Submarine laser communications

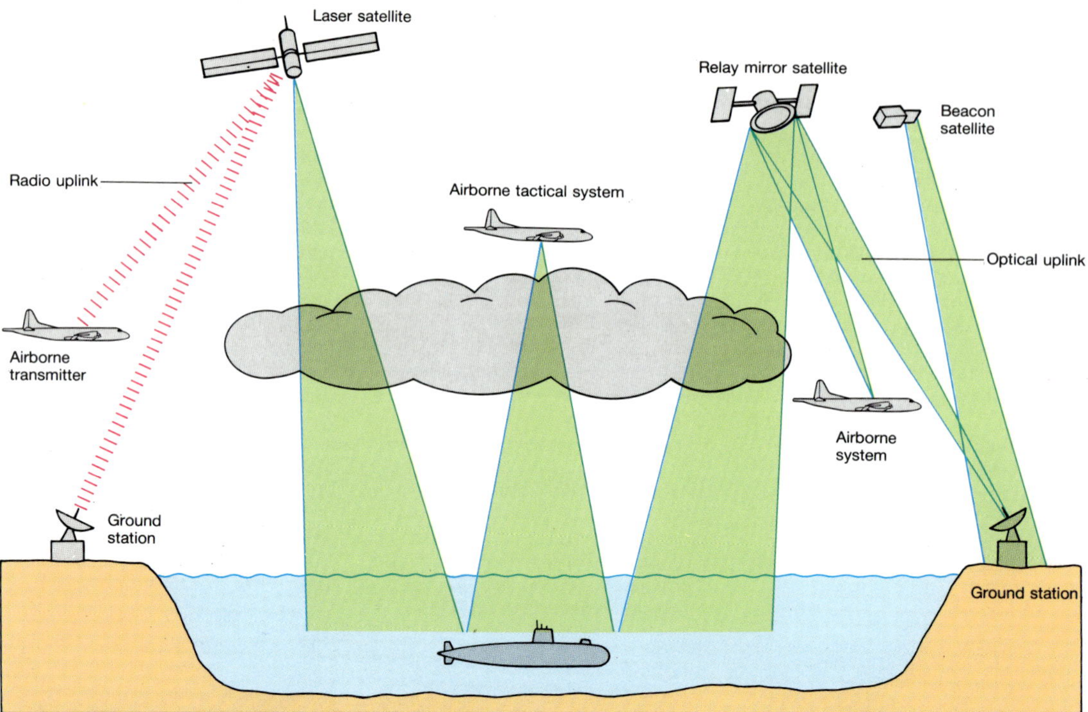

Above: For strategic communications to subs, the Americans propose to use space-based (left) or ground-based (right) blue-green lasers to penetrate the ocean.

submarine revealing its position. Mounted in a standard A-sized sonobuoy, the DLC buoy can be launched from any suitably equipped aircraft, or simply thrown overboard from a surface ship. The message, consisting of a maximum of four groups of three characters, is programmed into the buoy using a single push-button switch. On entering the water the buoy transmits the message once near the surface then descends to a predetermined lower depth where it transmits a second time, pauses for five minutes at the same depth, transmits a third time and then scuttles itself. The whole process from water entry to scuttling takes about 17 minutes.

BLUE-GREEN LASERS

There is an optical window in the blue-green part of the spectrum which enables transmissions to penetrate the ocean a substantial distance. The main problem is that the power requirements are considerable and satellites are not yet capable of carrying equipment of the necessary power. However, this difficulty may be overcome by using a ground-based laser in conjunction with a space-based mirror, with adaptive optics being used to produce a cohesive beam. Such a system could have a data rate up to 300 times better than that of an ELF system, but would not penetrate to the same depth. One interesting aspect of such a system is that while an aircraft which unintentionally passed though such a beam would not itself be in any danger, aircrew and passengers without laser glasses could suffer eye injuries.

COMMUNICATION FROM SUBMARINES

Any transmission, whatever part of the electromagnetic spectrum it uses, is liable to interception by hostile agencies and so risks giving away the submarine's position. For many years submarines could only transmit using the high frequency (HF) band (3-30MHz), which is relatively easy to intercept and to use for direction-finding (DF). The German Navy in World War II used

Sippican XSTAT operation

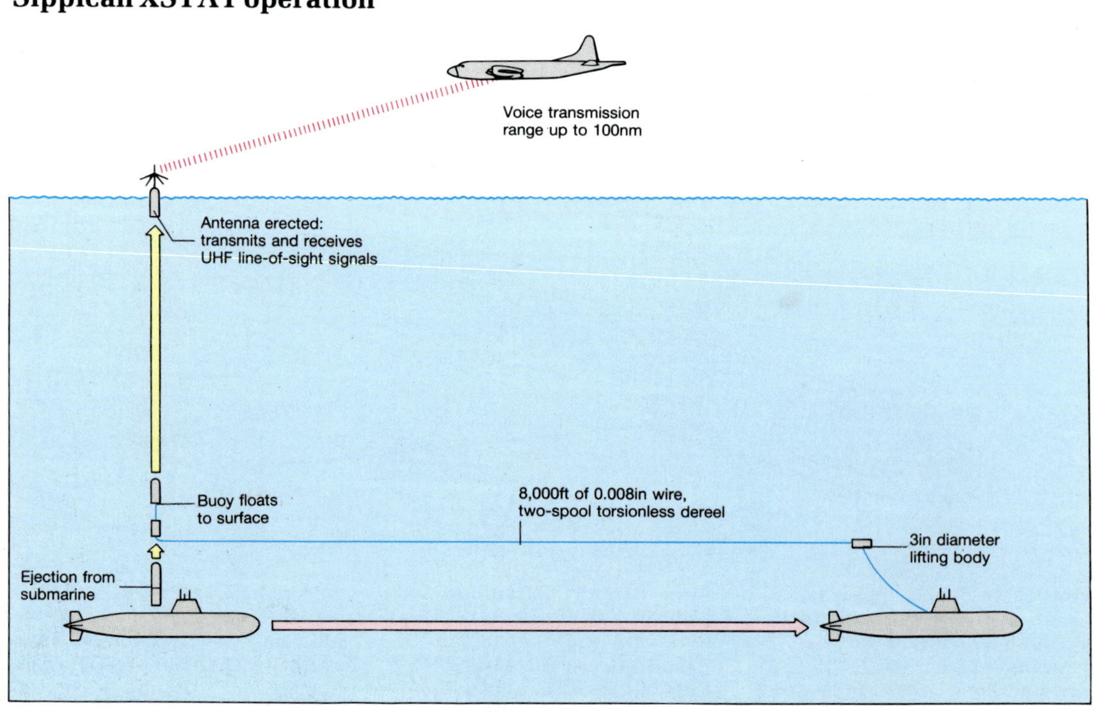

Left: A US Navy UH-1 helicopter hovers over the exposed periscope masts of a submarine, achieving optimum communications conditions.

Left: For the full range of standard radio communications submarines need mast-mounted antennas. Seen here under test at the UK National Maritime Institute is a hydrodynamic, non-hull penetrating integrated communications mast made of glass-reinforced plastic which the designers, Plessey Naval Systems, claim will improve communications performance and permit more flexible operating.

Below: Communications between submarines are particularly difficult; sonar can be used, but it reveals the submarines' presence. It is rare for two submarines to meet on the surface in mid-ocean, but this Soviet Victor III SSN (foreground) and Oscar SSGN did in the North Atlantic in 1985.

to exchange considerable amounts of radio traffic between its headquarters and the boats at sea; the transmissions from the HQ were monitored and, because the Enigma codes had been broken, the Allied hunting forces frequently knew as much about the U-boats' instructions as the latter did themselves. Further, because of the demands by Dönitz' HQ for information, the boats were forced to transmit at sea and could be DFed with ease and hunted down. Once the Germans appreciated this they took a variety of steps to minimise transmission times, some of them procedural but one of which was a technological means – the Kurier burst transmission system – whereby the information was compressed electronically and then transmitted in a very short squirt transmission. Such HF burst transmissions are still used; they are by no means undetectable, but they do make the interceptors' job much more difficult. The HF antennas are mounted on extending masts carried in the submarine's fin.

Satellite communications in the UHF and SHF bands are a boon to submarines, as transmissions are much less easy to detect from ground monitoring stations, although they can be detected by suitably equipped aircraft and by other satellites. Most submarines now carry mast-mounted satellite antennas which can be used when running on the surface or at periscope depth.

If real-time communications are not essential then transmitting buoys such as the US Navy's BRT-1 can be used. Containing a cassette recorder and radio transmitter, this device is released by the submarine and when on the surface transmits a message of up to four minutes' duration, with a preset delay of between 15 and 60 minutes. With a one-hour delay in transmission, a submarine travelling at 20 knots could be anywhere in an area of 1,664 square miles (4,310km^2) by the time transmission takes place.

Communications to surface ships and to other submarines are just as much of a problem. Buoys such as the BRT-1 can be used to pass messages which are not time-urgent to ships, and in certain circumstances acoustic underwater telephones can be used. Otherwise, communications to other submarines, must be passed back to base for retransmission on the normal fleet broadcast services.

Surface Antisubmarine Warfare

There is considerable discussion in most navies on the most effective way of combating submarines. Submariners themselves are almost unanimous in their view that the best anti-submarine platform is another submarine, while surface mariners and aviators tend to maintain that a combination of warships and aircraft in conjunction with area surveillance systems such as SOSUS give the best results. The use of submarines in anti-submarine warfare is described elsewhere; this chapter deals with the technology of surface warships and aircraft in the ASW battle.

ACTIVE SONAR

The primary means used by surface warships over the last 30 or so years to find submarines has been active sonar. The sonar dome in a warship is mounted either in the bow or under the ship's keel and a particular problem for such hull-mounted sonars is the self-noise generated by the relative movement between the acoustic transmitter-receiver and the water surrounding it.

Active sonar systems comprise large numbers of transducers mounted in arrays. Surface ships use flat circular or rectangular arrays; a typical modern system, the US Navy's SQS-26, has 576 transducer elements in a cylindrical array, housed in a large bulbous dome at the foot of the stem. The presence of such a bow-mounted sonar is usually indicated by a sharply overhanging bow, as on most US and Soviet ASW ships, whereas a less acute bow angle, such as those seen on British ships, normally indicates a sonar dome mounted in the keel. All these arrays are fixed and beams are formed electronically to give directional resolution, while Doppler shift in the return signal gives moving target indication.

Developments in active sonar for surface ships are aimed at maximising its excellent detection capabilities while trying to reduce its characteristic and revealing signature. The principal methods under investigation are spread-spectrum transmission, parametric sonar as described in the chapter on sensors.

PASSIVE SONAR

The major drawback of active sonar has always been that it reveals its presence to the target. A submarine will normally detect a surface warship's active sonar transmissions long before the warship itself realises a target is there, and while the presence of an anti-submarine aircraft is very difficult for a submerged submarine to detect, its proximity immediately becomes apparent when an active sonar buoy starts to transmit. Passive sonar is, therefore, growing rapidly in importance since, because it makes no transmissions, it ensures that it does not betray the hunter's position.

Hydrophones are often deployed in towed arrays, which limit the speed and manoeuvrability of the towing ship, making it very vulnerable

Simrad SS242 sonar system

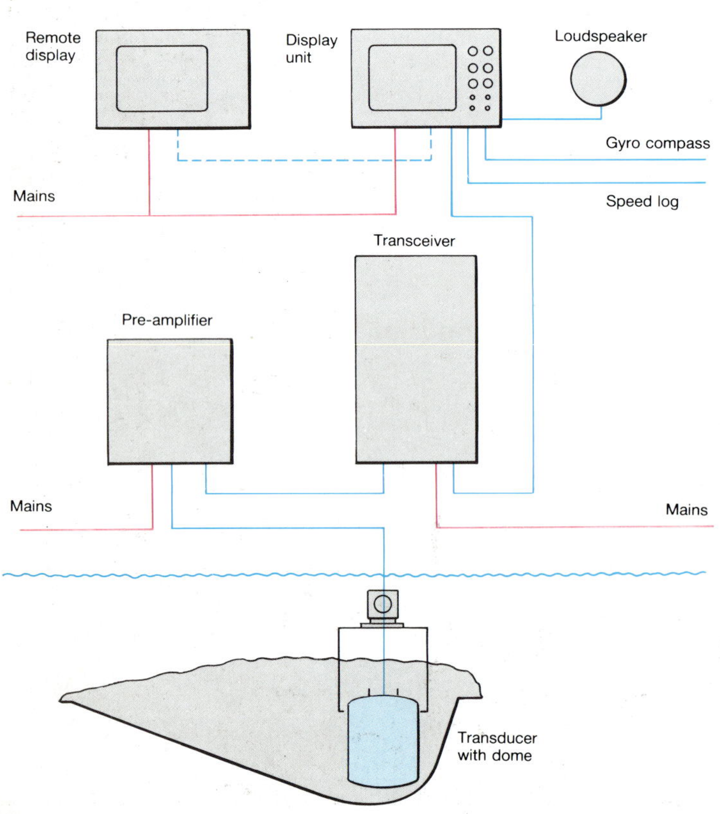

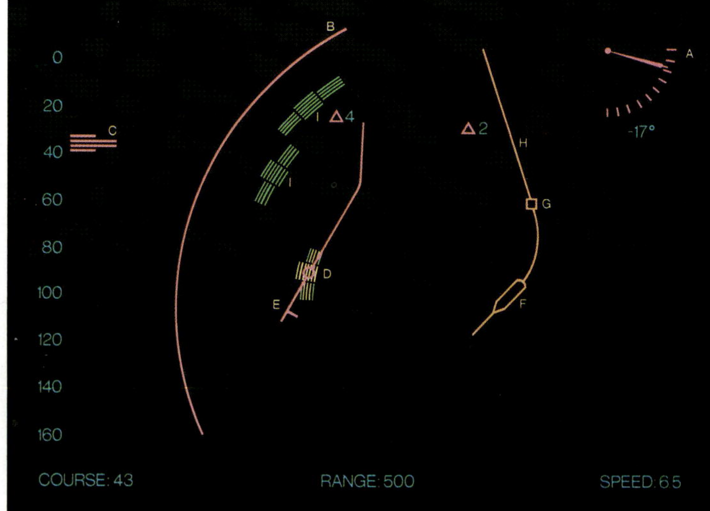

Left: Simrad SS240 series sonars are designed for installation in small surface ships. The transducer is mounted inside a dome and received signals are passed via a pre-amplifier to a transceiver. An operator's display unit and loudspeaker correlate inputs with data from the ship's gyro-compass and speed log, and remote displays can allow the situation to be monitored at other localities, such as the bridge.

Above: The multicolour display of a Simrad SS304 sonar, designed for installation in ships down to 150 tons. The −17° tilt angle (A) and 85° ping sector (B) of the sonar are shown, together with own ship's track (H), position marker (G) and actual position (F). The target's position (D), speed and direction (E) and depth (C) are also displayed, along with other underwater echoes such as fish shoals (I) and navigation data.

itself. The problem is heightened by the need for separation from the main body of a task group to maximise sonar performance: as was shown by British radar picket ships in the 1982 South Atlantic war, such isolated ships are highly vulnerable to air attack. Finally, the towed arrays themselves may give rise to detectable noise either from water-flow over the array or by the towing cable resonating at its 'natural' frequency, and processing electronics must be able to discard such signals.

NON-ACOUSTIC SENSORS

A submerged submarine moving through the water leaves a wake which is detectable by active sonar. This turbulence, conical in shape, eventually reaches the surface well astern of the boat, where it causes minute variations in the wave pattern. Both the USA and USSR are experimenting with over-the-horizon backscatter (OTH-B) radar in an effort to detect

Left: Graseby 750 sonar operators' console featuring three displays for (left to right) the Plan Position Indication, Doppler Display and Hydrophone-effect Passive Search Subsystems. Displays are stabilised geographically and supplemented by audio systems.

Above: Transducer arrays are mounted in hydrodynamic glass-reinforced plastic domes to minimise flow noise; the domes may be mounted either at the bows or on the keel amidships. This example is manufactured by Plessey Naval Systems.

Above: Plessey PMS 40 series surface ship sonar array, with 12 transducers in each vertical stave. This array provides omnidirectional simultaneous active and passive operation, and the electronics allow automatic tracking of up to ten active contacts.

Below: The three-man operators' console of the Plessey Type 2016 sonar system, current major fleet escort sonar of the Royal Navy. Electronic analysis and presentation of information is essential to enable the crew to make proper assessments of target data.

Plessey COMTASS (Compact Towed Array Sonar System)

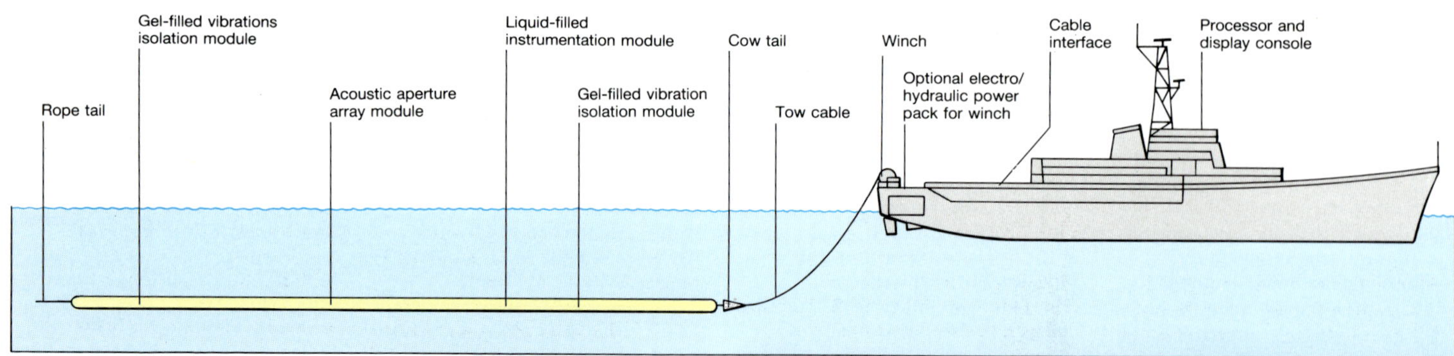

Above: The British Compact Towed Array Sonar System (COMTASS) provides a passive ASW capability for surface ships and submarines. Towed arrays are very effective, though they limit the speed and manouevrability of the towing ship.

Right: HMS *Cleopatra* with her Type 2031 towed array deployed. Such arrays need large stern installations, and her sister ships needed sponsons to mount the winch, adding 3ft (1m) to their length, but *Cleopatra*'s installation is within existing deck space.

this phenomenon at considerable ranges. Depending on the depth of the submarine and the prevailing oceanic conditions the wake turbulence may also force colder water to rise and mix with warmer water at the surface, causing a temperature differential detectable by satellite or aircraft-borne sensors.

When a submarine is travelling near the surface there is a tiny but perceptible rise in the surface level of the water above the hull which is potentially detectable by satellites. The USSR is known to be interested in this technique and the USA has at least one satellite, SEASAT, whose radio altimeter has a vertical resolution of 3.9in (10cm) and could be used in this role.

Submarines are also detectable by the electrical and magnetic fields they create. According to a Soviet writer there are electro-chemical processes on a submarine hull which generate varying electrical potentials with currents flowing between them using seawater as the conducting medium. The rate of change of the consequential electrical and electromagnetic fields is detectable by sensitive devices, among which would be very large seabed coils.

A submarine hull is a mainly ferrous body which moves through the lines of force of the Earth's natural magnetic field, creating a magnetic anomaly which is detectable by airborne magnetic anomaly detector (MAD) equipment. MAD units are mounted in extensions behind the tails of fixed-wing aircraft or in aerodynamic bodies, or birds, towed by cables behind helicopters. All advanced anti-submarine aircraft are fitted with such devices, including the American P-3 Orion and S-3 Viking, British Nimrod, French Atlantic and Soviet Il-38 May. MAD devices normally have a maximum detection range of about 1,000ft (305m) and are, therefore, unsuitable for area searches, but they are invaluable for the precise

EDO SQR-18A(V)1 TACTAS (Tactical Towed Array Sonar)

Below: The widely used SQR-18A TACTAS towed array system consists of three subsystems. The towed subsystem itself comprises an armoured cable, with an array of acoustic modules, and is shown here in its (V)1 form attached to an existing VDS (variable depth sonar) sonar body; in the (V)2 form, for ships with no VDS, the length of cable in relation to the ship's speed determines array depth. The tow cable spatially isolates the array from own-ship noise. The handling and storage subsystem comprises a hydraulically driven winch and operator's console installed in a stern compartment below decks, while the electronics sub-system provides the control and display functions. A signal conditioner provides gain and equalisation and converts the analogue signal to digital; the beam-former forms multiple search beams and also cancels out own-ship interference. The signal then passes through processors and a tracker to a mass memory, before being displayed to the operator in the ship's operations centre.

Towed array

VDS body

Above: The receiver array of the BAe Active Towed Array Sonar. Hydrophones and associated electronics are housed in a 65.6ft (20m) long, 3.46in (88mm) diameter flexible tube. Signals are passed to shipborne electron-ics as a single serial data stream.

location of underwater targets detected by other means, such as SOSUS. However, the use of titanium hulls in the Soviet Alfa class introduces a new factor, as titanium is a non-magnetic material and cannot be detected by MAD sensors. Fortunately for the users of MAD, titanium is so expensive, and the fabrication techniques involved in its use are so complex, that only a very small proportion of the world's submarines are ever likely to be constructed of this metal.

UNDERWATER OPTICS

Seawater is an efficient light absorber, but there is a window in the blue-green portion of the visible spectrum. Efforts are being made to exploit this for communication purposes with blue-green lasers, using satellites to project the beam onto the target area, as described in the previous chapter. A similar technique could be used to detect submarines, either by detecting minute return reflections from a satellite-borne sensor or by mounting a blue-green laser and suitable detectors in an ASW aircraft. In the latter case laser detection could well be complementary to MAD, and would overcome MAD's inability to detect titanium hulls.

ELECTRONIC WARFARE

It has been described elsewhere in this book how diesel-electric submarines are inherently vulnerable to detection, because they must approach the surface and expose their snorkel heads at regular intervals to recharge their batteries and replenish their life support systems. Nuclear-powered submarines do not have to expose snorkel masts, but they share with diesel-electric submarines the problem of communications, and surface anti-submarine forces are naturally quick to exploit this weakness. The primary means of communicating with a totally submerged submarine is by VLF radio, but the long towed antenna essential for reception is detectable by surface warships and aircraft. Not surprisingly, major efforts are being made to develop new communications systems for submarines.

Radio transmissions by submarines are, of course, immediately detectable by electronic surveillance using platforms such as satellites, shore-based monitoring stations, surface warships and aircraft. All will seek first to pinpoint the site of the transmission, then to identify the transmitter and finally to analyse the content of the signal. One way submarines endeavour to overcome this is by detaching transmitters in buoys which are released at normal operating depths and do not transmit until they reach the surface.

Thorn EMI degaussing range

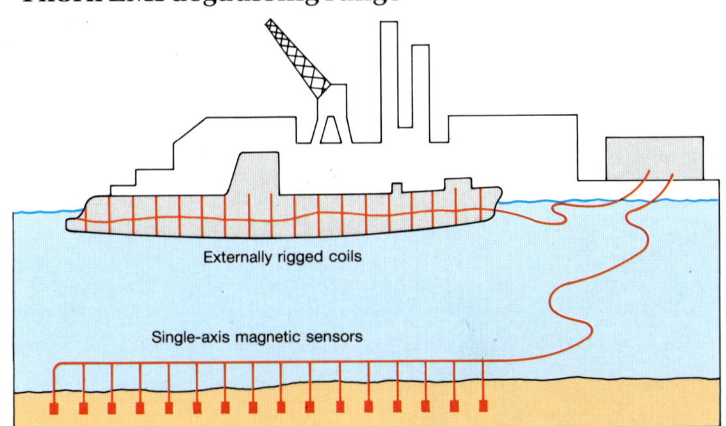

Above: During ship construction and in normal operation a ship or submarine becomes magnetised, with the three major elements being vertical, longitudinal and athwartships. It is therefore essential that they be treated on a degaussing range, one type of which is shown here, using sheltered water near a naval base so that handling facilities and electrical power can be utilised.

Above: Not surprisingly, the US Navy's silencing facilities for its submarine fleet are much more sophisticated and expensive than those shown on the left. Here USS *Ohio* (SSBN 726) is seen inside a huge, purpose-built structure being treated to reduce her magnetic and other signatures to the lowest feasible level, prior to going on an operational patrol. The Soviets have similar facilities.

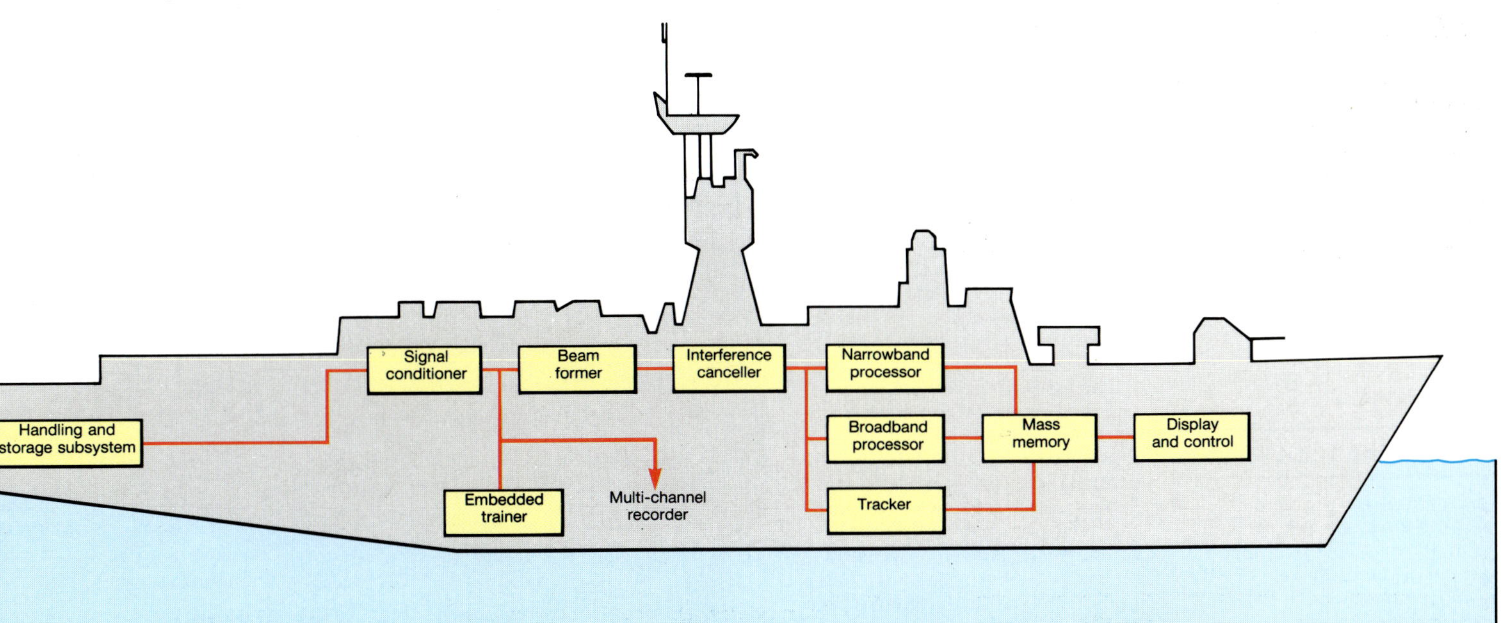

ANTI-SUBMARINE ROCKET LAUNCHERS

Many navies mount anti-submarine rocket launchers on surface warships, despite the inherent disadvantage – shared with depth charges – that their short range allows the target to come too close. The Soviet Navy has a series of devices designated *Raktenaya Bombometnaya Ustanovka* (rocket depth-charge launcher) whose designation suffixes indicate their range in metres. The most elaborate is the RBU-6000, which consists of 12 vertically loaded barrels arranged in a horse-shoe shape, on a mounting which can be both trained and elevated. The rockets are fired in a paired sequence; their maximum range is 6,562 yards (6,000m) and the warhead is 121lb (55kg) of high explosive. RBU-6000 is fitted in ships ranging in size from Kiev class aircraft carriers to Grisha class corvettes. Others in the series are the RBU-2500 (16 barrels), RBU-1200 (five barrels), RBU-1000 (six barrels) and RBU-600 (six barrels).

The only similar device in wide-scale use is the Swedish Bofors 375mm ASW rocket-launcher, which uses two types of rocket: one has a range bracket of 656-1,750 yards (600-1,600m) and the second of 1,750-3,940 yards (1,600-3,600m), the former designated Erika and the latter Nelli. The Bofors launcher comes in two-, four- and six-tube versions, and the six-tube version is used by the French firm of Creusot-Loire as the basis of its Model 1964 launcher.

MINES

Mines have a major role in anti-submarine warfare, though the days of the moored or bottom-sitting mine are probably numbered. Far more effective is the US Navy's Captor (Encapsulated Torpedo), which is designed exclusively for attacking submarines. Captor consists of a Mk 46 torpedo housed in a tube; laid by submarine, aircraft or surface ship, it sits on the ocean floor and monitors all passing maritime traffic using passive sonar equipment with a range of some 3,000ft (1,000m) which is gated to exclude surface traffic. On identification of a submarine target the active sonar is switched on, optimum launch time is computed and the torpedo is launched. No IFF is fitted, so friendly submarines must be kept clear of any Captor minefields.

STAND-OFF WEAPONS

To overcome the problem of reaching the target submarine before it can attack its hunter a number of stand-off weapons have been developed which deliver a depth charge or a torpedo by a carrier missile or rocket. The US Asroc consists of a Mk 46 acoustic homing torpedo with a strap-on rocket motor, and somewhat similar weapons are made in France (Malafon), Australia (Ikara) and the USSR (FRAS-1 and SS-N-14). Ranges are not great; that of Asroc, for example, is estimated to be between 1.25 and 6.2nm (2-10km).

The US Navy is developing a common successor to Subroc and Asroc known as Sea Lance (formerly ASW-SOW). Designed to combat the threat posed by such submarines as the Soviet Alfa and Sierra classes, and with a range estimated at between 35 and 100 miles (56-160km), Sea Lance will be launched vertically from surface ships and expelled from standard torpedo tubes in submarines. The system comprises a common

Above: Virtually all Soviet Navy surface warships are fitted with some of the numerous models of *Raketnaya Bombometnaya Ustanovka* (rocket depth-charge launcher). This is the 12-barrel RBU-6000, a device with a 6,561yd (6,000m) range which is fitted in ships ranging from Kirov battlecruisers to Grisha corvettes.

Below: Projected Franco-Italian ASW weapon designed to deliver a torpedo over ranges in excess of 22nm (40km) with in-flight updating capability.

Plessey PMW 49A deck launcher system

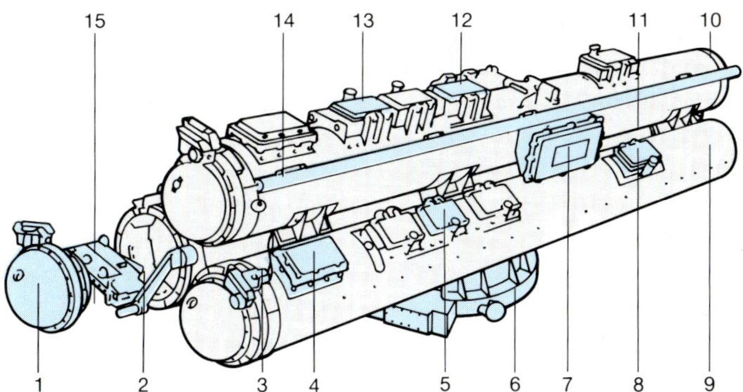

1 Breech assembly
2 Training handle
3 Locking ring and control lever
4 Control box
5 Hatch No 3 (Mk 46 lanyard solenoid unit)
6 Training mechanism
7 Starboard distribution box
8 Hatch No 1 (Stingray lanyard solenoid unit)
9 Tube No 3
10 Tube No 2
11 Tube No 1
12 Hatch No 2 (Stingray battery port cover remover)
13 Hatch No 4 (containing plug puller unit)
14 Charging hose
15 Torpedo securing beam

Above left: British PMW 49A triple torpedo launcher for lightweight torpedoes such as US Mk 46, British Stingray or Italian A.224S. The tubes are made of epoxide resin embodied with filament-wound glass fibre and have fire-retardant additives.

Above: The STWS antisubmarine torpedo launcher from which the PMW 49A was developed. One of the lessons of the Falklands War was the need for swinging bulletproof plates; these are now fitted outboard of the warhead end of the tubes.

Whitehead A.244/S Mod 1 shipborne system

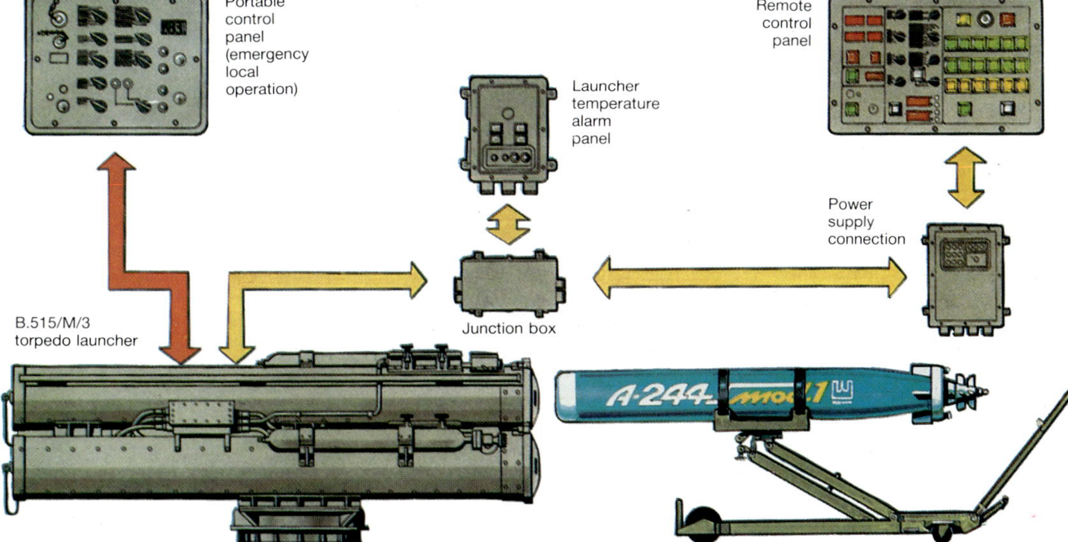

Above: This lightweight torpedo system by the Italian Whitehead organisation is designed for small ship use and is similar in function to the PMW 49A at the top of the page. The electrically propelled A.244 is 8.86ft (2.7m) long with a diameter of 12.7in (324mm).

Below: Launch of a lightweight torpedo from the STWS (ship's torpedo weapon system) tube aboard a Royal Navy warship.

missile carrying either the Advanced Lightweight Torpedo or a nuclear depth charge. The latter would almost certainly be a new common device to replace the W55, B57 and W44 nuclear warheads currently in service with the US Navy.

TORPEDOES

The general question of torpedoes is discussed elsewhere, their basic problem being lack of speed. Even with helicopters and stand-off delivery systems such as Asroc there is a need for much faster torpedoes; the US Advanced Capability (ADCAP) programme for the Mk 48 torpedo will raise its speed to 55 knots (63mph), while the next-generation British surface warship- and aircraft-launched torpedo – Spearfish – uses a gas turbine and a pump-jet to attain even higher speeds.

Warhead design is critical, particularly in the case of lightweight aircraft-launched torpedoes which, by their very nature, have small warheads and are most unlikely to cause any damage to stronger submarine hulls. In general terms the capabilities of current torpedoes lag behind those of the sonars that support them: they are slow, lacking in range and extremely noisy.

DEPTH CHARGES

The typical World War II surface warship ASW weapon, the depth charge is now little used by surface ships since to allow a modern submarine within launcher range – about two miles (3.2km) – would be very hazardous. However, depth charges are used by ASW helicopters; a good example is the British Mk 11 which contains 180lb (81.6kg) of Torpex. Far more effective, but with major political implications and therefore tactical limitations, is the nuclear depth bomb, though tactical nuclear weapons could be used more readily at sea than on land.

NUCLEAR WEAPONS

Above: USS *Cochrane* (DDG 21) launches an Asroc missile. Such delivery systems are essential if a surface ship is to have any hope of destroying a hostile submarine before it destroys her.

The traditional method of attacking a submerged submarine is by detonating an explosive charge on or near its hull. Because the submarine is already in a pressurized and hostile environment, the charge does not need to be big enough to cause a complete collapse of the hull on its own – it needs only cause a relatively minor amount of penetration and then leave the water pressure to effect a totally catastrophic collapse.

A successful attack on a submarine involves delivering a charge of sufficient explosive force within lethal range too quickly to allow the boat to take adequate evasive action. The difficulties are compounded by the relative slowness with which weapons can approach submarines, the increasing effectiveness of submarine sensors, the enhanced agility and speed of the targets and the growing strength of their hulls. Clearly there is a trade-off between the various factors involved, but one way of overcoming the difficulties is to produce an explosive charge so powerful that it need not be particularly close to the submarine to achieve its desired effect, an obvious candidate for such a role being a nuclear weapon. As with acoustic effects, however, the use of nuclear weapons under water is not entirely straightforward.

Documentation of the effects of underwater nuclear explosions is highly classified, because such explosions would have only military applications and effects, and consequently very sparse. However, it is known that the USA carried out a series of underwater tests prior to the imposition of the Nuclear Test Ban Treaty, including Test Baker: carried out in July 1946 at a depth of 200ft (61m) in a lagoon, its main aim seems to have

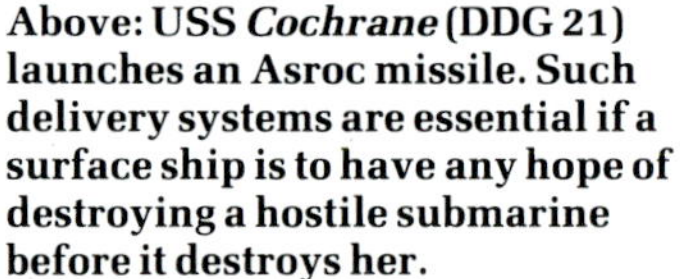

been to assess the effects on surface warships. Test Wigwam, carried out in 1958, was of unspecified yield at a depth of 2,000ft (610m), while Test Wahoo, carried out in 1958 at a depth of 500ft (152m), occurred over deep water.

In general terms, a deep underwater nuclear explosion results in limited thermal or nuclear radiation; the principal effect is the formation of a hot steam bubble centred on the explosion. This bubble rises through the water, expanding at a diminishing rate until a maximum size is achieved, and provided it does not touch the bottom or the

Below: Shadowgraph of a shaped-charge warhead detonating under water; the forward projection of the molten jet – the Monroe Effect – is clearly visible.

All Western antisubmarine weapons may soon have to rely on such warheads to penetrate the exceptionally strong hulls of some current Soviet submarines.

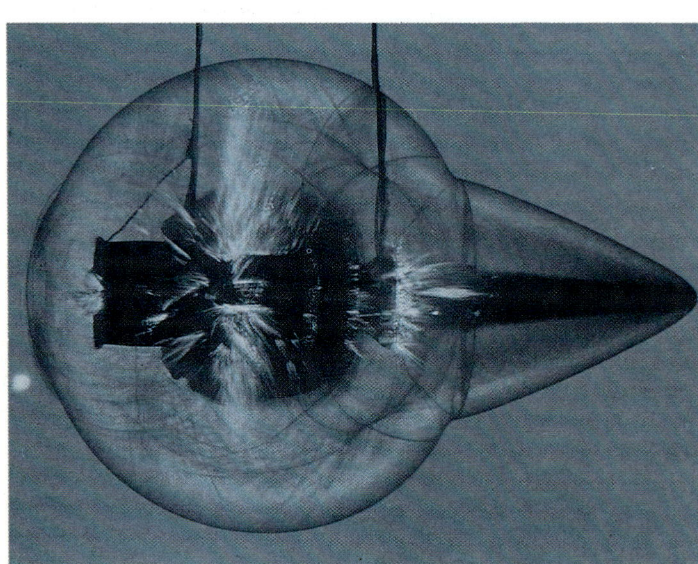

Below: Asroc uses a solid-fuel rocket to deploy a parachute-retarded Mk 46 torpedo or a 1kT nuclear depth charge over maximum ranges estimated at around 10,000 yards (9,600m).

surface, at this stage it is spherical in shape. As a result of the outward momentum of the water surrounding it, the bubble continues to expand until its internal pressure is below that of the ambient water pressure, whereupon the pressure outside the bubble forces it to contract. Now momentum forces it to contract to the point where internal pressure exceeds ambient pressure, some of the steam condenses and the bubble expands once again. Meanwhile, during the contraction phase, the bottom of the bubble tends to move upward more rapidly than the top, due to the difference in hydrostatic pressure, so as the bubble rises towards the surface, expanding and contracting as it goes, it generates a compression or shock wave with each expansion. Each compression is of a lower intensity but greater duration than its predecessor, and a total of three complete cycles seems to be the maximum.

During the pulsation and upward motion of the bubble, the water surrounding it acquires considerable upward momentum of its own, eventually breaking through the surface at a high velocity – 200mph in the Wigwam test. The very rapid expansion of the hot gas bubble results in a compression wave being sent out in all directions with a sharp rise in overpressure at the shock front, and this peak overpressure does not fall off as rapidly with distance as it would in air; for example, peak overpressure at 3,000ft (914m) from a 100kT deep-water burst is about 2,700psi (190kg/cm^2), whereas in air the peak would be only 2-3psi (0.14-0.2kg/cm^2). Conversely, the duration of the shock wave in water is much shorter than in air – two or three hundredths of a second as opposed to approximately one second.

There are also two forms of reflected wave and an induced wave. The first reflection is from the surface: where the water shock wave hits the surface it is reflected back as a negative pressure wave and below the surface the sudden change from positive to negative pressure is known as the surface cut-off. The second reflection comes from the bottom, and is a simple compression reflection. Where the bottom is rock or other hard material the shock wave may travel a short distance through this material before being reradiated back into the water. Both the latter shock waves are positive compression waves, unlike the surface reflection.

As in other areas, the nature of the ocean can cause vagaries in the wave paths. With a strong shock

Above: Surface emption caused by an early underwater nuclear weapon test at Bikini Atoll Numerous antisubmarine weapons are armed with nuclear warheads; effects are complex.

Subroc launch and trajectory profile

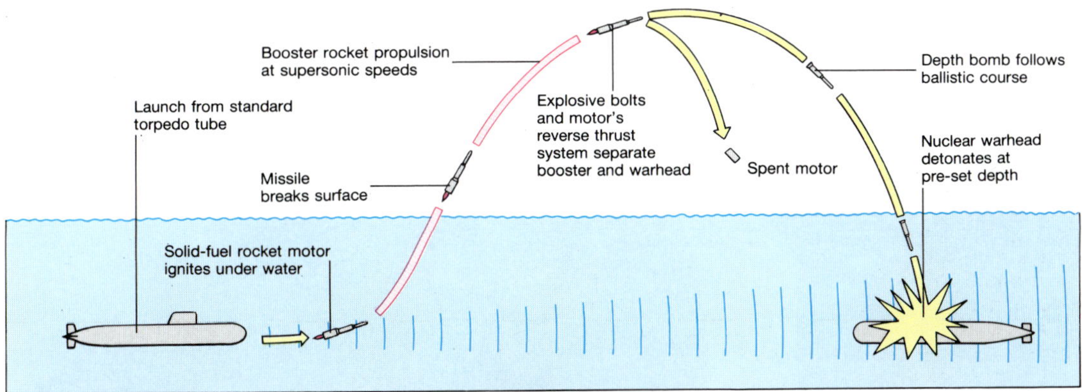

Above: Mission profile of a Subroc missile. Subroc is due to be replaced by the new Sea Lance antisubmarine stand-off weapon, which will operate on similar principles. Submarine sensors have long had greater ranges than their weapon systems; missiles are gradually righting the imbalance.

Below: Subroc powers away from the surface. In service since 1962, the weapon will remain operational into the 1990s because of delays with Sea Lance.

Above: Plessey Cormorant dunking sonar with the array elements folded away, an arrangement which facilitates rapid deployment.

Above: Cormorant's arrays deployed. Such extending arrays greatly enhance the performance of the sonar, giving greater range and improved definition.

intensity the surface-reflected wave tends to overtake the main shock front, because the latter sets in motion the water through which the following reflection wave is travelling. Also, as with acoustic waves, the variations in density, temperature and salinity can cause underwater shock waves to be refracted and thus either diverted from certain areas or, conversely, channelled toward or even focused on one area to produce a stronger than expected shock wave at some point at a great distance from the detonation.

The effect of an underwater nuclear explosion on a submarine is, therefore, the result of a complex series of activities. There may be up to three compression and rarefaction waves (called bubble pulses), as well as a negative shock wave reflected from the surface plus bottom-reflected and bottom-induced positive waves. The effect on an underwater target depends on the water depth, the explosive yield of the weapon, the nature of the bottom and the time interval between the direct and indirect shock waves, their magnitudes and their positive or negative natures. What is certain is that the sheer explosive power of a nuclear depth bomb or torpedo must give an attacker a much

Left: The reeling machine and transducer of the Bendix AQS-18 airborne sonar system, which is in service with Lynx helicopters of the West German Navy. The similar AQS-13F has been selected to equip the US Navy's new SH-60F Seahawk carrier-based antisubmarine helicopter. The transducer is not as small as it looks, being 49.4in (125.5cm) long, 13in (33.1cm) in diameter and weighing 193.6lb (88kg). The winch gives high deployment and retrieval rates.

Right: A Royal Navy Sea King Mk 5 recovers its Plessey Type 195 dunking sonar. Dunking sonar has advantages over expendable sonbuoys, not least being that its depth can be varied.

Above: Operators' console of the RN Type 195 sonar system. Two helicopters using dunking sonar can set up a search pattern that is hard for a submarine to evade.

OMERA ORB 3211 radar detection ranges

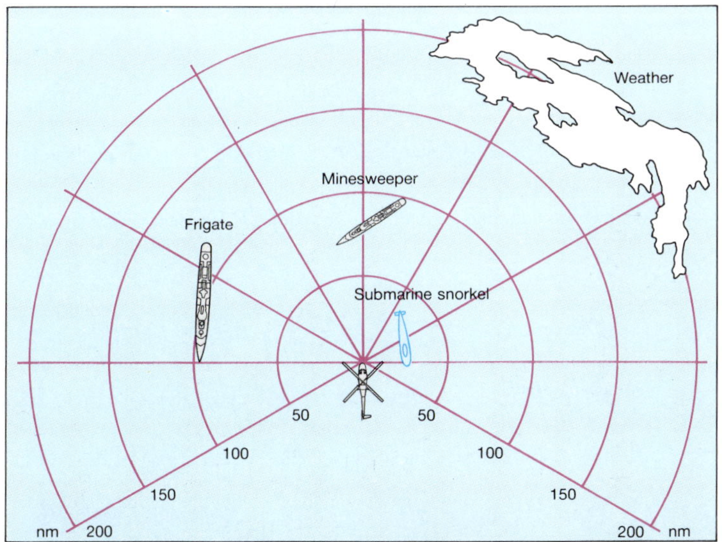

Left: The OMERA ORB 3211 radar is designed for installation in French Aérospatiale SA322 Super Puma helicopters. The detection ranges claimed by the makers range from 200nm for meteorological purposes to 25nm for a submarine snorkel, the latter figure underlining the risks involved in broaching the surface with any part of a submarine.

Below: This French Aéronavale Lynx is equipped with Heracles ORB 31W surveillance radar, Crouzet MAD and Alcatel dunking sonar, and is seen here with a prototype of the Murène antisubmarine torpedo.

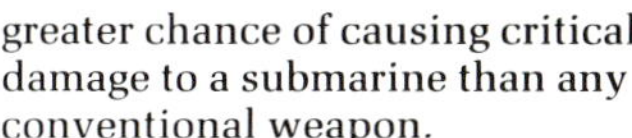

greater chance of causing critical damage to a submarine than any conventional weapon.

Nuclear warheads are used in anti-submarine torpedoes, depth bombs and stand-off weapons, a typical device being the US air-delivered B57 Mod 1 used by the US and various allied navies. Weighing around 510lb (231kg), the B57 Mod 1 is approximately 119in (302cm) long and 14.75in (37.5cm) in diameter and has a yield reportedly variable between five and ten kilotons. It is carried by US Navy S-3 Viking and P-3 Orion aircraft and SH-3 Sea King helicopters. Other US Navy nuclear weapons with ASW applications are Subroc, which has a W55 warhead with a 1-5kT warhead, and its successor, Sea Lance.

The Soviet Navy has a number of ASW nuclear weapons. The Whiskey class submarine which beached off the Karlskrona naval base in 1981 carried nuclear-armed torpedoes, and presumably Soviet anti-submarine aircraft carry nuclear depth bombs similar to the US B57.

CARRIER-BASED AIRCRAFT

Carrier-based aircraft can take the ASW battle to submarines in any part of the world's oceans, a factor clearly of high importance in the Soviet decision to build their own carrier fleet. ASW tasks are performed by aircraft such as the US Navy's S-3 Viking and the French Alizé, and many types of helicopter, such as the Soviet Ka-32 Helix and the US SH-60B Seahawk.

The principal requirements of an anti-submarine aircraft are the ability to transit rapidly between the aircraft carrier and the patrol line, long endurance on patrol, and the capability to detect, locate, identify and destroy submarine targets. It needs a variety of on-board sensors, including radar (for the detection and classification of surface targets), forward-looking infra-red, magnetic anomaly detectors, sonobuoys and electronic counter-measures equipment. All these sensors, plus inputs from the parent carrier and other ships and aircraft, produce so much information that substantial on-board data processing power is required. Finally, an ideal weapons load would include anti-ship missiles such as Exocet or Harpoon, homing torpedoes, rockets and both conventional and nuclear depth bombs. The only aircraft currently capable of all these tasks is the US Navy's Lockheed S-3 Viking; older aircraft still in service such as the Alizé and S-2 Tracker are much less capable. The Soviet Navy clearly requires a Viking-type aircraft to equip its new 75,000-ton carriers, but no suitable airframe currently exists.

An alternative to the fixed-wing ASW aircraft, albeit one with less range and endurance, is the helicopter. The earliest ASW anti-submarine helicopters offered no more than a means of delivering torpedoes rapidly in order to counter the speed of nuclear submarines, but as range and payload have increased ASW helicopters have become autonomous weapons systems in their own right. They also have the advantage of bringing an air capability to ships as small as frigates in size. The most advanced airframes currently in service are the US Navy's SH-60B LAMPS III (Light Airborne Multipurpose System), the British Sea King HAS.5 and Lynx HAS.3, and the Soviet Kamov Ka-32 Helix. For the future the most important aircraft currently in development is the European Helicopter Industries EH-101, a British/Italian Sea King replacement which will be equipped with Ferranti Blue Kestrel search radar, Marconi sonar systems, Decca ESM and AQS-81 MAD, all coordinated by a Ferranti data-handling system.

LAND-BASED AIRCRAFT

It is essential that there should be a land-based component of maritime-committed airpower. In virtually every country this is provided by naval aviators, except in the United Kingdom where, for historical reasons, the role is carried out by the RAF. The primary roles of land-based aircraft are anti-submarine patrol and maritime strike in support of the naval battle. Land-based aircraft provide effective and virtually all-weather support, but there are limits to their coverage, as was shown in the 1982 South Atlantic War, when the Royal Navy Task Force eventually got beyond the range of its land-based air support on Ascension Island.

The most important of the land-based types are the large ASW aircraft such as the Lockheed P-3 Orion, British Aerospace Nimrod, Dassault-Breguet Atlantic, Shin Meiwa PS-1, Kawasaki P-2J, Ilyushin Il-38 May and Tupolev Tu-20 Bear-F. Only three of these airframes were designed specifically for the ASW mission – the Atlantic, PS-1 and P-2J – another three being particularly successful ASW conversions of relatively unsuccessful commercial airliners, the Nimrod (Comet), P-3 Orion (Electra) and May (Il-18 Coot) while the last, the Bear-F, is a modified strategic bomber. The Japanese PS-1 is an interesting concept, the idea being that it can alight on water for the search and localization phase of its ASW patrol and use its powerful on-board sonar, rather than expend masses of sonar buoys. The idea has not caught on, however; the only other nation to try the idea is China, and the Japanese themselves have returned to land-based ASW aircraft with their large fleet of Kawasaki P-2Js, licence-built, updated versions of the Lockheed P-2 Neptune, and Lockheed P-3 Orions.

These aircraft are used for long-range, long-endurance ocean patrols to detect and track submarines in peacetime and to destroy them in war. In particular, they are required to follow up and classify submarine contacts made by the US Navy's SOSUS and SURTASS surveillance systems and the Soviet equivalents. Their on-board sensors include radar, forward-looking infra-red, low-light television, sophisticated ECM suites and MAD equipment, and they deploy expendable sonobuoys with radio uplinks to give them a sonar capability. Their weapons include torpedoes, conventional and nuclear depth bombs and air-to-surface missiles, making them similar in most

Above: The Il-38 May forms the mainstay of the Soviet fixed-wing antisubmarine aircraft force, and like nearly all such aircraft is a military conversion of a civil airliner. Note the MAD tailboom.

Below: The standard British sonobuoy, the Jezebel receives sounds generated by submerged submarines and relays them to ASW aircraft. Passive sonobuoys are undetectable by submarines.

SSQ 904 Jezebel sonobuoy deployment

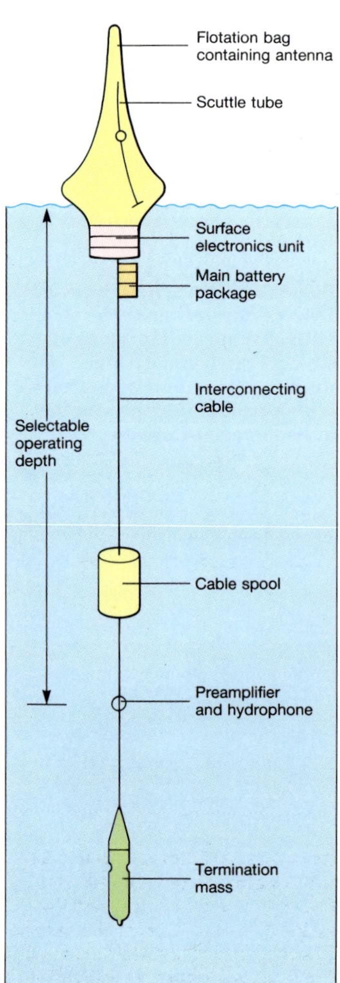

Below: An RAF crewman aboard a Nimrod prepares to launch an SSQ 954 DIFAR sonobuoy. This provides target bearing information in addition to the basic signal provided by the Jezebel.

respects to the carrier-based S-3 Viking, but they have much greaater endurance and payload and, with bigger crews, are able to conduct more protracted operations. Published figures for patrol times are 18 hours for the Atlantic, 12 hours for Nimrod and May, and 16 hours for the P-3 Orion. The endurance of the S-3 Viking is nine hours, though exponents of carrier-based airpower argue that because it is already at sea, and therefore much nearer the scene of action, the Viking spends much less time in transit and just as much time, or perhaps even more, on patrol.

Many navies use shore-based helicopters in a short-range ASW role. These are normally simply land-based versions of sea-going anti-submarine helicopters, but the USSR has developed a unique type, the Mi-14 Haze, specifically for the shore-based ASW role.

Another special type developed by the Soviet Union, the over-the-horizon targeting aircraft, provides mid-course guidance for submarine-launched missiles such as the SS-N-3 and SS-N-12; the Tu-95 Bear-D certainly and the Tu-16 Badger-D possibly have such a role. Bear-D has a massive radome in its weapons bay, together with some 40 other antennas, blisters and fairings along its fuselage, wings and tail. Bear-Ds appear to be deployed in pairs in this role, and while they are clearly vital to the missile systems deployed aboard Soviet surface ships their chances of survival and of achieving coordinated timings with submarines seem remote.

Right: The operators' consoles of the Atlantique 2 present information from all the common sensors used to detect submarines. The two sonobuoy operators' positions (foreground) receive hard copy of the information displayed on the screens above them. Next is the tactical coordinator's station, with the radar/IFF operator's position further forward and, finally, the electronic warfare officer/MAD operator's station.

Dassault-Breguet Atlantique 2 internal arrangement

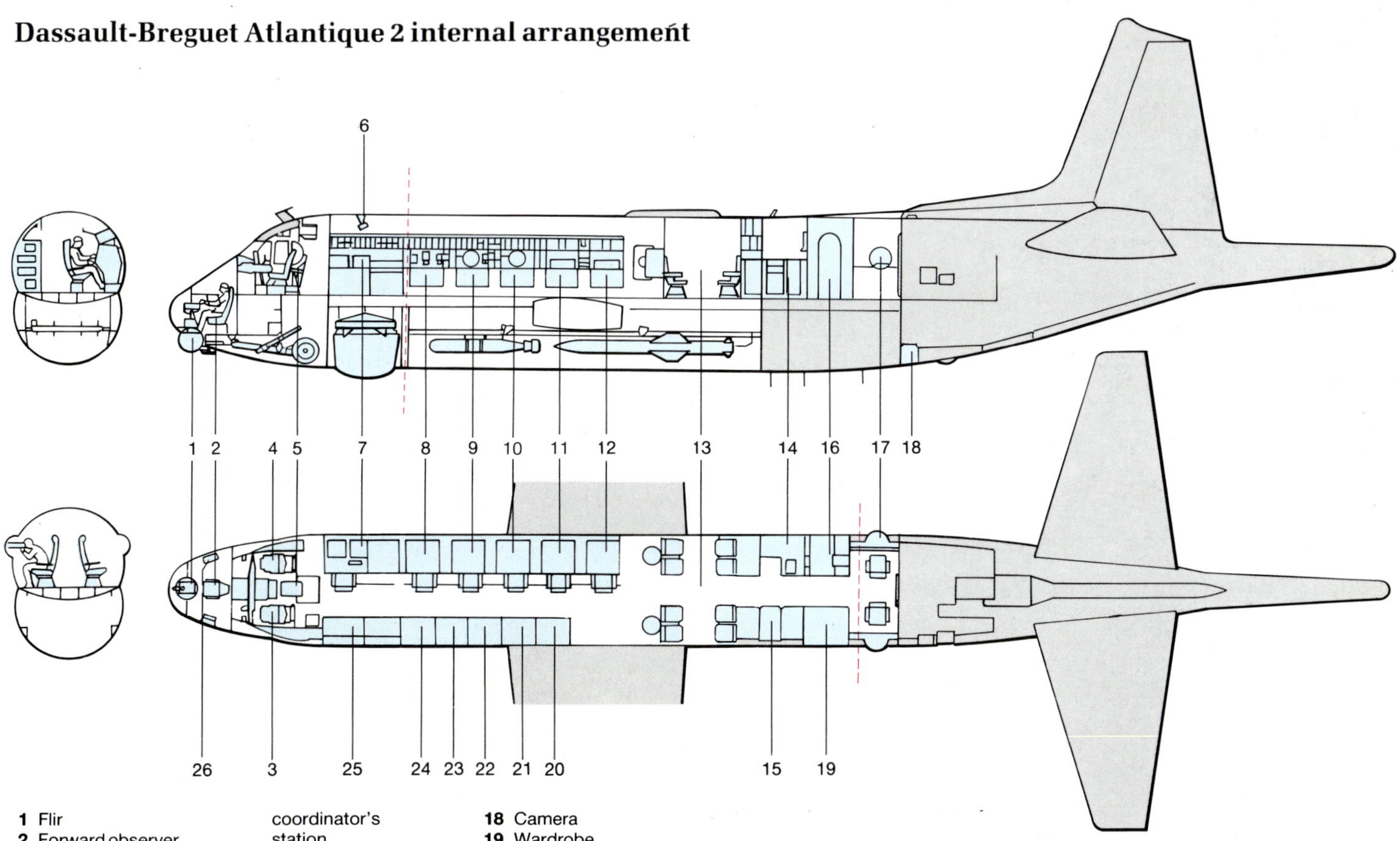

1 Flir
2 Forward observer
3 Pilot
4 Aircraft commander
5 Flight engineer
6 Sextant
7 Radio-navigation station
8 ESM/ECM/MAD station
9 Radar/IFF station
10 Tactical coordinator's station
11 Sonobuoy operator No 1
12 Sonobuoy operator No 2
13 Rest compartment
14 Galley
15 Crew room (table and seats)
16 Lavatories
17 Rear observer
18 Camera
19 Wardrobe
20 Radio equipment
21 Radar/IFF equipment
22 Sonobuoy receiver
23 Computer
24 Navigation equipment
25 Electrical circuits
26 Side-looking camera

Above: The Atlantique 2 is a well laid-out aircraft developed after many years' experience with the earlier Atlantic. Aircrew have to undertake lengthy missions, most of which are flown at low levels in turbulent conditions, typical examples being an eight-hour patrol 600nm from base or five hours at 1,000nm; for such lengthy tasks good facilities for crew comfort are essential.

Accidents and Rescue

The possibility of a submarine being damaged, either by attack in war or by accident at any time is clearly an important consideration both in submarine design and in a submariner's life. Accidents can result from a variety of causes, such as internal explosion, and failure of the hull through exceeding the maximum permissible depth after a loss of control or collision, particularly with surface ships. Since internal bulkheads have far less pressure resistance than the hull a major collapse of the hull at depth would almost certainly be catastrophic and, as was the case with USS *Thresher*, rescue would be pointless as there would be no survivors. Between collapse depth and approximately 650ft (198m), however, rescue by an external vessel is feasible, and at depths of less than 650ft escape without external assistance is possible given suitable equipment.

SUBMARINE LOSSES

The British have lost only three submarines since the end of World War II: HMS *Truculent* collided with a merchant ship in the Thames estuary in 1950, HMS *Affray* sank in the English Channel in 1951 and HMS *Sidon* foundered in harbour in 1955, following an internal explosion. The *Truculent* sinking illustrated a particular hazard for submarine escapers in that a number of men used the proper escape apparatus and reached the surface successfully

Above: The Kockums rescue sphere after a successful first ascent from a depth of 260ft (80m). The ventilation mast has been raised and a dinghy has arrived from HDW's tender *Pegasus*.

IKL/HDW rescue sphere

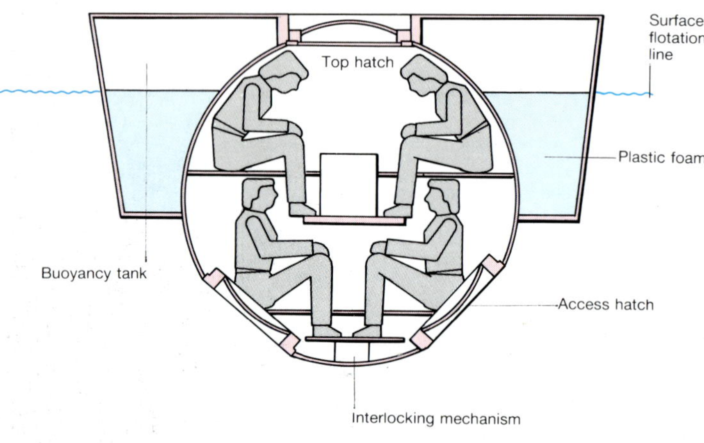

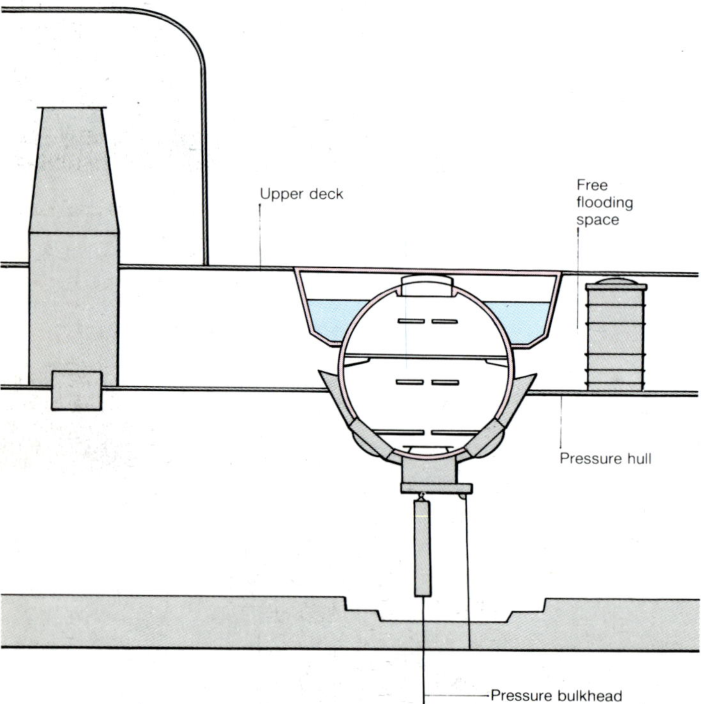

Above: The West German firm of Ingenieurkontor Lübeck (IKL) devised this rescue system, which is built into the Indian Navy's HDW Type 1500 submarines. In an emergency the crew enter the sphere, which is surrounded by a large buoyancy tank and contains enough air to enable 40 occupants to survive for up to 9 hours without fresh air. When the sphere reaches the surface a ventilation mast is raised, and in calm conditions the top hatch can be opened. When rescuers arrive and the crew have been transferred the sphere can either be towed at up to four knots by means of a pre-attached towing line, or hoisted to the deck of a rescue ship.

Below: Following the test the Type 1500 submarine surfaces, with the gap in the upper deck showing where the rescue sphere had been installed. This new system seems to be the most effective yet.

Below: The submarine's crew inside the rescue sphere as seen through the top hatch. There are two decks, with the crew sitting on circular benches. The sphere comes complete with survival kit to sustain the occupants for six days and is equipped with an emergency radio transmitter. The survivors can take it in turns to exercise on the platform of the buoyancy tank.

only to be swept out into the North Sea by the tide.

The US Navy has had two major submarine disasters in the same period. USS *Thresher* (SSN-593) was lost on April 10, 1963, while on deep diving trials following her first major refit: control was lost and she dived suddenly, totally out of control; before the situation could be rectified she had exceeded her crushing depth and the hull collapsed, primarily as a result of weld failure. The hull broke up and came to rest on the bottom at a depth of some 8,400ft (2,560m), but there has never been any trace of radioactive leaks. Her crew of 108 men plus four naval officers and 17 civilians on board for the trials were lost.

In a second disaster USS *Scorpion* (SSN-589) was lost on about May 27, 1968, along with her entire crew of 99 men. She was some 200nm (370km) southwest of the Azores, travelling from the Mediterranean to Norfolk, Virginia, on a routine crossing of the Atlantic. Her loss illustrated the submariners' perpetual communications problem, since it was some days before it was realised ashore that she was overdue. *Scorpion* lies at a depth of some 10,000ft (3,048m), but again there has never been any abnormal radiation.

The Soviet Navy has also suffered major disasters, though it is doubtful whether full details will ever be published, even if they are known, in the West. It is believed that several Foxtrot class submarines have been lost over the years; surprisingly, no other diesel-electric patrol boat is known to have sunk, but one diesel-electric ballistic missile submarine was lost in the Pacific in April 1968. The Golf-II SSB was carrying her usual load of three SS-N-5 SLBMs and the American CIA mounted a highly ambitious clandestine operation to recover her, using the deep-sea recovery ship *Glomar Explorer*. As far as is known the forepart of the sunken submarine was recovered in 1974, but whether this included any missiles has never been made public.

Of the Soviet nuclear submarines, one November class boat was lost off Finisterre in April 1970: most if not all the crew were rescued and no nuclear contamination has ever been detected in the area. Other Novembers have been seen in difficulty on the surface, and have had to be towed to Soviet ports for repair, and one Charlie class SSGN sank in the Pacific near Kamchatka in June 1983 for reasons never made public. She was later salvaged by a Soviet recovery ship.

The only French postwar losses have been three Daphné class conventional submarines. The first, *Minerve*, was lost without trace in the Mediterranean on January 27, 1968, and *Eurydice* disappeared, again without trace, off Toulon on March 4, 1970. These losses caused considerable anxiety about the Daphné class, which was doing well in the export markets;

SOVIET NAVY SUBMARINE ACCIDENTS

1966	A radiation leak in a nuclear submarine near Polynarny, close to the submarine base in the Kola Inlet, reportedly caused the crew to panic and there were some deaths. (Jane's Defence Weekly, Jan 19, 1985)
1966-68	A fire on board a Soviet nuclear submarine transiting under the Arctic ice cap caused several casualties. (ibid)
1968	A Golf II SSB was lost in the Pacific: the CIA recovered at least part of the submarine in a clandestine operation in 1974, using the specially fitted-out *Glomar Explorer*.
1970	A November class SSN caught fire in the Atlantic. According to US sources the captain ordered his crew to abandon ship, but they refused; the fire then spread towards the reactor and the submarine was scuttled with great loss of life. (JDW)
February 1972	A Hotel class SSBN surfaced in the North Atlantic off the Newfoundland coast in serious trouble. (JDW)
December 1972	A nuclear weapon accident on board an SSBN off the US coast is believed to have involved a radiation leak from a nuclear-armed torpedo of the type designed to attack US harbour installations. Several men died and the majority of crew suffered some form of radiation sickness. (JDW)
October 1976	A nuclear submarine in the Atlantic suffered a fire, with three officers reported killed. (JDW)
1977	Twelve officers were evacuated from a nuclear submarine in mid-Atlantic and flown to Leningrad as a result of a medical emergency involving exposure to radiation. (JDW)
1977	A fire on board a nuclear submarine may have been caused by failure of an outdated reactor. (JDW)
September 1981	A nuclear submarine in the Baltic had an emergency and was towed to Soviet waters at night. Several sailors died from "severe nuclear poisoning". (JDW op. cit.)
June 1983	A Charlie I or II was lost off Kamchatka in the Pacific; her hulk was later recovered by the Soviet Navy.
November 1983	A Victor III was forced to surface about 470 miles off the South Carolina coast (in the so-called Bermuda Triangle) after fouling the towing cable of a US Navy frigate's variable-depth sonar. She wallowed on the surface for some time while a Soviet AGI stood by until a salvage vessel arrived from Cuba. (TIME, November 14, 1983)
June 1984	An Echo II which fouled her propellers with a wire some 500nm north-northeast of the Shetland Islands was spotted on the surface trying to clear them.
June 1984	A Whiskey class conventional submarine was caught in the nets of the Norwegian trawler *Bentin*. A Norwegian coastguard cutter dropped hand grenades to signal the submarine to come to the surface, which she did after a further two hours.
June 1985	A Victor I SSN transiting the Straits of Gibraltar collided with a Soviet tanker, possibly while trying to hide in the tanker's noise shadow. (The combination of warm and cold layer in the Straits make it difficult to maintain a set depth, especially where a sudden thermal gradient makes a submarine porpoise.)
September 18, 1985	A fire on board a Golf II SSB off the Japanese coast was probably caused by an electrical overload after the boat was caught in a Japanese trawler's nets; smoke was seen to be coming from missile hatches in the sail. The boat was given assistance by Soviet minesweepers and an oiler and eventually limped back to Vladivostok.
October 1986	Following a fire in one of the SS-N-6 Sawfly missiles on board, a Yankee class SSBN was forced to surface some 600nm north of Bermuda and 760nm from New York. She was taken under tow by a Soviet merchantman, but later sank. Three crewmen died and several were injured.

Above: Following an August 28, 1976, collision with USS *Voge* (FF 1047) a Soviet Echo II SSGN wallows with her sail barely awash. Such collisions are rare.

Below: Soviet Yankee class SSBN on the surface in October 1986, after a fire in one of her SS-N-6 missiles. On patrol off the US east coast, she sank after limping for several days on the surface.

Kockums URF submarine rescue vehicle

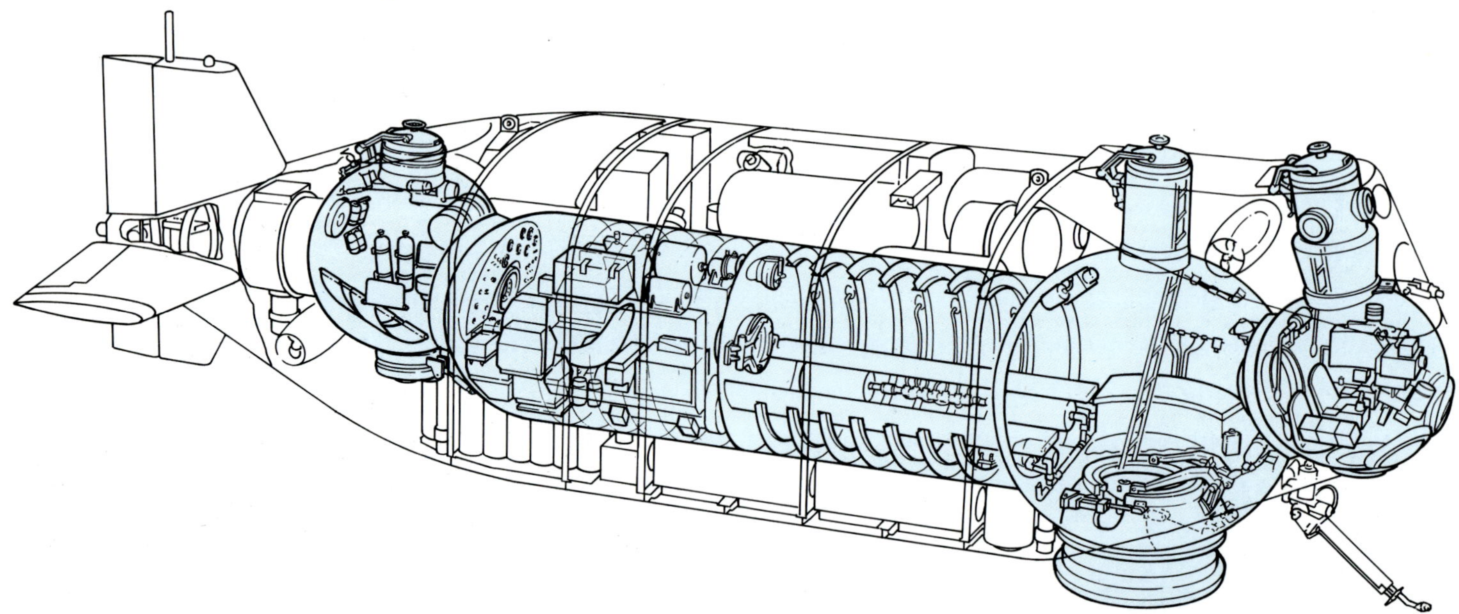

Above: The Swedish URF undersea rescue vehicle comprises a pressure hull (blue) surrounded by an outer casing. Two controllers sit in the operators' compartment forward; aft of this are, in turn, the rescue compartment, an auxiliaries compartment and the diving compartment.

then, in 1971, *Flore*'s snorkel system sprang a leak due to a faulty valve, but on this occasion an alert captain was able to take immediate remedial action and save his boat. Finally, on November 11, 1972, *Sirène* sprang a leak and sank, but she was later recovered and recommissioned and, presumably as a result of at last being able to identify the problem, no other members of the class have been lost. On the other hand, nor were any more export orders received.

ESCAPE TECHNIQUES

Escape from a sunken submarine is feasible in many circumstances, the most elementary being for the survivors of an accident to escape through specially designed hatches using various types of escape gear. British submarines have two single escape towers, one at each end of the boat, and each man has a hooded immersion suit, a system which has been proved down to 600ft (183m). The suit has a hood containing trapped air for the survivor to breathe during the ascent, and protects him from hostile conditions on the surface; in the escape tower the survivor plugs a built-in connector into a socket on the built-in breathing system, which provides pure air to inflate the lifejacket and fill the hood, and within about 16 seconds he is ready to leave. Sea pressure is then applied, the hatch is opened and the man immediately exits, ascending at 8ft/sec (2.4m/sec) and breathing normally as he does so. Once on the surface he unzips the hood, inflates the double-skinned survival suit and awaits the arrival of his rescuers.

At depths greater than 650ft a rescue vehicle is essential and several have been developed. The US Navy Deep Submergence Rescue Vehicle (DSRV) is, in effect, a small, air- and road-mobile submarine of which it was initially planned to build 12, each capable of carrying 12 survivors, but in the event just two, each capable of transporting four crewmen and 24 survivors, were constructed. They became fully operational in 1977 and have been tested in use with both US and British submarines; capable of operating at a maximum depth of 4,921ft (1,500m), the DSRV can withstand pressures equivalent to 9,022ft (1,750m). A normal propeller is capable of moving the craft at a maximum of five knots and two thrusters are fitted to manoeuvre it close alongside a sunken submarine. The vessel consists of two HY-240 steel spheres surrounded by a fibreglass hull, and is designed to be loaded into a USAF C-141 StarLifter, while the road transporter and additional support equipment travel in a second C-141. The DSRVs are taken to the scene of the rescue either on a special cradle mounted on the after deck of a suitably modified submarine or one of the two Pigeon class catamaran submarine rescue ships.

The Soviet Navy has arrived at a different and unusual answer to the same problem. It also has submersible rescue vehicles, each some 36ft (11m) long and with a shrouded propeller, but they are transported by the specially constructed India class submarines. These boats, of 4,800 tons submerged displacement, have large wells on their after casings, in which sit two of the submersibles, and they usually travel on the surface, submerging only when in the immediate vicinity of the sunken submarine. There are two India class submarines, one with the Pacific

Above: Built of HY 130 steel, the URF can operate at a maximum depth of 1,510ft (460m) – collapse depth is 2,953ft (900m) – and it can be docked with a submarine at angles of up to 45°. The vessel is moved by road on a low-loader then towed, on the surface or submerged, to an accident scene.

Below: Underwater view of the US Navy Deep Submergence Rescue Vehicle *Mystic* (DSRV-1), which is designed to operate at a maximum depth of 4,921ft (1,500m), with a collapse depth of 9,022ft (2,750m). Clearly seen here are the headlight, the duct for the bow thruster and the transfer skirt.

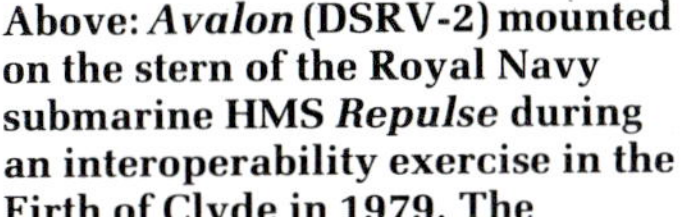

Above: *Avalon* (DSRV-2) mounted on the stern of the Royal Navy submarine HMS *Repulse* during an interoperability exercise in the Firth of Clyde in 1979. The exercise involved the transfer of 10 men and a quantity of stores from one submerged submarine to another. Twelve such vessels were planned, but only two were built.

Above: The Soviet Navy deploys two India class rescue submarines, one each in the Pacific and Northern Fleets. Designed to cruise on the surface, the Indias have large dorsal docking wells which carry two rescue submersibles, one approximately 40ft (12.1m) and the other about 37ft (11.3m) long.

DSRV general arrangement

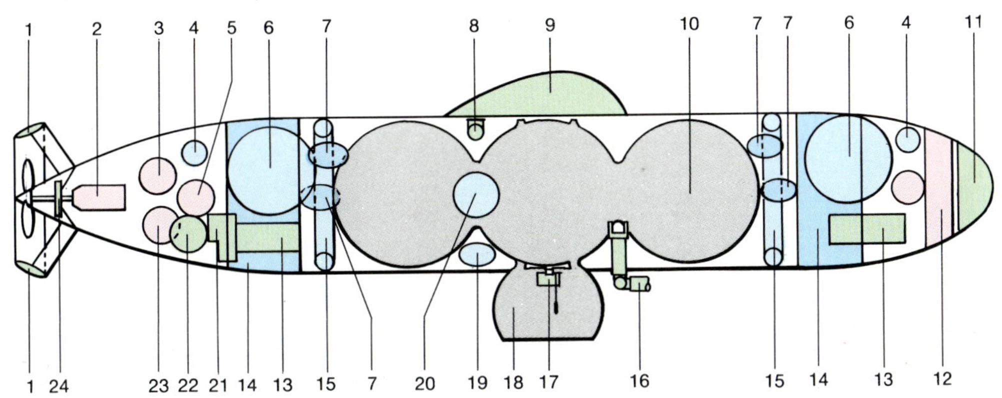

1 Tilting shroud
2 Main propulsion motor
3 Thruster controllers
4 Trim tanks
5 Thruster ducts
6 Transfer tanks
7 Variable ballast tanks
8 List pump
9 Access hatch canopy
10 Pressure capsule
11 Sonar dome
12 Forward thruster ducts
13 Battery banks
14 Ballast tanks
15 Toroidal tanks
16 Manipulator
17 Hauldown winch
18 Transfer skirt
19 Mercury tank
20 List tank
21 Hydraulic power pack
22 High-pressure air
23 Hydraulic and propulsion controllers
24 Shroud gimbal

Pressure capsule
Other tanks
Ballast tanks
Propulsion
Miscellaneous

DSRV sensors

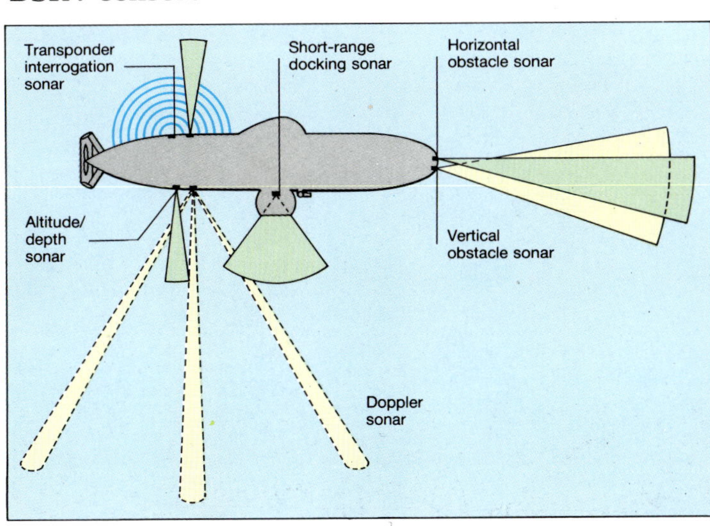

Above: The US Navy's DSRV is based on a three-sphere pressure capsule constructed of HY 140 steel which can accommodate the four-man crew and up to 24 survivors. The DSRV can be airlifted by Lockheed C-141 StarLifter, is road-mobile on a low-loader, and can be carried at up to 15 knots by any submarine with suitable mountings.

Left: Getting to the scene of an accident is one thing; finding a disabled submarine in the murky depths of the ocean is another. To cope with the hostile environment the DSRV is provided with a comprehensive range of sonars as shown, while optical systems include six television cameras, a 35mm still camera, flood and strobe lights and viewing ports.

Fleet and the other with the Northern Fleet.

The Soviet Navy also has a number of submarine rescue ships, including the 22,500-ton *Elbrus*, the only ship of her type in the world with an ice-breaking capability, presumably to support the latest SSBNs. Two submersibles are carried abaft the funnel and launched by gantries. The single 10,000-ton Nera class, eight 3,200-ton Prut class and 11 930-ton Valday class rescue ships have equipment and capabilities commensurate with their size.

Other navies are less well provided for. The Italian Navy has one salvage ship, the *Anteo* of 3,780 tons, which carries US-style submarine rescue equipment, including a McCann rescue bell. She also carries a 22-ton MSM-1/S submersible named *Usel*, which has a maximum operating depth of 1,970ft (600m). The French Navy has a similar ship, the 1,150-ton *Triton*, which is intended primarily for underwater research but has a rescue capability; her equipment includes a 13.5-ton tethered bell which can be used down to 820ft (250m) and a two-man submarine, the 16-ton *Griffon*, which can dive to a maximum of 2,000ft (600m). Japan has a rescue ship, the *Chiyoda* (4,450 tons), whose Japanese-designed, Kawasaki-built deep-submergence rescue vehicle is 39.4ft (12m) long and has a displacement of 40 tons.

Sweden, whose rescue missions are unlikely to be outside the relatively shallow Baltic, has a submarine rescue ship, the *Belos* (965 tons), which supports the 50-ton URF rescue submersible. The latter, constructed of HY-130 steel, has a maximum operating depth of 1,510ft (460m) and a collapse depth of 2,952ft (900m).

Submarines and their

Weapons

John Jordan

Below: A heavyweight torpedo is manoeuvred into position for embarkation through the weapons hatch of the Valiant class attack submarine HMS *Conqueror*.

Introduction

Above: The test launch of a UGM-84 Harpoon missile from a US submarine. Underwater-launched cruise missiles make it possible for the submarine to engage its targets at greater range.

Right: The Dutch submarine *Dolfijn*, one of the most innovative postwar designs, introduced the multi-pressure hull concept to modern submarine construction.

The following pages provide illustrations of the major classes of submarine currently in service, together with technical data and construction details. A large part of the text is devoted to the historical background of the class and to the prominent technical aspects of the design; other sections detail the various weapons carried by the submarines since their completion, and the location, designation and capabilities of the sensor arrays.

Although the number of submarines completed to each design is given, the names of individual units have been omitted. Two pages have been allocated to each class in order to provide consistency in layout and coverage, and the inclusion of names would have severely restricted the description of aspects of the design in the case of the larger classes, such as the US Navy's Los Angeles and Sturgeon.
As these types are among the most important designs dealt with it was felt that this would create a serious imbalance.

In a book such as this, it is never easy to decide which classes should be included and which should be omitted. As regards submarines the decision is made all the more difficult by the imbalance of construction, with small nations such as the Netherlands and Sweden building a succession of interesting designs in small numbers, while the United States and the Soviet Union build their own designs in classes of 30, 40 or 50. The author felt it was important to include any submarine type built in large numbers, but has attempted to compensate for this by discussing the design aspects of smaller classes which had to be omitted in the entries for other classes selected as representative of that country's construction. Thus Sweden's Sjöormen and Västergötland classes are covered in the entry for the Näcken class.

The final list of entries reveals the extent of Soviet submarine construction since World War II, with more than a third of the following spreads devoted to submarine types of Soviet design. In modern times no other country, even the United States, has ever had more than two types of submarine under construction simultaneously, yet in 1986 no fewer than seven different types, all of recent design, were under construction for the Soviet Navy.

The predominance of Soviet entries has created a number of problems both for the author and, more particularly, for the artists. We only ever see the uppermost part of a submarine's hull: the torpedo tubes, the propellers and the after control surfaces are beneath the water, while the torpedoes and missiles are carried within the hull and there are rarely tell-tale bulges to help us determine the configuration of the major sonars.

All submarines are designed for covert operations, and even the Western navies are less than forthcoming about major aspects of their submarine designs, particularly with regard to the precise designation, configuration and performance of sonar arrays. The Soviets guard their military secrets even more jealously, and the covert nature of submarine operations greatly facilitates their task: the only published photographs of Soviet submarines in dry dock depict elderly units of the Whiskey and Romeo classes, while data on Soviet submarine weapon systems and sonars comes exclusively from Western intelligence sources, is rarely complete, and is often unreliable and subject to correction as time passes.

Clearly there are serious implications for a book of this type. All drawings depicting the underwater configuration of Soviet submarines must be regarded as provisional, and the weapons depicted are those with which particular classes are credited by the major Western reference sources. The configurations of weapons such as the SS-N-3A anti-ship missile and the M-57 torpedo are based on published photographs, but those of more recent weapons must again be regarded as provisional. This is particularly true of the SS-N-15 and SS-N-16 anti-submarine missiles, whose configurations have been based of necessty on those of Western submarine-launched missiles of similar conception.

To attempt a serious comparison with contemporary Western submarines is clearly a major undertaking. Nevertheless, the author has made extensive use of the available reference sources in order to establish a consistent and logical overview of Soviet submarine development and weapon capabilities. The inclusion of all the weapon systems with which Soviet submarines are generally credited was considered essential to provide a complete picture, and these considerations largely outweighed any concern regarding visual accuracy.

Few submarine designs in this section of the book can be regarded as truly international. Drawings of submarines such as the German Type 209, which was designed for export, depict individual units in service with specific countries, together with their associated weapon systems, and any differences in the weapon and sensor outfits of boats in service with other countries are detailed in the text.

Left: A US Navy artist's impression of the Soviet Navy's Oscar-class cruise missile submarine (SSGN) published while the first unit was still fitting out at Severodvinsk. Although inaccurate in some respects, the drawing gets most of the detail right, including the number and position of the missile hatches, and the VLF buoy housing immediately abaft the fin.

Below: The real thing! The first unit of the Oscar class, seen here in northern waters shortly after completion. The Soviet Navy has apparently experienced some problems with the adhesion of the rubberized tiles designed to reduce the sonar signature of its latest submarines. A number of those applied to the curved sections of the hull casing are missing in this photograph.

Agosta class

Origin: France, first unit completed 1964
Type: Attack submarine, diesel-powered (SS)
Displacement: 1,490 tons surfaced; 1,740 tons submerged
Dimensions: Length 222ft (67.6m); beam 22ft (6.8m); draught 18ft (5.5m)
Propulsion: Diesel-electric drive on one shaft; two SEMT-Pielstick 16 PA 4 185 diesel generators, each 1,270bhp; one Jeumont-Schneider electric motor; 2,540bhp for 12.5kt surfaced, 2,990hp for 17.5kt submerged (see remarks)
Complement: 54
Background: With the loss of French Indochina in the early 1950s long range, which had been a primary requirement for the postwar Narval class, became less important. On the other hand, the Daphné class had proved to be on the small side for French maritime commitments, which by the late 1960s included a major presence in the Indian Ocean. Moreover, since the Daphnés had been designed there had been important new developments in submarine technology: the 'Albacore' hull-form had revolutionised underwater performance, while Modern torpedoes with sophisticated homing devices allied to computerized fire control made large salvos unnecessary, so fewer torpedo tubes were needed. The four attack submarines of the Agosta class, laid down between 1972 and 1974, were therefore not only significantly larger than the Daphnés, but of a completely new design.
Design: Double-hull construction was retained for these submarines, the space between the two hulls being used for ballast and fuel tanks, and for the sensing heads of much of the acoustic equipment. As with the earlier French designs, all deck protrusions retract to ensure a smooth waterflow. The pressure hull comprises a cylinder with cones fore and aft and is enclosed by a cylindrical outer casing which terminates in an oval-shaped bow housing the principal active and passive sonar arrays. In order to save weight, extensive use of plastics was made in the construction of the fin. The latter is positioned well forward, so that all the accommodation and messing spaces for the crew are grouped together abaft the control/attack centre. Beneath the control centre and the accommodation spaces are two battery compartments, each housing 160 Type N battery cells. This is double the number of cells

installed in earlier French submarines, and gives the Agostas exceptionally good underwater endurance. The diesel-electric propulsion plant allows for continuity of speed over the full power range. The main electric motor can produce 3,475kW (4,725hp) for short periods, boosting the maximum underwater speed to 20.5 knots. A separate creep motor can propel the submarine at 1.5 knots during silent patrol operations. It uses little power, enabling the submarine to remain submerged for long periods. The single five-bladed propeller is located

Below: *Hurmat*, the second of two Agosta class submarines in service with the Pakistani Navy. Originally ordered by South Africa, they were sold to Pakistan while under construction in 1977 as a result of a United Nations arms embargo. They were built by Digeon, Nantes, and entered service in 1979-80.

Above: *Galerna*, the first of four Agostas built under licence in Spanish shipyards. Two were completed in 1983, and a further pair in 1985. French technical assistance had previously been provided for the construction of four Daphné class boats also by Bazán, Cartagena.

abaft modern cruciform control surfaces. The forward hydroplanes are mounted close to the bow.

Armament: The traditional French 21.7in (550mm) calibre was adopted for the four bow tubes of the Agostas to enable them to fire existing torpedoes. However, the tubes were designed to handle both 21.7in (550mm) and more modern 21in (533mm) torpedoes. The L 5 21in (533mm) antisubmarine torpedo already well established as a surface-launched weapon, is free-running, employs active acoustic homing, has a maximum speed of 35 knots and a maximum range of 7,700yds (7,000m). It is now being superseded by the F 17, a wire-guided torpedo with electric propulsion and passive acoustic homing. The Mod.1 variant is an anti-ship weapon but an antisubmarine variant, designated the F 17P, has recently entered service. The Agostas currently carry a total of 20 torpedoes of both the L 5 Mod.3 and the F 17 types. Bévéziers conducted trials of the SM 39 Exocet submarine-launched anti-ship missile (see Rubis), and it is envisaged that the SM 39 will eventually be in service with all four boats of the class.

Electronics: The Agostas have a similar sonar outfit to the modernised boats of the Daphné class. Both DUUA 1 and DUUA 2 active/passive sonars are fitted, together with a DSUV 22 circular passive hydrophone array. There is a DUUX 2 passive ranging sonar, and DUUG/AUUD sonar intercept equipment. Torpedo fire control is provided by the DLT D-3 FC system linked to an Iris 35M computer. The system comprises a display of the tactical situation, based on inputs from the various sensors, a targeting display and a weapons control console. Simultaneous control of several torpedoes is possible.

Mast-mounted sensors include search and attack periscopes, a DRUA-33 surveillance radar, and ARUR and ARUD ESM intercept aerials.

Construction: Four submarines of the Agosta class were completed for the Marine Nationale between 1977 and 1978 and a further four were built under licence in Spain with French technical assistance between 1977 and 1985. Two Agostas were ordered from French shipyards by South Africa, but a United Nations embargo prevented these from being delivered, and they were re-sold to Pakistan. An order for a further two units from Spanish shipyards has yet to be confirmed.

Below: The Agostas have four bow tubes of 21.7in (550mm) diameter capable of accommodating older model torpedoes and more modern 21in (533mm) types. The current outfit consists of L 5 Mod 3 free-running anti-submarine torpedoes (1) and F 17 Mod 1 (2) wire-guided anti-ship torpedoes. Both types are now being superseded by the F 17 Mod 2, which has a dual seeker. The class is now being retro-fitted with the necessary fire control electronics for the SM 39 Exocet anti-ship missile (3). Weapons capacity is 20 torpedoes or missiles. Three TSM 3510 mines (4) can be carried in place of one torpedo.

Alfa class

Origin: USSR, first unit completed 1972
Type: Attack submarine, nuclear-powered (SSN)
Displacement: 2,900 tons surfaced; 3,680 tons submerged
Dimensions: Length 267ft (81.4m); beam 31ft (9.5m); draught 23ft (7m)
Propulsion: One liquid-metal reactor with turbo-electric drive on one shaft; two steam turbo-alternators, one motor; 47,000hp for 42-43kt max
Complement: 45
Background: Ironically, the original impetus for the development of the Alfa may have been provided by US official policy statements dating from the late 1950s to the effect that within the decade submarines would attain speeds of 45 knots and diving depths of 3,000ft (900m). The Soviets undoubtedly saw a use for such a submarine as a fast interceptor to be used against surface forces and hostile submarines detected by their ocean surveillance system. If the submarine were operated in a more offensive role, high underwater speed combined with a deep-diving capability would enable the submarine to evade Western antisubmarine defences by passing beneath them. Surface-launched ASW weapons such as homing torpedoes would take such a long time to reach the operating depth of the submarine that the latter would by then have passed out of range of the acoustic homing device. The decision to build the Alfa was followed by a prolonged development period during which the Soviets were always operating on the outer edge of technology. The development of a reactor employing liquid metal as a coolant cannot have been easy, to judge from US Navy experience with the submarine *Seawolf* (SSN-575) in the late 1950s: the *Seawolf* reactor was abandoned as unreliable within two years, and replaced by a conventional pressurized water-cooled model. The adoption of titanium for the Alfa's pressure hull in order to increase diving depth also posed serious problems. Titanium is much lighter than steel and has greater tensile strength, but it is difficult to roll and bend, and special welding processes had to be introduced. The prototype boat, completed in 1972, appears to have experienced serious cracking of

Above: The Alfa is one of the world's most remarkable submarines. The hull is constructed not of steel but of lightweight titanium, giving the Alfa an operating depth estimated at around 900m (3,000ft) while the unmanned propulsion plant, which is powered by a liquid-metal reactor, produces a maximum underwater speed in excess of 40 knots. However, slow series production was terminated after six production boats had been completed.

the welded joins, and following extensive trials in the Baltic had to be abandoned; she was broken up *in situ* in 1974. However, the Soviets persisted with the design and eventually resolved many of the associated problems, and series production began in the mid-1970s, the first boat being completed in 1979.

Design: The Alfa has a single reactor which employs a lead-bizmuth mixture as coolant. This results in a particularly compact propulsion plant, as only the reactor itself needs to be located within the containment shield. The adoption of a liquid-metal coolant also raises the temperature in the steam generator, enabling exceptionally high horsepower figures to be achieved for a reactor of moderate size. The propulsion machinery of the Alfa is highly automated, and it is reported that the engine room is entirely unmanned, but safety and accessibility standards are almost certainly far lower than would be permitted in the West. It is also reported that these submarines are exceptionally noisy at speed. This is hardly surprising given a combination of small submarine size and high power output, which almost certainly precluded 'rafting' or other methods of insulating machinery noise. Unlike other Soviet submarines, the Alfa appears to be of single hull construction, with a particularly smooth transition between the casing and the base of the streamlined fin. The single shaft is fitted with a seven-bladed propeller and there are conventional cruciform tail surfaces.

Armament: The Alfa is fitted with six bow tubes of standard 21in (533mm) diameter. These can fire conventional anti-ship or antisubmarine torpedoes, and the Alfa is probably also equipped to fire the SS-N-15 nuclear-tipped antisubmarine missile. There is no evidence to suggest that even the production boats are fitted with the larger 26in (650mm) tube. The distance between the bow and the fin is comparatively short, and this would appear to preclude installation of the larger tube and accommodation of the SS-N-16 missile together with its associated fire control consoles. There is undoubtedly less space available for torpedo stowage than on other contemporary Soviet SSNs, and a maximum figure of about 12 torpedoes/missiles seems likely.

Electronics: The Alfa has an active/passive bow sonar which is probably located above the torpedo tubes. The outfit of sensor masts is broadly similar to that of the Victor-class SSN and the Charlie-class SSGN: search and attack periscopes, Snoop Head/Bald Head combined surface surveillance/ESM, Park Lamp VLF reception, and aerials for HF and VHF communications. There are no hatches for VLF buoys, and no other visible towed arrays either for communications or for passive acoustic detection.

Construction: There is some disagreement about completion dates for these submarines, particularly for the prototype boat. The latter was built by the Sudomekh Shipyard, Leningrad, and is stated by some sources to have been completed as early as 1968. The six production boats were completed between 1979 and 1983 at Leningrad and Severodvinsk. Construction has now been terminated in favour of a larger titanium-hulled submarine, the Mike.

Left: The Alfa is credited with six bow tubes of standard 21in (533mm) diameter. These can handle long free-running anti-ship torpedoes with alternative conventional HE or nuclear warheads (1), and acoustic-homing antisubmarine torpedoes (2); two mines (3) can be carried in place of a single torpedo. It is thought that the Alfa is also equipped to fire the SS-N-15 nuclear-tipped antisubmarine missile (4), but there is no evidence to suggest that the type is fitted with the large-diameter 26in (650mm) tube.

Charlie class

Origin: USSR, first unit completed 1967
Type: Cruise missile submarine, nuclear-powered (SSGN)
Displacement: Charlie I: 4,000 tons surfaced; 4,800 tons submerged
Charlie II: 4,500 tons surfaced; 5,500 tons submerged
Dimensions: Charlie I: length 312ft (95m); beam 33ft (10m); draught 26ft (8m)
Charlie II: length 335ft (102m); beam and draught as Charlie I
Propulsion: One pressurized water-cooled reactor driving geared steam turbines; one shaft; 15,000shp for 24kt max
Complement: 90
Background: The development of a short-range, active radar homing missile which could be fired from underwater, the SS-N-7, promised to make the anti-shipping torpedo obsolete. Submarines thus equipped would be able to approach their targets undetected, launch their missiles outside the effective sonar range of the escorts, and make their escape without exposing themselves to enemy countermeasures. The Charlie is therefore the true successor of the torpedo-armed November class, the last unit of which was completed in the same year that the first of the new SSGNs was laid down. The threat posed by the pop-up launch mode of the SS-N-7 missile was taken very seriously by the US Navy, which was compelled to accelerate the development of close-in anti-missile weapons and electronic countermeasures (ECM). One of the primary missions of the US 'fleet submarines' of the Los Angeles class (qv) was to clear a path ahead of the carrier battle groups, where Soviet submarines might be lying in wait. These countermeasures appear to have influenced the Soviet Navy into a phasing out of the Charlie programme in the late 1970s.
Design: The Charlie belongs to the second generation of Soviet nuclear-powered submarines. The first of the class entered service in 1968, the year in which the first unit of the Victor class commissioned, and despite fundamental disparities in mission between the Victor and the Charlie, there are a number of striking similarities between the two designs. Length and beam are virtually identical, and the

Above: The broad bow of the Charlie houses eight vertical launch tubes for the SS-N-7 anti-ship missile. The SS-N-7 was the first Soviet anti-ship missile which could be fired from underwater: earlier Soviet SSGNs had to surface in order to launch their missiles, and were therefore vulnerable to attack by hostile aircraft. The submarine depicted is a Charlie I.

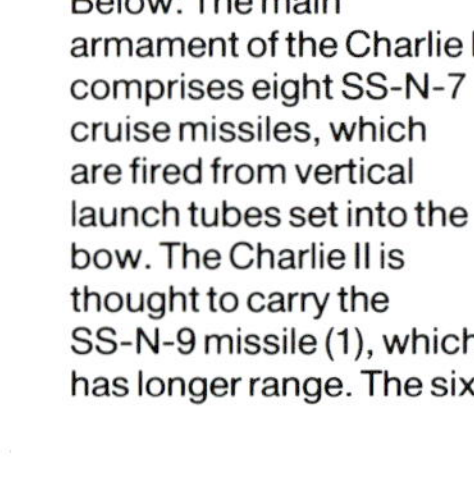

Below: The main armament of the Charlie I comprises eight SS-N-7 cruise missiles, which are fired from vertical launch tubes set into the bow. The Charlie II is thought to carry the SS-N-9 missile (1), which has longer range. The six 21in (533mm) bow torpedo tubes can fire a variety of weapons. In the Charlie II these include the SS-N-15 nuclear-tipped antisubmarine missile (2), plus a small number of antiship torpedoes (3).

propulsion system employs similar technology, with a single shaft driving a single, five-bladed propeller. They can be distinguished by the shape of the fin, the forward edge of which is angled in the Victor but vertical in the Charlie. The latter feature appears to have been not entirely successful, as a collar-shaped fairing is now being fitted at the base of the fin to improve hydrodynamic performance. The Charlie has cruciform after control surfaces, and retractable forward hydroplanes are mounted on the hull immediately abaft the missile tubes. The eight launch tubes for the SS-N-7 missile are located in the bow section between the inner pressure cylinder and the outer hull casing. They are covered by large square hatches some 14ft (4.25m) long, four on either side. The later variant, the Charlie II, which first appeared in 1973, is some 23ft (7m) longer than the Charlie I. An additional hull section has been inserted between the fin and the bow. The missile tubes are slightly farther aft, but contrary to early reports there has been no increase in their number, which remains at eight. The configuration of the fin and the after section of the later boats remains unchanged.

Armament: The SS-N-7 Siren is a conventional aeroplane-shaped missile with a length of about 23ft (7m). It employs solid-fuel propulsion, and has an estimated range of 30-35nm (55-64km). It can carry a nuclear or conventional warhead weighing approximately 1,100lb (500kg), making it particularly effective against large surface warships. It is reported that the Charlie II may carry the more advanced SS-N-9 missile, which is 6ft (2m) longer and has almost twice the range. However, the tactical value of such a long-range missile is questionable, given the significant increase in targeting problems and the absence of any facility for mid-course guidance. The diameter of the pressure hull in the bow section is necessarily reduced because of the need to accommodate the missile tubes. Consequently the torpedo armament is relatively small by the standards of other modern Soviet attack submarines. There are six torpedo tubes as compared with eight in the Victor, and it is estimated that a maximum of 12 torpedoes could be carried. The Charlie II is almost certainly equipped to fire the SS-N-15 nuclear-tipped antisubmarine missile, and 26in (650mm) tubes may eventually be retro-fitted to enable these submarines to fire the SS-N-16 missile.

Electronics: The Charlie is credited with a low-frequency active/passive bow sonar, plus conformal passive flank arrays. Mast-mounted sensors conform to those of other Soviet submarines of the period: search and attack periscopes, a Snoop Tray surface surveillance radar, Park Lamp VLF/LF reception, Brick Pulp ESM, and HF and VHF communications. The Charlie II variant has twin hatches abaft the fin for a VLF communications buoy.

Construction: Twelve submarines of the Charlie I class were completed between 1968 and 1972 at the inland Gorky Shipyard. They were the first nuclear boats constructed at Gorky, which had previously built only diesel submarines. They were followed by six Charlie IIs, completed at the same yard between 1973 and 1982.

Below: The hatches covering the eight missile launch tubes are particularly prominent in this view of a Charlie I. Abaft the missile hatches can be seen a narrow, angled hatch which marks the location of the retractable forward hydroplanes. In the Charlie II the length of the bow section has been increased.

Daphné

Origin: France, first unit completed 1964
Type: Attack submarine, diesel-powered (SS)
Displacement: 870 tons surfaced; 1,045 tons submerged
Dimensions: Length 190ft (57.8m); beam 22ft (6.8m); draught 15ft (4.6m)
Propulsion: Diesel-electric drive on two shafts; two SEMT-Pielstick 12 PA 1/4 diesel generators, each 615bhp; two Jeumont Schneider electric motors, each 790hp; 1,230bhp for 13.5kt surfaced, 1,580hp for 16kt submerged
Complement: 45

Background: Prior to World War II the Marine Nationale had established a clear distinction between long-range ('1st Class') submarines of 1,500 tonnes, and medium-range ('2nd Class') submarines of about half that size. This policy was to continue in the postwar period. The Narval, which was closely modelled on the German Type XXI, became the standard 1st Class type, and in 1952 the General Staff requested that design work should begin on a 2nd Class counterpart, which was to become the Daphné. Staff requirements included low noise, good manoeuvrability, a small crew and ease of maintenance -- all features of the tiny Aréthuse design which preceded the Daphné. The last two requirements would be met by employing extensive automation, and by adopting unit replacement techniques to minimize onboard maintenance. In addition, maximum speeds of 13 knots dived, 6 knots creep speed, and 7 knots snorkeling were demanded. Diving depth was to be greater than in the preceding classes, and there were to be at least six internal torpedo tubes (of which two were to be stern tubes for antisubmarine torpedoes) with

Below: *Daphné*, the name-ship of the class. Although lacking in endurance, these submarines have proved handy in the relatively shallow waters of the Mediterranean and they carry a heavy armament of torpedoes.

Daphné **(S 641)**

Above: The Daphné has an unusual arrangement of torpedo tubes reminiscent of French prewar practice. There are eight internal bow tubes, but the four stern tubes are external; two are directly above the stern, with the other pair angled out just forward of them. No reloads are carried. The torpedo tubes are of the traditional French 21.7in (550mm) calibre, and fire the older models of French torpedo. The E 14 and E 15 free-running anti-ship torpedoes (1) are complemented by the L 3 antisubmarine torpedo (2), which uses active acoustic homing. All three types are relatively slow by modern standards.

14 reloads and fire control on a par with the Narval class. These performance figures were generally exceeded in the final design, which incorporated no fewer than 12 torpedo tubes, of which eight were internal.

Design: The hull-form of the Daphné is conventional, with a prominent keel for improved stability during fast manoeuvres. The French continued to favour double-hull construction, with all fuel and ballast tanks outside the pressure hull. A maximum diving depth of 985ft (300m) is reported. Within the pressure hull there is a conventional single-deck layout. In keeping with French prewar practice all four stern tubes are external, the after pair being located directly above the stern with the other pair angled out just forward of them. Stern tubes were made possible by the adoption of a two-shaft machinery installation allied to conventional control surfaces. The diesel-electric propulsion system introduced with great success in the Aréthuse class was retained, and the name-ship of the class achieved 16 knots on trials – an increase of three knots on the original specification. The machinery is mounted on two levels, with the auxiliary machinery above the propulsion machinery.

Armament: The Daphnés have eight internal bow tubes arranged as two vertical rows of four, plus the four external stern tubes already mentioned. However, as the design was very tight, reloads were dispensed with in order to economise on space. All 12 tubes are of the non-standard French prewar calibre of 21.7in (550mm); they are therefore limited to torpedoes of indigenous design and manufacture. French torpedoes of the period shared many common parts in order to facilitate production and maintenance. The E 14 anti-ship torpedo is 14ft (4.3m) long and has a passive acoustic homing head. It is relatively slow by modern standards, having a speed of only 25 knots and a maximum range of 8,300yds (7,500m). The E 15 is essentially an E 14 with an additional section which increases maximum range to 13,200yds (12,000m). The L 3, which is presumably fired from the stern tubes, is a free-running antisubmarine torpedo with active acoustic homing. Its length, speed and range are identical to the E 14's, but it can be fired down to a depth of 985ft (300m), twice the maximum firing depth of the anti-ship torpedoes.

Electronics: As completed the Daphnés were fitted with a DUUA 1 active/passive scanning sonar, in a bulb above the stem; beneath the bow, in a larger dome, was a DSUV 2 circular passive array. The two primary sonars were complemented by a DUUX 2 passive ranging sonar for fire control, and an AUUD/DUUG 1 sonar intercept system to detect and analyse hostile sonar emissions. Torpedo fire control was provided by a DLT D-3 FC system. Search and attack periscopes were fitted, together with a Calypso surveillance radar and ESM intercept mast. Beginning in 1971 all except the name-ship, *Daphné*, underwent an extensive modernisation during which the submarines' electronics systems were substantially updated. The original DUUA 1 active/passive sonar was replaced by a DUUA 2 sonar housed in a prominent dome above the bow.

Construction: Eleven submarines of the Daphné class were completed for the French Marine Nationale between 1964 and 1970. Of these, *Minerve* was lost in 1968 and *Eurydice* in 1970. In addition, four were completed by French shipyards for Portugal between 1967 and 1969, three for Pakistan in 1970, and three for South Africa in 1970-71. One of the Portuguese boats was re-sold to Pakistan in 1975. Four further boats were built in Spain with French technical assistance and completed between 1973 and 1975.

Below: The Daphné has proved to be an attractive export design. Besides the eleven boats completed for the Marine Nationale, ten have been built in French shipyards for other countries, and a further four have been built under licence.

Delta class

Origin: USSR, first unit completed 1972
Type: Ballistic missile submarine, nuclear-powered (SSBN)
Displacement: Delta I: 11,750 tons submerged
Delta II: 12,750 tons submerged
Delta III: 13,250 tons submerged
Delta IV: 13,550 tons submerged
Dimensions: Delta I: length 456ft (139m); beam 39ft (12m); draught 29ft (9m)
Delta II/III: length 508ft (155m); beam and draught as Delta I
Delta IV: length 538ft (164m); beam and draught as Delta I
Propulsion: Two pressurized water-cooled reactors driving geared steam turbines; 2 shafts; 35,000shp for 24-25kt max
Complement: 120
Background: The early Soviet SLBMs had a relatively short range. Soviet ballistic missile submarines up to and including the Yankee therefore had to transit the NATO antisubmarine barriers in the Greenland/Iceland/United

Above: The Delta III carries the SS-N-18 Stingray missile, which is longer than the SS-N-8 Sawfly carried by the Delta I and II. The substitution has resulted in an unusually high casing around the missile section.

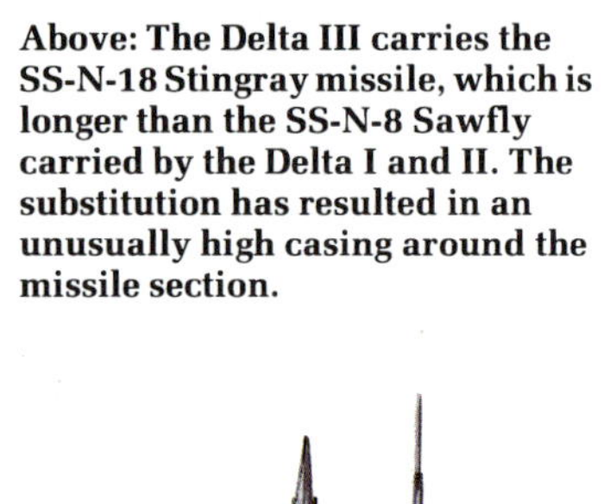

Above: The Delta III is equipped to launch 16 SS-N-18 Stingray ballistic missiles (1), which carry between one and seven reentry vehicles to a range of 3,500nm (6,500nm) or 4,350nm (8,000nm). Earlier Deltas have the SS-N-8 Sawfly, while the Delta IV has the SS-N-23 Skiff (see text for details). The Deltas have six bow tubes of 21in (533mm) diameter capable of handling both heavy-weight free-running anti-ship torpedoes (2) and the acoustic-homing antisubmarine torpedoes (3) which are standard aboard Soviet submarines.

Kingdom (GIUK) Gap in order to target the United States. As Soviet missile technology progressed the possibility emerged of developing a missile with a range exceeding 4,000nm (7,500km), sufficient to target all major US cities from the relative security of Soviet-dominated waters in the Arctic and the Northwest Pacific. The SS-N-8, first installed in submarines of the Delta class, was to became the Soviet Navy's primary strategic missile, and spawned a number of later derivatives.

Design: The Delta is essentially a modified Yankee. The forward section, up to and including the fin, is identical to that of the earlier boat, as is the stern section. The major structural difference is the enlarged missile section amidships. The SS-N-8 is a much larger missile than the SS-N-6, so the compartment in which the missiles are housed is longer, broader and higher than that of the Yankee. In spite of a 30ft (9m) increase in length the Delta I could accommodate only 12 missiles as compared with 16 in the Yankee. Shortly after the appearance of the first Delta a new variant, the Delta II, entered service with the Northern Fleet. The missile section of the Delta II was the same height as that of the Delta I, but was 50ft (15m) longer, enabling four additional SS-N-8 missile tubes to be worked in. This gave the submarines an extraordinary length to beam ratio which was to be repeated in later Delta variants. The after end of the missile casing was not stepped, as in the Delta I, but was angled down to join the after section. The Delta III, which followed in 1978, was of identical length to the Delta II, but the missile casing was 8ft (2.5m) higher in order to accommodate a new MIRVed missile developed from the SS-N-8, the SS-N-18. The latest (and probably final) variant, the Delta IV, made its first public appearance in late 1985, again in the Northern Fleet area. It is in many respects identical to the Delta III. The new missile carried, the SS-NX-23, is similar in size to the SS-N-18, so the missile casing is largely unmodified. The major external differences are related to the stern, which has the same low, angular fin as the second and third boats of the Oscar class (qv). Fin stabilisers are fitted on either side of the hull casing aft, suggesting that the increased height of the missile section from the Delta III onwards may have resulted in stability problems.

Armament: The SS-N-8 carried by the Delta I and II is a large, liquid-fueled missile about 43ft (13m) long with a diameter of 6ft (1.8m). It is armed with a single large nuclear warhead of 800kT. The earliest variant of the missile had a maximum range of 4,250nm (7,800km), but the later Mod 2 variant has a range of 4,950nm (9,100km). The SS-N-18 missile carried by the Delta III entered service around 1978 and was the first Soviet SLBM to have multiple independent reentry vehicles. The Mod 1 variant of the missile carries three 200kT MIRVs to a maximum range of 3,500nm (6,500km); the Mod 2 is fitted with a single 450kT warhead and has a range of 4,350nm (8,000km); and the Mod 3 carries seven MIRVs and has a range similar to the Mod 1's. The SS-NX-23 missile which is due to enter service in 1985-86 in the Delta IV is an improved version of the SS-N-18, with greater throw weight and improved terminal accuracy. It will probably be retro-fitted in the Delta III, but cannot be carried by earlier boats without structural modifications. All variants of the Delta are fitted with six bow tubes for standard 21in (533mm) torpedoes. The Delta IV may also have the large-diameter 26in (650mm) tube.

Electronics: The Deltas appear to have the standard active/passive bow array first fitted in submarines of the Yankee generation. The outfit of sensor masts is also standard for submarines of their period, but with one important addition: the cone-shaped Pert Spring satellite communications antenna. As with the Yankee, a variant of the Cod Eye radio sextant is housed in the upper section of the fin.

Construction: Eighteen submarines of the Delta I class were completed between 1972 and 1977 at Severodvinsk in the Arctic and Komsomolsk in the Pacific. The four Delta II variants were completed at Severodvinsk in 1974-75, and the first of the Delta IIIs followed in 1975. Fourteen had been completed by 1985, the year in which the first of the Delta IVs appeared. Construction of the latter is continuing.

Above: The first of the new Delta IVs is seen here running on the surface. The Delta IV is similar in most respects to the Delta III, but carries the more advanced SS-N-23 missile. External differences include only a single pair of hatches for a VLF communications buoy on the angled section of casing, and a modified tail fin with a tubular dispenser for a towed array.

Left: The variant depicted here is the Delta III, which has a particularly prominent missile casing reaching almost to the top of the fin. The Delta I and II, which carry the shorter SS-N-8 missile, have a lower casing above the missile section. The Delta II, which carries 16 missiles, is of identical length to the Delta III, but the Delta I has only 12 missile launch tubes and is accordingly 56ft (18m) shorter.

Echo II class

Origin: USSR, first unit completed 1962
Type: Cruise missile submarine, nuclear-powered (SSGN)
Displacement: 5,200 tons surfaced; 6,200 tons submerged
Dimensions: Length 380ft (116m); beam 32ft (9.8m); draught 25ft (7.5m)
Propulsion: Two pressurized water-cooled reactors driving geared steam turbines; two shafts; 30,000shp for 23kt max
Complement: 100
Background: The Echo was the Soviet Navy's first purpose-built cruise missile submarine, earlier types being conversions of existing diesel boats. The first variant, the Echo I, was fitted with six paired launchers for SS-N-3C nuclear land attack missiles. However, a major policy change in 1959-60, which saw the creation of the Strategic Rocket Forces as an independent arm of the Soviet armed services and the institution of a large programme of land-based ICBMs, resulted in the premature termination of the Echo I programme after only five submarines had been laid down. The nuclear land attack mission was taken away from the Soviet Navy, which would henceforth concentrate on defending Soviet territory against attack from the sea. A modified version of the SS-N-3 Shaddock (NATO designation SS-N-3A) was developed for use against surface ships and installed in a new, enlarged Echo variant, the Echo II. A large radar antenna for mid-course tracking and guidance of the SS-N-3A missile was installed in a lengthened fin. Heavy reliance was placed on off-board sensors to provide initial detection and tracking of the target. In response to data provided by specially-equipped maritime reconnaissance aircraft such as the Tupolev Tu-95 Bear-D and communicated via a central command post ashore, the Echo would take up position on the bow quarter of a carrier task force and launch its missiles at maximum range.
Design: The Echo design, like that of the contemporary Hotel-class SSBN, was derived from the Soviet Navy's first SSN, the November. It has the same propulsion plant, comprising two reactors in series, each producing approximately 15,000shp. This has proved notoriously unreliable in service, and Echo-class boats have undergone frequent breakdowns while on patrol. The hull of the Echo II was lengthened by 20ft (6m) as compared with the Echo I in order to accommodate an additional pair of SS-N-3 launchers. The launch tubes are set flush with the upper corners of the hull casing, and elevate in pairs to an angle of about 15 degrees for firing. Prominent indentations in the hull casing abaft the launchers serve to deflect the blast of the missile exhaust upwards and outwards. These create considerable drag and noise when the submarine is running underwater, making the Echo relatively easy to detect using passive sonar techniques. The Front Door/Front Piece tracking/guidance radar is housed in the forward section of the fin, which rotates through 180 degrees when the antenna is deployed.
Armament: The eight SS-N-3A missiles originally fitted in all submarines of this class are now being replaced by the more recent SS-N-12 Sandbox, which first entered service aboard the antisubmarine carrier Kiev in 1975. The SS-N-3A has an estimated length of 33ft 6in (10.2m), while the SS-N-12, at 38ft (11.7m), is slightly longer. By 1984 10 boats were reported to have undergone conversion, and the programme appears to be continuing. A major drawback with both the SS-N-3 and SS-N-12 missiles is that they have to be launched from the surface, where the submarine would be vulnerable to early detection and preemptive strike. Preparation and

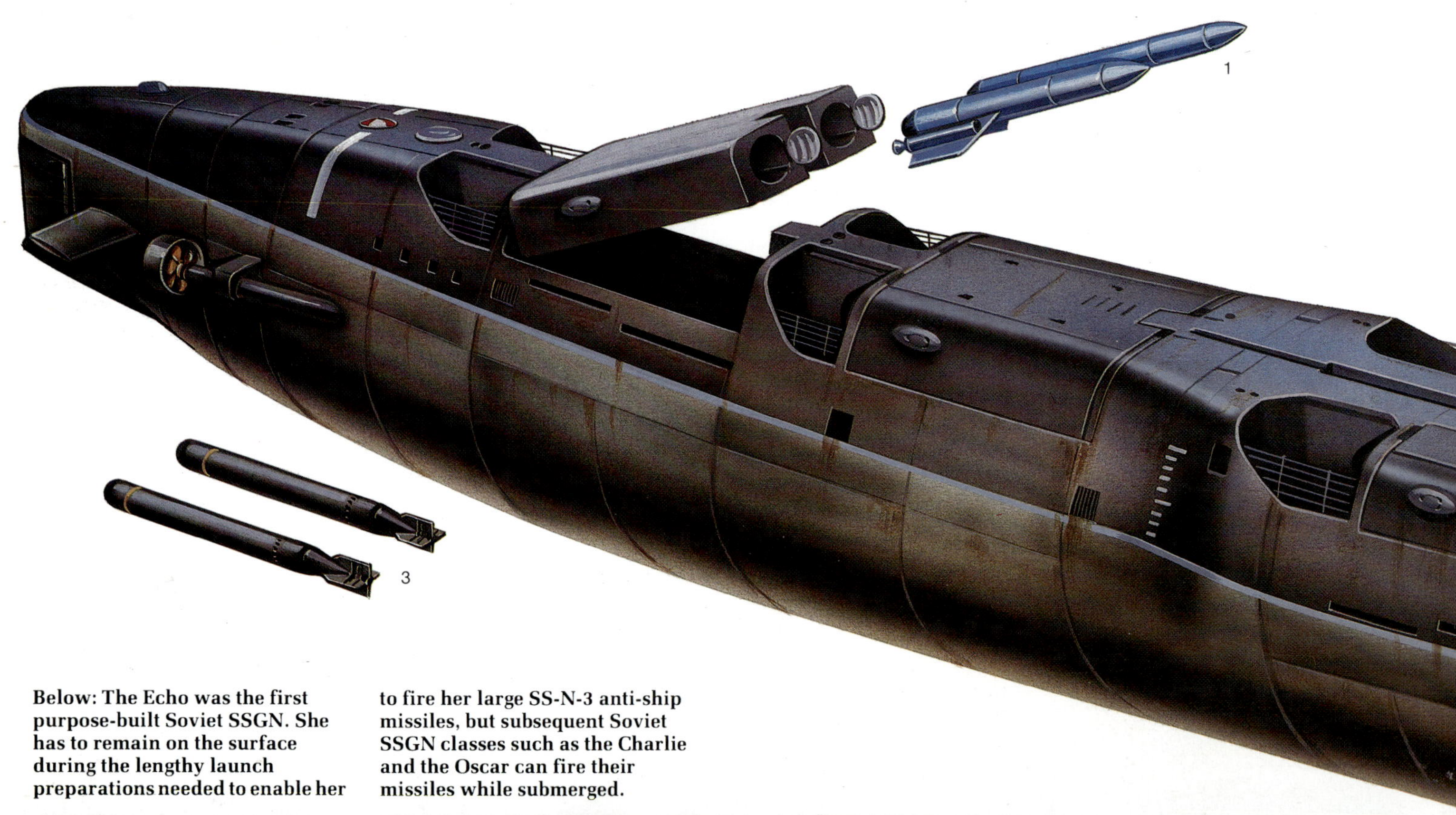

Below: The Echo was the first purpose-built Soviet SSGN. She has to remain on the surface during the lengthy launch preparations needed to enable her to fire her large SS-N-3 anti-ship missiles, but subsequent Soviet SSGN classes such as the Charlie and the Oscar can fire their missiles while submerged.

launch procedures take an estimated 25-30 minutes to perform, and the submarine has to remain on the surface to provide mid-course guidance. Six standard 21in (533mm) torpedo tubes in the bow can accommodate the standard anti-ship models, but in view of the age and primary mission of these submarines it is unlikely that they have received the fire control facilities necessary to accommodate more modern weapons. Four small stern tubes are fitted for 16in (400mm) antisubmarine torpedoes.

Electronics: As completed the Echo IIs were fitted with a passive Feniks bow array topped by a dome for the diminutive Hercules active sonar. The latter has been removed from all converted units of the class, and is also disappearing from unconverted boats. The sensor masts are fairly standard for Soviet submarines of the period: two periscopes, Stop Light ESM, Quad Loop DF, and HF and VHF communications aerials. However, in place of the customary surface surveillance radar the Echo IIs received a much larger air surveillance antenna, designated Snoop Slab. This was presumably necessary to provide warning of air attack while the submarine was surfaced and preparing to launch its missiles. It has been removed from converted units and replaced by the smaller Snoop Tray. Those boats fitted to fire the SS-N-12 missile have also received additional communications equipment, housed in bulged fairings on either side of the fin.

Construction: Twenty-nine Echo IIs were completed between 1962 and 1967; all but one remain in first-line service. Construction was shared evenly between Severodvinsk in the Arctic and Komsomolsk in the Pacific.

Above: The indentations in the outer hull casing are particularly prominent in this overhead view. They serve to deflect the missile exhaust, but cause considerable water turbulence around the hull. The missile launchers are paired, and are elevated for firing.

Left and below: The main armament of the Echo II comprises eight SS-N-3A Shaddock anti-ship cruise missiles (1) which are fired from elevating launchers stowed flush with the hull casing. Some units (variously reported as six or ten boats) have been modified to fire the SS-N-12 Sandbox missile, which is marginally longer and has a range of about 300nm (550km) as opposed to 250nm (460km) for the SS-N-3A Shaddock. Six bow torpedo tubes of 21in (533mm) diameter are fitted, and there are four smaller tubes of 16in (400mm) diameter in the stern. The bow tubes can handle standard free-running anti-ship torpedoes (2), which have either HE or nuclear warheads, while the stern tubes fire the short 400mm acoustic-homing torpedo (3), which would be used to defend the Echo against hostile submarines. Reloads are carried for both sets of tubes.

Foxtrot class

Origin: USSR, first unit completed 1958
Type: Attack submarine, diesel-powered (SS)
Displacement: 1,950 tons surfaced; 2,400 tons submerged
Dimensions: Length 300ft (91.5m); beam 25ft (7.5m); draught 20ft (6m)
Propulsion: Diesel/electric drive on three shafts; three diesels, three electric motors; 6,000bhp for 16kt surfaced, 5,300hp for 15.5kt submerged
Complement: 78
Background: The Soviet Navy had traditionally favoured a combination of large numbers of medium-range submarines for operations in Soviet coastal waters and a smaller number of long-range boats for scouting and reconnaissance. This policy found its classic expression in the Whiskey and Zulu classes of the 1950s, types which, in turn, found their natural successors in the Romeo and Foxtrot classes, the first units of which were completed in 1957-58. However, faced with a new threat from long-range carrier-based jet bombers capable of delivering a nuclear payload, the Soviet Navy was forced into premature termination of the medium-range Romeo in favour of larger submarines capable of intercepting hostile carrier task forces far from their bases. The Foxtrot and its nuclear-powered counterpart, the November, were ideal candidates to carry a newly developed torpedo with a nuclear warhead, designed for use against large formations of ships and port installations. In the event the November proved to be less than successful, and construction was shifted to the Echo-class SSGN (qv). The Foxtrot, on the other hand, proved to be a useful boat with a good general-purpose capability. It remained in production for the Soviet Navy until the late 1960s, and construction continued with a further 19 boats built for export to friendly countries during the 1970s and 1980s.
Design: In design terms the Foxtrot is essentially a refined Zulu. It retains the classic cigar shape of the German Type XXI, and the basic layout of machinery and torpedo tubes remains the same. However, whereas the Zulu was originally built with a stepped fin incorporating positions for small-calibre antiaircraft guns, the fin of the Foxtrot is altogether more streamlined. Moreover, the Zulu design made minimal allowances for the installation of modern sonar devices, whereas these are a major feature of the Foxtrot. Soviet reluctance to depart from the basic Zulu hull-form is, however, indicated by the installation arrangements for the passive sonar, which is incorporated into a specially-designed bulge above the traditional 'knife' bow. The retention of three shafts is also surprising, given that the centre shaft of the Zulu was thought to be associated with a closed-cycle propulsion system which was subsequently abandoned. Given a three-shaft arrangement and a slim, tapered stern it is difficult to see how the Soviet designers managed to accommodate the four standard stern tubes with which the Foxtrot is generally credited. Conventional after control surfaces are fitted, with a single large rudder incorporated in the stern, and the forward hydroplanes are fully retractable for surface operations in ice-bound waters.
Armament: The Foxtrot is reported to have a total of ten 21in (533mm) torpedo tubes, six of which are located in the bow and four in the stern. Anti-ship torpedoes with both conventional (HE) and nuclear warheads can be fired, and the Foxtrot can also presumably handle more recent antisubmarine models with acoustic homing. Stowage capacity is estimated at 22 torpedoes. These boats would be particularly useful for mining operations, for which each torpedo would be replaced by two mines. Some sources credit the Foxtrot with four small-diameter 16in (400mm) tubes for antisubmarine torpedoes in place of the 21in stern tubes, but it is not clear whether the smaller weapon was yet in service when the first Foxtrots were completed.
Electronics: The Foxtrot brought into service a new generation of Soviet sonar equipment. It has the classic combination of the passive Feniks array, housed in the bulged bow, and the active Herkules active attack sonar, topped by an underwater telephone in a small dome above it. There are also four fixed panels, each approximately 5ft (1.5m) square, disposed around the forward edge of the fin. These panels are also a feature of the contemporary November-class

Left: A Foxtrot operating with a missile destroyer of the Kashin class. The design has proved very successful, with more than 60 units completed for the Soviet Navy from 1958 to 1962 plus a further 19 units for export, but construction has now been terminated in favour of more modern types.

SSN and the Golf-class SSB, and are almost certainly components of a passive 'spot' hydrophone array, using the curve of the fin to obtain an accurate bearing on a contact. The sensor masts are standard for the period: search and attack periscopes, a Snoop Tray surface surveillance radar, Quad Loop direction-finding, Stop Light ESM, and aerials for VHF and HF communications. The latter is carried atop a hinged mast, as on the Echo and Golf classes, and folds back into a recess in the deck casing.

Construction: Sixty-two Foxtrots are estimated to have been built for the Soviet Navy, of which perhaps four have been lost. Construction has been exclusively at the Sudomekh Shipyard, Leningrad, which in the early 1970s merged with the Admiralty Shipyard to form the United Admiralty Shipyard. Soviet Navy construction probably ended in 1968. However, eight further boats of the class were completed for India between 1968 and 1974; subsequently eight have been delivered to Libya (1976-83) and three more have been supplied to Cuba (1979-84).

Above: The Foxtrot was the natural successor to the Zulu, which was in turn modeled on the German Type XXI. A traditional cigar-shaped hull was retained, the major difference between the two types being the adoption of more sophisticated sonar equipment. Note the rounded bow casing which houses the Feniks passive array, and the streamlined protrusion above it for the Hercules active sonar and the underwater telephone.

Below and opposite: There is some disagreement in standard Western reference sources as to the precise nature of the torpedo armament of the Foxtrot. All sources agree that there are six bow tubes and four stern tubes, but it is not clear whether the stern tubes are of standard 21in (533mm) diameter or whether tubes of the smaller 16in (400mm) diameter are fitted. This clearly affects any attempt to analyse the weapons carried. The six 21in bow tubes can fire heavyweight anti-ship torpedoes (1), with alternative HE or nuclear warheads. They can also handle acoustic-homing antisubmarine torpedoes (2) and mines (3). Two of the latter can be accommodated in place of each torpedo. The stern tubes can handle either 21in acoustic-homing torpedoes or the short 16in antisubmarine torpedo, depending on the precise diameter of the tubes.

Golf

Origin: USSR, first unit completed 1959
Type: Ballistic missile submarine, diesel-powered (SSB)
Displacement: 2,300 tons surfaced; 2,800 tons submerged
Dimensions: Length 321ft (98m); beam 28ft (8.5m); draught 21ft (6.5m)
Propulsion: Diesel-electric drive on three shafts; three diesels, each 2,000bhp; three electric motors, each 1,700hp; 6,000bhp for 17kt surfaced, 5,300hp for 12kt submerged
Background: Following World War II the Soviets acquired German rocket technology and developed missiles derived from the V-1 and V-2, and during the early 1950s experiments in towing a missile container behind a submarine – first undertaken by the Germans in 1944 – were revived; from these early experiments a new missile specifically designed for submarine launch was developed. The SS-N-4 Sark was a large three-stage liquid-fuelled rocket considerably larger than the early Polaris missiles of the US Navy and firing had to take place on the surface. The missile was fully 48ft (14.5m) long and was therefore too large to be accommodated in the submarine's hull. The solution adopted was to house the missile tubes in an elongated fin; this imposed serious constraints on the number of missiles which could be carried. The first Soviet ballistic missile submarines were converted boats of the Zulu class, the first of which entered service in 1958. The Zulu V, as it became known, had only two missile tubes, but it was followed by a purpose-built submarine, which became the Golf, with a larger fin housing three missile tubes. A nuclear-powered counterpart, the Hotel, was begun a year later, and parallel construction was established. However, the decision to establish the Strategic Rocket Forces resulted in early termination of the programme, and no more submarines of either type were laid down after 1960.
Design: The Golf is essentially a modified Foxtrot. The additional 25ft (8m) of length results from the need to accommodate three missile tubes in an elongated fin. Golf I-class boats modified for ballistic missile trials have been cut in half and have had an additional section inserted. The mast-mounted sensors are compressed into a relatively small space at the forward end of the fin, with the control/attack centre beneath. The diesel-electric propulsion system is identical to that of the Foxtrot, and the Golf has retained the Foxtrot torpedo tube arrangements.

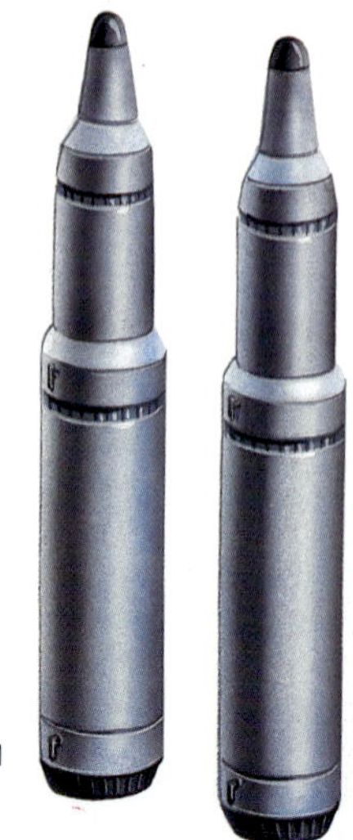

Left: A bow view of an SSBN of the Golf II class. Note the distinctive 'window' for the Feniks passive sonar wrapped around the bow, and the smaller sonar dome for the Herkules active attack sonar above it. The two square panels at the forward end of the fin, which are thought to be part of a passive ranging sonar, are particularly prominent in this view. Abaft the fin can be seen the housing for a VLF communications buoy which was added during the 1970s.

Armament: From 1963 onwards a limited modernisation programme was carried out which involved replacing the SS-N-4 Sark missile by the SS-N-5 Serb, which had twice the range and could be fired from under water. Thirteen of the 23 Golfs and all eight boats of the Hotel class were thus modified, the converted boats receiving the NATO designation Golf II and Hotel II respectively. The SS-N-5 Serb missile has a length of about 38ft (11.5m) and a diameter of about 5ft (1.5m), making it considerably smaller than its predecessor, the SS-N-4 Sark, and a 'sleeve' probably had to be inserted in the original missile tubes. Early versions of the missile had a maximum range of only 700nm (1,300km), but in a later variant this was extended to 900nm (1,650km). The Golf has six 21in (533mm) torpedo tubes in the bow, and a further four in the stern. Conventional anti-ship torpedoes can be fired, but it is unlikely that the submarines have been updated to handle more modern weapons.

Electronics: The Golf has a sonar outfit virtually identical to that of the Foxtrot, with a Feniks passive bow array complemented by a small Herkules HF active sonar atop the bow. There are also two square panels at the forward end of the fin. The mast-mounted sensors are identical to those of the Foxtrot – two periscopes, Stop Light ESM, Quad Loop DF, and separate masts for HF and VHF communications – but in contrast to later Soviet ballistic missile submarines, there is a total absence of electro-optical and satellite navigation equipment. However, all Golf IIs appear to have been fitted for VLF communications during the 1970s, with a prominent VLF buoy housing located either abaft the fin or atop the after deck casing.

Construction: Twenty-three submarines of the Golf class were completed between 1959 and 1962, 16 by the Severodvinsk shipyard in the Arctic, and the remaining seven at Komsomolsk in the Far East. Twelve of the 13 Golf IIs are believed to remain in service; six are in the Baltic, where they are a component of Soviet theater nuclear forces, and the remaining six are in the Pacific. The unconverted boats of the Golf I class have been scrapped or converted to other functions: three have served as trials boats for more recent ballistic missiles, and three have undergone conversion to special communications configurations (SSQ). Plans were also furnished to China, which launched a single submarine of this type in 1964, but the first missile launch from this submarine did not take place until 1982.

Above: A Golf II running on the surface off the east coast of Denmark. Six Golf-class SSBNs are currently based in the Baltic as part of the Soviet theatre nuclear forces. Their place in the other fleets has been taken by more modern nuclear boats.

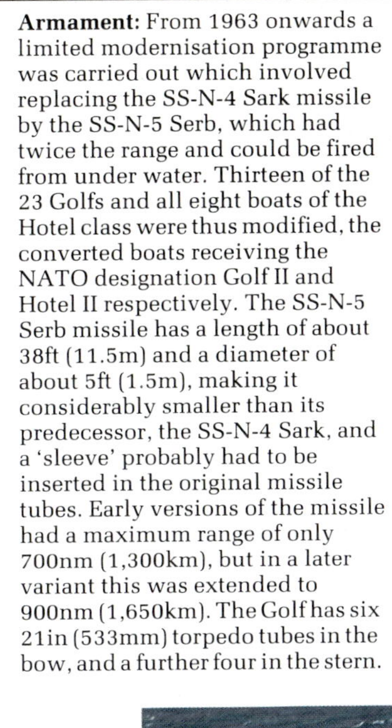

Above and right: The standard Golf II variant has three vertical launch tubes in the fin for SS-N-5 Serb missiles (1). These are now more than 20 years old, and even the later Mod. 2 variant has a range of only 900nm (1,650km). There are six bow torpedo tubes and four stern tubes, each of 21in (533mm) diameter.

The principal anti-ship weapon is probably the M-57 free-running heavyweight torpedo (2) carried by contemporary diesel attack boats. The Golf IIs may also have been retro-fitted to fire the wire-guided antisubmarine torpedo (3) which is reported to have entered service with the Soviet Navy during the 1960s.

India

Origin: USSR, first unit completed 1979
Type: Auxiliary salvage and rescue submarine, diesel-powered (AGSS)
Displacement: 3,900 tons surfaced; 4,800 tons submerged
Dimensions: Length 348ft (106m); beam 33ft (10m); draught unknown
Propulsion: Diesel-electric drive on two shafts; two diesel generators, two electric motors; 4,000bhp for 15kt surfaced, 5,000hp for 15kt submerged
Complement: Unknown
Background: Interest in deep submergence rescue vehicles (DSRVs) began in the United States following the loss of the submarine *Thresher* (SSN-593) in 1963. Two specially-designed DSRVs, *Mystic* (DSRV-1) and *Avalon* (DSRV-2), were completed in 1971 and 1972 respectively to provide a capability for rescuing survivors from submarines disabled on the ocean floor above their hull-collapse depth. The US Navy DSRVs were designed for launch either from another submarine or from a submarine rescue ship of the Pidgeon (ASR-21) class, with an alternative long-distance rapid-deployment mode using a C-141 transport aircraft. The DSRV concept clearly influenced Soviet ideas, but when the Soviet Navy decided to embark on the construction of similar submersibles in the mid-1970s it opted for a completely different mode of deployment. The Soviet DSRVs would be carried by a mother submarine, rather in the manner of the Japanese Kaiten-carrying submarines of World War II. Such a submarine would also be well-suited to 'special' missions, for which it might embark divers or Spetsnaz commando units who would operate from small inflatables or from other types of small submersible. Two purpose-built submarines of the India class were subsequently completed, one of which is attached to each of the two Soviet fleets which operate nuclear-powered submarines, the

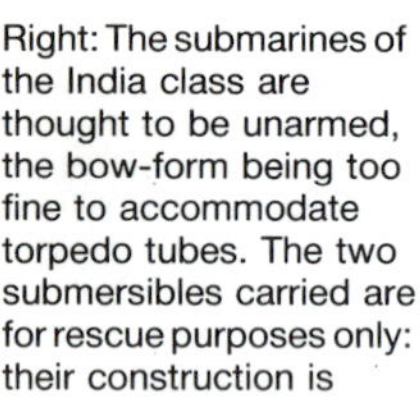

Right: The submarines of the India class are thought to be unarmed, the bow-form being too fine to accommodate torpedo tubes. The two submersibles carried are for rescue purposes only: their construction is probably based on two titanium pressure spheres. There is a small hatch atop the outer casing, and a larger circular mating hatch beneath to provide access to and from the submarine.

Left: One of the two auxiliary salvage and rescue submarines of the India class depicted during her transit from the Pacific to the Soviet Northern Fleet via the Arctic route; an ice guard is fitted over the bow to enable her to make the passage safely, and the two deck wells for submersibles set into the raised hull casing aft are covered by large steel plates. Note the bow-mounted diving planes.

Above: This view of the India shows the two rescue submersibles in place. They are semi-recessed in order to lower water resistance when the boat is running submerged. The outer hull casing of the India is lined with free-flood holes of a similar pattern to those of other conventional Soviet diesel boats such as the Foxtrot. A standard outfit of mast-mounted sensors is carried, including search and attack periscopes.

Northern Fleet and the Pacific Fleet.

Design: The India is a diesel-powered submarine of conventional double-hull construction. The basic configuration is reminiscent of the Foxtrot rather than the later Tango. The exceptionally fine bow, which is bulged above the water-line to accommodate a passive sonar, appears to have been adopted for high surface speed to enable the India to make a rapid transit to its operational area. It is probably too fine to accommodate torpedo tubes, so it seems likely that these submarines are completely unarmed. The long, relatively low fin is similar to that of the Yankee- and Delta-class SSBNs, and is located close to the bow. The India is the only type of Soviet submarine other than the Yankee and Delta to have its forward hydroplanes mounted on the fin. The after control surfaces are conventional, with a single vertical rudder beneath the stern. The two submersibles are carried semi-recessed in tandem deck wells abaft the fin. The deck wells are set into a prominent raised casing which extends almost to the stern. The submersibles mate with large circular hatches which give access to and from the submarine. When not in use the deck wells can be covered by large steel plates.

Equipment: Two different types of submersible have been observed in the deck wells of the India. Their distinctive colours (red/orange? and white stripes) mark them out as rescue vehicles. One is approximately 40ft (12.1m) long and appears to be powered by an electric motor driving a single shrouded propeller which is integrated with the cruciform control surfaces. The second is about 37ft (11.3m) long, and has small rotating propellers (also shrouded) on either side of its after section. These can presumably be angled in both the horizontal and vertical planes, and there are also cruciform tail surfaces. Both types have a large circular hatch beneath them to enable them to mate either with the mother submarine or with the submarine in distress. There is also a smaller hatch at the top of the submersible. Forward-looking optical viewing devices are fitted, and there are presumably also search and navigation sonars. The internal construction of the US Navy submersibles is based on three interconnected pressure-tight spheres made of HY-140 steel. The Soviet submersibles are somewhat shorter, and may therefore consist of two such spheres, probably of titanium. The forward sphere would house the controls and the two/three-man crew, while the after sphere would be able to accommodate 12-15 survivors. Other types of submersible may have been designed for clandestine operations, but none has yet been observed aboard the India. There has been some evidence of Soviet operations employing tracked submersibles in the coastal waters of Sweden, but neither of the two India-class submarines currently in service has deployed to the Baltic.

Electronics: The India has a medium-frequency passive array in the bow and presumably has an active high-frequency sonar located beneath the hull for location of a disabled submarine. A full outfit of sensor masts is carried: two periscopes, a Snoop Tray surface surveillance radar, Brick Pulp ESM, Quad Loop DF, and aerials for HF and VHF communications.

Construction: The first submarine of the India class was completed at Komsomolsk in the Far East in 1979, and a second unit followed in 1980. The same year saw the transfer of one unit to the Northern Fleet via the Arctic route.

Juliett class

Origin: USSR, first unit completed 1962
Type: Cruise missile submarine, diesel-powered (SSG)
Displacement: 3,000 tons surfaced; 3,750 tons submerged
Dimensions: Length 285ft (87m); beam 33ft (10m); draught 23ft (7m)
Propulsion: Diesel/electric drive on two shafts; two diesels, two electric motors; 4,000bhp for 12kt surfaced, 3,400hp for 8kt submerged
Complement: 80
Background: The Juliett is the diesel-powered counterpart of the Echo (qv). In the early 1960s only two Soviet shipyards (Severodvinsk in the Arctic, and Komsomolsk in the Pacific) were capable of undertaking the construction of nuclear-powered submarines. The Soviets would therefore continue to rely heavily on other submarine building yards to make up the numbers with conventionally powered boats. Moreover, the Echo and the Juliett conform to the traditional Soviet pattern which combines large, complex '1st Rate' naval vessels and smaller, cheaper '2nd Rate' units which can be produced in greater numbers. It is reported that 72 Julietts were initially projected, but that in 1962 it was decided to restrict construction to only 16 units. Diesel propulsion makes the Juliett best suited to deployment close to Soviet territory in the anti-carrier role, and until the early 1980s all 16 boats of the class served with the Soviet Northern Fleet. However, the endurance of these submarines is such that they have seen frequent deployments to the Mediterranean, where they have often combined with other missile units to shadow the carriers of the US Sixth Fleet, and to the Indian Ocean.
Design: The Juliett design is derived from the Foxtrot. In spite of the obvious external differences resulting from the very different missions of the two submarines, they have a number of features in common. Length is virtually identical, and the submarines probably share a similar internal layout. However, the Juliett has a

Right: The Juliett is the diesel-powered counterpart of the Echo II. Four SS-N-3 missiles are carried in elevating launchers which are stowed flush with the broad upper casing.

1

2

much broader outer casing in order to accommodate four launchers for SS-N-3A anti-ship missiles (half the number carried by the Echo II). The launchers are identical in configuration to those of the Echo, with the same prominent indentations in the hull casing behind them to deflect the blast of the missile exhaust. The fin is even longer than that of the Echo, as it has to accommodate a snorkel mast and diesel exhaust in addition to periscopes and the usual array of radar, ESM and communications antennae. It is, however, identical at its forward end, with a revolving section housing the Front Door/Front Piece missile guidance radar. The propulsion machinery installation is a down-graded Foxtrot plant, with only two diesels and two shafts. This has resulted in a significant reduction in maximum underwater speed. The standard 21in (533mm) stern tubes of the Foxtrot have been replaced by four small-diameter tubes for antisubmarine torpedoes.

Armament: The SS-N-3A Shaddock anti-ship missile is about 33ft 6in long (10.2m) and weighs 12,000lb (5,400kg). It has a conventional aeroplane configuration, and is powered by a turbojet with two solid-fuel boosters slung beneath. It has a maximum range estimated at 250nm (450km), and employs active radar homing in the terminal phase. It requires mid-course guidance if it is to attain its maximum range. A specialised maritime reconnaissance bomber, the Bear-D, transmits its radar picture via a video data link to the launch submarine, and course corrections are then relayed to the missile in flight. The submarine has to remain on the surface during these operations. The SS-N-3A has alternative conventional or nuclear warheads, each weighing approximately 2,200lb (1,000kg). The torpedo tube arrangements are identical to those of the Echo, with six standard 21in (533mm) bow tubes for anti-ship torpedoes, and four 16in (400mm) stern tubes for antisubmarine torpedoes.

Electronics: The Juliett has the same Feniks passive bow array as the Echo, and early boats have the same diminutive active ranging sonar topped by an underwater telephone above the bow. Later boats have a larger active sonar with a 3ft (1m) wrap-around 'window'. The outfit of sensor masts is identical to that of the Echo, and includes the Snoop Slab air surveillance radar used to detect hostile aircraft while the submarine is conducting its lengthy preparations for missile launch. However, the HF communications mast is incorporated into the raised section of the fin which houses the diesel exhaust, whereas the Echo has its own HF aerial atop a prominent hinged mast which folds down into a recess in the deck casing. A few boats of the Juliett class have recently been fitted with bulged fairings on either side of the fin; these are identical to those fitted in Echo-class boats modified to fire the SS-N-12 missile, and are probably for communications equipment. However, there is as yet no indication that the SS-N-12 update programme is being extended to the Juliett.

Construction: Sixteen Julietts were completed between 1962 and 1969 at the inland Gorky Shipyard. This shipyard had previously been responsible for construction of the Soviet Romeos.

Opposite and above: The main armament of the Juliett comprises four SS-N-3A Shaddock anti-ship missiles (1), which are housed in elevating paired launchers stowed flush with the hull casing. There is as yet no evidence that Julietts are being retro-fitted to fire the SS-N-12. The Julietts have six 21in (533mm) bow tubes for long anti-ship torpedoes (2), and four 16in (400mm) stern tubes intended to launch short antisubmarine homing torpedoes (3).

Right: The prominent indentations in the upper hull casing are to deflect the missile exhaust. The Front Door/Front Piece missile guidance radar is housed in the forward section of the fin, which rotates through 180 degrees when the radar is deployed. Preparations for missile launch have to be performed on the surface, thereby exposing the submarine to attack by aircraft.

Kilo class

Origin: USSR, first unit completed 1982
Type: Attack submarine, diesel-powered (SS)
Displacement: 2,500 tons surfaced, 3,000 tons submerged
Dimensions: Length 230ft (70m); beam 32ft (9.9m); draught 21ft (6.5m)
Propulsion: Diesel-electric drive on one shaft; two diesel generators, one electric motor; 4,000bhp for 12kt surfaced, 5,000hp for 16kt submerged
Complement: 60
Background: During the 1950s some 236 medium submarines of the Whiskey class were completed for the Soviet Navy. The Whiskey was followed by the improved Romeo design, but construction of this type was abandoned after only 20 had been laid down for the Soviet Navy. This appears to have been the result of a policy decision to terminate the construction of medium-range submarines in favour of the larger Foxtrot-class boat (q.v.), which was better suited to open-ocean operations. Nevertheless, the Whiskey was to remain the standard Soviet diesel boat throughout the 1960s, and was to prove its value in shallow-water operations in the Baltic and the Black Sea. Many were exported to friendly nations, including several of the countries belonging to the Warsaw Pact. However, by the mid-1970s most of the Whiskeys were more than 20 years old, and if their shallow-water mission was to be retained a replacement would have to be designed. This finally emerged as the Kilo, a comparatively large general-purpose submarine of conventional but modern design which would be built both for the Soviet Navy and for export.
Design: Externally the Kilo resembles modern Western diesel submarines much more closely than previous Soviet types. The hull is some 65ft (20m) shorter than that of the Tango, but beam has been increased by about 3ft (1m). The end result is a submarine remarkably similar in shape and size to the US Barbel and its Dutch derivatives of the Zwaardvis and Walrus classes, with an 'Alabacore' hull-form. There are, however, a number of subtle differences which mark out the Kilo as being of Soviet design and construction. The most important is the line of free-flood holes along the outer casing, which testifies to Soviet persistence with double-hull construction. The second difference is the longer fin, which is a feature of all Soviet submarines. A third difference is the position of the forward hydroplanes, which are located just beneath the deck casing immediately forward of the fin, not on the fin as in their US Navy and Dutch counferparts. The hydroplanes are fully retractable as on other Soviet boats to prevent ice damage during surface operations in northern waters. A rather more surprising feature of the Kilo is Soviet persistence with the after control surfaces employed in earlier diesel submarines such as the Foxtrot and Tango in preference to the cruciform tail surfaces now standard on their nuclear boats. The main rudder is beneath the stern, although there is a small 'tab' visible above the water. The function of the latter is not clear, although it may be a component of a hull-mounted passive array. In spite of the unusual rudder arrangement there is only a single shaft with a six-bladed propeller; all earlier Soviet diesel boats had a multi-shaft arrangement with the control surfaces abaft the propellers.
Armament: The Kilo has six bow tubes of 21in (533mm) diameter. These can fire the standard Soviet anti-ship and antisubmarine torpedoes. As an alternative payload, each torpedo can be replaced by two mines. It is not

Above: The new Soviet diesel-electric submarines of the Kilo class are being built to replace the elderly Whiskey and Romeo classes. They are, however, considerably larger and more capable than their predecessors, which were built in the 1950s.

clear whether the Kilo is fitted to fire the SS-N-15 antisubmarine missile. The latter can be fired from a standard torpedo tube, but the Kilo has a relatively limited weapons stowage capacity estimated at only 12 torpedoes, and it is in any case questionable whether the submarine's designed mission includes the engagement of hostile submarines with nuclear weapons. Nor is there any evidence that the Kilo is fitted with large-diameter 26in (650mm) tubes capable of firing the SS-N-16 antisubmarine missile or the Type 65 wake-homing torpedo.

Electronics: The Kilo is equipped with a low-frequency active/passive bow sonar, and is presumably also fitted with hull-mounted passive hydrophone arrays. However, there is no indication that a towed hydrophone array comparable to those of the more recent Soviet nuclear-powered attack boats is fitted. The mast-mounted sensors belong to an earlier generation of submarines. The elderly Stop Light ESM antenna is fitted in place of the more recent Brick Pulp, and Quad Loop DF in place of Park Lamp. In addition the Kilo is equipped with search and attack periscopes, a Snoop Tray surveillance radar, and HF and VHF communications aerials.

Construction: The first Kilo was completed by the Komsomolsk Shipyard in the Far East in 1982, and the class has since entered series production. Ten units have so far been completed for the Soviet Navy, and a further three are under construction. Production has now been extended to shipyards in the western USSR at Gorky and Leningrad (the United Admiralty Shipyard, formerly Sudomekh), and it is thought that the latter two yards will build the submarine for export customers such as India, reported to have placed orders for three boats in April 1984.

Right: In spite of her double-hull construction, the Kilo bears a striking similarity to contemporary Western diesel-electric submarines derived from the US Barbel class, being both shorter and beamier than earlier Soviet diesel boats. The class has now entered series production for the Soviet Navy, and is also being offered to friendly Third World countries.

Left: The Kilo has six bow tubes of 21in (533mm) diameter, and stowage capacity for an estimated 12 reloads. There is no evidence that these submarines carry antisubmarine missiles such as the SS-N-15, nor is there evidence to suggest that they have the larger-diameter 26in (650mm) tubes currently being fitted in Soviet nuclear boats. They are thought to be equipped only to fire conventional 'long' anti-ship torpedoes (1) and shorter antisubmarine homing models (2). Two mines (3) can be carried in place of one torpedo.

Lafayette class

Origin: USA, first unit completed 1963
Type: Ballistic missile submarine, nuclear-powered (SSBN)
Displacement: 7,350 tons surfaced; 8,250 tons submerged
Dimensions: Length 425ft (129.5m); beam 33ft (10.1m); draught 29ft (8.8m)
Propulsion: One S5W pressurized water-cooled reactor driving geared steam turbines; one shaft; 15,000shp for 20+kt
Complement: 140
Background: The first ballistic missile submarines built for the US Navy, the five SSBNs of the George Washington class, were converted Skipjacks with an additional 130ft (40m) missile section inserted abaft the fin. They were followed by five boats of the Ethan Allen class which, although generally similar in layout to their predecessors, were designed as SSBNs from the outset. They were also longer and had a number of features in common with the Thresher class SSNs, including superior silencing and a hull constructed of HY80 steel. The Ethan Allen was to form the basis of an improved design which became the Lafayette class. The Lafayette was the standard US Navy SSBN throughout the 1960s and 1970s, and had a major influence on the design of other Western SSBNs, notably those of the British Resolution and French Le Redoutable classes (qv).
Design: The early boats of the Lafayette class differed little from the Ethan Allen class in terms of their general layout and weapon/sensor technology. The major difference was in the missile tubes themselves, which were enlarged to accommodate future ballistic missiles of greater diameter than Polaris. This increased overall length by 15ft (4.5m), while the submarine's other dimensions remained unchanged. An essential part of the deterrence mission of the Lafayettes was the avoidance of hostile submarines. The sonar outfit was therefore biased towards detection rather than long-range fire control. The spherical bow sonar which was a feature of the Thresher design was not installed in US Navy SSBNs, which could therefore accommodate their torpedo tubes in the bow in the conventional manner. The S5W reactor is the same model as that installed in the SSNs, and the large size of the Lafayettes means that they are relatively slow. Quietness, however, has always been accorded much greater priority than high performance in US SSBN designs, and the last 12 units of the class (officially known as the Benjamin Franklin class), incorporated further improvements in machinery noise insulation. The large fin is based on that of the Skipjack, and carries the forward hydroplanes. One unit, the *Daniel Webster* (SSBN 626) was fitted with bow planes for evaluation.
Armament: The first eight units of the class entered service with the Polaris A-2 missile, which had a single nuclear warhead and a range of 1,500nm (2,800km). The remaining 23 boats received the A-3 variant, which had three MRVs

Below: The Lafayette class set the standard for Western ballistic missile submarines, both the British Resolution and the French Le Redoutable classes being based on these US Navy boats. The 16 launch tubes for the C-3 Poseidon missiles are located immediately abaft the fin. The unit depicted here, the *Nathaniel Greene* (SSBN 636), belongs to the earlier sub-group of the class: later units have been retro-fitted with the Trident missile.

Above and right: Earlier units of the Lafayette class retain the Poseidon C-3 SLBM, but the last 12 boats have been retro-fitted with the Trident-I C-4 missile (1). Sixteen missiles are carried in two rows each of eight launch tubes. All earlier models of torpedo have now been superseded by the high-performance Mk 48 (2), which can be used against surface ships or submarines. There are four bow tubes.

Above: The *Sam Rayburn* (SSBN 635), was the first submarine of the Lafayette class to be deactivated. This step was necessary in order to conform with the ceiling imposed on US SLBMs by the SALT II Treaty.

Lafayette class *Daniel Boone* (SSBN 629)

and a range of 2,500nm (4,600km). The A-3 missile was subsequently retro-fitted in the early boats. In 1970 the C-3 Poseidon missile entered service, and was to replace the A-3 in all submarines of the Lafayette class. Poseidon, a fatter missile than Polaris, with a length of 34ft (10.4m) and a diameter of 6ft 2in (1.9m), had a similar range to the Polaris A-3, but could carry ten 50kT MIRVed warheads. It remains in service aboard the surviving early units of the class, but since 1979 the 12 SSBNs of the Benjamin Franklin sub-group have been progressively converted to fire the Trident C-4 missile. The latter was designed to be compatible with the launch tubes of the Lafayette class, and has overall dimensions identical to Poseidon. It carries eight 100kT MIRVed warheads to a range of 4,000nm (7,400km). The increase in range has enabled submarines equipped with Trident to be withdrawn from forward-basing in Europe. The four bow torpedo tubes initially handled the same weapon mix as US Navy SSNs of the period (see Permit), although the Lafayettes were apparently not fitted to fire SUBROC. The early models of torpedo have now been superseded by the Mk 48.

Electronics: The sonar outfit installed at completion was essentially that of the Skipjacks: a BQS-4 active/passive sonar inside a circular BRQ-2C passive array in the bow, plus a conformal BQR-7 hydrophone array along the hull. The Lafayettes were fitted with Mk 88 missile fire control, and the standard Mk 113 torpedo fire control system. From 1974 onwards all submarines of the class underwent a sonar update programme. The BQR-2C passive array was replaced by the BQR-21 model, which has Digital Multi-Beam Steering (DIMUS), enabling five targets to be tracked simultaneously. A mast-mounted BQR-19 sonar was also fitted, to enable the submarines to avoid surface ships. The third element in the update programme was the BQR-15 towed array, which was installed for more effective detection of hostile hunter-killer submarines. Trident conversions have also received three Mk 2 SINS for more accurate navigation.

Construction: Thirty-one submarines of the Lafayette and Benjamin Franklin classes were completed between 1963 and 1967 at four different shipyards. Of these, three have now decommissioned to enable the United States to remain within SALT II Treaty limits.

Le Redoutable class

Origin: France, first unit completed 1971
Type: Ballistic missile submarine, nuclear-powered (SSBN)
Displacement: 8,000 tons surfaced; 9,000 tons submerged
Dimensions: Length 420ft (128m); beam 35ft (10.6m); draught 33ft (10m)
Propulsion: One pressurized water-cooled reactor with turbo-electric drive; two turbo-alternators driving one main electric motor; one shaft; 16,000hp for 20kt
Complement: 135
Background: In the early 1960s France embarked on the development of a Force de Dissuasion which was initially to be based on a force of five SSBNs. The programme not only served to reinforce the incipient political separation between France and the United States, but also marked the birth of an independent technology which would see the development of both nuclear reactors and ballistic missiles of French design and manufacture. The first reactor, the PAT 1, was produced in collaboration with the CEA (the French Atomic Energy Authority) and tested extensively ashore at Cadarache. Development of the missile took place simultaneously, the first French SLBM being launched from the experimental submarine *Gymnote* in 1968. Construction of the SSBNs posed a number of technical problems, including the development of high-tensile steel to cope with a required diving depth of 300m.
Design: The overall design was closely based on that of the US Navy's Lafayette class (q.v.), and these boats were the first French postwar submarines to have a single hull. They also have the fin-mounted forward hydroplanes and the cruciform after control surfaces of their US counterparts. the 16-missile SLBM compartment is located directly abaft the fin, with a three-deck acommodation layout forward and the machinery spaces aft; the torpedo handling room is in a smaller cone directly behind the four bow tubes. The propulsion system is unusual in that the single PWR reactor does not drive geared steam turbines, as in other Western SSBNs of the period, but drives two turbo-alternators, which in turn provide the power for a single large electric motor. An auxiliary SEMT-Pielstick 16 PA 4 850kW diesel generator provides sufficient power in an emergency to get the submarine back to its

Above: ***Le Redoutable*** **was the first of five SSBNs completed for the Marine Nationale during the 1970s. The nuclear reactors and the missiles were developed without US assistance.**

Le Redoutable class *Le Tonnant* (S 614)

home base. The fourth and fifth boats, *L'Indomptable* and *Le Tonnant*, have a metallic reactor core in place of the oxide cores of the earlier boats. The sixth boat, *L'Inflexible*, is of an improved type and is officially regarded as a separate class. Her missile compartment has been modified to accommodate the M 4 SLBM from the outset, and she has quieter machinery and more advanced electronics. *L'Inflexible* can be distinguished externally from her sisters by her re-shaped fin, with the hydroplanes mounted high on the forward edge.

Armament: The first two units of the class, *Le Redoutable* and *Le Terrible*, initially carried the M 1 missile, which comprised a two-stage rocket with a single 500kT nuclear warhead and a range of 1,350nm (2,500km). The M 1 was superseded in the third unit, *Le Foudroyant*, by the M 2, with a more powerful second stage which increased range to 1,600nm (3000km). The next two units, *L'Indomptable* and Le Tonnant, entered service with a mix of M 2 and M 20 missiles, the latter being identical in performance to the M 2 but carrying a thermo-nuclear warhead of 1MT. Since 1977 the earlier units have carried the same mix. Both the M 2 and the M 20 have a length of 34ft (10.4m) and a diameter of 5ft (1.5m). The M 4, which is about to enter service on the sixth boat, *L'Inflexible*, is a completely new missile employing more advanced propulsion and warhead technology; it has a length of 36ft (11.05m) and a diameter of 6ft 4in (1.93m). Range is 2,150nm (4,000km) in the current version, and this will be increased to 2,700nm (5,000km) in the M 4B. The multiple warhead comprises six TN-70 MIRVs, each of about 150kT. With the exception of *Le Terrible*, all the early boats of the class will be retro-fitted with the M 4 missile, beginning in 1985 with *Le Tonnant*. The four 21.7in (550mm) bow tubes can fire a combination of the L 5 Mod.3 antisubmarine torpedo and the F 17 dual-purpose torpedo; 14 reloads can be accommodated in the handling room. *L'Inflexible*, like the SSNs of the Rubis class, will have the smaller 533mm tube, and will be able to fire the SM 39 Exocet missile in addition to torpedoes.

Electronics: The first five units are fitted with the DUUV 23 panoramic passive array and the DUUX 2 ranging sonar, but *L'Inflexible* has the new DSUX 21 multi-function sonar in place of the DUUV 23, plus the DUUX 5 digital ranging sonar. It is envisaged that the DSUX 21 will be retro-fitted to the other boats during their M 4 refits. The submarines' position can be accurately determined by reference to three inertial navigation centres (CIN) ashore, and there is a periscope for terrestrial navigation.

Construction: The five units of the Le Redoutable class were completed between 1971 and 1980. *L'Inflexible* entered service in April 1985. All were built at Cherbourg Naval Dockyard. A larger SSBN of a completely new design is due to be laid down in 1988 for completion in 1994.

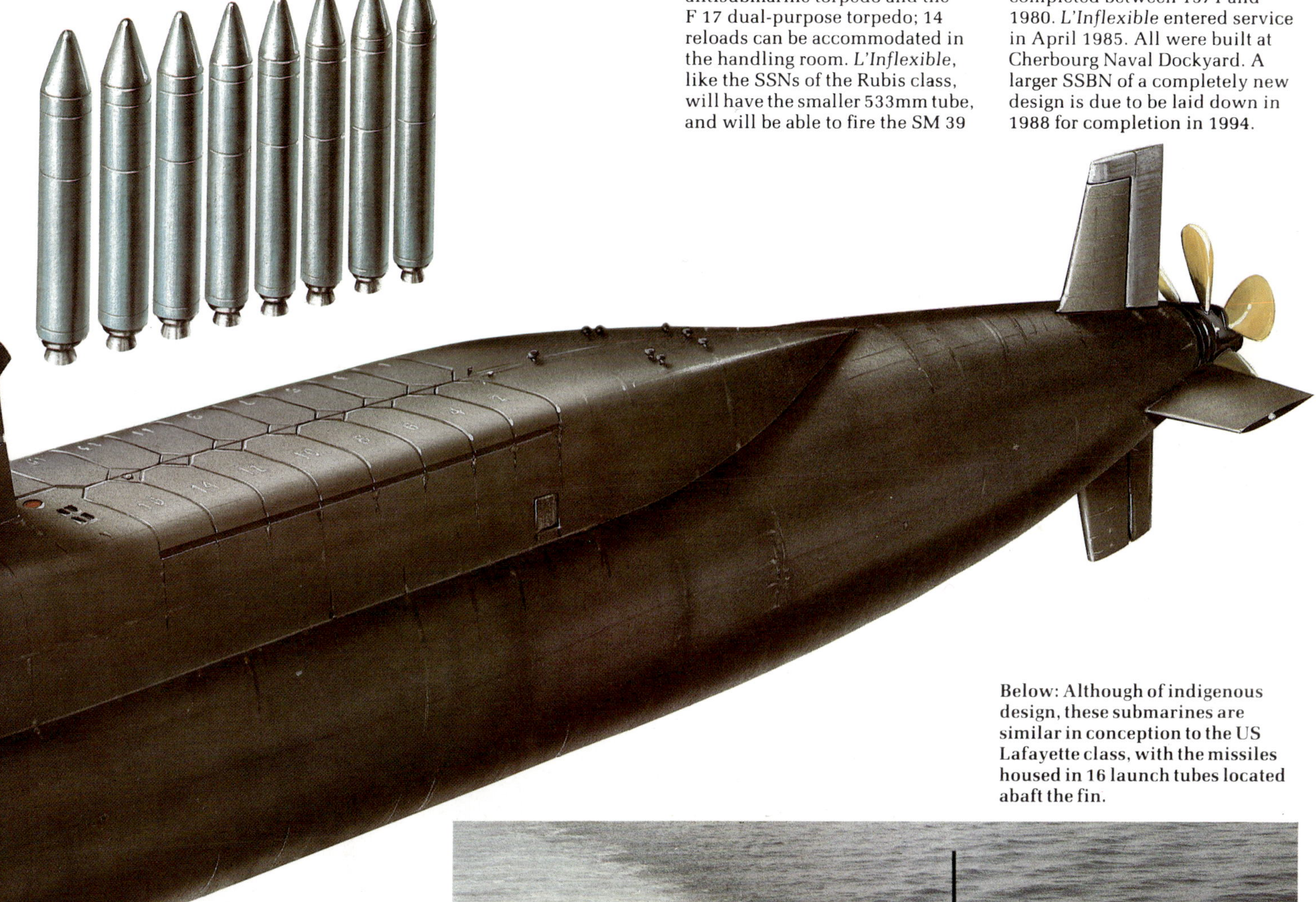

Below: Although of indigenous design, these submarines are similar in conception to the US Lafayette class, with the missiles housed in 16 launch tubes located abaft the fin.

Above and left: The first five units of the class carry a mix of M 2 and M 20 ballistic missiles (1). The two missiles are identical in appearance but the latter carries a larger 1MT thermo-nuclear warhead. The sixth unit. *L'œinflexible* has the M 4, a larger missile with greater range and a multiple-warhead capability. There are 16 vertical launch tubes in two rows of eight. A mix of L 5 Mod 3 antisubmarine torpedoes (2) and F 17 dual-purpose torpedoes can be fired from the four 21.7in (550mm) bow torpedo tubes.

Los Angeles class

Origin: USA, first unit completed 1976
Type: Attack submarine, nuclear-powered (SSN)
Displacement: 6,080 tons surfaced; 6,927 tons submerged
Dimensions: Length 360ft (109.8m); beam 33ft (10.1m); draught 32ft 4in (9.8m)
Propulsion: One S6G pressurized water-cooled reactor driving geared steam turbines; one shaft; 30,000shp for 31kt max
Complement: 127
Background: In the late 1960s the US Navy became increasingly concerned about the threat to its carrier battle groups posed by the new generation of Soviet submarines, and in particular the Charlie-class SSGN with its SS-N-7 'pop-up' missile. The most effective counter to Soviet tactics would be to station attack submarines ahead of the battle group to detect the Soviet missile boats as they took up their attacking stations: thus was born the 'close support' mission which provided the rationale for the development of the Los Angeles class. The ability to operate in conjunction with the carrier battle groups required high tactical speed, which in the Thresher/Permit and Sturgeon classes had been sacrificed in favour of quiet operation. However, the new submarine would also need to be at least as quiet as its immediate predecessors in order to engage in underwater combat with the Soviet SSGNs. The result was an exceptionally large boat with double the reactor power of earlier types.

Design: The Los Angeles design marked the final transition from the 'airship' hull-form of the Albacore and Skipjack to the cylindrical configuration which is a feature of all recent US submarines. The cylindrical middle body is almost as efficient as a continuously curved hull, and is much easier to build. The S6G reactor is a modified version of the D2G reactor used to power missile destroyers since the early 1960s. It employs natural circulation at low power ratings to minimize pump noise, but circulation pumps have to be switched on at higher speeds. This fits well into the pattern of 'sprint and drift' operations implied in the close support mission. The large size of the submarine has facilitated the effective isolation of noise-generating machinery from the hull, and the Los Angeles is probably the world's quietest nuclear submarine. The fin is relatively small in relation to the overall size of the submarine, thereby reducing resistance. The ability to rotate the fin-mounted hydroplanes to the vertical has, however, been sacrificed, placing limitations on under-ice operations. Later boats will have bow-mounted hydroplanes.
Armament: By the time the Los Angeles class entered service in the late 1970s the Mk 48 torpedo was in full production and had replaced virtually all the earlier types. The first 12 units received the Mk 113 fire control system and could therefore handle the SUBROC nuclear-tipped antisubmarine missile. Later units with the Mk 117 system could not handle SUBROC, but the Mk 117 is now being modified to make this possible. From 1978 onwards submarines of this class began to receive the Harpoon anti-ship missile. The trend towards tube-launched missiles continued with the first operational installation of the Tomahawk missile in 1983. Tomahawk (BGM-109), unlike Harpoon, was designed to be fired from a torpedo tube. It has a length of 20ft 3in (6.2m) and a diameter of 21in (533mm). It is powered by a turbojet sustainer motor with a solid-fuel booster and has a maximum range of 1,400nm (2,600km) in the land attack (TLAM) version, and 250nm (460km) in the anti-ship (TASM) version. The torpedo capacity of the Los Angeles class is no greater than that of the Sturgeons, although handling has been improved by the adoption of power transfer systems. The proliferation of tube-launched anti-ship missiles, allied to the retention of SUBROC, has resulted in difficult decisions regarding the appropriate weapon mix for a particular deployment. Later units of the class will therefore receive 15 vertical launch tubes for Tomahawk, located in the space between the bow sonar and the forward end of the pressure hull. Earlier units will eventually receive 12 similar tubes at scheduled refits.
Electronics: The Los Angeles class was designed from the outset to accommodate the BQQ-5 sonar suite. Like the BQQ-2 system

Right: The four midships 21in (533mm) torpedo tubes can fire the complete range of tube-launched weapons currently in service: the SUBROC antisubmarine missile (1), the Sub-Harpoon anti-ship missile (2), the dual-purpose Mk 48 torpedo (3), and the TLAM and TASM variants of the Tomahawk missile (4). Stowage capacity is currently limited to about 24 weapons, so later units of the class will carry their Tomahawk missiles in separate launch tubes.

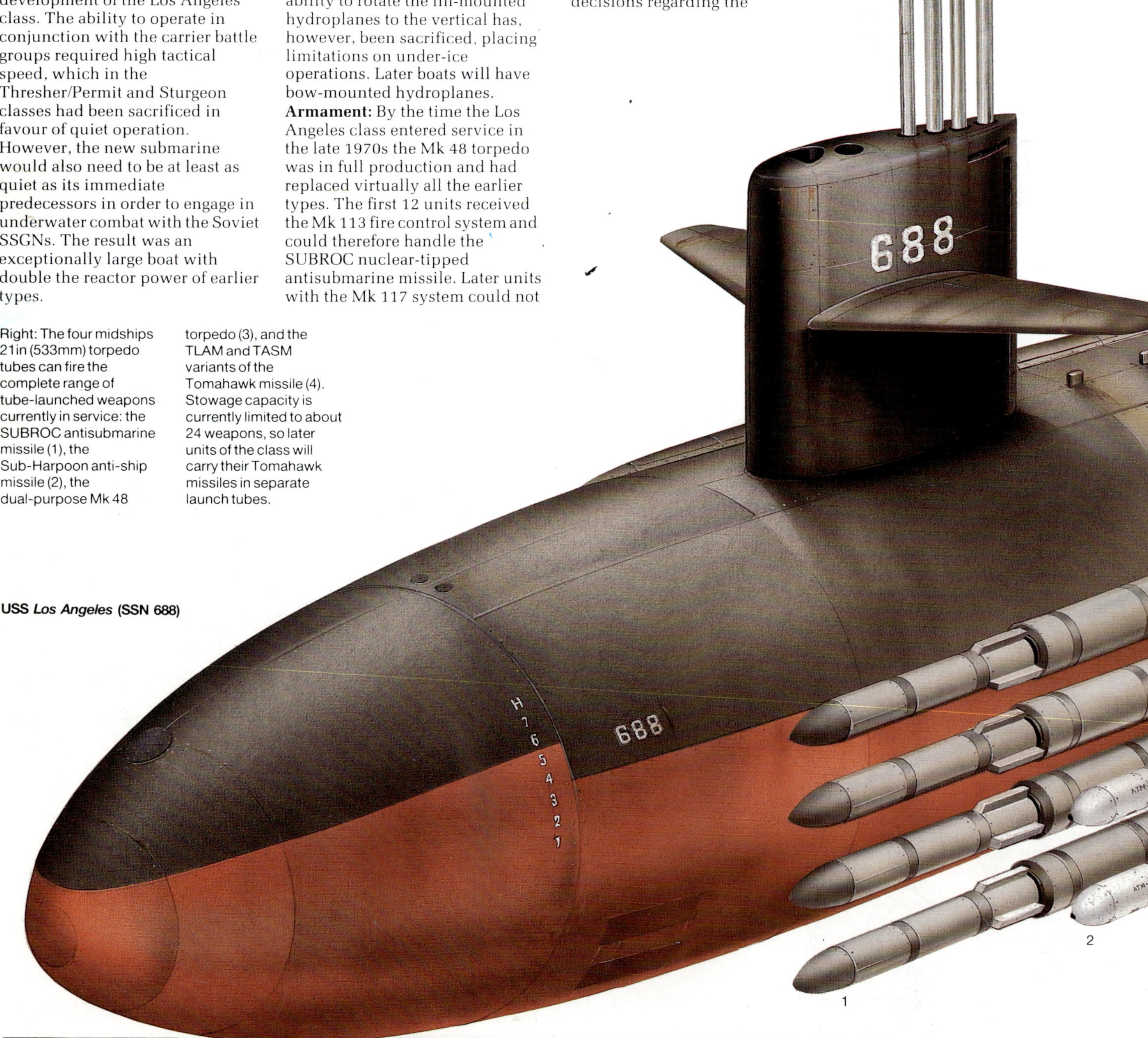

USS *Los Angeles* (SSN 688)

which it replaces, the BQQ-5 is based on a large active/passsive spherical bow sonar, a conformal passive hydrophone array, and a PUFFS fire control system. The BQS-11/12/13 spherical bow array incorporates Digital Multi-Beam Steering (DIMUS), which has superseded the mechanical scanning employed with earlier sonars and makes possible multi-target tracking. Another new feature of the BQQ-5 sonar suite is the addition of a towed array, which is stowed in a tube running along the hull casing. The model currently being fitted is the BQR-23 Submarine Towed Array Sonar System (STASS). Later submarines of the class will receive the Submarine Advanced Combat System (SUBACS), a new-generation integrated weapons/sonar control suite.
Construction: Thirty-four submarines of the Los Angeles class had been completed by the end of 1986, and a further 24 were under construction or on order, making this the largest class of nuclear submarine ever built.

Above: *Salt Lake City* (SSN 716) depicted during sea trials in 1984. The prominent fairing which runs the length of the casing houses the towed array, the winch being located between the bow and the forward end of the pressure hull. Note also the cylindrical hull-form, adopted in part to facilitate construction.

Below: A close-up of *Honolulu* (SSN 718). The small sail was adopted to minimize drag. Later boats will have 15 vertical-launch tubes for Tomahawk missiles fitted in a new section inserted between the bow and the forward end of the pressure hull.

Näcken class

Origin: Sweden, first unit completed 1980
Type: Attack submarine, diesel-powered (SS)
Displacement: 1,030 tons surfaced; 1,125 tons submerged
Dimensions: Length 162ft 6in (49.5m); beam 20ft (6.1m); draught 13ft (4.1m)
Propulsion: Diesel-electric drive on one shaft; one MTU 16V652 diesel generator; one Jeumont-Schneider electric motor; 1,800bhp for 20kt surfaced, 1,500hp for 20kt submerged
Complement: 19
Background: During the 1950s the Swedish Navy began the development of a series of small submarines of modern design intended for operations in the shallow waters of the Baltic. The primary mission of the early boats was anti-surface, but in recent years the anti-submarine mission has assumed greater importance, and the latest designs incorporate modern sensors, sophisticated noise reduction techniques, and both long (anti-ship) and short (ASW) torpedo tubes. The five submarines of the Sjöormen class, completed 1967-69, introduced the 'Albacore' hull-form and 'X'-planes to the Swedish Navy. They were followed by the three submarines of the Näcken class, an improved design developed following detailed design studies using computer analysis. Slightly smaller than their immediate predecessors, the Näckens featured a heavier torpedo armament and a new generation of automated machinery control and AIO/fire control systems.
Design: The Näcken is of single-hull construction with a prominent deck casing. The pressure hull, which is of high-yield steel, is cylindrical with a truncated cone aft. It is closed by flat bulkheads fore and aft, and there is a third pressure-tight bulkhead amidships, just abaft the fin. The internal layout is notable for its economical use of space. By shifting all batteries into the machinery spaces in the after part of the boat the designers have created a two-deck layout forward. The upper level houses the attack centre, which is immediately beneath the fin, and the accommodation spaces, which extend to the forward bulkhead. The torpedo tubes are on the lower level, with an extensive stowage and handling room abaft them. The machinery spaces are divided into three compartments. The forward compartment, which is on two levels, houses the highly-automated machinery control room and switchboard, with the 168-cell Tudor battery bank beneath. The centre compartment is also on two levels, with the single MTU diesel beneath and the auxiliary

Below: *Najad*, the second unit of the Näcken class, running on the surface. These compact submarines are of modern design throughout, and are ideally suited to the confined and shallow waters of the Baltic Sea.

Right: Näcken class boats have six bow tubes for 21in (533mm) torpedoes and two tubes for 16in (400mm) torpedoes. The current 21in torpedo is the Tp 61 (1), a high-performance anti-ship model which uses high-test peroxide propulsion. The short ASW torpedo fired from the 400mm tubes is the Tp 42, now being superseded by the Tp 43 (2).

***Näcken* (Näk)**

machinery above. The after compartment contains the main electric motor, which is a double-armature model by Jeumont-Schneider. The unusually high maximum speed of 20 knots on the surface enables these boats to make rapid transits in Swedish waters to meet any threat. Considerable attention has been paid to shock resistance and to silencing. The batteries and all propulsion and auxiliary machinery are on resilient mountings and have flexible couplings. The Swedish Navy was the first to adopt 'X'-planes operationally. They provide redundancy and fine control in both the horizontal and vertical planes, and an additional attraction for the Swedes was that they permitted 'bottoming' in the shallow waters of the Baltic. Somewhat surprisingly, the forward hydroplanes are mounted on the fin, as on the much larger US Navy SSNs. One unit of the class is being fitted with a Sterling closed-cycle engine.

Armament: Modern Swedish submarines have a mix of long anti-ship and short ASW torpedo tubes. In the Näcken class there are two horizontal banks of tubes, with reloads stowed abaft each tube.There are six positive discharge tubes of 21in (533mm) diameter for the Type 61 anti-ship torpedo, and two short 16in (400mm) tubes for the Type 42 anti-submarine torpedo. The swim-out method is employed for the latter to save space and provide for silent discharge. The Tp 61, which entered service in 1977, is a high-performance heavyweight torpedo with thermal (HTP) propulsion, capable of speeds in excess of 60 knots. It is wire-guided, and has a length of 23ft (7.1m) and a maximum range of 33,000yds (30,000m). The Tp 42 is a short (8ft 6in/2.6m) wire-guided acoustic-homing torpedo. The current Tp 422 model entered service in 1983, and will be superseded by the improved Tp 431 from 1987 onwards. FFV mines can also be launched from the torpedo tubes.

Electronics: The main active/passive attack sonar, which comprises a circular array of hydrophones, is located in the upper part of the bow casing, and may be a variant of the Krupp-Atlas CSU-3. The mast-mounted sensor outfit is unusual in that there is only a single Kollmorgen periscope for the search and attack functions. The Ericsson IDPS central data system, based on two Censor 932 computers, provides not only tactical data but also monitors the status of the machinery. The PEAB fire control system, which features two interchangeable consoles to provide tactical display and weapons control, allows the simultaneous tracking and engagement of multiple targets.

Construction: Three submarines of the Näcken class were completed between 1980 and 1981 at the Karlskrona and Kockums (Malmö) Shipyards.

Above: Three contemporary Swedish submarine types are featured in this photo. *Näcken* is outboard of *Sjöhunden* of the Sjöormen class, with *Vargen* of the older Draken class alongside the minelayer *Älvsborg*, which doubles in peacetime as a submarine tender. In the foreground is the stem of the first of four A-17 (Västergötland) class boats.

Nazario Sauro class

Origin: Italy, first unit completed 1980
Type: Attack submarine, diesel-powered (SS)
Displacement: 1,460 tons surfaced; 1,650 tons submerged
Dimensions: Length 209ft 6in (63.9m); beam 22ft 5in (6.8m); draught 18ft 9in (5.7m)
Propulsion: Diesel-electric drive on one shaft; three GMT A210 16 diesel generators, each 1070bhp; one Marelli electric motor; 3,210bhp for 14kt surfaced, 3,650hp for 20kt submerged
Complement: 49
Background: This was the second of Italy's postwar submarine designs. The first, the Toti, was a small coastal design comparable to the German Type 205/206. The Staff Requirements for the Nazario Sauro were for a larger boat with better endurance and improved habitability, capable of penetrating into waters controlled by a potential enemy. Operational conditions in the Mediterranean favoured a relatively small hull

Above: *Nazario Sauro*, the name-ship of the class. These submarines are a handy size for operations in the shallow waters of the Mediterranean; high underwater speed and good manoeuvrability were primary requirements for the design.

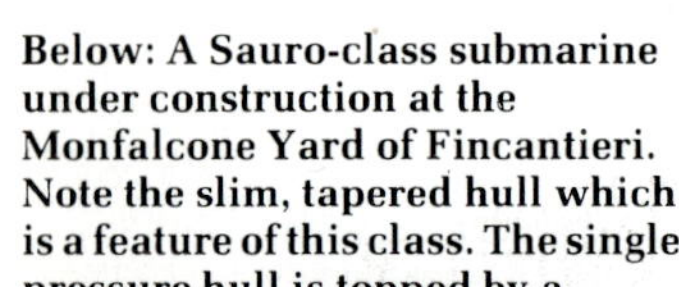

Below: A Sauro-class submarine under construction at the Monfalcone Yard of Fincantieri. Note the slim, tapered hull which is a feature of this class. The single pressure hull is topped by a prominent casing, while abaft the modern cruciform tail surfaces is a single, seven-bladed propeller. The forward hydroplanes are mounted on the fin, in the manner of US Navy submarines.

with high underwater speed and good maneouvrability, and further requirements were for a deep-diving capability, to take advantage of the thermal layers which plague sonar operations in the Mediterranean, and a low noise level. The first two units of the class were initially ordered in 1967, but budgetary problems resulted in cancellation and they were not reordered until 1972. Orders for a second pair were subsequently placed in 1976, but the completion of the first two units was again delayed because of defective batteries. This problem was finally resolved by purchasing batteries direct from Sweden, and a third pair with an improved weapon/sensor outfit was ordered in 1983.

Design: The Sauros have a modern 'tear-drop' hull-form with a single shaft and cruciform after control surfaces. The forward hydroplanes are mounted on the fin in the manner of US Navy SSNs, and single-hull construction was adopted to economise on weight. The pressure hull, which is cylindrical in the forward half of the boat but is tapered abaft the fin, is constructed of high-yield HY80 steel, giving these submarines a maximum diving depth in excess of 820ft (250m). It is closed at either end by hemispherical bulkheads. Beneath the fin there is a two-deck layout, with the control room and officer accommodation on the upper level, and the lower level occupied largely by the two 148-cell battery banks. Accommodation for the crew is located in the torpedo stowage room forward. The machinery spaces are divided into three sections. The forward compartment houses the three diesel generators, which are mounted abreast on a resiliently-mounted raft. The centre compartment houses the electrical switchboard with the auxiliary machinery beneath, and the after compartment is occupied by the large Marelli double-armature motor. The latter is air-cooled, and can produce 4,200hp for short periods. A speed of 19.3 knots was sustained for one hour on trials. Considerable attention was paid to silencing and shock resistance: not only is all machinery resiliently mounted, but there are flexible pipe connections and the machinery compartments are lined with noise-absorbent material, and the slow-turning seven-bladed propeller reduces cavitation at higher speeds. The snort tube has a particularly small cross-section and was designed to offer a low radar signature.

Armament: The submarines of the Nazario Sauro class have six bow tubes of standard 21in (533mm) diameter. Positive discharge enables them to fire torpedoes at maximum depth, and there is stowage for six reloads. The current Italian heavyweight torpedo is the Whitehead A.184, which is 19ft 8in (6m) long and can be fired against surface ships or submarines. The A.184 employs electric propulsion and is wire-guided, with an advanced active/passive acoustic homing head which controls both course and depth. A fast, 50-knot torpedo is currently under development: designated the A.290, it employs a lithium battery and a homing head developed from the short A.244 antisubmarine torpedo. In place of each torpedo, these submarines could carry two mines of the VS SM600 type. The VS SM600 is a sophisticated influence mine which can recognise the magnetic, acoustic and pressure signatures of a variety of surface ships and submarines. The fifth and sixth boats of the class will have longer tubes to enable them to fire the Sub-Harpoon anti-ship missile.

Electronics: The first four boats have the ELSAG/USEA IPD-70 sonar, which comprises a circular active/passive transducer with integral underwater telephone and passive intercept sonar, together with an ELSAG/USEA MD-100S conformal flank array. Mast-mounted sensors include Kollmorgen search and attack periscopes, the SMA SPS-704 radar, and ELT-724S passive ESM. The SEPA CCRG weapon control system can track four targets simultaneously. The fifth and sixth boats will have a more advanced electronics outfit based on the IPD-70S fully integrated sonar system.

Construction: The first four units of the Nazario Sauro class were completed by C.R.D.A., Monfalcone, between 1980 and 1982. The fifth and sixth units are being built by Fincantieri, the state-owned concern which has taken over the yard.

Below: The Sauros have six bow tubes of 21in (533mm) diameter. The current heavyweight torpedo is the Whitehead A.184 (1), a wire-guided weapon which can be fired against both surface ships and submarines. It will eventually be replaced by a 50-knot torpedo currently under development, the A.290. The fifth and sixth boats of the class will be fitted with longer tubes to enable them to fire the Sub-Harpoon anti-ship missile. In addition to the six weapons carried in the tubes there is stowage for six reloads; alternatively, two VS SM600 multi-sensor influence mines (2) can be carried in place of each torpedo.

Oberon class

Origin: United Kingdom, first unit completed 1960
Type: Attack submarine, diesel-powered (SS)
Displacement: 2,080 tons surfaced; 2,450 tons submerged
Dimensions: Length 290ft (88.5m); beam 26ft 6in (8.1m); draught 18ft 3in (5.6m)
Propulsion: Diesel-electric drive on two shafts; two ASR 16VVS-AS21 diesel generators, each 1,840bhp; two English Electric electric motors, each 3,000hp; 3,680bhp for 12kt surfaced, 6,000hp for 17kt submerged
Complement: 64
Background: Work on the first postwar British production submarine design, the Porpoise class, began in 1949. Like other contemporary western designs, it was heavily influenced by the German Type XXI. Draft staff requirements called for a speed of 17 knots to be sustained for 20 minutes, and for a maximum diving depth of 650ft (200m). The new submarines were designed for the ASW patrol mission, and featured a pair of stern tubes for short antisubmarine torpedoes. The Porpoise design proved particularly successful, and was succeeded by a modified design, the Oberon, which although virtually indistinguishable externally, incorporated a number of detail improvements.
Design: The Oberon has the conventional double-hull

Above: Although now more than 20 years old, the Oberons, represented here by *Otus*, continue to set a standard for quiet operation in the Royal Navy which only the very latest nuclear boats have exceeded. The Oberon design is essentially traditional, with a cigar-shaped hull flanked by ballast tanks, but they are large boats with good long-range performance on the surface, and have acquired a high reputation in service.

Above and right: The Oberons have six bow tubes of 21in (533mm) diameter, plus two shorter stern tubes of the same diameter. When these submarines were first completed in the 1960s they carried the Mk 8 anti-ship torpedo and the Mk 20(S) short anti-escort torpedo; the latter was fired from the stern tubes. From about 1970 the Mk 20 was replaced by the Mk 23 antisubmarine homing torpedo (1), which employed wire guidance. The Mk 23 was in turn superseded by the Mk 24 Tigerfish (2), a 'long' torpedo which can be fired only from the bow tubes of the Oberon. The stern tubes are therefore no longer used. Dual-purpose variants of Tigerfish were to have replaced the elderly Mk 8 torpedo, whose design dates back to the 1930s, but the latter remained in service in the late 1980s.

configuration of prewar British submarines. Advanced high-yield UKE steel was used in the construction of the pressure hull. In contrast, lightweight materials were used extensively in the construction of the fin and casing: the first unit completed, *Orpheus*, had a fin made of aluminium, but glass-fibre laminate was adopted for later boats. The long, single-cylinder pressure hull allows for a single-deck layout with the control room positioned centrally. Forward of the control room are the accommodation spaces, with the batteries beneath, and abaft it are the machinery spaces. US-type 'Guppy' batteries were adopted in order to simplify wartime supply. They are located in two compartments, each with 224 battery cells, and are linked in series to give 880v for short bursts. Not only did the Porpoise and Oberon types easily attain their designed underwater speed, but they have proved to be exceptionally quiet. A maximum range of 9,000nm (16,700km) on the surface enables them to undertake distant deployments, and although their primary patrol area is the North Atlantic, submarines of the class have regularly deployed to the Falkland Islands since the conflict of 1982.

Armament: The Oberons have six 21in (533mm) bow tubes, and two shorter tubes of the same diameter in the stern. When they were completed in the 1960s, they carried the Mk 8 anti-ship torpedo and the Mk 20(S) antisubmarine torpedo. The Mk 8, which is 22ft (6.7m) long, was designed in the 1930s but has proved so reliable that it was reported to be still in service in 1986. It is a straight-running weapon with a range of 5,000yds (4,500m) at a speed of 45 knots. The Mk 20 was developed in the 1950s as an anti-escort weapon and was designed to be fired from the stern tubes of the Porpoise and Oberon classes. It employed passive acoustic homing, was 13ft 6in (4.1m) long and had a range of 12,000yds (11,000m) at 20 knots. The Mk 20 was superseded from 1970 onwards by the Mk 23, which was essentially a Mk 20 with an additional section incorporating a wire-guidance casket. During the late 1970s both the Mk 20 and the Mk 23 began to be replaced by the Mk 24 Tigerfish (see Swiftsure). Tigerfish, unlike its predecessors is a long torpedo and has to be fired from the bow tubes of the Oberon. The short stern tubes are therefore no longer used.

Electronics: The original sonar outfit of the Oberons comprised a Type 187 active/passive scanning sonar, housed in a prominent dome above the bow, a Type 186 passive conformal flank array, and a Type 197 intercept array located at the after end of the fin. Type 186 was subsequently replaced by Type 2007, but the original sonar outfit remained otherwise unchanged into the 1980s. The decision to update these submarines with modern sonars was forced on the Royal Navy by delays in the Type 2400 (Upholder) programme. Nine boats are now to be retro-fitted with the Type 2051 Triton integrated sonar suite, which uses off-the-shelf equipment developed commercially. A new electronically-scanned active/passive array is housed in a streamlined sonar dome, and the suite includes a Type 2046 'clip-on' towed hydrophone array. The DCH tactical data system incorporates the latest compact computers with M700/40 microprocessors, and the fire control system will allow for simultaneous firing of two Mk 24 Tigerfish torpedoes. MEL Manta electronic warfare intercept equipment will be fitted.

Construction: Thirteen submarines of the Oberon class were completed for the Royal Navy between 1960 and 1967 and a further 14 have been built in British shipyards for other countries: three for Canada (completed 1965-68), six for Australia (1967-78), three for Brazil (1973-77) and two for Chile (1976). The Australian and Canadian boats are currently being refitted with new sensors, largely of US origin.

Above: *Oppossum* was the first of the British Oberons to receive the Type 2051 Triton integrated sonar, which is currently being fitted to a further eight boats of the class. The modernisation will include provision of a Type 2046 clip-on towed array and new fire control and electronic warfare systems. The remaining four unmodernised units are scheduled for disposal.

Ohio class

Origin: USA, first unit completed 1981
Type: Ballistic missile submarine, nuclear-powered (SSBN)
Displacement: 16,764 tons surfaced; 18,750 tons submerged
Dimensions: Length 560ft (170.7m); beam 42ft (12.8m); draught 36ft 6in (11.1m)
Propulsion: One S8G natural circulation reactor with turboeducation drive; one shaft; 60,000shp for 20+kt
Complement: 160
Background: The original requirement for the Ohio class came from a need to replace the SSBNs of the George Washington and Ethan Allen classes, which were incapable of conversion to fire the current Poseidon or the projected Trident missiles, and which by the early 1980s would be more than 20 years old. There was by the early 1970s concern regarding the dramatic growth in Soviet antisubmarine capabilities, which threatened many of the SSBN patrol areas favoured by the US Navy. Forward deployment from European bases, which exposed the US SSBNs to preemptive attack in wartime and to terrorist attack in peacetime, was also increasingly questioned. The Trident C-4 missile which was developed as a successor to Poseidon therefore featured a significant increase in range to 4,000+nm (7,400km). Available sea-space for SSBN patrol operations was thereby extended from three million to fourteen million square miles, and submarines armed with the missile would no longer have to operate from forward bases in order to target the major cities of the Soviet Union. Initially the new SSBN design was to have been an enlarged and improved Lafayette, employing the same S5W reactor for a maximum speed of only 19-20 knots. However, the US Navy was anxious to install a natural circulation reactor based on the model being tested in the *Narwhal* (SSN 671). The desire for sophisticated noise reduction techniques led in turn to a proposal that the expense involved in efficient quieting could be better justified if the missile complement was raised from the original 16 to 24. The result was a submarine more than twice the size of the Lafayette, with a 60,000shp reactor.
Design: The size of the Ohio was determined by the number of missiles to be carried. More than 24 would have made for too long a hull, with adverse consequences for the manoeuvrability of the submarine. The missile tubes are of larger diameter than those of the Lafayette to enable the Ohios to fire the Trident D-5 missile when the latter enters service in the late 1980s. The hull-form, like that of the Los Angeles, is essentially cylindrical for ease of construction. The propulsion machinery is extremely quiet in operation. The large S8G natural circulation reactor drives two sets of turbines, one for high and the other for low speed, via a turboeduction drive system. All noise-emitting machinery is raft-mounted and isolated from the hull. Sonar capabilities were accorded a higher priority than in earlier SSBNs, and the Ohios have a similar arrangement to that of US Navy SSNs, with a large spherical bow array complemented by amidships torpedo tubes. The large size of the hull has made possible a four-deck layout beneath the fin, with space for storage batteries below.
Armament: The Trident I C-4 missile has a length of 34ft (10.4m) and a diameter of 6ft 2in (1.9m). It comprises a three-stage solid-fuel rocket carrying eight 100kT MIRVed nuclear warheads. Since 1980 some missiles have had an alternative payload comprising eight Mk 500 Evader MaRVs (Manoeuvrable Reentry Vehicles) developed by Lockheed. Towards the end of the decade the Trident I C-4 will be superseded by the Trident II D-5 missile currently under development. The D-5 is a much larger missile than the C-4, with a length of 45ft 6in (13.9m) and a diameter of 6ft 11in (2.1m). Range will be a massive 6,000nm (11,100km) and a CEP of only 400ft (120m) is projected. The D-5 will carry up to 14 MIRVs of 150kT each, with an alternative payload of seven 300kT MaRVs. The four Mk 68 21in (533mm) torpedo tubes, which are located directly

Above: The Ohios are the largest submarines ever built in the West, and at 18,750 tons submerged displacement they are more than twice the size of their predecessors of the Lafayette class. They also are quieter, have more sophisticated sensors, and carry eight more ballistic missiles than earlier SSBNs.

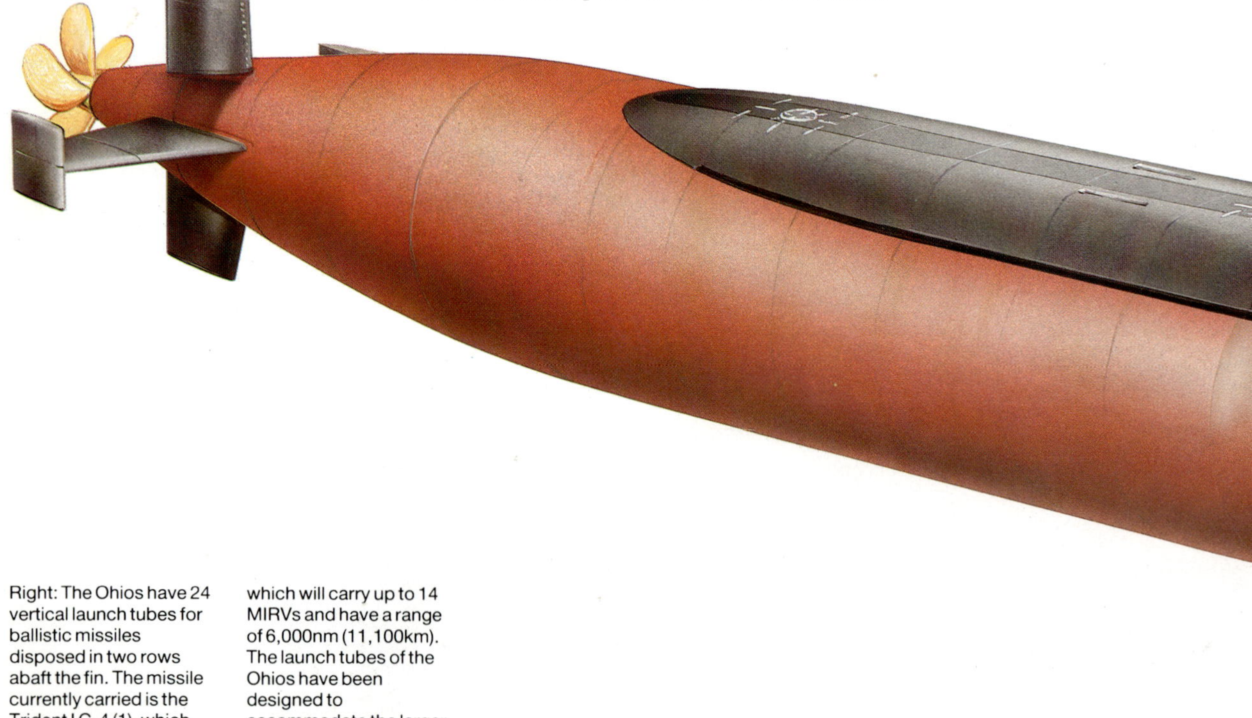

Right: The Ohios have 24 vertical launch tubes for ballistic missiles disposed in two rows abaft the fin. The missile currently carried is the Trident I C-4 (1), which has a range of more than 4,000nm (7,400km) and can carry up to eight independently-targeted reentry vehicles. In the late 1980s the C-4 will be superseded by the Trident II D-5 misile, which will carry up to 14 MIRVs and have a range of 6,000nm (11,100km). The launch tubes of the Ohios have been designed to accommodate the larger D-5 missile without modification. The four 21in (533mm) torpedo tubes are located directly beneath the fin, and fire the Mk 48 dual-purpose torpedo (2).

beneath the diminutive fin, fire the Mk 48 high-performance torpedo. As with the Los Angeles class, the torpedo transfer system is fully automated.

Electronics: The BQQ-6 sonar suite is similar to the BQQ-5 suite installed in the most recent SSNs, but without the active component. It comprises a spherical BQS-13 passive ranging sonar for fire control, a BQR-25 conformal hydrophone array, a PUFFS spot hydrophone array for fire control, and a BQR-23 towed array. There is also a BQS-15 sonar for under-ice operation, and a BQR-19 side-looking sonar for bottom-mapping. The Ohios have two Mk 2 SINS (Ship's Inertial Navigation System), and are fitted to receive data from navigation satellites to ensure that their missiles are accurately targeted. Missile fire control is provided by the Mk 98 digital computerized FC system, and the Mk 118 system is installed for torpedo fire control. The surveillance radar is a BPS-15A, and the WLR-8 (V) electronic warfare system is fitted.

Construction: *Ohio* (SSBN 726), the name-ship of the class, was completed three years late. Since that time, however, a further seven submarines of the class have been completed and the programme is now on schedule. Six units of the class are under construction or on order, and a four more are projected. All have been built by General Dynamics, Groton.

Above: *Florida* (SSBN 728), the third of eight Ohio-class SSBNs already in service; six further units are under construction, and four more are projected. They are the only US submarines capable of carrying the Trident II D-5 missile, which is significantly larger than its predecessors and will have a range of 6,000nm.

USS *Ohio* (SSBN 726)

2

Oscar class

Origin: USSR, first unit completed 1980
Type: Cruise missile submarine, nuclear-powered (SSGN)
Displacement: 11,000 tons surfaced; 13,500 tons submerged
Dimensions: Length 470ft (143m); beam 60ft (18m); draught 36ft (11m)
Propulsion: Two pressurized water-cooled reactors driving geared steam turbines; 2 shafts; 60,000shp for 25kt max
Complement: 130
Background: The Oscar is effectively a replacement for the ageing Echo-class submarines of the 1960s, and like its predecessor it is designed primarily for anti-carrier operations in sea areas relatively close to the Soviet Union. Its mission is to take up an advance position in the path of a US Navy carrier battle group, and to launch a multi-missile strike at maximum range. This would be coordinated with similar strikes by long-range maritime bombers and surface units in an attempt to saturate the defences of the carrier battle group. Initial target data would be provided by satellites or reconnaissance aircraft, creating a requirement for secure communications with a central command post ashore. Unlike the SS-N-3/12 missiles carried by the Echo, the SS-N-19 which equips the Oscar can be fired from beneath the surface. The submarine is therefore far less vulnerable to detection and preemptive attack.
Design: The Oscar is an exceptionally large boat, with a submerged displacement between two and three times that of contemporary Western nuclear-powered attack boats. The launch tubes for the 24 SS-N-19 missiles are located between the inner and outer hulls in the forward half of the submarine: there are six large rectangular hatches, each about 23ft (7m) long and concealing two missile tubes, on either side of the fin. The tubes are thought to be angled at approximately 45 degrees to the vertical. The outer hull casing is almost square in cross-section throughout the missile section, and there is a stand-off of about 13ft (4m) between the inner pressure cylinder and the outer casing. Abaft the missile section the outer hull tapers sharply, terminating in conventional cruciform after control surfaces. The second and third boats of the class have a more angular rudder-fin topped by a tubular housing for a towed communications array. The forward hydroplanes are close to the bow, as in the Typhoon, and are fully retractable. There is some disagreement as to the precise nature of the propulsion plant: because of the amount of space taken up by the SS-N-19 missile tubes, the pressure hull is relatively small in diameter (between 30ft and 36ft, 9-11m); a single large reactor is therefore unlikely. The length of the after section of the submarine suggests that two reactors are installed in series on the centre-line, with two sets of turbines driving two seven-bladed propellers. A total of 60,000shp would suffice to drive the Oscar at a speed of around 25 knots, which would be adequate for the projected mission of these submarines, given that they would take up position in advance of a task force and that noisy, high-speed operation on the flanks would therefore be unnecessary. As with other contemporary Soviet submarines, anechoic tiles have been applied over the entire hull casing.
Armament: The SS-N-19 anti-ship missile – the same model that equips the large nuclear-powered cruisers of the Kirov class – has a conventional aeroplane configuration, with folding wings for stowage in the launch tubes, and artists' impressions produced in the West show a turbojet sustainer motor slung under the missile fuselage flanked by twin solid-fuel boosters. The SS-N-19 has a maximum range estimated at 240nm (450km). Length is probably around 33ft (10m), and alternative high explosive (HE) and nuclear payloads can be carried. Eight torpedo tubes,

Left: The Oscar is the largest SSGN yet built, and surpasses in size all but the latest ballistic missile submarines. Her immense beam was generated by the need to accommodate large-diameter vertical-launch tubes for SS-N-19 anti-ship missiles outside the single pressure hull on either side of the fin. The six large square port-side hatches are particularly prominent in this close-up of the first unit of the class. There are two missile tubes beneath each missile hatch.

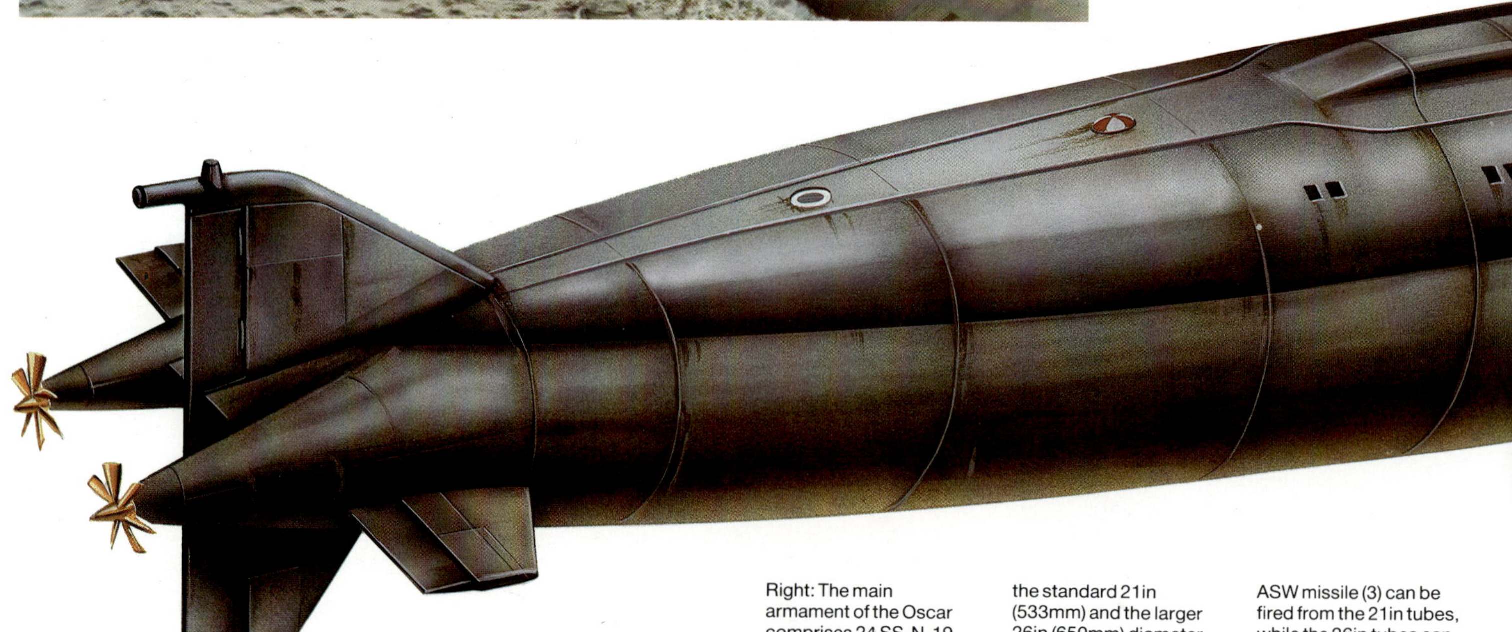

Right: The main armament of the Oscar comprises 24 SS-N-19 anti-ship cruise missiles (1) which are fired from angled launch tubes abeam the fin. Eight torpedo tubes, of both the standard 21in (533mm) and the larger 26in (650mm) diameter, are fitted, and there is stowage for 16 reloads. Antisubmarine homing torpedoes (2) and the SS-N-15 nuclear-tipped ASW missile (3) can be fired from the 21in tubes, while the 26in tubes can handle the SS-N-16 conventional ASW missile (4) and the Type 65 wake-homing torpedo (5).

including both the standard 21in (533mm) model and the large-diameter 26in (650mm) model, are fitted. These can handle the complete range of contemporary Soviet tube-launched weapons, including the SS-N-15 and SS-N-16 antisubmarine missiles.

Electronics: A large active/passive low-frequency bow sonar is fitted, together with an active medium-frequency ranging sonar; there are also passive arrays along the length of the hull. A single pair of large rectangular hatches immediately abaft the fin house buoys for VLF communications, and the second and third boats of the class also have a towed array for VLF (ELF?) communications which is deployed from the small tubular housing atop the vertical stabilizer. The low, streamlined fin houses an extensive array of masts including Snoop Pair/Rim Hat (surface surveillance/ESM), Park Lamp (VLF/LF reception), Pert Spring (satellite navigation) and Shot Gun (VHF communications). There are also numerous electro-optical sensors, including the Cod Eye radio sextant.

Construction: The first unit of the class was laid down at the Severodvinsk Shipyard in 1978, was launched in 1980, and ran her sea trials late in the same year. The second boat was not launched until 1982, and the third followed in 1985. Probably only the Severodvinsk Shipyard is capable of building submarines of this size, and although slow series production is proceeding, it seems unlikely that it will exceed a completion rate of one hull every two years.

Above: The second unit of the class photographed by the Norwegian Air Force in the area of the Soviet Northern Fleet. These large submarines would be deployed to counter US Navy Carrier Battle Groups. Note the distinctive tail-fin, topped by a cylindrical dispenser for a towed communications array.

Permit class

Origin: USA, first unit completed 1961
Type: Attack submarine, nuclear-powered (SSN)
Displacement: 3,750 tons surfaced; 4,300 tons submerged
Dimensions: Length 278ft 6in (84.9m); beam 31ft 8in (9.7m); draught 29ft (8.8m)
Propulsion: One S5W pressurized water-cooled reactor driving geared steam turbines; one shaft; 15,000shp for 27kt max
Complement: 106
Background: During the early 1950s US Navy tactical thinking favoured the parallel development of high-performance attack submarines for fleet work and slower hunter-killer submarines (SSKs) for deployment in antisubmarine barriers. A small experimental nuclear-powered SSKN, the *Tullibee* (SSN-597), was built to test the latter concept. The *Tullibee* employed turbo-electric propulsion for quietness, and was designed around a new sophisticated sonar suite, designated BQQ-1, which featured a large spherical bow sonar. This effectively displaced the torpedo tubes, which were relocated amidships. Even before the completion of *Tullibee*, however, it became apparent that the Navy could not afford two separate lines of development. The Thresher (now Permit) class which succeeded the Skipjacks was therefore biased heavily towards ASW, and a number of the systems developed for the *Tullibee* were incorporated.
Design: The Thresher was the first US Navy production submarine to have the revolutionary sonar/torpedo tube arrangement introduced by the *Tullibee*. This arrangement had the effect of minimising interference with sonar reception, and was adopted in all successive classes of US Navy SSN. First sketches of the design also show a turbo-electric propulsion plant, but the installation employed for the *Tullibee* produced insufficient power for a submarine the size of the Thresher, and a purpose-built plant would have taken too long to develop, so the US Navy persisted with the proven S5W reactor and conventional geared turbines. In the event a comparable level of quieting was achieved by isolating the propulsion machinery from the hull. The turbines and gearing were mounted on a 'raft' with resilient mountings. However, these measures had the effect of increasing the overall size of the submarine, and as the US Navy was by now committed to a reactor of fixed power, it would have to accept a loss of speed as compared with the Skipjack. Every effort was made to minimise this speed-loss. The size of the fin was reduced dramatically, so that it contributed only 8-10% of the total resistance of the submarine, as compared to 30% for the Skipjack. This resulted in problems in accommodating all the necessary sensor masts, and it was still not enough. Not until the Los Angeles class (qv) was the high speed of the original Skipjack design to be achieved again. The other innovation associated with the Thresher class was the use of HY80 steel in the construction of the single pressure hull. A maximum diving depth of 1,300ft (400m) is reported, but the introduction of high-yield steels was not without problems: the loss of the original name-ship of the class, *Thresher* (SSN-593), less than two years after her completion is thought to have been due to defective welding. However, improvements in construction techniques appear to have eliminated these problems in later boats of the class.
Armament: Because the bow position is occupied by the BQS-6 transducer array there are only four torpedo tubes, which are located beneath the fin and angled out at an angle of 10 degrees. The broad handling room can accommodate an estimated 18 torpedoes or missiles. As completed the Threshers were equipped to fire the Mk 14/16 anti-ship torpedo, the Mk 37 antisubmarine torpedo, and the Mk 45 ASTOR nuclear-tipped torpedo (see Skipjack). They were also designed from the outset to fire the SUBROC missile (see Sturgeon), which entered operational service in 1965. The earlier marks of torpedo have now been replaced by the dual-role Mk 48, and from 1976 onwards all units of the class were fitted to fire the Harpoon anti-ship missile.
Electronics: The BQQ-2 integrated sonar suite with which these submarines were initially fitted comprised the BQS-6 spherical active/passive array, the BQR-7 conformal passive array, and the BQG-3 PUFFS fire control sonar. The BQS-6 is capable of making detections out to the first convergence zone (30-35nm, 55-65km) using the bottom bounce or convergence zone modes of operation. The BQR-7 array comprises a 50ft (15m) triple row of 'spot' hydrophones for passive search and target classification. The BQQ-2 sonar suite is currently being replaced by the BQQ-5 (see Los Angeles). The original Mk 113 analogue fire control system has been replaced by the digital Mk 117 to enable the submarines to fire Harpoon. Mast-mounted sensors include search and attack periscopes, a BPS-15 surveillance radar, and the customary ESM and communications antennae.
Construction: Fourteen submarines of the Thresher/Permit class were completed at five different shipyards between 1961 and 1967. The last three units were built as prototypes for the succeeding Sturgeon class (qv), and have similar dimensions and displacement.

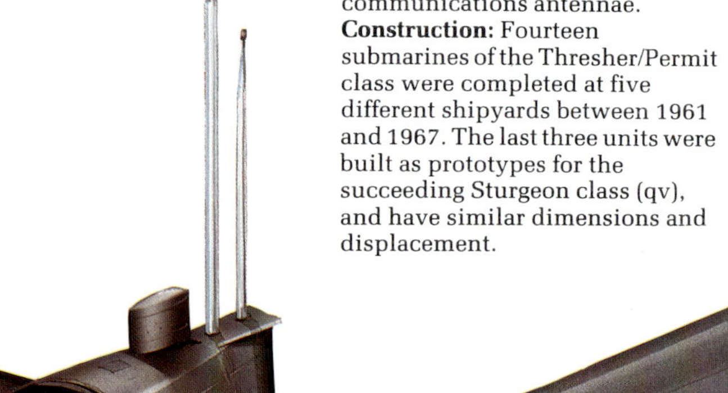

USS *Permit* (SSN 594)

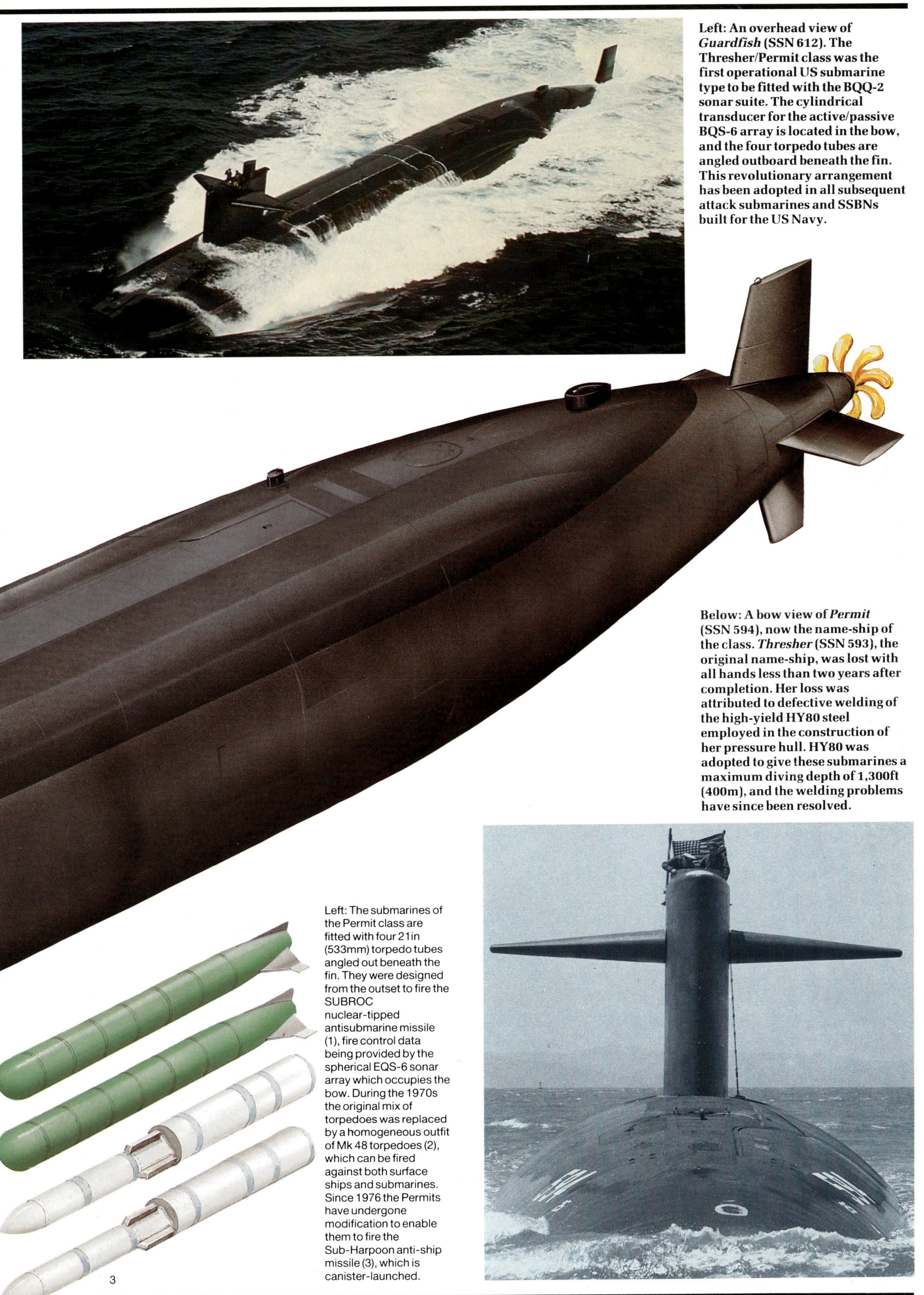

Left: An overhead view of *Guardfish* (SSN 612). The Thresher/Permit class was the first operational US submarine type to be fitted with the BQQ-2 sonar suite. The cylindrical transducer for the active/passive BQS-6 array is located in the bow, and the four torpedo tubes are angled outboard beneath the fin. This revolutionary arrangement has been adopted in all subsequent attack submarines and SSBNs built for the US Navy.

Below: A bow view of *Permit* (SSN 594), now the name-ship of the class. *Thresher* (SSN 593), the original name-ship, was lost with all hands less than two years after completion. Her loss was attributed to defective welding of the high-yield HY80 steel employed in the construction of her pressure hull. HY80 was adopted to give these submarines a maximum diving depth of 1,300ft (400m), and the welding problems have since been resolved.

Left: The submarines of the Permit class are fitted with four 21in (533mm) torpedo tubes angled out beneath the fin. They were designed from the outset to fire the SUBROC nuclear-tipped antisubmarine missile (1), fire control data being provided by the spherical EQS-6 sonar array which occupies the bow. During the 1970s the original mix of torpedoes was replaced by a homogeneous outfit of Mk 48 torpedoes (2), which can be fired against both surface ships and submarines. Since 1976 the Permits have undergone modification to enable them to fire the Sub-Harpoon anti-ship missile (3), which is canister-launched.

Resolution class

Origin: United Kingdom, first unit completed 1967
Type: Ballistic missile submarine, nuclear-powered (SSBN)
Displacement: 7,500 tons surfaced; 8,400 tons submerged
Dimensions: Length 425ft (129.5m); beam 33ft (10.1m); draught 30ft (9.1m)
Propulsion: One PWR 1 pressurized water-cooled reactor driving geared steam turbines; one shaft; 15,000shp for 24kt max
Complement: 143
Background: Until the early 1960s it had been envisaged that the Royal Air Force would continue to be responsible for the British nuclear deterrent. However, following the cancellation of the airborne Skybolt missile it was agreed at a joint Anglo-American conference at Nassau in 1962 that the United States would supply the Polaris missile system to the Royal Navy. After a careful study of refit schedules it was resolved that five submarines would be needed in order to guarantee at least one on patrol at all times. However, the fifth boat was cancelled by the Labour Government of 1964, which had entered office pledged to dismantle the entire programme and to complete those boats already laid down as attack submarines. The design was based on the US Navy's Lafayette class, but with British equipment and machinery. The Polaris A-3 missiles, the missile tubes, and the missile fire control systems were purchased directly from the United States. A special Polaris Executive was set up to supervise the construction of the SSBNs, and the creation of the necessary training and support facilities. In spite of its complexity the programme proceeded remarkably smoothly, and kept within its time schedule and projected cost.
Design: The Resolutions are generally similar in overall size and in appearance to the US SSBNs of the Lafayette class, the only major external difference being the location of the forward hydroplanes on the hull casing close to the bow. The British designers considered the adoption of fin-mounted planes, but maintained that the major advantage of better control at low speeds did not outweigh the disadvantages. The hydroplanes on the Resolution class fold upwards at their half-way point to

Below: The design of the Royal Navy's Resolution class was based on that of the US Lafayettes, and dimensions and displacement are virtually identical to those of the US Navy boats. The major external difference lies in the position of the forward hydroplanes, which are bow-mounted; they fold upwards to enable the submarines to come alongside. The internal layout forward and aft of the missile compartment is reminiscent of the Valiant-class SSNs, with which they share many common features.

Above and right: The Resolutions have 16 vertical launch tubes for the Polaris A-3TK missile (1), which has a range of 2,500nm (4,600km) and is now fitted with the British-developed Chevaline multiple warhead, comprising six reentry vehicles. There are six bow tropedo tubes of 21in (533mm) diameter, and the wire-guided Mk 24 Tigerfish torpedo (2) has now superseded the Mk 20/23 ASW torpedoes and the Mk 8 anti-ship torpedoes originally carried.

allow the submarine to come alongside. Internally, the layout forward and aft of the missile compartment is reminiscent of the SSNs of the Valiant class. The pressure hull is cylindrical throughout most of its length, and forward of the missile section there is a three-deck layout housing the control and accommodation spaces, terminating in a smaller cylinder containing the torpedo stowage room. The machinery spaces abaft the missile section are laid out in similar fashion to those of the Valiants (q.v.). However, the Polaris installation necessitated an increase in electrical generating power, so each of the two main turbo-alternators produces 1,700kW. As with the Valiants, a Paxman 4,000bhp diesel generator is available to provide emergency power in the event of reactor failure. During recent refits the noise signature of the auxiliary machinery has been reduced by 20%.

Armament: The Polaris A-3 missile has a length of 32ft 4in (9.85m) and a diameter of 4ft 6in (1.37m). It comprises a two-stage solid-fuel rocket with a maximum range of 2,500nm (4,600km) and was initially fitted with a single large nuclear warhead of British design. This is currently being replaced by six Chevaline multiple reentry vehicles (MRVs), each of around 150kT. Development was initiated in the early 1970s to improve penetration of Soviet missile defences around Moscow and the MRVs can hit targets 25 miles (40km) apart, but the all-British programme encountered serious technical difficulties and massive cost overruns. The first submarine to receive the improved missile (designated the A-3TK) was *Renown*, in 1982; *Resolution* followed in 1984, and *Repulse* in 1986. Work is now proceeding on re-motoring the missiles. In addition to their Polaris missiles the SSBNs of the Resolution class are fitted with six torpedo tubes of 21in (533mm) diameter. When first completed they carried the Mk 20 and Mk 23 antisubmarine torpedoes and the Mk 8 anti-ship torpedo, now replaced by the wire-guided Mk 24 Tigerfish.

Electronics: The original sonar outfit of the Resolution class was identical to that of the Valiants, with a Type 2001 active/passive chin array, a Type 2007 passive flank array, and a Type 197 sonar intercept array. Because of the decision to replace the Resolutions by four new Trident submarines of the Vanguard class beginning in the early 1990s, they will not have the Type 2001 array replaced by the Type 2020 sonar now being retrofitted in SSNs of the Valiant and Swiftsure classes. However, significant improvements have been made to the Action Information Organisation and Fire Control System, and the SSBNs have now been fitted with the Type 2019 intercept sonar and the Type 2024 towed hydrophone array. The latter was developed initially in collaboration with the United States and is based on the US BQR-15 towed array.

Construction: Four submarines of the Resolution class were completed between 1967 and 1968. Two were built by Vickers-Armstrong, Barrow-in Furness, and the other two by Cammell Laird, Birkenhead.

Above: The Resolutions continue to carry the Polaris A-3 missile. Recent modifications include the incorporation of six Chevaline multiple reentry vehicles developed in the United Kingdom, and re-motoring of the missiles will extend their service life until the new Vanguard class, armed with the Trident II D-5 missile, enters service in the 1990s.

Resolution class *Revenge* (S 27)

Romeo class

Origin: USSR, first unit completed 1958
Type: Attack submarine, diesel-powered (SS)
Displacement: 1,330 tons surfaced; 1,700 tons submerged
Dimensions: Length 254ft (77m); beam 22ft (6.7m); draught 16ft (4.9m)
Propulsion: Diesel/electric drive on two shafts; two Type 37D diesels, each 2,000bhp; two electric motors, each 1,500hp; 4,000bhp for 15.5kt surfaced, 3,000hp for 13kt submerged
Complement: 56

Background: The Romeo was designed in the mid-1950s as the natural successor to the medium-range Whiskey class, some 230 of which were completed between 1950 and 1957 to protect Soviet territory against the threat posed by the Western carrier task forces and amphibious landing fleets. The Romeo was essentially similar to the Whiskey in terms of its basic design, but would incorporate more advanced sensors. However, just as work on the first Romeos began there was a major change in Soviet naval policy. The defence of Soviet waters would henceforth be performed by submarines, surface craft and land-based aircraft armed not with torpedoes but with long-range cruise missiles. There was therefore no longer a requirement for a medium-range torpedo attack submarine, and construction of the Romeo was terminated after only 20 had been laid down. A number of the Soviet-built boats were transferred to friendly navies shortly after completion: six were delivered to Egypt 1966-69, two to Bulgaria 1971-72, and more recently two have been transferred to Algeria (1982-83) and two to Syria (1986). During the 1950s, however, the People's Republic of China was given access to the plans of the Romeo, and received sufficient technical assistance to begin construction. The first Chinese boat is reported to have been completed as early as 1960, but series production was established only in the 1970s because of technical and political problems. However, by the early 1980s more than 90 units had been completed, including a number for export.

Design: The hull-form of the Romeo, essentially that of the Whiskey, has the traditional 'cigar' shape common to most submarine types completed in the immediate postwar period. Control surfaces are also of conventional design, with twin propellers housed within circular propeller guards forward of horizontal hydroplanes and a single rudder. The forward hydroplanes retract into the upper part of the hull casing. The fin is also of similar size to that of the later Whiskeys, but there is a prominent fairing above it which houses the snorkel and the two periscopes and which serves to distinguish the Romeo from its predecessor. The major structural modification is to the bow, which has been redesigned to accommodate the Feniks passive sonar array and an additional pair of torpedo tubes. Internally, there are few changes. The single pressure cylinder allows for only one usable deck. The control room and the accomodation spaces are on the same level, with the batteries beneath. The machinery spaces comprise a main engine room housing the two Type 37D diesels, and a motor room housing the two electric motors. There are stowage rooms serving both the forward and the after torpedo tubes.

Armament: The Romeo has six bow and two stern torpedo tubes, all of 21in (533mm) diameter. In addition to the eight torpedoes carried in the tubes, an estimated six reloads can be accommodated. For an alternative payload each torpedo could be replaced by two mines. The standard torpedo employed by Soviet-built units is almost certainly an elderly

Above: A Romeo of the Soviet Navy photographed on the surface in 1979. The Romeo was originally intended as a successor to the Whiskey, but the construction programme was drastically curtailed as a result of policy changes which occurred in the late 1960s, and only 20 boats were completed.

1

free-running model dating from the 1950s. Some units may also have been updated to fire more recent torpedoes with an ASW capability, and the boats in service with the Soviet Navy will also undoubtedly also carry nuclear-tipped torpedoes (probably two). The Romeos in service with the North Korean and PRC Navies are probably equipped with an anti-surface torpedo derived from the early Soviet models. The Romeos built in China for the Egyptian Navy are apparently being fitted with Western fire control systems which would allow them to fire the more advanced torpedoes currently available for export.

Electronics: Both the Soviet and the PRC-built submarines are fitted with the standard Soviet submarine sonars of the late 1950s. The bulged casing in the upper section of the bow houses a Feniks passive array, and atop the bow there is a Tamir-5L active attack sonar housed in a small dome. Mast-mounted sensors comprise search and attack periscopes, a Snoop Plate surveillance radar, Quad Loop DF, Stop Light ESM, and aerials for HF and VHF communications. A Singer Librascope fire control system is currently being retro-fitted in some of the Egyptian boats.

Construction: Twenty Romeos were completed for the Soviet Navy by the Gorky Shipyard between 1958 and 1962. Eighty-four units were completed for the PRC Navy at the Wuzhang, Guangzhou, Jiangnan and Huludao Shipyards between 1960 and 1982. An additional seven units were built for North Korea and transferred between 1973 and 1975. Ten further boats have since been built in North Korea at the Mayang Do Shipyard. The six Romeos built in Chinese shipyards for Egypt were transferred from 1982 onwards.

Above and left: The Romeo has six bow torpedo tubes and two stern tubes, all of 21in (533mm) diameter; an additional six reloads can be stowed in handling rooms adjacent to the tubes. The Soviet boats are probably fitted to fire only the M-57 anti-ship torpedo (1), which has alternative HE or nuclear warheads. Romeos in service with China and the Warsaw Pact navies carry only the conventional model.

Right: An early view of a Soviet Romeo in the English Channel. Although these medium submarines lost favour with the Soviet Navy because of their relatively short range and because they lacked the necessary size to carry cruise missiles, the design was transferred to the People's Republic of China, which by the early 1980s had completed no fewer than 90 units. Because of the relative simplicity of the design the Romeo has proved popular as an export submarine.

Rubis class

Origin: France, first unit completed 1982
Type: Attack submarine, nuclear-powered (SSN)
Displacement: 2,350 tons surfaced; 2,630 tons submerged
Dimensions: Length 237ft (72.1m); beam 25ft (7.6m); draught 21ft (6.4m)
Propulsion: One 48MW pressurized water-cooled reactor with turbo-electric drive; two turbo-alternators driving one main electric motor; one shaft; 9,500hp for 25kt max
Complement: 66
Background: The first attempt by the Marine Nationale to build a nuclear-powered attack submarine dates from 1954, when the first feasibility studies were begun, and the first hull, number Q-244, was laid down at Cherbourg two years later. However, political friction between France and the United States led the latter country to deny France the enriched uranium needed to fuel the reactor. Development of a heavy water reactor using natural uranium was therefore begun, but this proved to be too large and heavy for submarine installation. The French then attempted to purchase a complete submarine reactor from the United States, but this request was also refused, and led to the abandonment of the project. French interest in SSN construction was re-established with the authorisation of a new type of boat in 1964, but this project was overtaken by the SSBN construction programme, which assumed priority. By the time the Marine Nationale returned again to the SSN project in the early 1970s, its constructors could call upon the valuable experience gained in the course of the SSBN programme. The result was an exceptionally compact design little bigger than the diesel-powered submarines of the Agosta class, and with many common elements with regard to weapons and sensors.
Design: The small size of the Rubis and her sisters is due to the development of a compact, integrated reactor-exchanger which takes up little internal hull volume and has had the effect of minimizing the weight allocated to shielding. Steam from the reactor is superheated before passing through two turbines. Each turbine drives one large and one small alternator. The large alternators generate power for the main electric motor, while the smaller alternators supply power to the auxiliary systems on board. The single shaft has a large-diameter five-bladed propeller. The cooling system uses natural circulation during normal running but is pump-assisted at higher speeds. There is an emergency diesel generator capable of driving the submarine for 50nm in the event of reactor failure. In contrast to the French diesel boats the Rubis has a single hull, which is closed by a hemispherical bulkhead at its after end and by a flat bulkhead pierced by the torpedo tubes at its forward end. This allows for a two-deck layout beneath the fin for the control and accommodation spaces. The pressure hull is constructed of Marel high-tensile steel, which gives the Rubis a diving depth of 985ft (300m), and the adoption of a positive discharge system for the torpedoes enables firing to take place at any depth. The forward hydroplanes, which are fin-mounted, and the cruciform after control surfaces are controlled by autopilot from a one-man console.
Armament: The four bow tubes are 21in (533mm) in diameter and can therefore handle only the most recent models of French torpedo. The L 5 Mod.3 acoustic-homing antisubmarine torpedo is carried, as is the new F 17. The latter is wire-guided and is produced in both anti-ship and antisubmarine (F 17P) versions. The F 17 has a length of 19ft 5in (5.9m), and has a maximum speed of 35 knots and a range of 20,000yds (18,000m). *Saphir*, the second unit of the class, was the first to carry the SM 39 Exocet anti-ship missile, and *Rubis* will be retro-fitted with the necessary fire control equipment in the near future. The SM 39, which is 15ft 5in (4.7m) long and has a diameter of only 14in (350mm), is too small to be fired from a conventional torpedo tube. The missile is therefore encased in a capsule for launch. The SM 39 has a range of 27nm (50km) and employs active radar homing. The small size of the Rubis has resulted in a somewhat reduced torpedo capacity: only 14 torpedoes or missiles can be accommodated, as compared with 20 in the diesel-powered Agosta.
Electronics: The sonar outfit of the

Rubis **(S 601)**

Above: *Rubis* is the smallest nuclear-powered submarine ever built. The design was made possible by the development of a particularly compact integrated reactor-exchanger, which has reduced the size and weight of the propulsion machinery. Note the adoption of fin-mounted hydroplanes on the US pattern.

Rubis class is essentially similar to that of the Agosta class, with an active/passive DUUA 2B attack sonar located in the upper part of the bow, and a DSUV 22 circular hydrophone array below the torpedo tubes. The DUUX 5 Fénelon passive ranging sonar, an advanced model which ran trials aboard the Daphné-class submarine *Doris* from 1977, has been installed in place of the DUUX 2 which equipped earlier boats. DUUG/AUUD sonar intercept gear is fitted, and there are TUUM HF and LF underwater telephones. Torpedo fire control is provided by the now-standard DLT D-3 system, and mast-mounted sensors include search and attack periscopes, a DRUA-33 surveillance radar, and ARUR and ARUD intercept aerials.
Construction: An ambitious construction programme which includes five submarines of the Rubis class plus a further five SSNs of an improved design is proceeding slowly, with only two boats completed to date. The fifth boat is due to enter service in 1990.

Below: The launch of *Saphir* at Cherbourg in 1981. The bow section housing the forward ballast tank and sonar arrays is yet to be fitted, all submarines of the class being launched with the pressure hull complete up to the flat forward bulkhead. Series production is proceeding slowly, with only two boats completed by early 1987 and three more scheduled for completion by 1990.

Left: The Rubis has four 21in (533mm) bow tubes and can stow 14 reloads. The L 5 acoustic-homing antisubmarine torpedo (1) is carried, as is the new wire-guided F-17 (2). A dual-purpose variant of the latter, the Mod.1, is now entering service. *Saphir* can also fire the SM 39 Exocet anti-ship missile (3), which has a range of 27nm (50km), and two TSM 3510 mines (4) can be carried in place of a single torpedo.

Sierra class

Origin: USSR, first unit completed in 1984
Type: Attack submarine, nuclear-powered (SSN)
Displacement: 6,000 tons surfaced; 7,550 tons submerged
Dimensions: Length 360ft (110m); beam 36ft (11m); draught 25ft (7.5m)
Propulsion: One/two pressurized water-cooled reactors driving geared steam turbines; one shaft; 40,000shp for 32kt max
Complement: 85

Design: The Sierra was one of three new Soviet attack submarine types which entered service in 1984-85. The Mike, which has a hull of titanium and may also have a liquid metal-cooled reactor, appears to be a high-technology development of the Alfa (q.v.). The Akula is a conventional steel-hulled boat with a pressurized water-cooled reactor, and in appearance closely resembles the Victor III. The Sierra is similar in overall size and construction to the Akula, thereby posing the question as to why the Soviets should choose to embark on the simultaneous construction of two separate types of SSN with similar capabilities. The Akula and the Sierra appear to be fitted with an identical outfit of sensors, and both are thought to be able to handle the full range of tube-launched missiles and torpedoes in the current Soviet inventory. One theory suggested is they are competing designs produced by different design bureaux, and that the Soviet Navy will embark on series production of either one or the other following extensive trials. However, given that the first Akula was built at the Komosomolsk Shipyard in the Pacific (which also participated in construction of the Victor III) and the first Sierra was built at Gorky in the western USSR, it may be that the designs are not so much 'competing' but regionally based, in the same way that the Kresta II and Kara-class BPKs were 'regional' designs. Only when a pattern of construction has been established will a more accurate assessment be possible.

Design: The Sierra is some 13ft (4m) longer than the Victor III, and has a broader beam. The latter is almost certainly related to measures intended to reduce machinery noise. The increase in beam would make it possible to isolate the propulsion machinery and its associated pumps and gearing from the hull by installing it on an insulated 'raft'. It is not yet clear whether two smaller reactors or a larger single reactor is employed, but a maximum speed in excess of 30 knots can be expected. The single shaft has a seven-bladed propeller which is also a feature of the Akula and the Mike. The fin is broad and squat in comparison to that of the Victor III, and is significantly shorter than that of the Akula. The forward hydroplanes, which are fully retractable, are mounted closer to the bow than was the case with earlier Soviet SSNs. The stern section terminates in the now-standard cruciform tail surfaces, with a teardrop-shaped pod identical to that of the Victor III atop the rudder fin. The lines of square free-flood holes along the outer casing testify to Soviet persistence with double-hull construction.

Armament: Six bow tubes are fitted. These are a mix of standard 21in (533mm) tubes and the new 26in (650mm) tube, although it is not yet clear how many of each there are. Standard anti-ship and acoustic-homing antisubmarine torpedoes can be fired from the 21in (533mm) tubes, which can also launch the SS-N-15 nuclear-tipped antisubmarine missile (see Victor) and the new SS-NX-21 cruise missile. The latter is similar in conception to the US

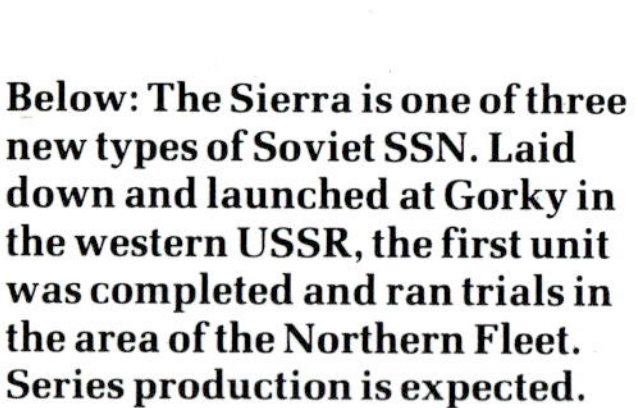

Below: The Sierra is one of three new types of Soviet SSN. Laid down and launched at Gorky in the western USSR, the first unit was completed and ran trials in the area of the Northern Fleet. Series production is expected.

Right: The Sierra has six bow tubes, with a mix of 21in (533mm) and 26in (650mm) diameters. All submarine weapons in the current inventory can be handled, including the SS-NX-21 land attack missile (1), which carries a nuclear warhead and can be fired from a conventional 21in tube. The 21in tubes can also fire the SS-N-15 nuclear-tipped antisubmarine missile (2) and conventional ASW homing torpedoes (3); mines (4) can be carried instead. The large-diameter tubes can fire the SS-N-16 conventional ASW missile (5) and the Type 65 wake-homing anti-ship torpedo (6).

Navy's Tomahawk. It has an estimated maximum range of 900-1,200nm (1,700-2,250km) and is probably fitted with a nuclear warhead. The current version is for land attack, although subsequent variants may have an anti-ship capability. The 26in (650mm) tubes can launch both the SS-N-16 torpedo-carrying antisubmarine missile and the new Type 65 torpedo, which has a range estimated at 54nm (100km) and homes on the wake of a surface ship.

Electronics: The Sierra has a large active/passive bow sonar, probably a development of the model installed in the Victor. Fire control capabilities will doubtless have been improved to enable the submarine to handle the full range of Soviet tube-launched weapons.

A towed hydrophone array is deployed from the pod-shaped housing atop the tail-fin. Mast-mounted sensors include: search and attack periscopes, the new Snoop Pair/Rim Hat surface surveillance radar/ESM combination, Park Lamp VLF reception, Pert Spring satellite navigation, and Shot Gun VHF communications. Other sensors have not been revealed. Curiously, the Sierra lacks the twin hatches for VLF buoys abaft the fin which are a feature of all other recent Soviet nuclear boats.

Construction: The first unit of the Sierra class was launched at the inland Gorky Shipyard in July 1983, and the incomplete hull was subsequently transferred via the White Sea Canal to Severodvinsk for fitting out. The submarine entered service in late 1984. There is as yet no evidence of series production, but it was expected that additional units of both the Sierra and Akula classes would be launched in 1986.

Right: The Sierra is slightly longer than the Victor III and has a broader, more cylindrical hull-form. Mast-mounted sensors include the distinctive Snoop Pair/Rim Hat surveillance radar/ESM combination. The prominent pod atop the tail-fin is thought to house a towed hydrophone array.

Skipjack class

Origin: USA, first unit completed 1959
Type: Attack submarine, nuclear-powered (SSN)
Displacement: 3,075 tons surfaced; 3,500 tons submerged
Dimensions: Length 252ft (76.7m); beam 31ft 6in (9.6m); draught 28ft (8.5m)
Propulsion: One S5W pressurized water-cooled reactor driving geared steam turbines; one shaft; 15,000shp for 30kt max
Complement: 114

Background: The US Navy's development of the nuclear-powered submarine proceeded rapidly following the completion of the *Nautilus* (SSN 571) in 1954. However, the Americans did not rush immediately into series production, preferring instead to evaluate a number of reactors of different design. At the same time, experiments were continuing with new hull-forms, the revolutionary *Albacore* having commissioned barely a year before *Nautilus*. The first US attempt at a production design, the Skate class, had a relatively small pressurized water-cooled reactor and a conventional hull based on the *Nautilus*. This limited underwater speed to a maximum of 20 knots. For the next class, however, the US Navy decided to combine the newly-developed S5W reactor (which was to become standard in US nuclear boats until the 1970s) with the hull-form of the Albacore. The result was a submarine with the exceptionally high underwater speed of 30 knots – a speed unequalled by any other operational submarine in the world until the Soviet Victor class appeared in the late 1960s. The performance of the Skipjacks was such that they continued to be regarded as 'first-line' submarines throughout their service lives.

Design: The Skipjacks were the first US nuclear-powered submarines to have a single hull. This had the effect of reducing overall size while maximizing internal volume. They were also the first nuclear boats to employ a single shaft, the five-bladed propeller being located abaft cruciform control surfaces. This arrangement was to set the standard for later nuclear submarines. It also precluded the installation of stern torpedo tubes, which were a feature of the twin-shaft Skate class. The reactor compartment is 20ft (6.1m) long, and all the other major components of the machinery installation are duplicated to provide redundancy. There are two heat exchangers, two pressurized-water coolers, two sets of turbines and two groups of turbo generators. Two small emergency motors linked to the single shaft and powered either by batteries or by two small diesel generators can bring the submarine home in the event of reactor failure. The Skipjacks have an exceptionally large fin which distinguishes them from later US nuclear boats, and they were the first operational submarines in the world to have their forward hydroplanes mounted on the fin. They were also the first US submarines, together with their diesel-powered contemporaries of the Barbel class, to have a centralised attack centre.

Armament: The Skipjacks have six Mk 59 bow tubes of 21in (533mm) diameter. During the 1960s these could fire a combination of the Mk 14/16 antiship torpedo, the Mk 37 antisubmarine torpedo, and the nuclear-tipped Mk 45 ASTOR. The Mk 14 and its hydrogen peroxide-powered derivative, the Mk 16, were straight-running torpedoes dating from World War II. They were 20ft 6in (6.25m) long, and had a diameter of 21in (533mm). The Mk 37 was developed postwar, and combined electric propulsion with active/passive acoustic homing. The Mod.0 and Mod.3 variants were both free-running, with a length of only 11ft 3in (3.4m), but the Mod.1 and Mod.2 variants were wire-guided, and therefore incorporated an additional section which increased length to 13ft 6in (4.1m); both types had a diameter of 19in (481mm) to enable them to swim out of 21in tubes. Discharge was therefore relatively silent. The small size of these torpedoes enabled two to be carried in place of a single large torpedo in the submarine's reload racks. The Mk 45 ASTOR was also wire-guided because US policy emphasised full control over nuclear weapons at all times. It was unpopular with US submariners because fire control for the torpedo implied active sonar operations which tended to

Right: The Skipjacks are fitted with six Mk 59 bow tubes of 21in (533mm) diameter. As completed these submarines were armed with three distinct types of torpedo; the Mk 14/16 anti-ship torpedo, the short Mk 37 ASW homing torpedo, and the MK 45 ASTOR, a large antisubmarine torpedo with a nuclear warhead. All three types have now been replaced by the Mk 48 (1), a fast-running heavyweight torpedo with optional wire guidance which can be used against both surface ships and submarines. Lacking the sophisticated fire control sonars of later US Navy attack submarines, the Skipjacks were never fitted to fire the SUBROC missile, and their advanced age has precluded the installation of more modern systems.

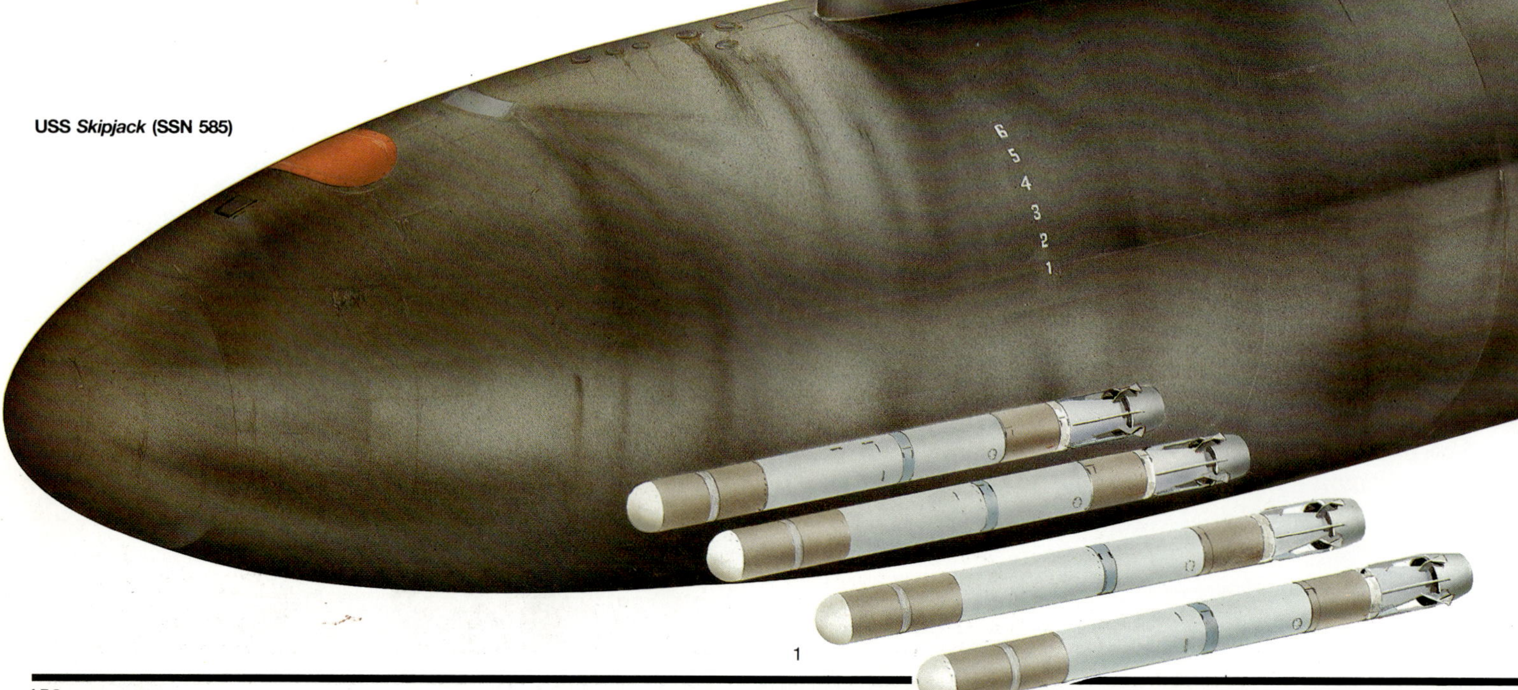

USS *Skipjack* (SSN 585)

give away the position of the submarine, and the weapon was duly discarded in the early 1970s. As production of the dual-purpose Mk 48 torpedo increased in the late 1970s, the Mk 14 and Mk 37 torpedoes were also progressively replaced.

Electronics: The Skipjacks have a modified BQS-4 active/passive sonar which transmits through a circular BQR-2C passive array. The BQS-4 can operate in the 'single-ping' or listening modes and has a maximum range of 6-8,000 yds (5,500-7,200m). The BQR-2 is a listening array which can operate in the searchlight or scanning mode and has a range of 10-13,000yds (9,000-11,700m). Mast-mounted sensors include search and attack periscopes, a BPS-12 surface surveillance radar, communications aerials, and direction-finding and ESM antennas. The original analogue Mk 113 fire control system has been replaced by the digital Mk 117, but no further updates are planned.

Construction: Six submarines of the Skipjack class were completed between 1959 and 1961 at four different shipyards. Of these *Scorpion* (SSN 589) was lost in May 1968, approximatly 400 miles southwest of the Azores, and *Snook* (SSN 592) was deactivated in 1986.

Above: The Skipjacks were the first US Navy attack submarines to combine the 15,000shp S5W pressurized water-cooled reactor with the revolutionary 'Albacore' hull-form. Underwater speed exceeded 30 knots, and the performance of these submarines was such that they remained in first-line service for over 25 years until they began to decommission in the mid-1980s.

Right: A bow view of *Scamp* (SSN 588); note the continuous curve of the hull-form and the prominent hydroplanes mounted on the fin. The high underwater speed of these boats was not to be equalled until *Los Angeles* commissioned in late 1976.

Sturgeon class

Origin: USA, first unit completed 1967
Type: Attack submarine, nuclear-powered (SSN)
Displacement: 4,250/4,460 tons surfaced (see remarks); 4,780/4,960 tons submerged
Dimensions: Length 292ft/302ft (89m/92.1m); beam 31ft 8in (9.7m); draught 29ft (8.8m)
Propulsion: One S5W pressurized water-cooled reactor driving geared steam turbines; one shaft; 15,000shp for 26kt max
Complement: 107
Background: The Sturgeons were the natural successors to the Thresher/Permit class boats. The latter suffered from a number of design compromises which were accepted in order to minimize underwater speed loss. These included a small fin with inadequate numbers of mast-mounted antennas, and limited electronics. The Sturgeon design was therefore enlarged to provide the necessary internal volume for more effective quieting and additional electronics, producing a boat which was to become the standard attack submarine of the period. However, the US Navy continued to produce experimental designs to investigate further improvements in submarine propulsion: the *Narwhal* (SSN 671, in service 1969) tested a natural circulation reactor, the S5G, which was to appear in an enlarged form in the SSBNs of the Ohio class (qv), and the *Glenard P Lipscomb* (SSN 685, in service 1974), tested a natural circulation reactor with turbo-electric drive. Both these submarines are operated as first-line units, and have similar

Below: *Richard B. Russell* (SSN 687), the last unit of the class to be completed. The later boats were 10ft (3m) longer to facilitate the installation of the BQQ-5 sonar suite, but the steady progression to larger submarines all powered by the same S5W reactor has resulted in some speed loss, and it was in part to restore this quality that the Los Angeles class was developed in the early 1970s.

Right: The Sturgeons are fitted with four 21in (533mm) torpedo tubes angled out beneath the fin and carry a similar mix of weapons to that of the Permit class. The normal weapon load is reported to be 15 Mk 48 dual-purpose torpedoes (1), four SUBROC antisubmarine missiles (2), and four Sub-Harpoon anti-ship missiles (3). Some units are being fitted to fire the long-range Tomahawk missile.

Above: ***Richard B. Russell*** **modified with a housing for a prototype communications buoy abaft the fin. No fewer than 37 Sturgeons were completed between 1967 and 1975, making them the standard US SSN of the period. The design was a modified version of the Permit class, with a larger fin to accommodate additional electronics.**

weapons outfits and electronics to the Sturgeons.

Design: The Sturgeon class follows the general arrangement of the Thresher/Permit class, with the bow occupied by the BQS-6 spherical array and the torpedo tubes angled out beneath the fin. An enlarged control room/attack centre, which extends aft from beneath the fin, accommodates additional computerised fire control consoles, enabling the Sturgeons to engage multiple targets. The machinery spaces were also lengthened for more effective noise insulation. The major external difference between the Sturgeon and the Thresher/Permit class is the substantially enlarged fin, which accommodates additional sensor masts for ESM. The fin-mounted hydroplanes are 38ft (11.6m) wide and can be rotated to the vertical to enable the submarines to break through ice packs. The last nine units of the class were lengthened by 10ft (3m) to facilitate the installation of the BQQ-5 sonar suite and its associated electronics, and as earlier units are retro-fitted with the new system they too are being lengthened.

Armament: Like the Thresher/Permit class, the Sturgeons are equipped with four 21in (533mm) Mk 63 torpedo tubes which are angled out beneath the fin. As first completed they carried a similar mix of anti-ship and antisubmarine torpedoes, plus the SUBROC missile. SUBROC (UUM-44A-2) entered operational service in 1965. It comprises a two-stage solid-fuel rocket with a ballistic trajectory and a nuclear warhead. A maximum range of 25-30nm (45-55km) is reported. SUBROC was to have been discarded as US Navy SSNs had their analogue Mk 113 fire control systems replaced by the digital Mk 117, but because of the absence of a natural replacement in the short term, Congress stipulated that the SUBROC fire control system be modified so that the missile could be kept in service. From 1972 the earlier models of torpedo were steadily replaced by the dual-purpose Mk 48. The latter is a high-performance torpedo using a liquid mono-propellant for propulsion to achieve a maximum speed of 55 knots. It is 19ft 6in (5.95m) long and has a maximum range of 40-45,000yds (35-40,000m). The Mk 48 was specifically designed to engage deep-diving submarines, and has a maximum operating depth of 2,500ft (760m). From the late 1970s Sturgeon-class boats began to receive the Sub-Harpoon anti-ship missile. Harpoon was designed primarily for surface-ship operation and is too small to be accommodated in a standard torpedo tubes; it is therefore launched inside a capsule from which it separates on breaking the surface. The missile itself is 15ft (4.6m) long and has a maximum range of 70-85nm (130-155km). At present submarines of this class are reported to carry 15 Mk 48 torpedoes, four SUBROC missiles and four Sub-Harpoon missiles. Some units of the class are currently being equipped to fire the long-range Tomahawk missile (see Los Angeles).

Electronics: As completed the Sturgeons received the BQQ-2 sonar suite, comprising the BQS-6 active/passive spherical bow array, the BQR-7 conformal passive array, and a PUFFS fire control sonar. The BQQ-2 installation is currently being upgraded to BQQ-5 status, and the BQR-23 towed array is being fitted. Mast-mounted sensors include search and attack periscopes, a BPS-14 or BPS-15 surveillance radar, UHF communications, and no fewer than four masts carrying DF and ESM antennae. There are also whip and floating wire aerials for communications, and in 1978 two units received an afterward extension to the fin for a towed communications array.

Construction: Thirty-seven submarines of the Sturgeon class were completed between 1967 and 1975 in six different shipyards.

Sturgeon class
***Richard B. Russell* (SSN 687)**

Swiftsure class

Origin: United Kingdom, first unit completed 1973
Type: Attack submarine, nuclear-powered (SSN)
Displacement: 4,200 tons surfaced; 4,900 tons submerged
Dimensions: Length 272ft (82.9m); beam 32ft 4in (9.8m); draught 27ft (8.2m)
Propulsion: One PWR 1 pressurized water-cooled reactor driving geared steam turbines; one shaft; 15,000shp for 30kt max
Complement: 97
Background: The Swiftsures were designed as the natural successors to the SSNs of the Valiant class. The weapon/sensor suite was little changed, and in the early units of the class was virtually identical to that of their immediate predecessors. However, the opportunity was taken for a complete hull redesign, and major modifications were made to the propulsion machinery in order to take into account experience gained with the Valiants and incorporate the latest quieting measures. This had the effect of reducing overall length by 13ft (4m) and the submerged displacement by 400 tons.
Design: In the Swiftsure and her sisters the cylindrical portion of the pressure-hull was extended as far aft as possible to eliminate structural transitions which had led to stress problems in the Valiants. The 'Albacore' hull of the earlier design has therefore been superseded by a broadly cylindrical hull-form with an exceptionally broad tail-cone. The shape of the forward half of the boat remains relatively unchanged, although here too the pressure hull has been broadened to accommodate a completely different layout of the torpedo tubes and torpedo handling room. As with the US Navy Permit/Thresher class, the height of the fin was significantly reduced in order to lower resistance. This led in turn to a reduction in periscope depth. As compensation the forward hydroplanes were lowered and made fully retractable. The torpedo handling room was relocated below the two main decks directly beneath the fin. Two of the five torpedo tubes are angled out on either side of the boat immediately abaft the chin sonar, in the manner of contemporary US Navy SSNs, and the fifth is presumably angled downwards on the centre-line and fires through the underside of the bow. This arrangement frees the bow for the sonar installation. The other major modifications concern the propulsion plant, which differs considerably in conception and layout from that of the Valiants. In the latter design the raft on which the main turbines and gearing were mounted had to be locked in when running at high speed. In the Swiftsures not only the turbines and gearing but virtually all noise-emitting auxiliary machinery is mounted on the raft, obviating the need for flexible couplings. The raft can therefore be isolated from the hull even at maximum power. As a further quieting measure, natural circulation was adopted for the reactor. Circular water scoops are located in the leading edges of the horizontal tail-fins, and these provide sufficient cooling through most of the power range, the coolant pumps being employed only at higher speeds. The improvements in quieting are such that the Swiftsures have dispensed with the separate main electric motor which was a feature of the Valiant propulsion plant. This has created a more compact layout in the machinery spaces and made it possible to reduce the overall length of the pressure hull. A small retractable motor, driven by a 112-cell battery charged by a 400bhp Paxman auxiliary diesel, is retained to provide power in an emergency.
Armament: The five bow torpedo tubes are of the standard 21in (533mm) calibre. An estimated 15 reloads are carried in the handling room. All units of the class were fitted to fire the Mk 24 Tigerfish antisubmarine torpedo from the outset. Tigerfish entered service in 1974, but numerous problems

Below: *Splendid*, the fifth boat of the Swiftsure class. The design has proved particularly successful, and the Trafalgar class currently in production is essentially evolutionary.

Right: The Swiftsures have five 21in (533mm) torpedo tubes, and an estimated 15 reloads can be accommodated. All six boats now carry the Mk 24 Tigerfish Mod.1 torpedo (2), which has a dual-purpose capability. A Mod.2 variant with improved guidance is undergoing trials. The class is also being retro-fitted to fire the Sub-Harpoon anti-ship missile (2). Two Stonefish (3) or Sea Urchin (4) mines can be carried in place of one torpedo.

were encountered both in development and after the weapon was deployed, and work on improved models has continued into the mid-1980s. The dual-purpose Mod.1 variant entered service around 1981 and has replaced the elderly Mk 8 anti-ship torpedo, and a Mod.2 variant with improved guidance has recently undergone trials. Tigerfish has a length of 21ft 2in (6.4m) and has a sophisticated two-way wire guidance system with automatic three-dimensional active/passive homing. It has a maximum range of 12,000yds (11,000m) at a speed of 40 knots. In addition to torpedoes, all units of the class will be refitted to fire Sub-Harpoon in the late 1980s.

Electronics: As completed the Swiftsures had a sonar outfit virtually identical to that of the Valiant: a Type 2001 active/passive 'chin' array, a Type 2007 passive flank array, and a Type 197 intercept array. Later boats of the class were fitted with the Type 2019 Passive/Active Range and Intercept Sonar (PARIS), a joint Anglo-Dutch-French development. The Type 2019 is now being retro-fitted to earlier boats. Fire control is provided by a DCB Action Information and Fire Control System. The Type 2026 towed array is currently being fitted, and it is envisaged that all units of the class will have their Type 2001 bow array replaced by Type 2020, beginning with *Superb* in 1985.

Construction: Six submarines of the Swiftsure class were completed at the Vickers Shipyard, Barrow-in-Furness, between 1973 and 1980.

Above: A bow view of HMS *Superb*. In this class the cylindrical portion of the pressure-hull was extended as far aft as possible to eliminate stress problems which had been experienced with the Valiant class. The forward hydroplanes are mounted low on the forward section of the hull and are fully retractable, permitting a reduction in the height of the fin.

HMS *Swiftsure* (S 126)

1

3

4

2

Tango class

Origin: USSR, first unit completed 1972
Type: Attack submarine, diesel-powered (SS)
Displacement: 3,200 tons surfaced; 3,900 tons submerged
Dimensions: Length 302ft (92m); beam 30ft (9m); draught 23ft (7m)
Propulsion: Diesel-electric drive on two shafts; three diesel generators, two electric motors; 6,000bhp for 15kt surfaced, 5,500hp for 16kt submerged
Complement: 72
Background: The large Foxtrot programme was completed in 1968, by which time the concept of the large ocean-going submarine with a primary scouting/torpedo attack mission had dated. The attention of the Soviet Navy, which until the early 1960s had been focused almost exclusively on the anti-surface mission, now turned towards antisubmarine warfare. The nuclear-powered Victor (qv) was the first Soviet submarine type to be designed for the ASW mission. However, the initial production rate was necessarily slow because of the greater priority accorded to the construction of SSBNs of the Yankee and Delta classes, which in the early 1970s were being built at the rate of five or six per year. Until the late 1970s, when the SSBN programme began to tail off, construction of the Victor was limited to a single shipyard, and the Soviet Navy therefore adopted its customary solution of designing a diesel-powered counterpart, which became the Tango. The new submarine would have similar weapons and sensors to the Victor, and great emphasis was placed on endurance, to enable the Tango to undertake lengthy patrols in defence of the Soviet 'bastion' areas.

Design: In profile the Tango closely resembles the earlier Foxtrot, but first appearances are deceptive. Whereas the Foxtrot has a traditional cigar-shaped hull-form based on the German Type XXI, the Tango has a hull-form which is essentially cylindrical, and while length remains virtually unchanged, these boats have 5ft (1.5m) more beam than the Foxtrot. Moreover, the cylindrical hull configuration is maintained throughout the length of the boats, whereas the hull-form of the Foxtrot is tapered towards the bow and stern. The improved hull-form

Above: The Tango succeded the Foxtrot in production in 1972. Although the two types are not dissimilar in profile, the Tango has a broader, more modern hull-form than its predecessor. The raised bow section is thought to be related to the provision of additional stowage space for the SS-N-15 antisubmarine missile and its associated fire control electronics.

1

2

3

4

is responsible for a substantial increase in internal volume, especially in the fully-rounded bow section, where the large low-frequency bow sonar is located. Greater space was also required in order to accommodate the SS-N-15 antisubmarine missile, together with the necessary fire control consoles, and battery capacity has been substantially increased over earlier Soviet diesel boats to give improved underwater endurance. The result is a submarine of 50% greater displacement than the Foxtrot. There is some disagreement regarding both propulsion machinery and the position and number of the torpedo tubes. US sources generally favour an arrangement similar to that of the Foxtrot, with one diesel and one motor on each of three shafts, and four stern tubes. However, other Western sources appear to favour a two-shaft installation with three diesel generators and two electric motors, with all torpedo tubes in the bow. This arrangement would conform more closely to that of the Victor, and therefore seems more logical given that the missions and weapon systems of the two types are virtually identical. Considerable emphasis has been placed on silencing, and the Tango is particularly quiet when operating on its electric motors: long slotted free-flood apertures have been adopted in preference to the more numerous limber holes of the Foxtrot, most of the deck fittings are recessed, and the hull has been sheathed in a sonar-absorbent rubber compound.

Armament: The six (possibly eight) bow tubes are all of the standard 21in (533mm) diameter. They can fire conventional or nuclear-tipped anti-ship torpedoes, antisubmarine torpedoes with acoustic homing, and the SS-N-15 nuclear-tipped antisubmarine missile. There is a relatively large stowage capacity for perhaps 16-18 missiles and torpedoes. There is as yet no evidence to suggest that the large-diameter 26in (650mm) tube will be retro-fitted although, given the primary ASW mission of the Tango, this must be considered a possibility for the future once the nuclear boats (which are presumably being given priority) have been modified.

Sensors: The Tango has a large low-frequency active/passive bow sonar - probably the same model installed in the Victor - and presumably has fixed conformal passive arrays along the hull. The outfit of sensor masts is standard, but there are minor variations between the early and later boats of the class. All have search and attack periscopes, a Snoop Tray surface surveillance radar, Quad Loop DF, and aerials for HF and VHF communications. Early boats have Stop Light ESM, but later units have a variant of the more modern Brick Pulp antenna which is a feature of Soviet nuclear-powered submarines of the Victor generation.

Construction: Nineteen Tangos were completed between 1972 and 1982 at the inland Gorky Shipyard, but production has apparently been terminated in favour of the Kilo.

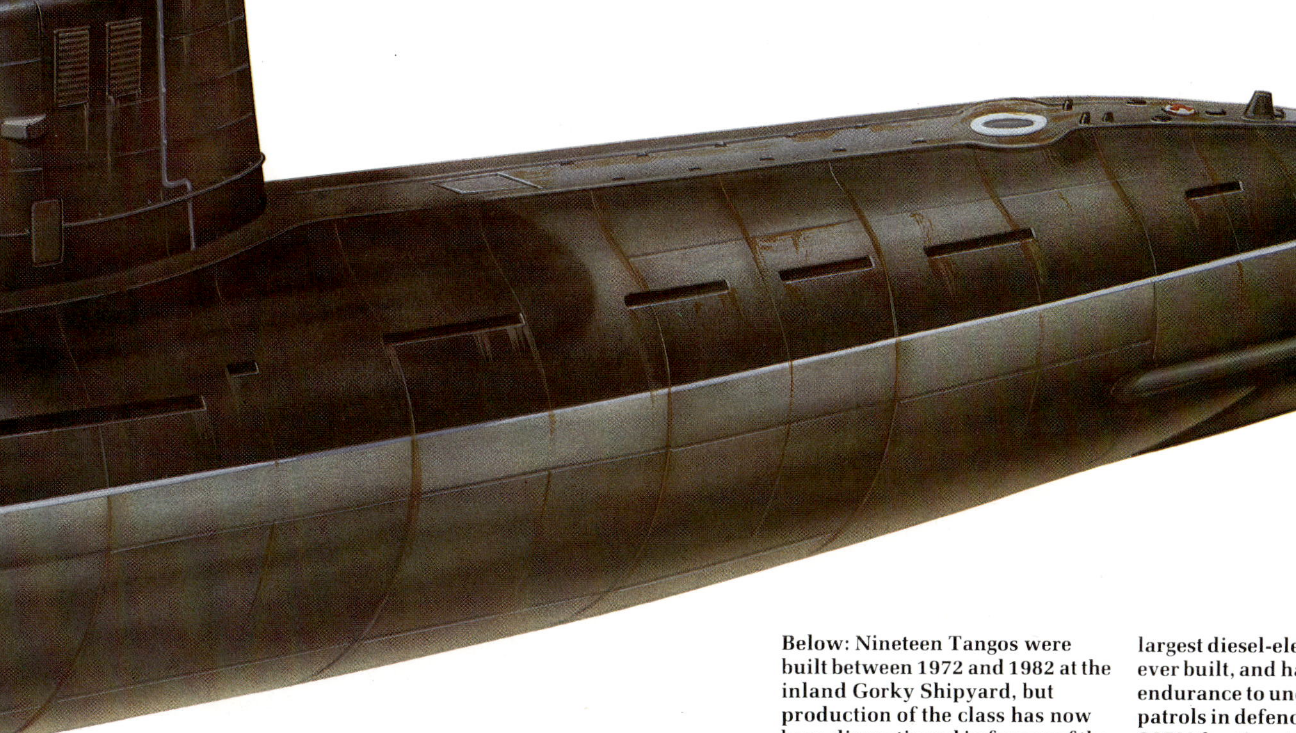

Below: The Tango has six (possibly eight) bow tubes each of 21in (533mm) diameter. The new large-diameter 26in (650mm) tube is not fitted, nor are there stern tubes as in the earlier Foxtrot class, and the weapons carried are thought to be identical to those of the early Victors, which have a similar mission. There are long 21in torpedoes (1) for use against surface ships; some of these will be fitted with a nuclear warhead. There will also be shorter 21in antisubmarine homing torpedoes employing acoustic guidance (2). The third major weapon is the SS-N-15 missile (3), which can be used against both submarines and surface targets; the SS-N-15 has a nuclear warhead and a range of about 22nm (40km). In addition to the six weapons carried in the tubes, the Tango has sufficient stowage space for an estimated 18 reloads. In place of each missile or torpedo two mines (4) could be carried.

Below: Nineteen Tangos were built between 1972 and 1982 at the inland Gorky Shipyard, but production of the class has now been discontinued in favour of the Kilo. The Tango is one of the largest diesel-electric submarines ever built, and has sufficient endurance to undertake lengthy patrols in defence of the Soviet SSBN 'bastions' in the Northern and Pacific Fleet areas.

TR-1700

Origin: Export design by Thyssen (FRG), first unit completed 1984
Type: Attack submarine, diesel-powered (SS)
Displacement: 2,115 tons surfaced; 2,265 tons submerged
Dimensions: Length 216ft 6in (66m); beam 24ft (7.3m); draught 21ft 4in (6.5m)
Propulsion: Diesel-electric drive on one shaft; four MTU 16V652 MB80 diesel generators, each 1,475bhp; one Siemens electric motor; 5,900bhp for 13kt surfaced, 8,970hp for 25kt submerged
Complement: 29
Background: Until the mid-1970s the Thyssen (formerly Rheinstahl) Nordseewerke Shipyard, Emden, had built submarines to IKL designs. Fifteen Type 207 (Kobben class) submarines were completed for Norway between 1964 and 1967, and orders were subsequently received for ten of the fifteen Type 206 boats for the Federal German Navy, the last being completed in 1975. In September 1973 the upper limit on displacement permitted to German shipyards by Treaty was raised to 1,800 tons standard, and Thyssen took full advantage of this development to design a high-performance ocean-going submarine which would appeal to Third World countries anxious to replace their elderly ex-US Navy 'Guppies' with modern construction. Unlike IKL's successful Type 209, which was essentially an enlargement of the Type 205/206 coastal submarines built for the German Navy, the TR-1700 was designed from the keel up. The hull and propulsion machinery are German, but the best in foreign technology has also been incorporated. The equipment is flexible to suit customer preferences, and the design itself has been developed both upwards (the TR-1700A) and downwards (the TR-1400 and TR-1000). However, the only order which has so far materialised is for Argentina, which ordered four TR-1700s in 1977. The first pair was to be built in Germany and the second pair under licence. An order for two smaller TR-1400s, also for Argentina, was cancelled in favour of two further locally-built TR-1700s in 1982.
Design: The Type 1700 employs single-hull construction. The 158ft (48m) pressure hull, which is of uniform diameter throughout except for a short tapered section aft, is of high-tensile steel, for a diving depth of 1,000ft (300m). It is closed by a hemispherical bulkhead forward and a flat bulkhead aft, and is divided into three sections, separated by two further transverse bulkheads. The forward section is on three levels, with the officer accommodation above the torpedo stowage compartment and the forward batteries beneath. The midships section has the central control room above the accommodation for the crew, with internal tanks below. A lock-out chamber in the fin allows for diver operations with the submarine submerged. The after section, which occupies more than half the length of the submarine, houses the exceptionally powerful propulsion machinery and the auxiliary machinery. The switchboard room is in the forward compartment, followed by a long central compartment which houses the four MTU diesel generators on the upper level with the after battery bank beneath. The third compartment is occupied by the large Siemens double-armature

Above: *Santa Cruz*, the first of the TR-1700s to be completed for the Argentinian Navy. A second German-built boat was delivered in 1985, and three further units are currently under construction in a specially designed shipyard in Buenos Aires.

TR-1700 *Santa Cruz* (Argentinian S 33)

electric motor, which can produce 8,000hp sustained, and 8,970hp for short periods. This gives the TR-1700 the remarkable maximum underwater speed of 25 knots. Power is provided by no fewer than eight 120-cell banks of Varta batteries. The adoption of extensive automation has made possible a complement of only 29 men, which is exceptionally small for a boat which approaches the size of the British Upholder and the Dutch Walrus class. The SAGEM diving controls are operated from a one-man console. In a departure from the IKL designs, the forward hydroplanes are mounted on the fin, and are complemented by cruciform tail surfaces.

Armament: There are six torpedo tubes of standard 21in (533mm) diameter, disposed in two banks of three. The capacious stowage room can accommodate 16 reloads. The Argentine Navy currently has in service the German SST-4 wire-guided anti-ship torpedo and the US Mk 37C short antisubmarine torpedo. Severe budgetary constraints make it unlikely that more modern torpedoes will be purchased in the short term, although the TR-1700 has been designed to fire a wide range of internationally-available types.

Electronics: An integrated active attack and passive search/intercept/ranging sonar suite has been installed in the Argentine boats. The precise identity of this equipment has not been revealed, but it seems probable that it is a development of the Krupp-Atlas CSU 3-4 multi-function array fitted in other recent German export submarines. The HSA SINBADS Action Information Organisation and Fire Control system is combined with a SAGEM plotting table. Mast-mounted sensors include Kollmorgen search and attack periscopes, surveillance radar and passive ESM.

Construction: The first two units for Argentina were completed at the Nordseewerke, Emden, in 1984-85. However, progress on the four locally-built units has been slow, and the precarious financial situation has led to rumours that the boats may be sold 'off the slipway'. The first was laid down only in late 1983, and work on the third was begun in 1985.

Above: One of the Argentinian TR-1700s under construction at the Norseewerke Shipyard, Emden. Unlike other German export submarine designs, the TR-1700 was designed from the keel up as an ocean-going boat with good long-range endurance. A maximum underwater speed of 25 knots can be sustained for short periods. Note the large propeller under canvas.

Opposite: The TR-1700 has six bow torpedo tubes of 21in (533mm) diameter. The torpedoes currently in service with the Argentinian Navy are the heavyweight SST-4 (bottom), which is an export development of the Seeal wire-guided heavyweight anti-ship torpedo, and the US Mk 37C short antisubmarine torpedo (top), which also employs wire guidance. It is not yet clear whether the Argentinian Navy will attempt to purchase the more recent SUT (Surface/Underwater Target) torpedo.

Trafalgar class

Origin: United Kingdom, first unit completed 1983
Type: Attack submarine, nuclear-powered (SSN)
Displacement: 4,800 tons surfaced; 5,300 tons submerged
Dimensions: Length 280ft (85.4m); beam 33ft (10.1m); draught 27ft (8.2m)
Propulsion: One PWR 1 pressurized water-cooled reactor driving geared steam turbines; pump-jet (see remarks); 15,000shp for 28-30kt max
Complement: 98
Background: The Swiftsure class proved particularly successful in service. The following design, the Trafalgar, therefore kept to the same basic hull-form and layout. However, some six years had elapsed between the two designs, and during that interval several major advances had been made in electronics and acoustic detection methods. The Trafalgar was to incorporate the latest quieting measures, and would be fitted with a new generation of underwater sensors.
Design: The Trafalgar is some 8ft (2.5m) longer than the Swiftsure, and submerged displacement has increased by 800 tons, suggesting that a significant quantity of additional equipment has been worked into the design. The hull-form and internal layout of the two submarines is virtually identical, but a number of detail improvements have been incorporated. The major modifications relate to the propulsion plant, the reactor featuring a new core (Core Z) with a longer life than earlier types. All main propulsion and auxiliary machinery, including the turbines, reduction gearing, pumps and condensers, is raft-mounted as in the Swiftsure. In the Trafalgar class, however, the raft is suspended from transverse bulkheads, not mounted on the hull, in order to provide more effective insulation. Natural circulation via water scoops located in the leading edges of the horizontal tail-fins has been retained, and the reactor coolant pumps are required only at higher speeds. However, in place of the conventional seven-bladed propeller of the Swiftsures, the Trafalgars employ a shrouded pump-jet. Pump-jets, which have already been used to propel torpedoes such as the US Navy's Mk 48, comprise a single multi-blade rotor turning relatively slowly against stator vanes in a duct. In effect the pump-jet is a high-pitch, low-revolution propeller. Pump-jets are significantly quieter than conventional propellers, but the installation brings with it a considerable cost in weight. This can be sustained in the Trafalgars largely because of the unusual 45-degree tail-cone angle, which provides additional buoyancy at the after end of the submarine. It is reported that the US Navy's new Seawolf (SSN-21) design will also have pump-jet propulsion. Development of the British pump-jet was not completed in time for installation aboard *Trafalgar* herself, which has similar shaft arrangements to the Swiftsures, and the second unit of the class, *Turbulent*, is believed to be the first Royal Navy submarine to be fitted with the system. A further innovation on the Trafalgar class is the adoption of anechoic hull tiles in order to reduce acoustic signature.
Armament: The Trafalgars have identical torpedo firing and handling arrangements to the Swiftsures, with five tubes of 21in (533mm) diameter firing through the sides and underside of the hull immediately abaft the bow sonar. Trafalgar was fitted from the outset to fire the Mod.1 dual-purpose variant of the Mk 24 Tigerfish torpedo, which entered service around 1981. This gave her a completely homogeneous torpedo outfit and enabled her to dispense with the elderly Mk 8 anti-ship torpedo. All Tigerfish torpedoes will shortly be brought up to the Mod.2 standard, which has improved guidance. The Trafalgars also carry the Sub-Harpoon missile, for which they have been fitted since completion. A further potential weapon is the Stonefish mine, specifically developed by Marconi Underwater Systems for deployment from a 21in (533mm) torpedo tube. Stonefish is an intelligent, programmable mine which uses the latest microprocessor technology for target assessment. It is of modular design, and can be allied to either a 660lb (300kg) or a 1,320lb (600kg) warhead according to the anticipated water depth.
Electronics: The Trafalgars are the first Royal Navy submarines to be

Below: *Turbulent*, the second unit of the Trafalgar class, is thought to be the first submarine to be fitted with a pump-jet instead of a conventional propeller.

Right: The Trafalgars are fitted with five 21in (533mm) torpedo tubes located just abaft the bow, and are armed with the Mk 24 Tigerfish torpedo (1), which now has a dual-purpose capability. They were also fitted from the outset to receive the Sub-Harpoon anti-ship missile (2), which is encapsulated for launch from a torpedo tube. Mines of various types can be carried, including the Stonefish (3), and Sea Urchin (4) programmable mines developed by Marconi Underwater Systems.

fitted with the advanced Type 2020 sonar on completion. The Type 2020 is a passive low-frequency array developed from the Type 2016 surface ship sonar installed in frigates of the Broadsword class. It is scanned electronically and gives full 360-degree coverage. The Type 2020 is now replacing the Type 2001 'chin' array in earlier Royal Navy SSNs. Besides Type 2020 the Trafalgars are fitted with a Type 2007 passive flank array, a Type 2019 sonar intercept array and the Type 2026 towed array. The latter has brought with it remarkable improvements in long-range detection and tracking capabilities. A DCB Action Information Organisation and Fire Control system is fitted.

Construction: Four submarines of the Trafalgar have been completed since 1983. Three further boats are under construction, but there will then have to be a pause in SSN construction for the Royal Navy to enable the new Vanguard-class Trident submarines to be built.

Above: *Trafalgar*, the name-ship of the class, is essentially a refined Swiftsure, from which she is virtually indistinguishable externally. Improvements include a new long-life reactor core, anechoic hull-tiling and a new generation of sensors. The Type 2020 sonar occupies the bow of the submarine, as in US Navy attack boats, and the torpedo tubes are angled out abaft the bow. The retractable sonar dome forward of the fin is for a Type 2019 sonar intercept array.

HMS *Trafalgar* (S 107)

1

4

2

3

Type 206

Origin: Federal Republic of Germany, first unit completed 1971
Type: Coastal submarine, diesel-powered (SSC)
Displacement: 456 tons surfaced; 500 tons submerged
Dimensions: Length 159ft 6in (48.6m); beam 15ft (4.6m); 14ft (4.3m)
Propulsion: Diesel-electric drive on one shaft; two MTU 12V493AZ diesels, each 600hp; one Siemens electric motor; 1,200bhp for 10kt surfaced, 2,300hp for 17.5kt submerged
Complement: 21
Background: In the immediate postwar period Germany was forbidden to build submarines. Subsequently, an upper limit of 350 tons was placed on submarine construction, and only conventional diesel-electric propulsion was permitted. These constraints taxed to the full the ingenuity of the German designers, who were compelled to rethink submarine design concepts *ab initio*. As the new submarines were primarily for operations in the Baltic, endurance assumed a low priority. Moreover, acoustic conditions in these shallow waters were poor. High-powered, long-range sensors were therefore of limited value. What was needed was a small, agile submarine capable of operating comfortably at snorkel depth for long periods , and with a powerful battery of torpedo tubes to cope with the multiple targets which might be expected in the event of an attempted amphibious landing by the forces of the Warsaw Pact. The earliest attack submarine design, the Type 201, quickly ran into problems when it was found that the anti-magnetic steel employed in the construction of the first three boats was subject to serious corrosion. The last nine boats of the class were therefore rebuilt as the Type 205. In 1962 the upper limit for tonnage was raised to 450 tons, and the German Navy embarked on the design of an improved class, the Type 206, which would take into account experience with the earlier boats and which would incorporate improvements in sensors and weapons.
Design: The hull design of Types 201, 205 and 206 is based on that of the wartime Type XXIII. The need to keep displacement to a minimum necessitated single-hull construction, with the main ballast tanks at the fore and after ends of the submarine. The large fin, which has a prominent conning tower at its forward end, is in part a concession to the need for surface transit in peacetime, but was also needed in order to accommodate a full outfit of retractable sensor masts. The bow is of near-circular cross-section, making possible an outfit of no fewer than eight bow tubes of the large-diameter, 'swim-out' type. This launch method saves weight, as positive discharge methods impose greater space and power requirements. Muzzle-loading is employed, so that the space normally required for torpedo handling and stowage is given over to the accommodation of the crew. In the forward half of the boat there is a single-deck layout, with the control room directly abaft the crew spaces and the battery compartments beneath. The silver zinc battery cell developed by Hagen/Varta for these submarines has twice the capacity of other battery cells of the period and a very fast reload cycle. This results in shorter snorkelling periods, thereby reducing demands on the crew and making the submarines more difficult to detect. A particularly ingenious solution was adopted to the provision of quick-reaction control surfaces. The forward hydroplanes are curved and fully retractable, and are used alternately, one to produce a bow-up and the other a bow-down angle. The after planes are integrated with the stabilisation fin. The rudder is abaft the single propeller.
Armament: The eight bow tubes are of 26in (660mm) diameter, but fire 21in (533mm) torpedoes. Early German postwar torpedoes were of the free-running type, but the Type 206 was designed to fire a new generation of wire-guided torpedoes. Seeal, a heavy-weight anti-ship torpedo, was 21ft (6.4m) long and had a range of 7nm (13km) at 35kt; Seeschlange, an antisubmarine torpedo based on the US Mk 37, had a length of 13ft 1in (4m) and a range half that of Seeal. Both torpedoes employed electrical propulsion and two-way wire guidance, but in the antisubmarine variant a 3-D sonar

Federal German Navy Type 206 *Emden* (U 16)

Above: U 29, the last but one of the 18 units built for the Federal German Navy. The Type 206 is an ingenious design which has turned postwar Treaty constraints to its advantage, and the class has not only proved successful in service with the FRG, but has also provided the basis for the Type 209 design which has dominated the export markets for the past 15 years.

replaced half the battery capacity. Seeal and Seeschlange have now been superseded by the SUT (Surface/Underwater Target) heavyweight torpedo, which has a length of 22ft (6.7m) and can be fired against both surface ships and submarines. In addition to torpedoes, these submarines can carry 24 mines in GRP containers strapped around the hull.

Sensors: The Type 206 has a comprehensive sonar outfit comprising an AN 5039A1 passive array, an AN 410A4 active ranging sonar, and a French DUUX 2 fire control sonar. An HSA Mk 8 Action Information Organisation and Fire Control System is fitted. Twelve out of the 18 units of the class are to undergo an extensive modernisation, beginning in 1989, during which a Krupp-Atlas CSU 83 (NATO designation: DBQS-21) integrated sonar system will replace the original sonar outfit, and the HSA Mk 8 combat system will be superseded by the SLW 83.

Construction: Eighteen units of the Type 206 class were completed between 1971 and 1974, construction being shared between Howaldtswerke, Kiel, and Rheinstahl-Nordseewerke, Emden.

Opposite: The submarines of the Type 206 class have no fewer than eight bow tubes of the large-diameter, 'swim-out' type. Initially the submarines carried a mix of Seeal heavyweight anti-ship torpedoes and Seeschlange 'short' antisubmarine torpedoes, both of which employed wire guidance. These have now been superseded by the SUT (Surface/Underwater Target) heavyweight torpedo shown, which can be used against both surface ships and submarines. Because of their small size the submarines of the Type 206 class have no space for reloads. However, a belt comprising glass-reinforced plastic mine containers has been specially developed for the type. The mine belt has a capacity of 24 mines.

Type 209

Origin: Export design by IKL (FRG), first unit completed 1971
Type: Attack submarine, diesel-powered (SS)
Displacement: Type 209/0: 1,105 tons surfaced, 1,230 tons submerged
Type 209/1: 1,180 tons surfaced, 1,290 tons submerged Type 209/2: 1,260 tons surfaced, 1,390 tons submerged
Type 209/3: 1,320 tons surfaced, 1,440 tons submerged
Dimensions: Type 209/0: length 178ft 6in (54.4m)
Type 209/1: length 184ft (56.1m)
Type 209/2: length 195ft 3in (59.5m)
Type 209/3: length 200ft (61m)
All variants: beam 20ft 4in (6.2m); draught 18ft (5.5m)
Propulsion: Diesel-electric drive on one shaft; four MTU 12V493 TY60 diesel generators, each 600bhp; one Siemens electric motor; 2,400bhp for 11kt surfaced, 5,000hp for 22kt (max) submerged
Complement: 30-33
Background: The completion of the Type 201/205 submarine programme for the Federal German Navy in the late 1960s coincided with the completion of 15 similar Type 207 (Kobben class) boats for Norway. The German shipyards, which had built up their design and construction capacity to a relatively high level, were faced by a prospective shortage of orders, and were compelled to turn to the export market. Treaty restrictions continued to limit (standard) displacement to a maximum of 1,000 tons. The designers Ingenieurkontor Lübeck (IKL), working in conjunction with the Howaldtswerke-Deutsche Werft shipyard, therefore proposed an enlarged version of the Type 205 coastal submarine which would incorporate the technologies developed for the German Navy's own submarine programme. The design proved particularly attractive to Third World countries with limited budgets, and the Type 209 has been ordered by no fewer than 12 navies, with construction both in Germany and under licence.
Design: The Type 209 has many features in common with the submarines of the Type 205 and Type 206 classes in service with the Federal German Navy. These include single-hull construction, eight 'swim-out' torpedo tubes disposed in a broadly circular arrangement, single-shaft propulsion with a five-bladed propeller, and retractable fixed-angle bow hydroplanes. However, full advantage has been taken of the increase in displacement to provide an enlarged fin, stowage capacity for torpedo reloads, and more powerful propulsion machinery.

Above: The Type 209 is the most successful export design of the postwar period. No fewer than 31 units – including the Colombian *Islay* shown here – have been ordered from the HDW Shipyard in the Federal Republic of Germany, and a further ten are being built under licence with German technical assistance.

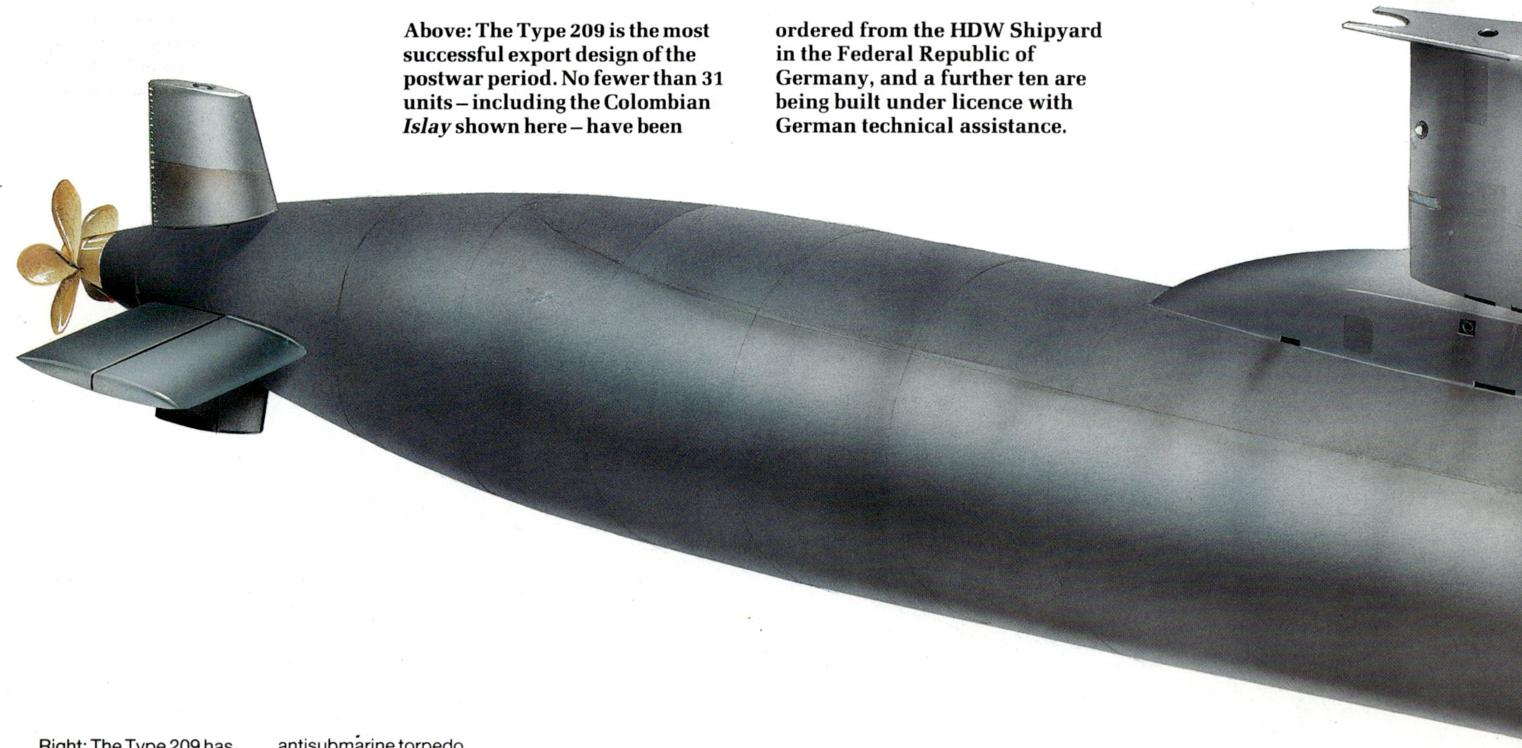

Right: The Type 209 has eight swim-out tubes capable of firing any torpedo of 21in (533mm) diameter. Most of the navies which have purchased the Type 209 employ two complementary types of torpedo: generally the 'long' SST-4 anti-ship torpedo shown here and the short NT-37C antisubmarine torpedo, which is of US origin. The German SUT dual-purpose torpedo is reported to be in service with the navies of Chile, Colombia, Ecuador amd Indonesia. Peru has recently ordered the Italian A.184, and Brazil apparently intends to purchase the British Mk 24 Tigerfish.

Power for the generators is provided by four MTU diesels, and the double-armature Siemens electric motor, which is resiliently mounted, has more than twice the output of the model installed in the Type 205/206. The Hagen/VARTA batteries are of tubular construction with GRP cell walls, and have 20% higher specific capacity than conventional plate cells, plus high resistance to underwater shock. The batteries have a 4-5 year life expectancy, and take up 25% of internal space. They give the submarines considerable underwater endurance and a maximum speed of 22-23 knots for short periods. The machinery is controlled from a fully-automated control room abaft the attack centre, the engine room itself being completely unmanned.

Armament: The Type 209 has eight 'swim-out' bow tubes capable of firing any torpedo of 21in (533mm) diameter. Six reloads can be accommodated in a stowage rack abaft the tubes. A number of the operating countries have purchased the German SST-4 (Special Surface Target) torpedo, which is the export version of the wire-guided Seeal anti-ship torpedo. The SST-4 is reported to be in service with the navies of Argentina, Greece, Peru, Turkey and Venezuela. In the Peruvian and Argentinian Navies it is paired with the US NT-37C short antisubmarine torpedo. Other countries have purchased the more recent German SUT (Surface/Underwater Target) heavyweight torpedo, which can be fired against both surface ships and submarines. The SUT is thought to be in service with the navies of Chile, Colombia, Ecuador and Indonesia. Peru has recently ordered the Italian A.184 for its Type 209s, and it is reported that the Brazilian boats will be equipped to fire the British Mk 24 Tigerfish Mod.1.

Electronics: Most Type 209s have the Krupp Atlas CSU 3-2 active sonar combined with a PRS 3-4 passive array. The latter is similar in conception to the British Type 2001, with a conformal 'chinstrap' array of hydrophones in triplet staves below the lowest tier of torpedo tubes. This is being superseded in recent construction by the CSU 3-4, an active/passive sonar with active intercept capability based on a circular array 10ft (3m) in diameter located inside the bow casing. Early Type 209s were fitted with the HSA Mk 8/24 combat system. Later boats are fitted with the HSA SINBADS combat system, and the Ferranti (UK) KAFS system is reported to have been selected for the new Brazilian boats.

Construction: Four Type 209/0s were completed for Greece in 1971-72, followed by four Type 209/1s in 1979-81. Two Type 209/1s were completed for Argentina in 1974, two for Colombia in 1975, and six for Peru in 1975-83. Three Type 209/1s were built by IKL for Turkey, and a further three have since been completed under licence at the Gölcük Naval Shipyard, with four more on order. Two Type 209/2s were completed for Venezuela in 1976-77, two for Ecuador in 1977-78, and two for Indonesia in 1981. Two Type 209/3s were completed for Chile in 1984, and five further boats of this type are being built for Brazil.

Above: The Type 209, essentially an enlargement of the Type 206 design in service with the Federal German Navy, has exceptional underwater performance for its size, and requires only a small crew. There are eight swim-out torpedo tubes disposed in a broadly circular arrangement, with six reloads.

Type 209/1 *San Luis* (Argentinian S 32)

Typhoon

Origin: USSR, first unit completed late 1981
Type: Ballistic missile submarine, nuclear-powered (SSBN)
Displacement: 25-30,000 tons submerged
Dimensions: Length 558ft (170m); beam 75ft (23m); draught 37ft (11.5m)
Propulsion: Two pressurized water-cooled reactors driving geared steam turbines; two shafts; 75-80,000shp for 24kt max
Complement: 150
Background: The original Yankee design on which the Soviet Delta-class SSBNs were based dated from the early 1960s. The nature of Soviet SSBN operations had changed considerably over that period due to the development of long-range SLBMs capable of targeting the territory of the United States from the security of Soviet-controlled waters. This placed a different set of requirements on SSBN design. High performance, which was previously regarded as essential because of the need to transit the NATO antisubmarine barrier in the Greenland/Iceland/United Kingdom (GIUK) Gap, now assumed less importance than endurance and firepower, for which a capacious hull was required. Because the submarines would be operating in relatively friendly waters, fewer hulls each with greater missile capacity were favoured. This fundamental change in operational philosophy has reportedly been accompanied by the introduction of a two-crew manning policy similar to the 'Blue/Gold' arrangement which is employed for all Western ballistic missile submarines.
Design: The Typhoon is a formidable submarine of a completely new design. Novel features include a multiple-hull configuration and the location of the missile compartment forward of the fin. The hull configuration apparently comprises two parallel pressure cylinders about 425ft (130m) long enveloped by a broad outer casing. This results in an exceptionally broad beam of some 75ft (23m), approximately twice that of the Delta. An estimated 6ft (2m) stand-off between the inner and outer hulls is thought to provide some protection against small Western antisubmarine torpedoes launched by surface ships or helicopters. A third, shorter pressure cylinder some 20ft (6m) in diameter is located directly beneath the fin, and houses the attack centre and command spaces. This arrangement is necessary to enable the periscopes and other sensor masts to be located on the centre-line in the conventional way. Each of the large twin pressure cylinders contains its own propulsion unit, comprising a single nuclear reactor and steam turbines driving a seven-bladed propeller. The two propulsion units are almost certainly capable of independent operation, and each presumably has its own machinery control centre and electrical switchboard. This would

Below and right: The Typhoon has 20 launch tubes for the SS-N-20 Sturgeon ballistic missile (1). The SS-N-20 is the first solid-fuel missile to go into series production for the Soviet Navy, the only other missile with solid-fuel propulsion being the SS-N-17 carried by the single Yankee II. The SS-N-20 has an estimated maximum range of 4,500nm (8,300km) and can carry between six and nine MIRVed warheads. The precise number of torpedo tubes is uncertain, but is probably eight, grouped as two sets of four at the forward end of the twin pressure hulls with stowage spaces behind. This suggests a stowage capacity of perhaps 40 missiles and torpedoes. The tubes are almost certainly a mix of 21in (533mm) and 26in (650mm), thereby enabling the Typhoon to fire all the submarine weapons in the current inventory. The SS-N-15 nuclear-tipped ASW missile (2) and short antisubmarine homing torpedoes (3) can be fired from the 533mm tubes. The 650mm tubes can handle the conventional SS-N-16 torpedo-carrying ASW missile (4) and the Type 65 anti-ship torpedo (5), which employs wake homing.

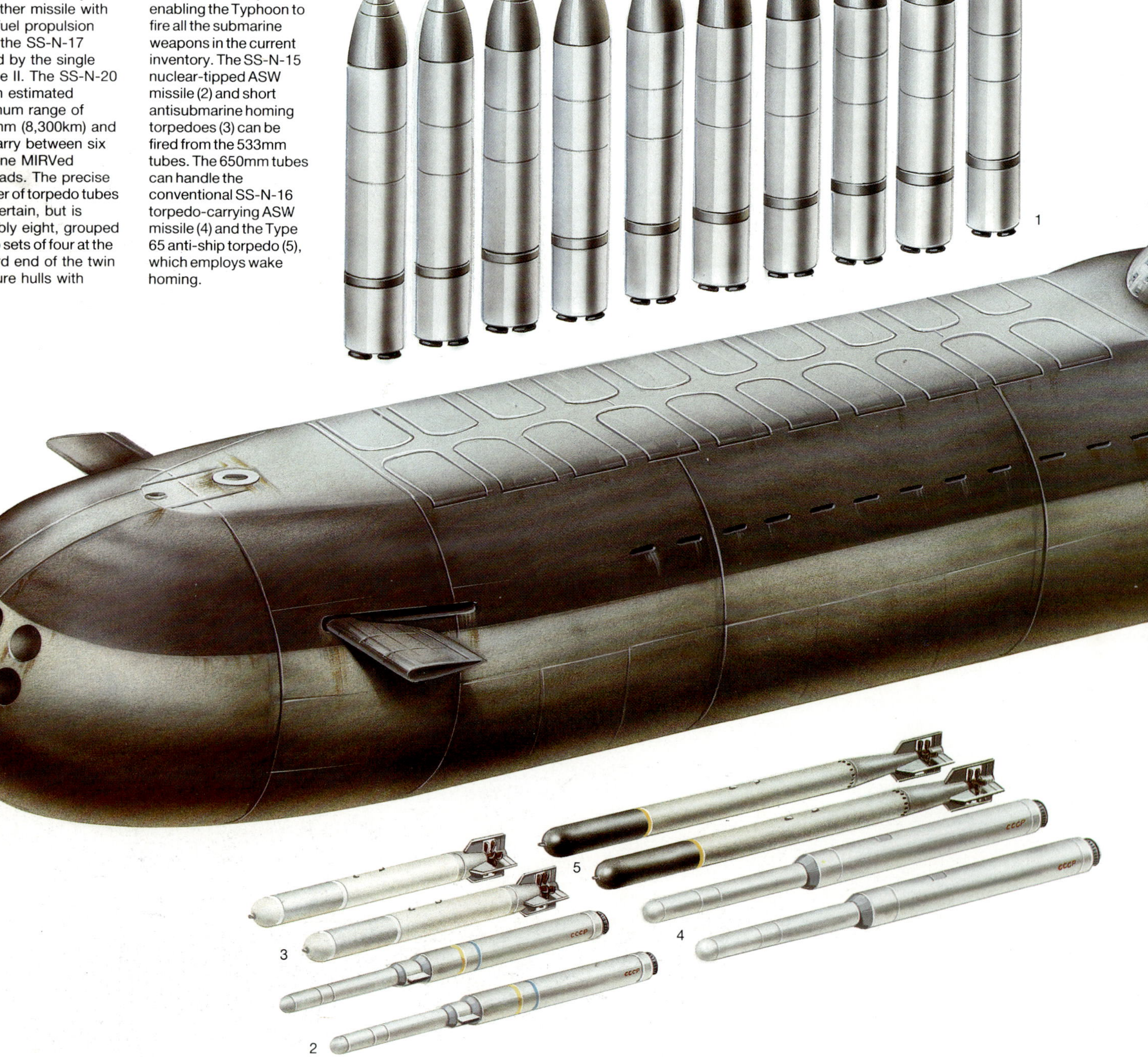

enable the submarine to continue operations even if a complete propulsion unit had to be closed down as a result of failure or action damage. The configuration of the fin and the sturdy tailfin/rudder assembly suggest that the submarine is designed for under-ice operations. The forward hydroplanes are located close to the bow, not on the fin as in earlier Soviet SSBNs. This maximizes control in the vertical plane. The hydroplanes are retractable as in Soviet attack boats, thereby reducing the risk of damage while travelling on the surface in ice-bound waters.

Armament: The Typhoon carries 20 SS-N-20 missiles in a large compartment forward of the fin. The unconventional position of the missile compartment may relate to the concentration of machinery weight in the short after section of the boat. The SS-N-20, a solid-fuel missile with an estimated length of around 50ft (15m) and a diameter of 7ft (2.2m), carries six to nine MIRVed warheads and has a maximum range of 4,500nm (8,300km). The missile could be launched from the Barents Sea or from beneath the Arctic ice pack. Little is known about the torpedo arrangements in the Typhoon. The twin-hull layout suggests four torpedo tubes in each hull with separate handling rooms. Some of these tubes may be of the larger 26in (650mm) diameter to enable the new Type 65 wake-homing torpedo or the SS-N-16 torpedo-carrying derirative of the SS-N-15 antisubmarine missile to be fired.

Electronics: The main active/passive transducer is probably located in the chin of the submarine, and there will undoubtedly be conformal passive arrays along the hull for detection and fire control. Large hatches located side by side abaft the fin house buoys for VLF communications. An extensive array of masts include search and attack periscopes, the distinctive Snoop Pair/Rim Hat surface surveillance/ESM combination, Park Lamp VLF/LF reception, Pert Spring satellite navigation, and Shot Gun VHF communications. There are also numerous unidentified electro-optical sensors.

Construction: The first unit of the class was laid down at the Severodvinsk Shipyard, appropriatly the world's largest submarine production yard, in 1977; she was subsequently launched in August 1980 and began trials in June 1981. The second boat was launched in October 1982 and began trials in June 1983. A third boat entered service in 1985, and a fourth in 1986. The large size of these boats suggests that only the Severodvinsk 402 Shipyard, which has extensive undercover construction halls, will be capable of undertaking their construction. It is therefore considered unlikely that production of Typhoon-class submarines will exceed the rate of one hull every two years.

Right: The Typhoon is the largest submarine ever built. Her length is virtually the same as that of the Delta IV and the US Navy's *Ohio*, but she has almost twice the beam of the latter vessels due to her unusual hull construction, which comprises two long pressure cylinders side by side within a broad outer casing. A third, shorter, pressure cylinder housing the command spaces is located within the hump at the base of the fin. The twin pairs of hatches in the after casing house VLF communications buoys.

Upholder class

Origin: United Kingdom, first unit to complete 1988
Type: Attack submarine, diesel-powered (SS)
Displacement: 2,215 tons surfaced; 2,365 tons submerged
Dimensions: Length 230ft 6in (70.25m); beam 25ft (7.6m); draught 21ft 4in (6.5m)
Propulsion: Diesel-electric drive on one shaft; two Paxman Valenta 1600 RPA 200SZ diesel generators, each 2,035bhp; one GEC electric motor; 4,070bhp for 12kt surfaced, 5,400hp for 20kt submerged
Complement: 44
Background: Following the completion of the Oberon programme in 1967 no further submarines with diesel-electric propulsion were contemplated by the Royal Navy. However, with the decision to build Trident submarines it became clear that there would have to be a gap of about eight years in the SSN building programme, because Vickers (Barrow) was the only remaining shipyard with sufficient nuclear construction expertise, and building capacity was limited. Moreover, the Oberons, by this time nearing the end of their service lives, had shown their value in routine patrol operations, and had proved to be inherently quieter than their nuclear counterparts. The Royal Navy therefore opted for a new diesel-electric design, employing as much of the technology developed for the SSN programme as it was possible to incorporate.
Design: The hull-form, which has an exceptionally high beam to length ratio, is closely modelled on that of the British nuclear boats. Single-hull construction has been adopted, and the cylindrical pressure hull is of NQ 1 (HY80-equivalent) steel for a maximum diving depth of 650ft (200m); the fin will be largely constructed of GRP. The large diameter of the pressure hull allows for a spacious two-deck layout. The control room, communications office and ESM office are grouped together beneath the fin, with the weapons stowage forward. The lower deck houses the accommodation and messing spaces, and there are two banks of Chloride lead-acid batteries beneath, each containing 240 cells. The propulsion and auxiliary machinery is located in a single-deck compartment abaft the accommodation decks. In the forward part of the machinery space are the two Paxman 16-cylinder diesel generators, which are mounted on a raft above the fuel tanks. The generator room is separated from the motor room by a transverse acoustic bulkhead. The GEC main motor comprises two motors in a common frame with two armatures on a common shaft. This arrangement makes possible series or parallel combinations, giving a continuous speed range between four and 20 knots. There is a separate motor generator for speeds below four knots. The Upholders have exceptionally high submerged speed, and their large battery capacity gives them an underwater endurance 45 per cent greater than that of the Oberon. They are also capable of sustaining 19 knots while snorkeling. Advanced automation, which includes an autopilot, has made it possible to reduce the complement to only 44 officers and men.
Armament: The six bow tubes are of the standard 21in (533mm) diameter and are disposed in two banks (two in the upper and four in the lower bank) in the upper section of the bow. Positive discharge is used to enable the torpedoes to be fired from any depth. Additional stowage, with hydraulic handling, is provided for a further 12 weapons. Initially the Mk 24 Tigerfish torpedo will be carried, but in the late 1980s this will be superseded by the heavyweight Marconi Spearfish which is currently under development. Spearfish, a high-performance torpedo designed specifically to counter the latest high-speed, deep-diving Soviet SSNs, has a length of 27ft 10in (8.5m), and weighs 4,400lb (2,000kg). Spearfish incorporates a Sundstrand turbine engine, and is reported to have achieved more than 70 knots on trials. Range will be in the region of 70,000 yards

Left: *Upholder*, the first diesel-electric submarine to be built for the Royal Navy for more than 20 years, is modeled on the latest nuclear-powered fleet submarines but costs less than half as much. Seen here at her launch at the Barrow-in-Furness Shipyard of Vickers, *Upholder* is due to enter service in 1988. Three further units have been ordered from Cammell Laird, and it is thought that the class will eventually total ten submarines.

(65,000m). Other weapons carried by the Upholder class will include the Sub-Harpoon anti-ship missile and Stonefish mines.

Electronics: The main active/passive sonar, designated Type 2040, was developed from the French Thomson-CSF Elédone. The passive array, comprising a triple-tier 48-stave circular transducer, is located in the chin of the submarine, while the active ('attack') component is housed inside the forward edge of the fin. Twelve targets can be tracked simultaneously. The Type 2040 will be complemented by the standard Type 2007 passive hydrophone flank array, the Type 2019 passive intercept sonar, and the Type 2026 towed array. The DCC Action Information Organisation and fire control system, developed from the DCA/DCB systems in service aboard Royal Navy SSNs, is based on two FM1600E computers with a digital data bus linked to three dual-purpose consoles. Up to 35 targets can be tracked, and automatic guidance can be provided for four torpedoes against four separate targets.

Construction: The name-ship of the class was laid down at the Vickers Shipyard, Barrow-in-Furness, in November 1983 and is due to enter service in 1988. Three further units were ordered from Cammell Laird in January 1986. The class may eventually total 10 submarines, and it is reported that the fifth boat may be of a 'stretched' 3,000-ton design which will be capable of longer endurance.

Right: The Upholder class boats have single pressure hulls, cruciform tail surfaces and single seven-bladed propellers. The main ballast tanks are fore and aft of the pressure hull, as in contemporary SSNs. Internally there is a multi-deck layout with a large modern control room, and the latest sensors will be fitted, including a Type 2026 towed array and the Type 2040 bow array, under wraps in this photo of the launching ceremony.

Below: The Upholders will be capable of firing the full range of weapons carried by the latest Royal Navy nuclear-powered hunter-killer submarines and will have six bow tubes of 21in (533mm) diameter. Initially the Mk 24 Tigerfish Mod.2 (1) torpedo will be carried, but this will eventually be superseded by the Spearfish torpedo (2) currently being developed by Marconi. Both types can be used against either surface ships or submarines, but Spearfish will be faster and will have a more sophisticated homing system. The Upholders will also be fitted with the necessary fire control electronics to handle the Sub-Harpoon anti-ship missile (3), which is launched from a canister designed to fit a standard 21in torpedo tube. In place of each torpedo or missile, two Marconi Stonefish mines (4) can be accommodated in the stowage racks. A total of 18 full-size weapons can be carried.

Valiant class

Origin: United Kingdom, first unit completed 1966
Type: Attack submarine, nuclear-powered (SSN)
Displacement: 4,200 tons standard; 4,900 tons full load
Dimensions: Length 285ft (86.9m); beam 33ft 3in (10.1m); draught 27ft (8.2m)
Propulsion: One PWR 1 pressurized water-cooled reactor driving geared steam turbines; one shaft; 15,000shp for 28kt max
Complement: 103
Background: The first British nuclear-powered submarine, HMS *Dreadnought*, was completed in 1963. Because of delays in the British military reactor programme, she was built around an American S5W reactor, which was purchased direct from Westinghouse. The US reactor section was grafted onto a forward section of British design, and British equipment and propulsion machinery were employed. A completely new generation of underwater sensors and combat systems were designed for *Dreadnought*, and these were to be incorporated in later British SSN designs. Meanwhile work proceeded on an all-British reactor at the Admiralty Reactor Test Establishment at Dounreay. This was to be incorporated in a modified design which became the Valiant class. The British SSNs, unlike their US Navy counterparts, are designed to operate in close support of a task force or a convoy, and are designated Fleet Submarines by the Royal Navy.
Design: *Valiant* was slightly larger than *Dreadnought* in order to accommodate the new British PWR 1 reactor, which was bulkier than the American S5W. Single-hull construction was again employed, but the 'Albacore' hull-form was smoother, less disjointed than that of Dreadnought. High-yield UKE

Above: The Valiants were the first nuclear submarines of exclusively British design, *Dreadnought* having been completed with an S5W reactor purchased directly from the United States. They are designated 'Fleet Submarines' by the Royal Navy.

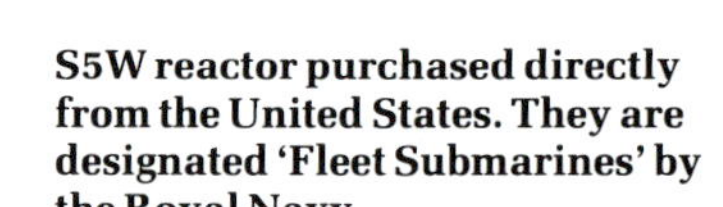

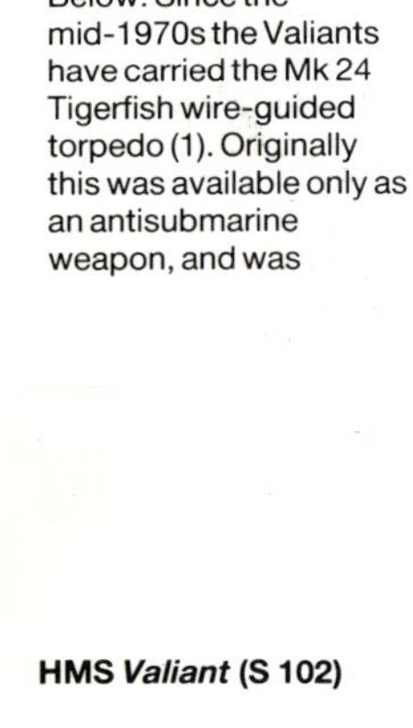

Below: Since the mid-1970s the Valiants have carried the Mk 24 Tigerfish wire-guided torpedo (1). Originally this was available only as an antisubmarine weapon, and was complemented by the elderly Mk 8 anti-ship torpedo, but the Mod.2 variant of Tigerfish currently in service has a dual-purpose capability. The Valiants are currently being retro-fitted to fire the Sub-Harpoon anti-ship missile (2). They can also launch Marconi Stonefish (3) and British Aerospace Sea Urchin (4) mines from their torpedo tubes.

HMS *Valiant* (S 102)

steel gives the submarine a diving depth of 1,000ft (300m). At the forward end of the boat there is a two-deck layout housing the control and accommodation spaces, and a smaller cylinder housing the torpedo stowage and handling arrangements. The after end of the submarine is occupied exclusively by the reactor and machinery spaces. *Dreadnought*, like the US Skipjacks, incorporated little or no sound insulation. In the Valiants, however, the main turbines and gearing were mounted on a raft insulated from the hull by flexible mountings. A novel feature of the class was the inclusion of a separate propulsion motor, located abaft the geared turbines and coupled directly to the single shaft. This arrangement permits three possible propulsion modes. For moderate speeds, such as might be required for support of a task force or convoy, power is provided by the geared turbines and the raft is isolated from the hull. At very high speeds, which would be used for interception or evasion, the raft is locked into place. And at creep speed, during barrier patrol or other such ASW operations, the boat is powered by the independent electric motor. A 112-cell battery, charged by a Paxman diesel generator, provides emergency power in the event of reactor failure. Unlike their US Navy counterparts, the British SSNs have their forward hydroplanes mounted close to the bow; they fold upwards to enable the submarine to come alongside without sustaining damage.

Armament: There are six bow torpedo tubes of the standard 21in (533mm) diameter, and the torpedo handling room has stowage capacity for 20 reloads. Early units of the class commissioned with the elderly Mk 8 anti-ship torpedo and the Mk 20 acoustic-homing antisubmarine torpedo. From 1970 onwards the latter was superseded by the Mk 23, essentially a Mk 20 with wire guidance. *Churchill*, the third unit of the class, was the first to be fitted to fire the Mk 24 Tigerfish wire-guided antisubmarine torpedo, which entered service in 1974. The guidance systems of the early models of Tigerfish were not particularly well-suited to anti-ship operation, and reports that the Mk 8 torpedo had been taken out of service in the early 1970s were conclusively refuted when the submarine *Conqueror* used two Mk 8s to despatch the Argentinian cruiser *General Belgrano* in 1982 during the Falklands conflict. *Churchill* evaluated both the Sub-Harpoon anti-ship missile and the US Mk 48 Mod.3 torpedo prior to the adoption of the former by the Royal Navy. *Courageous* was the first of the class to deploy Sub-Harpoon operationally, in 1981, and the other boats are currently being retro-fitted with the missile.

Electronics: As completed the Valiants had an advanced sonar outfit comprising a Type 2001 low-frequency active/passive array (strapped around the outside of the 'chin' of the submarine), a Type 2007 passive flank array, and a Type 197 intercept array. A well-equipped attack centre was based around the DCA Action Information Organisation and Fire Control System. Beginning with *Courageous* in the late 1970s, the class began a series of long refits during which major updates were made to the electronics. The Type 2001 chin array is being replaced by the Type 2020 electronically scanned array which entered service on the Trafalgar class, and a Type 2026 towed hydrophone array is being fitted. These modifications will be extended to all units of the class except *Warspite*.

Construction: Five submarines of the Valiant class were built for the Royal Navy between 1966 and 1971 at the Vickers Shipyard, Barrow-in-Furness and at Cammell Laird, Birkenhead. The programme was delayed by work on the Polaris submarines of the Resolution class.

Right: *Warspite*, the second unit of the class to be completed. The Valiants have a more curved hull-form than later British nuclear-powered submarines and a taller, more angled fin, and unlike their US Navy counterparts they have their forward hydroplanes mounted close to the bow. The current update programme includes provision of a Type 2026 passive array and modifications to the fire control electronics to enable these submarines to fire Sub-Harpoon.

Victor class

Origin: USSR, first unit completed 1968
Type: Attack submarine, nuclear-powered (SSN)
Displacement: Victor I: 5,100 tons submerged
Victor II: 5,700 tons submerged
Victor III: 6,300 tons submerged
Dimensions: Victor I: length 312ft (95m); beam 33ft (10m); draught 23ft (7m)
Victor II: length 328ft (100m); beam and draught as Victor I
Victor III: length 348ft (106m); beam and draught as Victor I
Propulsion: One/two pressurized water-cooled reactors driving geared steam turbines; 1 shaft (see remarks); 30,000shp for 29-30kt
Complement: Victor I & II: 80
Victor III: 85
Background: In 1960 the first US Navy ballistic missile submarine, *George Washington* (SSBN-598), entered service. This new development was to compel the Soviet Navy to rethink its maritime strategy. Antisubmarine warfare, which had previously been neglected, assumed a new importance, and the Soviet Navy embarked on an ambitious surface ship construction programme headed by the Moskva-class antisubmarine cruisers; almost simultaneously the first Soviet nuclear-powered submarine with a primary antisubmarine mission, the Victor, was laid down. Fitted with a newly developed LF active/passive bow sonar, the Victor was initially charged with hunting down Western SSBNs. In theory this meant that the Victor would attempt to pick up the SSBN as it sortied from its home port, and would shadow it throughout its patrol. These tactics appear to have met with little success, and in the early 1970s they were superseded by a 'pro-submarine' mission in support of the Soviet Navy's own SSBNs. With the advent of the Delta class and the 4,250nm (7,800km) SS-N-8 ballistic missile, Soviet SSBNs would increasingly operate in defended 'bastion' areas where they would be protected by a combination of surface ships, aircraft and submarines like the Victor. In 1972 the first of a new variant, Victor II, entered service; it introduced the SS-N-15 nuclear-tipped antisubmarine missile to the Soviet Navy. In 1978 this variant was superseded in turn by the Victor III, which was fitted with improved sensors, and large-diameter torpedo tubes which enabled it to fire the SS-N-16 antisubmarine missile.

Design: The Victor was a completely new design which owed little to the only previous Soviet SSN, the November, its tear-drop hull being 50ft (15m) shorter and slightly broader. An improved type of nuclear reactor was fitted, and some attempt was made to quieten machinery noise. From the Victor II onwards, the hull casing was covered with an anechoic rubber sheathing. The six torpedo tubes are all forward, the 16in (400mm) stern tubes of earlier Soviet nuclear boats being abandoned in favour of cruciform tail surfaces. The Victor was the first Soviet submarine with a single shaft. The Victor I and II variants are reported to have a single five-bladed propeller, with two small auxiliary propellers for manoeuvring. However, the Victor III has an unusual eight-bladed propeller, comprising two tandem four-bladed propellers which co-rotate. Each of the two later variants of the class shows an increase in length over its immediate predecessor: in both cases an additional hull section has been inserted between the fin and the bow, indicating that an increase in space was required for new weapons and fire control systems.

Armament: The Victor I was initially armed only with conventional anti-ship and acoustic-homing antisubmarine torpedoes, but the Victor II variant introduced the SS-N-15 antisubmarine missile into Soviet service. The missile is similar in conception to the US Navy's SUBROC. It has a nuclear warhead to compensate for guidance inaccuracies, and has a maximum range estimated at 21nm (40km). It can be fired from a standard 21in (533mm) torpedo tube, and the necessary fire control equipment may therefore have been retro-fitted in some Victor Is. The SS-N-16 antisubmarine missile carried by the Victor III did not enter service until about 1980. It carries a homing torpedo payload in place of a nuclear warhead, and is therefore of greater diameter than the SS-N-15. The SS-N-16 is fired from a special 26in (650mm) tube which can also handle the new Type 65 wake-homing torpedo.

Below: The Victors can fire a wide variety of weapons from their six bow tubes. In the Victor I the tubes are thought to be of uniform 21in (533mm) diameter; these can fire the SS-N-15 antisubmarine missile (1), which has a nuclear warhead, and an antisubmarine homing torpedo (2) thought to have entered service in the mid/late-1960s. In place of each of the torpedoes and missiles, two mines (3) can be accommodated in the racks. In the Victor II and III some of the torpedo tubes are of 26in (650mm) diameter, enabling them to fire the SS-N-16 antisubmarine missile (4), which carries a small homing torpedo, and the high-performance Type 65 anti-ship torpedo (5), which is thought to home on the wake created by a surface ship.

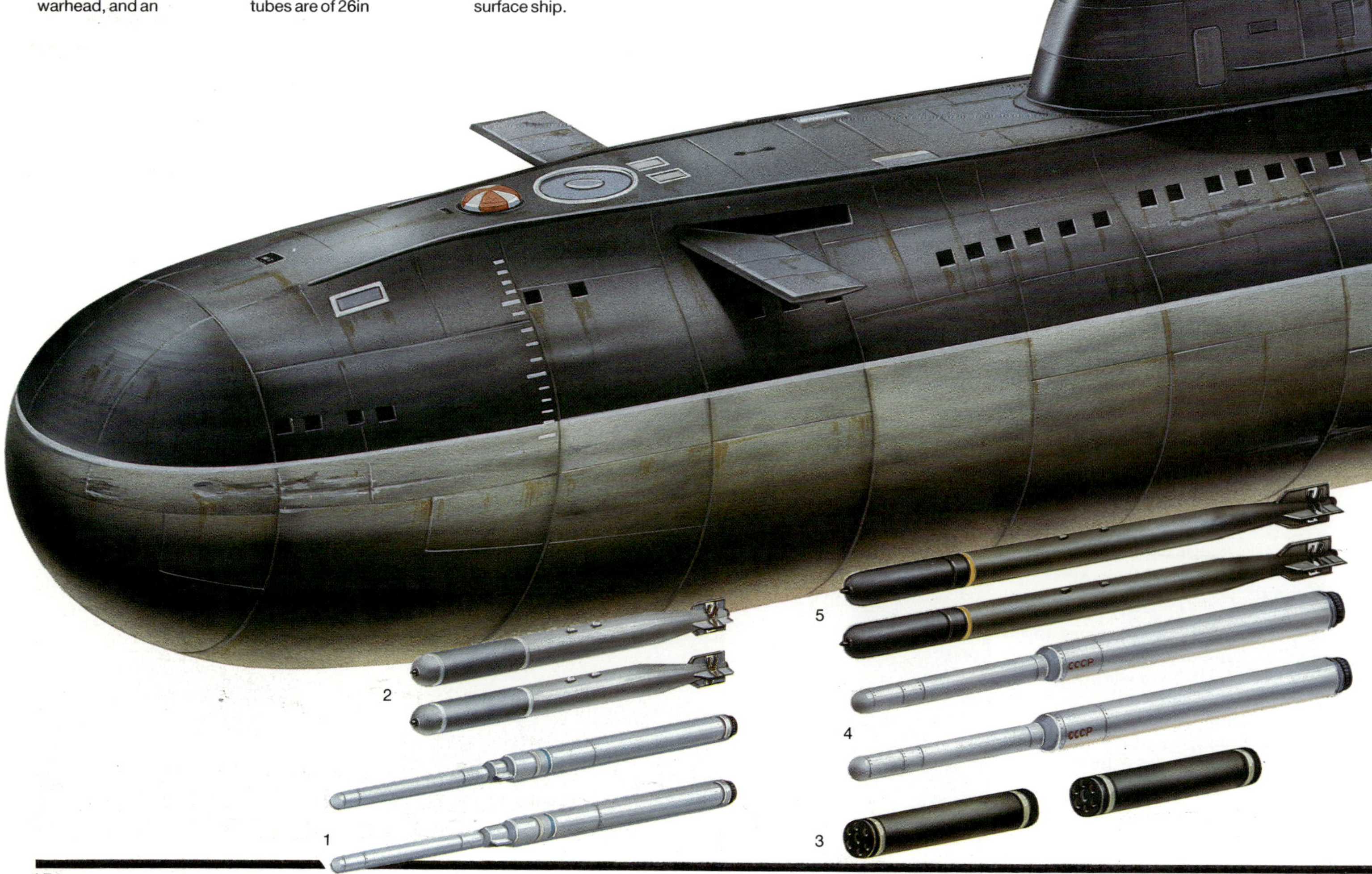

Electronics: All three variants of the Victor are fitted with a large active/passive LF bow array capable of detecting hostile ships at considerable distances under favourable sonar conditions. In addition, the Victor III can deploy a towed hydrophone array from the teardrop-shaped pod atop the tail-fin. The sensor masts are standard for their period and comprise search and attack periscopes, a Snoop Tray surveillance radar, Brick Pulp ESM, Park Lamp VLF reception, and aerials for HF and VHF communications. The Victor III also has Pert Spring for satellite communications. Both the Victor II and the Victor III have twin hatches abaft the fin for a VLF communications buoy.

Construction: Sixteen Victor Is were completed by the Admiralty Shipyard, Leningrad, between 1967 and 1975. Seven Victor IIs were completed by the same shipyard between 1972 and 1978. The first Victor III was completed in 1978, and since that time a further 20 have entered service, with a second production line being opened up at Komsomolsk in the Pacific. The Victor is now being phased out in favour of the similar, but slightly larger, Akula.

Above: A submarine of the Victor III class in trouble off the East Coast of the United States. Note the distinctive pod atop the tail-fin, thought to house a towed passive hydrophone array, and the co-rotating four-bladed propellers.

Right: An early view of a Victor I running on the surface. These are thought to have been the first Soviet submarines designed primarily to hunt other submarines and a number of innovatory features were incorporated in the design, including Western-style cruciform tail surfaces and a single propellor shaft. The Victor proved so successful that production continued for more than 15 years, and the design has only recently been superseded by the Akula.

Yankee class

Origin: USSR, first unit completed 1967
Type: Ballistic missile submarine, nuclear-powered (SSBN)
Displacement: 8,000 tons surfaced; 9,600 tons submerged
Dimensions: Length 430ft (130m); beam 39ft (12m); draught 29ft (9m)
Propulsion: Two pressurized water-cooled reactors driving geared steam turbines; two shafts; 35,000shp for 27kt max
Complement: 120
Background: When the Strategic Rocket Forces were formed in 1960 the Soviet Navy's land attack mission was suspended pending the development of powerful land-based ICBMs. Construction of the Hotel-class SSBNs was terminated after only nine had been laid down, as was construction of the Golf-class SSB. By 1964, however, the Navy had regained a limited nuclear land attack role and the first of a new type of SSBN, the Yankee, was on the slipways. The SS-N-6 missile with which these submarines were equipped could be launched from under water and had almost twice the range of its immediate predecessor, the SS-N-5. Nevertheless, the Yankees would still need to patrol relatively close to the East and West coasts of the United States in order to target all the major cities. This involved lengthy transits to their patrol areas, and Yankees serving with the Northern Fleet would have to pass through the NATO antisubmarine barrier in the Greenland/Iceland/United Kingdom (GIUK) Gap. A number of theories have been developed to explain the construction of these submarines. Some commentators have advanced the view that the Yankees have a second-strike mission, and at the start of a conflict would be held back in defended sea areas ('bastions') for nuclear war-fighting. Another possible explanation is that forward-deployed Yankees would target specifically naval installations such as ports and airfields.
Design: The Yankee belongs to the same generation as the Victor-class SSN and the Charlie-class SSGN; the hull-form and propulsion plant are therefore more advanced technologically than those of first-generation Soviet nuclear boats. Soviet missile technology had made comparable advances by the early 1960s, and in spite of its markedly superior performance the SS-N-6 missile was significantly smaller than the SS-N-4 Sark missile for which the Hotel and Golf were designed. There was therefore no longer any

1

Below: An overhead view of a Yankee I, showing clearly the raised section of casing housing the SS-N-6 missiles. Note the fin-mounted diving planes and the distinctive sonar 'window' around the top of the bow. The unit depicted is one of several with an angled base to the fin.

Above: A Yankee I running on the surface. Note the large rectangular apertures along the sides of the hull casing: these are evidence of double-hull construction, which continues to be favoured by Soviet designers. Thirty-four Yankees were completed for the Soviet Navy between 1967 and 1974.

need to accommodate the missile tubes in the fin, a design feature which in earlier classes had restricted the number of missiles to three. For the Yankee the Soviets adopted the arrangement standard in US Navy SSBNs (hence the NATO name for the class), with 16 missile tubes in two rows of eight abaft the fin. Another feature copied from the US boats was the hydroplane and rudder arrangement; the forward planes were mounted on the fin for the first time in the Soviet Navy, and combined with cruciform control surfaces aft. The major difference between the Yankee and Western SSBNs of the period was Soviet persistence with double-hull construction and twin-shaft propulsion. The need to transit sea areas dominated by NATO antisubmarine forces appears to have influenced the Soviets in favour of relatively high speed for the Yankee, which has more than twice the installed horsepower of contemporary Western SSBNs. A prototype conversion, the Yankee II, was modified in the mid-1970s to fire 12 SS-NX-17 missiles, but the SALT II Treaty prevented further conversions.

Armament: The SS-N-6 missile is around 38ft (11.5m) long and has a diameter of 5ft 5in (1.65m). The earliest variant of the missile carried a single nuclear warhead of about 1MT and had a maximum range of 1,300nm (2,400km). It was followed in 1972 by a Mod.2 variant with a range of 1,600nm (2.950km). A Mod.3 variant, which may have entered service one year later, had similar range but carried two reentry vehicles. The SS-NX-17 evaluated in the single Yankee II conversion is a somewhat larger missile, with a length of perhaps 40ft (12.5m) and a diameter similar to that of the SS-N-8 (hence the reduction from 16 to 12 missile tubes). It is reported to be more accurate than the SS-N-6 and is the only Soviet ballistic missile apart from the SS-N-20 to have solid-fuel propulsion. The Yankees have six bow tubes for standard 21in (533mm) torpedoes. Both long anti-ship and short antisubmarine torpedoes can be fired

Electronics: The Yankee has a large active/passive bow sonar with a distinctive wrap-around 'window' some 13ft (4m) deep. Mast-mounted sensors are identical to those of the Victor and Charlie classes, but there is also a Cod Eye radio sextant for navigational accuracy housed in the top of the fin.

Construction: The first Yankees were completed in 1977, and the programme was then accelerated, with parallel construction at Severodvinsk in the Arctic and Komsomolsk in the Pacific. A total of 34 submarines of the class were in service by 1974, but of the earlier Yankee Is have now had their missile tubes deactivated to enable the Soviets to stay within SALT II Treaty limits. One of these deactivated boats was recommissioned in 1982 to serve as a trials platform for a new long-range land-attack cruise missile, the SS-NX-24.

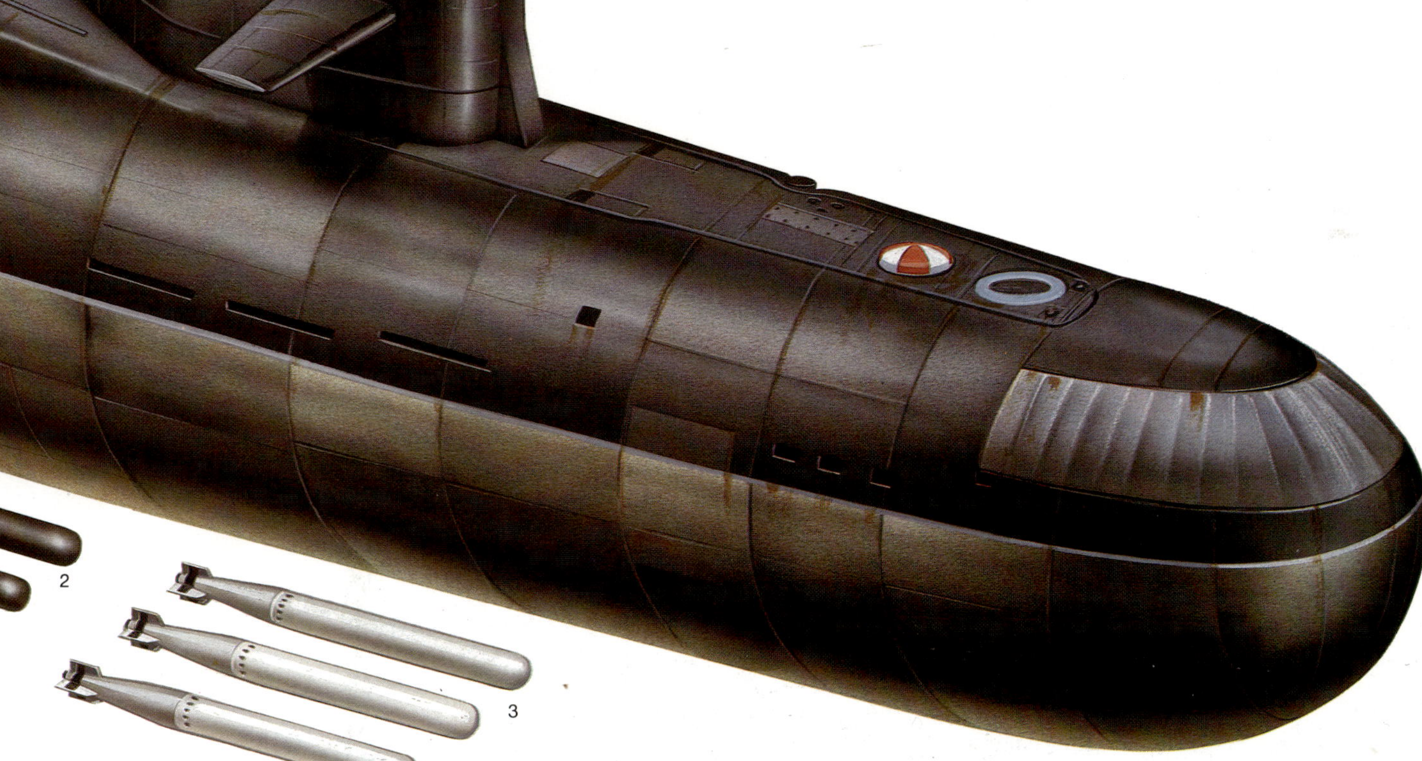

Left and below: The launch tubes of the Yankee house 16 SS-N-6 ballistic missiles (1). These are thought to be a mix of the Mod 2 variant, which has a range of 1,600nm (2,950km) and a single 1MT nuclear warhead, and the Mod 3, which has a similar range but carries two smaller reentry vehicles. A single unit of the class, designated Yankee II, was modified to carry 12 SS-N-17 missiles. Conventional long anti-ship torpedoes (2) of 21in (533mm) diameter can be fired from the six bow tubes, and there is probably also a shorter 533mm homing torpedo (3) for use against submarines.

Yuushio class

Origin: Japan, first unit completed 1980
Type: Attack submarine, diesel-powered (SS)
Displacement: 2,200 tons surfaced
Dimensions: Length 250ft (76.2m); beam 32ft 6in (9.9m); draught 24ft 6in (7.5m)
Propulsion: Diesel-electric drive on one shaft; two Kawasaki-MAN V8/V24-30 AMTL diesel generators, each 1,700bhp; one Fuji electric motor; 3,400bhp for 13kt surfaced, 7,200hp for 20kt submerged
Complement: 80
Background: The first fleet submarines to be built postwar for the Japanese Maritime Self-Defence Force (JMSDF) were the five units of the Ooshio class, which were completed between 1965 and 1969. The Ooshios were of conservative design, with a traditional hull-form, two shafts, and six bow and two stern tubes. They were quickly overtaken by new technology, and were decommissioned in the early 1980s. The Ooshio was succeeded by the Uzushio, a completely new type incorporating all the latest features of US Navy construction. The Uzushio was the first Japanese submarine with an 'Albacore' hull-form, and an internal layout similar to that of contemporary US SSNs was adopted, with the bow occupied by a large passive sonar array and six torpedo tubes angled out amidships. The Uzushio was designed for high underwater speed, and proved particularly sucessful; seven units were

Above: *Mochishio*, the second unit of the class. Seven submarines of this type have so far been completed, and a further seven are building or projected. Based, like their immediate predecessors of the Uzushio class, on the US Barbel design, the Yuushios have a large sonar array in the bow with the six torpedo tubes angled out beneath the fin, as in contemporary US Navy SSNs. They are large, sophisticated boats, with good endurance.

Right: The Yuushios are fitted with six 21in (533mm) torpedo tubes. They are angled out in two banks of three beneath the fin in the manner of US Navy attack boats, which also have a sonar occupying their bows. The Japanese Maritime Self-Defense Force currently has in service the US Mk 48 heavyweight dual-purpose torpedo and the 'short' US Mk 37C antisubmarine torpedo (1). The Mk 48 will eventually be superseded by a new high-performance torpedo of Japanese design and manufacture, the GRX-2 (2). The fifth unit of the class, *Nadashio*, was fitted from the outset to fire the Sub-Harpoon anti-ship missile (3), which will be retro-fitted to earlier boats.

completed between 1971 and 1978. The Yuushio type which followed is essentially an improved Uzushio, designed for deeper diving and with an improved electronics outfit.

Design: The Yuushio has a hull-form reminiscent of the US Barbel. Unlike its US Navy counterparts, however, the Japanese boat has double-hull construction, the pressure hull being framed externally, and high-tensile NS-90 steel has superseded the NS-60 steel employed in the construction of the Uzushio class, thereby increasing diving depth from 650ft (200m) to 1,000ft (300m). The maximum diameter of the pressure hull is amidships, where there is a three-deck layout. Forward of the fin there is a smaller cylinder in which the six torpedo tubes are located. There are six tubes, disposed as two vertical banks of three and angled out at 10 degrees to the submarine's axis, leaving the bow section free for the large passive sonar array. Immediately abaft the tubes there is a stowage room on three levels, with the reloads in line with the tubes. Above the stowage room is a combined control and attack centre, and accommodation for the officers and men is abaft the control centre and the torpedo stowage room respectively, arranged on two levels. The lower deck level is occupied exclusively by the submarine's batteries. The after section houses the propulsion and auxiliary machinery spaces together with the switchboard. The diesel engines are manufactured by Kawasaki under licence from MAN (FRG). The powerful electric motor, which can produce a maximum of 7,200hp for an underwater speed of 20 knots, was designed and manufactured by Fuji. The control surfaces of both the Uzushio and Yuushio classes are patterned on those of contemporary US Navy SSNs, with the forward hydroplanes mounted on the fin and cruciform tail surfaces forward of a single seven-bladed propeller. The Japanese boats have an automated steering system which features automatic control of both depth and bearing.

Armament: The six torpedo tubes are of standard 21in (533mm) diameter. No details are available of weapons capacity, but the layout of the stowage room suggests 12-15 full-length torpedoes shared between the three levels. It is reported that the JMSDF operates both the US Mk 48 wire-guided heavyweight torpedo, which can be used against surface ships or submarines, and the Mk 37C short antisubmarine torpedo. Two of the latter can be accommodated in place of one of the larger Mk 48s. A new high-performance torpedo of Japanese design and manufacture, the GRX-2, is currently under development. The fifth unit of the class, *Nadashio*, which was completed in March 1984, was the first to be fitted to fire the Sub-Harpoon anti-ship missile, which will eventually be retro-fitted in earlier boats.

Electronics: The sonar outfit of the Uzushio and Yuushio classes is based on the ZQQ-4 passive array located in the bow. The ZQQ-4, apparently a Japanese development of the US Navy's BQS-4, comprises three circular transducer arrays stacked one above the other. This arrangement serves to reduce the vertical beam of the sonar and to reduce the signal to noise ratio. The ZQQ-4 is complemented by an SQS-36J active (attack) sonar, and the electronics outfit is completed by a full array of mast-mounted sensors, which include attack and search periscopes, a ZPS-6 surveillance radar, and numerous masts for electronic warfare (EW) and communications.

Construction: By the end of 1986 seven units of the Yuushio class had been completed at the shipyards of Mitsubishi (Kobe) and Kawasaki (Kobe), with seven further units building or projected. A follow-on design, incorporating an advanced weapon control system by Hitachi, is currently being prepared.

Yuushio **(SS 573)**

Zeeleeuw class

Origin: Netherlands, first unit to complete 1989.
Type: Attack submarine, diesel-powered (SS).
Displacement: 2,450 tons standard; 2,800 tons submerged.
Dimensions: Length 222ft (67.7m); beam 28ft (8.4m); draught 23ft (7m).
Propulsion: Diesel-electric drive on one shaft; three SEMT-Pielstick 12 PA 4V 200 diesel generators (see remarks); one Holec electric motor; 3,950bhp for 12kt surfaced, 5,430hp for 21kt submerged.
Complement: 50.
Background: The Walrus class was designed in the late 1970s to replace the elderly triple-hull boats of the Dolfin class. Initially, the design was to have been based closely on that of the two submarines of the Zvaardvis class completed in 1972. However, as detailed design work proceeded so many modifications were incorporated that the Walrus became a separate type. In order to preserve the design teams and labour force at the RDM shipyard construction was brought forward, and the first steel was cut even before the contract for the first boat was signed in June 1979. However, a change in the Netherlands Navy specification, requiring a 50% increase in diving depth, led to major redesign and consequent delays in the construction of the first two boats. A second pair was ordered in January 1984, and a third pair his projected.
Design: Like the preceding Zvaardvis class, the Walrus has an 'Albacore' hull-form based on that of the US Barbel design. The forward hydroplanes are mounted on the fin, as in US Navy submarines, but the cruciform after control surfaces of the Zvaardvis have been superseded by 'X'-planes on the Swedish model (see Näcken). The adoption of high-tensile French MAREL steel for the pressure hull necessitated a reduction in the number of welded joints and hull apertures. The consequent increase in diving depth to 985ft (300m) brought further design modificatfons, including changes in the torpedo launching systems, a pressurized fuel system, a 'wet' exhaust system, more sophisticated hydraulics and additional emergency blowing systems. The pressure hull comprises a large-diameter cylinder amidships, with smaller-diameter cylinders fore and aft. The hull configuration is therefore an unusual mix of single- and double-hull construction. The larger cylinder amidships allows for a spacious three-deck layout with the control centre and officer accommodation on the upper deck and the accommodation for the crew on the second deck. The lower deck is occupied by the three 148-cell battery banks. The smaller cylinder forward houses the torpedo stowage room, while the smaller cylinders aft house the propulsion units and auxiliary machinery. In the forward machinery compartment are the three diesel generators, which are disposed abreast on a resiliently-mounted raft. The central compartment is divided into two decks, with the switchboard on the upper level and the auxiliary machinery below. The third compartment houses the main electric motor. The latter is a double-armature Holec model of Netherlands design and manufacture, but for the diesels the Dutch had to turn to the French, as the Werkspoor model which was employed in the Zvaardvis class was no longer in production. However, the second pair of submarines in this class will have the Brons-Werkspoor O-RUB 215X12 diesel currently under development. Control of the machinery is highly automated, and this has made possible a

Above: The Zeeleeuw class is a development of the Zwaardvis design depicted here which was based in turn on the US Barbel. The latest Dutch boats are all of modern design, employing an 'Albacore' hull-form, and the forward hydroplanes are mounted on the fin in the manner of their US counterparts.

Hr Ms *Zeeleeuw* (S 803)

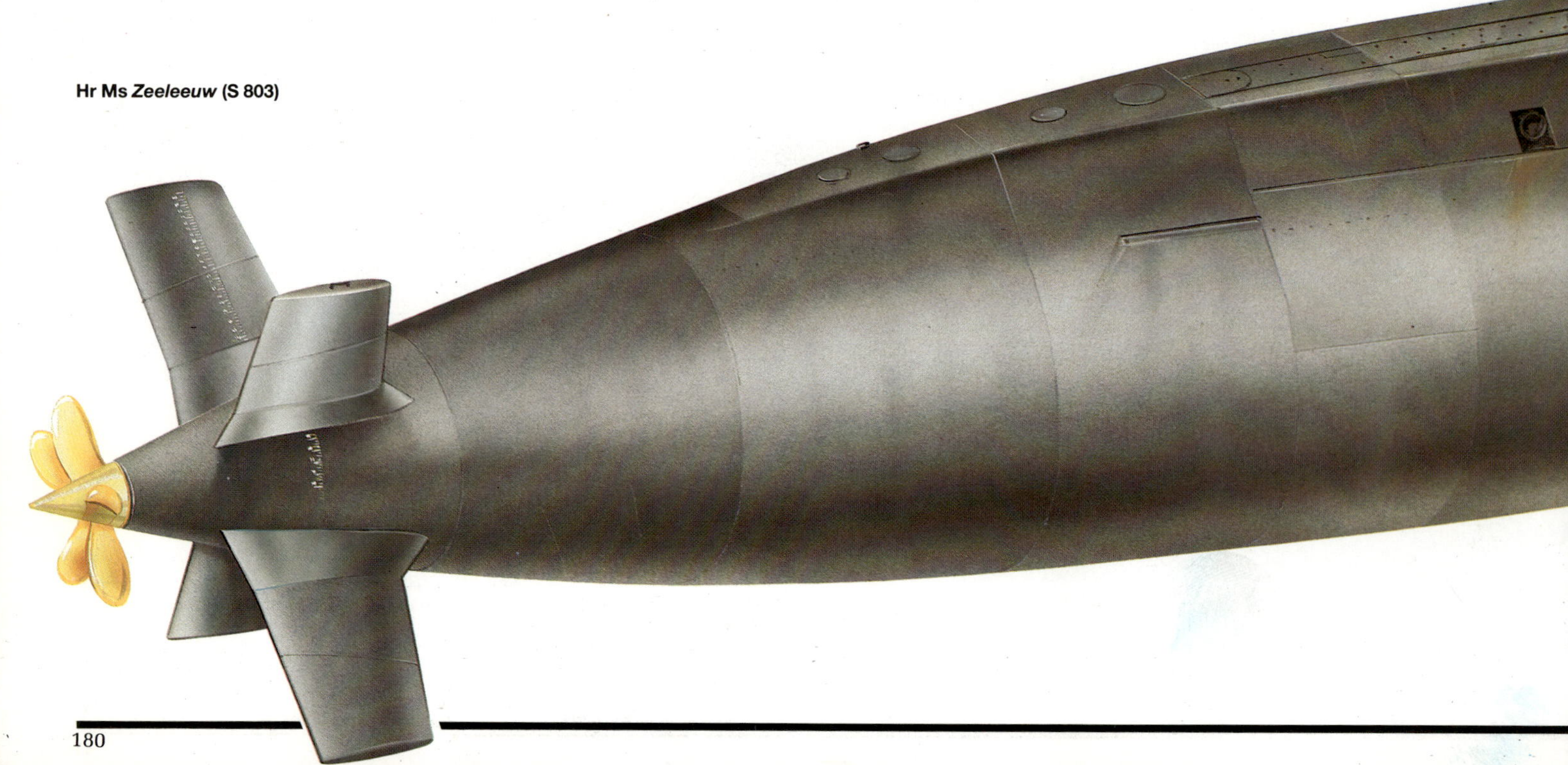

reduction in the complement to only 50 men.
Armament: The four 21in (533mm) bow tubes are of the positive discharge 'water-slug' type, which enables them to fire torpedoes at any depth. The capacious torpedo stowage room has a maximum capacity of 20 torpedoes or missiles. The torpedoes currently in service with the Royal Netherlands Navy are the Northrop NT-37C and -37D antisubmarine models and the US Mk 48 Mod.4 heavyweight torpedo. The improved NT-37E is currently being purchased, and it is envisaged that the Walrus class will also fire the Mk 48 Mod.5 ADCAP when the latter becomes available. They will be fitted from the outset with the necessary fire control facilities for the Sub-Harpoon anti-ship missile.
Electronics: The electronics outfit represents a marked advance on the earlier Zwaardvis class. The large Octopus active/passive circular bow array is based, like the Type 2040 currently being fitted in the British Upholder class (q.v.), on the Thomson-CSF Eledone sonar. The other major sonar array will be the British Type 2026 towed hydrophone array. The intercept sonar will be the Passive/Active Range and Intercept Sonar (PARIS) developed jointly by France, Britain and the Netherlands, which first entered service in 1978. The Walrus class will have a SEWACO VIII computer-based Action Information Organisation and Fire Control System. The Sperry Mk 29 Mod.2A inertial navigation system will be fitted, together with a NAVSAT (Navigation Satellite) receiver.
Construction: Completion of *Walrus* has been delayed following a serious fire at the RDM Shipyard, Rotterdam, and the class has been renamed Zeeleeuw after the second boat, which will complete on schedule in 1989. The third and fourth boats will follow in 1992 and 1994 respectively.

Above: The most notable innovation of the Walrus (now Zeeleeuw) class is the adoption of X-planes in the place of the conventional cruciform tail surfaces. X-planes give finer control of depth and bearing and permit 'bottoming'.

Above: The Zeeleeuw class will have four 21in (533mm) bow torpedo tubes of the 'water-slug' type. The Royal Netherlands Navy currently has in service the US Mk 48 heavy-weight dual-purpose torpedo (1) and the NT-37C/D/E short antisubmarine torpedo. These boats will also be fitted from the outset with the necessary fire control facilities for the Sub-Harpoon anti-ship missile (2). Besides the four weapons carried in the tubes, there is stowage for 16 reloads.

Underwater Warfare

Tactics

David Miller

Below: The Italian destroyer *Artigliere* breaks in two and sinks after being hit by a Whitehead A.184 heavyweight wire-guided torpedo in May 1983.

Introduction

A submarine's mission profile generally follows one of three mainpatterns, depending on its type and role, but all submarines must start by leaving base on or very near the surface, a manoeuvre which is almost always detectable by direct visual means, radio intercept – for example, of harbour control frequencies – or satellite observations. Unless they are confined to an area such as the Baltic they must then transit through the shallow waters of the continental shelf, where they are relatively easy to detect, before reaching the open ocean. And Soviet submarines must pass through choke points, where detection is particularly easy. In the deeper ocean, however, the three missions diverge.

When it is clear of the continental shelf a ballistic missile submarine will usually go deep and travel reasonably fast to its patrol area, taking every precaution to ensure that it is not being trailed by SSNs; in its patrol area it will cruise at about three knots, hiding itself from detection by varying its depth to match prevailing oceanic conditions. However, it must expose itself to the risk of detection when it needs to communicate with its national command authority or update its inertial navigation system. Nuclear powered attack submarines, being faster and more agile, operate at greater depths, but they too must communicate from time to time with their base or with cooperating task groups.

Conventionally powered submarines must surface as a matter of routine to run the diesels that recharge their batteries, and to expel the diesel exhaust. They can do so by exposing only the head of a schnorkel tube, but even that is a relatively easy target for modern radars and infra-red sensors, and the exhaust fumes can be detected by the sniffers mounted on most types of anti-submarine aircraft.

In considering submarine tactics there is one unique factor that should always be borne in mind, namely the solitary nature of the submariner's existence and fight for survival. In almost every other type of warfare units operate in groups, manoeuvring in cooperation and in regular communication with each other, with flanking and supporting units and with superior headquarters. The submariner, on the other hand, can, within certain well defined limits, receive communications from outside and communicate with his base, and he may, in some circumstances, operate in very loose coordination with other surface or submarine units, mainly on the basis of being given an exclusive zone within which he can operate, but in the final analysis he is on his own, and must fight and survive in isolation.

Above: Mk 46 torpedo launched from a Mk 32 launcher on board a destroyer. The effectiveness of surface warships against submarine targets is a subject of discussion in most navies; many hold that submarines and aircraft are the most effective platforms.

Left: Periscope view from HMS *Oberon* of a Westland Sea King dunking. ASW aircraft, both fixed- and rotary-winged, are very effective in the ASW role, especially when using passive sonar, as they are virtually undetectable by the submarine.

Top right: Royal Navy Lynx HAS.3 carrying two Mk 46 antisubmarine torpedoes. Such small shipborne helicopters have brought a much-needed enhancement to surface warships' ASW capabilities, though aircraft size is growing.

Right: The control room on board HMS *Trafalgar*, lead boat of the latest class of British SSN. The submarine provides a unique operational environment, being almost totally self-contained, and dependent on its own resources and capabilities for survival.

Submarine Tactics

The sole utility of ballistic missile submarines lies in their strategic capability and their tactical use must, therefore, be viewed in their strategic context. Since the 1950s US and (probably) Soviet strategic thinking has been based on the concept of a nuclear triad of long-range bombers and land-based and submarine-launched ballistic missiles, the last being the ultimate deterrent in that they provide an assured response to a first strike by ICBMs with a massive attack on the aggressor's cities. This strategic theory of deterrence was enhanced when both the USA and the Soviet Union had a proportion of their nuclear armouries deployed in such a way as to be immune to a first strike by the other side, but two factors suggest that this equation may be altered in the near future: the first is the dramatic increase in the accuracy of SLBM warheads; the second is the steady increase in the effectiveness of present-day anti-submarine warfare techniques.

The accuracy of a warhead dictates the role of the missile that launches it, since a highly accurate warhead can be used in a first-strike attack on an opponent's ICBM silos while a less accurate warhead can only be used against unprotected area targets such as cities. The accuracy of the latest warheads on US and Soviet SLBMs is giving both sides at least the potential for a counter-force role, provided they are attacking fixed targets of known location. However, the deployment of the Soviet rail-transportable SS-X-24 and road-mobile SS-25, with their 6,250-mile (10,000km) ranges and ability to change locations, has negated the advances in US warhead accuracy.

Ballistic missile submarine bases

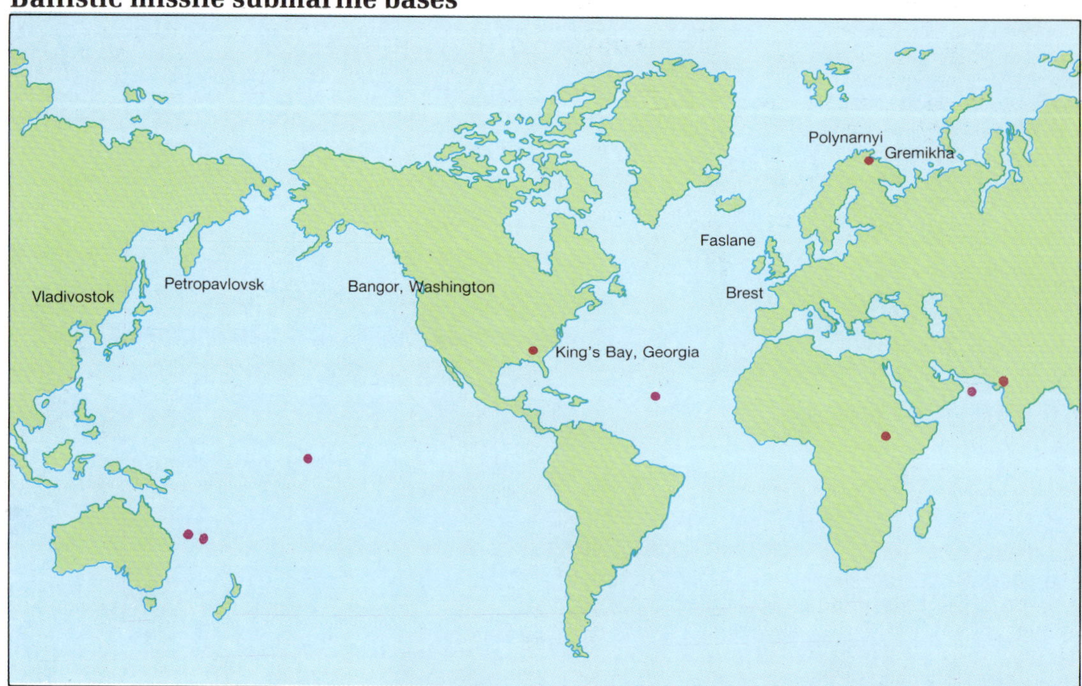

Above: Ballistic missile submarines seek the security of the ocean depths while on patrol, but must begin and end their missions at bases whose locations are known.

Right: Us DoD artist's depiction of a new Soviet submarine base. The underground pens whose entrances are clearly shown are designed to ensure the survivability of SSBNs.

Below: The British submarine base at HMS Dolphin, Gosport. Used by conventional submarines, this base is also the home of Flag Officer Submarines (FOSM), who commands the UK force.

Right: US strategic underwater detection capability, showing coverage given by sea-bed arrays such as SOSUS and land-based ASW aircraft. Tactical detection is the job of submarines, and ships.

US strategic underwater detection capability

Sea-bed sonars

Sea-bed sonar coverage

P-3 surveillance areas

About a third of any naval force is in port at any one time for maintenance, repair, exchange of crews or major refit. Thanks to good management and reliable equipment the US Navy is able to keep 65 per cent of its Ohio class submarines at sea, an improvement on the figure of 55 per cent for the earlier classes, but the Soviet Navy seems to have more problems with its SSBN fleet and usually maintains no more than 15 boats on patrol at the same time; an alarm signal would be given to the US if large numbers of Soviet SSBNs were to put to sea in a short period. The British guarantee to keep an absolute minimum of one SSBN at sea at all times; the French have two; and one Chinese SSBN is probably deployed most of the time.

NATO's submarine-based strategic nuclear forces are unusual in that they are operated by three different navies, under three entirely separate national controls. Ballistic missile submarines are the most survivable of the current strategic nuclear systems when on patrol at sea, and there is no doubt that the US and Soviet SSBN forces pose the major second-strike threats to each other. The great strategic benefit of the British and French SSBN fleets is that they provide second and third nuclear decision-making centres in Western Europe, and their value is enhanced by the fact that each country has total control over its SLBM warheads. The USSR is, therefore, faced with the fact that if she were to attack Western Europe, even if the USA held back, the UK and France, either collectively or individually, could inflict an unacceptably destructive blow in retaliation. The strategic equation is further complicated for the USSR by the existence of another entirely independent nuclear force on its eastern flank.

Because of the special facilities required for ballistic missile submarines the location of their bases is easily identifiable and well known to potential opponents, and contemporary surveillance devices such as satellites and electronic monitoring enable their arrival and departure to be closely observed. Their departure is accompanied by characteristic and easily identifiable behaviour by escort vessels as they are checked for noise and magnetic signature and, in many cases, their clip-in towed arrays are fitted. Nor need such surveillance be necessarily confined to sophisticated space-based or electronic monitoring: British SSBNs, for example, have no choice but to leave their Scottish base at Faslane through the narrows at Rhu just north of Helensburgh, in full public view, while French SSBNs have a similar problem leaving Brest.

Having crossed the continental shelf a submarine is able to dive deep and seek shelter in the most suitable layers of the ocean. Early SSBNs, many of which are still in service, had to approach the surface periodically to update their inertial systems, exposing satellite communication antennas to do so, but more recent systems do not need such regular updates. Patrol areas depend on national strategies, geographical factors and, ultimately, the range of the missiles themselves.

Below: USS *Ohio* (SSBN 726) transits the Hood Canal en route to the western Trident submarine base at Bangor, Washington. There are two Trident bases; the other is at King's Bay, Georgia.

Above: *Alexander Brykin*, lead ship of a new class of Soviet SSBN tenders, as depicted by a US DoD artist. Missile replenishment in protected waters will greatly enhance survivability.

Left: A Soviet Delta IV surfaces in the Arctic to launch its SS-N-23 SLBMs. The Arctic has become a major potential battlefield and nuclear submarines roam under the ice-cap as a matter of routine.

Potentially hostile SSBNs are, inevitably, priority targets for opposing anti-submarine forces, even in peacetime. Even so, the dilemmas that would confront the commander of a ballistic missile submarine and a hostile attack submarine tracking it in time of tension – the one facing possible destruction of his deterrent load, the other confronted by the possibility of allowing it to be launched, and neither daring to break off the engagement to communicate with higher authority – are such that it would be a poor navy that did not have standing procedures to deal with the eventuality.

SOVIET STRATEGY

It seems clear that the Soviet Navy, if not the Soviet leadership, regards its ballistic missile submarine fleet as its most important single naval asset, just as it regards the US Navy's SSBN fleet as one of the most critical threats to its own homeland. It would also appear that the Soviet surface fleet has been designed with the primary task of protecting the SSBN fleet, rather than conducting independent forays into the North Atlantic which may nevertheless remain as a secondary task.

The Soviet Navy's early SSBNs, the Yankees, carried missiles whose range necessitated patrols close to the North American seaboard. Many are still in service, as was demonstrated all too clearly as recently as October 1986, when a Yankee was forced to surface following a catastrophic explosion in one of its SS-N-6 missiles some 600nm due north of Bermuda and thus some 750nm from New York and a similar distance from Washington, DC, both well within the 1,600nm range of its missiles. Although the Yankees are inherently vulnerable so close to the US mainland, the very short flight-time of their missiles enables them to threaten time-urgent targets such as the Strategic Air Command bomber bases on or near the Atlantic coast.

Other Soviet SSBNs are concentrated in two areas: the Sea of Okhotsk in the Far East and the Barents Sea in the west of the USSR. The US Navy and its allies are consequently forced to send submarines, surface warships and anti-submarine aircraft into these Soviet-dominated areas.

The original western Soviet SSBN base at Polynarnyi, on the Kola Peninsula, caters for the Yankee and earlier Delta class submarines but appears to be too small for the Typhoon class boats, and a totally new base for them, with protective pens blasted out of the adjacent cliffs, is being built at Gremikha. The Soviet SSBNs in the Far East are based at Petropavlovsk on the Kamchatka Peninsula and at Vladivostok.

Soviet Pacific Fleet Pacific exit

Above: Soviet submarines leaving Vladivostok are forced to transit the Sea of Japan and the Kunashir Passage between Kunashir Island and Hokkaido before they can reach the Pacific. This is one reason why the Soviets retain the Kurile Islands so tenaciously.

US AND ALLIED STRATEGY

The US Navy's ballistic missile submarine fleet is armed with a mix of Poseidon and Trident missiles. With the shorter ranged Polaris and Poseidon missiles some elements of the fleet had to be forward based at Rota in Spain and Holy Loch in Scotland, but with the introduction of Trident it has become possible to pull back to

Above: Crewmen in the control room of USS *Ohio*. Ballistic missile submarines form part of the strategic deterrent, and their crews must face the daily possibility that they may be called on to unleash a nulear holocaust.

Below: HMS *Resolution*, one of the Royal Navy's four current ballistic missile submarines. The British strategic nuclear capability is a major domestic political issue, and while a new class of SSBN is already building at the Vickers yard at Barrow the future cancellation of the programme remains a possibility.

two bases on the coast of the continental USA: Bangor in Washington State and King's Bay, Georgia.

Little information has ever been given about US Navy SSBN patrol areas, but it can be assumed that with Trident and Poseidon missiles maximum use is made of their longer range to enable the submarines to patrol in the Indian, Pacific and Atlantic Oceans, at maximum range from Soviet ports to exacerbate the Soviet anti-submarine problem but still threatening the major industrial and population complexes in the European and Far Eastern USSR.

The British SSBN base is at Faslane, on the Gareloch, off the River Clyde. Four submarines carry out patrols of approximately 70 days each, and the role of their Polaris missiles is publicly stated to be to threaten counter-value strikes against industrial and civilian complexes in European USSR; as the missiles' range is around 2,895nm it can be assumed that their patrol areas will probably be in the northern and western Atlantic. The French SSBNs, based on Brest, are generally similar to their British counterparts and can be assumed to have a similar targeting policy.

CHINESE STRATEGY

China has one operational Xia class SSBN, three more under construction and a further two planned; each carries 12 CSS-N-3 SLBMs. It can be assumed that China's operational deployment policy will be similar to that of France and the UK, but until SLBMs of much greater range are developed only targets in the Soviet Far East can be threatened. There are some very high value strategic targets in this area, although none is critical to the survival of the USSR.

The consequence of China joining the SSBN club is that European USSR is threatened by three seperate nuclear forces, those of the USA, UK and France, and the Far East is threatened by the USA and China, thus adding to the strategic uncertainty facing the Soviet leadership and strengthening deterrence. Each of the other five nuclear powers is only threatened by the USSR. The location of the Chinese SSBN base has not been publicly announced, but is probably in the vicinity of Huludao on the Yellow Sea.

CRUISE MISSILE SUBMARINES

The tactical handling of submarine-launched cruise missiles depends to a large extent upon the mission of the submarine and its weapons. While Soviet cruise missile submarines are intended primarily for use against US Navy carrier-based task groups, American SLCMs have three basic missions: anti-ship, anti-submarine and land attack.

For many years the Soviet Navy's primary task was to deal with the US Navy's aircraft carrier-centred task groups, whose nuclear-capable attack aircraft had the potential to operate against targets deep inside the USSR. The tactical problem was that the submarine needed to fire its missiles from a relatively safe distance – estimated to be about 200nm – while ensuring that they attacked the crucial carrier rather than some much less important target in its protective screen. The answer was to use shore-based radio intercept stations to locate the task groups and signal the information to the submarine and to a naval air station; two Bear-D aircraft would then be sent to find and observe the task group, transmitting radar pictures to the surfaced submarine, whose SS-N-3 sent back its own post-launch radar picture to the launch vessel, where the radar operator matched the two pictures, identified the carrier and informed the missile, which then homed on the designated target.

The system had a number of major shortcomings: the survivability of a pair of Bear-Ds in the vicinity of a US carrier task group would appear to be low, and since the SS-N-3A had the general physical and flying characteristics of an aircraft it is quite likely that it would be brought down by the task group's air defence systems. The submarine was also vulnerable for a relatively lengthy period and would be an ideal target for an anti-submarine aircraft.

The Charlie class submarines are able to launch their SS-N-7 or SS-N-15 anti-ship missiles while submerged, which implies that they are capable of reaching a firing solution based on their sonar and that the missile must have sufficiently sophisticated on-board devices to enable it to home on the appropriate high-value targets without any external inputs. The SS-N-19 carried by Oscar class boats has a range of the order of 250nm, is smaller than its predecessors, flies lower, and probably uses satellite data inputs to provide targeting information.

These missile systems give the Soviet Navy a very effective capability against NATO task groups. In a period of tension SSGNs would shadow NATO fleets, and it would be very difficult for NATO forces to detect and shadow all of them all of the time, so they would possess the initiative, being able to launch at will as hostilities started, while their missiles would be very difficult to counter.

No other navy has an equivalent dedicated cruise missile submarine, although the US Navy now uses the Tomahawk submarine-launched missile in an anti-ship role. The tactics would be similar, with launch taking place

Tomahawk over-the-horizon anti-ship attack profile

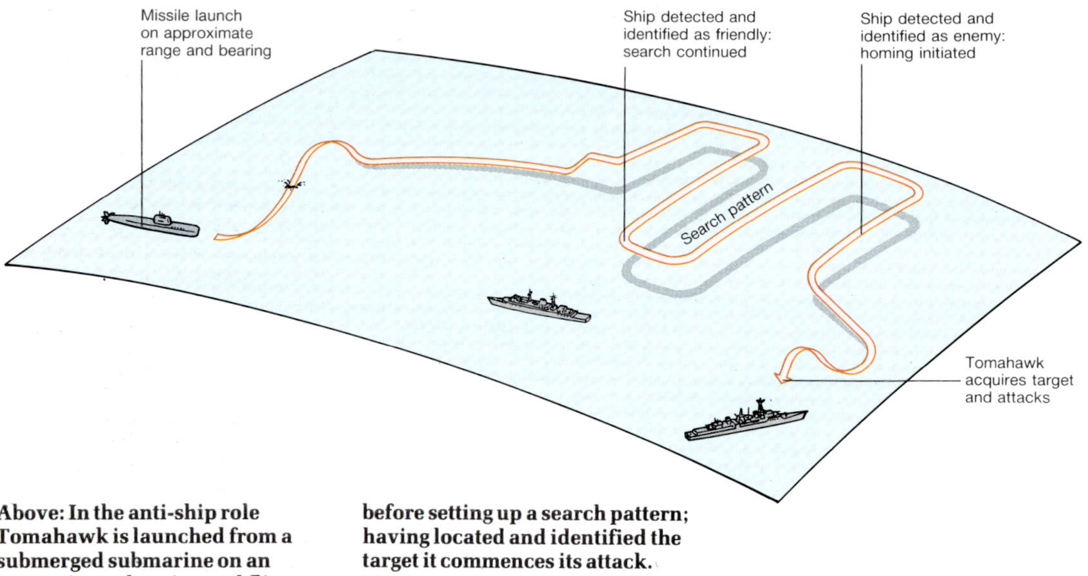

Above: In the anti-ship role Tomahawk is launched from a submerged submarine on an approximate bearing and flies towards the area of the target before setting up a search pattern; having located and identified the target it commences its attack. Maximum range is approximately 330nm (450km).

Above: Views through the periscope of a Dutch Walrus class submarine of a van Speijk class frigate on its attack run during a national exercise. In general terms, submarines can detect and attack surface warships at greater ranges than the ships can detect and attack them, unless the ships carry ASW helicopters.

Right: The ability of a submerged submarine to reach the torpedo danger zone (TDZ) of a surface target depends on the speed and bearing of the target and the submarine's own speed. For example, if the target is proceeding at 21 knots, then a 9-knot submarine can reach a launching position on the TDZ only if her initial position is within 38° of the target's bows, while a 15-knot submarine can approach from a larger area and an angle of up to 64°. A diesel submarine's battery endurance reduces rapidly with speed.

Submarine approach areas

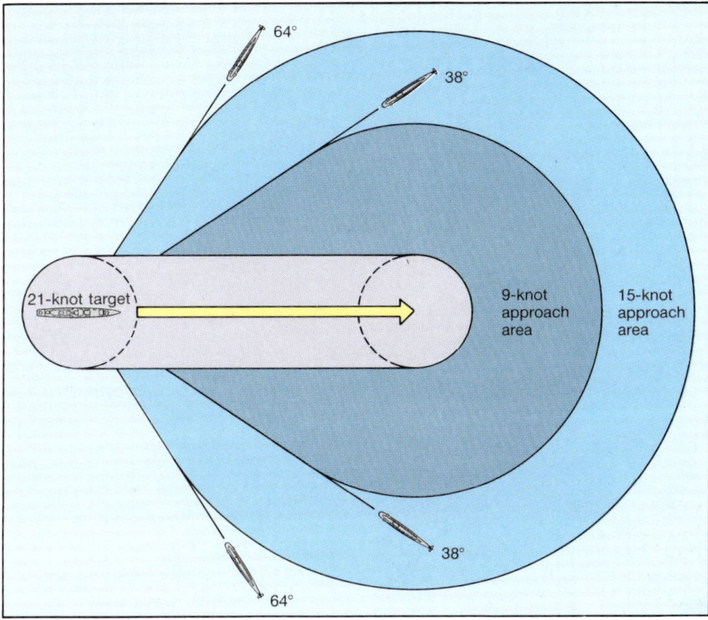

Tigerfish tactical employment

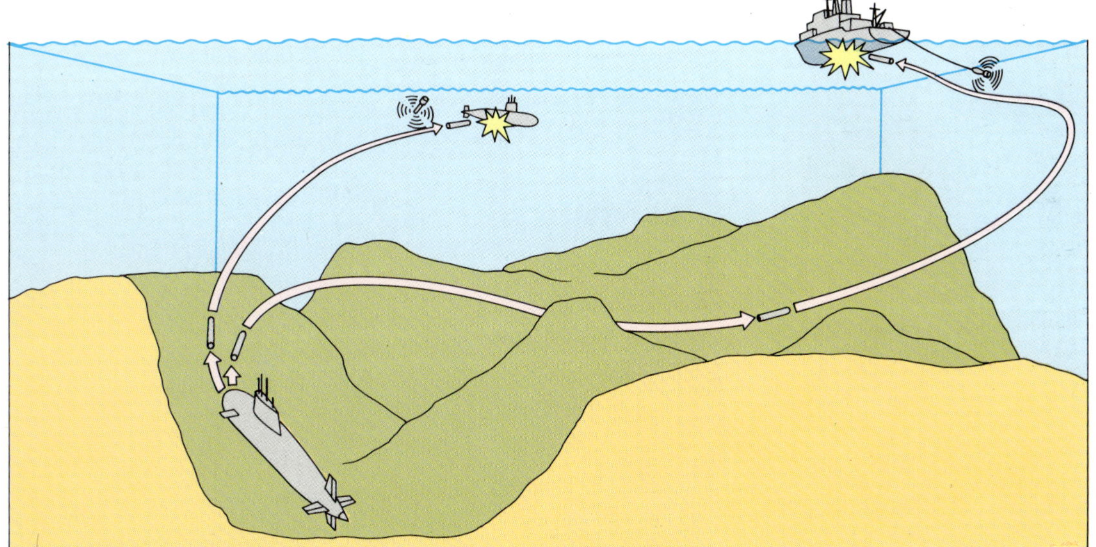

Left: A Soviet Victor III SSN shows the unique rudder-mounted pod whose function has not been published in the West. The ability of such vessels to travel at high speed, manoeuvre at high rates and remain submerged for protracted periods means the era of the submarine dogfight is here.

Above: An underwater ambush using the terrain of the sea-bed to hide the presence of a submarine is now a feasible operation. The scenario depicted here utilises the tactical flexibility of the Marconi Tigerfish torpedo to show how surprise attacks could be carried out against surface or submerged targets. This weapon uses wire guidance in the initial stages of the attack up to the point where the torpedo's on-board active/passive 3D sonar homing system can assume autonomous control for the final run to the target; the on-board computer helps it avoid seduction by noise-makers.

from behind the horizon against a high-value Soviet target such as a Kiev class carrier or a Kirov class battlecruiser.

ATTACK SUBMARINE TACTICS

Attack submarines, whether nuclear or diesel-electric powered, can be used for a variety of missions, including operating as escorts to friendly SSBNs; carrying out barrier patrols in the approaches to choke points; keeping clear ocean lanes for task groups or convoys; acting as part of the screen for such task groups or convoys; following up contacts made by other means, such as SOSUS; pursuing independent missions against specific targets such as hostile SSBNs in sanctuaries; and conducting general ocean search.

In a barrier patrol a submarine is likely to operate at very low speed with its sensors in the passive mode. It would normally only use its sensors actively to give a final confirmation of a target's range and bearing, perhaps with a single pulse which would certainly alert the target but without giving away the range and direction of the threat. The problem for the hunter is that if he cannot detect any possible targets he will want to move to another area, which normally involves the possibility of detection. Many submarines, therefore, adopt sprint-and-drift tactics, moving at maximum speed to the new area and then returning to a silent search mode.

A further dilemma for the submarine captain is that while his survival depends on remaining undetected, his role as an attack submarine is to sink hostile submarines or surface vessels and a successful attack immediately confirms his presence.

CLANDESTINE OPERATIONS

Because they can move about the oceans and approach hostile coasts unseen, submarines have long been used for clandestine operations such as the delivery and retrieval of men to and from the shore and ferrying miniature submarines or submersibles to the vicinity of their targets. The US Navy, in particular, has found submarines ideal for such operations, especially in the wide reaches of the Pacific, and in World War II its submarines were used both to transport raiding parties and to deliver supplies to guerrilla forces. In August 1942 the converted minelayer *Argonaut*, along with the *Nautilus*, delivered a raiding party of no fewer than 211 marines to Makin Island in the Gilbert Archipelago, where they killed all 70 members of the Japanese garrison and destroyed a seaplane base. In another raid on May 11, 1943, *Nautilus* and *Narwhal* delivered a different unit to Attu Atoll with equal success. The British also used submarines effectively on clandestine operations, both around the coasts of Nazi-occupied Europe and in South-East Asia.

The Italian Navy made excellent use of its submarines to deliver miniature submarines and frogmen to the vicinity of enemy bases. Two boats of the Adua class were converted to carry watertight containers for three assault craft, and two Flutto class boats had four such containers; trials were also carried out with miniature submarines intended for use against ports in Africa and America, and the submarine *Da Vinci* was temporarily converted to carry one on the foredeck. Using such underwater craft the Italian Navy sank or seriously damaged some 63,000 tons of warships and 50,000 tons of merchant shipping.

Since the war many navies have used submarines for covert missions. Virtually any attack or patrol submarine can be used for such purposes, but diesel-electric submarines have proved particularly suitable because of their exceptional underwater quietness. The two largest navies are, however, able to afford specialised submarines for these tasks.

The Soviet Navy frequently uses its large fleet of diesel-electric submarines for covert tasks and considerable resources are devoted to such missions, and in 1981 a Soviet Whiskey class submarine ran aground off the Swedish Kalskrona naval base.

It would appear that any task which has to be performed outside the parent submarine is carried out by men of the naval Spetsnaz units. These Spetsnaz units receive high priority for equipment, the vast majority of which is kept very secret in the usual Soviet way, but one important type of equipment which has recently become public knowledge in the West is the tracked miniature submarines used by naval Spetsnaz units in a blatant reconnaissance of the Swedish naval bases in the Stockholm archipelago in October 1982. These vessels have twin tracks and large single propellers and are taken to the vicinity of their targets by mother-ships, probably the India class submarines which had previously been thought to be intended solely for underwater rescue missions.

Incredibly, it subsequently came to light that a photograph of these

Above: A Royal Navy rating working at a plotting board on board HMS *Trafalgar*. Lacking visual references, submarine crews must maintain and continually update a three-dimensional picture of the tactical environment utilising inputs from all available sensors.

Saab ELMA ASW system

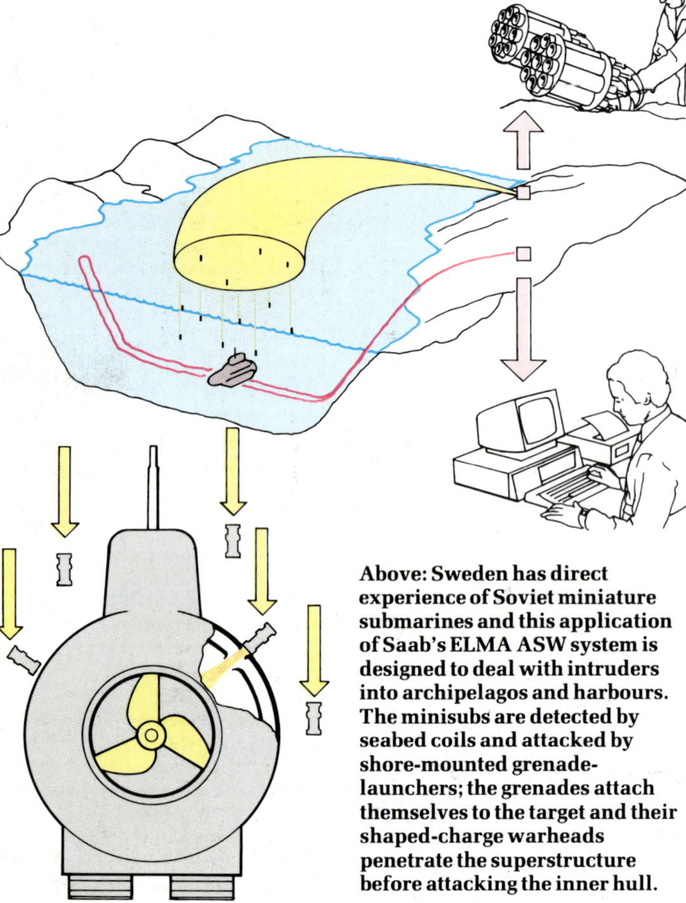

Above: Sweden has direct experience of Soviet miniature submarines and this application of Saab's ELMA ASW system is designed to deal with intruders into archipelagos and harbours. The minisubs are detected by seabed coils and attacked by shore-mounted grenade-launchers; the grenades attach themselves to the target and their shaped-charge warheads penetrate the superstructure before attacking the inner hull.

Below: This Marconi 360° area defence sonar is designed to detect intruders into harbours, landing sites and other sensitive zones. Frequency can be varied for detection of divers or small submersibles, and the sonar can be integrated with night vision devices in a coherent system.

tracked mini-subs was openly published in Pravda in the mid-1970s; they were said by the Soviet authorities to be in use for a search for the lost city of Atlantis, a somewhat fanciful explanation. Unfortunately, nobody in the West seems to have appreciated their possible military significance. Such mini-submarines could be put to a number of uses apart from reconnaissance, such as laying nuclear mines at the exit points from NATO nuclear submarine bases and interfering with NATO seabed installations such as the SOSUS network. One question that inevitably arises is whether other reconnaissance missions have been carried out by these machines – could they, for example, have reconnoitred the British nuclear submarine base at Faslane in Scotland, the French base at Brest, or the many US naval bases?

The British Royal Marines include the Special Boat Squadron, which has over 40 years' experience of operating from submarines, and has in the past few years seen service in Oman and Borneo as well as in the South Atlantic War of 1982. In the last conflict one SBS unit flew from the UK in a C-130 and then parachuted to a submarine in the South Atlantic; this took them to South Georgia, where they were the first British troops ashore. A Royal Navy diesel-electric submarine, HMS *Onyx*, operated in the area throughout the conflict and is probably the boat which undertook most of the clandestine operations. The Army's Special Air Service (SAS) is also believed to have at least one unit capable of operating from submarines, but the Royal Navy has no specialised submarines for these tasks, finding its normal diesel-electric submarines adequate.

Above: The amphibious transport submarine USS *Grayback* (LPSS 574). Capable of carrying 67 swimmers, she has been replaced by two former SSBNs, *Sam Houston* and *John Marshall*.

Below: US Navy two-man Swimmer Delivery Vehicle operated by an Underwater Demolotion Team (UDT). UDTs are combined with SEALs in two Special Warfare groups.

US Navy amphibious units include two types of special forces: Underwater Demolition Teams (UDT) and Sea-Air-Land (SEAL) teams. UDTs were raised in World War II: they perform the traditional beach reconnaissance missions as well as destroying specific targets such as roads and bridges in coastal areas and carrying out underwater demolitions. All potential members of SEAL teams come from the ranks of the UDTs and they receive special training to prepare them for their new tasks. This advanced training is needed because they are expected to operate with little support and in restricted waters or on land in a combat environment where they may become involved in encounters with enemy forces.

To fulfil their mission SEALs may be carried to the hostile shoreline by submarine and disembark either on the surface or underwater. Each SEAL team comprises 27 officers and 156 enlisted men formed into five platoons, each capable of independent operations. SEAL teams can be expected to carry out similar tasks to the submarine-borne special warfare units of other nations, including reconnaissance, sabotage and demolition. In the conventional phase of a future war they could be used to reconnoitre hostile nuclear installations such as SSBN bases, and to destroy them or inhibit their use in the nuclear phase.

Following its successful use of submarines in raiding operations during World War II the US Navy has always maintained a few transport submarines in service. USS *Grayback*, built as a cruise missile carrier, was converted in 1967 to carry seven officers and 60 troopers and was home-based at Subic Bay in the Philippines, which clearly brought the coastline of most of Asia within her range. The latest move is to convert two former SSBNs of the Ethan Allen class, *Sam Houston* and *John Marshall*, to this role, with cement ballast in the missile tubes and missile-related electronics removed. With virtually unlimited range and operating depths exceeding 984ft (300m), they carry the same passenger load as the *Grayback*, though presumably in greater comfort and for longer distances, and with the potential for a greater amount of specialised equipment to be carried on board.

Antisubmarine Tactics

Anti-submarine warfare can be divided into four capability areas according to the platform type and mission – submarine, surface, airborne and surveillance – but each involves similar difficulties, the greatest and most intractable of which is the nature of the ocean itself. If submarines have problems, their enemies, the anti-submarine forces, have an even harder time.

A typical anti-submarine engagement goes through six stages: search, contact, approach, attack, close combat and disengagement. The search may be either general, as part of the protective measures for a convoy or surface group, or directed by information gained from other sensors, such as SOSUS or satellites. The search phase will usually be carried out by the hunting platform – aircraft, surface warship, or submarine – as a patrol following a general search pattern, or as a component of a task group in a designated area. In the latter case, both surface ships and submarines are faced with the problem that the ideal speed of the group may well be greater than the optimum search speed. At this stage, also, the hunter needs to avoid detection, so wherever possible he will use passive sensors coupled with inputs from other platforms.

Contact comprises two elements, detection and classification. Detection is the indication that a possible target is actually in the search area; it will usually be accompanied by a general bearing and followed by classification, the refining process which seeks to confirm that the contact really is a submarine and not a merchant ship, whale or other harmless object, and then to identify it. Examination of the contact's acoustic signature and comparison with the hunter's data bank can lead not only to a broad classification but also to type, class and even, under certain circumstances and with modern equipment, an individual submarine. The approach stage begins with tracking, ideally accomplished by passive means to avoid alerting the target, followed

Variable-depth sonar advantages

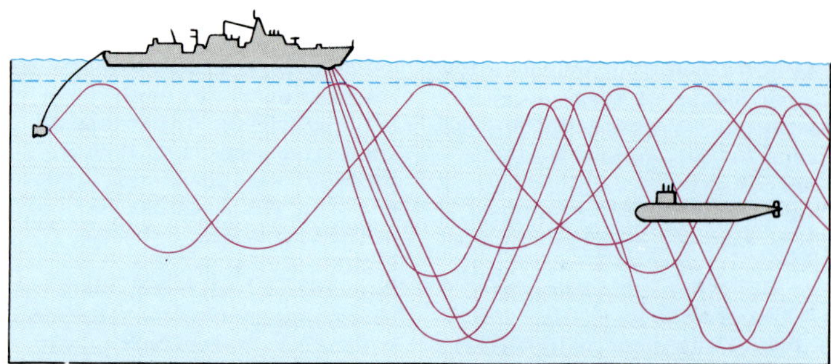

Above: Bow-mounted arrays suffer a number of problems: own-ship noise, pitch due to ship motion and possible shadow zones. Many of these can be overcome by a variable-depth sonar, which operates below the surface layer, where it is separated from own-ship noise and avoids shadow zones.

Below: HMS *Phoebe* with her Westland Lynx ASW helicopter, the winch for her Type 2031 towed sonar array and port triple STWS torpedo tubes clearly shown.

Above: HMCS *Iroquois* (DDH-280) with one of her two CHSS-4 Sea Kings on the flight-deck and, at the stern, the SQS-505 variable-depth sonar. Although surface-to-surface and surface-to-air weapon systems will be replaced under a modernisation programme, the antisubmarine systems will be retained.

Asroc fire control

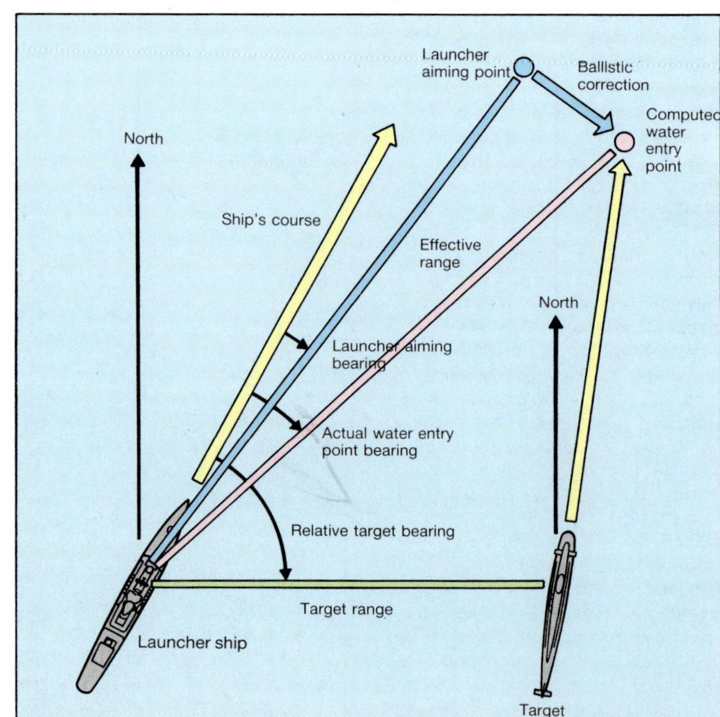

Above: The US Navy's Underwater Battery Fire Control System (UBFCS) Mk 114 for Asroc computes the relative speeds and positions of the launch ship and underwater target then aims the missile on a course which will bring it to the optimum water entry point, having compensated for ship pitch and roll and wind.

by localization, when the hunter manoeuvres into an attacking position.

In the culmination of the hunt, the attack stage, the hunter must be able to launch its weapons with a fair degree of confidence that the target will be hit, and the primary cause of uncertainty for most navies is weapon, especially torpedo, performance. Consequently, normal submarine practice is to fire torpedoes at about half their theoretical effective range, nominally about 10 or 12 nautical miles, which in relative terms is very close indeed. Even though most modern torpedoes carry their own acoustic sensors, and many have wire-guidance links back to the launcher, there are still many limitations which affect their chances of a successful engagement.

If the initial attack is a failure a close-combat phase ensues in which the protagonists seek to eliminate one another. In the case of submarine-versus-submarine engagements this resembles two fighter aircraft wheeling and manoeuvring in a dog-fight, identifying and evading hostile weapons while trying all the time to deliver the fatal blow themselves. This is the one phase of anti-submarine warfare in which the mechanical excellence of the submarine is the primary factor.

The final stage – disengagement – takes place in a return to the previous conditions of quiet, undetected operation, and a resumption of the search phase.

SURFACE ASW

The aim of anti-submarine warfare, to deny the enemy the effective use of his submarines, can be achieved either by destroying the vessels or by adopting tactics and manoeuvres that render their operations ineffective. Of all the types of naval warfare this is the one that most occupies the thinking of contemporary naval strategists and tacticians. New ASW platforms, weapon systems and sensors are continuously being developed and the majority of today's navies devote the major part of their expenditure to this discipline.

Modern attack submarines have two main roles: first, to search for and destroy enemy surface vessels, both warships and civilian, and secondly to attack other submarines. To achieve these ends effectively, they are fast, able to take maximum advantage of ambient oceanic conditions by operating effectively at various depths, and capable of spending prolonged periods at sea without outside support. Most importantly, they are fitted with detection systems capable of locating targets at considerable distances and carry weapons that are able to destroy their enemies with the minimum risk to themselves. All these qualities contribute to the submarine's greatest asset, its

Submarine sensor and weapon systems

Below: Plessey outline of a typical submarine sensor and weapon control fit. Inputs from acoustic, radio-frequency, optical and imaging sensors are recorded and displayed, along with other data, in the command and control centre, and used for navigation, target acquisition and surveillance and fire control. Expendable buoys would be used to supplement the mast-mounted communications antennas, and electronic support measures (ESM) provide air or surface threat warning.

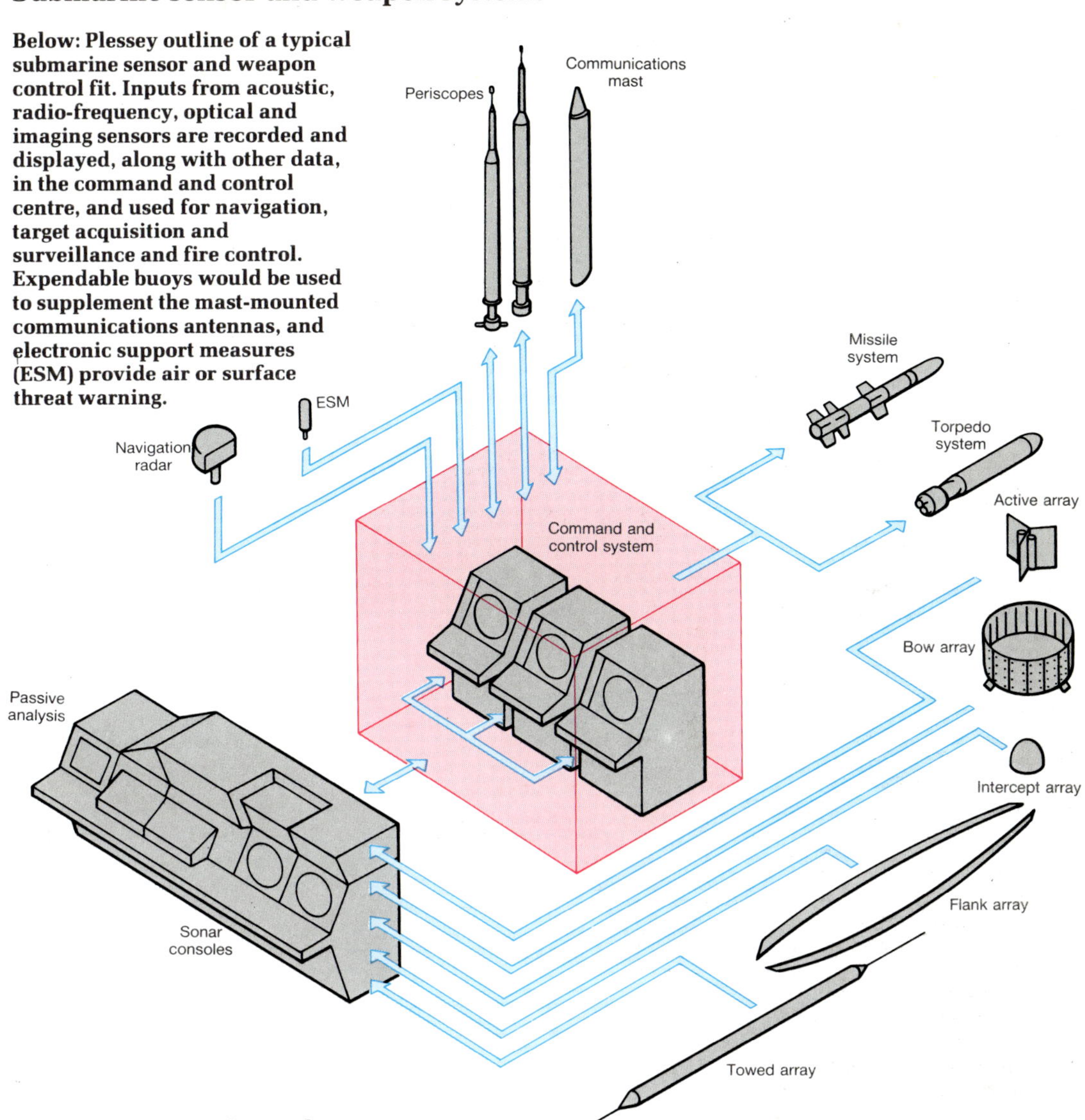

Stingray tactical employment

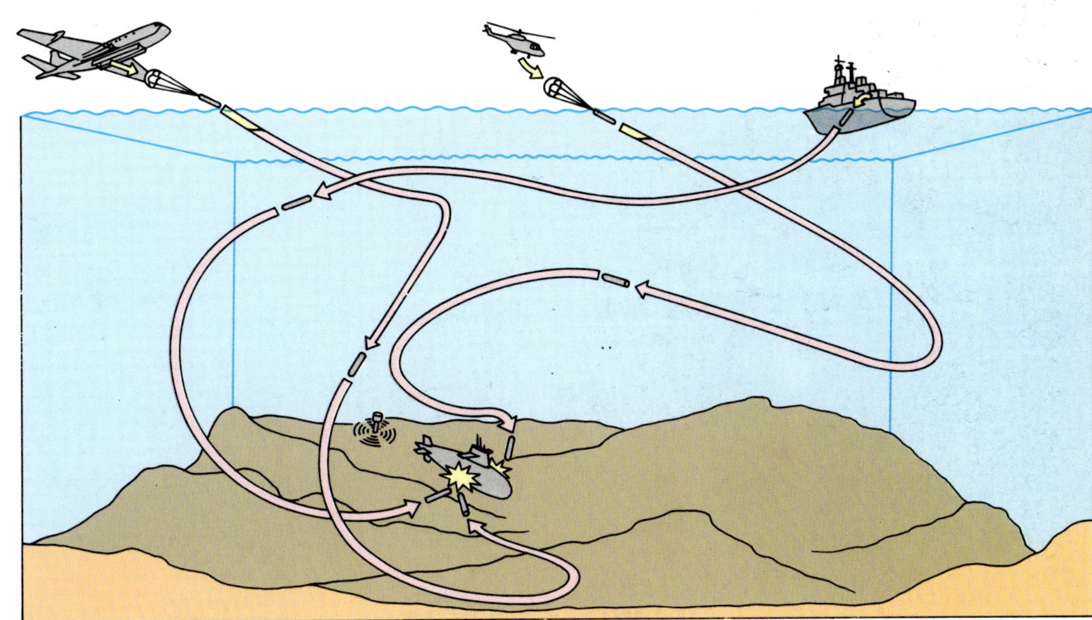

Above: The Marconi Stingray lightweight antisubmarine torpedo can be launched from fixed-wing aircraft such as the Nimrod depicted here, ship-based helicopters or surface vessels. Because it is inert until it reaches the water – normally stabilised by a parachute – it can be launched immediately a target is detected, which in the case of MAD detection systems is essential, and its on-board computer can discriminate between its target and expendable decoys.

ability to remain undetected, and make it an increasingly difficult target for surface ships.

The parallel development of nuclear power and the streamlined Albacore-type hull have enhanced submarine performance to the point where there are serious doubts about the ability of surface ships to detect SSNs before they attack. In the view of many, the most effective weapon to use against a submarine is another submarine, since it works and fights in the same environment and is therefore able to take advantage of the unique peculiarities of the sub-surface world, and SSNs have come to be used in support of surface forces. Nevertheless, surface task forces must be capable of their own effective ASW operations.

Traditionally, and especially during World War II, captains of anti-submarine ships have set great store by identifying with the thoughts of their opponents. Great stress was placed on knowing how submarines were fought, to the extent that the strengths and weaknesses of individual submarine captains were carefully assessed and their particular tactics were studied in great detail. In a modern ASW action this type of mental battle may still be significant, though it may be more difficult for a modern captain, comfortable and warm in his operations room surrounded by electronic plots, digital radar displays, the glow of dulled red lighting and the constant chatter of voice nets on headsets, to project his thoughts into the thinking of the submarine captain. Nevertheless, it remains important to make the attempt. 'Know your enemy' is a philosophy that serves the military commander well.

Above: One of the most effective of current ASW helicopters, the Royal Navy's Sea King can use radar, dipping sonar or sonobuoys such as the one seen here on its way down, to detect and locate hostile submarines. A squadron of nine of these aircraft operates from each of the RN's ASW carriers and one is usually operational from each of the Fort Grange class RFAs.

Right: A crewman aboard a Royal Navy Sea King prepares to let go a passive sonobuoy. The buoys are laid in patterns, the return signals being analysed to give a precise fix on a target.

There are few commanders at sea today in any navy who have had the experience of actually hunting a submarine in a hostile environment with the ultimate intention of sinking it. There are, of course, exceptions: both the British and Argentinian navies gained some invaluable experience in the South Atlantic War of 1982, and live anti-submarine operations were also conducted during the Indo-Pakistan war of 1969. It should not be forgotten, however, that, virtually alone among military activities, ASW and counter-ASW tactics can be tested on the high seas between the opposing forces in peacetime with a relatively low risk of escalation, albeit without the intention or the likelihood of destruction.

Submarines still use some of the old techniques, especially those that are enhanced by the speed of the modern boats. One example is the sprint-and-drift tactic, in which a nuclear submarine makes a noisy high-speed dash followed by a period of total silence as it drifts towards its target.

DEFENCE OF SURFACE FORCES

There are two basic situations in surface ASW: the defence of purely military forces and the protection of merchant shipping. The main areas of naval conflict in any future war are likely to be the North Atlantic – particularly the Norwegian Sea – the Baltic and the Mediterranean as far as NATO and the Warsaw Pact are concerned, and the northern and central Pacific in a conflict involving the

Task force protective screen

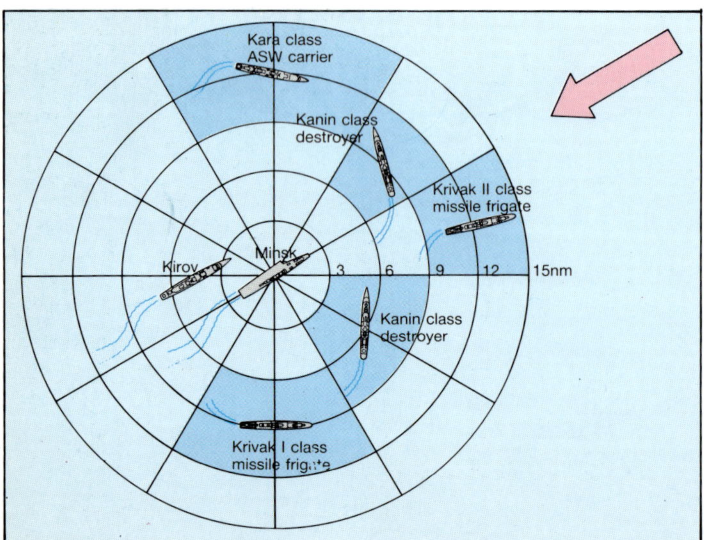

Above: Typical disposition of a Soviet task force, with the main body (*Minsk* and *Kirov*) changing course every few minutes to reduce the submarine threat, while the outlying escorts are allocated patrol sectors of some 60-72sq miles (155-185km²) each.

ASH-3H ASW mission profile

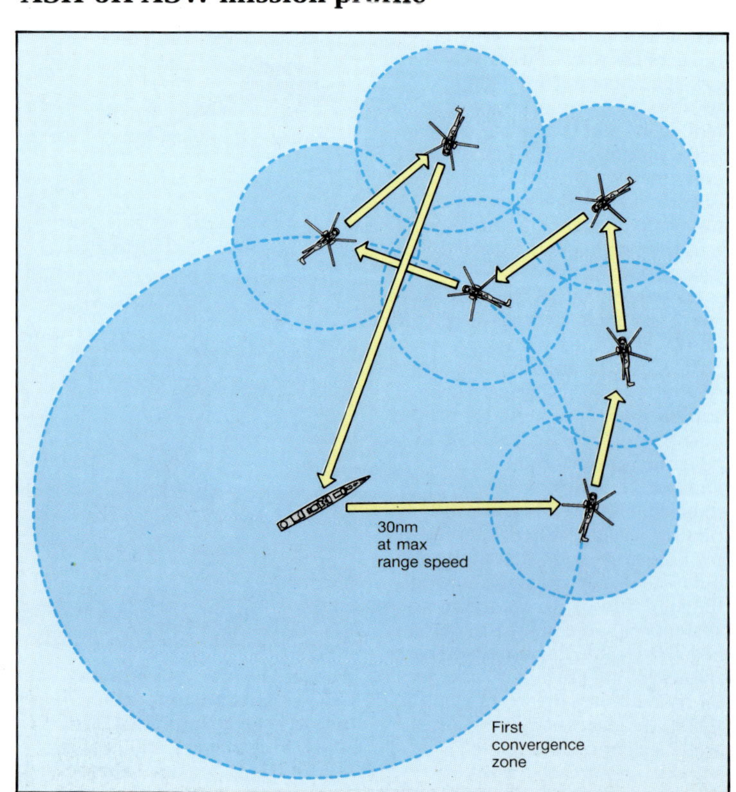

Right: With a total time on station of 3hr 40min an Italian Navy Sea King can spend half its time hovering to deploy its AQS-18 sonar, which has a maximum range scale of 20,000 yards (18,500m), and half transiting at max endurance speed.

USA and its allies and the USSR.

It is important to consider how a large task force would proceed. The concept of the protective screen around the main body is all-important, as it seeks to ensure that the specialisation of each unit, whether surface or airborne, can be exploited to the full. In the inner protection zone are the active-sonar frigates and helicopters and to allow control and to ensure that the area is fully sanitised each vessel and helicopter is given a defensive sector, normally of about 60-72 square miles in area, and each ship manoeuvres constantly to deny attacking submarines the information they need to set up a firing solution for their weapons. Ships use mainly hull-mounted sonars, while many units, particularly the larger ones, tow noise-makers to decoy any possible acoustic torpedo attack.

Outside this inner zone, the next area is patrolled by ships and aircraft using passive sonar devices. Surface ships use towed arrays such as the American TACTAS system, while helicopters are more likely to use sonobuoys because of their passive capabilities and their ability to cover wider sectors than dipping sonars. Next comes the outer zone where, well in advance of the main body, long-range maritime patrol (LRMP) aircraft utilise the full range of detection devices, including radar, both directional and non-directional sonobuoys, MAD and the Mark 1 eyeball to feed constant information into the aircraft's computer system. Such aircraft are armed with torpedoes, missiles and depth charges for

Above: Inside an RN Sea King, with the control panel for the Type 195 dipping sonar on the right and the sonobuoy operator's position on the left. An advanced processing and display system helps streamline operations.

Below: A Soviet Navy Mi-14 Haze ASW helicopter approaches a Kashin class destroyer. The Mi-14 is not normally seen operating from ships, but deploys from land bases. It has a chin-mounted search radar and a MAD bird, and almost certainly uses sonobuoys.

prosecuting an attack if a submarine is detected.

Further out still are the hunter-killer nuclear-powered submarines, well away from their own surface units and the noise of their cavitating propellers, where they are free to manoeuvre. Commanders of such submarines must be able to assume that anything detected moving is an enemy. With the main body carrying out a zigzag course astern of them, restricting its overall speed of advance to probably no more than about 10 knots, the SSN is able to make the most of its speed advantage to cover large areas of sea, although the higher its speed the greater is its noise and consequently the possibility of its detection by an enemy.

With such a screen around him, the task force commander proceeds towards his objective. He must be constantly aware of all the information available to him, both from his own forces and from external sources such as satellite surveillance and intelligence reports, and possible submarine contacts near the main body will demand instant reaction. Attacks can be carried out by a variety of weapons, depending on the target's distance from the fleet: submarines at more than five miles would be dealt with either by helicopters using homing torpedoes or by ships released from their sectors to form a coordinated and independent attack unit. Such attacks would probably proceed according to general pre-planned tactics, with each ship operating within a designated sector based around the submarine's suspected datum. Frigates and destroyers in this situation would launch their helicopters armed with torpedoes.

It must be remembered that positive sonar contact with submarines is notoriously difficult to establish. Ships can search in vain for a long time, either because the contact was spurious in the first place or because the enemy submarine has managed to slip

Countermeasures to torpedo attack

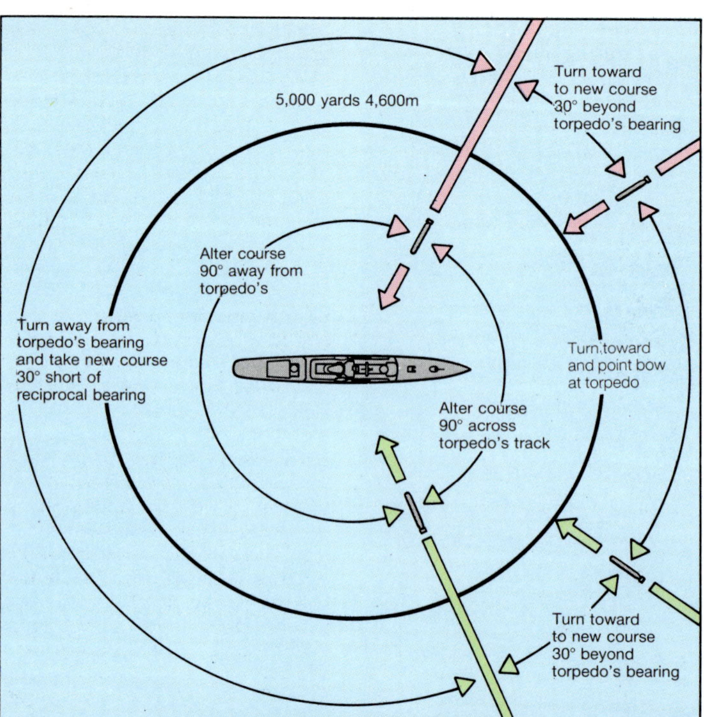

Left: A submarine's aim is to present a surface ship with a situation where it cannot evade an incoming torpedo. Surface ships must take immediate evasive action on detecting a torpedo to have any change of success, and manoeuvres must be carried out at full speed, as the time available is short – indeed, a 45-knot torpedo detected at 5,000 yards (4,600m) is just 200 seconds from impact, so any evasive manoeuvre must be a virtual reflex action. The ship's aim is to present incoming weapons with the narrowest profile, while also displacing the ship's position as rapidly as possible. If a torpedo is detected at less than 5,000 yards the manoeuvres are slightly different, as there is even less time. The exception to these tactics is if the ship is towing a noise-maker, when an injudicious turn could place the ship between the decoy and the torpedo. Technology is making evasion by surface ships more difficult: many modern torpedoes have wire-guided, acoustic and non-acoustic modes, as well as on-board computers.

Above: Royal Navy frigate HMS *Andromeda* demonstrating her manoeuvrability. Warships need good sensors to detect torpedoes as far out as possible, but quick reactions, high speed and turning ability are also essential to successful evasive actions, and the modified broad-beam Leander is considered to be one of the best.

Task force reaction to submarine contact

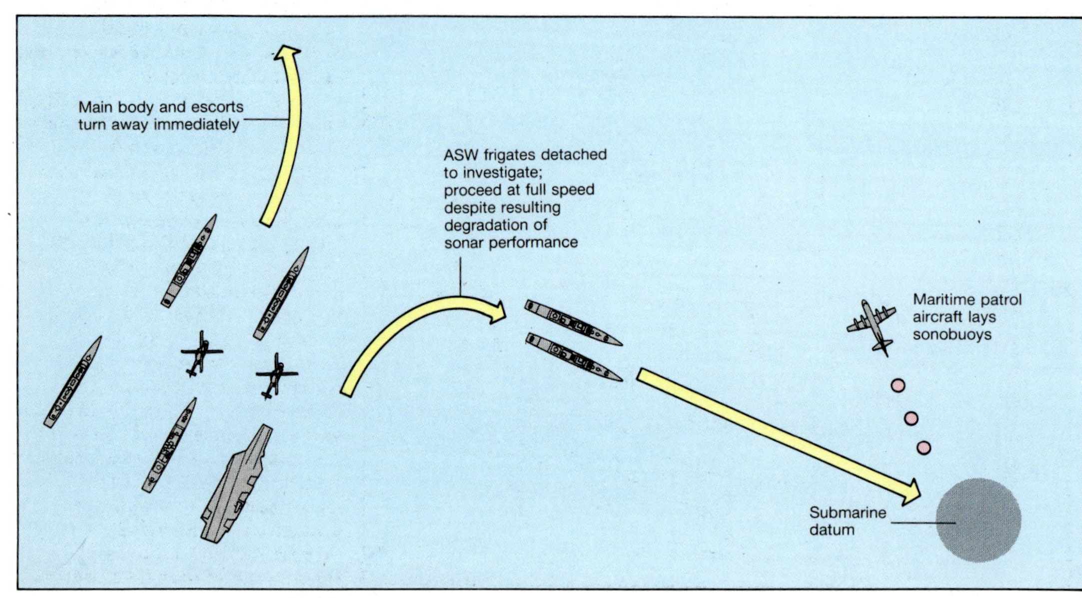

Left: If a submarine is detected approaching a task force and assessed as representing a possible threat, the task force will investigate and seek to destroy it. The most likely immediate reaction of the surface group commander would be to turn the main body away from the direction of the threat while at the same time detaching suitable ASW units – ships or aircraft – to proceed at full speed towards the enemy submarine's estimated position.

away undetected; its commander is, after all, more interested in attacking the main body than the patrolling frigates.

As soon as a submarine contact is made by any unit in the task force, the main body will turn away from the estimated position of the enemy vessel, and at all times zig-zag plans will be maintained. Normally such plans are predetermined, though they can also be varied by the local commander to take account of existing tactical conditions; based on the desired course to be made good, they will allow the ships of the group to alter course together without any further signal communication, and plans can be drawn up to take account of the estimated capabilities of particular types of enemy submarine. Vessels out in the screen, however, are unlikely to follow pre-set zig-zag patterns, though they would need to know the manoeuvres of the main body in order to maintain their correct station.

DANGER ZONES

Obviously, the force commander cannot afford to take evasive action every time a submarine contact is reported. Instead, he will normally have to establish areas of danger relevant to the main body, based on his estimate of the capabilities and tactics of the enemy's submarines. For example, even a nuclear submarine commander will prefer to be ahead of his target when he prepares for an attack, and he will have to close to within range of its weapons, two considerations which set certain limits on its area of manoeuvre, and the surface commander can estimate this area, normally referred to as limited lines of submerged approach. Such estimates clearly contain an element of risk, but so do most tactical decisions, and unless he is to manoeuvre his ships all over the sea the naval commander has little option but to make informed guesses. Within these lines can be estimated the torpedo danger zone, and certain defensive actions can then be planned for implementation if a submarine is detected in any given area.

The development of the high-speed, deep-running, well protected submarine has led to demands for ASW weapons with much greater destructive power than the lightweight torpedo, which is simply too small to carry a useful warhead. The nuclear powers have therefore developed nuclear depth bombs capable of being carried by long-range maritime patrol aircraft, ship-borne helicopters and surface ships, which need only be dropped in the vicinity of the submarine to produce a kill. By their very nature, such small nuclear devices exploded underwater produce little or no nuclear fallout, but their use is likely to be restricted by political considerations as well as by the more obvious concern of a commander for the safety of his own submarines.

Norway is of crucial strategic importance to both NATO and the Warsaw Pact. It is important in NATO strategy because it stretches northward toward the Soviet Union's main Atlantic naval bases, and it is of prime importance to the Russians since it could provide forward bases from which ships and aircraft could easily harass trans-Atlantic support for the Western Alliance. In a World War III scenario control of the Norwegian Sea, which measures approximately 1,000nm by 800nm, would probably be one of the major areas for naval engagements, and naval forces would have to secure the lines of communication across this sea in support of land and air forces fighting the battle ashore.

Tactically, this could be achieved in two ways: by saturating the area with aircraft and ships and accepting the consequences of a set-piece battle; or by attempting to disrupt the enemy's plans for concentration by keeping forces widely dispersed with greater latitude for manoeuvre, a course more likely to

Limiting lines of submerged approach

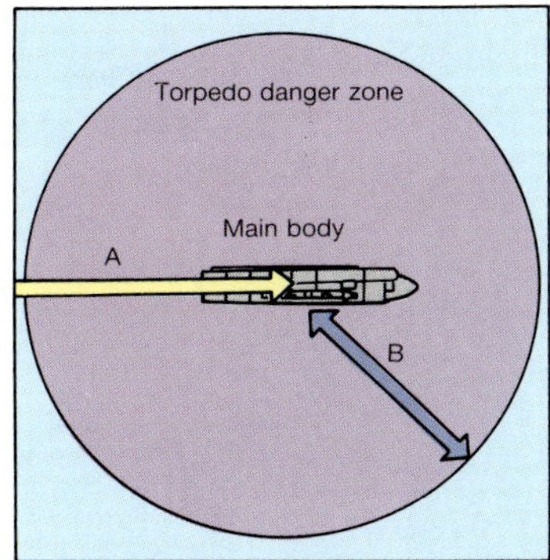

Left: Submarines pose a continuing threat to any body of surface ships and surface group commanders must be prepared to make instant decisions on whether or not detected submarines pose immediate threats to their forces. A set of criteria for assessing potential threats have therefore been established. These are normally represented as the limiting lines of submerged approach; previously produced as overlays on plotting tables, they are computerised on modern warships so that an assessment can be presented instantly on a commander's attack information screen. The first step is to plot an advanced position based on the centre of the main body and allowing for the running time of an attack torpedo (A). Around this advanced point, a circle designated the Torpedo Danger Zone is created; its radius (B) is the range at which it is anticipated that torpedoes would be fired. This circle advances with the main body.

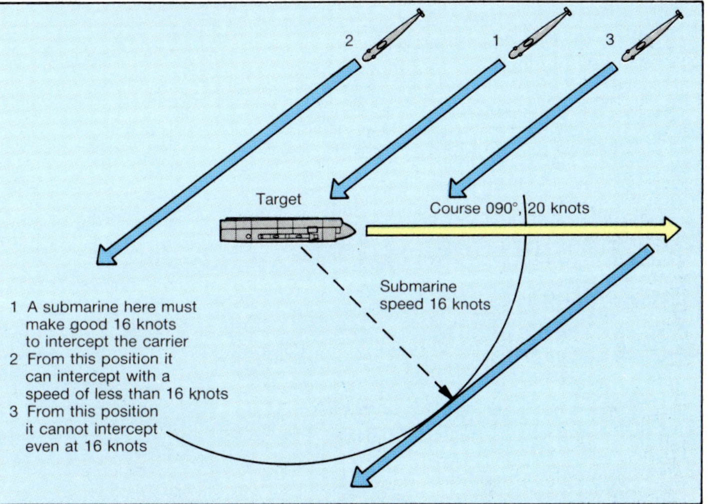

Left: To assess whether a detected submarine can actually intercept the main body some assumptions have to be made. Although the maximum speeds of different types of submarines vary, during an attack a submarine will always proceeds as slowly as possible to minimise noise and so reduce the risk of detection. Once the speed has been estimated, an arc with this speed as its radius can be drawn (16 knots in this example), and at the same time the main body's course and speed can be plotted (090°, 20 knots). A line drawn from the 20nm mark as a tangent to the arc of the submarine's speed gives the relative course the submarine must make good at 16 knots.

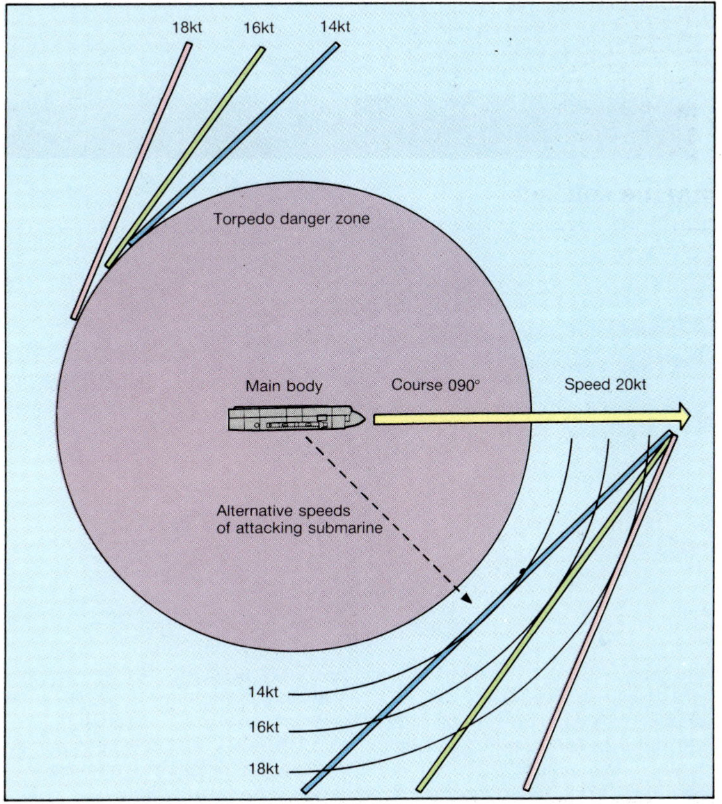

Left: In fact, that the submarine does not actually have to intercept the ship directly in order to reach an attacking position – it needs only manouevre to within torpedo range. In practice, therefore, the two diagrams above are combined as shown here. In addition, several relative courses can be prepared to cover differing submarine speeds – in this example, 14, 16 and 18 knots – and instead of drawing the submarine's relative course direct to the aircraft carrier at the centre it can now be drawn to the periphery of the torpedo danger zone. It can be seen that any detected submarine with an estimated speed of less than 18 knots and a position to the right of the relative courses drawn represents a threat to the carrier. It is also possible to estimate the limitations on the courses a submarine would have to steer from its detected position to close the carrier, thus enabling the force commander to decide with some accuracy where to place his airborne units for maximum protection. (Note that the submarine tracks shown are relative rather than true courses.)

The GIUK gap: NATO's ASW barrier and the Soviet response

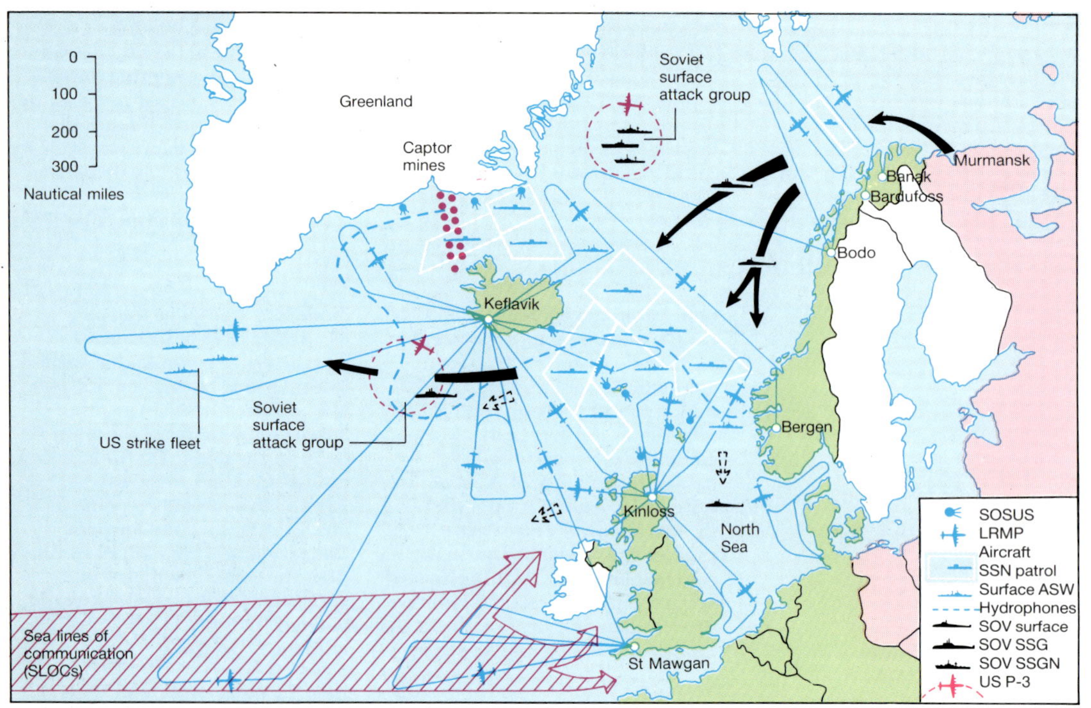

Left: Should an East-West conflict start ships and submarines from the Soviet Northern Fleet could be expected to attempt to break out of northern waters into the Atlantic through the Greenland-Iceland-UK (GIUK) gap and into the North Sea, while submarines and surface vessels would also attempt to reach the North Sea through the Skagerrak. These sea passages are designated choke points by NATO, and a great deal of effort has been put into attempting to seal them. They would be covered by a series of layers involving antisubmarine aircraft, fixed monitoring devices such as SOSUS and patrolling submarines. Further, during a period of rising tension US and European strike fleets could be expected to enter the area. This map, taken from Soviet sources, shows a possible NATO deployment. It should be noted that NATO long-range maritime patrol aircraft would be expected not only to cover the choke points but also to support strike fleets shadow Soviet surface groups.

Soviet Summerex 85 naval exercise

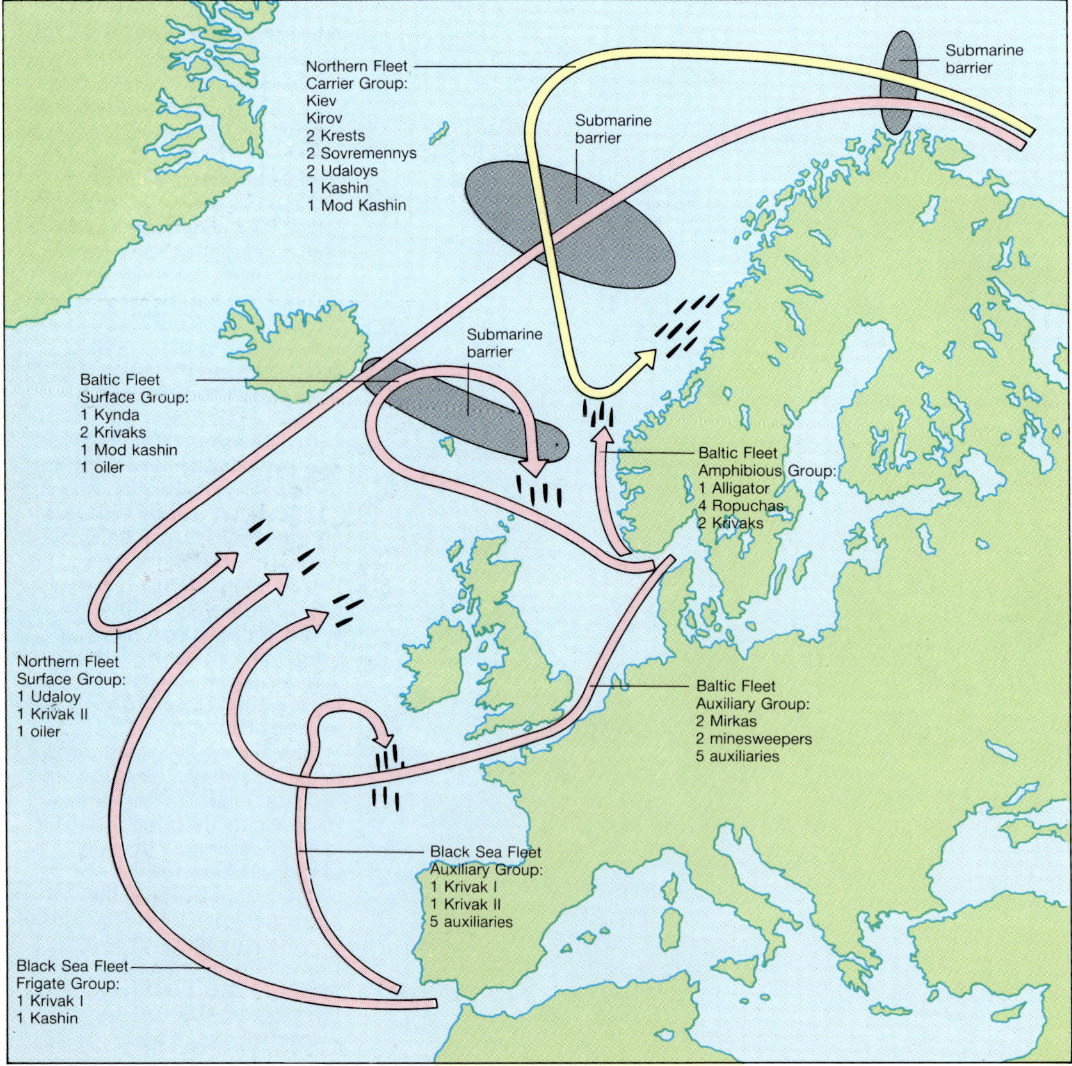

Above: Since 1980 the USSR has carried out naval exercises in the Norwegian Sea, the GIUK gap and the waters to the west of the British Isles. These are designed to rehearse Soviet operations into the North Atlantic and also to practise their response to the deployment of a UK/Netherlands amphibious force, which would be NATO's response to a crisis on the northern flank. In Summerex 85 the Soviets set up submarine barriers in the same areas as those they claim would be used by NATO, especially southeast of Iceland, which could lead to a major underwater battle.

avoid a battle and to result in a series of engagements. The size of the Norwegian Sea would demand two or three carrier battle groups, probably in support of amphibious forces. The demands on the control of such a dispersed attacking force would be considerable, but there would be distinct advantages in terms of anti-submarine warfare. Detection of enemy submarines is paramount, and a fast-moving and constantly manoeuvring task force would more easily confuse and deceive the enemy and might well impose on him unwanted manoeuvre and therefore possible exposure.

DEFENCE OF MERCHANT SHIPS

The protection of merchant shipping against submarine warfare is also of vital importance, especially to the Western Alliance. More than 99% of the world's trade is still carried by ships, and every day about 120 ocean-going ships arrive in Western Europe where they discharge three million tons of cargo; in addition, approximately 30 million tons of crude oil are delivered every month to Europe and America. It is estimated that in a major conflict in Western Europe 1,000 ship loads per month would have to arrive to meet the minimum civilian and military requirements, and another 500 ship loads of military stores, equipment, ammunition, fuel and men would have to cross the Atlantic.

The traditional method of protecting merchant shipping in a war environment is to form the vessels into convoys: this permits better control and coordination and allows the defending forces to make efficient use of their limited resources. It should not be thought, however, that convoying is a passive and purely defensive

tactic. On the contrary, it is an aggressive and offensive measure because it forces the submarine to come to the protected convoy and thus fight in the area of the surface force's choosing, rather than vice versa. It also leaves vast empty areas of ocean which the submariners must search fruitlessly.

Many question whether, in an age of nuclear weapons and fast merchant ships, convoying is still viable, but it is perfectly possible to plan for convoys which are spread out over very large areas of sea. Up to 40 ships spaced at five-mile intervals, while still constituting a coherent and controllable group, would cover an area 750 square miles (1,940km^2), and it would require nine or ten 5MT tactical nuclear weapons, all precisely placed, to destroy such a convoy.

Above: The Standing Naval Force Atlantic (STANAVFORLANT) is made up of ships of several NATO navies which work together routinely to develop ASW drills and ensure close coordination in time of war.

Increasing the space between the ships also makes the attacking submarine's task considerably more difficult, since after an attack on one ship the submarine commander would have to transit several miles before he was in a position to start setting up a new fire control solution. Moreover, having attacked the first vessel he would know that the defending forces would be aware of his location and hunting for him. During World War II it was usual to space ships in a convoy at half-mile intervals; increasing the interval to one mile enlarged the defence area for the escorts by 50 per cent but the risk of loss reduced to about one quarter. Increasing the interval yet again to two miles reduced the risk of loss by a further one-sixteenth, but only increased the convoy perimeter by two and a half times.

Whatever its formation, there are two main ways that a convoy can be protected: by providing it with its own dedicated escorts or by sailing it through areas already occupied and tactically dominated by other supporting groups. The latter is the more likely to be used in a modern war, as it allows more efficient use of limited naval resources and – most importantly – permits passive sonar operations in quiet areas of sea before the fast-moving and noisy merchant vessels arrive. Such support groups would include ships with towed arrays, helicopters and, hopefully, LRMP aircraft, and ideally each group would have at least one SSN in support.

Convoys are normally routed to cause maximum confusion to the enemy, thus minimising the risk of exposure. For example, long-leg

Convoy support groups

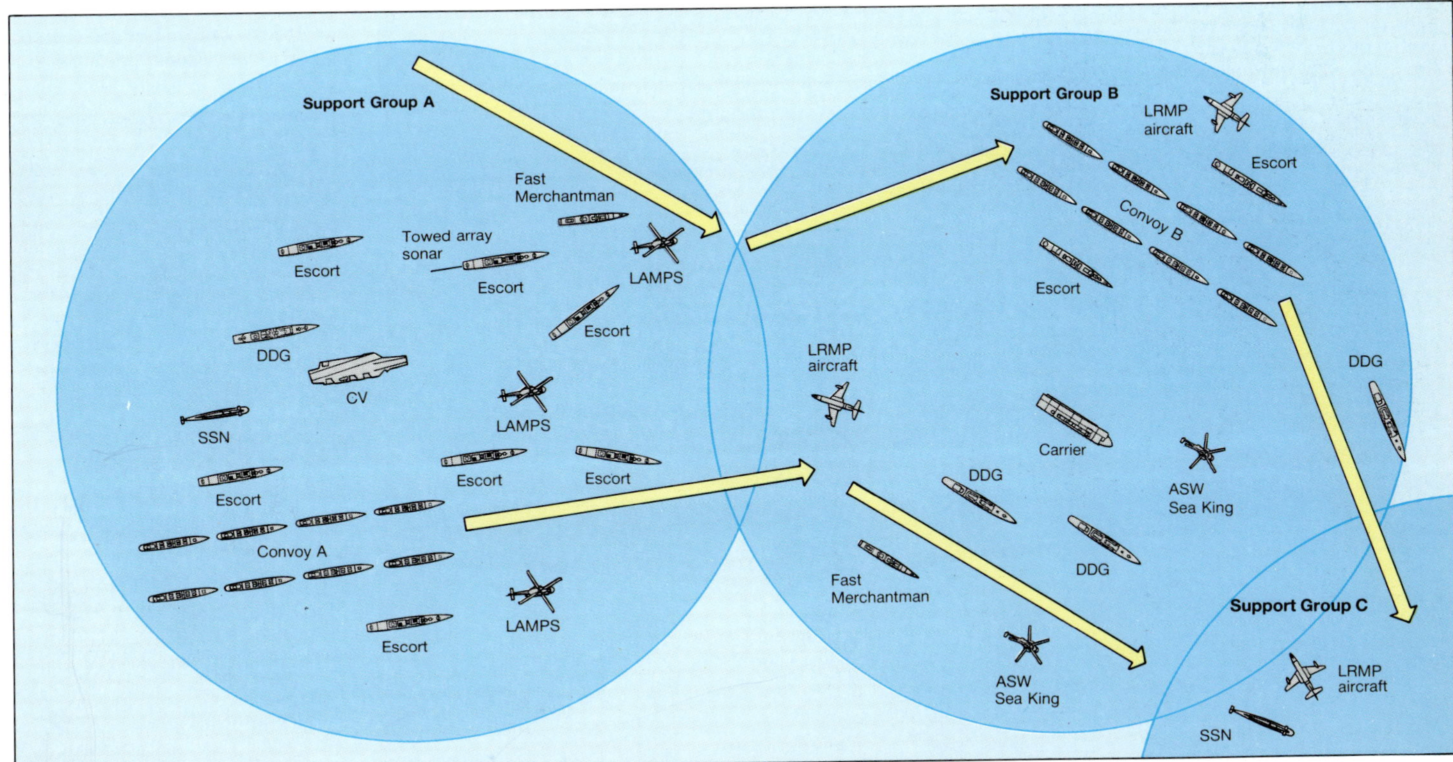

Above: If an enemy uses convoy tactics he forces a hunting submariner to go to him, rather than vice versa. Conversely, the submarine threat compels the enemy to devote considerable resources to protect his convoys. In the case of NATO's supply routes across the Atlantic, the routing of convoys would have to optimise the use of limited naval resources. This diagram shows support groups being used to sanitise areas in advance of transiting convoys. The merchant vessels would have only a minimum number of accompanying escorts; indeed, there might only be ASW helicopters based on one or two of the merchantmen themselves. For their part, the support groups would only be dedicated to a convoy while it passed through.

zig-zags, each 10-12 miles (18-22km) in length, with alterations of course of 30-40°, make it particularly difficult for an attacking submarine to get into the grain of a convoy, while the support groups advance their positions as necessary. In addition, groups should have their own air cover, which should aim to destroy any shadowing aircraft in order to deny the enemy as much information as possible and thereby force him to reveal his whereabouts.

In order to reach a firing solution, a submarine captain has to sort out what is going on on the surface. Shore authorities will pass on any available information, provided by satellite and air reconnaissance and other intelligence sources, but this is inevitably out of date by the time it reaches him. Moreover, the submarine's own on-board sonar information may well be confused, especially as fast-moving convoys make a good deal of noise, which would often be augmented by acoustic deception equipment. To resolve such anomalies the submarine may be forced to approach the surface to use its radar, which will almost certainly be detected by the defenders' ECM equipment and give them a bearing on the submarine's position extremely quickly. And the submarine will certainly use its periscope, which can be detected by the radar of a long-range maritime patrol aircraft.

If a submarine has to transit at high speed to close a convoy, the risk of detection is again increased. In the last war submarines enjoyed a speed margin of 16:6 over the convoy, but only when the submarine was running on the

Hammerhead tactical employment

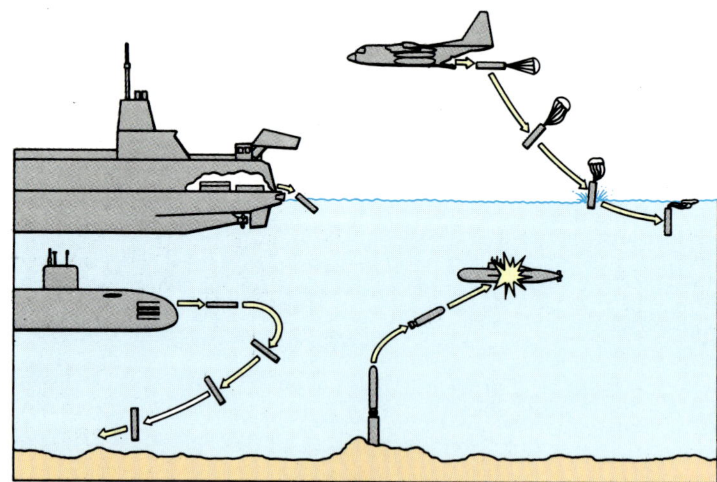

Left: The Marconi/Loral Hammerhead advanced sea mine concept involves an antisubmarine torpedo contained in a 21in (533mm) diameter tube and is designed for offensive and defensive use against both submarine use surface targets. Intended to be able to be positioned beyond the continental shelf and to be laid by aircraft, surface ships or submarines, it is designed to sink to the ocean floor and rest there in a vertical attitude, lying in wait with the torpedo sonar operating in the passive mode. When a target has been detected, tracked and classified the torpedo will be released at the optimum moment to ensure maximum lethality closing on its target with active sonar.

Whitehead A.244/S search pattern

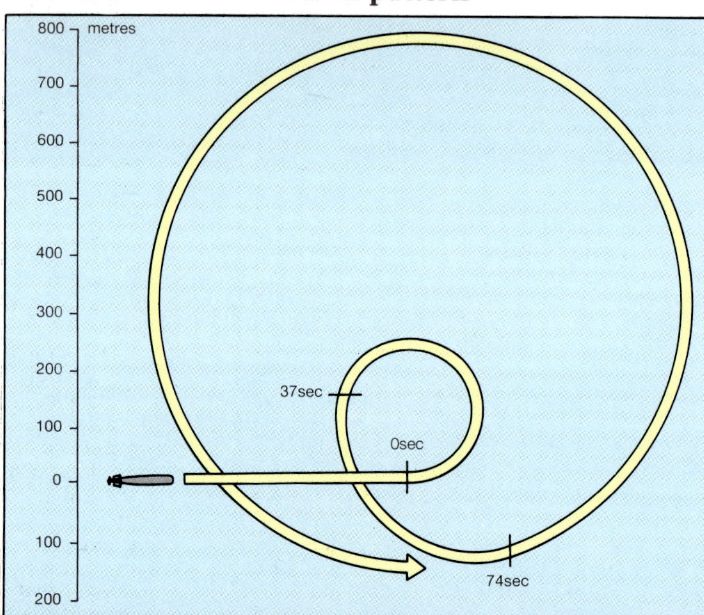

Left: For many years torpedoes simply followed a straight course after launch, which meant that if the initial alignment was wrong or if the target detected the approaching missile and took evasive action, it missed. Modern torpedoes' though still aimed at the target, have an autonomous search capability which enables them to carry out their own search pattern if no target is encountered. The Italian Whitehead A.244/S torpedo, for example, is launched when the ship has manoeuvred into a launch area that gives the required hit probability and travels on a pre-set bearing and at a pre-set depth with its acoustic head activated and searching for the target. After a straight run of predetermined length, if the torpedo has not acoustically acquired the target it initiates a curvilinear search pattern which can be either a constant-depth spiral (shown here) or a helix.

surface. Today that margin is approximately 30:17 with the submarine submerged – and over 40:17 in the case of some Soviet submarines – but whereas 17 knots is a speed easily sustained by a modern warship, a speed of 30 knots submerged makes a submarine very vulnerable to detection.

THE MISSILE THREAT

Torpedo-firing submarines are only one type of threat. Convoys are also liable to attack from missile-firing submarines such as the Soviet Echo class using target acquisition information passed to them either by satellites or reconnaissance aircraft. The range of the Echos' SS-N-3 Shaddock missiles could be as much as 300nm (555km), but the submarine would have to surface before it fired and would therefore make itself vulnerable to detection. The Soviet Charlie class boats can launch SS-N-9 Siren missiles while still submerged, but their range is one-third that of the Shaddock. Either threat should be more easily containable in the support group type of convoy screen, where point defence systems such as Seawolf can provide cover in case of missile attack and electronic counter measures will aid confusion and deception.

The essential principle of tactical defence of a convoy depends on confusion of the enemy, which in turn will force that enemy to show himself, however briefly. Then, as in all naval warfare, once detected the submarine should be destroyed before it can manoeuvre into an attacking position.

Above: A Soviet Victor III caught on the surface by a patrolling Lockheed P-3 aircraft. Well over 600 P-3s have been built for the US and many foreign navies and the type will be in service well into the next century.

AIRBORNE ASW OPERATIONS

The use of aircraft in the ASW battle started in World War I and has continued to grow in importance ever since. Two types of operation are mounted: independent area search tasks under control of a maritime headquarters, and support operations in conjunction with a naval force at sea. The aircraft, whether carrier-borne, land-based or amphibian, fixed-wing or helicopter, is by far the most rapid and effective method of turning a frequently vague long-distance contact into a definite localized target and then conducting the attack. An additional advantage of aircraft is that their presence is very rarely detected by a submerged submarine, which means that in a well conducted airborne ASW operation the first the submarine captain should know about an attack is when he hears the propellers of a high-speed torpedo closing rapidly on his boat.

FIXED-WING AIRCRAFT

The modern maritime patrol aircraft (MPA) is a unique and highly effective package of sensors, search and target analysis capability, and weapons. All current types are land-based, apart from the US Navy's carrier-based Lockheed S-3A Viking and the few remaining amphibian types, the Soviet Be-12, Japanese PS-1 and Chinese PS-5.

In normal circumstances magnetic anomaly detection is used to give positive confirmation of tracks detected by other means, though in choke points such as the Straits of Gibraltar it can also be used as a primary detection system. MAD can also be used to assist in refining the attack solution, though it is, of course, ineffective against titanium-hulled submarines.

Radar is used to detect surface targets, and even the smallest objects, such as a periscope or the tip of a diesel-electric submarine's snort tube, can now be picked up at great distances. Modern radars are also capable of displaying radar profiles, thus giving virtually instantaneous identification of the target, while periscopes and snorts can also be detected by infra-red devices.

Since sonobuoy performance is so dependent upon the ambient conditions a bathythermograph buoy will frequently be dropped first. This consists of a float which automatically lowers a device which reads temperature and salinity as it goes, the information being transmitted by the surface buoy to the aircraft overhead. Selection of the sonobuoy and its operating mode can then be made:

Atlantique typical ASW mission

8 hours on patrol at 170 knots
Reserves: 5% total fuel + 5% consumed fuel + 20 minutes
32min
94min at 30,000ft and 290 knots
9min
9min
92min at 25,000ft and 290 knots
Patrol altitude: 80% at 2,000ft, 20% at 300ft
Total time: 12 hours 31 minutes
35min
Ramp weight: 97,600lb (44,300kg)
Fuel: 33,535lb (15,225kg

Left: One of the most effective antisubmarine weapon systems is the maritime patrol aircraft, of which the British Nimrod is a good example. Long endurance and ample accommodation for sensors are essential.

Above: Typical ASW reconnaissance sortie by a French Atlantique aircraft: an eight-hour patrol more than 600nm from base is possible with standard antisubmarine mission armament of four torpedoes plus more than 100 sonobuoys and a variety of markers and pyrotecnic devices. The speed with which such aircraft reach their patrol area, the size of the area covered, and their ability to switch patrol areas quickly are significant.

sonobuoys can be either directional or omnidirectional and either active or passive. In all cases hydrophone operating depth, surface-to-air transmission frequencies, buoy life and operating mode are set in the aircraft prior to release, though in some modern sonobuoys operating depth can actually be altered after the sonobuoy has entered the water in order to follow a target into a different temperature layer.

The many complex inputs from all these sensors are correlated and controlled by a computerised central tactical system. Such a system is also used to propose weapons solutions and to conduct weapons release.

Maritime patrol aircraft operate either independently on area search tasks, or in support of a maritime force at sea. In the latter case they are normally under the tactical control of the force commander and will usually be deployed as part of the defensive screen at some distance from the surface force itself. They can operate alone on a designated patrol line or, more usually, in conjunction with ASW helicopters from the force's own ships.

In area search tasks the MPA operates independently, usually under the control of a shore-based maritime headquarters. It is normally given a specific area to search, which will frequently be part of an ASW barrier such as that established by NATO in the GIUK gap.

Once a hostile target has been identified the MPA conducts an attack. Most carry various types of torpedo and depth bombs with either conventional or nuclear

Above: An Italian Navy ASH-3D launches a Whitehead A.244/S torpedo. When dropped by a helicopter out of sonar contact the torpedo will be set to start its search pattern immediately.

Right: An SH-2F LAMPS I ASW helicopter deploys its ASW-81 MAD bird. Aircraft usually detect and classify targets with sonobuoys and then make a MAD pass prior to weapon launch.

Below: A Westland Lynx of the Federal Germany Navy with its AQS-18 dunking sonar deployed. The transducer is on a 1,000ft cable and operating modes include moving target indication.

Below right: A Royal Navy Lynx deploys a Stingray lightweight torpedo. The parachute will lower it vertically to the water, where the torpedo will start its search for its submarine target.

Dipping sonar: typical ASW operation

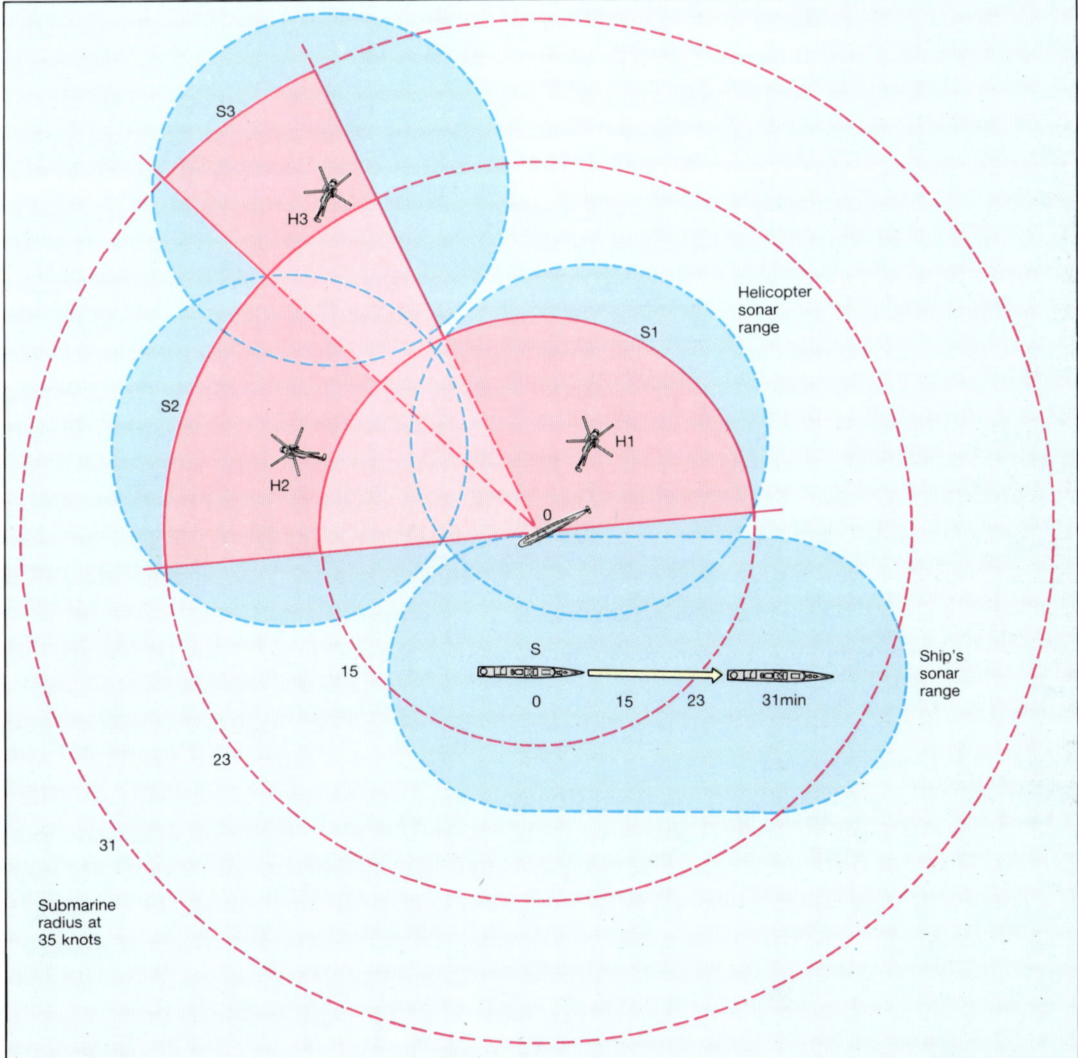

Above: Active sonar in ship S moving at 12.5 knots detects an SSN moving at 12 knots; the SSN accelerates to 35 knots. Ship's helicopter at 10 minutes notice deploys at 120 knots to H1, taking two minutes to hover and deploy its sonar to 200m. Contact to operation at H1 takes 15 minutes. Blue circles are areas covered by the helicopter's sonar; solid red lines mark the diminishing areas where the submarine might be: at H1 the helicopter will detect the SSN if it is in S1; if not it moves 9 miles (15km) in 8 minutes to H2 and will detect the SSN if it is in S2; if not, it should be in S3.

warheads. The torpedo has frequently proved to be the weakest link in the entire system and, as described elsewhere, vast sums have been expended on torpedo development programmes in a number of countries.

ASW HELICOPTERS

Helicopters have great tactical value in the ASW battle in that they can confer a major and relatively long-range ASW capability on even small surface warships and enable navies who cannot afford expensive, complex and manpower-intensive aircraft carriers to take their own air power to sea. The early ASW helicopters were simple extensions of their ships' sensor and weapon delivery systems, but some modern types are fully autonomous ASW hunter-killers.

A surveillance device unique to the helicopter is the dunking sonar, which is deployed by a winch from a hovering helicopter. When in the hover a helicopter should ideally face into the wind to avoid weather-cocking; it also uses fuel at a much increased rate, and when it is necessary to move to a new search position the dunking sonar must be withdrawn from the water, thus breaking contact. Then, if a submarine track has been firmly established, the sonar must again be withdrawn for the aircraft to start the attack. These problems handicap an ASW helicopter acting alone but they are overcome if two such aircraft can work as a team, since one can always have its sonar in the water, holding the contact, while the other can use its MAD gear under the guidance of the aircraft in contact to establish the submarine's course and then launch an attack, the standard weapons being homing torpedoes or depth bombs.

Dunking sonar has certain advantages over sonobuoys. In some areas, such as the Mediterranean, there are discrete layers of water of differing temperatures, and the interface between them – the thermocline – acts as a barrier to acoustic signals. The dunking sonar, however, can often be lowered through these layers to seek and locate targets which might otherwise have escaped detection.

The passive mode is preferable in certain situations, particularly where it is believed the submarine has no reason to suspect that he has been detected at all and is thus unlikely to take evasive action. The active mode is normally used when time is of the essence – that is, when the submarine is rapidly taking up an attack position against surface targets, or when he knows that he has already been detected. In any case, being hunted by a pair of ASW helicopters using active dunking sonar is a daunting experience for a submarine captain, since he can never be quite sure whether they are still in contact or from which direction the next ping will come.

Index

Classes of Submarines are indexed by class name and country or origin. Individual boats are indexed by name and pennant number. Page numbers in bold type refer to subjects of illustrations or captions.

M

N

O

P

Q

R

S

T

Picture Credits

Endpapers: Kockums Page 1: MoD/Navy 2/3: FRC/*Naval Forces* 4/5: MoD/Navy 6/7: Kockums 8: (upper left) US Navy; (lower left) Howaldtswerke-Deutsche Werft; (right) FRC/*Naval Forces* 9: US Navy 10/11: US Navy 13: (upper) Dassault-Breguet; (lower) Kockums 14: (top) US Navy; (remainder) MoD/Navy 15: (all) Imperial War Museum 16: (top and bottom) Imperial War Museum; (centre) US Navy 17: (both) Imperial War Museum 18: Imperial War Museum 19: MoD/RAF 20/21: (top) FRC/*Naval Forces;* (bottom left) MoD/Navy; bottom right) US Navy 22/23; (top and bottom left) US Navy; (bottom right) FRC/*Naval Forces* 24: MoD/Navy 25: (bottom) US Navy 26/27: (all) Imperial War Museum 28/29: Imperial War Museum 30: Imperial War Museum 31: US Navy 32/33: US Navy 34: (both) US Navy 35: (bottom) US DoD; (remainder) US Navy 36: Imperial War Museum 37: Imperial War Museum 38/39: (top, centre and bottom left) US Navy; (remainder) Imperial War Museum 40: US Navy 41: US Navy 42: US Navy 43: US Navy 45: (top) Jet Propulsion Laboratory; (bottom) US Navy 46: (top) Sippican; (bottom) US Navy 49: (bottom left) Hollandse Signaalapparaten; (bottom right) US Navy 51: (top left and right) MoD/Navy; (centre) US Navy 52: US Navy 53: (top) US DoD; (centre) US Navy; (bottom)FRC/*Naval Forces* 55: US DoD 56: (top) Vickers Shipbuilding & Engineering; (bottom) US Navy 57: (top) US Navy; (bottom) MoD/Navy 58: (bottom) US Navy; (remainder) MoD/Navy 59: (top) MoD/Navy; (centre) US Navy; (bottom) Thyssen Nordseewerke 61: (top left) MoD; (top right) DCN 62: (top) Brons Industrie; (bottom) Paxman Diesels 63: (top left) Marconi Command and Control Systems; (remainder) Thyssen Nordseewerke 64: (top) US Navy; (bottom left) E and TV Films; (bottom right) US Air Force 65: (top right) US Navy; (top right) MoD/Navy 66: (bottom left) US DoD;(bottom right) US Navy 67: (both) US Navy 68: (top) US DoD; (bottom left) Aérospatiale; (bottom right) US Navy 69: US Navy 70: (top and centre left) MoD/Navy; (centre right) US Navy 71: (top, centre and bottom right) US DoD; (bottom left) Aérospatiale 72: MoD/Navy 73: (centre left) Thomson Sintra; (bottom) MoD/Navy; (remainder) Krupp MaK 74: (bottom) Whitehead; (remainder) Marconi Underwater Systems; (remainder) MoD/Navy 78: (top left and right) Barr & Stroud; (centre) MoD/Navy 79: (top) MoD/Navy; (centre) FRC/*Naval Forces* 80/81: (top) US Navy; (remainder) Boeing Aerospace 82: Sippican Ocean Systems 83: (top) US Navy; (centre) Plessey Naval Systems; (bottom) US DoD 84: (upper) Graseby Dynamics (lower) Simrad Naval Systems 85: (all) Plessey Naval Systems 86: MoD/Navy 87: (top) British Aerospace; (centre) US Navy 88: (top) TASS; (bottom) Matra 89: (top and bottom) MoD/Navy (centre) Whitehead 90: (top and bottom right) US Navy; (bottom left) Hunting Engineering 91: (top) Library of Congress; (bottom) Goodyear Aerospace 92: (top left and centre) Plessey Naval Systems; (bottom left) Bendix Aerospace; (bottom right) MoD/Navy 93: (top) Plessey Naval Systems; (bottom) Thomson Sintra 94: (top) US Navy; (bottom) Plessey Naval Systems 95: Dassault-Breguet 96: (all) Howaldtswerke-Deutsche Werft 97: (top) US Navy; (bottom) US DoD 98: (centre) Kockums; (bottom) US Navy 99: (top left) US Navy; (top right) MoD 100/101: MoD/Navy 102: (top) MoD/Navy; (bottom) US DoD 103: (top) Royal Netherlands Navy; (bottom) US DoD 104: DCN 105: US DoD 107: US Navy 108: US Navy 109: US Navy 110: ECP-Armées 111: Wright & Logan 112: US DoD 113: US DoD 114: MoD 115: MoD 116: US Navy 117: MoD 118: US Navy 119: US Navy 120: US Navy 121: MoD 122: MoD 123: MoD/Navy 124: US DoD 125: US Navy 126: US Navy 127: US Navy 128: ECP/Armées 129: ECP/Armées 131: (both) US Navy 132: Kockums 133: Kockums 134: (both) Fincantieri 136: MoD/Navy 137: MoD/Navy 138: US Navy 139: US Navy 140: US DoD 141: US DoD 143: (both) US Navy 144: MoD/Navy 145: MoD/Navy 146: MoD 147: Skyfotos 149: (both) SIRPA-Marine/MARS 150: US Navy 151: US Navy 153: (both) US Navy 154/55: (both) US Navy 156: MoD/Navy 157: MoD/Navy 158: MoD 159: US Navy 160: Thyssen Nordseewerke 161: Thyssen Nordseewerke 162: MoD/Navy 163: Vickers Shipbuilding & Engineering Ltd 165: HDW 166: HDW 167: HDW 169: US DoD 170: MoD/Navy 117: MoD/Navy 172: MoD/Navy 173: MoD Navy 175: (top) US DoD/Mitsuo Shibato; (bottom) PPL 176: MoD 176/77: US DoD 180: RDM 181: RDM 182/83: Whitehead 184/185: (all) MoD/Navy 186: (centre) US DoD; (bottom) MoD/Navy 187: US Navy 188: (both) US DoD 189: (top) US Navy; (bottom) MoD/Navy 190: FRC/*Naval Forces* 191: MoD/Navy 192: (top) MoD/Navy; (bottom) Marconi Underwater Systems 193: (both) US Navy; 194: (centre) Plessey Naval Systems; (bottom) Canadian Forces 196: MoD/Navy 197: (top left) Dowty Electronics; (top right) MoD/Navy; (bottom) US DoD 198: MoD/Navy 201: MoD/Navy 202: MoD/Navy 203: US Navy 204: (top) Whitehead; (bottom left) Westland Helicopters; (bottom right) MoD/Navy 205: Kaman Aerospace

Above: Launch of the *Västergötland* by Kockums, Malmö, September 1986.